METHODS and STRATEGIES for TEACHING STUDENTS with MILD DISABILITIES

A CASE-BASED APPROACH

Joseph Boyle

Rutgers, The State University of New Jersey

David Scanlon

Boston College

WADSWORTH
CENGAGE Learning

Australia • Brazil • Japan • Korea • Mexico • Singapore • Spain • United Kingdom • United States

WADSWORTH
CENGAGE Learning

Methods and Strategies for Teaching Students with Mild Disabilities: A Case-Based Approach
Joseph Boyle and David Scanlon

Acquisitions Editor: Chris Shortt

Senior Development Editor: Lisa Mafrici

Assistant Editor: Diane Mars

Editorial Assistant: Linda Stewart

Media Editor: Mary Noel

Marketing Manager: Kara Parsons

Marketing Assistant: Ting Jian Yap

Marketing Communications Manager: Martha Pfeiffer

Project Manager, Editorial Production: Cheri Palmer

Creative Director: Rob Hugel

Art Director: Maria Epes

Print Buyer: Rebecca Cross

Permissions Editors: Katie Huha and Jennifer Meyer-Dare

Production Service: Macmillan Publishing Solutions

Text Designer: Marsha Cohen

Photo Researcher: Kate Cebik

Copy Editor: Heather McElwain

Illustrator: Macmillan Publishing Solutions

Cover Designer: Janice Moore

Cover Image: © Collier Campbell Lifeworks/ CORBIS

Compositor: Macmillan Publishing Solutions

For product information and technology assistance, contact us at **Cengage Learning Customer & Sales Support, 1-800-354-9706.**
For permission to use material from this text or product, submit all requests online at **www.cengage.com/permissions.**
Further permissions questions can be e-mailed to **permissionrequest@cengage.com.**

Library of Congress Control Number: 2008942565

Student Edition:

ISBN-13: 978-0-618-39689-4

ISBN-10: 0-618-39689-6

Wadsworth
10 Davis Drive
Belmont, CA 94002-3098
USA

Cengage Learning is a leading provider of customized learning solutions with office locations around the globe, including Singapore, the United Kingdom, Australia, Mexico, Brazil, and Japan. Locate your local office at **www.cengage.com/international.**

Cengage Learning products are represented in Canada by Nelson Education, Ltd.

To learn more about Wadsworth, visit **www.cengage.com/wadsworth**

Purchase any of our products at your local college store or at our preferred online store **www.ichapters.com.**

Printed in Canada
1 2 3 4 5 6 7 12 11 10 09

Dedication
To Carole, Joshua, and Ashley—with love.
                                                    J. R. B.
To Candace Bos—friend and teacher.
                                                    D. J. S.

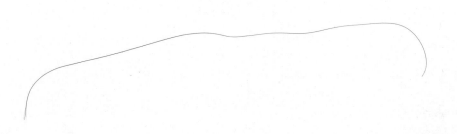

Brief Contents

PART I
Foundations for Teaching Students with Mild Disabilities

PART II
Teaching Methods for Specific Content Areas

PART III
Comprehensive Special Education Practices

Contents

PART II
Teaching Methods for Specific Content Areas

PART III
Comprehensive Special Education Practices

About the Authors

Joseph R. Boyle is a former elementary special education teacher. In his special education classroom and other settings, he taught students with mild to moderate disabilities. These students included students with learning disabilities, mild to moderate cognitive disorders, traumatic brain injury, attention deficit/hyperactivity disorder, autism, and Asperger's syndrome. As a special education teacher, he has collaborated and co-taught with general education teachers and other school professionals. He received his PhD in special education from the University of Kansas. Through research at various universities, he has developed a number of classroom interventions for students with mild disabilities in the areas of reading and note taking.

Joseph R. Boyle is currently an associate professor of special education at the Graduate School of Education at Rutgers, The State University of New Jersey. He has taught or currently teaches courses for university students in undergraduate to doctoral programs. The courses he has taught at Rutgers and other universities include methods and materials for special education, collaboration and consultation, introduction to special education and special education law, assessment in special education, special education behavior management, language disabilities, critical issues in special education, and technology in special education classrooms. He has also taught several courses online and in other web-based formats. His current research interests include examining the effectiveness of teaching techniques among students with mild disabilities, particularly in the areas of reading and note taking. He has coauthored three special education casebooks and numerous journal articles. Over the past several years, he has been involved with the Virginia Council for Learning Disabilities, as well as most recently with the national organization, Council for Learning Disabilities (CLD), serving as vice president, president-elect, president, and past-president from 2005 to 2009.

David Scanlon is a former high school and community college special education teacher. In his high school resource room, he taught students with a variety of disabilities; some were mainstreamed and others took most or all of their academic courses with him. In the community college, he taught basic literacy courses and assisted with advising students with disabilities. He received his PhD in special education and rehabilitation from the University of Arizona. Following his graduation he worked as an assistant research scientist at the University of Kansas Center for Research on Learning (CRL). There, he and his colleagues developed strategic interventions appropriate to the inclusive content-area classroom context. While at the CRL, David served as director of intervention research for the National Adult Literacy and Learning Disabilities Center. The Center was funded to identify best curricular practices in adult basic education.

David Scanlon is currently an associate professor of special education in the Lynch School of Education at Boston College. He teaches courses for students ranging from undergraduate to doctoral students. Among the courses he teaches are an introductory special education class, special education methods for regular education teachers, methods for special education teachers of students with mild disabilities, and investigations into scientific and social theories on the nature of learning disabilities and special education practice. He continues to research effective interventions for children and adolescents with mild disabilities, including focuses on content-area literacy and transition, and, most recently, Asperger's syndrome. He has coauthored several learning strategies, in addition to curricular materials and nearly fifty research publications and book chapters. He is the past chairperson of the Special Education Research Special Interest Group of the American Educational Research Association, past chairperson of the Research Committee of the Council for Learning Disabilities, former associate editor of the *Journal of Teacher Education*, and current editor of the *Learning Disability Quarterly*.

Preface

Welcome to the first edition of the textbook, *Methods and Strategies for Teaching Students with Mild Disabilities.* We have combined our experiences as educators with our knowledge of best instructional practices to write this book and are excited to share the first edition with you.

Why We Wrote This Book

Our own experiences as former elementary and high school teachers—and now as teacher educators and researchers—have helped us shape the content, features, and pedagogy found in this book. Having taught graduate and undergraduate education students for more than a decade, we found many special education methods textbooks lacking. Some textbooks offered too few practical instructional methods, or represented dogmatically narrow approaches to teaching and learning. Most were a compendium of methods and techniques, often to the detriment of student learning. Our students often complained to us that their textbook had too many techniques that were presented in a superficial manner and that lacked sufficient depth for use in the classroom. We observed that students knew the features of the techniques, but didn't quite understand how to use them with their students.

We therefore developed this textbook with student learning at the forefront. We wanted to develop a text that would reflect first-rate pedagogy. We also wanted students to be able to apply their knowledge soon after learning it. As a result, *we designed this textbook around a common core of knowledge that we believe all special education teachers should know, and then designed activities and cases to support the learning of it.*

Who Should Use This Book?

This textbook was designed for students studying to be either special education or general education teachers. It describes the current inclusive context of K-12 schooling. It also presents teaching practices appropriate to both roles. It addresses the continuum of placements and services for students enrolled in special education. Readers of this textbook will learn best instructional practices and how to participate in all aspects of the special education process (for example, RTI, multidisciplinary teams, IEPs, working with families, co-teaching, accommodations, and progress monitoring) for students with mild disabilities.

The introductory chapters provide a link between traditional methods courses and other "introductory" special education courses. Instead of simply providing a redundant introductory text, we present an overview of mild disabilities, with discussions of the special education process and various educators' roles, and theories of learning that influence instruction applicable across the mild disabilities, all from an applied perspective. Hence, this book is appropriate for methods courses that build from a regular/special education foundation, those that serve as students' only exposure to practices appropriate for their students with mild disabilities, and inclusion courses that provide strategies and techniques that can be used in inclusive settings.

How This Textbook Is Different From Others

As we explain here in greater detail, our textbook is unique and innovative for the following key reasons:

1. **Throughout the entire text, we link current educational research to practice.**

   At the heart of the book is our philosophy of *linking research to practice* so that teachers use effective strategies and techniques to constantly improve the learning (and lives) of students with disabilities. This text reflects the most current scholarship about teaching students with mild disabilities, but in a way that is accessible to preservice students and novice readers.

2. **This special education textbook interweaves compelling case studies and research-based special education teaching strategies and techniques.**

   We integrated cases into the text to connect theory and knowledge with practice. In each chapter, two cases are presented so that students can apply their knowledge of strategies and techniques. The cases reflect realistic special and regular education scenarios, lending insight into the experiences and perspectives of students, educators, and families.

3. **Instead of including every technique under the sun, each chapter focuses on several key, empirically validated teaching strategies.**

   This text takes a focused and integrated approach to teaching methods. Each chapter presents a limited number of teaching techniques, but with sufficient detail so that students can thoroughly learn them. As we explain each technique, we discuss typical challenges for students with mild disabilities.

4. **Equal attention is paid to each of the mild disabilities.**

   In every chapter, the unique learning needs of students with different mild disabilities are described. Effective practices and the research that supports their use with students with varying disabilities are also referenced.

5. **The relationship of student and family diversity to effective teaching and learning is presented.**

   Instead of addressing diversity in feature boxes or as a separate chapter, examples in each chapter directly show how to consider types of diversity such as sex, race, ethnicity, English language learners, economic class, family status, sexual orientation, and disability. Empirically supported evidence of how diversity impacts schooling and learning is presented, in addition to effective inclusive practices for all.

6. **As we explain in the next sections, we use reader-friendly features to alert readers to important text content and to relate content directly back to the cases.**

In doing so, we try to facilitate readers' learning and understanding of teaching strategies and techniques. The features and cases are structured to serve as examples that you can also use in your class teaching; however, they are not relied upon so heavily that you cannot make connections to your own perspectives or experiences.

Student Learning Features

Every chapter of this text offers the following features that were designed to enhance student learning. Each of these features represents effective pedagogic practices. They are designed to make this textbook not only informative, but a teaching and learning tool for your students.

Chapter Questions: To orient students to the information they are about to read, each chapter begins with chapter questions that represent the "big ideas" students should think about as they read.

Chapter Question Alerts: Margin notes throughout each chapter prompt readers to think back to the opening chapter questions. Students are reminded to think about the relevant chapter question while reading that section of the text.

Case Studies with Accompanying Case Questions, and a "Think Back to the Case" Feature: Each chapter contains two engaging case studies about real education issues for students to "solve." Each Case Study ends with questions about what teachers should do based on the case scenario. Those questions guide students to reflect on critical components of the cases as they read the chapter. As information appropriate to answer a case question is presented, a "Think back" box summarizing an answer to that question follows.

Video Case Connections Boxes: Using the award-winning Video Cases, readers are prompted at appropriate points in each chapter to use the Internet to view a Video Case that provides real classroom footage of the featured concepts. Each Video Case Connection is accompanied by a thoughtful question or brief activities designed to provoke student reflection.

Methods and Strategies Spotlight Boxes: In each of these special boxes, a specific practice is highlighted and discussed in depth.

Tips for Generalization Boxes: Because teachers need to learn how to generalize procedures they learn, we highlight examples of generalization practices. Readers can consult these boxes to learn ways that popular and validated practices can be properly generalized to meet the needs of individual students or unique setting demands.

Application Activities: To help students extend their learning of what they read, each chapter ends with three to five Application Activities. Each of these activities encourages students to apply practices they have learned. The activities are designed so that students may engage in them even if they are not in a student teaching situation when they read this book.

Technology Resources: Our text integrates coverage of technology throughout. Readers will find coverage of relevant technology within each chapter and a list of related technology resources at the end of each chapter. In this book, technology is treated as a standard form of practice, not an add-on to teachers' routines. We also include a full chapter on technology so that students can fully grasp the concepts behind technology usage today (universal design for learning and access to the curriculum, for example).

Coverage of the CEC 2009 and other Professional Standards: The Council for Exceptional Children 2009 Standards for entry-level educators are listed inside the front and back covers of the text. In each chapter, explicit reference is made to the CEC and other standards (for example, NCTE, NCTM, IRA). The purposes of the standards, how to use the standards, and ways to meet the standards are addressed throughout the entire book.

Text Organization and Coverage

We have organized this book into three main sections:

- The chapters within the first section, *Foundations of Teaching Students with Mild Disabilities,* provide background information about students with disabilities and current special education policies related to school-level practices; information on how to plan, teach, and monitor instruction; and information about learning theories that influence special education instructional approaches.
- In the second section, *Teaching Methods for Specific Content Areas,* readers will find chapters about current strategies used to teach in various content and basic skills areas.
- The chapters within the third section, *Comprehensive Special Education Practices,* provide students with knowledge and skills about specific components of the special education process such as technology use, transition planning, collaboration and consultation, and working with families.

Chapter Walk-Through

Part I, *Foundations of Teaching Students with Mild Disabilities,* begins with discussion in **Chapter 1** of the characteristics of students with mild disabilities, major legislation that affects today's schools and families, and current practices in the field (for example, responsiveness to intervention). Instead of being simply redundant with what many students may learn in an introduction to special education class, this chapter focuses on implications for practice. In **Chapter 2,** we describe how to plan, teach, and monitor instruction in the classroom. We take readers from the pre-referral process, through individualized education plan (IEP) development, lesson planning, and best practices in special education, and end with a discussion of ways to monitor the progress of students with disabilities, all focused on the roles and activities of effective regular *and* special educators. In **Chapter 3,** we discuss past and present learning theories in special education and techniques or methods that are derived from those theories to aid student learning.

In Part II, *Teaching Methods for Specific Content Areas,* we begin with **Chapter 4,** which addresses strategies and techniques for improving oral language. Next, we move on to the reading chapters. **Chapter 5,** *Early Reading: Strategies and Techniques,* describes early reading skills such as phonological awareness and word-attack skills; **Chapter 6,** *Later Reading: Strategies and Techniques,* covers fluency and comprehension skills and strategies. **Chapter 7,** *Written Language: Strategies and Techniques,* describes how to teach written language skills and strategies to students with mild disabilities. In **Chapter 8,** *Math: Strategies and Techniques,* we discuss how to teach math concepts and skills to students with disabilities, and how to implement strategies to help students overcome difficulties with problem solving. In **Chapter 9,** *Teaching in the Content Areas: Strategies and Techniques,* we describe ways to facilitate learning in the content areas, including content enhancement routines and techniques for helping students understand textbook information. Finally, **Chapter 10,** *Organization and Study Skills: Strategies and Techniques,* wraps up Part II by describing how to teach students with disabilities much-needed organizational skills, note-taking and study skills, as well as test-taking strategies.

In Part III, *Comprehensive Special Education Practices,* we begin with **Chapter 11,** *Technology and Teaching,* in which we describe how assistive technology can be used in today's classroom to bypass skill deficits or improve student learning in basic skill areas such as reading and written language. We also discuss how teachers can enhance their own teaching through technology, including using technology to manage their time by using electronic gradebooks and electronic IEPs. **Chapter 12,** *Transition,* describes how teachers can assist students with mild disabilities in the transition process as they move from high school to post-school settings. We cover post-school options in addition to college and the world of work, stressing the importance of transition planning. In **Chapter 13,** *Collaboration and Co-Teaching to Enhance Instruction,* we present readers with the latest information about collaboration. We also describe how teachers can augment their collaboration skills to become more effective co-teachers, and how co-teachers can teach effectively in today's inclusive classrooms. Lastly, we include a chapter on families, **Chapter 14,** *Working with Families,* because of the important role that families play in students' learning. This chapter discusses how a disability impacts not only the student but also the student's family. It also explains ways in which teachers can improve families' relationships with schools.

Supplements for Students and Instructors

A variety of exciting supplemental materials are also available to accompany the text.

Book Companion Website

The book-specific website at www.cengage.com/education/boyle offers students a variety of study tools and useful resources such as glossary, flash cards, web quizzes by chapter, web links by chapter, and more.

Premium Website The premium website offers access to the Video Cases, including exercises, bonus videos, and more. Go to www.cengage.com/login to register or purchase access.

Instructor's Manual Instructors will appreciate succinct chapter summaries, outlines, learning objectives, reflection questions, and additional suggestions for activities provided in the Instructor's Manual.

Test Bank The Test Bank contains multiple choice, fill-in-the-blank, and essay questions, as well as readily referenced teaching tips for each chapter. It is available electronically in the password-protected Instructor Resources section of the companion website, along with the Instructor's Manual.

PowerLecture This one-stop digital library and presentation tool includes preassembled Microsoft® PowerPoint® lecture slides by the authors. In addition to a full Instructor's Manual and Test Bank, PowerLecture also includes ExamView® testing software with all the test items from the printed Test Bank in electronic format, enabling you to create customized tests in print or online.

WebTutor™ on BlackBoard® or WebCT® Jumpstart your course with customizable, rich, text-specific content within your Course Management System. Whether you want to web-enable your class or put an entire course online, WebTutor delivers. WebTutor offers a wide array of resources including access to the Video Cases and more. Visit webtutor.cengage.com to learn more.

Acknowledgments

We are grateful to the many reviewers whose thoughtful feedback helped make this the best textbook possible. The following experienced general and special education teacher-educators suggested content and features that they know from experience are essential to our students' learning: Roger Bass, Carthage College; Robin D. Brewer, University of North Colorado; Steve Chamberlain, University of Texas at Brownsville; Carrie E. Chapman, Indiana University; Hollie C. Cost, University of Montevallo; Carol B. Donnelly, Worcester State College; Elaine Fine, Montclair State University; Joseph B. Fisher, Grand Valley State University; Gerlinde G. Beckers, Louisiana State University; Kimberly Grantham Griffith, Lamar University; Mary Beth Hendricks, Columbus State University; Celia E. Johnson, Bradley University; Ui-jung Kim, California State University, Los Angeles; Stephanie Kurtts, University of North Carolina at Greensboro; Loralee A. LaPointe, University of South Dakota; Robin H. Lock, Texas Tech University; Marc A. Markell, St. Cloud State University; Sharon A. Maroney, Western Illinois University; Maurice Dean Miller, Indiana State University; Yvonne Ridings Moore, Union College; Gerry Nierengarten, University of Minnesota, Duluth; Michie L. Odle, State University of New York, Cortland; Marion Panyan, Drake University; Mary B. Perdue, Oakland City University; Kathleen Puckett, Arizona State University; Barbara Ray, University of Tennessee at Chattanooga; Tess

Reid, California State University, Northridge; Colleen Klein Reutebuch, Texas Tech University; Joan P. Sebastian, National University; Martha Staton, University of Delaware; Roberta Strosnider, Towson University; Lisa P. Turner, Clarion University.

We are especially grateful to Dr. Joseph B. Fisher of Grand Valley State University, our expert reviewer, who provided detailed feedback on nearly every chapter of this text. We are also thankful for his contributions to the ancillary support materials that accompany this text. We also appreciate the editorial and production staff at Cengage Learning that includes Diane Mars, Jill Traut, Cheri Palmer, Ashley Cronin, Mary Noel, and Christopher Shortt. We are especially grateful to Lisa Mafrici, Senior Development Editor at Cengage; Shani Fisher, Senior Sponsoring Editor at Cengage; and Beth Kaufman, Consulting Editor; for their extensive reviews, feedback, and support throughout this entire project.

Finally, we wish to express our appreciation to our families, friends, and colleagues for being patient with us as we worked on this textbook, and for providing us with support and encouragement throughout the many phases of this project.

Providing Special Education to Students with Mild Disabilities

1

CHAPTER QUESTIONS

1. How do mild disabilities affect a student's academic and social skills?

2. What instructional practices have been proven by research to benefit students with mild disabilities?

3. Where do students with mild disabilities receive their education; who provides what types of services?

4. What are the major implications of legislation for how we serve students with disabilities?

5. What is RTI and how does it relate to traditional special education practices?

What makes special education "SPECIAL"?

This question has been asked time and again in the field of special education (for example, Dunn 1968; Will 1986). Most experts seem to agree that **special education** is an educational program that is designed to meet an individual's unique needs. The basic concept of **individualizing** a student's education is in essence what makes it "special" (Kavale and Forness 1999). Special education instruction is also typically presented at a slower, more intense pace, and is typically more structured than regular education instruction (Kauffman and Hallahan 2005). Although several other factors might contribute to the uniqueness of special education (for example, frequent reinforcement for correct performance, low teacher-pupil ratios, and differentiated curriculum), the instruction qualified educators provide is essentially what makes it unique. That is, in the majority of cases, *you* will be the defining factor that makes the student's education "special."

To teach students with disabilities, it is important first to understand the different types of disabilities and the characteristics of each type.

Practical Descriptions of the Mild Disabilities

Chapter Question

ALERT

In this section, you will find information that answers a Chapter Question:

1. How do mild disabilities affect a student's academic and social skills?

Throughout this book, we will refer to students with mild disabilities. The term **mild disabilities** refers to students who have learning disabilities (LD), mild levels of mental retardation (MR), emotional or behavioral disorders (EBD), and speech and language impairments[1] (SLI). These are four of thirteen disability categories served by the nation's special education law, the Individuals with Disabilities Education Act (IDEA) (see Table 1.1). (States use many different labels for disabilities, but they all correspond to the IDEA's 13 categories.) In addition to the mild/moderate disabilities, we address attention deficit/hyperactivity disorder (ADHD), because it closely resembles the four and, in fact, is often associated with one or more of those disabilities. Moreover, when IDEA was amended in 1997, the definition of other health impaired (OHI) was revised to include language about students with ADHD. Therefore, some students with ADHD are served by the IDEA under OHI.

States use a number of labels for disabilities. The terms *mild* and *moderate* are perhaps the most commonly recognized categorical terms for the students addressed in this book. The terms signify the degree to which the disabling conditions impact daily functioning in comparison to more severe disabilities (also known as "low incidence" or "intensive" disabilities). The designation *mild/moderate* is sometimes used because the level of impact of the disability can vary depending on context and the relative intensity of the condition for an individual. For the most part, however, the effects are mild in terms of learning and daily functioning. For example, students with mild disabilities are usually in an academic curriculum; whereas, students with moderate disabilities are in a **functional curriculum,** such as a life skills or vocational

---

[1] We will not directly address SLI in this text, as students with SLI are served primarily by trained speech and language pathologists.

TABLE 1.1: Disability Categories Currently Served under the IDEA, with Percentage of Special Education Population

Mild/Moderate Disability Categories	Intensive Disability Categories
Specific learning disability (45.3%)	Other health impairments (9.3%)
Speech or language impairments (19.0%)	Autism (3.2%)
Mental retardation (8.9%)	Multiple disabilities (2.2%)
Emotional disturbance (7.9%)	Developmental delay (1.3%)
	Hearing impairments (1.2%)
	Orthopedic impairments (1.0%)
	Visual impairments (0.4%)
	Traumatic brain injury (0.4%)
	Deafness-blindness (<0.1%)

Note: Percentages do not total 100 percent due to rounding.
Data from U.S. Department of Education. Individuals with Disabilities Education Act (IDEA) (Table 1.3). (Washington, DC: U.S. DOE. 2007. www.ideadata.org/PartBReport.asp).

training program. In practice, however, the term *mild* is typically used alone. (A label preferred by some is *high incidence* to signify the commonality of these disabilities.)

CASE 1.1　Three Elementary School Students: Maria, Sy, and Burton

Case Introduction

In this case, you are introduced to three students with mild disabilities in Yoko Yoshita's inclusive classroom. As you read the case, you will notice that they each have some difficulties in class, but so do some of their classmates. Teachers face the challenge of knowing when a learning difference is a disability and what to do about it when they suspect that it is. As you read the case, ask yourself what special education services the students need.

At the end of the case, you will find case questions. These questions are meant to serve as points for reflection. Of course, if you can answer them immediately, you should do so, but you may want to wait to answer them until you have read that portion of the chapter that pertains to the particular case question. Throughout the rest of the chapter, you will see the same questions. As you see them, try to answer them based upon that portion of the chapter that you just read.

Yoko Yoshita was starting her first year as a general education teacher in a third-grade inclusive classroom at Gamon Elementary School. She was surprised to find that some of her special education students performed as well or even better in certain areas than some of the typically developing students. Maria, Sy, and Burton were among the students with disabilities in Yoko's class of 21.

Maria was extremely shy. She would seldom ask for help, volunteer to answer a question, or participate in a fun activity. Maria also tended to sit still and observe her classmates when she was supposed to be partnering with them; sometimes she would work alone—seemingly unaware she was supposed to be participating with others. She had one "friend," whom Yoko noticed usually bossed Maria around. Maria typically withdrew from other students and remained silent if they tried to be social with her. While in second grade, Maria had been identified as having an emotional disturbance, specifically that she was experiencing depression. Yoko knew that shyness and demure behavior were common for Mexican American girls who lived in the community, so she was often confused as to when Maria's behaviors were related to her disability.

continued

Saed, who went by Sy, was a quiet student, but not shy like Maria. Sy's family had moved to the United States within the last year. He had learned some English when they still lived in Palestine, but his mother and father tended to speak Arabic at home. Understanding that language differences held him back, Yoko was comfortable with the amount of work and socializing that Sy did. At the same time, she noted that he seemed to have difficulty developing sight-word vocabularies and recognizing sounds made by letters and letter blends. Feeling that she was not meeting his needs, Yoko sought the help of a team of colleagues. That team included Sy's second-grade teacher, a teacher of English as a second language (ESL) whom Sy saw three times a week, and a special educator, all of whom worked closely with Yoko and Sy's parents. Together, they attempted different instructional activities and kept records of how the activities benefited Sy. Based on a referral by Yoko and her colleagues, Sy was identified as having a learning disability.

Burton was what Yoko's principal referred to as "all boy." It seemed like he always found excuses to move around the classroom; if something interested him more than what Yoko wanted him to attend to, for example the dinosaurs on the bookshelf or manipulatives for math time, he couldn't resist going after them anyway. The principal made her observation about Burton in late October when Yoko commented that he was a very nice boy but too disruptive and distracted compared to the other children in her room. Yoko kept careful observations of what he did and the results of different efforts she made to help him control his behavior. She also kept her principal informed and spoke to Burton's parents, whom she found were at their wit's end with his behavior at home as well. In early spring, Burton was identified as having attention deficit/hyperactivity disorder. Yoko asked her principal for an aide to help her manage Burton. The principal instead arranged for a district behavior specialist to visit the classroom every once in a while. This was not listed on the individualized education program of services for Burton.

Yoko's first year of teaching was challenging. She was prepared for the reality that first-year teachers spend a lot of evenings and weekends in their classrooms. She also knows that she still has a lot to learn, and is glad that she has colleagues on whom she may call as resources.

CASE QUESTIONS

1. In what ways could Sy's primary language impact the process of determining whether he has a learning disability?

2. In what ways could Maria's ethnic culture impact the process of determining whether she has an emotional disturbance?

3. For each student, what are common characteristics associated with their specific disability?

Learning Disabilities

The IDEA includes the category of disability as "specific learning disability," with "specific" meaning that it impacts people in specific categories of academic skill. The definition of specific learning disability cites a significant limitation in acquiring and/or expressing information in one or more of the following areas of using language: listening, speaking, reading, writing, spelling, mathematical calculations, or reasoning (Federal Register 2006), with approximately 80 percent of those with LD having difficulty with reading (Snow, Burns, and Griffin 1998). This is important to remember because if you are teaching students with LD, chances are good that you will be remediating their reading skills. You must also remember that, although some students with an LD are affected in just one area (for example, reading), most are impacted in multiple areas (for example, reading, writing, and memory).

Just as no two students learn alike, we have increasingly come to understand that no one cognitive disorder makes up a learning disability; rather, LD is a "heterogeneous group of disorders" (National Joint Committee on Learning Disabilities [NJCLD] 1989). That explains why one student with LD may have difficulty with beginning reading skills (for example, recognizing letters or letter blends), whereas another may have trouble with higher-level reading skills (such as discerning main ideas or inferring meaning). Still another student might have difficulties in writing, mathematics, or organization, but not in reading. The commonality that unites all students with LD is that they process information differently than others and experience low academic achievement because of it. Put simply, an LD is an unexplained failure to learn among students with average or above-average intelligence (Fuchs et al. 2003; Stanovich 2005).

What LD "Looks Like" and How It Is Experienced. Despite good instruction, students with LD have great difficulty processing information as they learn. This difficulty in processing is often evidenced in poor performance in academic areas such as reading, written language, and math. Although some learning difficulties are common among all students with LD (for example, phonological processing problems are among the most common problems for students with LD), there is no one type of learning disability, as we mentioned before.

As a consequence of slower learning rates and difficulties with comprehension and recall, students with LD tend to have a limited number of approaches for addressing a learning task, such as determining an unknown word (Hallahan et al. 2005; Meese 2001; Harris, Reid, and Graham 2004). For example, think of all the different strategies you can use when reading an unknown multisyllabic word. You can sound it out, examine prefixes, use context clues to guess what it means, look it up, or use one of several other effective practices. Students with LD typically have only one or two skills in their repertoire for dealing with the multisyllabic word. Thus, when they attempt to read an unfamiliar word and are not successful, they tend to laboriously persevere, trying the same approach over and over again, or they simply give up. The reason for this is that they lack sufficient control of the cognitive skills needed for this reading task.

Cognitive Processing Difficulties. This inefficient approach to learning for students with LD can be characterized as *nonstrategic* (Harris, Reid, and Graham 2004). A strategic approach to performing a task would involve recognizing the task demands (for example, reading an unfamiliar word), identifying options for how to approach the task (for example, using context clues, decoding), selecting an appropriate option, and following that plan for completing the task. While following the plan, strategic students monitor whether they have followed the steps to the plan and evaluate whether or not the plan is working. When necessary, the students must decide to stick with the planned strategy, select a new one, or alter the original version (for example, Pressley 2002; White and Frederiksen 2005). Not all successful approaches to task performance are strategic, because if any of those elements are missing the students probably take a "hit-or-miss" approach to solving the task or use a rote routine to solve the task. For students with LD, this nonstrategic approach often leads to the use of rote memory and typically ends in task failure or poor performance on the task (compare to Langner 1997).

When students are nonstrategic, they may lack strategies or the ability to think strategically. Being able to think strategically (described by some as executive control or **executive functioning;** Meltzer et al. 2001) is the coordination of all of the previously named skills that are involved in being strategic.

Strategic learners plan, execute, and evaluate task performance. Research supports our understanding of executive functioning as knowledge about how a strategy works (procedural knowledge), why a strategy works (declarative knowledge), and knowledge of when a strategy will be appropriate or need to be modified (conditional knowledge) (Flavell 1979; Pressley 2001). Students who fail to employ strategies they know may only have learned them as a collection of steps and not as a strategic process that they control. (See Chapter 3 for more on executive function, metacognition, and strategies.)

Many students with LD also have difficulties with cognitive organization (Mastropieri and Scruggs 2007), which is related to strategic planning. This means that they are not aware of relationships among facts or concepts and they do not discern between salient and noncritical information. Recognizing relationships, which includes inferring them, is essential to storing information in memory and comprehending concepts (Searlman and Herrmann 1994). By being inactive in their approach while receiving new information or thinking through complex thoughts, students with LD do not consider how a concept relates to other concepts they know. Without recognizing such relationships, new information is less relevant and meaningful, and more difficult to learn. Examples of this lack of cognitive organization include difficulty grasping new concepts or following directions, forgetting information they seemed to have learned, expressing themselves in disorganized fashions, presenting information out of logical order, excluding critical content, emphasizing what should be tangentially related information, and not fully expressing details.

Academic Skills Difficulties. Busy classroom teachers are likely first to observe evidence of problems in cognitive processes among students with LD as difficulties in listening, speaking, reading, writing, calculating, or problem solving.

Reading is the most common academic skill affected by a learning disability (Mercer and Pullen 2005). Reading comprises a complex array of skills (see Chapters 5 and 6) that range from recognizing letters to extrapolating and generalizing meaning of complex text. Written language and oral language skills rely on some of the same cognitive processes involved in reading and may result in difficulties with spelling, word choice, and organization of information for students with LD. In all of these academic skill areas, students may demonstrate difficulties with only a subset of a skill and perform well in other skill-related areas.

Students with LD may also have difficulty with attention and concentration. They may have difficulty initially attending to a task or may be easily distracted. In addition, some students with LD may exhibit hyperactivity and impulsivity. Learning disabilities and ADHD can be comorbid conditions (that is, they are both present in an individual and are related to one another) (Riccio, Gonzalez, and Hynd 1994; Smith, Dowdy, et al. 1997). Although those with learning disabilities face a variety of academic difficulties, they can also be average learners in many other areas and may even excel in some areas (see the following Methods and Strategies Spotlight).

Social Skills Difficulties. In addition to their academic strengths and weaknesses, those with LD can be socially fragile. Some students report having few friends (Donahue, Pearl, and Bryan 1980; Mehring and Colson 1990), and observational

METHODS AND STRATEGIES SPOTLIGHT

Gifted and LD

Learning disabilities are often thought of in terms of deficits, or the things students cannot do well. Consequently, we can form negative views of students' potential. So much of the focus of special education for LD is on remediating what students have difficulty doing that we tend to forget LD is a learning *difference*, not an *inability*. We can even find ourselves forgetting that an LD impacts only certain areas of a student's cognition and achievement. A particular subgroup of those students with LD should remind us just how heterogeneous learning disabilities are: students who have an LD but are gifted. Such students are sometimes referred to as **twice exceptional.**

Students who are twice exceptional have the following three characteristics:

- A significant discrepancy between aptitude and achievement
- Evidence of a cognitive processing deficit
- An outstanding talent or ability (Mills and Brody 1999), such as music, writing, or mathematics

Twice exceptional learners have been estimated to represent between 2 percent to 5 percent of all school students (LD Online, 2007). We often have difficulty recognizing the dual exceptionalities of these learners. Sometimes their cognitive and academic difficulties "compete" with their cognitive strengths, and they are not able to demonstrate what they are capable of (for example, a student with significant reading difficulties will have difficulty in a math class that relies heavily on reading and writing skills). In other cases, we observe the low achievement that results from their LD and fail to notice their exceptional abilities that are a sign of giftedness (Mills and Brody 1999; see also Ferri, Gregg, and Heggoy 1997).

Although researchers disagree little as to whether LD and giftedness can coexist, it is relatively uncommon for schools to recognize both conditions in a student (Gardynik and McDonald 2005). This may be because school personnel do not accept that students with LD can also excel intellectually (Gardynik and McDonald 2005). Such thinking represents a fundamental misconception of the condition of learning disabilities.

Once educators get past their shortsightedness about whether LD and giftedness can coexist, they should find providing appropriate interventions easy. Many of the same intervention approaches appropriate to serving those with LD are appropriate for gifted students. Effective approaches include the following:

- Matching instructional level and pace to the individual student's interests and learning needs
- Varying instructional levels for subject or topic areas across the curriculum (for example, the student participates in an English language arts curriculum below the level of classmates and in a mathematics curriculum above classmates)
- Using technology to help students progress at a personally appropriate pace (see Lovett and Lewandowski 2006, for source citations and further details)

When twice exceptional students receive services appropriate to both their giftedness and their LD, they tend to be more motivated, to have high self-esteem, and to improve academic performance (see Gardynik and McDonald 2005).

evidence indicates that their classmates do not wish to associate with them academically or socially (Donahue, Pearl, and Bryan 1980). Why this happens is not well known; however, some students with LD can appear socially awkward, in part because of the social rejection they experience, and because they have difficulty processing social cues. Moreover, some students may not be actively processing while in social situations and may not know how to conduct themselves in certain contexts (for example, cooperative groups, whole class participation, recess, the cafeteria, or locker room) (Hutchinson, Freeman, and Berg 2004). Still, some students with LD are well liked, in both social and academic settings. This is probably because of the limited ways their LD affects them, because of their own coping skills, or because they use more positive social skills (Raskind et al. 1999). Sy is an example of a student who seems to be coping well in all regards but reading.

Depending upon how the LD affects these students, how well the students cope with it, and how well it is supported, the students may signal their difficulty in a variety of ways. In addition to exhibiting skill difficulty, the student may not complete work, may always earn below-norm grades, may appear frustrated, or may act out aggressively or as the class clown in an attempt to avoid uncomfortable situations. Dropping out of school is another possibility for students with LD, particularly for those who become frustrated with school (Scanlon and Mellard 2002; Wagner 1991).

THINK BACK TO THE CASE with the three students: Maria, Sy, and Burton . . .

1. *In what ways could Sy's primary language impact the process of determining whether he has a learning disability?*

Sy demonstrated slow development of a variety of reading skills normally expected of a third grader. The cultural adjustments and limited English instruction Sy faced certainly could have been factors in his slow reading development. Focusing solely on those factors, however, could obscure attention to any cognitive difficulties he may be having. He seems also to have memory difficulties with language tasks. That could be a sign of a learning disability. Language differences could also confound accurate assessment of his language and cognitive abilities (Haager 2007).

Sometimes teachers are slow to observe or believe a student's skill difficulties. Some teachers may attribute poor performance to lack of effort. Teachers may think this in the case of students who actually have LD because they may appear average in every regard, including academic performance, with the exception of the skill area affected. Take, for example, a student with LD who has excellent analytic skills, is an average speller, and who produces an excellent outline for a paper assignment, but who then turns in an essay that is nearly incomprehensible at the sentence and paragraph levels. This is an example of someone who may have an LD. Moreover, the student may have a persistent difficulty with expressing what she or he knows and planned to express, or with expressing in general or unique to writing. In this example, a specific skill area is affected. Students with LD are also prone to *learned helplessness*. This means that they have low motivation to persevere in academic tasks that are challenging to them, and they may avoid attempting them.

Attention Deficit/ Hyperactivity Disorder

Like LD, attention deficit/hyperactivity disorder (ADHD) is considered to be a cognitive disorder intrinsic to the individual. It can include difficulty gaining and/or sustaining attention; it may additionally or alternatively include difficulty regulating one's own behavior, which appears as hyperactivity and impulsivity. There is variation across individuals with ADHD in terms of how they are affected. Thus, people who have ADHD have one of three subtypes: (a) predominately inattentive, (b) predominately hyperimpulsive, or (c) combined inattentive and hyperimpulsive. According to the *Diagnostic and Statistical Manual* (DSM) definition, ADHD critically impacts functioning, occurs in two or more settings, and has its onset before the age of seven (American Psychiatric Association [APA] 1994; 2000). Unlike LD, ADHD is diagnosed by a medical doctor, not an educational psychologist and team of educators.

A common misconception is that students with ADHD cannot receive services under the IDEA. The IDEA states that students with ADHD are entitled to services under the other health impairment (OHI) category (see Sec. 300.8 (c)(9)(i), 46757). The definition for this category includes the criterion "chronic or acute" problems. Historically, that standard has caused confusion as to when students with ADHD satisfy the eligibility criteria because judging the level of ADHD-type behaviors in that way is subjective; in fact, all students engage some of these behaviors some of the time (Hallahan et al. 2005). In response, the United States Department of Education has clarified that students with ADHD can be eligible for IDEA services for the condition "ADD/ADHD," when categorized within OHI or when coexisting with another eligible disability (Davila, Williams, and MacDonald 1991; Wodrich 2000). Both learning disabilities and emotional/behavioral disorders are sometimes comorbid with ADHD. Because students with ADHD are counted under different disability labels, just what percentage of the population is served can only be estimated. The National Institute of Mental Health (2006) reports that perhaps less than half of children and adolescents with ADHD have cases that meet the criteria for the IDEA. An estimated 3 percent to 5 percent of the school-age population may have ADHD (APA 2000).

Students with ADHD may be entitled to services under Section 504 because it relies on a general definition of "disability," instead of naming and defining qualifying disabilities as the IDEA does.

What ADHD "Looks Like" and How It Is Experienced. Being easily distracted, daydreaming during class, feeling the urge to get up and walk around, or becoming interested in another student's work are some examples of behaviors that can characterize "typical" students. Yet, these rather benign behaviors are the very same classic traits of people with ADHD. Benign behaviors become those associated with ADHD when they occur at chronic or acute levels and the individual has difficulty regulating them. A good way to judge whether the behaviors are inappropriate and whether the students are having difficulty regulating them is to compare their performances to that of their peers (for example, same age, same gender, same topic). See Table 1.2 for examples of common behaviors of students with ADHD at different age levels. In addition, educators should observe carefully whether the behaviors in question interfere with the students' positive academic and social performances. In Case 1.1, Yoko used exactly that

TABLE 1.2: Example Characteristics of Students with ADHD at Different Age Levels

Preschool		
Accidents due to acting independently Non-compliance	Resists routines Aggressive in play	Excessive talk Easily upset
Elementary/Middle School		
Fidgeting Out of seat	Interrupting Inconsistent productivity	Dependence on adults Poor social skills
Middle/Senior High		
Restless Substance use	Low self-concept Procrastination	Impulsive Difficulty following directions

Reprinted with data from M. Fowler, *Ch.A.D.D. Manual.* (Fairfax, VA: CASET Association, 1992), and S. E. Shaywitz and B. A. Shaywitz, "Attention Deficit Disorder: Current Perspectives," in *Learning Disabilities*, ed. J. F. Kavanagh and T. J. Truss (Parkton, MD: York. 1988, 369–523).

process to document that Burton was more active than would reasonably be expected.

ADHD behaviors that can be more difficult to notice are distractibility and inattentiveness associated with the ADHD-inattentive subtype. Distractibility means students' attention can easily be diverted from important tasks. Distracted students chronically attend to what others are doing, routinely get off task by focusing on something else, or instantaneously stop paying attention, even in the middle of one-on-one conversations. They are the students who have difficulty focusing their attention in the first place, seem never to get started with a task, or do not pay attention to details. Typically, distractibility and inattentiveness occur in combination in students with ADHD.

Cognitive Processing Difficulties. The unique cognitive processes of students with ADHD have been characterized as problems with *inhibition* (Barkley 2000). Typical, nondisabled students do not act on their impulses; rather they control them—their inhibitions prevent them from acting on their thoughts. From this perspective, those with ADHD simply do not self-regulate their thought processes. When they get an idea, they impulsively act on it, instead of evaluating its appropriateness. If they detect a distraction in their environment, they attend to it instead of channeling their focus. Uninhibited cognitive processing is believed to be a form of limited executive function. Different from the limited executive function in those with LD, the appropriate cognitive behavior for students with ADHD may be within their repertoire; however, it merely is not selected.

Barkley (2000) has suggested that people with ADHD are uninhibited specifically in the areas of *time awareness* and *time management*. He suggests that they do not consider the relation of time to themselves; instead, they act spontaneously rather than delay or regulate their actions. Moreover, they do not organize tasks based upon priority or take into account the proportion of time or effort necessary to complete a task efficiently. In addition, individuals with ADHD may have difficulties with working memory (ibid.). For example, they do not retain and attend to information in working memory, or they fail to attend to salient information, which results in poor comprehension.

Academic Skill Difficulties. Although there is a cognitive explanation for ADHD behaviors, the learning difficulties associated with ADHD are, in effect, secondary consequences. It is the consequence of being distracted or inattentive that results in students missing important information or producing poor quality work (LeFever et al., 2002; Salend and Rohena 2003). Academically, students with ADHD do not achieve commensurate with their peers (Stubbe 2000) because they do not fully learn information. They often rush through assignments and do not check their work. When confronted with the consequences of being off task or doing low-quality work, these students will often respond in a panic mode to redo and catch up on their work, resulting again in a low quality or quantity of work. Effective intervention responses address both regulating behavior patterns and remediating academic content and skills.

Social Skills Difficulties. Socially, the status of students with ADHD depends on how the condition manifests itself. The students' distractibility behaviors may be barely noticed by their peers, or at least not be of a concern to them. Those with hyperimpulsive behavior are more likely to be noticed. They might garner a reputation for being the class clown if their off-task and out-of-seat behaviors constantly cause them to be viewed as "goofy," or they might get a reputation as class rebel if they come across to their peers as defying the teacher's attempts to have them participate in activities. Peers are more likely to resent students with ADHD if the students' behaviors bring negative consequences to the peers (Merrell and Wolfe 1998; Ratey, Hallowell, and Miller 1997); other students in the class may be distracted from their own work, penalized by the student for not fulfilling expected contributions to a group task, or offended or even harmed by the student's actions.

Mild Mental Retardation

Those not familiar with the subtypes of mental retardation might be surprised that it can be included under the category of mild disability. The subtypes constitute a range of mental retardation, divided into four levels of functioning (mild: IQ 50–55 to approximately 70; moderate: IQ 35–40 to 50–55; severe: IQ 20–25 to 35–40; and profound: IQ below 20–25). The DSM-IV (APA 1994; 2000) states that the distinctions among the four levels relate to intelligence quotient (IQ) and adaptive functioning; however, in practice, the labels are typically assigned based on IQ alone. (Visit this textbook's website for a description of an alternative labeling system endorsed by many mental retardation professionals but not adopted by the IDEA.) Mild mental retardation (MMR) is the highest functioning level of retardation; it is the only one of the four considered mild.

To have mild mental retardation means that a person's overall cognitive functioning is impaired to a degree that significantly limits age-appropriate functioning (note that "significantly" differs from "severely"). Cognitive functioning encompasses abilities such as comprehension, reasoning, abstract thinking, and memory.

People with mental retardation have limitations in multiple areas of cognitive functioning. Unlike those with LD, who need support in using their cognitive skills efficiently, or those with ADHD who are impulsively distracted from employing appropriate skills, those with mild mental retardation are thought to have limited aptitude in terms of cognitive skills. Especially in the MMR subtype of retardation, the notion of limited capacity does not mean an absolute limit to what an individual is capable of learning. Those with retardation at all levels are always capable of learning new things. They typically learn slowly and in very concrete ways, needing constant review and support to apply their knowledge (Miller, Hall, and Heward 1995).

The label *mild* is the hardest part of MMR to define. Those with MMR function well in the regular education environment and can be semi-independent in daily living. Conversely, those with profound retardation perform cognitively at very low levels, including in their ability to learn, and, hence, need almost constant assistance. The difficulty in defining "mild" is in operationally defining it.

What MMR "Looks Like" and How It Is Experienced. Because MMR is a cognitive disorder, physical indicators or characteristics may not always accompany it (for example, those with Down syndrome often exhibit physical characteristics such as an almond shape to the eyes, shorter limbs and digits, and protruding tongue). Indeed, students with MMR can have such proficient social skills and independent living skills that one may not realize that they have MMR.

Academically, students with MMR will likely be behind others in the class by roughly two or more years in skill levels (for example, reading or math). In addition to academic skills, students with MMR may also be delayed in the areas of social, emotional, and independent functioning skills. Students with MMR will also learn new skills and concepts at a much slower rate than classmates, particularly as the complexity of the skills or concepts increases. Thus, the older the students, the further behind they will be. Students with MMR also tend to forget skills and concepts that are not routinely reinforced by drill and practice.

Cognitive Processing Difficulties. Students with MMR have difficulties gaining and sustaining attention, in a different manner than the attention difficulties of students with ADHD. Because students with MMR do not discern where to focus their attention, they may observe a procedure (for example, for an arithmetic calculation), but not identify the critical actions of each step or the order in which to perform the steps. They may also pay attention to extraneous information rather than to critical information. As part of the difficulty with regulating their attention, they may shift their attention to extraneous information either because they found it interesting or were unable to distinguish it as unimportant information. It appears that students with MMR do not have the executive control to remain focused on critical content.

Students with MMR also have difficulties with the three stages of memory: short-term, working, and long-term. Short-term memory is particularly difficult for them (Bray, Fletcher, and Turner 1997). As a consequence of not attending to details and recognizing relationships that help give new information significance, information tends to be poorly grasped. Although students with MMR are prone to forgetting information in long-term memory, especially when not regularly rehearsed, their long-term memory capacity is not as limited as their short-term capacity (ibid.).

Academic Skills Difficulties. Due to their lack of attention to salient details and their poor comprehension, those with MMR typically require more exposure to content and more practice opportunities to comprehend and recall information accurately (Miller, Hall, and Heward 1995). Actual processing time can be slower for students with MMR as well. Thus, they will require a longer time to think about an appropriate response or to recall a needed skill, as well as guidance with the process in many cases.

Typically, students with MMR need to learn new tasks in concrete ways. Tasks that require abstract reasoning, drawing complex relationships, or constructing inferences can be challenging for them. Thus, "lower-level" skills are learned more efficiently. In reading, skills of word calling and reading of "comfort-level" passages that do not include complex concepts will be more successful than more abstract skills such as passage comprehension. In math, simple operations will be performed with greater success than problem-solving activities.

Generalization (also referred to as transfer) is also a challenge for those with MMR. This means the ability to apply knowledge or skills to tasks similar or different from those with which the skill was learned. Whereas other learners may learn a skill in drill and practice and then readily apply it (for example, generalizing arithmetic facts to word problems), students with MMR may need to learn the skill in context so that little transfer of learning is involved.

Social Skills Difficulties. Along with cognitive and academic skills difficulties, students with MMR can experience social skills difficulties. Often, children and adolescents with MMR report dissatisfaction with the quality of friendships they have, and adults similarly perceive fewer and poorer friendships among students with MMR (Hughes et al. 1999; Siperstein, Leffert, and Wenz-Gross 1997). In other words, their friendships tend to lack intimate sharing and spontaneous interactions (Siperstein, Leffert, and Wenz-Gross 1997). Social difficulties are due in part to their concrete ways of thinking, which extend to a limited capacity to take into account the interests of others and to express oneself fully. Also, those with MMR do not always present themselves in socially appealing ways. For example, coming across as stubborn or aggressive when they are frustrated with a task (Cook and Semmell 1999) may not be an appealing trait to other students. In addition, as they progress into the adolescent years, their friendships tend to decline (Hughes et al. 1999).

Some peers may not wish to associate with students with MMR for fear it will cause them to be socially ostracized. In other cases, students without disabilities will befriend those with MMR, not so much out of personal bonding, but out of wishing to do a good deed. Although true friendships can flower from such arrangements (for example, the Best Buddies program; www.bestbuddies .org), it can be the basis for an unequal relationship where the "friend" with MMR is treated differently than a nondisabled friend. In the case of academics, classmates with MMR may not be welcome by peers when working on group projects for fear those with MMR will prevent the group earning a good grade. However, although they may have fewer friends and more strained friendships than others, those with MMR also do have genuine friendships with peers who care about them just as they would any other friend. Also, despite potential obstacles to including students with MMR in regular education classrooms, their presence has increased over the years and has resulted in positive academic and social outcomes for all students (Williamson et al. 2006).

Emotional or Behavioral Disorders

Emotional or behavioral disorders (EBD) can be thought of as distinct from one another. One concerns emotions (or feelings and moods), whereas the other relates to actions a person makes. In a practical sense, however, both aspects are often present in a person with EBD. Those with EBD may have emotional problems that manifest as behavioral problems. Therefore, an appropriate response would address the emotional needs as well as the behavioral needs.

There is considerable professional disagreement as to the nature of this disorder. The disagreements are highlighted by the differences of opinion about what to call it. Even the way the IDEA 2004 names this disability is confusing. After first naming the condition as "serious emotional disturbance," the IDEA then states "referred to . . . as 'emotional disturbance'" (*Federal Register*, August 14, 2006, (300.8)(a), 46756). The term *serious* is one point of contention, with some professionals arguing that the word is pejorative and that an adjective (that is, serious) is not used in any other disability category under the IDEA. Likewise confusing, many professionals today prefer to use the term *behaviorally disordered* (BD), noting that the term *emotional* carries many negative connotations that tend to influence perceptions and service options. Citing concerns that the disability may nonetheless have something to do with an emotional disorder or a combined condition, the Council for Children with Behavior Disorders (CCBD)—a division of the special education professional organization the Council for Exceptional Children (CEC)—proposed instead to refer to the condition as **emotional or behavioral disorder** (*Federal Register, 59 (131), February 10, 1993*) (see also Forness and Knitzer 1992). Since then, the label EBD is fairly commonly used among school-based professionals.

Despite the controversy about which specific label to use, most professionals broadly recognize that students with EBD have similar characteristics. Students with EBD have chronic difficulties in one or more areas involving socialization with others, unusual behaviors or emotions under normal circumstances, a general mood of unhappiness or depression, and physical or emotional reactions such as fearful responses to school or personal problems. In addition, these chronic problems adversely affect educational performance and are often not easily treated.

What EBD "Looks Like" and How It Is Experienced. Some of the indicators of EBD are far more obvious than others. The distinction, however, is not based on emotional versus behavioral type. The different types of EBD are traditionally separated into those categories that are primarily **externalized**—or overt outward performances—or those that are **internalized**—or characterized by withdrawing and acting toward the self, including by self-neglect (Lambros et al. 1998). See Table 1.3 for partial lists of common externalized and internalized behaviors.

TABLE 1.3: Common Externalized and Internalized Behaviors of Students with EBD

Externalized Behaviors	Internalized Behaviors
Violent outbursts	Isolated play
Angered reactions	Frequent claims of being ill
Emotional mood swings	Depression
Physical or aggressive actions	Cutting or mutilation of self
Tantrums	Extreme shyness
Destructiveness	Disregard by peers
Disrespectfulness and noncompliance	Anorexia
Sexual promiscuity	Panic attacks

Cognitive Processing Difficulties. Those students who have EBD have cognitive processing difficulties that interfere with academic functioning. They may become profoundly depressed at times, obsessed about their own body image, or filled with deep rage, that they are not able to focus on academic tasks. Although a subset of those with EBD miss a large amount of school (Bauer and Shea 1999), many miss out on schooling by not fully attending cognitively because of these emotional or behavioral problems. Many of these students develop gaps in skills, such as performing well in reading, but not math. Unlike students with ADHD, students with EBD do not have limited ability for *performing* needed cognitive skills for learning per se, but rather have difficulty *regulating* their cognitive skill performance. As a result, they often score below average on tests of intelligence and achievement (Coleman and Webber 2002; Kauffman 1997). The answer as to whether interferences with cognitive processes lead to their diminished scores or vice versa likely depends on the individual student in question. What is certain is that those with EBD have difficulty attending, perceiving information correctly, and making logical deductions and decisions.

Academic Skill Difficulties. One indicator of an EBD is poor academic performance due to gaps in knowledge and skills (Gresham, Lane, et al. 1999). There are not specific skills that students with EBD are most likely to have difficulty with; rather, they merely have problems in some skill areas. Some of the specific disabilities that fall within the EBD category can directly relate to limited comprehension or memory skills, for example. More often, however, students with EBD experience gaps in their learning because of the interruptions to learning caused by their condition. Students like Maria might not be able to concentrate because they are distracted by their depression. Regardless of whether they exhibit internalizing or externalizing behaviors, they will miss out on instruction and skills practice because of their condition. Indeed, students with EBD are often removed from the classroom because they are disruptive to other students, they need privacy to deal with emotions, they need additional support for their own personal safety or the safety of others, or they need to receive related services.

⏩ ▶ ⏪

VIDEO CASE CONNECTIONS BOX

━━⚪━━━━━━━━━━━━━

Watch the Video Case entitled *Handling a Student with Behavior Problems*. Make a list of the specific ways that Peter's behaviors can result in gaps in his learning. Next, watch the bonus video, *Classroom Management Challenges Experienced by Most New Teachers*. Note which of Peter's behaviors on your list distinguish students with EBD from the types of challenging behaviors most typically developing students present from time to time.

Social Skills Difficulties. Students with EBD tend to be unpopular (Kauffman 1997) among peers regardless of whether they have internalizing or externalizing behaviors. On the one hand, those with primarily internalized behaviors might more accurately be described as *unnoticed*. For example, students with eating disorders often go a long time before others realize they have a problem. Depressed students like Maria in Case 1.1 can be thought of as only shy, unless her shyness turns into chronic and acute withdrawal from others. In Maria's case, her withdrawn behavior can easily be overlooked in the busy milieu of a school. On the other hand, because of the mood swings and atypical behaviors of students with EBD, classmates may find them "odd" and not wish to interact with them; unfortunately, teachers may also avoid interacting with these students (Feldman et al. 1983).

Externalized behaviors are considered far more problematic in schools because of their disruptive nature. These behaviors are "in your face," may pose a threat to the climate of the classroom, and may place the student or others in danger. Students who lash out in anger, bully others, or break down are easily noticed and hard to ignore. For the sake of safety and personal privacy, externalizing behaviors are also likely to garner more immediate responses, such as removing the student from the classroom so as not to prolong others witnessing these actions or expelling the student from school for serious acts.

Students with EBD make themselves known primarily in association with their internalized or externalized behaviors. Sometimes they "grow into" the

THINK BACK TO THE CASE with the three students: Maria, Sy, and Burton . . .

2. *In what ways could Maria's ethnic culture impact the process of determining whether she has an emotional disturbance?*

Cultural behaviors, such as the shyness and demure behavior that Yoko observed among Mexican American girls, can confound the evidence possibly indicating an EBD. Latinas and Native American students are sometimes reticent to assert themselves in school, even in such expected ways as answering questions, demonstrating their knowledge, or asking for help (Sparks 2000). In contrast, Webb-Johnson (2002) observed that culturally typical expressive behaviors of African American students with EBD were often discouraged. As a consequence, the students either acted out more than they would in a culturally responsive environment or focused more on behavioral compliance than on academic engagement.

behaviors, so indicators such as the depression-linked behaviors Yoko saw in Maria should be carefully considered so that difficulties do not escalate.

In conclusion, of all the students with mild disabilities, those with EBD are the most likely to be removed from the regular education classroom or building because of their disability (U.S. Department of Education 2006). Often they are considered to be among the most challenging students to teach. Like all students with disabilities, they do challenge teachers who, unlike Yoko, fear academic diversity and consider it beyond their capability or job description. However, when teachers collaborate with other educators, service providers, and parents and use the student's individualized education program (IEP) to guide them (read on to the next section of this chapter), they can be successful in including students with EBD in the general education classroom and, in the process, help those students manage their disability.

Chapter Question
ALERT

In this section you will find information that answers a Chapter Question:

2. What instructional practices have been proven by research to benefit students with mild disabilities?

Meeting the Learning Needs of Students with Mild Disabilities

There is a phrase that we special educators often hear. Almost as often as someone asks what we do for a living, we hear, "you must have a lot of patience." That is very telling of what people think about students with disabilities and what it takes to teach them. There might be some truth to it, but it misses by a mile what special education teaching is all about. Special educators do have some methods of teaching that are different from what general educators typically use, but, for the most part, we teach the same content and skills that general educators do. The special education student's knowledge outcomes are typically the same too, which is to say they know many of the same things and can do most of the same things as other students.

Each of the mild disabilities was explained to you as a difference in how students process information during the stages of acquiring, constructing, and expressing knowledge. Special educators employ principles of effective practice that are based upon the strengths and needs of students with mild disabilities. What is different about special education students is that, more so than their regular education peers, they exhibit gaps in skills and they are less likely to benefit from traditional teaching methods used in regular education classrooms. Students with mild disabilities tend to have a limited range of learning strengths and, therefore, need to be instructed in specific ways if they are going to benefit fully from a lesson.

THINK BACK TO THE CASE with the three students: Maria, Sy, and Burton . . .

3. *Given the learning challenges that Maria, Sy, and Burton present, are there generally effective teaching practices Yoko should use with them?*

Yes. The following are facts about the ways students with mild disabilities learn best. They are translated into important **principles of effective instruction.**

Principles of Effective Special Education Practice

Researchers have identified the following practices as effective for students with mild disabilities. Their regular education peers also benefit when these practices are used. So, special *and* general educators can use these practices in pull-out or inclusive settings.

Clear and Explicit Instruction. To provide clear and explicit instruction means that teachers are unambiguous and leave no doubt as to what they are communicating to students (Good and Brophy 2003). Some students with mild disabilities have poor attention and distractibility. They may not pick up on essential details during instruction. Students with mild disabilities even more commonly have difficulties with short-term memory and recognizing how information is organized. They are typically not efficient at making inferences and drawing relationships between and among knowledge and skills. Students with such difficulties may become confused if content and skills are presented in a disorganized fashion. Those students benefit from instruction that is *clear* and *explicit*.

Students in general education classrooms are expected to make assumptions about what they hear or read, make connections to prior knowledge as well as among the new knowledge they are acquiring/constructing, and think about the demands of the task. General education students can more often perform those operations automatically and without hesitation. Conversely, students with mild disabilities perform those cognitive skills poorly—in quality and consistency. In other words, students with mild disabilities need to be taught how to perform them and need frequent cues to help them remember to use those newly learned skills and strategies.

To be clear and explicit, teachers should first think carefully about whether their explanations (or directions) name a topic (for example, say: "You are to *write an essay* that *tells me* . . ." or "When your numerator, *remember that's the number on the top, the one you are dividing into*, is bigger than your denominator . . ."). They should also consider whether each of the major concepts or discussion points is stated overtly and clearly (for example, "Remember, an essay is at least five paragraphs and it contains . . ." or "When people started to work in factories during the Industrial Revolution they had to leave some old work skills behind. Where did they work before factories and what kind of skills did they have that wouldn't be needed in a factory?"). Teachers should also get into the habit of asking themselves, "Do they know what I mean?" It can be helpful to ask students to repeat directions back to be sure that they fully understand them or to restate concepts "in their own words" to check for clarity.

Frequent and Intensive Instruction. Hearing information once is not likely to lead to it being transferred to long-term memory. Exposure, whether to content or skills, needs to occur multiple times, and those multiple exposures should occur in close proximity to one another (Gleason, Carnine, and Vala 1991). Frequent instruction involves providing multiple opportunities to practice new content or skills. It could mean working on the same information for three successive class sessions, instead of once during the same three-week period, for example. Intensive instruction means that students are exposed to the concept or skill a number of times within a lesson, including practice sessions. Within each of the frequent lessons, the students have multiple practice opportunities. Although drill and practice have benefits (ibid.), lessons do not need to be overly repetitive. Any concept or skill can be incorporated into further iterations of the topic, and practice activities should be varied (for example, Bulgren et al. 2000). Furthermore, because of memory difficulties and the complexities of building comprehension, students with mild disabilities are particularly prone to gaps in comprehending information and forgetting important facts when they experience delays between exposures to content or skills (Mastropieri and Scruggs 2007).

Effective learning involves contemplating knowledge and applying it. When teachers show students a new skill, the logical next step is to have them practice it. One purpose of multiple practices with informative feedback is so students can eliminate mistakes, develop proficiency, and encode the information to long-term memory. To have students develop fluency of skills, some special education techniques call for fast-paced, intensive practice (for example, Direct Instruction: Carnine, Silbert, and Kame'enui 1997; and Strategy Intervention Model: Ellis et al. 1991). Although the necessity of speedy practice can be debated, the benefit of providing students with mild disabilities with intense lessons is well established. The more frequency and intensity, the more likely new lessons can build on previous lessons instead of repeating them.

Modeling and Examples. To **model** is to demonstrate a skill or task. To provide an example is to show or explain what something is like. Students with mild disabilities particularly benefit from modeling and examples because they remove one potential source of confusion about what is being learned. With a mental image in mind, the students have a better chance of replicating the skill or comprehending a concept (Uberti, Scruggs, and Mastropieri 2003). Without a mental model or concrete representation, students would have to guess at what the expectations were and would have nothing against which to judge the quality of the product (or process) they produced. For students who have difficulty monitoring their own cognitive processes, a model used as a reference can be a tremendous help.

Think-alouds are another example of effective teaching, particularly when the task involves modeling a series of steps for students. In addition, think-alouds are important for good modeling of cognitive processes (Lenz, Ellis, and Scanlon 1996), such a cognitive strategy. In think-aloud modeling, teachers not only overtly show expected behaviors (for example, the steps of a mathematical calculation or for writing a complete paragraph), but they also demonstrate for the students what they are thinking while performing the task. This helps students to "see and hear" the cognitive thought processes involved in completing the task. Students with mild disabilities typically have inefficient cognitive processes, so modeling more appropriate thought processes is essential for them to learn the skill or task. A teacher modeling how to write a good paragraph might demonstrate clearing the desk and holding the paper and pen at the proper angles while saying, "Now that I have my paper and pen ready, I need to plan. So first I will think of the main idea of my paragraph. Let's see, I know that I am supposed to write about the life of factory workers in England during the Industrial Revolution. That's a big topic, so I need to make a specific point about it.

One thing that I think is interesting is . . ." Think-aloud modeling includes labeling the parts of the process as well. In this example, the teacher cued students to first prepare their materials and writing environment, next to plan, then to execute the plan, and so on.

Practice/Application Opportunities. Along with the principle of *frequent and intensive instruction*, providing practice through application activities is another essential component of learning. Offering multiple exposures is not enough; students need multiple chances to practice and/or apply what they have learned. This may be the point at which learning truly occurs, because it is through their use of knowledge or a skill that students come to "own" it. Students with mild disabilities may not fully appreciate a concept that they merely read about but never discuss, and they may not understand directions or a skill that they only hear about or observe. However, through practice, they come to understand and assimilate the knowledge into long-term memory.

It is almost intuitive that students will need to practice new skills; the same is true for applying concepts they learn. Application can be a low-level cognitive process such as actively thinking about something, or it can be higher-level manipulation of information that students need to comprehend, store, and later recall.

Informative Feedback. At the very least, feedback by itself tells students whether they got something right or wrong. Even more effective is feedback that is *informative*. **Informative feedback** tells students what was right or wrong from their performance of a task, or it tells them why something did or did not work and what they should change to correct their actions. A teacher might say to a student, "The reason you got that right was because . . ." or "What you want to do differently on your next attempt is . . ." These types of informative feedback statements provide students with clear, specific feedback on their performance.

Because students with mild disabilities tend to be inefficient at monitoring, modifying, and abandoning inappropriate approaches to completing a task (for example, Harris, Reid, Graham 2004), informative feedback can be valuable at helping them to correct their actions.

If teachers are unable to provide students with informative feedback due to time constraints or other limits on their instruction, they should at least provide them with **consequated feedback** (that is, telling them the consequences of their performance—right or wrong, or a total score). In doing so, students can at least judge whether they are getting the content correct or not. However, whenever possible, use informative feedback with students so that they can better gauge how well they are doing and take corrective actions to improve future performance.

Instruction within the Student's Range. Effective instruction is instruction given on a student's cognitive and instructional level. As students with mild disabilities get older, a gap can develop between what is expected of them and what they know/can do well (Baker, Gersten, and Scanlon 2002; Bulgren and Scanlon 1997/1998). As this gap continues to grow, students with disabilities may become frustrated because the skills that they are currently learning, based upon their *grade level*, may not be the same as their *knowledge level*. In those cases, they need first to learn prior knowledge and prerequisite skills.

Because students with mild disabilities are typically less proficient in abstract reasoning and understanding relationships among new and known information, they are less likely to benefit from instruction that is beyond their current knowledge of the topic. Instead, by working within their instructional level—what they are able to learn with supports—they can gradually increase the sophistication of their knowledge or skill. The cognitive psychologist Lev Vygotsky (1978) referred to this as the "zone of proximal development" (ZPD). Vygotsky suggested that students can gradually increase the "ceiling" of their capabilities, developing the potential to learn successively new and more complex information, when teachers provide appropriate supports or scaffolding.

The challenge for teachers is to try to gauge the zone for a particular student. Teachers often rely on grade-level calibrated curriculums to guide them; however, this can be a challenge when teaching students with mild disabilities that differ in cognitive processing, knowledge, and skill gaps. It can be particularly valuable for teachers of students with disabilities to conduct a pretest to determine their baseline (that is, starting level) knowledge or skills. The process can be as simple as making informal observations with careful reflection, ideally supported by student work samples. In some cases, students could give a demonstration or explanation, complete practice exercises, or a test—be it a quick probe or a comprehensive standardized measure. Information from students' IEPs should also be helpful to serve as starting points for teaching them.

Structured Instruction. Often, students aren't sure why they are learning certain bits of information, other than because the teacher said so. It would be far more instructive if students knew what they were learning and how it related to things that they previously learned or to events in their life (Lenz, Marrs, et al. 1993).

Because of inefficient or distracted learning traits, students with mild disabilities often have difficulty seeing the "big picture" of a lesson or reading. For them, it can seem like a collection of random facts and concepts. In some cases, teachers may have to present an overview of what students will learn prior to teaching. Virtually any theory of learning explains how information is understood, remembered, and recalled for usage by forming associations to other information in long-term memory (for example, schema theory, information processing theories, social constructivism; Schunk 2004; Snowman and Biehler 2006). When teachers make the organization of content overt, all learners, especially those with mild disabilities, understand its relationship to prior knowledge and better understand how it links to new knowledge.

To reveal the structure of instruction, teachers can do things as simple as orienting students to what they will be learning and why (for example, Lenz, Marrs, et al. 1993). Basically, this can occur by sharing the day's agenda with the students. Too often, teachers treat their lesson plans on a need-to-know basis with students. A much better practice would be to discuss what they will learn and how it relates to previous lessons. To further improve instruction, teachers could also discuss why the day's content matters, including how it relates to previously

Special education services should be provided in the regular education classroom whenever feasible. The special educator and regular educator need to collaborate to coordinate services in the inclusive classroom.

▼

Chapter Question

ALERT

In this section you will find information that answers a Chapter Question:

3. Where do students with mild disabilities receive their education; who provides what types of services?

learned information. When students know what is expected of them, both in terms of actions and products, the outcomes of a lesson are more likely to be achieved.

Supporting Technologies. Students with mild disabilities can benefit from the use of **instructional technologies.** These technologies can help to make the content visible, including abstract aspects of the content, such as relationships among key concepts, through the use of maps and organizers (Bulgren and Scanlon 1997/1998; Englert et al. 2007; Scanlon et al., forthcoming) or through the use of grids to help students understand the concept of place value. They also provide opportunities for students to practice technology skills as they learn about the actual skills (for example, learning how to use spell-checker properly can help students understand that spelling, punctuation, and grammar are important aspects of written compositions).

The term *technology* here means the wide range of materials that support instruction (Scanlon, forthcoming; Swanson and Hoskyn 1998). It does not have to be only those things that require a power source to operate. From this perspective, lists or figures on the chalkboard constitute technology, as do graphic devices (see Baker, Gersten, and Scanlon 2002) or laptop computers loaded with specialized hardware for reading text to students. (See more about technology in Chapter 11, "Technology and Teaching.")

The CEC standards for effective special educators (forthcoming; also see the inside cover of this text) identify additional important practices for teaching students with special needs.

The Special Education Process

CASE 1.2   **The Role of the Special Educator**

Case Introduction

In Case 1.1, you read about three students with disabilities and their regular education teacher. Now you will read about Marco, their special education teacher. As you read about

Marco, think about the role of a special educator. If students with disabilities are enrolled in an inclusion classroom, does that mean they do not need the support of a special educator? What should a special education teacher be doing all day?

continued

Should Marco function to support the regular education curriculum, or is there a separate special education curriculum for which he is responsible?

Marco is a special education teacher in Gamon Elementary, where Maria, Sy, and Burton attend. When people ask him what he teaches, he likes to reply, "It should be in-line skating, since I spend all day racing all over the building." He is commenting on the fact that he is expected to serve a number of different students, in different classrooms, and consult and collaborate with a variety of teachers every day.

When Yoko first became concerned about Burton, she asked Marco to observe her classroom a few times. Marco's observations were very helpful in assessing Burton for ADHD. At the same time, Marco already had a caseload of students in special education for which he was responsible.

Yoko just wasn't prepared for Maria's depression, and she found herself challenged. Marco came to observe and quickly determined that he needed to schedule even more time with Maria in the classroom, to try and better understand her situation. He was also able to provide Yoko with some helpful tips when she began to have difficulties teaching Sy. Their collaboration led to identifying Sy's learning disability. Yoko also needed advice on what she should be doing to work with Burton. The behavior specialist only offered general tips, and Burton had not shown any signs of improved behavior.

Marco's job is also to provide special education to a number of students, with the priority placed on students already identified with a disability. Several of those students come to see Marco in the learning center for instruction in specific skills, such as reading, math, and organization. Marco is also responsible for supporting several students who take most or all of their classes in regular education classrooms. That means that he needs to consult regularly with the classroom teachers to keep abreast of what they are doing in those rooms. He also needs to be in those rooms on a regular basis so that he can participate in setting expectations and fully know what is going on. The students also need to work closely with Marco frequently to review critical skills or for more individualized help.

Marco co-teaches math four days a week with the second-grade teacher. Four of his students are in that room.

In addition to in-line skates, Marco could use a cloning machine. He is challenged two to three times a week by being called out of his schedule. A teacher might ask for an observation or consultation, as Yoko did; a situation might arise where a child's behavior requires immediate intervention from Marco; and very often teachers send students out of class to find Marco so that he can give those students needed extra support on an assignment or test. Marco particularly resents that a few teachers in the building believe he is there only to support their teaching.

CASE QUESTIONS

1. Why do some students receive special education services seemingly indirectly in the regular education classroom whereas others go to a separate setting for their individualized instruction?
2. What should be done about students being sent to see Marco without advance notice to him? Is this just a scheduling problem?

Where Special Education Is Provided

In the early days of special education, students with mild disabilities were often segregated from their peers, both physically and in the curriculum used to teach them. Much has changed since then, and now you are more likely to find students with disabilities in general education with their special education supports being provided to them in the classroom. Some of those students are "pulled out" from time to time to receive more intensive interventions (see Table 1.4).

The Regular Education Classroom. According to the U.S. DOE (2006), 48.2 percent of all special education students aged between 6 and 21 receive at least 80 percent of their education in a regular education classroom; approximately 47 percent of those with LD and 29 percent with EBD were in regular classrooms at least 80 percent of the time (statistics for those with MMR and ADHD are not readily disaggregated from the broader disability categories in which they

TABLE 1.4: Where Students with Mild Disabilities Receive Their Education, Percentage by Disability Category

	Regular Classroom	Resource Room	Separate Classroom	Separate School	Residential School	Homebound or Hospital
Specific Learning Disability	54.5	33.7	10.9	0.6	0.2	0.2
Other Health Impairments*	56.0	28.0	12.8	1.6	0.3	1.3
Mental Retardation*	14.1	29.1	51.2	4.7	0.5	0.5
Emotional Disturbance	34.7	21.6	26.8	12.6	3.0	1.2

*Note: Recall that many students included in these IDEA categories do not have mild disabilities.
Source: Data from U.S. Department of Education. Individuals with Disabilities Education Act (IDEA) (Table 2-2c). (Washington, DC: U.S. DOE, 2007. www.ideadata.org/PartBReport.asp).

are counted). For the most part, those students with mild disabilities receive their instruction from the regular education teacher, although others (for example, special education teachers, speech and language pathologists) may also be involved. As such, students with mild disabilities participate in the general education curriculum. (See Chapter 2 for a discussion of instructional accommodations for the general education classroom.) A special educator or classroom aide may be assigned to collaborate with the general educator to teach all students in the class.

THINK BACK TO THE CASE about Marco and the Role of the Special Educator . . .

1. *Why do some students receive special education services seemingly indirectly in the regular education classroom whereas others go to a separate setting for their individualized instruction?*

Students enrolled in special education who participate in the regular education classroom and curriculum still have an individually designed education program that indicates what types of special instruction they need to benefit from their education. Depending on how much the individualized education program deviates from the general education curriculum and classroom routine, the general educator might be responsible for delivering the special education components of the program. Common examples include ensuring that students needing special instruction personally understand directions given to the whole class, reviewing foundational knowledge or skills for the lesson's topic with those students, or adjusting expectations for quality or content of completed assignments. Students who need more intensive review and practice or have a significant skills gap may benefit more from individualized instruction in another setting.

Aides and paraprofessionals are often assigned to provide academic assistance. If a student needs more intensive or unique instruction in the general curriculum, a special educator might accompany the student to the class and provide the instruction there. Marco, for example, visits some students' classrooms on a regular basis to provide them with their special education. A special educator may always accompany a student with special needs to certain classes and provide daily special education instruction right in that room. Depending on what the student's teachers and parents have planned, the special educator might also provide instruction to others in the class at the same time. Of course, special educators sometimes consult with general education teachers and observe in their classrooms, but do not directly teach the special education students present. That is yet another way that special education can be provided in the regular education classroom.

The Learning Center and Resource Room. The special education classroom has no universal name. In some schools, it is called the special education room, but it is most typically called the learning center or resource room. The distinction between the latter two, if any, depends on the school. In some schools, a distinction is made between a room where students only sporadically visit for support—the learning center—and where students attend on a routine schedule—the resource room. As a general rule, the more differentiated the curriculum or instructional practice, the more likely it will be taught in a resource room.

Sometimes students in special education need to receive their education outside of the regular education environment. That may be because they are working on a curriculum that is substantially different from the general education curriculum, they cannot work with peers in their regular education class or even grade level, they may need to work with peers who have similar learning needs, or they may simply like more privacy as they receive their specialized instruction. For example, students who are significantly behind their peers in reading may be more comfortable practicing their skills outside of the view of others (compare to Elbaum, Schumm, and Vaughn 1995).

More Restrictive Settings. Some students receive their education in "substantially separate" placements, which are often in a separate building. Typically, these students have more severe disabilities. Of students with mild disabilities, only those with EBD are likely (in percentages) to be placed in programs more restrictive than the general education school environment (U.S. DOE 2003). This usually occurs in the cases of students who are prone to highly disruptive and injurious behaviors (to self or others), and to those whose internalizing behaviors pose a significant threat to themselves, such as self-mutilation or suicidal tendencies. As distracting as Burton in Case 1.1 can be, he is not likely to be placed outside of the general education environment. Some experts in the field of special education see this as a disparity based on the fact that those with EBD make others more uncomfortable than do those with ADHD, despite the fact that both are disruptive to the classroom (see Hallahan et al. 2005).

THINK BACK TO THE CASE about Marco and the Role of the Special Educator . . .

2. What should be done about students being sent to see Marco without advance notice to him? Is this just a scheduling problem?

Marco was frustrated that teachers often interrupted his teaching schedule by sending students to him for extra help with little advance notice. Although a system of more advance notice would help the situation, it is not really a good solution to the problem. The real problem is that he is supposed to be helping students to develop necessary knowledge and skills, and his work is being regularly disrupted. The problem in Marco's school is that the teachers (and he) treated his role as strictly support to the general education teacher. It is true that Marco needs to support students learning in the general education classroom, but he also has students with specialized curriculums assigned to him. If special education is going to be about more than getting students through to the end of the school day, then the learning center should be more than a glorified study hall (Deshler et al. 2001). By this, we mean that students with disabilities need to be taught the skills to be independent learners. Both general education and special education teachers need to understand what curriculums they are to teach and how they can support one another.

What Is an Inclusive School?

There is no official definition and there are no criteria for what constitutes an **inclusive school**. Although virtually all public schools have some students with disabilities enrolled, the term *inclusive school* is used to signify a school that proactively includes students with disabilities into the regular education classes and curriculum, instead of segregating them. Some districts use this term, and others do not because they adopt a more de facto attitude about including students with and without disabilities together under the same roof. Three immediate questions come to mind when discussing inclusive schools:

- Which students with disabilities are being placed in the inclusive classes?
- Which classrooms will be inclusive?
- What should students with disabilities learn in the inclusive classroom?

Inclusion schools typically include students with mild disabilities and students with severe disabilities in some cases. Depending on the students' academic needs, they may be placed in inclusive classrooms for all subject areas or just for those in which they can participate with minimal support. Some inclusion schools provide co-teachers, paraprofessionals, and a special educator with a designated schedule of when they will be in the classroom together. In some cases, inclusion schools offer classes with a reduced number of students, as a sign of their support of inclusive education. If the school is truly "inclusive" and does not just offer a seat in the classroom, then the classroom teacher directly interacts with students with disabilities. (More about inclusion schools can be found in Chapter 13.)

Research Evidence

When Inclusion Works. Using data collected annually on participation in special education, the U.S. DOE (2006) reported that 48.2 percent of students served by the IDEA, between the ages of 6 and 21, spend less than 21 percent of their school day outside of the general education environment. Of those students, 46.9 percent of those with LD spend less than 21 percent of their schooltime outside of general education settings; those with MR (mild, moderate, severe, and profound levels are not distinguished in the report) spend 10.9 percent of their time outside of the general education setting, and 28.8 percent of students with EBD are removed from general education less than 21 percent of the school day. (Remember that students with ADHD are not counted separately from all of the other students in the other health impairments category, so their participation is not stated in the report. Inclusive of all disability conditions within the OHI category, 49.5 percent of those students are removed less than 21% of the time.) These data reflect increases from the level of general education participation reported in the same report even ten years previous. Thus, many students with mild disabilities are included in the general education environment for a significant portion of the school day.

Despite the fact that many teachers have reported apprehension about inclusion, they have been found to be supportive of the practice (Bulgren and Lenz 1996; Scruggs and Mastropieri 1996; Vaughn et al. 1996; Vaughn et al. 1999). Indeed, research findings show that inclusive approaches can be effective (Rea, McLaughlin, and Walther-Thomas 2002). Studies of the instructional accommodations that teachers are willing to provide reflect that inclusion is most effective when the needs of students with special needs can be addressed using teaching procedures that are also appropriate for their general education classmates (Schumm and Vaughn 1991) and when the teachers believe they have been properly prepared and supported (DeSimone and Parmar 2006; Scruggs and Mastropieri 1996).

Implications of Laws Pertaining to Special Education

Three major federal laws call for disability-related education services in schools. They make distinct contributions to how we provide special education. In addition, each state has its own laws governing special education practices, and the Federal Americans with Disabilities Act (ADA) requires schools to protect the civil rights of students with disabilities. The three major laws that we will discuss are IDEA, Section 504, and No Child Left Behind (NCLB).

Chapter Question
ALERT
In this section you will find information that answers a Chapter Question:

4. What are the major implications of legislation for how we serve students with disabilities?

Individuals with Disabilities Education Act (2004)

The **Individuals with Disabilities Education Act** (2004) is the primary law pertaining to special education. It is the law that dictates in the greatest detail how special education services should be provided. Through its regulations (most recently updated in 2004 and known as the Individuals with Disabilities Education Improvement Act), this education act prescribes how special education will be provided.

The law complements the comprehensive NCLB (see later in this section) by requiring that all students in special education have access to the general curriculum and that they be included in accountability measures (Flowers, Browder, and Ahlgrim-Delzell 2006).

The Six Major Provisions of the IDEA in Practice. The expansive IDEA has maintained six major provisions since its inception in 1975, as Public Law 94-142, The Education for All Handicapped Children Act. Some of the major provisions of the IDEA deal more with protections for families and schools and less with specifically what goes on during daily instruction. Still, they are all vital to ensuring that students with disabilities are properly served and their rights to an appropriate education are protected. The following are the six provisions:

1. The **zero reject** provision makes clear that no student with a disability may be denied an education.
2. The **due process** provision provides families with rights and recourse when decisions are being made about their child's education.
3. The **parent and student participation** provision ensures that parents and students are informed and invited to participate in the special education planning, implementation, and evaluation process. In fact, special education services cannot begin until parents have signed an individualized education program affirming their consent for the special services.
4. **Nondiscriminatory identification and evaluation** is a provision based on a long history of discriminatory practices in referring students to be assessed for disabilities and special education eligibility. Cases involving nonnative English speakers (for example, *Diana v. California State Board of Education,* 1970) and racial/ethnic minority students (for example, *Larry P. v. Riles,* 1972) who were wrongly identified as having disabilities demonstrate that both the process for identification and the actual evaluations are possibly biased. The nondiscrimination provision is not limited to initial identification, however. The IDEA requires regular evaluation of progress, as well as triennial assessments of the status of disabling conditions. Nondiscriminatory practices in those activities are provided for as well. Despite this provision, questions continue as to whether members of minority groups are still overrepresented in special education (Harry and Klingner 2006).
5. **Free and appropriate public education** means that students with a qualifying disability are eligible for an education at public costs as long as they are enrolled in public education. Moreover, their special education must be "appropriate," which means the educational program must be designed so that the students benefit from it.
6. Finally, the place where special education is provided must be the **least restrictive environment,** which is the physical location closest to the classroom the students would be in if they had no disability and no special education. The intent is to minimize the segregation of students with disabilities (see Lipsky 2005). The IDEA 2004 regulations emphasize that every effort should be made to have the regular education environment be the least restrictive environment (LRE), but the regulations still do not *define* it as the regular education classroom.

Section 504 of the Rehabilitation Act of 1973

When revised in 1973, the Rehabilitation Act included **Section 504,** which pertains to those with disabilities enrolled in programs that benefit from federal funding. Over years of reauthorization, Congress and the courts have affirmed that it pertains to students with disabilities enrolled in school, regardless of whether they have been found eligible under IDEA.

The primary contribution of Section 504 is its provision for access to education for students with disabilities. To put this in context, think of an everyday example: An old school building has entrances only at the tops of stairs. It would be difficult for a student who uses a wheelchair to enter the building. What should the school do? Send that student home? Should they tell the parents to come build a ramp if they want their child to receive an education? Should they send a teacher down to the bottom of the steps to work there with the student? Unfortunately, all of those suggestions reflect common practices prior to the passage of Section 504 and Public Law 94-142. IDEA and Section 504 tell schools that they should build a ramp themselves or find some other way to get that student into the building. That is providing access to an education.

No Child Left Behind Act (2001)

The **No Child Left Behind Act** (2001) is a comprehensive education act that directs a variety of school practices and applies to special education as well. Three components of the NCLB Act stand out for their relevance to daily instruction of students in special education: (a) the requirements for high standards, (b) expectations for "scientifically-based" instructional practices, and (c) that teachers must become "highly qualified." The NCLB Act requires that all students be held to high standards for learning and achievement (the IDEA 2004 includes text affirming that high standards apply to students in special education). The notion of "high standards for all" represents a belief that all children are capable of learning (Honig and Hatch 2004). It also represents an assumption that, pre-standards, schools were not sufficiently challenging students (Nolet and McLaughlin 2000). To monitor whether all students are being held to and succeeding at appropriate high standards, the NCLB Act mandates assessments of performance in language arts, mathematics, and science. Students with mild disabilities must pass the same high-stakes tests as other students to be promoted or to graduate (although a limited portion may pass an alternative version of the test [Gerber 2005]), or face the same consequences as others.

To ensure that high standards are met, states are mandated to set curriculum and outcome standards. The standards identify knowledge and skills that students should attain. Each state department of education is responsible for ensuring that standards guide instruction in each curriculum area. In many instances, states rely on professional organizations, such as the National Council of Teachers of English, the International Reading Association, and the National Council of Teachers of Mathematics, to devise the content standards they adopt. Those standards apply to students in special education as well. Consequently, annual individualized education goals should be formulated with the standards in mind.

The NCLB Act also requires that teachers employ scientifically based practices. In short, that means practices that have been researched to validate their effectiveness. The definition of science behind scientifically based has been controversial, with some questioning if the emphasis on positivist experimental designs is overly restrictive (National Research Council [NRC] 2001), particularly because it excludes many research design options appropriate for small samples of research participants (Sideridis and Greenwood 1996). In the classroom, the scientifically based practices expectation means that teachers should primarily use practices with a published record of research to support them or that include data-gathering activities to assess their effectiveness. The U.S. DOE's Institute of Education Sciences' website, the What Works Clearinghouse (www.whatworks.ed.gov), is a primary resource for validated practices. The NCLB Act also requires that teachers earn the designation of "highly qualified" in the subject areas they teach. States set the criteria for highly qualified, which typically include passing exams that may be required for licensure as well. This is a confusing and problematic requirement for special educators because special education teaching has no "highly qualified" requirement beyond being "fully licensed" (IDEA 2004), but special educators are expected to be highly qualified in all content areas they teach[2] (King-Sears 2005). Thus, the IDEA stipulates that teachers of special education can be designated highly qualified by one route if they only provide consultative services to general educators and do not teach in a core subject area, or by satisfying the NCLB requirements for highly qualified in a particular core subject area if they have teaching responsibilities in that area.

VIDEO CASE CONNECTIONS BOX

Watch the Video Case entitled *Foundations: Meeting the Demands of Educational Legislation* to hear perspectives of a principal and teachers regarding expectations to comply with educational legislation. After you watch the video, list at least one learning goal for each of the major education legislations (IDEA, Section 504, NCLB) that you hope to accomplish as you read the remaining chapters of this textbook (for example, "I wish to understand the distinction between a special education intervention and a related service," or "How can students with mild disabilities be prepared to participate in mandated high-stakes assessments?").

The IEP: The Blueprint for Individualized Education

Students receive special education when identified as having a disability and shown that they are not able to benefit from "regular" education (professionals commonly use the term *regular* to describe the typical curriculum and general school environment). When a student is enrolled in special education, an IEP must be designed. The parents and the school must describe and agree to how the student's education will differ from the general education.

A team develops the IEP. The IDEA mandates who must participate on the team: (1) a special educator, (2) at least one of the student's general educators from a class where the disability poses an impact (thus, at the secondary level, not every teacher the student has throughout the day has to participate, for example), (3) a school administrator, (4) a parent or legal guardian, (5) the student (when appropriate), (6) someone qualified to interpret assessment results if any will be considered, and (7) other service providers as appropriate (for example, related service providers, classroom aides, or representatives of institutions to which a student will be transitioning). With their diversity of expertise and perspectives,

---

[2] The Council for Exceptional Children (CEC forthcoming) has identified ten standards that all special educators should satisfy to be effective educators. See the inside cover of this book for a list of the CEC standards.

the team has the task of identifying what needs to be different in the student's education and working out a plan for what will be done.

A paper or digital plan must be written to keep a record of what the team decides. The document is the IEP; in fact, many assume the "P" stands for plan. The IEP can be thought of as a "blueprint for special education" because it must clearly state what the special education will be.

The IEP should be written plainly enough so that parents who are not professional educators can understand it. A great variety of information must be recorded on the IEP. The IEP must state which disability the student has and the ways in which the disability interferes with the student benefiting from the regular education (for example, "Due to Maria's clinical depression, she often misses important information in class, and she is not developing appropriate skills for socializing with peers"). That information would logically lead into what special instruction and services are planned for the student. Thus, it must also state what instructional goals will be accomplished in the ensuing year, and where and by whom services will be provided.

To ensure that the IEP becomes a plan that is followed, the team must recommend the nature of special instruction to be offered. Thus, Maria and Sy's completed IEPs identify how they will be supported instructionally to meet their annual goals. They also name where the LRE is for each of the specified activities and what type of professional will provide the services (for example, special education teacher, general educator, reading specialist). To view samples of student IEPs, please visit the website for this book.

Responsiveness to Intervention: A New Approach to Special Education for Students with Learning Disabilities

A recent development in special education practice for students with learning disabilities impinges upon the conceptualization of learning disabilities, its definition, assessment, and instructional interventions. The **responsiveness to intervention** (RTI) model is significantly altering how students are identified as having learning disabilities and served. As the terms indicate, how a student *responds* to instructional interventions (for example, does or does not make intended learning progress) serves as the basis for determining the student's instructional needs. If the student responds as desired, instruction continues; if the student does not respond satisfactorily after a reasonable amount of time or after a number of opportunities has passed, then the teacher should change instruction to better meet the student's needs. So, the RTI model is an approach that commences instructional responses to a student's needs as soon as academic difficulties are first suspected. This is in contrast to the traditional IDEA eligibility process, which requires students to meet the operational definition for specific learning disabilities—you should recall that it includes identifying a discrepancy between cognitive aptitude and achievement. Critics of the discrepancy formula and conventional IDEA referral process argue that it does not reliably distinguish learners with a true LD from other low achievers, that it is not useful for determining who needs specialized services (for example, Stanovich 2005), that it delays providing needed services (for this reason the referral process has been nicknamed the "wait to fail" approach (for example, Vaughn and Fuchs 2003), and that it may be biased against minority populations (Harry and Klingner 2006).

Chapter Question
ALERT

In this section you will find information that answers a Chapter Question:

5. What is RTI and how does it relate to traditional special education practices?

There is no one model of RTI, just certain principles that make it RTI. Even the three tiers are not a given. That is by design, so that the best model(s) may emerge from practitioners and researchers working in the field to determine what procedures work best. (For more on how educators participate in RTI models and RTI's relationship to the IEP planning process, see Chapter 2.)

TIPS FOR GENERALIZATION ▶

Common Approaches for Enacting RTI

The National Joint Committee on Learning Disabilities (NJCLD; 2005) has summarized popular approaches to implementing RTI (see Figure 1.1). The following are the four major steps.

1. The process begins with universal screening for difficulties. In **universal screening,** all students are assessed for how well they are achieving. One approach to universal screening is to test all students in a classroom, grade level, or school at early and midpoints in the school year, as well as part way into the final third of the year. The screening process may involve either standardized or informal assessments; however, individual students' performances should be compared to the class, grade, school, or standardized norm. The purpose of universal screening is to find potential academic difficulties early, certainly before they hinder academic performance.

2. If any students in the screening sample are found to be having academic difficulties, then it can be assumed that instruction has not met their needs. Others who were not detected in the screening may also, or soon will, need more support. Thus, beginning in **tier 1** of three possible "tiers" of intervention, all students in the group are to receive intensified "**effective instruction,**" as called for in NCLB (2001) and codified in the IDEA (2004).

    Through the RTI process, students' learning problems are addressed with effective interventions as soon as they are noticed. Also, in addition to avoiding serious delays in enrolling the students in special education for individualized intervention, inappropriate disability identification and special education placements can be avoided (Fuchs et al. 2003). Throughout tier 1, educators conduct regular **progress monitoring** (see Chapter 2) to determine whether individual students are benefiting from the effective instruction. Those who are not making sufficient progress enter into tier 2.

3. Students participating in **tier 2** receive intensified effective instruction in addition to the effective instruction they and their peers are already receiving. In tier 2, someone trained specifically in the procedures being used must provide the intensive instruction. The students who participate in tier 2 may receive the additional instruction in small group or pull-out settings. Some RTI proponents suggest that pull-out instruction should be avoided in tier 2 because it is inconsistent with the philosophy of RTI to provide appropriate intervention within the regular classroom instructional routine. Progress monitoring continues in tier 2. Those students who do not make sufficient gains in tier 2 proceed to tier 3 interventions.

4. Tier 3 instruction is more likely to occur in a pull-out setting; however, that is not a given. In **tier 3,** more intensive and individualized scientifically based practices must be used, and progress monitoring to document effectiveness continues. In some versions of RTI, entering a student into tier 3 constitutes providing special education. In other versions, students may enter special education if tier 3 efforts are documented as ineffective. The IDEA regulations make clear that the entire RTI process is not special education. Further, when a student is moved from the RTI approach to special education, the traditional referral process and documentation of an LD using the discrepancy approach must be employed.

FIGURE 1.1

NJCLD's (2005) Commonly Identified Stages (Represented as Tiers) of Responsiveness to Intervention Models

1. **Tier 1:** High-quality instructional and behavioral supports are provided for all students in general education.
   - School personnel conduct universal screening of literacy skills, academics, and behavior.
   - Teachers implement a variety of research-supported teaching strategies and approaches.
   - Ongoing, curriculum-based assessment and continuous progress monitoring are used to guide high-quality instruction.
   - Students receive differentiated instruction based on data from ongoing assessments.

2. **Tier 2:** Students whose performance and rate of progress lag behind those of peers in their classroom, school, or district receive more specialized prevention or remediation within general education.
   - Curriculum-based measures are used to identify which students continue to need assistance, and with what specific kinds of skills.
   - Collaborative problem solving is used to design and implement instructional support for students that may consist of a standard protocol[1] or more individualized strategies and interventions.
   - Identified students receive more intensive scientific, research-based instruction targeted to their individual needs.
   - Student progress is monitored frequently to determine intervention effectiveness and needed modifications.
   - Systematic assessment is conducted to determine the fidelity or integrity with which instruction and interventions are implemented.
   - Parents are informed and included in the planning and monitoring of their child's progress in Tier 2 specialized interventions.
   - General education teachers receive support (e.g., training, consultation, direct services for students), as needed, from other qualified educators in implementing interventions and monitoring student progress.

3. **Tier 3:** A comprehensive evaluation is conducted by a multidisciplinary team to determine eligibility for special education and related services.
   - Parents are informed of their due process rights and consent is obtained for the comprehensive evaluation needed to determine whether the student has a disability and is eligible for special education and related services.
   - Evaluation uses multiple sources of assessment data, which may include data from standardized and norm-referenced measures; observations made by parents, students, and teachers; and data collected in Tiers 1 and 2.
   - Intensive, systematic, specialized instruction is provided and additional RTI data are collected, as needed, in accordance with special education timelines and other mandates.
   - Procedural safeguards concerning evaluations and eligibility determinations apply, as required by IDEA 2004 mandates.

[1] D. Fuchs et al. (2003) used the term *standard protocol* to refer to an approach in which students with similar difficulties (e.g., problems with reading fluency) are given a research-based intervention that has been standardized and shown to be effective for students with similar difficulties and uses a standard protocol to ensure implementation integrity. The term is used in this sense in this report.

From National Joint Committee on Learning Disabilities. 2005. NJCLD Position Paper: Responsiveness to Intervention and Learning Disabilities. *Learning Disability Quarterly* 28:249–60.

CHAPTER SUMMARY

Students with mild disabilities are a diverse group. Although certain characteristics unite all of those with the same disability label, all individuals are unique in terms of how the disability impacts them, as well as in what is needed for academic success. The four mild disabilities are learning disabilities, mild mental retardation, emotional or behavioral disorders, and attention deficit/hyperactivity disorder.

Children and adolescents with mild disabilities are as capable of benefiting from education as is any other student. Cognitive processing difficulties distinguish them from regular education students. Their academic and social development is often at a slower pace than their peers, and achievement is often documented to be lower as well. Effective instructional practices for students with mild disabilities are based upon their specific cognitive strengths and needs. Principles of effective practice include, in addition to holding them to high standards and expectations, research-validated practices that directly respond to their unique

cognitive processing and behavioral traits. Such practices include using clear and explicit instruction, providing models and examples, and scaffolding practices that are within the student's ranges of capabilities.

Children and adolescents with disabilities are entitled to a free, public education just like any other student. Two of the four major laws concerning the rights of students with disabilities, the IDEA and Section 504, most directly inform special education and related service practices in schools. In accordance with those laws, students who have mild disabilities most typically participate in the regular education curriculum and school environment. That requires that the educators involved have clearly defined roles and that they support one another in those roles. Thus, both regular and special educators must collaborate in providing effective special education. The IEP process is used to devise an individually appropriate curriculum and to inform all parties involved of what is expected educationally for the student with the disability.

KEY TERMS

Consequated Feedback, 20
Due Process, 28
Effective Instruction, 32
Executive Functioning, 5
Externalized, 14
Free and Appropriate Public Education, 28
Functional Curriculum, 2
Generalization, 13
Inclusion School, 26
Individualizing, 2
Individuals with Disabilities Education Act, 27

Informative Feedback, 20
Instructional Technologies, 22
Internalized, 14
Least Restrictive Environment, 28
Mild Disabilities, 2
Model, 19
No Child Left Behind Act, 29
Nondiscriminatory Identification and Evaluation, 28
Parent and Student Participation, 28
Principles of Effective Instruction, 17
Progress Monitoring, 32
Responsiveness to Intervention, 31

Section 504, 28
Special Education, 2
Tier 1, 32
Tier 2, 32
Tier 3, 32
Twice Exceptional, 7
Universal Screening, 32
Zero Reject, 28

APPLICATION ACTIVITIES

The following activities were designed to help you apply knowledge that was presented in this chapter. Using information from the chapter, complete the following activities.

1. Review the first case, with Maria, Sy, and Burton. For each of the three students, brainstorm how the IDEA provisions for *nondiscriminatory identification and evaluation, free and appropriate public education,* and services in the *least restrictive environment* could be fulfilled in Yoko's classroom.

2. Among students with mild disabilities, those with EBD are the most likely to be removed from the general education classroom. For each internalized and externalized behavior associated with EBD listed in Figure 1.1, recommend a related service that might enable a student exhibiting the behavior to stay in the regular classroom (recall that related services are different from individually designed special education interventions).

3. Develop a lesson plan (see Appendix A on the book-specific website for a lesson plan format) for a single student or a whole class. Identify in the plan how you will incorporate each of the principles of effective practice. (If you cannot think of a topic for your lesson plan, watch the Video Case entitled *Reading Comprehension Strategies for Elementary School Students: Questioning Techniques* and develop a plan for teaching Liz Page's elementary students what an interpretive question is; or watch *Using Information Processing Strategies: A Middle School Science Lesson* and develop a plan for teaching E. J. Beucler's students the definition of physical change.)

4. Read Deshler et al. (2001). Thinking of a special education student you have worked with, list special education and related services you believe the student should receive and then identify which level of service from Deshler et al. is best suited to providing those services.

WEBSITE RESOURCES ON MILD DISABILITIES

The following are some of the numerous websites for teachers interested in meeting the needs of students with mild disabilities.

American Association on Mental Retardation
www.aamr.org

The website of the AAMR includes a variety of resources for parents, teachers, and other scholars interested in mental retardation policy and practices. In addition, question-and-answer sections are included. Downloadable publications may also be found.

Council for Exceptional Children (CEC)
www.cec.sped.org

The CEC is a professional organization for teachers, researchers, administrators, and parents concerned for children and adolescents with disabilities. The

Council includes a number of divisions devoted to specific areas of special education; some of the following pertain to serving students with mild disabilities:

Council for Children with Behavior Disorders (CCBD)
www.ccbd.net

Division for Research
www.cecdr.org

Division for Learning Disabilities
www.teachingld.org

Division on Developmental Disabilities
www.dddcec.org

Teacher Education Division (TED)
www.tedcec.org

Council for Learning Disabilities
www.cldinternational.org

CLD is another professional organization for professionals in the field of learning disabilities. Helpful resources include "InfoSheets" on special education policy and effective practice. A section on the "science of learning disabilities" provides an introduction of the role science and research plays in identifying effective practices. Guidelines for being a good "consumer" of science are also included.

LD OnLine
www.ldonline.org

This website is designed for parents and teachers of students with learning disabilities. It provides great resources for helping children and adolescents with disabilities improve their skills in many academic areas. Students, parents, and teachers may participate in interactive forums regarding effective practices and other topics of interest.

Special Education Research Special Interest Group (SIG) of the American Educational Research Association (AERA)
www.aera.net

The AERA is the largest organization of educational researchers in the world. The Special Education Research SIG includes leading researchers in

mild disabilities. The website provides information about the organization and its members.

What Works Clearinghouse
www.whatworks.ed.gov

This interactive website was developed by the U.S. Department of Education's Institute of Education Sciences. It includes definitions and criteria for "scientifically based practices." Interventions that "work" based on the IES standards are reviewed by topic area.

U.S. Department of Education
www.ed.gov

This site has information on education policy, extensive information on the No Child Left Behind Act, including resources to facilitate compliance, and special sections directed toward students, parents, teachers, and administrators. This is also a portal for many other education-related U.S. DOE websites.

U.S. Department of Education, Office of Special Education and Rehabilitative Services
www.ed.gov/about/offices/list/osers

This site has information specifically on special education policy and practices. You may download resources on all aspects of IDEA compliance. *The Annual Report to Congress* provides extensive data on the implementation of the IDEA. The full regulations for the implementation of IDEA 2004 are also available.

Visit the book-specific website at www.cengage.com/education/boyle for a variety of study tools such as web links, tutorial quizzes, glossary/flash cards, bonus material not included in the text, and more.

The premium website offers access to additional materials, including the Video Cases. Go to www.cengage.com/login to register or purchase access.

Planning, Teaching, and Monitoring Instruction

CHAPTER QUESTIONS

1. When students begin to experience learning problems, how should educators work together to address their needs?

2. What information should be included in an individualized education plan, and how does it help educators to meet a student's special learning needs?

3. How can teachers plan effective lessons for special education students?

4. What research-based techniques are effective for teaching students with mild disabilities?

What do you think is the biggest concern of educators who work with students with disabilities in inclusive classrooms?

The biggest concern among regular education teachers who have students with disabilities in their inclusive classes is the adverse effects those students may have on statewide testing results, followed by the need for more professional development to know how to teach them (Idol 2006).

Despite the fact that most students with mild disabilities spend the majority of their day in regular education classrooms (U.S. Department of Education 2006b), many regular education teachers report that they are willing to teach them, but are unprepared to do so (Lopes, et al. 2004; also see Cass, Scanlon, and Walther-Thomas 2006). Special educators work with regular education teachers and the students in their classrooms, as well as work with small numbers of students outside of the classroom. Special and regular education colleagues can become successful teachers of students with mild disabilities if both become knowledgeable about mild disabilities and carefully plan and teach using proven, effective practices. In this chapter, you will learn about proven practices for planning, teaching, and monitoring learning while you use the instructional practices presented in the chapters that follow.

Chapter Question
ALERT

In this section, you will find information that answers a Chapter Question:

1. When students begin to experience learning problems, how should educators work together to address their needs?

How and Why to "Plan, Teach, and Monitor" for Students with Mild Disabilities

Effective teachers think carefully about what they are going to teach, which involves considering the learning needs of their students and how best to teach the content. Effective teachers also collaborate with their colleagues, especially when their students are struggling. The Council for Exceptional Children (CEC) provides standards for educators working with students with special needs. These standards emphasize skills of planning and collaboration (CEC 2009; also see the inside cover of this textbook).

| **CASE 2.1** | **Getting to the Bottom of Albert's Learning Needs** |

Case Introduction

As you read about Albert, ask yourself why he may be having difficulties with assignments. Could the explanation be related to how Penny teaches him, or could there be some cognitive or social explanation? Ask yourself what a special educator would suggest be done to address Albert's learning needs.

At the end of the case, you will find case questions. These questions are meant to serve as points for reflection. Of course, if you can answer them immediately, you should do so, but you

may want to wait to answer them until you have read that portion of the chapter that pertains to the particular case question. Throughout the rest of the chapter, you will see the same questions repeated. As you see them, try to answer them based upon that portion of the chapter that you just read.

Shortly after the school year began, Albert's family moved into the school district, and he joined Penny's fifth grade classroom. Penny knew that the content and skills that

continued

Albert knew might differ from what students in her class knew. She also realized that Albert would need some time to adjust to his new school and community.

Two months passed and Penny realized that Albert had persistent difficulty completing assignments independently. Once Penny realized this, she started to think more carefully about the nature of Albert's difficulties. When the class started working on assignments, he would often look confused or start work in a way that was clearly wrong. For example, if they were to read aloud with a partner, he would begin to read silently; once he tried to rewrite story problem questions in his own words when they were supposed to be solving the math problem. On rare occasions, he would raise his hand and ask for help. If Penny asked, "What are you supposed to be doing?" he almost always answered, "I don't know."

When Penny told Albert what he was supposed to be doing, he would understand and get to work. Still, she considered the quality of his work low compared to that of his peers in the room. Penny also found it necessary to check in with Albert while he worked, often having to remind him of the correct way to complete the assignment.

Finally, Penny decided to meet with and explain Albert's problems to Martha, the head special education teacher in the building. Penny suggested that Albert might have a learning disability. Martha acknowledged that a disability was a possibility, but said she felt it prudent first to observe Albert in Penny's classroom to analyze what exactly happens when Penny gives Albert step-by-step directions, and why Albert doesn't comprehend directions as the other students do. Martha also said that an important first step would be to contact Albert's parents to ask what information they could share about his learning history and

any other insights into why he is having difficulties or what to do about them. Martha also noted that it was appropriate to be in touch with the parents now, just in case they needed to be informed later that the school suspected a possible disability.

Martha also discussed different methods of presenting directions to Albert. After Martha observed Albert in the classroom, the two teachers sat down to discuss the observation. In their discussion, Martha noted that Penny's instructions to Albert might be more successful if she named the steps overtly (for example, "First you . . . Second, you need to . . ."), and that writing down the steps in order was particularly helpful for most students like Albert.

After she tried Martha's suggestions, Penny felt she was beginning to do a better job teaching Albert because he comprehended assignments better and was beginning to perform tasks better. Penny appreciated the support Martha had provided. She and Martha noted, however, that the data they were keeping on Albert's performance showed he was making only minimal progress. Martha suggested they contact the school's Teacher Assistance Team so that other colleagues in the building could consult with them on the case.

CASE QUESTIONS

1. How can a team of educators help Penny and Martha identify Albert's needs and come up with an appropriate instructional plan?
2. If Albert does need special education, how should the team determine whether his curriculum should change from the regular fifth grade curriculum Penny teaches?

Collaborating When Students Begin to Struggle

Among the problems Penny faced with Albert was a lack of information. She did not know much about his academic history, because his family was new to the district. She did not know what kind of expectations he had been held to in his last school, and she could not consult teachers in the building who had taught him the years before. Penny also was not able to get much information directly from Albert as to why he was having difficulty. She needed to know more about what was happening with him. She also needed more concrete plans for how she should help him.

Pre-Referral: The First Stage. Before a student can be enrolled in special education and receive an individually appropriate education, that student must be identified as (1) having a disability covered by the IDEA, and (2) needing special education (review Chapter 1). As a preliminary stage to determining whether a student such as Albert satisfies those two generic special education eligibility criteria, a pre-referral process must be completed. Pre-referral is a helpful process for determining how to provide a student with appropriate academic or behavioral supports while the student is still in the general education classroom.

In a **pre-referral** process, both theories as to why the student is having difficulties and possible instructional remedies are explored. The emphasis is on instructional remedies, instead of immediately looking for a possible disability (Burns 2006; Marston, et al. 2003). So although Penny was right that Albert's behaviors could be symptomatic of some disability, it makes more sense first to learn more about the behaviors and determine if they are readily resolved before testing him for a disability. (Also, without considerably more information, it would be difficult to know for what disability to assess him.) Observing a student's learning patterns, reteaching, teaching in a different way, and responding to a student's affective needs are all pre-referral activities focused on instructional remedies. A student may have difficulty learning certain content for various reasons (for example, low interest, inadequate prior knowledge, ineffective teaching for that individual, absences, or social and other personal stresses). If the source of the problem is that the student is not motivated to learn the content or that the teacher has not been effective in teaching that student, then activities are designed to correct the learning problem. By exploring why the student is having difficulty and altering instruction, the "problem" might be addressed, and a full evaluation for special education may not be needed.

In the case of Albert, in addition to Martha's advice to try clear and explicit direction (giving and writing down the steps of instructions for Albert), Penny might also have investigated whether Albert had mastered certain pre-skills or knowledge; if she found that not to be the case, she could reteach in those areas or reconsider what she was teaching him. Penny could also have Albert use think-alouds to complete assignments, or have him paraphrase directions back to her. She could also teach him how to underline key components of written directions. She might even consider whether he may need to have his seat changed because he is easily distracted. In short, a near-endless variety of pre-referral activities may be tried. They should be simple attempts to see if the problem can be alleviated; they are not major instructional interventions such as teaching a student an elaborate learning strategy.

Observing the student's learning patterns and trying to teach in different ways are just good teaching behaviors that teachers should routinely use. However, when a student does not seem to be benefiting from instruction that is generally effective for others, it is imperative that teachers seek to understand why the student is not learning and explore the use of differentiated teaching methods to teach the student. If you find that some of your students are not learning as expected, you should immediately question whether you could be teaching differently to better meet their needs.

Your colleagues can be great resources for helping you think about ways to vary your teaching. If the problem is not quickly and easily resolved, you should follow your school's procedures for formally initiating the pre-referral process, which typically involves a team of educators who will work with you to resolve the student's problems.

VIDEO CASE CONNECTIONS BOX

Brainstorm reasons you might not want to consult your colleagues when you are having difficulty teaching a student (for example, it is embarrassing, time-consuming, might count against me in my annual review). Then watch the video *Collaboration with Colleagues* to hear why teachers appreciate collaborating with one another. Next to each item on your list, write a way you can overcome each problem (for example, *embarrassing:* "Be sure to show off the good ideas I thought of myself"; *might count against me:* "Inquire about other new teachers' experiences with making pre-referrals").

The team of educators that becomes involved upon formally initiating a pre-referral process is typically known as the **Teacher Assistance Team** (other common names include Child Study Team, Support Team, and Pre-referral Intervention Team) (Buck et al. 2003) (see Figure 2.1). Members of the Teacher Assistance Team can include the classroom teacher experiencing the difficulty, a special educator, a teacher coach, behavior specialists, administrators, and others who have relevant expertise. The team should inform the parents that they are working on behalf of their child and consult the parents for their perspective on the source of the student's learning or behavioral difficulty. The parents might have ideas on how to respond to the problem as well. Throughout this process, the team documents the learning problem and offers suggestions to the classroom teacher. In some cases, two general educators consult, a special educator may observe and offer tips, another teacher may come in to model different teaching practices, or a counselor might talk with the student. The nice thing about teacher assistance teams is that colleagues come together to support one another; it is not a court judging your competence as an individual teacher, it is colleagues joining together to problem solve. Indeed, the team is most successful when the participants perceive one another

FIGURE 2.1

Mandated Teams for the Special Education Process

Pre-referral					504 Plan
	Screening				
		Referral:			
		Assessment			
			Eligibility Determination		
				Individualized Education Planning	
Pre-Referral Team (*e.g.*, Teacher Assistance Team)			Multidisciplinary Team	Individualized Education Plan Team	504 Team

Note: Pre-referral, multidisciplinary, and IEP teams are mandated by the IDEA. Section 504 mandates 504 teams.

as collaborators, instead of as administrative or authoritative experts judging each other (Rafoth and Foriska 2006).

Historically, large numbers of students have been incorrectly identified as having disabilities and subsequently placed into special education when in fact regular education could have been more appropriate for them. Likewise, some students who would have qualified as having disabilities were denied special education because they were not accurately identified (Harry and Klingner 2006; Stanovich 1999; 2005). Research has shown that students of color, those from lower socioeconomic backgrounds, and English language learners have been particularly vulnerable to misidentification (Figueroa 2005; Haager 2007; Harry and Klingner 2006). This misidentification is likely due to educators not understanding the student's language and culture, rather than to teacher bias. Teachers who engage in pre-referral activities are less likely to refer students for special education based on sociocultural factors; they instead are more likely to refer a student based upon learning problems (Drame 2002).

THINK BACK TO THE CASE) of Penny, Martha, and Albert. . . .

1. How can a team of educators help Penny and Martha identify Albert's needs and come up with an appropriate instructional plan?

The pre-referral process does not end with recommendations being made by the Teacher Assistance Team. The teacher and the rest of the team implement their plan, gather data, and observe whether their attempts have been successful (for example, Marston et al. 2003). Through the team process, the extent of a "problem" is determined, understanding of the causes may be achieved, and doable solutions are implemented. The team does not finish its process until it has satisfactorily addressed the problem.

You will recall from Chapter 1 that both the No Child Left Behind (NCLB) Act (2001) and IDEA (2004) call for teachers to use **"scientifically based" intervention practices.** Beginning in the pre-referral process, data should be collected documenting that scientifically based intervention practices were used and what their effects were (*IDEA* 2004). This data collection is to ensure that teachers have tried research-proven teaching practices, and that the learning problem persists, despite teachers' best efforts. Should the teacher and team determine to proceed toward assessing whether a disability is present and whether special education is warranted, the effects of using scientifically based practices will need to be documented prior to the actual referral for special education evaluation (see Referral: Stage Three). See the following Tips for Generalization Box on guidelines for identifying scientifically based practices. (The Responsiveness to Intervention approach also calls for using scientifically based practices to identify learning disabilities and/or alternative service delivery that is now allowed under the IDEA. See Chapter 1 for a detailed description of that process and its implications.)

TIPS FOR GENERALIZATION

How to Identify "Scientifically Based" Practices for Special Education

The NCLB Act (2001) defines "scientifically based" intervention practices as having "reliable evidence that the program or practice works" (U.S. DOE 2006). Identifying scientifically based practices can be time-consuming, and it is not quite as simple as looking for practices that come with a claim of having been researched. There are standards for what constitutes "scientifically based." First, be aware that the majority of teaching practices that are promoted, both commercially and passed down by tradition are not adequately tested through research to determine their effectiveness (Carnine 2000; Odom et al. 2005). To help determine which practices satisfy the standards of "scientifically based," the NCLB Act and IDEA clarify that practices published in peer-reviewed publications (typically, professional journals) or otherwise reviewed by a panel of independent experts are reliable sources. The two laws specify that, ultimately, the research should include *rigorous experimental research procedures*, including "well conducted randomized control trials and regression continuity studies, and secondarily quasi-experimental studies of especially strong design" (Institute of Education Sciences 2006).

What to look for

There is no simple checklist to follow when determining whether an intervention is sufficiently researched. Claims by researchers and evidence of their methodological rigor must be evaluated. The following resources will be helpful in learning what standards satisfy the expectation for "scientifically based research":

Exceptional Children 71, no. 2 (2005)

Five articles detail appropriate evidence of sound research practices for documenting effective intervention practices. Also see: Cook, B. G., Tankersley, M., & Landrum, T. J. (Eds.). (forthcoming). Determining evidence-based practices in special education [special issue]. Exceptional Children for five studies that apply the evidence standards named in this volume.

Teacher Education and Special Education 24, no. 4 (2001)

A theme issue discusses bridging the gap between research and practice in special education. Although many of the articles address matters of teacher education, they include useful information on what constitutes effective research.

What Works Clearinghouse website http://ies.ed.gov/ncee/wwc

The U.S. Department of Education, Institute of Education Sciences, maintains this website that includes detailed guidelines that Clearinghouse evaluators use to determine if research evidence supports specific practices. A section of the website provides reports on their evaluations of specific interventions.

R. J. Shavelson and L. Towne, eds., *Scientific Research in Education* (Washington, DC: National Academy Press, 2002)

This report by the National Research Council criticizes the "scientifically based" standards as inappropriately narrow for education research and includes suggestions for additional appropriate research practices.

Screening: The Second Stage. During the pre-referral process, the Teacher Assistance Team may begin to suspect that the student's learning problem is due to a disability. Before rushing to assess the student for a disability in that case, the team assesses the *probability* of the student having a disability first, through the screening process. This process can also be useful for narrowing down the list of possible disabilities to consider. Be cautioned that even though you or other members of the team may suspect a disability even before beginning pre-referral interventions, proceeding to the screening stage should be a data-driven process. Team members should still consult one another and employ scientifically based practices with data collection to monitor whether or not the practices are effective. Anecdotal and research-based data (for example, Harry and Klingner 2006; MacMillan and Siperstein 2001) indicate that the student is more likely to be inappropriately referred and identified when educators prematurely presume the student has a disability.

In the **screening** process, indicators of a disability are looked for using the combination of informal and formal observations. For example, if a teacher suspects an attention problem, the teacher might then try observation checklists, conversations with the student about attention habits, and moving the student's seat to prevent distractions. Teachers who suspect difficulty with mathematical reasoning might review the student's work samples and ask the student to model a few mathematical procedures, in addition to having the student complete a published math skills test that is the norm for the student's grade level, to see if direct evidence of a reasoning problem is present. Because screening is a continuation of the pre-referral process, the teacher should also attend to other factors such as deficits in prior knowledge that are easily corrected through instruction.

Referral: The Third Stage. Should attempted instructional remedies during pre-referral prove to be insufficient, and the screening evidence indicate that a disability is a reasonable possibility, then a **referral** for (1) assessment for a disability, and (2) evaluation to determine the need for special education is warranted. Rinaldi and Samson (2008) note that educators sometimes delay referring students who are English language learners (ELL), believing they need more time to develop English language proficiency. Rinaldi and Samson note that although language development is an important factor in learning, delaying referral for those who likely do have a disability will only make the eventual task of remediation more difficult; they advocate following an RTI model (review Chapter 1) to speed needed interventions to the ELL student. The referral is made to a Multidisciplinary Team. The **Multidisciplinary Team** (sometimes known as a Collaborative Problem Solving Team) is composed of a variety of professionals from the school district who have professional strengths to contribute based on the student in question (IDEA 2004). The team members must employ a variety of approaches to assessment, in part to ensure that the IDEA provision for non-discriminatory identification and evaluation is not violated. The team will also review the information collected from various sources during the pre-referral and screening processes. The impact of cultural and language bias is reduced when multiple data sources are used (de Valenzuela and Baca 2004).

Once parents have been notified of the pre-referral "findings" and have provided their written consent, **assessment** for a possible disability may begin. The outcome of the assessment process is a declaration as to whether the student has a disability, and if so, what type of disability.

If a disability is found, a team continues the pre-referral process to determine whether the student with a disability is eligible for special education. The eligibility criteria include that the student has a disability covered by the IDEA, and that the student needs special education (sometimes phrased as would "benefit from" special education). Members of this team must include the student's parents and special educators (*IDEA* 2004). If the outcome of this **eligibility determination** process is that the student should be enrolled in special education, the team must plan an individualized education program.

The Individualized Education Plan

Chapter Question

ALERT

In this section you will find information that answers a Chapter Question:

2. What information should be included in an individualized education program (IEP), and how does it help educators to meet a student's special learning needs?

To help ensure that you and your colleagues provide students with disabilities with an individually appropriate education, the IDEA requires that a written plan for that "special" education be developed. The resulting document is the individualized education program (**IEP**). (Recall from Chapter 1 that educators commonly call the written plan "the IEP," even though the *P* technically stands for "program.") Keep in mind that students in special education are entitled to an individualized education *program*, not just a *plan* for one or some disjointed services. (From birth until age three, an eligible child is covered by an Individualized Family Services Plan [**IFSP**] that also provides services to family members necessary to support the child's development.) The purpose of the IEP is to identify students' unique learning needs, relevant history of learning, instructional goals, procedures that help students attain those goals, and the settings where they will participate in various services, among other things.

The IDEA regulations (2004) specify the minimum required content of an IEP. See Box 2.1 for a list of IDEA-required content for all IEP forms. Those most explicitly related to educational planning may be considered as organized into four major categories: *the present level of academic achievement and functional performance, instructional goals, specially designed instruction*, and the *service delivery plan*.

PLAAFP   The IEP must include a statement of the student's **present level of academic achievement and functional performance (PLAAFP)**. In the PLAAFP section, the teacher provides information describing how the student's disability relates to participation and learning progress in the regular education curriculum. The content must pertain specifically to achievement in major academic skill areas such as reading, writing, and mathematics (to be consistent with NCLB Act expectations for achievement to be used as an index of student learning) (Gibb and Dyches, forthcoming); however, the student's functional skills need to be considered as well. Examples of functional performance include socialization, self-care, employment skills, and ability to use public transportation.

The necessary information concerning academic achievement and functional performance includes statements of the student's current level of ability. These statements should be summarized from formal and informal assessments of the student. Observations from teachers, related service providers, parents, and the student may be incorporated. Both the student's current levels (typically meaning "strengths") and needs should be documented. A useful PLAAFP statement includes specific information that can be informative to planning instruction to meet the student's needs (for example, "decodes at 3.1 grade level

---

BOX 2.1

CONTENTS OF WRITTEN INDIVIDUALIZED EDUCATION PLANS AS SPECIFIED BY IDEA 2004 REGULATIONS*

1. Statement of child's** present levels of academic achievement and functional performance, including how disability affects involvement and progress in regular education curriculum
2. Measurable annual goals, including academic and functional goals that enable the child to be involved and make progress in regular education curriculum or meet other educational needs
3. Description of how progress toward meeting annual goals will be measured, and when periodic reports of progress will be made
4. Statement of special education and related services and supplementary aids and services; and statement of program modifications or supports to school staff to enable the child to:
   i.   Advance toward annual goals
   ii. Be involved in and make progress in the regular education curriculum, and to participate in extracurricular and nonacademic activities
   iii. Be educated and participate with other children with and without disabilities
5. Explanation of extent to which child will not participate with other children while engaged in services stated in (4)
6. Statement of individual accommodations needed to participate in state and district-wide assessments of academic achievement or functional performance, and statement of why a child cannot participate in the regular assessment and attesting that the selected alternate assessment is appropriate for the child
7a. A projected date for the beginning of services and modifications, as well as the frequency, location, and duration of them
7b. Appropriate transition goals and needed services, beginning no later than with the IEP in effect at age 16
7c. Statement informing stakeholders one year in advance of rights transferring to the child upon reaching the age of legal majority.

---
*Paraphrased from IDEA (2004) regulations, §300.320.
**The term *child* is used in the law.

---

and comprehends passages at 2.4 grade level," as opposed to "reads at a 2nd to 3rd grade level").

Instructional Goals

The heart of the IEP is the statement of **annual goals.** The annual goals respond to the information in the PLAAFP and are the basis for determining what accommodations and specially designed instruction will benefit the student. Simply said, the annual goals are outcome statements that name what the student will accomplish in one year. For each academic area impacted by the student's disability (as stated in the PLAAFP), the IEP should contain at least one goal stating what the team expects the student to be able to learn in one calendar year. When written appropriately, the goal will state an observable outcome. If the goals are written with overly general wording, there is no guarantee that the teacher and everyone else who works with the student will have the same outcome in mind. Instead, a goal statement should name precisely what will be observed if the goal is accomplished. Consider the two examples of good goal statements from Box 2.2: although there will always be room for some questioning of what a goal statement intends, all stakeholders know fairly specifically what outcomes are expected for Rena and Jae-Su. In the case of Jae-Su's goal statement, there is room to question how much the quality of her composition matters and what "*conform to* English Language Arts standards #3, 7, and 8" means, but there is enough specificity that all stakeholders can share understanding of the goal.

Historically, **short-term objective** statements have had to accompany annual goal statements; however, IDEA (2004) now requires only objectives, or benchmarks, for students who participate in alternative assessments that correspond to alternative achievement standards. When used, short-term objectives should be accomplished in the process of attaining an annual goal. In some cases, students would master the objectives sequentially, in the order they are listed under the goal statement. A traditionally worded objective statement includes an observable behavior, the condition under which the behavior will be performed, and the standard by which performance will be judged (most commonly a proficiency level). Previous IDEA reauthorizations allowed using **benchmark** statements in place of short-term objectives. Recognizing that many goals are not accomplished by lockstep attainment of discrete skills (objectives) and that progress can be assessed without discrete measurements, benchmarks instead represent markers of progress toward goal attainment (see Box 2.3).

BOX 2.2

EXAMPLES OF GOOD AND POOR IEP GOAL STATEMENTS

GOOD GOAL STATEMENTS

"Rena will recognize 50 words on sight from the second-grade level of the Dolch word list."

"Jae-Su will compose five-paragraph essays on class topics; essays will conform to English Language Arts standards #3, 7, and 8."

POOR GOAL STATEMENTS

"Stuart will improve his social skills."
   [What does "improve" mean? Which social skills or how many? In what context?]
"Anwar will use grade-level math strategies."
   [Which strategies? For what math skills?]
"Felicia will pay attention for five minutes without getting distracted or fidgeting."
   [Pay attention to what? In what setting?]

BOX 2.3

EXAMPLES OF SHORT-TERM OBJECTIVE AND BENCHMARK STATEMENTS

GOAL

"Rena will recognize 50 words from the second-grade level of the Dolch word list, on sight and in grade-level appropriate contexts."

Objective #1: Given a list of ten randomly selected words from the Dolch first-grade–level list, Rena will correctly read eight of the words aloud.

Objective #2: Given a list of ten randomly selected words from the Dolch second-grade–level list, Rena will correctly read eight of the words aloud.

Objective #3: Given a grade 2-level controlled reading passage, Rena will read aloud sections including at least 8 Dolch second-grade list words, without error.

GOAL

"Jae-Su will compose five-paragraph essays on class topics; essays will conform to English Language Arts standards #3, 7, and 8."

Objective #1: Jae-Su will prepare a TREE outline for essay planning that conforms to an essay topic assigned for a social studies topic.

Objective #2: Jae-Su will compose paragraph-length "essays" that conform to a TREE outline she develops.

Objective #3: Jae-Su will compose five paragraph essays that conform to a TREE outline she develops, for a topic assigned in any of her content classes.

How Jae-Su's objectives may be rewritten as benchmark statements:

Benchmark #1: By the end of January, Jae-Su will develop appropriate TREE outlines for content classroom topics without being prompted for content.

Specially Designed Instruction

The **specially designed instruction** portion of the IEP includes descriptions of any skills or content instruction that the IEP team determines the student must receive to attain goals (for example, use of a particular basal reading series or instruction in a reading technique such as Orton-Gillingham). Even when a student will receive instruction that is planned as part of the regular education curriculum anyway, it should be specified in the specially designed instruction section. That way, if the classroom teacher decides to alter the curriculum, the special education student will still receive the needed instruction. This section is also the place to record any specific instructional approaches that need to be used with the student (as specific as "orthographic approaches to writing" or "use corrective and informative feedback with frequent praise"). The information in the specially designed instruction section sometimes pertains to individual goals (for example, the orthographic approach to writing would be used during instruction on the skills of writing, but maybe not during a social studies class), and to all instruction for the student in other cases (for example, use feedback and praise).

Another aspect of specially designed instruction involves related services. **Related services** include transportation and developmental, corrective, or other support services that a student needs to receive and benefit from an education. Examples of related services include speech and language tutoring, physical or occupational therapy, social work support, psychological services such as counseling, and transportation to and from school. These services may be considered to provide students with access to their education. They are not educational interventions. The only related services that may be provided under the IDEA are those that are needed for students to benefit from a special education. In accordance with Section 504, however, related services must be provided to support general or special education.

The specially designed instruction section of the IEP is also the place to identify **instructional accommodations** students should receive. An accommodation is a minor change in how teachers present information to the student or in how the student learns or performs. The change does not alter overall learning expectations. To accommodate a student with ADHD, for example, the teacher might give that student preferential seating away from distractions or the teacher might give the student a rubber toy to squeeze to alleviate a desire to fidget. Other accommodations relate more directly to the teaching-learning process; the teacher might give the student print copies of directions that everyone else only receives orally, as Penny did for Albert in Case 2.1, or the teacher may give the student extra time on exams to compensate for distractibility. Note that, in all of these examples, the student still learns, or is tested on, the same content or skills as nondisabled peers. (For much more on accommodations, see Chapter 9.)

THINK BACK TO THE CASE of Albert and Penny . . .

2. *If Albert does need special education, how should the team determine whether his curriculum should change from the regular fifth-grade curriculum Penny teaches?*

Once Albert's IEP team has determined his annual goals and any short-term objectives or benchmarks, the members must review Albert's learning profile and discuss the learning tasks demanded by the curriculum they have planned. From this conversation, they should identify if and how to change his regular education instruction for him to succeed. The varied expertise of team members will be useful for determining the most beneficial option for Albert. They will need to remember that IDEA regulations encourage as little alteration of the regular education curriculum as possible. The regulations also encourage the team to try to keep the student in the regular education environment whenever feasible. Thus, the team begins by discussing accommodations and then specially designed instruction and related services that Albert may need.

Service Delivery

Once the goals and specially designed instruction are stated, the IEP must include a **service plan.** This section of the IEP identifies the following:

- The types of professional(s) (for example, special educator, general educator, therapist) who will provide specific services (for example, classroom instruction, one-on-one tutoring, counseling)

- Where those services will be provided (the least restrictive environment)
- The duration of the services (for example, how frequently per week, for what portion of the calendar year)
- How each goal is addressed by one or more of the specified services

The service plan section also includes an area to specify **testing accommodations** that the student will receive during standardized and high-stakes testing, as well as during classroom testing. Just like instructional accommodations, testing accommodations are minor changes in how the student is tested or in how the student performs the test; testing accommodations do not alter the overall testing expectations. Among common testing accommodations for students with mild disabilities are extra time, a scribe, taking the exam in a study carrel or private setting, being able to use a calculator, and being allowed to write directly on the exam, even if others have to write answers on a separate answer sheet.

To be effective, the testing accommodations identified should be consistent with the instructional accommodations the student receives (Burns 2006). The accommodations will be of limited usefulness on tests unless the student uses the accommodations daily. It makes little sense to teach a student to do a task one way (for example, completing math problems using a calculator), and then assess the student's abilities in other ways. Completing this section of the IEP is very important. In the case of some standardized and high-stakes tests, accommodations that are not certified as necessary on an official document such as an IEP may be denied to students. Some standardized exams (for example, SAT and GED) have approved lists of acceptable accommodations. IEP teams should consider them for students who will eventually take those exams.

The 504 Plan   A different plan is developed for students with disabilities when they do not need special education services under IDEA, but still require reasonable accommodations. A plan specifying needed accommodations and related services, commonly known as a "**504 Plan,**" is developed instead, in accordance with provisions of Section 504 of the Rehabilitation Act (1973). Like an IEP, a 504 Plan needs to include sufficient information for educators to understand why specified services are needed, what those services should be, and how they should be provided (for example, who is responsible and in what settings). In the case of students who require special education in addition to related services, the requirements for Section 504 are satisfied by compliance with IDEA procedures, and the IEP form includes all content that would otherwise appear on a 504 Plan. To qualify for 504 services, a student must have a physical or mental impairment that substantially limits a major life activity or is regarded as a handicap by others. Many students with ADHD in particular satisfy this criterion but do not meet IDEA eligibility criteria (Barkley 2000).

Section 504 does not specify what content should be included in a 504 Plan (nor, technically, that a plan be written). However, a useful 504 Plan specifies what related service(s) a student should receive, who will provide it, and how its impact will be monitored (see Burns 2006; Smith 2001). See Figure 2.2 for an example of a 504 Plan.

FIGURE 2.2

Sample 504 Plan

Name: _____ Albert C. _____ School/Class: _____ Fifth _____

Teacher: _____ Penny Margolis _____ Date of Plan: _____ 10–29 _____

General Strengths:

Albert performs math skills on grade level and is doing well during Math. His problem-solving skills (mathematical and otherwise) are also strong. He has excellent penmanship. Socially, he is appropriate with his peers and has made friends since moving into the district.

General Weaknesses:

Albert reads below grade level, showing difficulties with decoding as well as with comprehension. He makes frequent spelling errors in essay papers and assignments. A significant difficulty for Albert is comprehending and following directions.

Accommodation 1

Provide explicit directions for all assignments and back them up with written step-by-step directions.

Class:

All

Person Responsible for Implementing Accommodation:

Classroom teacher and any aides

Accommodation 2

Review instructions with Albert by having him paraphrase or explain them.

Class:

All

Person Responsible for Implementing Accommodation:

Classroom teacher or aide

Accommodation 3

When reading is not an instructional goal, provide easy-to-read version of materials or either read aloud or allow group reading.

Class:

All

Person Responsible for Implementing Accommodation:

Classroom teacher or aide

Individuals Participating in Development of Plan:

Penny Margolis–classroom teacher
Martha Bender–special educator

Source: Format for blank form reprinted with permission from T. E. C. Smith. Section 504, the ADA, and public schools (*Remedial And Special Education* 22(6)(2001):335–43).

The Team Develops the IEP

The team that comes together to compose the IEP represents the various stakeholders who play a role in the student's education. The following people are named by IDEA 2004 as members of the team:

Parent(s)
Student–whenever appropriate*
Special education teacher
Regular education teacher(s)
Representative of local education agency, who is:

- Qualified to supervise provision of services
- Knowledgeable about regular education curriculum
- Knowledgeable about resource availability

Professional to interpret instructional implications of evaluation results**
Transition agency representative**
Others deemed appropriate by the parent or education agency and consistent with IDEA and state and local requirements**

Parents and students can feel like outsiders at a team meeting (see Summers et al. 2005). When teachers use professional jargon that is unfamiliar to or assumed to be common knowledge it is easy for parents to feel devalued and unable to contribute. Educators have an obligation to make parents feel that their input is valued, because families have valuable insights and goals for their child that can easily be overlooked in the process (Gonzalez et al. 2001; Moll, et al. 1992). In the case of parents for whom English is not a comfortable language, the IDEA requires that a translator be present at the meeting and that all relevant documents be shared in translated forms, including the IEP document that the team develops. In the same ways that parents may feel like outsiders to the IEP process, students who are present in IEP meetings tend to remain silent, with their input rarely solicited (Arndt, Konrad, and Test 2006). With preparation to participate, however, they too can make valuable contributions regarding their educational experiences and goals (Test et al. 2005). Students who participate in their own IEP meetings in meaningful ways tend to be more motivated to succeed in the education they and their teammates plan (Arndt, Konrad, and Test 2006). (See Chapter 12 for more on student participation on IEP and individualized transition plan [ITP] teams.)

Chapter Question

ALERT

In this section, you will find information that answers a Chapter Question:

3. How can teachers plan effective lessons for special education students?

Relating Education Plans to Regular Education

To be consistent with NCLB (2001), the IDEA requires that all students in special education participate "in the regular classroom, to the maximum extent possible, in order to . . . meet developmental goals and, to the maximum extent possible, the challenging expectations that have been established for all children" (*IDEA* 2004, §1400(c)(5)). When such participation is not appropriate, the goals specified for these students should focus on meeting the curriculum standards of their nondisabled peers (Allbritten, Mainzer, and Ziegler 2004).

---

*Must participate upon achieving legal age of majority, or if transition planning is to be discussed
**As needed

The charge from the IDEA is clear: teams should plan an individually appropriate education that maximizes a student's participation in regular education (Turnbull, Huerta, and Stowe 2006). All regular education curricula have **"curriculum standards."** The standards identify the learning experiences or outcomes expected of all learners who participate in the curriculum (Popham 2006). Curriculum standards shape the mandated regular education curriculum at the state and local levels. In accordance with NCLB requirements, all students' performances on the standards must be directly assessed, which is typically accomplished through exams. In a majority of states, those exams are "high stakes," meaning that performance on them is tied to whether students are promoted to the next grade or graduate. The NCLB requires all state-level departments of education to publish publicly their curriculum standards; many states' standards are readily available via their DOE websites. For most curriculum areas, states adapt standards proposed by professional organizations in the various curriculum areas. (The *Website Resources on Planning, Teaching, and Monitoring Instruction* section at the end of this chapter includes the names and web addresses for professional organizations offering standards in the major curriculum areas.) The standards reflect the opinions of experts regarding what skills and knowledge students should possess. Some standards identify exact and observable skills or knowledge (for example, "As a result of activities in grades K–4, all students should develop understanding of . . . life cycles of organisms . . ." [*National Science Education Standards*, National Research Council, 1996]), whereas others identify more global expectations (for example, "Students read a wide range of . . . texts to build an understanding of texts, of themselves, and of the cultures of the United States and the world . . ." [*Standards for the English Language Arts*, National Council of Teachers of English and the International Reading Association, 1996]).

Standards and Students in Special Education

Students enrolled in special education are expected to participate in the same standards as their peers in regular education; there are no separate curriculum standards for special education. The primary support that students in special education receive when they participate in the regular education curriculum standards occurs through accommodations. Through provision of accommodations, students can work on the same content and skills as their peers, using the same (or highly similar) materials. So, students with a mild disability who are expected to "read a wide range of texts to build an understanding of the cultures of the United States and the world" may read a text written at a different level but that covers the same content as their classmates read, for example.

Students with mild disabilities who perform certain academic skills significantly below grade level are expected to keep up with the regular education content to the greatest extent possible while they work on those academic skills. Whenever possible, they should learn grade-level appropriate skills, even though other more basic skills proficiencies still need to be developed. Thus, if asked to read a Shakespeare play, a student who reads well below the comfortable reading level required might be accommodated in reading the play (for example, receiving assistance with comprehension, using an alternative version of the text), while also receiving supplemental instruction in more basic reading skills.

Although students with mild disabilities typically benefit from the same high learning standards as other students, they do sometimes need to be taught differently or are expected to perform in ways that differ from what the standards expect. In such cases, the specially designed instruction section of the IEP is where the different methods of instruction or performance are recorded.

No matter the content-area standards being addressed for students with mild disabilities, certain effective teaching practices may be used to help them

CASE 2.2   Planning for Special Education in Relation to Inclusion and Standards

Case Introduction

In this case you meet Rosa, a special educator who works with some students in a pull-out setting and other students in regular education classrooms. In her resource room, she faces the challenge of working with students who have different IEP goals at the same time. When Rosa works in regular education classrooms, she finds that she has to collaborate differently with each regular education teacher whose classroom she shares. In some cases, they share the teaching; in other cases, they merely share space. As you read the case, you will see that Rosa must plan what she will teach and how best to teach it in each of these varied contexts.

As a special education teacher, Rosa played a major role in developing the IEPs for each of her students. Rosa coordinates most of the consulting with the Teacher Assistance Team and Multidisciplinary Team, and generates most of the ideas the teams adopt for the IEPs. In addition, she actually writes up the IEPs following team meetings, and she serves as the special educator identified in the service delivery section of those plans. All of her efforts on behalf of students give her useful insights into how best to work with them.

One of Rosa's students is Paula. Paula is an eighth grader with mild mental retardation. Her least restrictive environment for English and social studies is the resource room. There, Rosa and Paula work together on basic literacy skills; however, they are obligated to work on the regular education English and social studies curricula as well. Paula's reading and writing skills are at approximately a fourth-grade level. Developing literacy skills is a slow process and Paula needs frequent review of skills she has learned previously. When Paula is in the resource room with Rosa, four other students for whom Rosa is responsible are present as well.

Another of Rosa's students is a ninth-grader named Taylor who has both a learning disability and attention deficit/hyperactivity disorder-inattentive subtype. Rosa accompanies Taylor to his pre-algebra and English classes, where she works with him and several other students.

In both pre-algebra and English class, the students spend a good portion of the time practicing skills they are learning. In ninth-grade English, the focus is on grammar and composition, which the classroom teacher teaches from a perspective of mastering rules of composition, instead of focusing on quality of expression, for example. Although the English teacher respects Rosa, he has a different perspective on their co-teaching. He believes that Rosa is there to support his lesson with Taylor and a few other special education students. He wants Rosa to step in and teach Taylor and the others whenever he is ready to move on with the rest of the class. Even though Rosa and the special education director try to get him to understand Rosa's role, he remains resistant. So, in that room, Rosa tends to "stand by" while the regular education teacher leads the whole class, then she typically works directly with Taylor and a few other students with IEPs who are all seated near one another.

The pre-algebra teacher is much more welcoming of Rosa as a co-teacher. They plan their roles together. Even though he does all of the full class instruction, Rosa sometimes interrupts him to help make a point clear; she freely wanders about the room helping all students as needed. In fact, although the students can observe that she frequently works with Taylor and a few other students, they are not aware that she is there because of Taylor. She is careful to attend always to Taylor, but the class teacher is also able to work routinely with him with this arrangement.

CASE QUESTIONS

1. How can Rosa and the regular education teachers she works with create productive working relationships to meet Paula's and Taylor's needs?
2. How can sharing lesson plans with Taylor and his regular education classmates enhance their active learning?
3. What are effective teaching practices that Rosa can use in both the resource room and regular education classroom?

meet the standards. The first step of effective teaching, however, is planning an effective lesson.

Lesson Planning

There is no one best approach to planning, just as there is no one best format for lesson plans. Planning a lesson helps to ensure that a teacher has carefully thought through the following:

- What the student(s) should learn
- Why the student(s) should learn it
- What the student(s) will need to be able to do to have success
- Ways the lesson may need to be modified
- How the teacher will know if students have success
- How the classroom will be configured

Effective teacher collaboration requires teachers to plan together as well as evaluate their working relationship and the student learning outcomes that result.

A good plan will also guide teachers in evaluating how effectively they taught and how efficiently the students learned. Having a good plan is essential to having a good lesson.

Schumm et al. (1995) suggested that there are three interrelated phases of lesson planning. The **preplanning phase** includes thinking about topics such as those previously listed and setting the plan for both what will be taught and how it will be taught. Curriculum standards are a useful guide for determining what to teach. Teachers often rely on state- or district-level curricula or those supplied with textbooks when preplanning their lessons (Vaughn and Schumm 1994).

The preplanned lesson plan can be considered an outline or a script for the lesson. In addition to responding to the topics previously listed, the plan takes into account the resources available to teachers, the amount of time they have for lessons, and their background knowledge of the student(s). (In the section that follows, you will read about the essential components of a useful lesson plan.) See Appendix A on the book-specific website for a sample lesson plan.

The **interactive planning phase** is the ongoing planning that occurs while a lesson is happening. Effective teachers monitor how well their students are learning during a lesson, and they make adjustments to their instruction as they teach. They are constantly planning what they will do next, based on what they see happening during the lesson. In the process of teaching, teachers may decide to give a few more practice examples, skip or reorder certain activities, or alter the amount of time planned for the lesson, for example. It is important to realize that teachers (a) can alter lessons as they go, based on thoughtful monitoring of student progress, and (b) have a preplanned lesson plan that will guide in making alterations consistent with theories of learning (see Chapter 3) and targeted lesson outcomes. It can be particularly valuable for teachers to be willing to "deviate from the script" for students with special needs in the regular classroom who need an individual accommodation (for example, immediate feedback during practice exercises or clarified directions).

Finally, in the **postplanning phase,** which follows the lesson, teachers review the appropriateness of their plans by considering how well the plans were followed, how effective the plans and teaching were, and how well students performed. To ensure accuracy, teachers should use data collected during the lesson, in addition to recalling personal observations from the lesson. They can review their lesson plans to see if certain activities took appreciably less or more time than allotted; they can also look at student work products to determine if explanations of content were clear. Postplanning concludes with (a) making notes on the completed lesson, for when it is next taught, and (b) updating plans for ensuing lessons based on what was learned (for example, begin the next lesson with a review of the completed lesson, build in more time for practice).

According to Schumm et al. (1995), three factors influence planning at the three planning phases: the teacher, the environment, and student-related factors (see Figure 2.3). The **teacher factor** involves how carefully the teacher is inclined to plan, the teacher's knowledge and skills, and awareness and ability to make accommodations for individual students; all influence the quality of lesson plans produced at any of the three phases. **Environmental factors** include the physical environment and the scholarly climate of the school community. The physical layout of the classroom is a factor; the teacher must consider how the layout will affect grouping, "traffic patterns," and access to viewing media such as a demonstration video. The scholarly climate of the school community relates to academic factors that influence a teacher's planning. Some principals require lesson plans to be filed on a weekly basis; other schools have a culture among faculty that is tantamount to peer pressure to plan, or not. How schools prescribe a curriculum, particularly as it relates to standards, is another academic factor that shapes the scholarly climate. Among **student-related factors** are the prior knowledge individual students bring to the lesson, their motivation,

FIGURE 2.3

Factors Influencing the Three Planning Phases

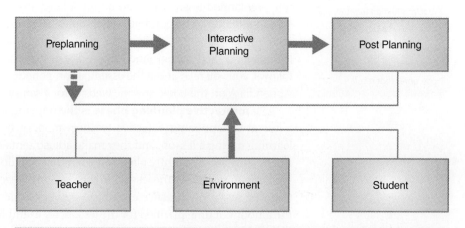

Reprinted with permission from J. S. Schumm, S. Vaughn, D. Haager, J. McDowell, L. Rothlein, and L. Saumell. "Regular Education Teacher Planning: What Can Students with Learning Disabilities Expect?" (*Exceptional Children* 61(1995):335–52 (particularly 337)).

TABLE 2.1: 14 Lesson Plan Components Recommended for Teacher Planning

Student objectives*	Materials required*	Time required
Prerequisite skills	Seating arrangement	Anticipatory set
Instructional steps*	Checks for understanding*	Guided practice*
Independent practice*	Summary/closing	Evaluation of student outcomes*
Follow-up activity*	Self-evaluation of lesson presentation	

*Components beginning special educators most need to include in their lesson plans. Reported by **Searcy and Maroney (1996)** as recommended by greater than 55 percent of survey respondents.

and how well they attend. The students' academic skills are also student-related factors, as are their ability to participate in accommodations and their behavior during the lesson.

Components of a Lesson Plan. Traditional components of a lesson plan include objectives, materials, procedures, and assessments (Albert and Ammer 2004).

Searcy and Maroney (1996) identified 14 components of lesson plans that professional literature recommends teachers use. Those marked with an asterisk in Table 2.1 are components special educators most strongly recommended for beginning special education teachers to include in their lesson plans. (See Callahan, Clark, Kellough [1998] for other recommended lesson plan components.) Ultimately, what makes a lesson plan useful is that it contains all of the information a teacher needs to get through a lesson.

The Challenge of Planning. Making time to plan is one challenge to planning. Fighting the inclination to "plan in your head" is another. Even though experienced teachers recommend that beginning teachers develop lesson plans, most novices do not; indeed, most experienced teachers report that they do not either (Arends 1998; Searcy and Maroney 1996). The greater the number of students for whom they were responsible, the more likely they were to write plans, however. Even though the teachers surveyed typically did not write out their lesson plans, they did plan. They reported planning consciously but without writing plans down. They also reported interactive planning by following habit or instinct during teaching.

THINK BACK TO THE CASE of Rosa and her students . . .

1. *How can Rosa and the regular education teachers she works with create productive working relationships to meet Paula's and Taylor's needs?*

Working together in a teaching relationship is not as easy as coming together for an IEP meeting. **Co-teaching** requires being able to plan together (across all three planning phases), communicate ideas and concerns to one another, and teach in ways that are compatible (Cook and Friend 1995). Co-teaching and collaborating can be

continued

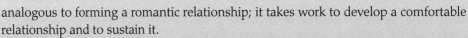

analogous to forming a romantic relationship; it takes work to develop a comfortable relationship and to sustain it.

Friend and Bursuck (1999) offer seven tips for nurturing a successful co-teaching relationship: (1) plan, including how you will work together; (2) discuss your views on teaching and learning; (3) attend to details such as rules, routines, and grading; (4) prepare parents for what to expect from co-teachers; (5) avoid the trap of treating one teacher as the "paraprofessional"—it is usually the special educator; (6) talk out disagreements; and (7) go slowly—grow into relying on one another as your relationship develops.

To determine compatibility, potential co-teacher partners can ask each other the following questions (selected items paraphrased from Vaughn, Bos, and Schumm 2000):

How do you help new students feel comfortable in your classroom?
What kind of practice activities do you use?
What are your basic classroom rules? What are the consequences?
How can we give each other constructive feedback as our relationship develops?

If Rosa and her colleagues consider themselves incompatible but still have to work together, these questions serve as an outline of factors they will need to address together. (Co-planning and co-teaching are discussed in more detail in Chapter 13 on collaboration).

Making Use of Lesson Plans. Students will benefit from teachers that share lesson plans with them in the form of advance organizers (Lenz, Alley, and Schumaker 1987; Ellis and Lenz 1990). In the 1960s, Ausubel (1963; Ausubel, Novak, and Hanesian 1968) suggested that advance organizers help orient learners to the topic and task expectations in ways that boost participation and learning outcomes; more recent research has corroborated that idea (Bulgren and Lenz 1996; see also Swanson and Hoskyn 2001).

THINK BACK TO THE CASE   about Rosa . . .

2. *How can sharing lesson plans with Taylor and his regular education classmates enhance their active learning?*

Using a lesson planning organizer (Lenz et al. 1993) that the students participate in developing, the teacher can preview the planned lesson topic and content as well as major activities.

In Figure 2.4, a teacher completes a lesson organizer for a lesson on women in U.S. history. The teacher begins by orienting students to the lesson. First, she explains the lesson topic (similarities and differences between Harriet Tubman and Sojourner Truth) and how it relates to the larger unit (famous women in American history). Now the students have a sense of what the lesson has to do with anything else they are studying.

FIGURE 2.4

Shared Planning Lesson Organizer: Women in History

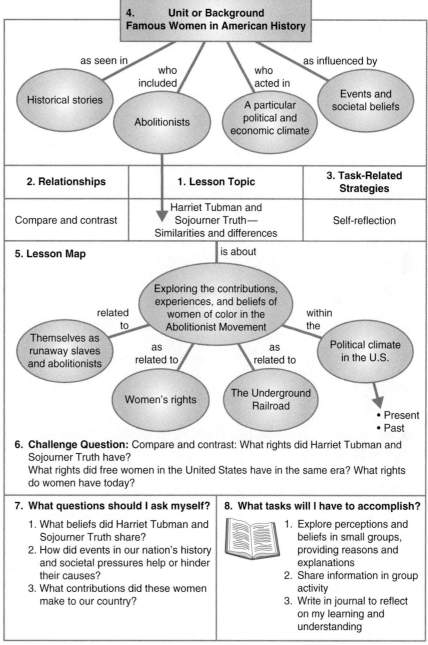

Reprinted with permission from L. R. Albert and J. J. Ammer. "Lesson Planning and Delivery." In *Teaching Content to All*, ed. B. K. Lenz, D. D. Deshler, and B. R. Kissam. (Boston, MA: Allyn & Bacon, 2004, 205).

The web is the central feature of the lesson organizer. It identifies key concepts and vocabulary that will be addressed in the lesson, as well as how they all fit together to address the lesson topic. The teacher should walk the students through reading the web, and all portions of the organizer, by narrating the information represented. To keep the students actively involved, the narration should become an interactive dialogue in which the students share their prior knowledge about the lesson topic and web content. They can also generate questions they want to answer during the lesson, or they can predict answers to questions the teacher poses. In this way, they participate in developing the plan for what they will study. The lesson organizer serves to inform students as to what will be learned, activate their prior knowledge, preview vocabulary and concepts, indicate relationships among vocabulary and concepts, and motivate students to think about the content.

The organizer sections titled "Challenge Question" and "What questions should I ask myself?" are places to indicate the "big ideas" of the lesson. The questions cue students to the types of information and relationships among concepts they will be studying. They are also cued to which information is particularly important to attend. The questions are designed to prompt thinking. So a good question on a lesson organizer does not ask a student merely to recall a fact, but rather to synthesize or otherwise act on content from the lesson (Lenz et al. 1993). The questions can be referred to periodically throughout the lesson.

Although the lesson organizer is useful to help launch a lesson by orienting students to the topic, it can also be a useful organizational tool throughout the lesson. The "tasks to accomplish" section can include a record of when assignments are due or when certain activities will take place. In the Figure 2.4 lesson organizer, students can see that they will have a small group activity and journal writing for which they are responsible. To help them remain organized, students should have copies of the lesson organizer that they can keep in their notebooks and refer to as needed.

Chapter Question
ALERT

In this section you will find information that answers a Chapter Question:

4. What research-based techniques are effective for teaching students with mild disabilities?

Using "Best Practices" in Special Education Teaching

As the term suggests, *best practices* are those instructional techniques that are considered most often to be effective for students with mild disabilities. There are two main sources that inform us on best practices. First, standards identify knowledge and/or skills that teachers should possess. As you will read, using teacher standards is mandated by NCLB, but the standards themselves are developed by a variety of professionals. The second source of best practices is research. Educational researchers design experiments to "test" instructional practices and publish their findings; in the second half of this section, you will read how to judge the findings of such research. (Most professionally recommended standards are for practices supported by research.)

Standards for Special Educators

Just as there are curriculum standards for what students should learn in school, there are standards for what teachers should know. Standards exist for educators by school level for the lower grades; for example, the Council for Exceptional Children's Division for Early Childhood published *Recommended Practices* for preschool through age five (Sandall et al. 2005), and the Association for Childhood Education International produced *Elementary Education Program Standards* for the elementary years (ACEI 2000). Standards also exist by subject areas for teachers at all levels. The NCLB Act mandates that licensed teachers achieve standards in the areas of their licensure. Examinations are commonly used to determine whether teachers meet the expected standards. The NCLB Act also mandates that teachers be **"highly qualified"** to teach in the area(s) in which they are licensed. States have the responsibility for determining how "highly qualified" status is attained. Commonly, meeting the state's teacher standards is included in the requirements for "highly qualified."

The CEC Standards. The Council for Exceptional Children (2003) has identified standards of practice for special educators (the publication is commonly known as "The Red Book"). Various stakeholders in special education collaborated to identify topic areas for special educator standards as well as the standards within each of those areas. They have developed standards for entry-level special education teachers, including by certain disability categories (and gifted and talented), for special educators preparing for advanced roles such as diagnostician and administrator, and for special education paraprofessionals. (In addition, they have identified a "code of ethics and standards for professional practice for special education".)

The "knowledge and skill base for all entry-level special education teachers of students with exceptionalities in individualized general curriculums" pertains to virtually all beginning special education teachers of students with mild disabilities. There are ten of these standards (see the inside cover of this book). Within each standard, there are specific competencies for knowledge and skill. The competencies for specific knowledge represent the breadth of knowledge a special educator should have, such as the following:

Standard #2: Development and Characteristics of Learners
Typical and atypical human growth and development
Family systems and the roles of families in supporting development

Standard #4: Instructional Strategies
Sources of specialized materials, curricula, and resources for individuals
    with disabilities

Likewise, the skills standards identify what a special educator should be able to do, such as the following:

Standard #4: Instructional Strategies
Use strategies to facilitate maintenance and generalization of skills across
    learning environments

Standard #6: Language
Use communication strategies and resources to facilitate understanding of
    subject matter for students whose primary language is not the dominant
    language
Plan instruction on the use of alternative and augmentative communication
    systems

In a recent survey study (Zionts, Shellady, and Zionts 2006), special educators reported that they appreciate the importance of the CEC standards but find them difficult to implement. Crutchfield (2003) has identified a four-step process to use the standards to monitor and improve your own practice.

1. Identify the appropriate set of CEC standards (for example, for entry-level educators).
2. Rate your mastery level for each standard (using Crutchfield's self-evaluation forms).
3. Note which standard areas are your strongest and weakest.
4. Choose a domain(s) to work on and plan your professional development course of action.

"Best" Instructional Approaches in Special Education

Although the CEC standards represent overall knowledge and skills a special educator should possess, they are not all that a special educator needs to know to be an effective teacher. Effective special educators need to know which specific instructional practices are most beneficial for their students, as well as how to use them. As discussed in Chapter 1, most students with mild disabilities learn the same content and skills as other students. Particular instructional practices, validated by careful research on their effectiveness, are commonly used with special education students, regardless of the content or skills they are learning, however. Many of those practices are effective for all learners, but are considered by some to be essential for students in special education (Kauffman 2002; Harris and Graham 1996; compare to Heshusius 1991).

Research Evidence

"Best Practices" in Special Education. Several researchers have conducted rigorous statistical analyses to identify which instructional practices have been the most effective for those with mild disabilities (for example, Vaughn, Gersten, and Chard 2000; Vellutino et al. 2000; Swanson and Hoskyn 1998). Perhaps the most comprehensive of all of these has been a meta-analysis conducted by H. Lee Swanson and his colleagues in the 1990s (for example, Swanson and Hoskyn 1998; Swanson, Hoskyn, and Lee 1999). Swanson first identified published research studies from a 30-year period that satisfied rigorous criteria for identifying who the participants were (for example, documentation that they satisfied the definitional criteria for a specific learning disability and for special education enrollment), studying one or more interventions, and for fully reporting the analyzed data. Swanson then applied meta-analytic statistical procedures to identify trends across study findings (Swanson and Hoskyn 1998). He identified the following nine instructional components (ibid., 303) that the body of published research can support as effective for students with mild disabilities:

- Sequencing
- Segmentation of information
- Augmentation of teacher instruction (e.g., homework)
- Drill, repetition, practice
- Technology
- Directed questioning/responding
- Controlling task difficulty

- Small interactive groups
- Strategy cuing

In a further analysis of effectiveness for adolescents (defined as between 11 and 19 years of age), two components were found to have the most impact: advance organizers and explicit instruction (Swanson and Hoskyn 2001). Two instructional approaches that incorporate high percentages of these components, Direct Instruction and Learning Strategy Instruction, are commonly used in special education teaching.

Direct Instruction/Explicit Instruction. **Direct Instruction** (commonly known as DI) is a published series of curricula (for example, Carnine, Silbert, and Kame'enui 1990; Engelmann 1980). Traditional components of DI instruction include carefully sequenced learning goals and lesson content, teacher-cued student participation, scripted lessons, and rapid-paced student responding. Some educators consider DI to be too limiting on teachers as instructional decision makers and to promote isolated skill performances that are of limited utility for application in practice (Heshusius 1991; Poplin and Rogers 2005). Some teachers embrace some of the principles of DI but not the carefully constructed DI curricula. The critical principles of Direct Instruction include the following:

- Sequenced skill objectives
- Sequenced lesson activities
- Review of pre-skills/prior knowledge
- Reteaching
- Intensive practice
- Frequent practice
- Errorless learning
- Corrective feedback

Instructional approaches that borrow from the principles of Direct Instruction are sometimes known as direct instruction spelled with a lowercase "d" and "i," but more commonly as **directive instruction** or **explicit instruction.** Many of the principles of DI are incorporated, but some practices are relaxed or omitted (for example, unison student responding when the teacher cues). DI/explicit instruction is research-validated as effective for students with mild disabilities learning both academic and behavioral skills. Swanson's meta-analysis findings included that DI/explicit approaches are among the most effective for students with mild disabilities. Swanson and Hoskyn (1998) state, "a combined direct instruction and strategy instruction model is an effective procedure for remediating learning disabilities relative to other models" (303) (Note: They use the term *direct instruction* to mean the same thing as "DI/explicit instruction," and not exclusively the published curriculum series.) You will read about instructional practices that incorporate DI/explicit instruction principles throughout this book.

Learning Strategies Instruction. In **Learning Strategies Instruction,** students are taught skills as part of skill systems that address all aspects of performing a meaningful task. The focus in learning strategies instruction is on performance of the overall task, instead of on individual component skills. For example, in the paraphrasing strategy (Schumaker, Denton, and Deshler 1984)—a classic reading comprehension strategy—students learn to identify reading tasks that call for the strategy (for example, comprehend a multiparagraph reading and recall its key content), analyze the reading paragraph by paragraph for main ideas and important details to recall, and then paraphrase that information as a check of their comprehension (also see Ellis 1996). The strategy includes cognitive cues that remind students of what to do and why (Ellis et al. 1991).

By being taught learning strategies, students not only learn specific skills of a task (for example, reflecting at the paragraph level and identifying a main idea), but they learn how those skills fit together into a comprehensive process. Thus, instead of building up incremental skills of the reading process to the point where fluid reading with comprehension is eventually realized, students learn the overall process of reading for comprehension.

The Relationship Between DI/Explicit and Learning Strategy Instruction. Swanson and Hoskyn (1998) reported that Learning Strategies Instruction alone was more effective than DI/explicit instruction alone. However, both were rated as "highly effective." The two are not diametrically opposed approaches to teaching. Many of the principles of DI/explicit are incorporated into research-validated strategy instruction models. Likewise, updates to the DI curricula include application of skills to meaningful tasks even when more incremental skills of the overall process have yet to be mastered (for example, Carnine, Silbert, and Kame'enui 1990). In fact, Swanson's meta-analysis indicates that the combination of Direct Instruction/explicit instruction and learning strategies instruction is more powerful than either approach alone (Swanson and Hoskyn 2001).

Progress Monitoring. Teachers can enhance their use of Direct Instruction/explicit instruction, Learning Strategies Instruction, or most any approach to teaching by incorporating progress monitoring. They will also be in compliance with legal expectations for effective practice. The NCLB Act requires that states document their schools' progress toward achieving NCLB goals. A major way in which progress is monitored is charting students' adequate yearly progress (AYP). The premise of this requirement is that all students, including those with disabilities, can achieve the standards set by NCLB if progress is monitored and effective instructional decisions are driven by that data (Allbritten, Mainzer, and Ziegler 2004). The IDEA also requires that student progress be monitored, specifically, for individual students in a way that reflects progress toward their IEP goals. Progress monitoring can be effective in improving teaching practices and student learning (Safer and Fleischman 2005). If data shows progress to be minimal, or too slow, then changes to improve performance should be made; otherwise, the data can confirm that teachers should stick with the practice they are using.

METHODS AND STRATEGIES SPOTLIGHT

C-BM for Monitoring Student Performance

Another popular instructional approach in special education for students with mild disabilities is **Curriculum-Based Measurement** (**C-BM**). C-BM is virtually synonymous with progress monitoring. It has its origins in Curriculum-Based Assessment (Deno 2003a; 2003b; 1992), which is an approach to assessment that relies on evaluations of student performance using content from the student's curriculum instead of, for example, standardized achievement tests. In C-BM, teachers routinely sample student performance at the end of lessons to inform ongoing lesson planning. A particular benefit of C-BM is that it helps teachers to chart a student's progress on long-term learning goals, not just day-to-day short-term objectives (Stecker 2006).

In the graph in Figure 2.5, Rosa has drawn a **goal line** at 80 percent, indicating the level of correct performance she is working to help Paula achieve. By plotting Paula's performance data on daily tests of reading rate and accuracy, Rosa can see that Paula is making progress toward the goal (observe her accelerating **trend line**). However, the **rate** at which she is progressing is too slow, as evidenced by the **slope** of the line. Rosa believes that Paula should be progressing at a faster rate. Rosa could visually inspect Paula's rate and slope of progress by drawing an **aimline** on the graph as well. The aimline should be a straight line that begins where Paula's first performance is plotted and then extends to the place where the goal line intersects the date by which Rosa expects Paula to accomplish the goal. Once drawn, the daily data points should fall very close to the aimline, to indicate that the progress is occurring as planned. By continuing to use Paula's daily graph, Rosa and Paula will be able to monitor what types of learning progress ensue when Rosa modifies her instructional practices.

FIGURE 2.5

Paula's Daily Reading Rate and Accuracy

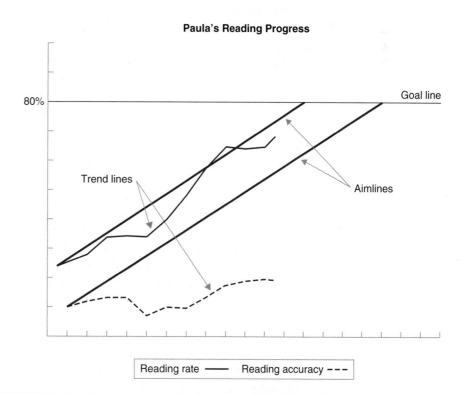

THINK BACK TO THE CASE about Rosa . . .

3.   *What are effective teaching practices that Rosa can use in both the resource room and regular education classroom?*

Direct instruction/explicit instruction and learning strategies instruction approaches are flexible enough that they can be taught to individual students or groups of students. Rosa may use both approaches with flexibility in a variety of contexts. Progress monitoring can also be used along with either approach, and is amenable to a variety of learning contexts and goals.

In the following section, two structured approaches to students working together are described. They too can be used in the range of special education placements and instructional contexts where Rosa and her students can be found.

Peer Tutoring and Cooperative Learning

If you have ever worked with a partner or in a group where someone did all of the work and somebody else got the credit, you know that there is more to getting students to cooperate than just telling students to work together. In peer tutoring and cooperative learning, students take active roles in the learning process by helping each other to learn. The two approaches are sometimes criticized; some charge that the approaches hold back more knowledgeable peers and they deprive students of the teacher's expertise. When conducted properly, neither is the case. We reference both of these approaches throughout this book.

Peer Tutoring. Peer tutoring is an effective way for students to practice using new skills and content. Among the benefits of peer tutoring is enhanced social standing for students with disabilities (Fuchs et al. 2002). By being paired, students with and without disabilities can interact in positive ways and come to appreciate one another as students pairing can lead to friendships as well.

One of the most extensively validated approaches to peer tutoring for students with disabilities is **classwide peer tutoring** (Greenwood and Delquadri 1995). In the general education classroom, all students in the room are assigned to tutoring pairs. Each student learns how to be an effective tutor and an appropriate tutee. Students learn how to prompt one another, how to politely correct, how to ask for assistance, and how to monitor their on-task behavior (Mathes et al. 1994), for example. Each pair in the class has a responsibility for simultaneously practicing an academic skill and using good tutoring behaviors. This approach to classwide teaching incorporates the Direct Instruction principles of intensive and rapid-paced practice, and of receiving informative feedback. The tutor prompts the tutee and then the tutor provides correction with feedback; the two then work together to make the corrections. Following the first round of practice, the two switch roles and continue practice. When one member of the pair is more skilled than the other, typically that peer tutors first (Fuchs and Fuchs 2005). Research findings clearly demonstrate the benefits of classwide peer tutoring to students with disabilities (Greenwood and Delquadri 1995).

Mastropieri et al. (2003) teach students to refer to each other as "admirals and generals" when they participate in peer tutoring. The students learn that they are of "equal rank." The teacher can easily determine who will be an admiral or general for a given lesson based on relative strength, and then announce, "Today, generals will tutor first." Although classwide peer tutoring was developed for elementary grade classrooms and is most often employed for practicing basic skills, it has been successfully applied to content learning in secondary-level classrooms as well (for example, Maheady, Sacca, and Harper 1988; Mastropieri et al. 2003; Spencer, Scruggs, and Mastropieri 2003).

In **peer-assisted learning strategies (PALS)** (for example, Fuchs et al. 1997; McMaster, Fuchs, and Fuchs 2006), peers tutor each other in a process based on classwide peer tutoring. The pairs are composed of stronger and weaker students in the skill. To form the pairs, the teacher composes two rank-ordered lists, one of the strongest students in the class for the skill and the other of the weakest; then the top names on each list are paired, followed by the second names, and so on. Like classwide peer tutoring, students interact as tutor and tutee, each taking a turn in each role. Also like classwide peer tutoring, hallmarks of the PALS process include a high level of engagement by both partners, regardless of role, and informative feedback. Each PALS pair is assigned to a team. Pairs earn points for their team based on the quality of their skill performance, as well as by earning "bonus points" based on the teacher observing them using good cooperative tutoring skills. At the elementary level, new PALS pair teams are created every four weeks, to keep pairings based on relative skill levels appropriate and the competition exciting. At the high school level, pairs are reformed daily, in response to both absentee rates and interests in working with a variety of peers (McMaster, Fuchs, and Fuchs 2006).

Research has demonstrated that PALS benefits both students with mild disabilities and their peers in inclusive classroom settings (Fuchs et al. 1997). Positive effects have been found for social skills as well (Fuchs et al. 2002). Those findings are reported for both elementary and secondary level students (see McMaster et al. 2006 for a summary). Interestingly, research into why some students do not benefit from PALS as much as their peers has indicated that limited pre-skills are likely contributing factors, but alterations to address their specific needs have only produced mixed effects (Al Otaiba and Fuchs 2002; McMaster et al. 2005). (You can read more about the PALS strategy used with reading in Chapter 4.)

METHODS AND STRATEGIES SPOTLIGHT

Teaching Students to Work Together

To be successful peer tutors, the students must learn how to perform their role(s) appropriately. **Cue cards** that list the steps of the procedures or necessary behaviors for each role can be made. You should also plan to monitor your students periodically to be certain they are interacting appropriately. Students can earn participation points based on how well they perform, regardless of the quality of their skill learning.

Students can participate in naming and defining the behaviors they should engage to help them understand their roles. The information they generate can be posted on a T-chart (Johnson, Johnson, and Holubec 1991). To make a **T-chart,** list the behaviors inside the left side of the T (see Figure 2.6), and write a description of what the behavior "looks and sounds like" on the right side. The students can participate with the teacher in naming the skills and describing the performance criteria. The completed chart can then be hung on the classroom wall as a ready reminder.

However students are reminded about good cooperative skills, they must be taught those skills directly, using effective teaching practices. Thus, especially when they are first learning cooperative skills, students should receive supportive instruction and feedback on their skill performance. They may be graded on their cooperative performances as well. Because they are busy learning new skills, they should not be faced with challenging content the first few times they try them (Ellis et al. 1991).

FIGURE 2.6

Sample T-Chart for Teaching Social Skills

SKILL	LOOKS/SOUNDS LIKE
Contribute ideas	"I think . . ."
Request information	"What does that mean?"
Listen carefully	Don't be doing other things when someone is talking to you.
Summarize	"So, what we decided was that . . ."
Encourage others to participate	"Tell us what you think."
Check for understanding	"Is this what you mean?" . . . "Do you get it?"

Reprinted courtesy D. Scanlon. "Social Skills Strategy Instruction," In *Teaching Adolescents with Learning Disabilities*, ed. D. D. Deshler, E. S. Ellis, and B. K. Lenz (Denver, CO: Love, 1996).

Cooperative Learning. The two factors that distinguish cooperative learning from peer tutoring are (a) more students are involved, and (b) the task is typically a joint effort to solve a challenge or to produce a product. The benefits of cooperative learning are much the same as they are for peer tutoring, however. When cooperative learning works correctly, students with and without disabilities benefit by being actively involved in the learning process, social relationships are enhanced, and all participants learn academic content from the experience (Slavin 1991; also see Tatayama-Sniezek 1990).

Cooperative learning does not always work. Some students get excluded, others do a disproportionate share of the work, not everyone involved learns the same things, and social relationships are damaged. In fact, some group activities do not even qualify as "cooperative learning." It is merely "group work" if certain essential factors are not present, factors that render the process cooperative. Researcher Robert Slavin analyzed published research on cooperative learning to identify the essential factors for effective cooperative learning.

The following are Slavin's (1991) **five essential factors for cooperative learning** that must be incorporated into the group process for it to be cooperative:

- Common goal—valued by both the group and individual members
- Group interdependence
- A structured schedule of instruction
- Individual accountability
- Group rewards based on individual members' achievement

According to Slavin's review, the combination of all factors is necessary for effective cooperative learning. Thus, cooperative learning activities need to be structured in such a way that all members of the group are invested in the process and that all members are accountable for their own performance as well as that of all group mates so that certain specified learning activities occur.

VIDEO CASE CONNECTIONS BOX

Watch the Video Case entitled *Cooperative Learning: High School History Lesson*. Identify instances of the five essential factors for cooperative learning being incorporated or violated.

To demonstrate the necessity of the five essential factors, Slavin modified a popular approach to cooperative learning that did not satisfy all five, and hence, according to his research review, was not a consistently effective approach to cooperative learning. That original approach was Jigsaw (Aronson et al. 1978); Slavin termed the version that incorporated the five elements "Jigsaw II" (Slavin 1991). In Jigsaw II, the teacher divides the topic by the number of teams that can be formed in the class. Each home team has the same number of members as the topic has been divided into. In the first step, all members of the home team go to a different table to become experts on their part of the topic. At that individual's topic table is one member each of every other home team in the room. For the sake of the home team, each representative at a topic table must work hard to learn the information and bring it back to the home team. While working with members of other home teams at the topic table, the student should use effective cooperative skills to be sure to benefit as much as possible from studying the topic (sabotaging other home team's representatives will not work because the topic table members must cooperate to learn their information). When students return to their home teams, they each have to teach their teammates about the content they studied. To end the activity, each member of the home team takes a quiz on all content studied at each of the topic tables. The score for the quiz is a team score, compiled from the individual group members' performances. In this way, each home team member has an obligation to help all teammates fully learn the content each brought back to the team.

VIDEO CASE CONNECTIONS BOX

Brainstorm a list of reasons teachers would like to use cooperative learning that included students with mild disabilities; also brainstorm a list of reasons they might not. Then watch the Video Case entitled *Cooperative Learning in the Elementary Grades: Jigsaw Model,* and compare your lists to the reasons teacher Ilene Miller likes the Jigsaw approach.

There are three levels of working together: teaming, cooperation, and collaboration (Damon and Phelps 1989). When students team, they partner to perform an activity, but do not truly need to rely on one another to learn. It may just be more efficient to study via teaming. In cooperation, the students do need to rely on each other; each needs to learn from the others and to help the others learn. In truth, however, cooperative learning can also just be more efficient than individualized learning. If students cooperate to identify important women in U.S. history, for example, they are helping each other to think about the concepts and are each taking roles in gathering information or completing aspects of the task, but ostensibly, none are learning something that they could not learn on their own. (Because Damon and Phelps are making reference to how individuals interact cognitively, the term *cooperative* applies equally to peer tutoring and cooperative groups.) By contrast, in **collaboration,** each member of the team contributes to a collective knowledge set (ibid.), an understanding no one could have constructed alone. Thus, in collaboration, participants jointly construct knowledge by incorporating each other's understandings with their own. Collaboration could occur in most cooperative learning configurations.

Based on disability-related student variations, cooperative learning or peer tutoring will not go well if students are not prepared to work well together (McMaster and Fuchs 2002). Without having a clear procedure in which each participant can feel successful and be successful in the eyes of peers, animosity may develop, the essential activities of effective cooperative learning will not occur, and poor learning will result (Gillies and Ashman 2000; Pomplun 1997). As Slavin's (1991) research documents, students must be accountable for their cooperative roles in addition to the learning outcomes.

CHAPTER SUMMARY

Planning to provide an appropriate education to students with disabilities begins with determining their educational needs. Historic rushes to identify disabilities and place students in special education have proven unnecessary, and may have contributed to overidentification of some student populations and overlooking others who should have been identified and appropriately served (Harry and Klingner 2006). Teachers may prematurely judge special education to be the correct response for students with possible disabilities due to a lack of resources for guiding their daily practices with students who challenge them (Skrtic 2005). The pre-referral process required by the IDEA helps to assure that teachers have collegial support to investigate the nature of a student's learning difficulties, and to identify workable responses.

In the case of students for whom special education is deemed to be the right option, teachers continue to collaborate by participating in a team process to develop an individualized education program. The IEP document that the team generates serves as a "blueprint" for all educators and service providers who will work to provide the student an appropriate education. The IEP should guide the teacher's instructional planning process. Teachers still need to develop lesson plans for students receiving special education, regardless of where those students receive their education (the LRE) and how many students or professionals are involved in the lesson. Lesson plans help teachers to fully prepare and can guide their process during the lesson.

When teachers collaborate in teaching, they may merely consult with one another, as can be the case when students receive some of their education in the regular classroom environment and other parts in a more restrictive setting. There are a variety of configurations for how teachers can co-teach.

Research evidence (for example, Swanson and Hoskyn 1998; 2001) supports the notion that some instructional practices are more effective than others for students with mild disabilities. Typically, those practices include orienting students to lesson goals and tasks, providing clear and explicit instruction, keeping students actively engaged in the learning process, supporting practice, and providing informative feedback. Along with standards for teacher practice, such practices should guide teachers' work with students who have mild disabilities. Fortunately, these practices can be applied in any setting or curriculum where a student with special needs may be placed. By committing to informed planning and following plans, all educators who serve students with mild disabilities can participate in providing them with an appropriate education.

KEY TERMS

504 Plan, 50
Aimline, 65
Annual Goals, 46
Assessment, 44
Benchmark, 47
Collaboration, 70
Co-Teaching, 57
Cue Cards, 67
Curriculum-Based Measurement (C-BM), 65
Curriculum Standards, 53
Eligibility Determination, 45
Environmental Factors, 56
Five Essential Factors for Cooperative Learning, 68

Goal Line, 65
Highly Qualified, 61
Instructional Accommodations, 49
Interactive Planning Phase, 55
Multidisciplinary Team, 44
Peer-Assisted Learning Strategies (PALS), 67
Postplanning Phase, 56
Preplanning Phase, 55
Pre-referral, 40
Present Level of Academic Achievement and Functional Performance (PLAAFP), 45
Referral, 44
Related Services, 49

"Scientifically Based" Intervention Practices, 42
Screening, 44
Service Plan, 49
Short-Term Objective, 47
Specially Designed Instruction, 48
Student-Related Factors, 56
T-Chart, 67
Teacher Assistance Team, 41
Teacher Factor, 56
Testing Accommodations, 50
Trend Line, 65

APPLICATION ACTIVITIES

Using information from the chapter, complete the following activities that were designed to help you apply knowledge that was presented in this chapter.

1. Gather three different blank IEP forms (for example, from local school districts or from the education websites of various states' departments). Using a completed IEP (for good examples, see Gibbs and Dyches, forthcoming), transfer the content onto each of the three forms. Note differences in criteria for recording the same information, what information is not required across all forms, and any features or content unique to one or two that you consider to be appropriate for all IEP forms.

2. As a student preparing to become a special educator, you should not expect to be a proficient special educator yet. Using Crutchfield's (2003) evaluation guides, self-identify the CEC standards on which you are close to competence and those you most need to work toward.

3. Prepare two different C-BM graphs for addressing the same IEP goal for a student. One graph should reflect a DI/explicit instruction approach to addressing the goal. The other graph should reflect a Learning Strategies approach to instruction. (Hint: The layouts of the graphs may look the same, but what is plotted will likely vary.) Based on the two graphs, consider whether the lesson would best suit your student's learning needs if it were taught via DI/explicit instruction, strategy instruction, or a combined approach.

4. Review the procedures for Jigsaw II (p. 69). Identify how each of the five essential factors for effective cooperative learning (Slavin 1991) is accounted for in the process.

WEBSITE RESOURCES ON PLANNING, TEACHING, AND MONITORING INSTRUCTION

Numerous websites are useful to teachers for planning, teaching, and monitoring their instruction. The following list provides a sample of choices in websites, from those that provide research articles and materials to those that are informative websites.

Academic Benchmarks
www.academicbenchmarks.com

This website provides direct links to all states' standards.

Council for Exceptional Children's Professional Standards website
www.cec.sped.org

This website provides downloads of the CEC Standards, as well as background information on the standards, their development, and application.

National Middle School Association
www.nmsa.org

The National Middle School Association website includes a link to standards for middle school–level educators and for middle school programs.

Education World
www.education-world.com/standards/national/index.shtml

This commercial website includes links to the websites of most professional organizations that have recommended content-area standards (for example, National Council of Teachers of Mathematics, National Geographic Society, Center for Civic Education, and the consortium of National Arts Education Associations). The site also provides links to all state's standards.

Educational Software Directory.net
www.educational-software-directory.net

This site includes links to planning tools and to IEP development and monitoring tools. Both commercial and public usage resources are listed.

U.S. Department of Education Assistance to States for the Education of Children with Disabilities and Preschool Grants for Children with Disabilities
http://idea.ed.gov/explore/home

This link provides access to U.S. DOE resources for understanding and conforming to IDEA 2004 regulations.

Visit the book-specific website at www.cengage.com/education/ boyle for a variety of study tools such as web links, tutorial quizzes, glossary/flash cards, bonus material not included in the text, and more.

The premium website offers access to additional materials, including the Video Cases. Go to www.cengage.com/login to register or purchase access.

Learning Theories: Past and Present

3

CHAPTER QUESTIONS

1. What is a theory, and why are theories useful?

2. How can different theories help us become better teachers?

3. What is one application of each theory?

Why do educational theories matter—especially in an era when achievement outcomes seem to be what is most important about education?

The No Child Left Behind (NCLB) Act and the Individuals with Disabilities Education Act (IDEA) both stress the importance of students *achieving* high standards. How students are taught influences how they learn and how well they achieve, and theory guides how you teach. Some educators disdain their theory courses as the least valuable part of their teacher preparation program, and do not consider theory as relevant to their day-to-day practices. Education theories, however, explain why certain effective teaching practices work as they do. Education theories also represent our best explanations as to how students learn. Whether we are conscious of them or not, our theories guide how we teach. Whenever you read about a strategy or technique in this book that you like, your theories of teaching and learning are informing your opinion. Theories also drive the work of researchers and policy makers and, in turn, the techniques that are used in classrooms.

Chapter Question
ALERT

In this section, you will find information that answers a Chapter Question:

1. What is a theory, and why are theories useful?

Why Learn about Theories?

As the very first CEC (Council for Exceptional Children) standard for entry-level special education teachers states, effective educators of students with mild disabilities need to know "models, theories, and philosophies that form the basis for special education practice" (forthcoming). Because theories serve to inform teachers and guide their teaching, effective educators need to be familiar with major theories and how they influence their practices.

What Is a Theory?

A **theory** is a framework that is used to describe an event or set of events; it makes generalizations about observations and consists of an interrelated, coherent set of ideas and models. Nicolaus Copernicus developed a theory that the sun is the center of our universe, Sigmund Freud asserted theories of conscious and unconscious minds, and a number of cognitive psychologists and educators have evolved theories about how people learn. A theory is testable. If one aspect of the theory, a *hypothesis*, is confirmed through research or testing, the theory is strengthened. If a hypothesis is rejected, the theory is weakened and may need revising. Hypotheses are tested and confirmed through research. Continual hypothesis generation and testing helps theorists to revise, modify, or eventually reject a theory.

In his book *A Brief History of Time* (1988), Stephen Hawking wrote "a theory is a good theory if it satisfies two requirements: It must accurately describe a large class of observations on the basis of a model that contains only a few arbitrary elements, and it must make definite predictions about the results of future observations." He goes on to state that, "any physical theory is always provisional, in the sense that it is only a hypothesis; you can never prove it. No matter how many times the results of experiments agree with some theory, you can never be sure that the next time the result will not contradict the theory. On the other hand, you can disprove a theory by finding even a single repeatable observation that disagrees with the predictions of the theory" (33). Sound and solid one day, a new theory can rock our world. It can literally change the way that we see things. In the history of educational theory, some theories have forever impacted educational practice, whereas others have influenced us for a short period of time and then were quickly discarded.

What makes for a "useful" theory? A useful theory should summarize or explain observable events, generate hypotheses that can be empirically verified, and create new research (Hergenhahn and Olson 2001). A good theory should help teachers explain how learning occurs and, when used with students, should result in improved learning or teaching.

CASE 3.1 **The Heart of the Highway**

Case Introduction

In this case, you will read about a health sciences teacher, Ned Massori, who used theory to help shape his teaching. He thinks about the learning objectives for his lesson; in that way, he arrives at effective teaching practices to use. As you read the case, you will see how he uses both direct teaching and an analogy to help students learn new content.

At the end of the case, you will find case questions. These questions are meant to serve as points for reflection. Of course, if you can answer them immediately, you should do so, but you may want to wait to answer them until you have read that portion of the chapter that pertains to the particular case question. Throughout the rest of the chapter, you will see the same questions. As you see them, try to answer them based upon the portion of the chapter that you just read.

Ned Massori taught a unit on the functions of the human heart last year, and was very disappointed with the outcome. Last year, his students first drilled on the key vocabulary associated with the heart (for example, *ventricle, artery, muscle*), and students had to write definitions for the terms. Following that drill, he used an oversized plastic heart model to point out the various parts of the heart on which students had been drilled. While the students watched his demonstration, they labeled parts of the heart on a diagram he had passed out. Finally, they viewed a short movie that showed both how cartoon and real hearts operate. The video narrator repeated many of the things Ned had said while he taught students with the plastic heart model.

As he reflected on last year's lesson, Ned recalled that a few students couldn't memorize the key terms and their definitions. Still a few more knew most of the terms but had mixed up which definitions belonged with which terms. He was most vexed that although the majority of the class correctly learned the heart vocabulary, they had little understanding of what it all meant. Test questions that required students to explain how the heart works or to problem-solve common heart ailments proved to be too challenging for most.

Ned realized that his teaching activities did not match the types of comprehension outcomes he had planned for the unit. He also realized that although he did want his students to memorize key concepts—on the assumption that memorization is necessary for fully thinking about them—he also wanted them to be able to think *with* those concepts.

After careful reflection on what happened during last year's lesson, as well as on what he wanted students to know, he was ready to begin anew. This time he did not start with drill and practice of key vocabulary; instead, he wanted his students to learn about them in context right from the start. He thought that the terms would be better recalled if students could relate them to the functioning of the heart.

So Ned Massori began this class with, "Today we are going to discuss the human heart, so I thought I would bring along my map of the Beltway around Washington, DC, to help me explain it."

As students at Kennedy High School, in a Virginia town not far outside the beltway, Ned's students were all too familiar with the highways around Washington, DC. As he drew the Beltway, Ned highlighted the main roads around the DC area. It looked like the following:

continued

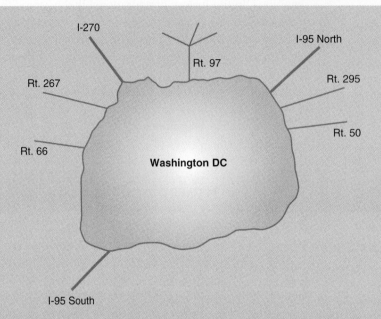

He began asking the students to think of the cars as red blood cells traveling on the highway, or major arteries. He told them, "I-95 South represents the inferior vena cava. I-270 represents the superior vena cava. Route 97 represents the aorta. Routes 295 and 267 are pulmonary arteries, and Routes 50 and 66 are the pulmonary veins." As he went on, the students filled in the same handout he had used last year.

"What happens when we have plaque buildup in an artery?" he asked them. Yosef raised his hand and said, "There is a blockage."

"Yes, you're correct," replied Mr. Massori, "just like a blockage that is caused by a car accident."

Mr. Massori then explained that an ambulance comes to help when there is an accident, just as humans have white blood cells to help. He made several other analogies between parts of the heart and the highway system. As the class filled out the diagram, he questioned students around the room, checking for accuracy of the diagram and asking about analogous parts.

Following this lesson, he asked students to work on memorizing the concepts by writing definitions in their own words. Ned theorized that they needed to memorize the concepts to master them and that they should do better than last year's students because they learned how the heart relates to a highway system and how the different components of the heart function.

CASE QUESTIONS

1. In his revised lesson, Ned Massori still wanted his students to memorize key concepts about the heart. How could this help them to "think *with*" the concepts?
2. Why would an analogy serve as an effective method for teaching students the names of the heart's parts and their functions?
3. If Ned had instead given his students a list of key concepts and definitions, and then asked them to apply them to a drawing of the DC Beltway without explaining the analogy for them, could the students have figured out the analogy?

Knowledge about how to teach comes from multiple sources. These sources can be personal experiences, advice or testimonials from others, or knowledge from learning theories or research. These sources of *teaching knowledge* are often deeply ingrained in our "belief system." These beliefs support our acceptance of a technique or theory and explain a teacher's continued use of a technique. Likewise, to encourage teachers to use a new technique, personnel preparation trainers must demonstrate to teachers that the new technique is worth replacing their current method. How well the new method matches the teachers' personally held theories of teaching and learning influences whether they will adopt the practice (Gersten, Chard, and Baker 2000; Scanlon et al. 2005). Of course, teachers can decide to use new techniques for any number of reasons, but perhaps the best reason is that the new techniques have been shown through research or learning theory to be more effective than prior methods.

Origins of Our Own Teaching Knowledge

One of those sources of how to teach probably comes from how we were taught as children and from our own personal experiences (Good and Brophy 1994). In their first teaching situations, novice teachers often rely on their own knowledge and experiences of how they were taught, though these memories may be distant. For many, this is a reflexive response and does not reflect the best methods for teaching students or managing their behavior.

A second source of teaching knowledge is advice or testimonials from others. Novice educators are recipients of many bits of wisdom passed down from veteran teachers. The teachers' lounge serves as the perfect environment for stories and lessons learned from others. Some of this knowledge may be effective, but new teachers should be wary of any suggested teaching method unless it is backed up by research, rather than just hearsay. Although experienced teachers do have practical wisdom, many practices employed in classrooms have little research backing (ibid.). Similarly, testimonials from producers of educational materials should be viewed with caution. Some of these new techniques or materials may be accompanied by testimonials from other teachers or administrators who used them and vouch for their effectiveness. You should remember that manufacturers of educational materials are in the business of sales and, although a new technique may follow common logic, it may not be effective if it is not accompanied by research. Other research-based techniques may be more effective.

Learning theories or research make up the third source of teaching knowledge. This is the best source when looking for effective teaching techniques. Research-based techniques typically have been well scrutinized and have gone through extensive reviews by professionals in the field (see for example the What Work's Clearinghouse; http://ies.ed.gov/ncee/wwc). Typically, teaching methods that have been researched are detailed, and the procedures for using them are explicit. Moreover, teaching techniques drawn from sound theories provide a basis for developing a wide variety of other new techniques. In addition, using techniques that are drawn from theory and research allow teachers to understand how they work and provide them with the best hope of improving skills or behavior in their students.

Theories of Learning Influential to Special Education Practices

An accurate count of all the teaching theories that have been generated may never be calculated. Some theories are better known than others, some have been quickly rejected following hypothesis testing, while still others are slight

▼

Chapter Question
ALERT

In this section, you will find information that answers the following Chapter Questions:

2. How can different theories help us become better teachers?

3. What is one application of each theory?

variations of earlier theories. In this section, we describe several theories and models of learning. Over the years, some of these theories have been more useful than others; yet at any one time, each theory was used to explain how humans learn and grow. Furthermore, each of these theories has been particularly influential to twentieth- and twenty-first-century special education practices in North America. Although some theories have been discredited or are no longer widely used, other new theories have spun off from the originals. Read each carefully and try to understand how each explains the process of learning.

Although the theories featured here are only a small sample of the many theories that have influenced regular and special education, they represent three major domains of education theories: behavioral, cognitive, and constructivist. Historically, each of the three domains influenced an era of educational practice, in the order we name them; each, undoubtedly, influenced the theories that followed.

Behavioral Theory

A very influential theory that has guided much of education practice in the past 50 years is **behavioral theory.** Behavioral theory looks at the effects of different external stimuli to help us understand why we behave the way we do. Its application to teaching is often referred to informally as behaviorism. There are multiple facets to behavioral theory, some focusing on reinforcing behaviors, others on extinguishing behaviors. The various facets may be employed in teaching individually or in combinations.

Behaviorism. From a behaviorist viewpoint, all behavior is learned and has been learned through the use of reinforcement, punishment, or extinction. Singing, talking, walking, and determining one's political perspectives are all learned behaviors developed to produce positive effects in our environments. Toddlers who take a few steps find walking fun and expedient; as well, they receive praise for it, so the behavior is reinforced and continues. Based on experiences people have had, they form political views that earn them labels such as "liberal" or "conservative" and that process explains why they support certain candidates. Educators can capitalize on the effects of reinforcers, punishers, and extinction to shape students' learning and behaviors.

Behavior modification is a technique based on the work of renowned psychologist B. F. Skinner. Using behavior modification, teachers extinguish an undesirable behavior and replace it with a desirable behavior. Based upon Skinner's principle of **operant conditioning,** any response that is followed by a reinforcing stimulus tends to be repeated, and any response that is followed by punishment or by ignoring tends not to be repeated (Hergenhahn and Olsen 2001). In other words, individuals learn a behavior to *operate* in their environments (make a certain response to their environment) to acquire or avoid a consequence—hence the term *operant.* Skinner believed that to understand behavior, we should look only at overt responses to find out why the behavior is occurring, has decreased, or has stopped. It is not that Skinner did not believe in cognition and thinking as mediating factors to explain why people behave as they do, but he believed that the best way to understand behavior was to examine it in terms of overt responses and consequences (Hohn 1994). The following explanations of components of operant conditioning include examples of behavioral principles in action.

Reinforcement

According to Skinner, a consequence is a reinforcer when it serves to increase the probability of the recurrence of the response. What is a reinforcer? A **reinforcer** is anything that increases the rate with which an operant response occurs. Praising a student for good work (for example, solving a math problem, conjugating a verb, behaving appropriately) is very likely to be reinforcing to the student; in turn, the student will repeat the behavior to receive more praise. However, what is reinforcing to one person may not be reinforcing to another person. Also, what was reinforcing at one point in time may not be reinforcing during another time in that person's life. It is important to remember that a reinforcer works only when it increases the probability that the response will occur again. One other important fact about reinforcement is that if you want the response to occur again, you must provide the reinforcer only when the response occurs—this is known as **contingent reinforcement.**

Reinforcers can be either negative or positive. A **positive reinforcer** increases behavior when presented immediately following the response. A *negative reinforcer* increases behavior when removed. Therefore, a negative reinforcer is not punishment; it is instead removal of something (relief) that the student does not appreciate (for example, erasing the student's name from a list of students at risk for being kept after school, or decreasing the number of homework problems for students who achieve a high percentage of correct performances during in-class practice).

THINK BACK TO THE CASE about Ned's lesson about the heart . . .

1. *In his revised lesson, Ned Massori still wanted his students to memorize key concepts about the heart. How could this help them to "think <u>with</u>" the concepts?*

We most often think about behaviorism as applied to "behaviors" such as sitting appropriately in class and speaking politely, but the same principles apply to learning content. From a behavioral theorist's perspective, students need to be reinforced for thinking about concepts, including their definitions, accurately. They can also be reinforced for applying, or thinking *with* them.

Types of Reinforcers. A **primary reinforcer** is something that is needed for survival, like food, water, or sex, and increases a response rate (Skinner theorized that breathing, seeking food and drink, and sex drive are the only innate human behaviors). Primary reinforcers work because they are not taught or learned: everyone needs them for survival. When a neutral stimulus is paired with a primary reinforcer, the neutral stimulus begins to take on the reinforcing value of the primary reinforcer. The neutral stimulus (now reinforcing) is known as a **secondary reinforcer** or **conditioned reinforcer.** Points or tokens that can be traded for a primary reinforcer are secondary reinforcers. Praise or attention can also serve as secondary reinforcers when paired with a primary reinforcer. When a secondary reinforcer has been paired with more than one primary reinforcer, it becomes a **generalized reinforcer.** Money is the best example of a generalized reinforcer because it can be used for many different types of primary reinforcers. Even when the primary reinforcer is gone, generalized reinforcers usually remain strong reinforcers. For example, students may respond to money even though they cannot use it. Students may respond well to praise even though the primary reinforcement is no longer present. Teachers can use a variety of secondary reinforcers or make new ones such as praise, pats on the back, or smiles, if paired with primary or even generalized reinforcers such as money.

Punishment

Whereas reinforcement increases behavior, punishment decreases the probability of the occurrence of a behavior (response) temporarily. According to Hohn (1994), punishment can occur in one of two ways. One, punishment can present an aversive (for example, a spanking, yelling, incarcerating) or remove a positive reinforcer (for example, removing tokens, points, or recess time). In order to be considered punishment, punishment has to *decrease* the student's behavior when applied. If the punishment is applied (for example, a spanking) and the child continues the inappropriate or dangerous behavior, either the punishment is not punishment (that is, it is a neutral stimulus) or another reinforcer may be present that is maintaining or increasing the behavior. An example would be if a parent were to slap his child on the back after the child burped, yet other people in the room laughed at the child. If the child continues "burping" behavior, it could be that the behavior is actually being reinforced (that is, laughing), rather than decreased (that is, slapping). Remember that unlike punishment, negative reinforcement *increases* the response, whereas punishment *decreases* the response. Another distinction is that with negative reinforcement the teacher removes the stimulus (for example, nagging) once the behavior increases. Punishment occurs when the teacher applies an aversive stimulus to decrease behavior. Keep in mind that punishment only reduces the behavior temporarily. Even Skinner claimed that punishment only suppresses the response while it is being applied, and that it is likely to reappear after withdrawing the punishment (Hergenhahn and Olson 2001).

Punishment has various side effects: it may (1) lead to avoidance behaviors, (2) lead to retaliation or negative feelings toward the punisher, (3) teach students what not to do, (4) result in the student experiencing negative emotions, and (5) not generalize across settings.

In the first effect, punishment may lead to avoidance or escape behaviors. Students who are constantly punished for inappropriate behavior may avoid coming to class or may try to escape from the situation or setting when it comes time to receive the punishment. In the second effect, teachers who give punishment may be the target of retaliation or, at the very least, may be viewed negatively by students. Students who are punished by being given extra English assignments may then develop negative feelings toward English. In the third effect, punishment teaches a student *what not to do* rather than teaching what to do. In some cases, students may become confused and frustrated because he or she does not know what to do to receive positive reinforcement or feedback. The fourth effect of punishment is that it may generate negative emotions. Emotionally, students may develop feelings of fear, sadness, or depression, or may learn that inflicting pain on others is acceptable (ibid.). The fifth effect of punishment may result in not generalizing to all settings. Although punishment may work for a teacher during math, it may not work during other subjects or in other settings.

Again, just think of punishment as suppressing the behavior. Under what conditions should punishment be used? Probably never. Punishment is really not a viable solution to addressing inappropriate student behavior. In certain situations, you may feel a need to punish a student because alternative behaviors for reinforcement are not apparent, the student has clearly broken a policy, or you are afraid of the precedent that may be established by not publicly punishing the student. Punishment is potentially legitimate in such circumstances, but the effects will be short-term at best. The more ideal solution is to arrange the situation so that you are able to reinforce the student for behaving appropriately in ways that prevent the student's inclination to act inappropriately. Some students seek punishment because punishment is better than receiving no attention at all.

In the following sections, we discuss the use of differential reinforcement of incompatible (DRI) behavior or differential reinforcement of alternative (DRA) behavior as useful alternatives to punishment.

Time-Out

Time-out is another procedure that attempts to decrease the probability or the occurrence of a behavior (response) temporarily. **Time-outs** are the withholding of reinforcement for all behaviors. Typically, they are used with younger students. In some cases, the child may be moved to a quiet area of the classroom; in other cases, the child may be removed from the classroom. When using time-outs, teachers should avoid nagging or scolding children, speaking to them in an angry voice, or looking at them while in time-out.

Just as there are problems with punishment, there are also problems associated with time-outs. First, removal from the classroom may constitute a change in placement for the child and may require administrative approval. In some cases, if time-outs are overused, they become seclusion. Teachers should always check with their supervisors before using time-outs. Second, if the classroom is not a positive reinforcing environment, removing the child may serve no purpose. Hence, the teacher can expect the inappropriate response to continue in the time-out setting. Moreover, if the classroom is not a reinforcing environment, the child has no incentive to come back to it. Related to this point, teachers have to be certain that leaving the classroom is not a reinforcing experience in itself. If a child is placed in the principal's office and the principal or other office staff inadvertently provide reinforcement while the child is in the office, the child may want to leave the classroom on a more frequent basis to go to the office. The same might be true of using the hallway as a time-out setting. Third, similar to punishment, time-outs may only teach the child *what not to do* rather than what to do.

Extinction

Extinction means to eliminate a behavior by withholding reinforcement. Whereas time-outs involve removing the student from a reinforcing environment, extinction involves withholding reinforcement for an inappropriate response.

With extinction, it helps to identify the reinforcement that is associated with the student's response. For example, when students call out answers to questions rather than raise their hands, the teacher probably inadvertently reinforced calling out the answer by giving attention to the student (or even using positive reinforcement in the form of responding to the student's answer). In this case, to use extinction, teachers must make it clear that they will not accept any answers that are called out; instead, they will only accept answers from students who raise their hand.

Alternatives to Punishment and Time-Out. Use of **differential reinforcement of incompatible (DRI)** behavior and **differential reinforcement of alternative (DRA)** behavior serve as good alternatives to punishment. With these techniques, teachers reinforce appropriate behaviors. With DRI, the teacher identifies the inappropriate behavior and an incompatible or mutually exclusive behavior as a replacement behavior. For example, if the inappropriate behavior is getting out of the seat, an incompatible target behavior would be sitting in the seat. Similarly, DRA looks for alternative behaviors—these are *not* mutually exclusive, and it might be possible for both incompatible and target behavior to occur at the same time, like raising a hand and calling out an answer. However, teachers should identify target behaviors that are unlikely to occur simultaneously, such as teasing and complimenting. All students have appropriate behaviors in their repertoire—it is simply a matter of finding them and reinforcing them. Again, be sure that you have reinforcers at your disposal that are reinforcing for the student. Just because you view an item or event as reinforcing does not necessarily mean that your student will find it reinforcing.

DRI or DRA involves the following steps:

1. Identify the inappropriate behavior and then identify an incompatible (target) behavior (for DRI) or an alternative (target) behavior (for DRA) with which to replace it. In other words, an incompatible behavior is one that cannot occur simultaneously with the inappropriate behavior or a mutually exclusive behavior.
2. Try to use a target behavior that students already have in their repertoire.
3. If possible, choose a behavior that can be maintained by environmental reinforcers (for example, smiles or conversations).
4. As soon as you observe the target behavior, reinforce it. Use extinction with the inappropriate behavior.

METHODS AND STRATEGIES SPOTLIGHT

Targeting Behaviors for Change

Not all rule-breaking behaviors that students exhibit need to be changed. For example, wearing a hat, tapping a pencil or pen on the desk, chewing gum or eating candy, expressing anger, fidgeting in the seat, or speaking without permission are some behaviors that may violate school rules; however, not *all* teachers would agree that they need to be obeyed. In the case of students such as those with EBD, teachers may view getting through the school day as enough of a challenge that they will relax certain rules.

So just how do you know if a behavior needs to be targeted for change? Kaplan (1995) devised a set of guidelines to help teachers determine if a questionable behavior needs to be changed.

Classroom Rules. Teachers love rules—some teachers more than others, particularly those who either have too many rules for students to follow or have rules that shouldn't be rules at all. Are students allowed to chew gum? Are students allowed to swear in the classroom? (If so, which words constitute a "swear" word?) Are students allowed to disagree with a teacher? These are just some of the rules that might be called into question. In other words, choose your rules carefully, and be prepared to defend them.

Control Issues. Some teachers enjoy total control in their classroom. We have been in classes in which students were not permitted to talk or even whisper to other students. For some teachers, controlling the behavior of others can be an obsession. Many of these teachers use too many rules (both written and unwritten) to control the behavior of others. Although control is an important aspect of classroom management, overly controlled classrooms can be stressful learning environments for both the students and the teacher. When teachers develop a rule, consider whether it benefits the students.

The So-What Test. Kaplan defines the "so-what" test as a measure to determine whether a student's inappropriate behavior interferes with his physical, emotional, social, or academic well-being. If it does interfere, it might be a behavior to target for change. When applied to each individual, a behavior may be acceptable for one student but unacceptable for another student. For example, if a student taps a pencil on her desk so loudly that it disrupts other students, the other students may get angry and pick on her. This behavior might be appropriate for changing. Conversely, if a student has a nervous habit of tapping his pencil on his desk, others are not bothered by it, and the student is academically performing well in the class, then it is probably not a behavior that needs to be targeted for change.

Sociocultural Considerations. For all students, it is important to consider the individual's culture when deciding whether to change behavior. Some behaviors may be bound by the student's particular culture. For example, in certain Asian cultures, when a youth has used inappropriate behavior and is being reprimanded, it is customary for the child or adolescent to turn away from the person doing the reprimanding, because of feeling ashamed. Therefore, it may not be appropriate to have the child look at you (that is, maintain eye contact) while being reprimanded for an inappropriate behavior. Time is a concept that differs from culture to culture for students. Therefore, having a student come to class at a specific time each day may be difficult for certain children, and it may take a while for them to adjust to the new culture's sense of timeliness. Reprimanding is not an appropriate response in such a case.

Cognitive Behavior Modification

Cognitive psychologists and education theorists valued many of the principles of behaviorism offered by Skinner and others, but rejected the notion that we should restrict ourselves to addressing observable behaviors. They believed that we are capable of theorizing cognitive activities, and that understanding how the mind works is essential to addressing fully the thinking and learning process. They proposed and tested a second behavioral theory, cognitive behavior modification.

Cognitive behavior modification (CBM) refers to using cognitive skills to help control one's behavior. Cognitive behavior modification grew from the belief that people do in fact use cognitive skills and that psychologists and others can modify or change behavior by having individuals think about their behavior. CBM represents a merging of the cognitive field with the behavior field. CBM incorporates self-talk or self-monitoring for students to monitor their own behavior. The two main types of CBM are self-instructions and self-monitoring.

Donald Meichenbaum developed one of the earliest studies that used self-instruction training to teach coping strategies to children with ADHD. Self-instruction includes several steps for students to verbalize statements of self-coping, self-evaluation, and self-reinforcement. These steps are meant to help students think through and solve problems. Meichenbaum (1977) taught children with hyperactivity the following skills:

1. Define the problem ("What is it that I have to do?").
2. Focus attention and response guidance ("Carefully . . . draw a line.").
3. Use self-reinforcement ("Good, I'm doing fine.").
4. Use self-evaluative and coping skills ("That's OK. Even if I make a mistake, I can keep going.").

After students were trained in these skills, they used them with various fine motor and problem-solving tasks. Meichenbaum (1977) reported that this training was successful at helping children with hyperactivity and children with impulsivity to improve their performance on complex and time-consuming cognitive tasks.

In another example of self-instructional training, Burgio, Whitman, and Johnson (1980) developed self-instructions for students with mental retardation. The students used the following question-and-answer steps to remain on task during independent seatwork:

The child asks her or himself:

1. The child asks, "What does the teacher want me to do?"
2. He or she answers, "My teacher wants me to work on my math worksheet."
3. He or she asks, "How am I supposed to do this?"
4. He or she answers, "I need to start with problem number one."
5. Starting the work, he or she self-reinforces, "I'm doing a good job working."
6. Using a self-monitoring statement, he or she ignores distractions, saying, "I hear people talking but I am going to keep working."
7. He or she uses a coping statement, saying, "I messed that one up, but I will do better on the next one."

Of course, teachers cannot just provide the self-instructions and then expect students to become proficient at using them, so Meichenbaum and Goodman (1971) developed a five-step sequence for training students to use self-instructions. These steps are often used in various self-instructional training programs today. Of the steps, the crucial first step, now called think-alouds, are frequently used in strategy programs and aid students in understanding the teacher's internal thoughts while they are performing the task. The following are the five steps of the Meichenbaum and Goodman model:

1. Cognitive Modeling—An adult model performs a task while thinking aloud.
2. Overt External Guidance—The student performs the same task while the model verbalizes the steps and provides guidance.

3. Overt Self-Guidance—The student performs the task while saying the steps aloud.
4. Faded Overt Self-Guidance—The student whispers the steps while completing the task.
5. Covert Self-Guidance—The student performs the task while silently reviewing the steps.

Another cognitive behavior modification technique is called *self-monitoring*. When teaching students to use self-monitoring, there is initially a cuing system (for example, a bell or tone) that prompts the students to stop what they are doing to record self-behavior on a self-monitoring card (see Figure 3.1) (Boyle and Hughes, 1994). The tone or bell sounds at random intervals from 15 seconds to 120 seconds. Once students hear the tone, they stop the task and ask, "Am I working?" (or "Am I on task?"). If on-task, students place a mark under the "Yes" and keep working. If the answer is "No," students record a mark under "No" and tell themselves, "I need to get back to work." This self-monitor training program was used with elementary students with mental retardation. Figure 3.2 presents a self-monitoring card used with older students. Using this card, students record a + or 0 when the tone sounds. Figure 3.2 also includes a cheat sheet to remind students of examples of on-task and off-task behavior.

FIGURE 3.1

Self-Monitoring Card

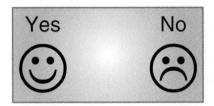

FIGURE 3.2

Self-Monitoring Cheat Sheet and Cue Card

Source: Reproduced by permission from J. Kaplan, *Beyond Behavior Modification: A Cognitive-Behavioral Approach to Behavior Management in the School* (Austin, TX: PRO-ED, 1995).

Cognitive Theories

Building on the sentiments of CBM theorists, other psychologists further rejected behavioral theories that refused to consider cognitive processes. Cognitive theorists believe that we can understand cognitive processes and even theorize thinking operations based on careful examinations of how people go about completing various cognitive tasks. We present five influential cognitive theories: information processing, schema theory, metacognitive theory, social learning theory, and perceptual theory.

Information Processing Model. Today, perhaps the most influential model that drives research in education and special education is the information processing model. The information processing model (see Figure 3.3) examines how information is processed during learning. Most models of information processing contain the following three main assumptions:

1. Information is processed through stages. In other words, new information is processed in each stage or component in the model. For example, in the sensory register, we temporarily store specific bits of information that we view as important enough to pass on to short-term memory.
2. Each stage is limited in how much information can be processed at any one time. In each stage, only a limited amount of information can be processed and passed on to the next component or encoded into long-term memory.
3. Information is lost at each stage through decay, interference, or lack of usefulness. Because of the limited capacity of each stage, only a limited amount of information can be processed. We must decide what information we will

FIGURE 3.3

Information Processing Model

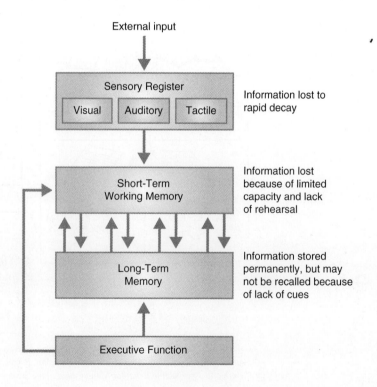

pay attention to, and pass that information on to be processed. In addition, if we do not use rehearsal strategies or manipulate information, it will be lost to decay.

Psychologists believe that people process information in stages, and that each stage or store has limits in terms of how much information can be processed at any one time. Moreover, as critical information is selected to be passed on to the next store, irrelevant information is discarded. From your own experiences, you are aware that you can only deal with a certain amount of information at any one time; otherwise, you become "overloaded" with information (remembering the digits of a phone number may be a good example). Atkinson and Shiffrin (1968) developed one of the earliest information processing models that sought to explain how information is processed and has been used and expanded upon in many other models of information processing. In Figure 3.3, a box represents each of the memory stores; however, keep in mind that information is flowing through these stores instantly and that simultaneous interactions are occurring in each of theses stores. Moreover, consider that this model represents symbolically what is believed to be occurring in the human brain and is a mere abstraction (that is, it is an attempt to draw a model of a theorized and nonobservable process). Psychologists believe the purpose of each store is to receive, temporarily store, organize, and encode information. That information is then passed along to the next store when it is at capacity or when a sufficient amount of information has been acquired.

The Sensory Register

Information from external stimuli comes in through the senses and enters the **sensory register.** Incoming information, in the form of external stimuli, bombards us through our auditory, visual, or tactile senses. The function of the sensory register is to take in information from the environment, store it briefly, and then determine the relevance of it and whether it needs to be transferred to the next store. Information is stored very briefly, a few hundred milliseconds to a few seconds in duration at most, and then it is either processed or it decays rapidly. Rapid decay is important because, without it, images or sounds would interfere with the input of new stimuli. Verbal sensory stores are sometimes referred to as echoic memory because the last bits of information that we hear will sometimes linger (or echo) for a brief period of time. Imagine, for example, that you are taking notes during a lecture and your professor speaks so quickly that you just barely have time to record the lectures points. You have probably experienced remembering the last bits of information spoken because the words were still in your ears (that is, auditory sensory memory) after the professor stopped speaking.

Psychologists believe that when information enters your sensory register, two other constructs are at work, helping you sift out the important information. One component is **attention,** and the other is **perception.** In expanded models, attention and perception are often represented as separate boxes or stores where information lingers before being passed on to short-term memory. Despite these boxes lacking in our model, attention and perception appear to be two very important components that play a major role in our ability to perceive crucial information for processing. Because we have so many stimuli bombarding our senses, we need some way to determine the important information to attend. Attention helps with this task, by allowing us to focus in on those important bits of information that are crucial for learning or functioning. In doing so, we focus our attention on one thing at the expense of other things. For example, if we are busy working on a project in a loud classroom, we use attention to focus on the important information of the task and ignore the other noises. However, if someone suddenly calls your name, you may instantly look in the direction from where the voice came. In part, our attention alerted us to stop the task and look toward the voice. Similarly, perception is the component that helps us use part of the new information to see if it matches up with something we know (that is, information stored in long-term memory). Perception is responsible for helping us find a recognizable pattern from the incoming stimuli, and then deciding if that recognizable stimuli is worth processing, based upon matching patterns from our memory. If the pattern is important, we focus attention to that part of the stimuli and disregard other parts of the stimuli.

Many of the learning challenges that students with mild disabilities face represent difficulties at the sensory register stage of the information processing theory. Students with ADHD or EBD have difficulty attending to pertinent information because they are easily distracted (for example, Teicher et al. 1996; Lauth, Heubeck, and Mackowiak, 2006). Students with learning disabilities and mild mental retardation have difficulties with distinguishing important from unimportant information, which involves an aspect of attention, and they also tend to have problems organizing information that they process.

Short-Term Memory

Information from the sensory register that is not decayed is coded and then sent to short-term memory. Short-term memory is just that—short-term. It is believed that information remains in short-term memory for about 15 to 20 seconds and, without rehearsal or further encoding with long-term memory, is lost. When rehearsed, the information may remain in short-term memory for up to 20 minutes.

Again, short-term memory is limited in its capacity to hold large stores of information. Psychologists believe that it can hold seven plus or minus two bits of information. This came to be known as Miller's magic number, after the famous psychologist who performed his experiments in the 1960s and found that individuals can remember between five and nine bits (or items) of information (Miller 1956). Despite this magic number, psychologists today believe that the capacity may be closer to five plus or minus two bits of information when trying to remember information. Bear in mind that this

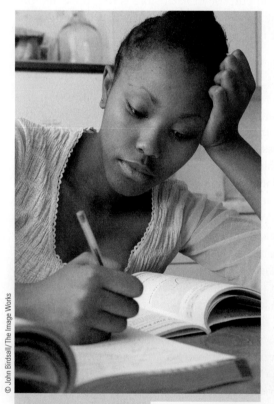

Encoding information from short to long-term memory occurs when students use rehearsal strategies

depends upon the familiarity of the information and whether we are able to manipulate or rehearse the information in short-term memory to keep it there. For example, if we were given a list of 12 items, we might be able to categorize or group them so that we could remember the information longer and remember all 12 items (that is, associate them via a story or a rhyming method such as peg word) (Krinsky and Krinsky 1996; Scruggs, Mastropieri, and Levin 1986), or by chunking them, such as when we remember the phone extension "1-1-8-0" as "11-80".

What exactly is a *bit* of information? A bit can be thought of as a small amount of information. In some cases, one bit equals one number, such as those found in telephone numbers. In other cases, a bit can be a word, phrase, or small chunk of information. As you could guess, the larger the bits the fewer of them that can be held in short-term memory. Because of its limited capacity, new information may often bump out information already in this store, or it may simply drop out as time progresses. For students with disabilities, short-term memory is even more limited than seven plus or minus two bits of information. The belief is that students with certain types of disabilities (for example, mental retardation or learning disabilities) have poor or limited short-term memory. The implications for these students include that we need to break information down into smaller chunks and practice rehearsal strategies to transfer this information into long-term memory.

Short-term memory is often referred to as **working memory** because this is the place where various activities occur such as organizing new information, retrieving information from long-term memory, and encoding new information with information from long-term memory. Whereas long-term memory is strictly for storage, working memory is really the place where all the processing occurs. When we use clustering or rehearsal strategies, we are using these in working memory, usually with the intent to either encode information for long-term storage or keep it for a short period of time. If information is not encoded to long-term memory during this stage, it is lost forever.

Rehearsal. Rehearsal serves two purposes: for short-term use and for longer use so that we transfer the information over to long-term memory. In the first case, we can use **maintenance rehearsal** to keep information in memory for a short period of time—such as repeating a telephone number until we can dial the number. In the latter case, we typically use **elaborative rehearsal** to encode the information into long-term memory. Elaborative rehearsal works by elaborating on information from long-term memory to associate it with new information. To do this, we must bring information from long-term memory into working memory and then connect the two together by adding (or elaborating on) bits of new information with the previously learned concept. When teaching older students, connecting new with prior knowledge may not be a problem because older students have lots of experiences and knowledge already in long-term memory. However, younger children may not have much prior knowledge about the new concept that you are about to teach; therefore, you need to find ways to tap into the limited knowledge they do have about the concept that you are teaching.

Chunking. **Chunking** is another strategy that we use to remember information. Like rehearsal, we can use chunking to keep information in short-term memory longer, or we can use it to transfer information into long-term memory. With chunking, we look for common associations between and among the items being learned so that we can clump similar items into groups or chunks. The organized information is now easier to remember, in part because of the similarities in each group and in part because each item in the group serves to cue us to remember other items in a group. Teachers can help students clump information together to remember it by organizing it ahead of time and then showing students the relationships among the items in each group. We often cluster information without realizing we have done so. For example, if we go shopping without our grocery list, we may have trouble remembering the items. One technique to recall the items is to compartmentalize the store into sections such as meats, produce, bakery, and dairy products. We then use these areas to remember items from our grocery list—such as milk and eggs in dairy, oranges and pears in produce, hamburger and lunch meats in meats, and bread and donuts in bakery.

Long-Term Memory

Once information is encoded from short-term memory with information in long-term memory, it is stored in long-term memory forever. Psychologists believe that it never fades or is lost except for injuries, such as stroke, traumatic brain injury, or other brain traumas. Anecdotal evidence from a neurologist named Wilder Penfield (1969) suggests that this is, in fact, true. Penfield was a neurosurgeon who performed thousands of procedures on patients. During his operations, he would use an electronic probe to stimulate different parts of his patients' brains. Having done this, his patients reported back that they recalled long-forgotten memories that they believed had been lost. The same is true for us. Often when given the proper recall cue such as an odor, sound, or picture, we remember a flood of memories from long ago. For some people, walking into a school for the first time since they graduated and smelling that distinct "school smell" brings back memories, both pleasant and unpleasant. These memories have not been lost, but were simply stored away in long-term memory. In fact, the levels of processing theory has provided some research to attest to the fact that we actually "know" more than we can easily recall. According to the levels of processing theory (Craig and Lockhart 1972), when information is processed it can be processed at varying levels of depth. Information that is remembered for its meaning is stored deeper than information that is stored based upon visual (seeing it) or acoustic (hearing it) cues. Thus, the deeper the level of processing, the more the person would remember the information. This implication means that if you want to ensure deep processing of information in students, you need to make it meaningful to them. Rather than just explain and tell them about a concept, the levels of processing theory tells us to have students elaborate on the concept and relate it to what they already know about the concept and—organize new information with prior knowledge from long-term memory.

Long-Term Memory Units. According to cognitive psychologists, knowledge is stored and arranged in units (Anderson 1990). These units can be defined as declarative knowledge, procedural knowledge, or conditional knowledge. **Declarative knowledge** is knowledge about facts and things—the knowledge of *what*. When we learn that Christopher Columbus sailed to the new world in 1492, we are creating declarative knowledge. **Procedural knowledge** is knowledge about steps or procedures—the *how* of knowledge (for example, how to throw a football and the steps involved in long division). **Conditional knowledge** is knowledge about *when* to use certain bits of declarative knowledge with procedural knowledge. Some theorists believe that learning strategies (review Chapter 2) are part of conditional knowledge (Mayer 1987); while others consider them part of procedural knowledge (Gaskins 2005). It is quite possible that the strategies are initially learned as procedural knowledge, and as students become more proficient at using them with different types of content and material over time, the strategies become conditional knowledge.

Schema Theory. Cognitive psychologists also theorize that information in long-term memory is arranged into knowledge structures. Each knowledge structure is called a **schema** and contains information about a particular concept. Schema theorists believe that we possess schemata (the plural of schema), and that these schemata consist of both declarative knowledge and procedural knowledge (Gagne 1985). For example, if you discussed golf with another person, you might be discussing popular PGA players and the rules of golf (declarative knowledge), as well as how to swing a driver versus how to swing a wedge (procedural knowledge). According to schema theory, when students have a well-defined schema about a concept that they are learning, they can easily access the schema, elaborate on it, and become more knowledgeable about the concept. On the other hand, when they have poorly developed schema, learning becomes slow and tedious as they try to grasp the concept. Regardless of which theory you espouse, it is important to remember to tap into prior knowledge before teaching new knowledge. Remember, learning involves making connections between what is known and what is being learned.

THINK BACK TO THE CASE   about Ned's lessons about the heart . . .

2.   *Why would an analogy serve as an effective method for teaching students the names of the heart's parts and their functions?*

Both information processing theories and schema theory suggest that students learn concepts by forming relationships among them. Ned Massori's analogy to the DC Beltway should therefore help his students to relate the functions of the heart to something already familiar to them. Likewise, they will be able to relate the parts and various functions of the heart to one another, because they all relate to each other to tell the story of the Beltway/heart functioning.

Executive Function

Knowing when to use a strategy or procedure based upon the type of task requires knowledge beyond the memory stores presented in our model. Using planning and goal-setting skills, being flexible when solving problems, directing attention to the appropriate parts of the task, and using self-regulatory behaviors to control emotions and impulses during tasks all require control from a larger, overarching system (Meltzer and Krishnan 2007). In the information processing system, this overarching, supervisory mechanism is typically referred to as **executive function.** There has been a "lack of clarity" between the use of the terms *executive function* and *metacognition* (Meltzer and Krishnan 2007). For some, executive function and metacognition mean the same thing (Snowman and Biehler 2006). Keep in mind that, to date, there is still no clear distinction made in professional literature between the two concepts (Meltzer and Krishnan 2007). For the sake of clarity in this textbook, we will use the term *executive function* as a broad umbrella term that describes how to control many different cognitive processes and encompasses metacognition, self-regulation (for example, planning and self-monitoring), attention, and regulation of our memory systems. Although executive functioning involves metacognition, it also refers to attention and self-regulation of learning in general. When applied to students, executive function refers to selecting appropriate goals, beginning work, organizing information, prioritizing tasks, memorizing information for later use, shifting strategies dependent upon the tasks and situation, and self-monitoring and checking (Meltzer and Krishnan 2007). Conversely, we will use the term **metacognition** to mean knowledge of tasks and strategies, and the flexible use of a strategy. We will intentionally limit this term as it applies to tasks, strategies, and strategy use.

Another way to think of executive function is as a mechanism that "orchestrates cognition" in the brain (Neisser 1967). The main purpose of the executive function is to direct the traffic of managing multiple tasks, particularly when working memory becomes taxed from trying to complete too many tasks at once or from trying to complete complex, difficult tasks. Executive function is responsible for allocating and directing attention to tasks when too many demands are made on memory and processing. Think of executive function as the dispatcher in a taxicab company. The cabs are analogous to strategies, and the dispatcher decides when and where to send them as the calls (that is, learning demands) come in. The dispatcher must match up the best strategy with the demands of the task. For instance, if the task is to remember someone's telephone number long enough to dial it, the dispatcher might send a rote memory strategy, whereby the individual simply verbally repeats the number several times until it is dialed. If, on the other hand, the learning task is to remember all five Great Lakes, then the dispatcher might send a first-letter mnemonic strategy, whereby the individual remembers the names using the acronym HOMES (Huron, Ontario, Michigan, Erie, and Superior). The dispatcher must pay attention to feedback and self-monitor the strategies that are used to determine if the best, most efficient strategy has been dispatched and if the strategy led to successful task completion.

Metacognitive Theory and Strategy Use. Flavell (1976) claimed that metacognition involves how to use a strategy, where to employ a strategy and support its use, and when to employ a strategy based upon the task or situation. A **strategy** is a set procedure or series of steps for successfully completing a task. Ellis et al. (1991) define it as "an individual's approach to a task." More than likely, these strategies are stored in long-term memory as procedural knowledge or conditional knowledge (Ellis et al. 1991; Mann and Sabatino 1985). As procedural knowledge, the strategy allows the student to work through a series of steps and substeps on the task. As conditional knowledge, the student is able to modify and adapt the strategy for different learning situations.

Students with mild disabilities have several problems associated with executive functioning in general, and more specifically, metacognition and strategy use. These students often lack effective strategies or, in some cases, know about effective strategies but fail to use them for the task at hand (Mann and Sabatino 1985). Indeed, students with mild disabilities have problems in strategy selection and use (Butler 1998). In terms of metacognitive skills, these students do not know when and where to use certain strategies. It is not that they lack metacognitive skills, but they simply use less sophisticated metacognitive skills (Wong 1996). For example, a student might be aware that she needs to study for an upcoming test on Friday; however, the night before the test, she decides simply to read over her notes (a common study strategy used by students with mild disabilities). Although this strategy has worked well in the past on quizzes, there is too much content to remember for this particular study strategy to be effective on the upcoming test. In this case, the student has failed to recognize that the task demands have changed and to adjust accordingly (that is, use a more effective strategy). Some students with mild disabilities may have problems selecting appropriate strategies to match task demands or have problems actually implementing the strategies that they set out to use (Butler 1998). At other times, they do not monitor task performance and fail to make adjustments in strategy use based upon feedback and performance (Wong 1991; 1996). Some of these problems are the result of weak or inadequate metacognitive skills; however, some of the problems are due to poor attention and self-regulation of cognitive skills (Meltzer and Krishnan 2007).

VIDEO CASE CONNECTIONS BOX

Watch the Video Case called *Metacognition: Helping Students Become Strategic Learners*. Listen to teacher Julie Craven describe the metacognitive learning goals that she has for her students. Then, rewatch the video and identify instances of her teaching behaviors that should help her students develop metacognitive skills.

Social Learning Theory. A third theory builds on ideas present in both behavioral theory and information processing theory. This model, developed by Albert Bandura (1977), is called **social learning theory.** According to this theory, learning occurs as the result of an interaction of three factors: physical characteristics of the person (P), environmental contingencies (E), and the person's behaviors (B) (see Figure 3.4). From this perspective, students learn new behaviors by observing others and then responding to those observations. Much of Bandura's early work, referred to as **observational learning,** examined how young children would change their behavior after observing a model who was either reinforced or punished for the behavior. Bandura believes that, through observations, students see and learn the consequences of the behavior

FIGURE 3.4

Bandura's Model of Social Learning Theory

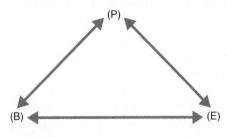

(P) Person The physical characteristics (for example, race, gender) of the person include expectations, beliefs, knowledge, and values. The physical characteristics also include metacognition or the ability to plan and monitor learning.

(E) Environmental contingencies Environment refers to the student's social and physical environment. This component includes interactions with and influences of others, as well as the nature of the task.

(B) Person's behavior The person's behavior refers to how the person responds to and modifies behavior in light of what is learned. This component not only includes current behaviors, but the ability to regulate behavior based upon self-observations and self-evaluation.

of others and then decide whether to use this information to change their own behavior when they are placed in similar situations.

The following is an example of how social learning theory works, based on how a person's expectation might affect how he would respond in a given situation. George is a poor math student (P) and is working on a math worksheet (E) with a good student, Sandra. George's expectation (P) might be that he will not do well, so he gives up easily when he comes to difficult problems (B). Sandra, however, intervenes and shows him a strategy for solving the problems (E). As a result, George can solve the difficult problems (B) and feels better about his math skills (P).

According to Bandura, the following components are essential to observational learning:

1. **Attention** is needed to observe a model and determine which actions and responses are important to remember. It helps to break down complex tasks into subtasks, so that attention can be focused on the salient parts of each subtask.

2. **Retention** is crucial for remembering information from observations. Bandura claims that we store observational information in two forms: verbal descriptions or images. Physical activities, such as how to roll a bowling ball or form letters when writing, are probably stored as images. On the other hand, how to balance a checkbook might be stored as verbal descriptions, as this procedure is usually a series of steps. Despite the distinction between the two types, representations of observed events more than likely contain both verbal descriptions and images.

3. **Production** refers to the translation of stored images and verbal descriptions into actions. In some cases, we may rehearse in our mind before we actually perform the actions. During production, we frequently compare our actions with a model and then use self-observation and self-correction to modify our actions or behaviors. If a student is demonstrating a new behavior or skill, it is important to have a teacher observe and give immediate feedback to the student. During later stages, students use self-observations and self-correction to further correct their actions.

4. **Motivation** occurs through reinforcement in observational learning. Bandura believed that reinforcement serves to motivate people in three ways: (1) people see the model reinforced for their actions and they like it; (2) people believe that, if they act like the model who was reinforced, they too will be reinforced; and (3) people perform the actions and enjoy (that is, internal reinforcement) performing the actions. The belief is that these three ways serve to motivate students to perform the same or similar actions.

The "Self" Component

As you can see, the "self" components are important in Bandura's view of social learning theory. Self-regulation, self-control, self-reflection, and self-efficacy all serve to help us better understand and use new skills, actions, and behaviors. **Self-regulation** involves developing personal standards to evaluate our performance, deciding whether we met those standards, and deciding whether we should be rewarded for meeting those standards. For example, Tom just learned how to play golf, in particular, how to drive the golf ball. He has decided that his goal is drive the ball 300 yards. After one successful night at the driving range, 15 of the 30 golf balls that he drove went 300 yards or longer. **Self-control** is our ability to control our behavior or actions, even when others are not around to judge us (with rewards or punishment). In some cases, we delay gratification for our actions until we can earn a larger reward. For example, after earning an "A" on a quiz, Nerbay decides to continue studying hard for the next few nights until he takes the test. After he takes the test and finds that he has earned an "A," he decides to take a couple of nights off from studying and watches TV. **Self-reflection** is an important skill to possess because it encourages us to reflect and judge past actions. In doing so, we are able to make adjustments to our actions to better our behavior or performance. In some cases, our self-reflection and judgments help us improve our actions, but we might also use moral standards to judge our actions or behaviors.

In some cases, our self-morality keeps our behavior and actions in check, particularly when dealing with other people. For example, Marcy has just yelled at her class for being too loud. Upon reflection, Marcy realizes that she was upset about a fight she had this morning with her boyfriend and that according to her moral code, she was wrong to take out her frustrations on her students. **Self-efficacy** is a person's beliefs about what he or she is capable of doing. How successful the people perceive themselves to be at a particular task often determines whether they will persevere through tough times or give up on the task. Comparing our performance to others and failing or succeeding at a task often determines our *level* of self-efficacy (for example, I'm good at golf), but not necessarily our *accuracy* of our self-efficacy (for example, I actually shoot 120 per game). In other words, one's perceived self-efficacy may or may not match real self-efficacy (Hergenhahn and Olson 2001). Accordingly, if one has low perceived self-efficacy, when in fact he or she is doing well, this individual may become overwhelmed and give up on difficult tasks. On the other hand, people with highly perceived self-efficacy may get in over their heads on tasks because, in fact, they are not good at the task.

Perceptual Theory. This theory has been influential in the history of special education practice, particularly for serving students with LD. However, the theory has been largely discredited in more recent years (see for example, Kavale and Forness 1999; Poplin 1988). We describe it briefly here because you are bound to see reflections of it in special education information and materials that you come across in your professional life. The theory is perceptual motor theory, which we will simply refer to as perceptual theory, because most motor theories have a perceptual component to them. For example, early learning theories by Ayres (1972), Barsch (1967), and Getman (1965) each had components of perceptional ability separate or combined with motor abilities, along with other abilities such as visual and auditory abilities (Mann and Sabatino 1985). Because many motor theories often encompass perceptual skills, there is often much overlap and similarity between these theoretical areas.

Many of these perceptual theories postulated one or more of the following:

1. In some cases, remediation of the perceptual abilities (for example, perceptual, visual perceptual, auditory perceptual, motor form perception, and perceptual motor skills) should result in improved cognitive skills.
2. In some cases, remediation of perceptual abilities should occur prior to and separate from cognitive skill remediation.
3. In some cases, perceptual ability training should begin at the level at which the child can handle perceptual training and then progress upward through the area in which the child has the perceptual problem.
4. In some cases, perceptual motor training is not meant to remediate the actual underlying processes, but is meant to enhance the brain's ability to learn how to do things.

In some cases, despite the students' ages, they would practice gross motor skills such as creeping, running, or crawling (for example, the Delacato method; Delacato 1959). In other cases, students worked on hand-eye coordination with activities such as throwing and catching a ball. Still, in other cases, students worked at pulling and pushing objects. The belief was that deficiencies in lower level (that is, basic) foundation abilities (for example, walking, running, and skipping,) would result in later learning disorders. At first, children would be assessed in these skill areas and then receive remediation in those areas that they performed poorly. Again, the belief was that students would need to master these skills before more advanced cognitive skills could develop, or that remediation of these skills would help reduce the severity of the learning problems (Ayres 1972).

Jean Ayres (1972) believed that a "disordered sensory integration" accounted for certain aspects of learning problems in children with disabilities and that enhancing sensory integration, through tactile and vestibular stimulation, would make academic learning easier for these children. Moreover, through the use of her test, Southern California Sensory Integration Test (SCSIT) (Ayers 1972), children would be assessed on the following areas: figure-ground perception, kinesthesia, crossing the midline of the body, motor accuracy, and standing balance, to name a few. Once these deficient areas were determined, therapy would begin. Therapy for these children consisted of tactile stimulation or vestibular stimulation. Tactile stimulation therapy would consist of brushing the child's skin with a dry washcloth or soft brush. Vestibular stimulation would consist of spinning or swinging the child while the child is seated in a net hammock that has both ends attached to a single point overhead. Other types of stimulation (that is, proprioceptive stimuli) therapy were also recommended. These included muscle contractions during locomotor activities (for example, the child would lie in the prone position on a skateboard and would push himself around the room while lifting his head, arms, and legs) or postural activities (for example, the child would balance on a large ball or balance board).

Despite the logic of perceptual theories, a number of problems have been associated with them and we caution against the use of perceptual theory to teach children with mild disabilities. The first problem is associated with the tests used to assess perceptual and perceptual motor skills. The majority of perceptual tests are unreliable or otherwise technically inadequate (Salvia and Ysseldyke 2004; Ysseldyke, 1973), often having low reliability and question-able validity. However, the remaining problems negate the value of seeking to develop more stringent assessments. Second, perceptual ability appears to be an elusive construct that has never been adequately proven to exist nor has never been proven to exist in its pure form (Larson 1976). Third, the use of perceptual training to remediate academic deficits has been called into question. Hammill and Larson (1974) point out that the effectiveness of such training is essen-tially "nonvalidated" (411). In their 1974 study, they found inconclusive evidence to support the notion that children with perceptual (for example, visual percep-tual) problems perform poorly in school. Moreover, the efficacy of training stu-dents in perceptual skills has not been effectively demonstrated by the research (Hammill and Larson 1974). Kavale and Mattson (1983) further extenuate this point with their findings from a meta-analysis of perceptual motor training. They found that students who received perceptual motor training made gains that were only slightly better than chance and, overall, the "perceptual-motor interventions are not effective treatments for exceptional children" (171). Fur-thermore, in a follow-up analysis of various perceptual training methods (that is, movigenic training, perceptual motor training, neurological patterning, visual perceptual training, visuomotor training, and perceptual training), Kavale and Forness (1999) reported, "there is no indication of positive effects" (22). Despite the apparent findings and evidence, perceptual and process training persists in special education as viable training methods (Kavale and Forness 1999).

Constructivist Theory

Each of the previously mentioned behavioral and cognitive theories has been influential in the fields of special and regular education, but continue to be prom-inent, particularly in special education research and practice. Perhaps indicative of the differences between special education and regular education (see Poplin and Rogers 2005), one theory has been considerably more influential to regu-lar education research practice than to special education. The current preemi-nent theory of learning in regular education is **constructivism** (sometimes more formally known as social constructivism) (see Moll 2004). Constructivists focus less on the behavioral and cognitive aspects of learning, and instead address the social nature of learning and comprehending, including the importance of meaningfulness for learning.

The Russian psychologist Lev Vygotsky first proposed the principles of con-structivist theory. According to Vygotsky (1978), learning is a social process in which learners interact with others in their environment to learn concepts and skills and gradually internalize them. Constructivist theory also has origins from the work of Jean Piaget, with contributions from other education theo-rists (Poplin 1988). Constructivists believe that students learn through a process of *actively constructing knowledge*. Whereas constructivist principles have been commonplace in regular education classrooms for the past couple of decades, it has only been within the past decade that special education has begun to apply these principles to develop teaching techniques for students with disabilities

---

BOX 3.1

CONSTRUCTIVIST PRINCIPLES

1. All students are active learners. Always search for constructing knowledge.
2. The best predictor of what is learned is based on what students already know.
3. Form follows function in learning.
4. Learning occurs best when it goes from whole to part to whole.
5. Errors are essential to learning.
6. The end goal is construction of knowledge, not transmission of it.

Source: Adapted from M. Poplin (1988). Holistic/Constructivists Principles of Teaching/Learning Process: Implications for the Field of Learning Disabilities (*Journal of Learning Disabilities* 7(21):401–16).

(Poplin and Rogers 2005). This construction process involves making connections between new information and prior knowledge (Good and Brophy 1994). More specifically, the construction of new knowledge comes about through the processes of transformation and self-regulation (Poplin 1988). **Transformation of knowledge** occurs when students learn new knowledge (or new experiences), and their prior knowledge is then transformed into new knowledge. This construction of new knowledge occurs not by simply adding new information, but by the students assimilating the new knowledge and, in doing so, changing the way they now understand the concept. For example, early on, a child learns the concept of a cow as a large creature with horns. Living next to a dairy farm, the child sees many different types of cows. Then one day while on a walk in the woods with his father, the child sees a deer foraging on small bushes and immediately calls the deer a "cow." The father corrects him, telling him that a deer is skinnier and has antlers, not horns. According to constructivist theory, the child must now reconstruct his knowledge about cows as he learns more about deer. This new experience with a deer transforms his knowledge about cows. However, if the concept of a deer is too much for the child to accept, the child may reject the notion of deer and continue to call deerlike animals cows. In this case, the child self-regulates what he learns and refuses to learn. Box 3.1 illustrates six principles of constructivist theory (Poplin 1988).

The following elaborates upon the six constructivist principles. In the first principle, according to constructivists, students are always active learners, always searching to learn new information, as long as it is of interest to them. Constructivists believe that students are always trying to make sense of the world around them. In doing so, students first judge whether the topic/concept is of interest or value to them. If it is something worthwhile to learn, they will then construct knowledge of this topic.

In the second principle, the best predictor of what someone will learn is often what they already know. As self-regulated learners, students will search out to learn more about those topics that interest them and about which they have prior knowledge. If students have no prior knowledge about a topic, learning about the topic will be very difficult unless it is linked to some related prior knowledge.

The third principle states that form follows function in learning. This tenet refers to the fact that students will learn some new skill or topic in their own manner because they are more concerned with the function of the skill or content than the exact form; that will come later. For example, when students learn to write, they often follow natural developmental or emergent stages (Lipson and Wixson 1997); however, they will scribble on paper and, when asked what they are writing, they will read back to you a logical sounding message, despite the fact that what was written is illegible (or nonsense). Over time, students begin to use letters that are parts of the word, and, still later, the correct letters (in the correct order) to form actual words that make up a "real" message. Only over time and with much practice will students master the correct form (that is, writing legible letters/words) of the message (function).

Under the fourth principle, learning occurs best from whole to part to whole. Some constructivists claim that, when teachers reduce a task to their individual components, the task itself loses its meaning; it simply becomes a collection of parts or steps. Moreover, teachers should try to help students understand the meaning or purpose of concepts or skills first so that when broken down, the students can scaffold the parts to something that is meaningful. Constructivists claim, and rightly so in many cases, that teachers are often so busy teaching the specifics of learning tasks that they often forget to explain to students why they are learning the task in the first place (Poplin 1988).

The fifth principle states that learning errors are important. Rather then penalize students when they make errors, constructivists claim that we should help students understand their errors so that they can correct them and, in the process, learn.

In the sixth principle of constructivist theory, teachers are no longer the ones who *transmit* facts or other bits of unrelated knowledge to students; instead, teachers help students construct knowledge—knowledge that is *meaningful* to each student (see Table 3.1). Because students personalize and make the information meaningful as they learn, they will remember it longer and recall it when

THINK BACK TO THE CASE about Ned's lessons about the heart . . .

3. *If Ned had instead given his students a list of key concepts and definitions, and then asked them to apply them to a drawing of the DC Beltway without explaining the analogy for them, could the students have figured out the analogy?*

From a constructivist perspective, the students could have used their expert knowledge about the DC Beltway to construct an understanding of the functions of the heart, about which they are currently novices. Ideally, they would problem-solve the analogy in a social context. For example, they could work in small groups, or Ned could be an expert who gives them hints and answers questions they ask. Through dialogue, students would model their ideas for each other and refine the analogy they construct by talking it through. Seeking how to solve an authentic problem, such as Beltway congestion or heart disease, might help the students.

TABLE 3.1: Transmission of Information Versus Social Construction of Knowledge

Transmission view	Social construction view
Knowledge as fixed body of information transmitted from teacher or text to students	Knowledge as developing interpretations coconstructed through discussion
Texts, teacher as authoritative sources of expert knowledge to which students defer	Authority for constructed knowledge resides in the arguments and evidence cited in its support by students as well as by texts or teacher; everyone has expertise to contribute
Teacher is responsible for managing students' learning by providing information and leading students through activities and assignments	Teacher and students share responsibility for initiating and guiding learning efforts
Teacher explains, checks for understanding and judges correctness of students' responses	Teacher acts as discussion leader who poses questions, seeks clarifications, promotes dialogue, helps group recognize areas of consensus and of continuing disagreement
Students memorize or replicate what has been explained or modeled	Students strive to make sense of new input by relating it to their prior knowledge and by collaborating in dialogue with others to co-construct shared understandings
Discourse emphasizes drill and recitation in response to convergent questions; focus is on eliciting correct answers	Discourse emphasizes reflective discussion of networks of connected knowledge: questions are more divergent but designed to develop understanding of the powerful ideas that anchor these networks; focus is on eliciting students' thinking
Activities emphasize replication of models or applications that require following step-by-step algorithms	Activities emphasize applications to authentic issues and problems that require higher-order thinking
Students work mostly alone, practicing what has been transmitted to them in order to prepare themselves to compete for rewards by reproducing it on demand	Students collaborate by acting as a learning community that constructs shared understandings through sustained dialogue

Source: Reprinted with permission from T. Good and J. Brophy, *Looking in Classrooms* (New York: Harper Collins College Publishers, 1994).

Chapter Question

ALERT

In this section you will find information that answers a Chapter Question:

3. What is one application for each theory?

needed. In this type of learning, teachers move away from having students remember facts and other unrelated bits of knowledge, and teachers instead focus on reflective discussions and the implication of content or skills learned (Good and Brophy 1994).

Using Theories in Teaching

Now that we have discussed several theories of learning, we will discuss their applications to learning. Think back to each theory as you read about the applications, and try to understand how the application was derived from that theory.

Application of Behavioral Theory

Applications of behavioral theories rely upon stimulating the learning processes that behaviorists believe underlie cognition. We provide examples of some the most commonly utilized practices in special education (see Swanson and Hoskyn 2001, for example): reinforcement, task analysis and group contingencies.

CASE 3.2   **Math Problem Problems**

Case Introduction

Now that you have worked through the first case in this chapter, you should feel comfortable addressing issues in a second case. In this case about math teacher Vernon Jackson and his student, Linda, see if you can find evidence of how the various education theories described in the first half of this chapter are enacted in an everyday teaching scenario. Ask yourself what the implications are of Vernon's and Linda's thoughts and actions for the type of learning that results for Linda.

Vernon Jackson told students to read the first problem on the worksheet as he handed it out. He then told them, "I will tell you how to do the first problem, and you will do the rest." In front of him, Linda looked over the ten problems on the worksheet and let out a depressing sigh. "Not again," she said to herself, followed up with, " I hate doing these problems."

When Mr. Jackson reached the last row, he continued, "OK. Read the first problem while I tell you how its done." Writing it on the board, he was cognizant of his students' general dislike of word problems and listened for disparaging remarks about the assignment. Linda didn't attend to the directions and instead, began to write a note to her friend Cory Franks.

Mr. Jackson then described how to complete the problem, "For this problem, you will need to use only the important information and disregard the rest of the information." As Linda glanced at the first problem, which was about camping, she remarked to herself, "Great, I don't even like camping."

"Linda," Mr. Jackson asked, "How many campers like hotdogs?" Linda, surprised that he called on her, responded with a blank look on her face. "OK," Mr. Jackson continued, "look at the problem and tell me how many campers are eating hotdogs out of 20 campers?"

Linda then responded, "12?"

"Good," Mr. Jackson remarked, while leaning against his desk. He then continued, "If each student eats three hotdogs, how many hotdogs are needed?"

As Linda looks around, students are busy writing down what Mr. Jackson had said; however, because she missed what was said, she scribbled out her own computation. "Ah, 27?" Linda responds.

"No, Linda," Mr. Jackson replies. "Blaine, how many hotdogs are needed?" Blain correctly responds "36," and Mr. Jackson smiles and tells him he is correct.

"Finally, if hotdogs are 30 cents a piece, how much money is needed to purchase hotdogs for the campers?" Mr. Jackson asks the class.

In a chorus of voices, they respond, "$10.80."

"Now, you do the rest," he instructs his class, despite the fact that many students have already begun working on the second word problem. It's not surprising than many of the students are working independently because they have been reviewing word problems for the past two weeks.

Mr. Jackson then lets the students work on the remainder of the problems while he sits at his desk and looks for worksheets for the next portion of his lesson. Mr. Jackson likes to tell students how to complete problems. He feels that students understand his directions because he is a verbal person who believes that all students need to become auditory learners if they hope to progress into the higher grades.

To Linda, a student with a learning disability, completing math word problems is just about the worst thing. In addition to her reading problems, she does poorly in math, often failing to pick up concepts that other students easily understand. Over time, despite the different math teachers, Linda has grown to dislike math and often avoids anything relating to math. For example, when Mr. Jackson informs students that they can complete one extra worksheet per week for bonus points, Linda flatly refuses, in spite of her borderline grade of a "D."

CASE QUESTIONS

1. From behavioral theory, what could you do to help Linda improve her math skills?
2. What components of social learning theory could you use to teach this math lesson?
3. What could you do to help Linda with her self-efficacy for solving work problems?

Reinforcement. Reinforcement serves as a strong tool for teachers to use in the classroom. Teachers can use various forms of environmental reinforcers such as smiles, verbal comments, winks, or pats on the back to initiate or maintain appropriate behaviors in students. In many cases, the teacher's attention serves as a form of reinforcement for students. However, teachers should be cautious because there may be times when their attention inadvertently serves to reinforce a student's inappropriate behavior. Pointing out misbehaviors in some students can serve to reinforce a particular behavior and maintain it or even increase its frequency. When introducing new behaviors to a student's repertoire, teachers should reinforce those new behaviors immediately and frequently. Once the behaviors are established, teachers can use reinforcers less frequently, as well as use less intense reinforcers (that is, move from primary to secondary reinforcers). Whenever teachers use primary reinforcers, they should always pair them with a secondary reinforcer, such as praise or attention so that teachers can begin using more natural reinforcers that are commonly found in the student's environment.

Steps for improving behavior involve:

1. Choose an inappropriate (that is, undesirable) behavior that needs to be changed.
2. Decide which new or alternate behavior you want to see increase in frequency and replace the inappropriate behavior.
3. Decide how to measure the new target behavior, and begin taking data to determine its current level.
4. Decide when and how you will begin reinforcing the target behavior, and determine which reinforcers you will use.
5. Keep data to ensure that target behavior is increasing. Once you see increases and know that the behavior has been established, decide how you want to change, if any, the reinforcement or frequency of reinforcement.
6. Once the behavior has been established over a long period of time, decide how you want to fade out external reinforcers or move to a self-monitoring system.

Task Analysis. Using a **task analysis** to examine complex behavior changes or complex tasks often helps students. A task analysis involves breaking down a large task into smaller subtasks or steps. Once tasks are broken down, students are taught to perform these smaller steps before being asked to complete the larger overall task. Typically, students must master each step before being taught the next step. For example, washing hands involves several smaller steps. In the first step, you turn the water on. Next, you wet your hands. Next, you put soap on your hands. Next, you lather the soap in your hands. This would be followed with rinsing off the soap. Next, you dry your hands. Finally, you turn off the water. In this example, each step would be taught individually or in conjunction with other steps. Some children can learn multiple steps, whereas other children need to be taught each individual step.

Group Contingencies. A group contingency is a system in which the receipt of reinforcement for the entire group depends upon the behavior of its group members. A group contingency is a behavior management technique that is used to control the behavior of large groups of students. For example, the "marbles in a jar" technique has been used to help control group behaviors. Using this technique, the teacher has two jars, one full of marbles, and one empty. The first jar should contain a sufficient number of marbles so that the teacher can give periodic reinforcement over a few days. Periodically, the teacher reinforces positive classroom behaviors by moving a marble from one jar to the other. In some cases, the teacher explains why she is moving marbles from one jar to the other and at other times, no explanation is given. Initially, the teacher should explain to students which positive classroom behaviors are being reinforced (for example, quiet behavior, on-task behavior, using cooperative skills with one another). Although this group reinforcement technique might be a consistent technique, teachers should supplement this form of management with other types of reinforcement, such as verbal praise or smiles for appropriate classroom behaviors.

THINK BACK TO THE CASE about Linda's math skills . . .

1. From behavioral theory, what could you do to help Linda improve her math skills?

From a behavioral perspective, Mr. Jackson could break down the skill of solving word problems into steps and then list these steps so that Linda could refer to them while working on word problems. He could also use positive reinforcement to shape Linda's behavior until she begins to use the problem-solving steps correctly.

Applications of Cognitive Theories

As we have discussed previously, cognitive theories attempt to explain how students think and learn. As you read each section on application of cognitive theories, think about how each could improve the thinking and learning skills of students with mild disabilities. We begin with *cognitive* aspects of learning and end with more *social* aspects of learning.

Application of the Information Processing Model in Teaching. Several applications have derived from the information processing model. While reading this section, think about how each application might assist your students in storing new knowledge in long-term memory—the ultimate goal of learning. Of course, this involves pulling down knowledge from long-term memory into working memory so that new knowledge can be encoded and then stored in long-term memory.

Attention

Attention is a process used to decide what is critical to remember and process and then send this information on to the next memory store. Prior to any lesson, teachers should direct students' attention to the task at hand (for example, see the lesson grabber activities described in Chapter 10). If giving oral directions, it is important first to have students stop what they are doing and look at you as you describe the directions. Using selective attention, students pay attention to you and your words as you describe each step. *Gaining* their attention is one aspect of attention; the other aspect is *sustaining* their attention over a period of time. Sustained attention is a difficult process for some students with disabilities. Teachers can improve students' sustained attention by using activities such as "20 Questions" or "I-Spy". For students with attention problems, it is important to reduce distractions (for example, excessive noises or visual clutter), break large tasks into manageable parts, present multistep directions one step at a time, emphasize key parts to a task or key information in a learning unit, and reinforce students when they focus and sustain attention to task.

Chunking

Chunking involves combining similar or like items together for the purpose of learning or remembering them. Chunking is a particularly helpful strategy with unorganized information or lists of items. Students can learn to organize lesson content into a web or other graphic that depicts how discrete concepts are related and then use the category label to recall them, for example. Of course, prior to presenting it to students, teachers can organize information into helpful chunks of knowledge based upon a category. These useful chunks of related knowledge will help students remember the information better, particularly if the chunks are distinct categories. For example, teachers can chunk types of triangles into equilateral, isosceles, and scalene, and they can chunk types of polygons into rectangle, quadrilateral, parallelogram, and rhombus.

Meaningfulness

Meaningful learning occurs when students link new knowledge with prior knowledge (that is, from long-term memory). They are not just chunking the information, they are forging schematic relationships. With the technique KWL (know, want, learn), students determine what they already know about the topic prior to learning and then linking it up with new information as they learn (for a detailed description, see Chapter 6). Figure 3.5 is an example of a KWL Plus chart. This chart includes the letter "S," which represents *things you STILL want to know about*. Other ways of connecting new with prior knowledge involve using an advance organizer. An advance organizer is given at the beginning of a lesson and involves tapping into prior knowledge in the form of a review of content already learned, a discussion of information about a known topic, or review of recently learned information. For example, prior to learning about double-digit addition with carrying over, students might review math problems that do not involve carrying over. Once they practice a few of these, students then learn the new concept of carrying over.

Analogies

Analogies represent another method of tapping into long-term memory to bring the prior information into working memory so that new knowledge can be encoded to it. For example, biology students often use the analogy of the cell function with that of a factory (see Table 3.2). Of course, students have to be familiar with the first part of the analogy or they will be learning two new concepts.

Strategies

Strategies are a set of procedures or steps that are used to complete a task. With any given task, some strategies may be more successful than others. We often

FIGURE 3.5

KWL Plus Chart on Estuaries

K	W	L	S
In this column, list things you already **know** about estuaries	In this column, list things you **want** to know about estuaries	In this column, list things you **learned** about estuaries	In this column, list things you **still** want to know about estuaries
• _____ _____ _____ _____	• _____ _____ _____ _____	• _____ _____ _____ _____	• _____ _____ _____ _____
• _____ _____ _____ _____	• _____ _____ _____ _____	• _____ _____ _____ _____	• _____ _____ _____ _____
• _____ _____ _____ _____	• _____ _____ _____ _____	• _____ _____ _____ _____	• _____ _____ _____ _____

TABLE 3.2: Analogy Between Cell Functions and a Factory

Plant Cell	Factory	Function
Cell wall	Border fence	Protection
Nucleus	Copy room	Makes DNA copies
Endoplasmic reticulum	Conveyor belt	Transports materials
Ribosomes	Assembly line	Assembles proteins
Mitochondrion	Power station	Makes energy
Chloroplast	Solar panels	Gathers energy
Vacuole	Waste pond	Stores wastes

use strategies without even consciously thinking about them. However, for many students, particularly students with disabilities, strategies must be directly taught. The most effective strategies are those that are tied to a specific task (for example, reading comprehension, solving math story problems, or studying lists of items) and/or content area. The strategies that need to be taught to students are those that are more than mere rote rehearsal strategies.

Effective strategies are tied to a specific learning task and are taught along with metacognitive skills (that is, knowing when and where to use the strategy). Rather than use rote rehearsal to remember vocabulary words and their definitions, students could use specific study strategies, such as the IT FITS strategy (King-Sears, Mercer, and Sindelar 1992; see Box 3.2) or the LINCS strategy (Ellis 1992; see Figure 3.9, for example. A number of other strategies are described throughout this book.

BOX 3.2

IT FITS STRATEGY FOR REMEMBERING VOCABULARY

I Identify the term.
T Tell the definition of the term.
F Find a keyword.
I Imagine the definition doing something.
T Think about the definition doing something with the keyword.
S Study what you imagined until you know the definition.

BOX 3.3

LINCS STRATEGY FOR REMEMBERING VOCABULARY

L List the parts.
I Imagine a picture.
N Note a reminding word.
C Construct a LINCing story.
S Self-test.

TIPS FOR GENERALIZATION

Metacognition and Strategy Flexibility

Any strategy training should include metacognitive components. In particular, Wong (1996) pointed out that training should promote self-awareness and self-regulation. That means teachers should nurture their students' self-awareness by making them aware of the task demands and how the strategy will help them address these demands for success. Self-awareness of task demands means that students know why they are completing the task (that is, the purpose of the task) and they are also aware of the steps needed to achieve the goal. Self-regulation, on the other hand, refers to self-monitoring of accurate strategy use and self-checking of work for accuracy. Other researchers go beyond these definitions and suggest that metacognitive skills should include *flexibility* of strategy use for new situations and an *internalization* of the strategy steps so that students can put into their own words why the strategy is effective for them.

In terms of training for *generalization* of a strategy, teachers should train students to use the strategy with new, similar tasks (for example, use the reading strategy with a newspaper article and with a textbook, rather than with just short passages), and should teach students to internalize the strategy by helping them understand why the strategy works for them. Through internalizing (Wong uses the term "mediating student mindfulness"), students can understand which aspects of the strategy lead to their success. By using the strategy with novel materials, students gain practice at flexibility of the strategy as it applies to these new materials.

Application of Social Learning Theory. Whereas information processing models address the mechanisms of cognitive processing, social learning theory is applied by focusing on both social interactions and the cognitive processing that students engage to navigate and learn from those social interactions. Social learning theory relies on modeling and various opportunities to learn in cooperation with others.

Models

As you read about social learning theory, you probably saw that the use of models is an important component in changing behavior. The use of peer models is particularly helpful for students when they are learning new tasks or need feedback about incorrectly performed tasks. Models serve to show students how to perform a task and provide a concrete and realistic example of performance. Whenever possible, teachers should try to model a behavior for students, rather than just describe it. Although descriptions are important prior to modeling, modeling provides students with an explicit example of the behavior or performance. Once teachers model a behavior, it is important for students to practice that new behavior while receiving with feedback. Using guided practice, students can practice modeling the behavior for each other while the teacher circulates around room providing feedback on their performance.

Cooperative Learning and Peer Tutoring

Cooperative learning and peer tutoring are often associated with one another. Although both involve students working together to learn, there are typically differences between the two sets of approaches. Cooperative learning involves students working to complete a tasks in groups, in which they can be dependent on one another in several possible ways. In peer tutoring, two students take turns performing the roles of tutor and tutee.

Cooperative learning consists of organizing students into heterogeneous groups of four to five students. Within each group, students are responsible for achieving both an individual and group goal (Putnam 1993; Slavin 1990). Individual efforts within a cooperative learning group help contribute to the group goal. By contributing positively to a group goal, individuals develop self-efficacy. Moreover, as others in the group are rewarded for their actions, students may become confident that they too are capable of successfully completing the task. Teachers can also provide encouragement and feedback to students as they work in groups. Teacher feedback serves as another source that will enable students to develop accurate self-efficacy skills about the task that they are working on.

Classwide peer tutoring (CWPT) is a popular peer tutoring method to help students learn from one another. In peer tutoring, students directly assist or teach other students skills or knowledge. The act of teaching others often builds self-confidence in students, because they must know the material well enough to teach it. In doing so, students remember the content in meaningful ways that help them retain and recall the information in long-term memory. To get the most out of the tutoring experience, teachers should take care to match up tutors with tutees. Good models have appropriate coping skills to deal with the demands of the task. Those skills, such as verbalizations (for example, "I need to calm down to complete this task." or "I need to go slower over the tough parts."), serve to improve the self-efficacy skills of those being tutored. Even though adults can model the correct completion of tasks for students, students may wonder whether they are capable of performing like an adult to complete the task. Instead, peer models can provide a more realistic example of how to complete a task for the student being tutored (Hohn 1994).

THINK BACK TO THE CASE) about Linda's math skills . . .

2. What components of social learning theory could you use to teach this math lesson?

From a social learning perspective, Mr. Jackson could pair Linda up with a model who could show her how to solve word problems. Mr. Jackson could then reinforce the students who correctly model the problem-solving steps. Another option would be to place Linda within a cooperative learning group where other students would work together to help her solve word problems.

3. What could you do to help Linda with her self-efficacy for solving work problems?

Linda needs to develop higher levels of self-efficacy for solving word problems and better self-regulation skills. Mr. Jackson can help with these "self" skills by making sure that she completes problems successfully. He can model for her by thinking aloud while he solves problems. He could use positive self-talk and use self-reinforcing statements to help her with self-regulation skills.

Application of Constructivists Theories

As we noted, students participating in general education classrooms are likely to encounter constructivist-based teaching and learning; and certainly it can be found in popular special education practices today as well (for example, Mariage 2001; Montague 2003). Constructivist lessons very often involve a social component such as dialogues with a teacher or a peer, teaming, or group work. Because the process of constructing knowledge relies on active cognitive engagement, constructivist lessons tend to be focused on meaningful or authentic tasks, such as solving a problem of interest to students (for example, using mathematics to determine a plan for equitable distribution of relief resources following a natural disaster, as opposed to "mindlessly" solving practice problems).

In a social, or dialogic, process, the student receives information and tries to construct meaning about the new information, which can include trying to use it (for example, you might ask questions or try to explain new information to someone who is helping you learn about it). Through an exchange in which the learner is actually problem-solving how to comprehend new concepts, understanding is constructed. The student less familiar with the information is termed a **novice.** The more knowledgeable partner(s) is the **expert.** Vygotsky (1978) referred to the range between a student's present problem-solving developmental capability and what the student is capable of when guided by an expert as the **zone of proximal development (ZPD).** Through social interactions with experts, the novice gradually becomes an expert on a particular concept. This theory of how people learn is often thought of as distinct from behavioral practices that emphasize drill and practice to mastery (for example, Direct Instruction), although the two can work together (Harris and Graham 1996; Poplin and Rogers 2005).

Social interaction during constructivist lessons is only a vehicle for the process of knowledge construction within a student's ZPD. Through such social activities as peer editing and presenting one's writing from the "author's chair" (Englert and Mariage 1991), students interact with experts to think actively about content. The sharing of ideas and attempting to comprehend others' perspectives cause students to grow in their understanding.

VIDEO CASE CONNECTIONS BOX

Watch the Video Case *Cooperative Learning: High School History Lesson.* Listen to high school student Jake discuss the benefits of talking about content with cooperative learning group mates. Restate his explanation using the previous information about constructivist teaching and learning activities.

To be effective experiences, constructivist lessons cannot simply be open-ended opportunities for teams of students to explore whatever interests them. Without direction, students may not think about the critical aspects of a concept or may simply elect to not investigate things that are not of interest to them. Without guidance, students may even come to firmly "learn" misinformation (Mayer 2004). Scaffolded instruction is an effective approach to supporting student learning as they gradually assume "ownership" of ideas (Hogan and Pressley 1997). By **scaffolding,** teachers support students by directing their learning. Teachers might provide the students with specific questions to answer, outline the process the students are to follow for their own knowledge construction, or model procedures when scaffolding (Baker, Gersten, and Scanlon 2002; Reiser 2004).

When constructivist lessons include scaffolded support, they can be effective for learners with mild disabilities—who have been found to benefit most from explicit instructional practices (review Chapters 1 and 2). Typically, students with mild disabilities benefit from explicit instruction to help them firmly master foundational concepts and skills (Gersten 1991; Swanson and Hoskyn 2001). Others have noted that a balance of constructivist and more explicit instruction is more likely to benefit those with mild disabilities (for example, Harris and Graham 1996; Poplin and Rogers 2005).

CHAPTER SUMMARY

We hope that you now have a new appreciation for learning theory and can approach learning tasks from different perspectives after reading this chapter. Because a sound theory is a framework used to describe events, it can be used to describe how students with mild disabilities learn and why they exhibit certain behaviors—both appropriate and inappropriate. Theories serve to help you become better teachers. We have described different theories and provided applications of each to help you understand how they are used in teaching.

In the field of special education today, behavioral (including cognitive behavior modification) and cognitive (including the use of strategies and metacognition) theories represent the predominant theories, and constructivist theories are becoming increasingly influential. Special education teachers and their colleagues use applications of these three theories daily. If you visit any classroom that includes students with mild disabilities, you will see popular techniques derived from these theories, such as learning strategies, mnemonic instruction, self-monitoring, self-instructions, peer tutoring, and cooperative learning. The rest of this book will discuss different teaching techniques and strategies that have been derived from the theories and that are research-based techniques. We hope that this book will not be the first or last time that you read about these theories, because many of them are much too complicated to be presented in a few short pages; instead, we hope that you will read other sources for expanded views on the different theories.

KEY TERMS

Attention, 87	Executive Function, 92	Scaffolding, 109
Behavior Modification, 78	Expert, 108	Schema, 91
Behavioral Theory, 78	Extinction, 81	Secondary Reinforcer, 79
Chunking, 90	Generalized Reinforcer, 79	Self-Control, 95
Classwide Peer Tutoring (CWPT), 107	Maintenance Rehearsal, 89	Self-Efficacy, 95
Cognitive Behavior Modification (CBM), 83	Metacognition, 92	Self-Reflection, 95
	Motivation, 94	Self-Regulation, 95
Conditional Knowledge, 91	Negative Reinforcer, 79	Sensory Register, 87
Conditioned Reinforcer, 79	Novice, 108	Social Learning Theory, 93
Constructivism, 97	Observational Learning, 93	Strategy, 92
Contingent Reinforcement, 79	Operant Conditioning, 78	Task Analysis, 102
Cooperative Learning, 107	Perception, 87	Theory, 74
Declarative Knowledge, 91	Positive Reinforcer, 79	Time-Outs, 81
Differential Reinforcement of Incompatible (DRI), 82	Primary Reinforcer, 79	Transformation of Knowledge, 98
	Procedural Knowledge, 91	Working Memory, 89
Differential Reinforcement of Alternative (DRA), 82	Production, 94	Zone of Proximal Development (ZPD), 108
	Reinforcer, 79	
Elaborative Rehearsal, 89	Retention, 94	

APPLICATION ACTIVITIES

Using information from the chapter, complete the following activities that were designed to help you apply the knowledge that was presented in this chapter.

1. You have a student who constantly curses in your classroom. Because this is a behavior that you have targeted for change, describe what you could do to change this behavior. Describe the new behavior, how you will reinforce it, what you would do if cursing continues, and how you will monitor the student's performance. Review your answers and identify which theory(s) they most reflect.

2. Using the information processing model, describe one concept and how you could teach it using an analogy. Describe what information would tap into prior knowledge and how you would link new knowledge about the concept with prior knowledge.

3. Think of a concept or skill that you will teach when you become a teacher (or if you cannot think of one, use the concepts: theory and hypothesis). Identify how you could teach the same thing from each of the three domains of behavioral, cognitive, and constructivist theories.

TECHNOLOGY RESOURCES FOR UNDERSTANDING AND USING THEORIES

The *What Works Clearinghouse* website
http://ies.ed.gov/ncee/wwc/

This website is maintained by the U.S. Department of Education, Institute of Education Sciences. It includes detailed guidelines that Clearinghouse evaluators use to determine if research evidence supports specific practices. A section of the website provides reports on the evaluations of specific interventions.

The *Doing What Works* website
http://dww.ed.gov/

This website, like the What Works Clearinghouse website, is a sister site that the U. S. Department of Education maintains. It provides examples of possible ways educators might apply research findings and how to use teaching techniques. In addition, this website offers tools and resources that can be applied to diverse groups of students, including ESL students.

The *Iris Center* website
http://iris.peabody.vanderbilt.edu/index.html

This website provides high-quality resources for college and university faculty and professional development providers in the form of training materials such as case-based activities, video clips, and teaching modules.

The *National Center for Education Evaluation (NCEE)* and *National Center for Special Education Research (NCSER)* websites
http://ies.ed.gov/ncee/ and http://ies.ed.gov/ncser/

These companion websites are sponsored by the Institute for Education Sciences and provide reports about research-based techniques and strategies for teachers, along with the effectiveness of these techniques and guides or data products relating to the research.

Visit the book-specific website at www.cengage.com/education/boyle for a variety of study tools such as web links, tutorial quizzes, glossary/flash cards, bonus material not included in the text, and more.

The premium website offers access to additional materials, including the Video Cases. Go to www.cengage.com/login to register or purchase access.

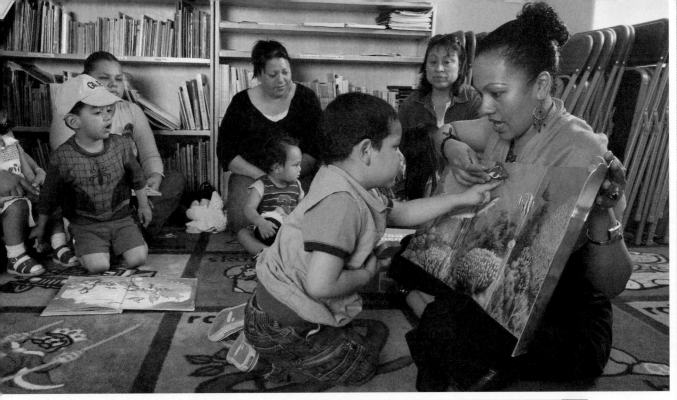

© Michael Newman/PhotoEdit Inc.

Oral Language: Strategies and Techniques

4

CHAPTER QUESTIONS

1. Why is oral language important to teach, and what are the components of oral language?

2. How are models useful in describing how language develops in children?

3. How does language normally develop in children, and what are some common language difficulties among students with mild disabilities?

4. How do oral language skills influence reading and writing skills?

5. What strategies and techniques are effective for improving language skills?

Do you think language problems are common among students with disabilities?

If you answered *yes*, you are correct. Among students with disabilities, 96 percent had one or more types of a communication deficit; of those students, 90 percent had a language impairment, and 23 percent exhibited articulation disorders (Gibbs and Cooper 1989; Wagner and Blackorby 2002). The American Speech-Language-Hearing Association (ASHA) 2006 Schools Survey confirms these numbers by reporting that approximately 70 percent of speech language pathologists (SLPs) regularly serve students with mild disabilities (for example, learning disabilities and mental retardation) in public schools. Because of the high number of students with disabilities who also have concurrent language problems, the Council for Exceptional Children (CEC) has specifically addressed understanding language development and language problems as standards that all special education teachers should acquire (CEC 2003) (see the inside cover for specific CEC standards).

In this chapter, you will learn how to teach oral language skills to students with mild disabilities. We will present information about components of language, models of language development, and milestones for normal language development. In addition, we will discuss the language problems of students with mild disabilities, and techniques, skills, and activities for improving the oral language of students.

CASE 4.1 — **Short Supply of Words**

Case Introduction

In this case, you will read about a student who has language difficulties. As you read the case, you will see how his problems affect his communication with others and his academic skills. Think about how you could help him if you were his teacher.

At the end of the case, you will find case questions. These questions are meant to serve as points for reflection. Of course, if you can answer them immediately, you should do so, but you may want to wait to answer them until you have read that portion of the chapter that pertains to the particular case question. Throughout the rest of the chapter, you will see the same questions. As you see them again, try to answer them based upon the portion of the chapter that you just read.

Sammie Mattati grew up in the suburbs of Philadelphia, Pennsylvania. His parents, Kakie and Sabot Mattati work in center-city Philly as successful lawyers at a large law firm. When Sammie was born, his parents didn't really notice that anything was different about him at first. Often too busy to spend much time with him during the day, they relied upon their nanny, Sophie, for reports of Sammie's progress. Even Sophie didn't notice problems as she cared for him. In all, his first two years of life were rather uneventful. During the latter part of Sammie's second year, however, Sophie and his parents began to notice that, while other children Sammie's age were speaking, he remained void of words and instead communicated using gestures and sounds. Despite the delay, Kakie and Sabot didn't worry because Sabot himself did not speak until he was almost three years old. Even when Sammie began to use words, he still relied heavily on gestures to help him communicate. When he turned four, his parents noticed that his speech was still behind that of his playmates and decided it was time to seek help.

Working with their local school division, Markel School District, Sammie's parents scheduled him for a speech and language evaluation; they determined that Sammie was delayed in the areas of language and sound production. Within a few weeks, Sammie was receiving speech services from the Speech Language Pathologist (SLP) at his local preschool. These services continued when he entered kindergarten and are continuing even today, now that Sammie is in fifth grade. In addition to receiving special education services for speech and language, he also qualified under the category of specific learning disabilities in third grade because of reading problems. To receive assistance in reading, Sammie leaves his fifth grade class and walks to the special education resource room twice a week.

Now in fifth grade, Sammie's language problems continue, particularly in the area of word recall. On one recent day, Mrs. Laptia, his special education teacher, asked him to identify some common objects found around the room. Sammie had particular difficulty with certain objects, such as the wall clock. When his teacher asked him to name the object, he first had to describe its shape, size, and characteristics before finally calling it by its name: a clock. He has similar problems recalling specific vocabulary words and uses this technique whenever he cannot immediately think of the name. Often, he has similar problems in his written assignments. In addition, class discussions are particularly difficult for Sammie because he has trouble keeping track of who is talking and has difficulty contributing to the discussion. In reading, he also has some difficulty

recognizing new vocabulary words, particularly those that have multiple syllables. When he comes to a word that he can't pronounce, he will either skip it or replace it with a similar sounding word.

During his language services, his SLP works with him in the speech clinic. In the room, they review worksheets to improve his vocabulary, particularly for vocabulary words in upcoming chapters or stories, and work on his reading aloud. She also works with Sammie on writing stories from memory and using synonyms when he can't come up with the correct word. His classroom teachers also help by using word walls and allowing Sammie to use technology to aid his writing. Although these techniques help Sammie, he still has problems writing stories or with on-the-spot responses.

CASE QUESTIONS

1. What area of remediation would you target for Sammie?
2. In addition to oral language, what other skills would you, as the teacher, address?
3. Name and describe two types of oral language activities or techniques that you could use to remediate Sammie's language problems.

As you can see from the case, Sammie's language problems interfere not only in how he communicates, but in other academic areas as well. Oral language serves as the primary means of communication in most classrooms, particularly elementary ones, yet it is rarely part of the formal curriculum. Typically, teachers only address oral language skills when students have speech and language difficulties. At other times, teachers simply refer the child to an SLP for services. In this chapter, you will learn about oral language and methods that you can use to improve the oral language skills of students with mild disabilities, like Sammie.

▼

Chapter Question
ALERT

In this section, you will find information that answers a Chapter Question:

1. Why is oral language important to teach, and what are the components of oral language?

The Importance of Oral Language

Oral language skills are important for several reasons. Oral language skills allow students to communicate effectively. Oral language skills are used on a daily basis in the classroom and are essential skills as they are the primary means by which teachers and students communicate for learning. Language skills are also useful as students answer teachers' questions about information that is learned, participate in classroom discussions, initiate and maintain conversations with peers and adults, and express ideas and feelings about various topics. Language skills have been linked to academic development, particularly in the areas of reading and written language (Catts and Kamhi 2005). Among bilingual students, oral language skills play a critical role in reading (Miller et al. 2006). Language difficulties can be discouraging for a student like Sammie, because the difficulties affect both him and those with whom he is trying to communicate. For students like Sammie, communicating with others can be a frustrating experience.

Oral language is not addressed directly in the classroom, despite its importance, for varying reasons, some of which include the following:

- Some believe that most children develop language skills naturally and do not require remediation.
- It may be difficult to determine language proficiency in children who are shy or withdrawn.
- Oral language skills may be difficult for teachers to break into subskills that can be taught effectively.
- Most schools emphasize academic skills and may not consider oral language as part of the academic curriculum.
- Most educators believe that children will simply outgrow language difficulties. (Polloway and Smith 2000)

Although emphasizing academic skills over oral language skills may be valid for prioritizing content taught in classrooms, oral language skills remain the primary means of communication in elementary classrooms. Whether teachers are giving verbal directions for completing worksheets or students are listening to a lecture on science, oral language skills form the basis of classroom communication. Because of the importance of these skills for school and beyond, language skills should be incorporated into the curriculum, especially for students with mild disabilities.

Oral Language and Its Components

Language is defined as "a socially shared code, or conventional system, that represents ideas through the use of arbitrary symbols and rules that govern combinations of these symbols" (Bernstein and Tiegerman-Farber 1997, 6). Not only are most people familiar with the written symbol *B* in the English language by its name *bee*, but most are also familiar with the letter-sound association of it: *ba*. The letter name and letter sound both represent a "shared code" that two people need to understand for effective communication. The same is true of spoken words and sounds (that is, phonemes) that we use.

Furthermore, to communicate, there must be a **sender** of a message, a **receiver** of the message, a **shared code** of understanding of the message, and a shared **intent** of the message (Kuder 2003), as illustrated in Figure 4.1. Typically, when two people are having a conversation, a sender and receiver are trying to convey a message. For these two to understand the message, both need to understand the shared code (that is, both speak English), and both should understand the subtle nuances of the message or intent of the message. For example, if you were speaking to a child as she pulled out a bag of cookies and began eating them, you might say, "Mmm . . . those cookies look good." If the child responded that, "Yes they are good," then there would be a misunderstanding as to the intent of your message. In this case, your intent was that you wanted to eat one of the cookies. Lastly, speech, although not necessary, is

FIGURE 4.1

Parts of Communication

Sender   Message   Receiver

useful for communication to occur. Speech is "the neuromuscular act of producing sounds that are used in language" (Kuder 2003).

Categories of Language

Language is typically broken down into two categories: expressive or receptive. **Expressive language** refers to spoken words that are produced from speech. **Receptive language** refers to an understanding or comprehension of spoken words. Children can have problems in either expressive or receptive language, or both. Expressive language problems can occur in a person's ability to pronounce phonemes, words or sentences, or to express thoughts or feelings. One of the most common expressive language problems is with articulation. For people with articulation disorders, speech can be difficult to produce.

Students with receptive language difficulties typically have problems with tasks that involve the understanding of sounds, words, or sentences. For example, children may exhibit problems with (1) discriminating between similar phonemes (for example, *mat* and *nat*), (2) determining the correct ending of spoken words (for example, is it correct to say, "we goed to the store?"), (3) determining the correct sentence structure (for example, which would be better to say, "hitting Sue" or "Bill hit Sue"), (4) knowing the correct meaning of spoken words (for example, "He was a precocious boy. What does precocious mean?"), or (5) understanding the rules of a conversation (for example, if you are having a conversation with another person and he begins to check his watch and speak less often, what might he want to do? Bring the conversation to a close?).

Components of Oral Language

In addition to classifying language problems as receptive and expressive, oral language is also divided into five components: **phonology, morphology, syntax, semantics,** and **pragmatics.** The five components of oral language are illustrated in Table 4.1.

Phonology refers to the system that defines each sound and the rules for how the sounds can be combined together. A **phoneme** "is the smallest linguistic unit of speech that signals a difference in meaning" (Bernstein and Tiegerman-Farber 1997). To determine if a sound is a different phoneme, simply change the phoneme in a word. If the sound creates a new word that you recognize, then the sound is a different phoneme from the original.

Morphology refers to how words are constructed from morphemes. A **morpheme** is "the smallest linguistic unit that has meaning" (ibid.). In other

TABLE 4.1: The Five Components of Language

Component	Expressive Example	Receptive Example
Phonology	Showing a child a picture of a rabbit, the child says the word (*rabbit*, not *wabbit*).	You ask the child to tell you if the words *bat* and *back* are the same or different.
Morphology	*I am kicking the ball. Yesterday, I _____ the ball.*	*Look there is a wolf. Now look, there are two wolfes.* Is that correct?
Syntax	Use the words *tall, is, Matt, boy,* and *a.* Make a sentence using these words.	Does this sentence make sense? *The jumped in and boy swam.*
Semantics	*Which word means to jump very high?* (leap)	Show me what you would do if I asked you to *scrawl* something on a piece of paper.
Pragmatics	*I once saw a snake and it scared me. Have you ever seen something scary?*	*Can you circle the cat in the picture and draw a line under the dog?*

words, a morpheme is the smallest part of a word that has meaning and cannot be broken down further because it would lose its meaning. For example, *boy, run,* and *bat* are morphemes because each has meaning by itself. This type of morpheme is commonly referred to as a **free morpheme** because it can stand alone and has meaning. Another type of morpheme is called a **bound morpheme** (for example, *ly, pre,* and *ed*). A bound morpheme only has meaning when connected to a free morpheme or another bound morpheme that is connected to a free morpheme. Prefixes (for example, *re*), suffixes (for example, *tion*), past tenses (for example, *ed*), present tenses (for example, *ing*), possessives (for example, *'s*), and plurals (for example, *s* or *es*) all represent examples of bound morphemes.

Syntax is the system of rules that help us determine the correct structure of words and phrases to form sentences. Syntax also guides how to transform sentences into new similar sentences or completely different sentences. For example, a child could say, "Billy and Natasha were playing with the toy," or "The toy was played with by Billy and Natasha." Both sentences have similar meaning, yet the sentence structure has changed slightly. If the child said, "Billy hit Natasha with the toy," then the sentence structure changed, as well as its meaning. As children grow older, they use syntactic rules to form new, complex sentences. Children begin to use interrogation and negation to form sentences to ask questions and state sentences in the negative.

Semantics refers to the meaning of language and is usually measured by looking at a student's use of vocabulary. Semantics also involves the set of rules that determine whether certain words can go with other words and still make sense. For example, because most teachers are adults, the *three-year-old teacher* would not make sense. Nor do the following words *north cars rain and walk,* when arranged in this order. Although the words may be structurally correct (that is, noun plus verb), they simply do not make sense the way they are stated. Moreover, the *context* in which words are used also helps us to understand the meaning of the sentence. If we were to say that, *Roger was flying today.* Depending upon the context in which it is used (or what has already been said about it), it could mean that Roger flew on a plane, Roger ran really fast, or Roger was driving very fast. The meaning of the sentence depends upon whether we were talking about his flight, talking about seeing Roger at a track meet, or talking about seeing Roger at a car race.

The last element of language is pragmatics. **Pragmatics** refers to "the use of language in social contexts" (Bernstein and Tiegerman-Farber 1997). Pragmatics refers to the use of language during conversations, during narratives or stories, or in everyday situations to understand and make requests for our wants and needs. Pragmatics involves knowing the rules and skills for using language in social situations. For example, knowing when to take turns in a conversation, how to initiate and end a conversation, and knowing when to ask questions for clarification are all important aspects of pragmatics. Moreover, because students use pragmatic skills in a wide variety of social situations, they will need to draw on their knowledge of language conventions (for example, sentence structure and grammar) as they adjust their speech to respond to the needs of specific audiences, purposes, and situations (IRA/NCTE 1996). (See the National Council of Teachers of English (NCTE) website at www.ncte.org, for more on teaching standards relating to speech and writing.)

Implications for Diverse Students

Within the English language are dialectic traditions that vary by culture. African-American children who speak African-American English at home, for example, are confronted by expectations to comprehend and use different rules for the five components of language (Washington 2001). They may use nonstandard rules for syntax that hinder their communication skills in school. Further, African-American children from low-income households have learned different language traditions than those expected in traditional classroom learning, such as not being familiar with responding to "wh" questions (for example, where, when, why, and what) (Washington 2001). As Washington suggested, students who are not familiar with the dominant language or dialect must be supported when using language for learning. Teachers should consider all five language components when examining the oral language skills of children, particularly those students who have language difficulties due to disabilities, English language learner (ELL) status, and/or cultural variations.

VIDEO CASE CONNECTIONS BOX

For an example of a culturally responsive lesson that engages students in oral and written language activities, watch the Video Case entitled *Culturally Responsive Teaching*. Note the ways that the teacher engages the students in conversation by asking them to share information about their own culture. Also note the ways that the teacher models and corrects language usage in ways that are encouraging to the students.

Chapter Question
ALERT
In this section, you will find information that answers a Chapter Question:

2. How are models useful in describing how language develops in children?

Different Models of Language Development

The following four different models describe how language develops in children: behavioral, psycholinguistic, semantic-cognitive, and pragmatic. Although no one model seems to account for all language development, each model makes a contribution to our understanding of language development. A shortcoming in one particular model can often be explained by another model.

Behavioral Model

According to the behavioral approach, language is learned (Skinner 1957) like other skills and behaviors. That is, learning occurs through modeling, imitation, reinforcement, punishment, or extinction. As children learn sounds and words, reinforcers in the environment help to shape those sounds into words; when reinforcement is applied for an approximation or the correct pronunciation of words, those words are repeated. Slowly, children begin to acquire more phonemes and use them as they pronounce words. According to this theory, children's use of verbal language is reinforced, usually by natural reinforcers such as smiles, pats on the back, or other environmental or natural stimuli; hence, as language skills are reinforced, they are used more frequently. Accordingly, teachers and parents can provide positive reinforcement to a young child if they are interested in increasing the child's use of language. For example, some parents do not give their child food or drink (reinforcer) until they use words like *juice* or *drink* (behavior).

Psycholinguistic Model

According to this model, all children are born with a universal learning mechanism called a **language acquisition device** (LAD). Analogous to RAM memory that is built into a computer, the LAD is "built in" and allows for children to learn language easily. The LAD consists of the rules or general set of principles for sentence structure and a mechanism for discovering how this set of sentence structure rules applies to a child's particular language. According to this theory, the LAD explains why children are capable of learning language so quickly and why children can learn such large amounts of language within a short period of time.

Semantic-Cognitive Model

According to the semantic-cognitive model that came about from the work of Jean Piaget and Lois Bloom, the language development of young children is very much dependent on their cognitive development. Similarly, as children acquire more experiences about a particular topic, their language about that topic becomes more complex and sophisticated. Therefore, when building vocabulary, teachers should focus on providing rich experiences from which children can draw meaning. In the same manner, concepts should be learned through rich experiences. In some cases, teachers may look for "learning moments" to stop the class and teach a particular concept. For example, if children find a caterpillar during recess, the teacher might encourage them to bring it back to the class and then teach children about the stages of metamorphosis as it applies to the life cycle of a butterfly.

Pragmatic Model

According to this model, children develop language through the need to communicate and interact with others. Children also learn that communication can direct the behavior of others in their environment to have their own needs met (Bruner 1983). Under this model, language develops through the more functional aspects of language such as making and understanding requests. Early on, as parents attempt to meet the needs of their children through communication, children begin to use language to have their needs met. Social interaction, particularly through language, is self-rewarding. With young children, parents very often adjust their language through "motherese." Parents using "motherese" often speak to children in short, concrete sentences spoken at a slower rate. In this way, parents adjust their language so that children can understand the intent of their communication.

Typical Language Development

Chapter Question
ALERT

In this section, you will find information that answers a Chapter Question:

3. How does language normally develop in children, and what are some common language difficulties among students with mild disabilities?

In most children, language follows a natural course of development. Generally, we say that children have typical language development if they are following a developmental path defined by a set of language milestones aligned in a hierarchal order based upon age. However, milestones simply provide a range of skills and are more or less a general approximation of where a child's language should be by a certain age. The Learning Disabilities Association of America (1999) has defined milestones using the chart provided in Table 4.2. However, the authors of the chart also caution that children do not typically master all of the items in each box until reaching the upper age in the range.

How Do I Know When Child Has a Language Problem?

Although milestones may provide an approximation of a child's language development, teachers should consider other factors to determine if language difficulties are problematic enough to warrant a referral for a speech and language evaluation (Kuder 2003). The first factor relates to academic difficulties that the child might be having. Is the child's oral language problem interfering with any other academic skills such as reading and writing? If so, the child's language problem may possibly be contributing to these difficulties. A second factor concerns how the child's language problems affect his or her relationships and interactions with peers and others. Because language problems may interfere in the child's ability to communicate clearly, they could affect the child's ability to make friends and socialize. A third factor is the child's ability in the classroom to interact with the teacher or other professionals who work with the child. For example, if the child does not follow verbal directions or participate in discussions, this may hinder his academic performance. The fourth factor is a lack of progress in language and one of the previously mentioned areas. Students who are learning the English language can present some of the same difficulties, due to language differences (Swanson et al. 2004); thus, educators should use multiple and dynamic approaches to assess whether they are observing English language learning difficulties and/or more generalized language difficulties (Laing and Kamhi 2003). As a rule, if the child's language problem is getting progressively worse and the child has a problem in one or more of the three areas previously mentioned, then the child should be referred for a speech and language evaluation. Finally, American Speech-Language-Hearing Association (ASHA) provides useful resources on its website (www.asha.org), such as "Your Child's Communication Development: Kindergarten Through Fifth Grade," which details the speaking, listening, reading, and writing skills that students should be able to do at each grade level.

Language Difficulties and Implications in the Classroom

Language disorders are especially prevalent among students with mild disabilities. Despite documented evidence of language problems, it should be noted that only 6 percent of these students receive services by a speech language pathologists (Gibbs and Cooper 1989). Whether in comprehension or

TABLE 4.2: Hearing and Talking Milestones

Hearing and Understanding	Speaking
Birth to 3 Months	**Birth to 3 Months**
Startles to loud sounds Quiets or smiles when spoken to Recognizes parent voice and quiets if crying Increases or decreases sucking behavior in response to sound	Makes pleasurable sounds (cooing and gooing) Cries differently for different needs Smiles at familiar faces
4 to 6 Months	**4 to 6 Months**
Moves eyes in direction of sounds Responds to changes in tone of voice Notices toys that make sounds Pays attention to music	Makes babbling sounds more speechlike (includes *p*, *b* and *m*) Vocalizes excitement and displeasure Makes gurgling sounds when left alone and when playing with you
7 Months to 1 Year	**7 Months to 1 Year**
Enjoys games like peekaboo and patty-cake Looks in direction of sounds Listens when spoken to Recognizes words for common items like "cup," "shoe," "juice" Begins to respond to requests ("Come here," "Want more?")	Makes babbling sounds with both long and short groups of (cv) sounds, such as "tata upup bibibibi" Uses speech or non-crying sounds to get and keep attention Imitates different speech sounds Has one or two words (*bye-bye, dada, mama*), although they may not be clear
1 to 2 Years	**1 to 2 Years**
Points to a few body parts when asked Follows simple commands and understands simple questions ("Roll the ball," "Kiss the baby," "Where's your shoe?") Listens to simple stories, songs, and rhymes Points to pictures in a book when named	Says more words every month Uses some one or two word questions ("Where kitty?" "Go bye-bye?" "What's that?") Puts two words together ("more cookie," "no juice," "mommy book") Uses many different consonant sounds of the beginning of words
2 to 3 Years	**2 to 3 Years**
Understands differences in meaning ("go/stop," "in/on," "big/little," "up/down") Follows two requests ("Get the book and put it on the table.")	Has a word for almost everything Uses two- to three-word "sentences" to talk about and ask for things Speech is understood by familiar listeners most of the time Often asks for or directs attention to objects by naming them
3 to 4 Years	**3 to 4 Years**
Hears you when called from another room Hears television or radio at the same loudness level as other family members Understands simple, "who, what, where, and why questions	Hears you when called from another room People outside family usually understand child's speech Uses a lot of sentences that have four or more words Usually talks easily without repeating syllables or words

TABLE 4.2: (*Continued*)

4 to 5 Years	4 to 5 Years
Pays attention to a short story and answers simple questions about it Hears and understands most of what is said at home and in school	Voice sounds clear like other children's Hears and understands most of what is said at home and in school (e.g. "I like to read my books") Communicates easily with other children and adults Says most sounds correctly except a few like *l, s, r, v, z, ch, sh, th* Uses the same grammar as the rest of the family

Source: Adapted from Learning Disabilities Association of America, "Speech and Language Milestone Chart" (http://www.ldonline.org/article/6313, 1999).

production, language problems can prevent students from being successful in the classroom and may interfere with academic skills (Seidenberg 1997). In the classroom, these students may not feel comfortable in social situations and may not want to participate in groups. At other times, these students may be reluctant to speak or may speak in a quiet voice when interacting with peers. ELL students and others for whom English is not their primary language face similar learning challenges and consequences, regardless of whether they have a specific language impairment (SLI). Approximately 69 percent of ELL students at the middle and secondary levels are second- or third-generation immigrants who have been enrolled in American schools since at least kindergarten (Calderon 2007). Like students with mild disabilities who have language difficulties, ELL students need intensive support, as well as recognition of their language learning needs across several school years. Of course, some students are both students with mild disabilities and ELL students (Baca and Cervantes 2003). Just as annual IEP goals should address language development for students with mild disabilities, the No Child Left Behind Act (2001) requires that schools make progress in developing the English language proficiency of all students.

For students with disabilities, language or communication may prove to be a difficult or frustrating task. Among students with mental retardation, language problems are considered one of the most detrimental aspects of adaptive behavior (Owens 1997). These students exhibit both quantitative and qualitative differences in their language that affect their communication and interactions with others. According to Bernstein and Tiegerman-Farber (1997), the language development of students with mental retardation before the mental age of ten is similar to the development of nondisabled students; it differs only in **mean length of utterance** (MLU) (for example, quantity of language). After the mental age of ten, the language of students with mental retardation differs qualitatively; their sentences are shorter, more concrete, and may be difficult to understand. Owens (1997) and Kuder (2003) have summarized some of the general difficulties that students with mental retardation exhibit to include the following:

1. Problems understanding phonological rules
2. Delayed acquisition of morphological rules

3. Poor vocabulary
4. Lack of understanding of pragmatic rules

Problems in Phonology, Morphology, and Syntax

As noted, many students with mild disabilities have difficulties with phonological awareness, particularly in processing language sounds. Research has also shown that students who have difficulty with phonological awareness also have problems with reading. Students with mild disabilities have problems with morphological knowledge, particularly word parts. In addition, these morphological problems often occur with more complex or higher-level morphological components such as irregular word endings, noun derivatives, and understanding of prefixes (Wiig and Semel 1984). In regard to syntax, students with mild disabilities often use shorter, less complex sentences with fewer elaborations. In fact, their syntactic development may plateau at a certain age and may limit their use of sentence structure and sentence length (Kuder 2003).

Problems in Semantics and Pragmatics

As you could guess, students with mild disabilities also typically have problems in semantics, particularly in the area of expressive and receptive vocabulary. Often they use limited vocabulary, use more concrete vocabulary in conversations, and have difficulty understanding abstract or figurative language (Owens 1997). In the area of pragmatics, students with mild disabilities have delayed understanding of requests and commands, a less active role in conversations, and poor understanding of conversational rules (for example, taking turns, making significant contributions to a conversation, and using conversational repair strategies).

THINK BACK TO THE FIRST CASE with Sammie . . .

1. What area of remediation would you target for Sammie?

As you have read, oral language encompasses five main areas: phonology, morphology, syntax, semantics, and pragmatics. From the case, you can see that Sammie has problems in word recall that could be considered an aspect of semantics. He also has trouble with tracking speakers during class discussions, which could be considered an aspect of pragmatics. These two areas would be appropriate for remediation.

Chapter Question
ALERT

In this section, you will find information that answers a Chapter Question:

4. How do oral language skills influence reading and writing skills?

Oral Language and Reading and Writing

The association between language problems of students with mild disabilities and reading and writing problems is complex; however, a link does exist between language disabilities and reading or written language disabilities (Friel-Patti 1999). Deficits in oral language could result in problems in reading and written language (Sturm and Clendon 2004), as illustrated by Table 4.3. Longitudinal studies have found that children who develop language impairments at an early age often have continued problems during adolescence in oral language, literacy, and academic achievement (Aram and Hall 1989). In particular, children who lack phonological awareness appear to have problems in early reading

TABLE 4.3: Oral Language and Reading and Written Language

Language Domains	Implications for Reading	Implications for Writing
Phonology		
• Demonstrated delays in phonology (e.g., Berninger & Gans, 1986; Vandervelden & Siegel, 1999)	• Phonological skills are related to the development of phonemic awareness and decoding	• Phonological skills are related to spelling development
Morphology		
• Difficulties with production of morphemes (e.g., Binger & Light, 2002; Kelford Smith, Thurston, Light, Parnes, & O'Keefe, 1989; Sutton & Gallagher, 1993)	• Knowledge of morphology is needed to comprehend sophisticated meaning changes in text	• Morphology is critical to conventional writers who communicate subtle word meanings through text
Semantics		
• Restricted experiences and background knowledge (e.g., Carlson, 1981; Light, 1997) • Vocabulary delays (e.g., Berninger & Gans, 1986; Udwin & Yule, 1990)	• Background knowledge and vocabulary are needed to effectively comprehend text • Vocabulary is needed to communicate during a range of reading lessons	• Background knowledge and vocabulary are central to content generation • Categories of knowledge support retrieval of content • Vocabulary is needed to communicate during a range of writing lessons
Syntax		
• One- to two-word utterances predominate (e.g., Harris, 1982; Udwin & Yule, 1990) • Prevalence of simple clause types, word order deviations, and word omissions (e.g., van Balkom & Welle Donker-Gimbrere, 1996)	• Knowledge of sentence structure and sentence connections is needed to process the range of sentences encountered in text	• Knowledge of sentence structure is needed to compose simple, compound, and complex sentences and to support cohesion between sentences
Pragmatics		
• Impaired pragmatic skills (e.g., Light, Collier, & Parnes, 1985a; O'Keefe & Dattilo, 1992; von Tetzchner & Martinsen, 1996) • Typically respondents (e.g., Basil, 1992; Harris, 1982, Light et al., 1985a; O'Keefe & Dattilo, 1992; von Tetzchner & Martinsen, 1996) • Restricted range of speech acts (e.g., Light, Collier, & Parnes 1985b; Udwin & Yule, 1991)	• Pragmatic skills are related to understanding author's intention • Pragmatic skills are needed to understand classroom participation structures of reading activities	• Pragmatic skills are related to understanding audience • Writing requires children to generate text independently often with an absent audience • Pragmatic skills are needed to understand classroom participation structures of writing activities • Children ask questions and comment on peers' compositions
Discourse		
• Greater number of communication experiences with conversational discourse (Nelson, 1992) • Restricted experiences with classroom discourse (e.g., narrative discourse or expository discourse) (Nelson, 1992; Sturm, et al., 2003a)	• Knowledge of the discourse structures of text is needed to support text comprehension • Knowledge of the discourse structures of reading lessons (e.g. small group reading, large group discussion) is needed to participate effectively in classrooms	• Knowledge of the discourse structures of text is needed to organize a coherent composition • Knowledge of the discourse structures of writing lessons (e.g., peer and teacher conferences, large group lessons, sharing) is needed to participate effectively in classrooms

Source: Adapted from J. Strum and S. Clendon, "Augmentative and Alternative Communication, Language, and Literacy: Fostering the Relationship," (*Topics in Language Disorders* 24(1):77, 2004).

(Adams 1990). In addition to this link, researchers have found other skills, both oral language and print skills, that correlate with later reading skills. For example, the language skills of expressive vocabulary, oral language proficiency, and recall of sentences or stories are three skills that have been shown to predict reading achievement. All of this information points to the role that oral language skills, including phonological awareness, play in reading development, as well as other literacy aspects such as awareness of print (for example, concepts of print and letter identification) (Scarborough 2005). As children get older, other skills beyond phonological skills contribute to decoding and comprehension. For example, students who have difficulty with semantic skills also have problems with vocabulary words and reading comprehension (Nation 2005). Other language skills such as listening comprehension are also related to reading skills. Students with poor listening comprehension also performed poorly on measures of reading comprehension (Nation and Snowling 1997). Moreover, weaknesses in certain aspects of oral language may lead to or be causally linked to problems in reading and written language (Nation 2005); students with language disabilities or spoken language delays often perform poorly in other areas, such as spelling and vocabulary (Snowling 2005).

THINK BACK TO CASE 4.1) **with Sammie . . .**

2.   *In addition to oral language, what other skills would you, as the teacher, address?*

Because word recall could create problems for Sammie during written language, it might be a good area to address. In terms of written language, Sammie's word recall problems might create frustrating situations for him when he is asked to write responses to short-answer or essay questions on worksheets or tests, or to compose written essays or compositions. Keep these problems in mind as you read about oral language skills and techniques.

Chapter Question
ALERT

In this section, you will find information that answers a Chapter Question:

5. What strategies and techniques are effective for improving language skills?

Strategies and Techniques for Teaching Oral Language Skills

Using the four previously discussed models, the following are some basic principles for teaching oral language. These practices can and should be used both when directly teaching language skills and when teaching for content learning, as oral language skill is essential for learning and using content knowledge (Moje et al. 2004).

1. From the behavioral perspective, use imitation and modeling for the proper use of language. Provide a sentence or word, and ask the child to say it. Provide positive reinforcement in the form of a smile or praise if the student says the word or sentence correctly. If a student is using incorrect syntax in class, the teacher should simply rephrase aloud what the student was trying to say. For example, the response to a student who says, "We goes to the car now?" should be "Yes, we are going to the car now."

2. From a semantic-cognitive approach, teach language skills in context whenever possible. If you are discussing concepts or vocabulary, teach them in context. For example, if teaching students about different animals, teach them by visiting the zoo.

3. From the psycholinguistic perspective, teach rules for using language. If teaching sentence structure, teach students first to differentiate between complete and incomplete forms of sentences (for example, She in the yard played versus she played in the yard), then to finish partially completed sentences (for example, The dog ate the ___.), and, finally, to produce their own complete sentences.

4. From the pragmatic approach, teach language within a group dynamic. Use other children as models for the correct use of language and to encourage the target child to participate with others during small group discussions. Also, when using groups, be careful that you promote tolerance for language differences among others in the group. In fact, exposure to language differences makes others more tolerant and open (Wilby 2004).

5. Use games or other activities to teach target skills. Students enjoy learning and are more engaged when taught using games or other motivating language activities.

6. Focus on expressive and receptive language skills. Language involves more than just speaking words and sentences. Receptive skills are often overlooked and include following oral directions, listening for new vocabulary words, reading a story and having the students predict the ending, playing listening games (for example, Simon Says), or playing a song and having the children listen for verses to sing aloud.

7. When teaching younger children, gain their attention before beginning an activity, and use tactile and fun materials to maintain their attention throughout the activity.

8. Use sufficient wait-time when you ask questions and after the student responds to your question (Rowe 1986). Teachers should use a minimum three seconds of wait-time when they ask children a question before prompting them for more information (Rowe 1986), particularly for young children (Medcalf-Davenport 2003). Wait-time allows children time to consider the question, search long-term memory for information, and formulate an appropriate response. When teachers wait three seconds or more after asking a question, the amount and quality of discussion increases (Roberts and Zody 1989). Similarly, when teachers wait three seconds or more after the student has responded to the question, there are also improvements in the student's use of language and logic (Rowe 1986).

9. Use structured lesson plans that include aspects of Direct Instruction. If teaching a new skill, model the proper response, use guided practice so students can perform the skill while you provide feedback, and then assess by having the child demonstrate the skill independently.

10. Teach for generalization. If children are taught a language skill in school, have them practice the skill for homework and report back when and where they used the skill.

Improving Language Skills in the Classroom

To improve oral language skills, children must be given opportunities to practice and use the skills that they have been taught. Often, classrooms are tightly controlled environments in which students are expected to work quietly with very little interaction with other students. However, scheduled breaks during the day (for example, lunch or recess) could serve as opportunities for students to practice and use language skills. Throughout the day, teachers could use routines as opportunities for students to practice communication skills (Creaghead 1992). Many of these routines are typically accompanied with scripts that students use to communicate. Routines include the following:

1. Beginning the day
2. Transition between subjects
3. Lunch
4. Recess
5. Free choice time
6. Ending of the day
7. Classroom lessons
8. Reading groups
9. Tests
10. Getting, doing, and returning homework
11. Working independently
12. Studying from workbooks

During these times, students could be taught the scripts (that is, a set of typical communication skills) that could be used on a daily basis. For example, as students enter the classroom during the beginning of the day, they should say, "hello," and use other appropriate greetings for the teacher such as, "It looks like a cold/hot day today, Mrs. King." These routines provide cues for students to use communication skills. Of course, teachers may have to use more explicit prompts to get students to use communication skills (Creaghead 1992). Over time, many of these prompts could be phased out.

Students from underrepresented communities in the school and school district, including those with limited English proficiency, can benefit from the literacy instructional activities previously described, merged with critical literacy practices. For example, they can be asked to use language to describe experiences unique to their identity group (Herrero 2006). Examples include discussing family activities, community traditions, or ways in which American society reacts to their group(s) (Harry, Klingner, and Hart 2005).

Andreanna Seymore/Stone/Getty Images

Language skills play an important role in a child's education

METHODS AND STRATEGIES SPOTLIGHT

Supporting Speech and Language in the Classroom

If possible, classroom-based language interventions should be a collaborative effort between the speech-language pathologist (SLP) and the classroom teacher. A collaborative effort provides advantages for everyone involved in the class. SLPs often can advise teachers on what materials and methods to use to help students develop language skills. Classroom teachers can provide an ideal teaching environment for the SLP because of the ample supply of models (that is, those students who can correctly use language skills) and because the classroom can provide plenty of interaction among students. In other words, the classroom is a natural environment for language development to occur.

The following template is useful for teaching communication lessons in the classroom (Dodge 2004):

Target skill: Identify a specific target skill. Use a previous assessment to help identify a specific language skill or language-related social skill the student needs to develop.

Opening question: Use an opening or intriguing question to gain students' attention. This question should be tied into the content or activities of the lesson. For example, "You are busy working on a science worksheet and you want to know what the term *igneous* means. What could you do to find the information?"

Model: The teacher should model the appropriate script (that is, the language and actions). Show students a few different examples of correct and appropriate responses to this situation (for example, how to ask the teacher a question).

Role-play: As with learning any new skill, students should practice. One of the best ways to simulate reality is to practice the skill through a role-play scenario. Pair up students and allow them to practice role-playing the example.

Carry over: Plan with students how they could be reminded to use their script. In some cases, the teacher could cue the student to use the script. In the same case, the teacher could use a nonverbal cue, such as a raised finger, or a verbal cue such as "wait and think" to remind students to use the appropriate script before responding.

Wrap-up: During wrap-up, ask students to think about one time during the day that they will be able to use their new communication skills. Ask them to remember the situation and script to be used during that time, and state that you will check with them tomorrow to see how well they used their new communication skills.

Challenge and follow-up: Challenge your students to use the new skills in the agreed-upon situation and in other situations. Follow up by checking to see if students actually used the targeted communication skills and if they need to make modifications in the script that they used.

Creating Opportunities for Students to Use Communication Skills

Teachers should try to *create* opportunities for student interaction by forming cooperative learning groups during class. As discussed in Chapter 2, cooperative learning involves having students work in small groups of three to five students. Each student works toward a common goal, and each student is individually accountable, as well. During cooperative learning, students are interdependent (Johnson, Johnson, and Holubec 1990; Putnam 1993) upon one another to complete the task and achieve the goal.

The following is an example of a cooperative learning lesson that encourages language-based interactions. The teacher has assigned students to write a report about a dinosaur and then present it to the class (**goal interdependence**). They need to present where the dinosaur lived, its diet and characteristics, and illustration, along with other facts. One group chose Tyrannosaurus. Each student is assigned a role (**role interdependence**). Nathan was designated the illustrator; Jacob, the researcher; Sammie, the writer; and Kaytlyn, the presenter. All students need to complete their parts with the help of others. Jacob needs to research (**task interdependence**) the dinosaur with the help of others. Jacob might begin looking on the Internet for information and then ask the others in the group to go to the library to find information. Before Sammie can write the report, he needs the research from his classmates. Jacob needs to use the computer for research (**resource interdependence**), but must share it with Nathan to find pictures to illustrate and with Sammie to write the report. Each student not only receives a grade for individual contribution, but the group will also receive a group grade for the report and presentation (**reward interdependence**).

Listening Skills

Language, like other academic areas, should be taught to students with mild disabilities. Some students may require intense instruction, whereas other students may simply need direct instruction in language skills only when they encounter problems. When teachers consider language skill instruction, they should think broadly to include language skills such as listening skills as well as more traditional language skills such as words and word ending.

Because most of the information given in classrooms, particularly elementary, is in verbal form, listening skills are important for students to learn. Listening requires focusing attention on the speaker, selecting the important parts of the message, and remembering those parts. Listening is more than just hearing; it involves processing and understanding the message. Because these skills are so important, they should be taught directly, particularly to young children.

When providing directions to a child, Wiig and Semel (1984) suggest strategies such as asking the child to *repeat the steps overtly* and *rehearse* the directions by repeating them silently, *printing* critical words from the directions on cards that the child can use while carrying out the task, or having the child *write* them down as the directions are given aloud.

To aid students with mild disabilities in remembering components of effective listening skills, use the following acronym in Box 4.1:

BOX 4.1

PLAN TO LISTEN

P **P**ay close attention to what is being said.

L **L**isten to the message and remember the steps or parts.

A **A**sk questions if you don't understand.

N **N**ame the steps or parts of the message.

Say them again to yourself or write them down.

BOX 4.2

WHOLE CLASS DIRECTIONS

Use the following suggestions when providing directions to the entire class:

- Begin by gaining everyone's attention. Prompt students to stop working and watch you. Use verbal prompts such as, "Eyes on me" or "Watch and listen."
- Do not give directions until you have everyone's attention, even if that means standing quietly in front of the class until everyone is watching you.
- Provide verbal reinforcement for students who are paying attention (for example, "Good, Lashonda is watching me and paying attention.").
- Write the directions on the board prior to giving them verbally and then point or refer back to the directions as you give them.
- Be very explicit and provide examples to illustrate each point in your directions.
- Before students begin the task, ask them if they have any questions.
- After students begin the task, monitor to make sure they are following your directions correctly. If they are not following the steps, stop everyone and review or model the directions again.

A teacher can also facilitate the effectiveness of giving directions to a student by (1) gaining the child's *full attention* prior to giving any directions, (2) maintaining *eye contact* while giving directions, (3) keeping directions *short* and straightforward, (4) using *vocabulary* that is commensurate with the child's cognitive level, (5) *pointing* to objects or pictures to help the student understand parts of the directions, when appropriate, (6) *modeling* what the child should do, (7) asking the child to *show* you what to do, (8) *asking* the child if he understands the directions or has any questions, and (9) using *cues* to prompt the child to the most important parts of the directions (for example, "The most important part to remember is . . ." or "The three things you need to remember are . . ."). When providing directions to the *entire class*, the suggestions in Box 4.2 might be useful.

Listening Activities

The following listening games and activities could be used to strengthen students' listening skills:

- **Teacher Says** This game is similar to Simon Says; however, students in class will follow the directions. The teacher asks students to complete different motor skills, such as jumping up, walking around the room, or jumping up and down. Students have to listen closely and should perform only those skills that are preceded by the words *Teacher says* (for example, "Teacher says, touch your toes."). The purpose of this game is to train the students to listen to and follow your directions.

- **Same or Different** Students listen to the teacher read a pair of words to determine whether they are the same or different. Begin with words that are discernibly different when spoken (for example, rock – ball); gradually use word pairs that are similar (for example, ran – rat).

- **Last is First** The teacher says a word aloud and the child says a new word that begins with the last letter (for example, *bag, girl, lost, top, pan, now*).

- **Scrambled Story** The teacher reads parts of a story that is scrambled up, and asks students to put the parts in the correct order.
- **Story Chain** Elementary students love this activity. Start by giving students a story starter such as, "One day I was flying my rocket home and...." Next, ask a child to add a part to the story. Once they add their part, another child adds a part, and so on, until everyone has participated in the story.
- **Word of the Day** Teachers choose a "word of the day" for students, particularly students in secondary classes. Students then try to use the word correctly in as many different sentences as possible. Students who can correctly use the word in the most sentences and can use the word in the best sentence (that is, provide the best example for use of the word) are awarded prizes.
- **Oral Reports** Older students can present information to other students in small groups or in class. These reports can be tied into content-area subjects, such as science, history, or literature. Working in small groups, each student is responsible for completing a portion of a report and then presents that portion verbally to others in the group or to the entire class.
- **TV Newscasts** Older students listen to an evening newscast. The students write down three to five unknown words from the newscast, bring them to school, and find out the meaning of the words from either a dictionary, a student work group, or the teacher. The student then has to use the term correctly in a sentence.

Directed Listening-Thinking Activity

To improve listening comprehension, teachers should use a directed listening-thinking activity (DLTA) (Cramer 2004). This activity can be used whenever the teacher reads or explains content to students. Using a DLTA, teachers tap into students' prior knowledge about the topic to make predictions, check for comprehension while reading or explaining, and discuss or elaborate on the topic after teaching.

The **DLTA** has the following three main components:

1. **Before listening,** teachers establish a purpose for listening. Teachers ask questions about the topic and elicit predictions based upon student input.
2. **During listening,** teachers periodically stop the activity (such as lecturing or reading) to ask students questions about what they are being told. These questions involve checking the accuracy of predictions and then modifying the predictions or confirming the accuracy of these predictions based upon supporting evidence.
3. **After listening,** follow-up activities are used to review vocabulary, check comprehension, or check the accuracy of predictions.

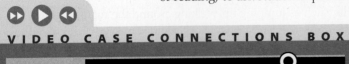

VIDEO CASE CONNECTIONS BOX

Watch the Video Case *Bilingual Education*. Teachers Sarah Bartels-Marrero and Sheila Donelan help their students discuss a task in two languages. State how the same activities could have been done in a monolingual classroom where language development is part of the curriculum as well.

Phonemic Skills

Phonemic awareness is the understanding that spoken words are made up of phonemes. Although phonemic awareness deals solely with sounds or phonemes, it is not the same skill as phonics (Rasinski and Padak 2004). **Phonics** refers to letter and sound correspondence. Phonics links the written symbol with phonemes. Phonemic awareness is the precursor to phonics and has been identified as an important pre-reading skill. Before children can understand sounds with their corresponding written symbols (phonics), they must first learn to recognize, remember, segment, and blend phonemes. (Chapter 5 also presents phonemic awareness activities for students.) Following are several phonemic awareness skills that Yopp and Yopp (2000) have identified for students to master.

- **Sound Matching** In sound matching games, students determine if two words that are spoken begin (or end) with same sound. Do these two words (*pass - pot*) begin with same sound? Do these two words (*sat – tap*) have the same middle sound? Do these two words (*fat – cot*) have the same end sound?
- **Sound Isolation** In sound isolation activities, children identify the sound that a word or words begin with. What sound do you hear at the beginning of the word *mat*? What sound do you hear at the end of the word *man*? What sound do you hear in the middle of the word *fast*?
- **Sound Substitution** In sound substitution activities, children substitute a sound within a word. What word would you have if you changed the *pa* in *past* to *ma*? (*mast*) What word would have if you changed the *nd* in *hand* to *rp*? (*harp*)
- **Sound Blending** In sound blending activities, children pair parts of words to determine new words. What word would you have if you put these sounds together: *par- ty*? What word would you have if you put these sounds together: *man – a – ger*? What word would you have if you put these sounds together: *f – a – st*?
- **Sound Segmentation** In sound segmenting activities, children segment letters or word parts into sounds. Tell me which parts you hear in the word *c – ost*? Tell me what sounds make up the word *cat*? How many different sounds do you hear in *sat*?
- **Sound Deletion** In sound deletion activities, children tell the teacher parts of words. Say the word *baseball* without the *base*? Say the word *power* without the *er*? What sound do you hear in *will* that is missing in *ill*? What would be left if the *r* sound were missing in *track*? (*tack*).

When teaching these skills, teachers should make these skills into games and activities that students can enjoy (Yopp and Yopp 2000). See which students can get the most correct, or pair students up and see which pair can get the most correct. Some tasks are easier than others so caution should be used to begin with easier tasks and progressively move on to more difficult tasks. For example, sound matching using the initial phoneme is easier than blending phonemes to produce words. If students are having problems, say the words slower and exaggerate the target sound that you want students to practice (for example, LLLLLLLittle). In some cases, students can tap out or clap the number of sounds in words to help them discriminate.

Understanding Word Parts

When teaching word parts or morphemes, remember that there are two types of morphemes: bound and free. These are often taught to students as part of spelling or language arts, and both free and bound morphemes can be taught to students with disabilities. Recall that a free morpheme can stand on its own as a word (for example, boy, bat, can), and a bound morpheme only has meaning when attached to a free morpheme (for example, ly, s, ed, est, anti). Bound morphemes can change the meaning of words when added to them. Wiig and Semel (1984) have categorized bound morphemes into three groups: prefixes, suffixes, and infixes.

Prefixes include *sub-* and *trans-*. In American English, the most common prefixes are: *un-, in-, dis-,* and *non-*.

Suffixes include *-er, -ly, -ed, -ness, -ing, -ate,* and *-tion*.

Infixes are words that have been changed by inserting or adding a morphological element, such as an affix. An *inflectional affix* adds a particular grammatical function to a word without changing the category of that word, but results in a variant of the word. Examples of inflectional affixes include: noun plurals (*-s* or *-es*), possessives (*'s*), present progressive (*-ing*), and past tense (*-ed*). Teaching children with disabilities about free morphemes is important because understanding word parts can help them break down spoken and written words to pronounce them or understand their meaning. Infixes with inflectional endings (for example, *-es, -ing, -ed*) should be taught first because they tend to be the easiest to learn. Next, teach the affixes through activities where children learn the affix, meaning, and how to use them with real words. If possible, tie these activities in with reading or writing affixes in context.

Different sources will list common prefixes and suffixes; however, lists both overlap and differ. In Tables 4.4 and 4.5, we have combined different lists to provide a list of prefixes and suffixes to teach students with mild disabilities.

TABLE 4.4: List of Recommended Prefixes

Prefix	Meaning	Examples
ab-	from; away	absolve; abnormal
de-	opposite; remove	deflate; demote
dis-	opposite; not	disgrace; disagree
en-, em-	cause to; into	emboss; enclosure
in-	in; not	install; indirect
mis-	bad; wrong	mistake, misplace
non-	not	nonresident; nonprofit
pre-	earlier than; before	prepare; preamble
re-	again; backward	recount; rewind
sub-	under; lesser	subject, submit
super-	above; greater	supersonic; supervisor
trans-	across; to change	transatlantic; transplant
un-	not	unskilled; uncover

TABLE 4.5: List of Recommended Suffixes

Suffix	Meaning	Examples
-able, -ble	having much skill at; capable	acceptable; credible
-al	relating to; action	personal; rehearsal
-er	one that performs; comparative	reporter; hotter
-ful	full of	peaceful
-ic	relating to	idiotic
-ion, -tion	act; process; condition	demolition; perfection
-ious, -ous	full of; having	cautious; poisonous
-ize	cause to be	visualize; specialize
-less	lacking	careless; joyless; homeless
-ly	like; similar	lovely; motherly
-ment	state of; process	amazement; involvement
-ty, -ity	condition of; degree	safety; rarity
-y	made of; state of	muddy; truly

Teaching Syntax and Morphology

Along with morphological skills, syntax is another area of oral language that may be a concern for students with disabilities (Polloway and Smith 2000). The following suggested guides for teaching morphological and syntactic aspects of oral language might be useful to cover (Wiig and Semel 1984):

1. Regular noun plurals
2. Noun-verb agreement of singular and plural regular nouns and verbs in present tense
3. Regular noun possessives in the singular and plural forms (for example, *cat, cats*)
4. Irregular noun plurals (for example, *leaf, leaves*)
5. Irregular noun possessives (*geese's food*)
6. Regular past tense of verbs (*walked*)
7. Irregular past tense of verbs (*fall, fell, fallen; eat, ate, eaten*)
8. Adjectival inflections for comparative and superlative forms (*big, bigger, biggest; good, better, best*)
9. Noun and adverb derivation (*sing* to *singer; slow* to *slowly*).
10. Prefixing (*write, rewrite*)

When teaching syntax or sentences structure, begin with short, simple direct sentences before moving on to more complex ones. Use concrete objects or pictures to illustrate sentences that students are having difficulty understanding. Provide plenty of examples for students to understand the new sentence structure. Wiig and Semel (1984) suggest that teachers use at least ten examples when teaching sentence formation. For example, because children with disabilities have difficulty understanding passive language (for example, "The ball was thrown by Judy."), you may need to present many examples that include illustrations or stick figures drawn on the board to help students understand passive sentences. Once students master a new sentence structure, use drill and practice (with feedback) to ensure that they master the new sentence structure. After students understand your examples of the new sentence structure, you can ask them to choose (discriminate) between two or three sentences to choose the new form. Once they can do this, you can ask students to give you examples of new sentences that they created. Often, oral language activities can be paired with written exercises.

Building Vocabulary and Improving Word Find

Because students with mild disabilities learn vocabulary at a slower rate than nondisabled students (Baker, Simmons, and Kame'enui 1998), teachers need to use a variety of techniques and activities to remediate deficits in this area. When teaching vocabulary, special education teachers should use several principles. First, introduce vocabulary words in context (for example, "*Erosion* is wearing down the granite on the statue."). Second, provide students with definitions that use examples in context. For example, erosion might be used in the following sentence: "The rain caused erosion that took the dirt down the hill and left a bare, muddy bank." Third, use pictures or real-life examples to illustrate the vocabulary word. Fourth, whenever possible, present multiple examples so that students master the word before introducing nonexamples. For example, present examples of erosion such as pictures of the Grand Canyon, mudslides, and smooth granite surfaces (for example, Washington Monument) before presenting nonexamples such as the sun fading the color on a piece of paper or cloth. Fifth, relate vocabulary words with information in students' prior knowledge to make deep connections during learning. Other techniques include using semantic maps, mnemonic strategies, or visual imagery, and teaching children to categorize items.

Semantic Classification and Categorization

To improve storage of information, students could learn to cluster information in semantically related categories (Wiig and Semel 1984). In other words, list similar words under one category. Students can be given review activities in which they have to categorize information such as parts of a cell, different types of biomes, or different types of cells. Moreover, when teaching content to students, organize information in different categories for students to record in their notes. Teachers should explain why items in a category are related and how, discussing the similarities and differences. In early grades, teachers could ask students to categorize pictures and, in later years, ask students to categorize words.

FIGURE 4.2

Word Map for Chlorophyll

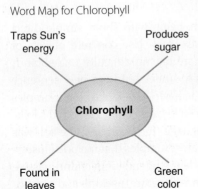

Semantic Maps. A *semantic map* (Bos and Anders 1990) or word map (Schwartz and Raphael 1985) is a type of map that helps students to understand a vocabulary word and its related characteristics. The visual display shows how words are related. To create a map, students use a vocabulary word and related words. A vocabulary word is placed in the center circle and then the students use words to describe the concept by drawing lines to it. When students first create word maps, it is best to keep them simple (see Figure 4.2).

Mnemonic strategies. Keyword and mnemonic methods are used to help students remember new information such as vocabulary because they

FIGURE 4.3

Mnemonic Method for Vocabulary the Word *Chlorophyll*

Green-colored dress

Phyllis Green making sugar cookies.

link new words or concepts to familiar words and images (Mastropieri, Scruggs, and Fulk 1990; Scruggs and Mastropieri 1990; Uberti, Scruggs, and Mastropieri 2003). By making these connections, unfamiliar words become more meaningful and concrete, and students are better able to recall the vocabulary words. Through linking unfamiliar vocabulary with familiar information, the vocabulary words can be more easily remembered. For example, to remember the word and function of chlorophyll—which is a green pigment, and makes sugars—students might pair up a picture of Phyllis Green making sugar cookies (see Figure 4.3).

Visual imagery. Visual imagery is another effective technique to increase recall of vocabulary, particularly if paired with keywords or mnemonic techniques. Using this technique, teachers provide students with a vocabulary word, a definition, and a keyword. Using imagery, students form an image in their minds of the keyword interacting with the definition. For example, if students are trying to study what the term *decibel* (a unit for intensity of sound) means and are given the keyword *bell*, they might imagine a large bell ringing so intensely that their eardrums are about to burst (see Figure 4.4).

Word Find Activities

Children with mild disabilities often have word retrieval problems. These problems can plague students well into adulthood. How information is stored in long-term memory often determines how well it can be retrieved. Remembering information from memory depends upon three things: acquisition, retention, and retrieval (Norman 1982). Acquisition refers to how you acquire or learn information. If you never really hear important information, then you have not really acquired it. The second component, retention, relates to how well you studied or learned the important information. Once you learned the information, did you rehearse or practice it? If so, you are more likely to recall it. Another way to retain information, probably the best way, is to relate or link new information with information that is already stored in your long-term memory. Linking new information this way will provide more cues for you to recall it later. The last component, retrieval, refers to cues that are present when you need to recall information. If the cues, key words, are present at the time of recall, then you are more likely to be able to retrieve information. Using these three components will not only help you recall more information, but will help your students as well.

FIGURE 4.4

Visual Imagery for *Decibel*

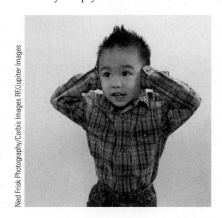

Ned Frisk Photography/Corbis Images RF/Jupiter Images

Jenny Solomon/Shutterstock Images

Facilitating Word Retrieval. Teachers can use the following techniques to help students with disabilities retrieve information quicker and more successfully (Wiig and Semel 1984):

1. Help a student retrieve a word (for example, *armadillo*) by providing *word cues* that belong to the same semantic class (for example, type of animal with a hard covering).
2. Use phonemic cues to assist students. In this case, the teacher can say the first phoneme or syllable of the word. At other times, the teacher can "mouth" the first phoneme or syllable of the word.
3. Use associative cues (for example, *army*) or synonyms to help the student retrieve the target word (for example, *military*).
4. Provide multiple cues to help the student retrieve the target word. For example, if the child were trying to retrieve the word *tanker*, the teacher could say, "Is it a ship, barge, or boat?"
5. Provide cues that are used to study the word to help with retrieval of a target word. For instance, if the child learned that a *pathogen* is an *agent* that causes a communicable *disease*, the teacher can cue the student by asking, "What is an *agent* of *disease*?" or state, "It has to do with a communicable *disease*."

THINK BACK TO CASE 4.1) **with Sammie . . .**

3. *Name and describe two types of oral language activities or techniques that you could use to remediate Sammie's language problems.*

As you have just read, teachers can provide students with word cues to assist them in word recall problems. As was discussed in Case 4.1, the teacher can use a word bank to help a student like Sammie. Teachers can also use semantic or mnemonic strategies that are discussed later in the chapter.

Improving Pragmatic Skills

As stated previously, students must be given opportunities to practice oral language skills in the classroom. Teachers can create opportunities by changing the response format of assignments (for example, from written to oral presentation) or by creating activities that encourage students to use oral language skills with others. For example, after reading a passage, teachers can ask students to tell orally what they read instead of having students write a summary of what was read. At other times, teachers can have students do oral reports or presentations to demonstrate their knowledge of content.

Another activity that allows students to practice oral language skills with other students is *role-playing*. There are two types of role-playing exercises: individual role-playing and interactive role-playing. During **individual role-playing,** students must take a side or play a role. In some cases, students can practice new language skills (that is, scripts) that they have recently learned. Typically, one student practices the skills with another student. For example, two children could role-play using persuasion to voice their feelings about something that they feel strongly about (for example, water conservation, recycling, attending a rally). The target child could be on one side, and the other child could play the role

VIDEO CASE CONNECTIONS BOX

In the Video Case *Philosophical Foundations of Education*, watch the segment on *Critical Theory in Action* for a discussion by different educators on why and how to use critical theory to help students find relevancy in the curriculum. Think about how the skills of conversation that you have read about so far are involved in students engaging in critical theory-based activities.

of someone with an opposing view. The second role-play type is **interactive role-playing.** In this type of role-playing, a few students assume a role and act out or ad-lib that role. If teaching a social skill, students could play roles in which the target student responds using the newly learned social skill. For example, a child could practice giving instructions to a group of students about how to play a new game or an older student could explain to others how to complete an assignment.

Conversation Skills. As children grow older, they learn the art of "holding a conversation." Conversation, like other aspects of language, have rules that most children learn incidentally. The rules for having a successful conversation include taking turns when speaking, choosing an agreed-upon topic, contributing bits of information about the topic, listening to the other person's contributions to the topic, and using appropriate nonverbal cues. Nonverbal cues that are used in conversations provide feedback to the speaker and listener about how the conversation is progressing and whether to end the conversation. These cues include facial expressions, eye contact, and distance between the speaker and listener. If one person becomes distracted or does not understand what the other person is saying, either one can use conversational repair strategies. **Conversational repair strategies** are used to get the conversation back on topic or to change topics. Conversational repair strategies include asking for clarification, asking to repeat something, or asking for more information (Konefal and Folks 1984). When the conversation is not progressing or is coming to a close, either party can provide verbal and nonverbal cues to end the conversation, such as looking at a watch, yawning, ending eye contact, or one party may simply say, "I have to get going." If children with disabilities are experiencing problems with conversations, teachers may have to teach rules explicitly and then practice those rules through role-playing.

Discussion Skills   Very often, teachers hold class discussions hoping to provide an engaging format with which students will make educated contributions and learn from the knowledge that is shared. However, for a lot of teachers, class discussions often do not succeed because students fail to listen or make meaningful contributions, or they are distracted by irrelevant activities occurring in the class. Likely, two key factors to the success or demise of a class discussion are the topic of discussion and how well students prepare (including having knowledge about the topic). Choosing familiar and interesting topics can increase the chances that the discussion will be successful. During discussions, students must use active listening to focus on the topic and follow who is speaking. Active listening involves leaning slightly forward toward the speaker, maintaining eye contact,

Hadi in the Hallway

Case Introduction

Now that you have worked through the first case in this chapter, you should feel comfortable addressing issues in a second case. In this case, Hadi Bakr is a first grade student who has receptive language problems, mostly in the area of listening skills.

Hadi Bakr was born to Abu and Amina Bakr in Detroit, Michigan. Hadi is an American citizen; however, his parents are citizens of Egypt. Originally from Cairo, Egypt, they moved to the United States after Abu was transferred to an architectural firm in Detroit. Hadi was born four years after his brother Talib, and the two children attend the same elementary school, Barker Elementary School. Hadi is now attending the full-day kindergarten, and Talib is in fifth grade. Talib would always watch out for his younger brother and would bail him out of fights with neighbors or trouble with their parents. Three years ago, Talib was classified as having learning disabilities (LD); however, he never exhibited behavior problems and was a model student.

Hadi's first year of formal schooling was difficult at best. During the previous year, he had been identified with ADHD and was placed on medication to help him control his impulsivity and inattention. In addition to these problems, Mrs. Trini Mendoza, his kindergarten teacher, felt that Hadi had language problems as well. At the start of this year, Hadi was referred for a speech and language evaluation, and Ms. Inez Pena found several areas of concern relating to receptive language, particularly with listening comprehension, receptive vocabulary, and understanding of verbal directions. Other areas such as mental retardation and hearing loss had been ruled out through testing.

Ms. Pena has been working with Hadi over the past two months on his receptive vocabulary problems but has made little progress. In the classroom, he still has many problems, despite taking medications for ADHD. Almost every day, Mrs. Mendoza has problems with Hadi, mostly because he does not pay attention or listen to directions. When Hadi becomes too much to handle, Mrs. Mendoza places him in the hall to calm down and regain his composure. She has tried various techniques such as moving his desk to the front of the room (which is closer to her), and she has called his parents on several occasions, but these efforts fail or don't last long.

Yesterday, while she was working with the reading group in the back of the room, she gave him a set of directions. "Hadi," said Mrs. Mendoza, "look at me." When Hadi looked up, she continued, "I want you to go to your desk, get out your pencil, sharpen it, put your name on your paper, and then go to the math group in the front of the room." Hadi was lost after she told him to go to his desk. He went to his desk and pulled out his pencil and crayons and began coloring on a worksheet. After several minutes of working with her group on round-robin reading, she turned around, only to find Hadi quietly sitting at his desk coloring. "Hadi," she yelled, "go to the math group in the front of the room. Why do I always have to yell at you?" Hadi replied that he was only doing what she had told him to do.

On other days, Hadi simply wanders out of his seat to play with toys in the corner. One morning illustrated Hadi's behavior. Mrs. Mendoza was busy working with the math group on adding while the rest of the students were busy working on a worksheet at their desks. She had given them explicit directions to complete the worksheet first, and then they were allowed to color. When Mrs. Mendoza last looked back at her class, they were busy at their desks working on either the worksheet or coloring. Hadi too had begun his worksheet, but when he saw the blocks in the play area, he couldn't resist. As the other children finished up their worksheets, Hadi quietly got out of his seat and went behind the bookshelf to play with the blocks in the play area. As Mrs. Mendoza finished up with her math group, she noticed that Hadi was nowhere to be found. "Hadi," she yelled out, but no one responded. Seeing the open door to the hallway, she rushed into the hallway, thinking that Hadi had left the room. He was still nowhere to be found. She walked up and down the hall several times, but she could not find him. "Great, I lost a kid," she thought to herself. Finally, when she peeked her head back in the room and heard giggles coming from the play area. She found that Hadi, who was amused by the incident, was playing with blocks. Again she yelled, "Hadi, out to the hallway."

Note: Mrs. Mendoza's reactions to Hadi's behaviors were ineffective; the same pattern repeated itself day after day. Instead of teaching him better skills, Mrs. Mendoza was simply reacting to Hadi's behaviors. If you reexamine the case, you will observe that most of Hadi's problem behaviors are related to his difficulties with receiving oral information. As Mrs. Mendoza works closer with Inez Pena, the pattern of promoting Hadi's inappropriate behaviors should cease.

CASE QUESTIONS

1. What specific skill would you try to remediate first?
2. Name and describe two types of activities/strategies that you would use with Hadi.

SLANT STRATEGY

S <u>S</u>it up
L <u>L</u>ean forward
A <u>A</u>ctivate your thinking
N <u>N</u>ame key information
T <u>T</u>rack the talker

and providing nonverbal feedback to the speaker, such as nodding one's head to agree or disagree and providing verbal feedback like, "Yes, I agree" or "I see how you could feel that way." One technique that has been shown to be effective at increasing student participation is the SLANT strategy (see Box 4.3) (Ellis 1989; also see Paxton-Burrsma and Walker (2008) for more information).

When using the SLANT strategy steps, students first **sit up** in an upright but relaxed position. Students then **lean forward** slightly in their chairs. The next step, **activate your thinking,** reminds students to activate the discussion by asking clarifying questions such as, "What is this about?" or "What do I need to remember?" As students are completing this step, they also need to answer their question, and ask the teacher questions about what they don't understand. The **name key information** step cues students answer the teacher's questions, share their ideas or comments, and add to other students' statements. Finally, the last step, **track the talker,** cues students to keep their eyes on the teacher as she speaks and to look at other students as they talk.

Training for the SLANT strategy occurs through the following steps (Deshler et al. 1981; see also Lidgus and Vassos 1996). In step one, the teacher introduces the SLANT strategy. In this beginning step, students discuss the rationale or positive outcomes of using SLANT, discuss when and where to use the strategy, and discuss what happens to students who choose to participate versus those who choose not to participate. During the second step, the teacher describes the five steps that make up the strategy. During the third step, the teacher models the strategy steps for students. During modeling, the teacher demonstrates the steps and slowly involves the students in the demonstration while providing feedback about their performance. In step four, the verbal practice step, the teacher rehearses the strategy with students and then assesses each student for mastery of the steps. In step five, the practice step, students target an academic class in which they will use the SLANT strategy, and they observe one another while providing feedback to each other. In step six, students are assessed on their knowledge of the SLANT steps. In the last step, the teacher instructs students to apply the SLANT strategy to a new class and periodically checks to see how they used the strategy.

Although the SLANT strategy enables students with mild disabilities to interact effectively in class discussions, it is also important to structure activities (for example, cooperative learning activities) so that students without disabilities develop positive attitudes about their peers with mild disabilities (Nowicki and Sandieson 2002). For teachers, this structuring means modeling and coaching students about how to work cooperatively with others, as well as making regular education students feel comfortable when interacting with students with disabilities. Furthermore, in some cases, maintaining positive attitudes may involve providing disclosure about the nature of the disability to enhance social interactions of students with and without disabilities (Maras and Brown 2000). Additionally, if regular education students view the interaction (that is, structured activity) as a threat to their social status or self-image, these students might very well reject or develop negative feelings toward students with mild disabilities (Hastings and Graham 1995).

TIPS FOR GENERALIZATION

Linking Oral Language Skills with Reading and Writing

When teaching oral language skills, plan to teach these skills directly in lessons, but also plan to integrate these skills into written language and reading. Because of the overlap of language skills in these areas, you can teach crossover skills in many different contexts. For example, if students have learned a new vocabulary word, you could integrate this word into a written language assignment, and they could read it in context in one of their textbooks.

Remember that there is no single method for teaching vocabulary; instead, teachers should combine methods and techniques. First, teachers should limit the number of vocabulary words to teach per class. Teachers should decide if the words are critical to learn or if the words are simply words that students may never see again. Second, students should be actively engaged during vocabulary instruction. Rather than just learn vocabulary through rote drill and practice, students should learn words in ways in which they can gain a deeper understanding of the words. Using visual imagery, understanding word parts (for example, prefixes and suffixes), and tying the word to context are different ways of learning vocabulary that provide for a deeper understanding of words. Third, provide multiple exposure of vocabulary words for students. Students should see the words in multiple contexts and used with a variety of activities. You may need to discuss and explain the vocabulary word in the new context because it may take on a slightly different meaning based upon its usage. Last, do not forget about using computer software and technology to assist students in learning vocabulary. A variety of software programs can be used to increase student vocabulary knowledge (see Technology Resources for Improving Oral Language Skills). Some software programs even allow teachers to enter their own vocabulary words.

Research Evidence   *Semantic Organizers and Cognitive Maps.* Semantic organizers have long been shown to be effective at increasing vocabulary use and comprehension of students who used them. In studies by Bos and others (Bos and Anders 1987; 1990; Bos et al. 1989; Scanlon et al. 1991), researchers demonstrated that students who used semantic maps outperformed students who learned vocabulary using a traditional approach (for example, a dictionary approach). These researchers also demonstrated that, when children used semantic maps and organizers while reading, they increased recall of vocabulary and reading comprehension. Moreover, a recent synthesis of research on semantic organizers and cognitive maps (Kim et al. 2004) supported the use of these techniques as effective tools for increasing reading comprehension, and pointed out the particular effectiveness of them on comprehension measures among children with mild disabilities.

Keyword and mnemonic strategies. The keyword or mnemonic strategy has been used in numerous studies to improve vocabulary learning in students. Veit, Scruggs, and Mastropieri (1986) used the strategy to improve dinosaur vocabulary in students with LD. In this study, students trained to use the mnemonic technique outperformed all other groups on immediate recall and delayed recall tests. In another study, Mastropieri, Scruggs, and Graetz (2003) taught students with LD to remember and recall vocabulary and facts about chemistry using the mnemonic strategy. Student with LD who were taught this technique outperformed students in the traditional learning group. Still in another study, Mastropieri, Scruggs, and Fulk (1990) taught students with LD to remember and recall abstract words using the keyword method. The keyword method resulted in the highest level of recall and comprehension of vocabulary words.

THINK BACK TO CASE 4.2) **with Hadi . . .**

1. *What specific skill would you try to remediate first?*

For Hadi, it would seem appropriate to address his ability to follow directions. To assist students in following directions, you might first want to establish eye contact before giving directions.

2. *Name and describe two types of activities/strategies that you would use with Hadi.*

For the skill of following directions, the teacher should show Hadi how to establish and maintain eye contact when someone is speaking to him. She could also teach Hadi to repeat the directions to her verbally, step by step, before actually completing the task. She could then reinforce him for using these skills. In this case, it might involve setting up a behavior management program to help him develop these and other social skills.

CHAPTER SUMMARY

Oral language often forms the basis for learning other subject areas such as reading, writing, and content areas. Oral language is important because it is the main form of communication in young children and is needed as children enter school. Early on, children learn language skills from parents or other caregivers. Over time, teachers become the primary facilitators for teaching language skills to students. Typically, teachers instruct students in one or more of the following five oral language components: phonology, morphology, syntax, semantics, and pragmatics. Models are useful for describing how language develops in children and can serve as a basis for teachers when teaching language skills in the classroom. In children, formal language (that is, words) normally develops along a continuum that was described in the milestone table (refer to Table 4.2). As we have discussed, students with mild disabilities often have a variety of language problems, from lack of phonology, to word recall and higher-level language problems (that is, difficulty understanding abstract or figurative language). Teachers should ensure that instruction in language skills occurs daily or every other day to build a base for future learning. Teachers could use many of the language techniques that we discussed (for example, word recall techniques or the SLANT strategy) or develop their own based upon the student's individual needs. Whenever possible, language skills should be taught in context and taught in environments that allow students to practice these skills.

KEY TERMS

Bound Morpheme, 118

Conversational Repair Strategies, 139

Expressive Language, 117

Free Morpheme, 118

Goal Interdependence, 130

Individual Role-Playing, 138

Intent, 116

Interactive Role-Playing, 139

Language, 116

Language Acquisition Device, 120

Mean Length of Utterance, 123

Morpheme, 117

Morphology, 117

Phonemic Awareness, 133

Phonics, 133

Phonology, 117

Pragmatics, 117

Receiver, 116

Receptive Language, 117

Resource Interdependence, 130

Reward Interdependence, 130

Role Interdependence, 130

Semantics, 117

Sender, 116

Shared Code, 116

Syntax, 117

Task Interdependence, 130

APPLICATION ACTIVITIES

Using information from the chapter, complete the following activities that were designed to help you apply the knowledge that was presented in this chapter.

1. Design a language lesson comprising different activities that will help children develop oral language skills. Be sure to include lesson objectives and one or two state standards in your lesson. (See Appendix A on the book-specific website for an example.)

2. You are assigned a new first grade student who has language deficits in syntax. Describe some activities that you could do in your classroom to improve her syntax.

3. Take one of the strategies/techniques that was presented in this chapter and describe how you would teach it to a child with a disability.

TECHNOLOGY RESOURCES FOR IMPROVING LANGUAGE SKILLS

Many different types of software programs and websites on language are available for students. Each software program covers different skills. Some programs cover multiple skills, and language skills are only part of them. Some of the websites are meant for teachers who want to further their understanding about language or language disabilities. Special education teachers should match up student skill deficits with those software programs. The following list provides websites for improving the language skills of students with mild disabilities.

Jumpstart Preschool
www.jumpstart.com

In knowledge adventure, children can work on simple activities that include skills such as listening, letters, pre-reading, phonics, and letter sounds. For students who perform poorly or get stuck on a certain activity, a tutorial opens and provides feedback and remediation of the skill.

Kaplan: Writing and Vocabulary Essential Review
www.kaplan.com

This program covers three topics: writing, vocabulary, and grammar. Pretests are provided for each of these topics so that students can determine which specific skill on which they want to be working.

American Speech Language Hearing Association (ASHA)
www.asha.org/default.htm

This website provides resources for professionals, students, and parents on numerous topics related to speech and language, including information about speech and language disorders, milestone charts, and research in the field.

The National Institute for Literacy
www.nifl.gov

This website provides materials for teachers about language, literacy, and reading. This educational and informative website site offers materials based upon the student's level (for example, childhood, adolescent, adult).

Learning By Listening
www.learningthroughlistening.org

This website was developed by Recording for the Blind & Dyslexic® (RFB&D®) and Center for Applied Special Technology (CAST) and includes strategies, activities, case stories, educator-developed lesson plans to improve students' listening skills, and information on how to use universal design to help all students benefit from learning.

Child Development & Parenting Information
www.childdevelopmentinfo.com/index.htm

This website provides information for parents about developmental milestones and different ways that they can assist their children in language development.

Mysterynet.com
www.mysterynet.com/learn

This website provides teachers with lesson plans that involve mystery. These lesson plans include listening skills, vocabulary, and reading and writing skills.

Visit the book-specific website at www.cengage.com/education/ boyle for a variety of study tools such as web links, tutorial quizzes, glossary/flash cards, bonus material not included in the text, and more.

The premium website offers access to additional materials, including the Video Cases. Go to www.cengage.com/login to register or purchase access.

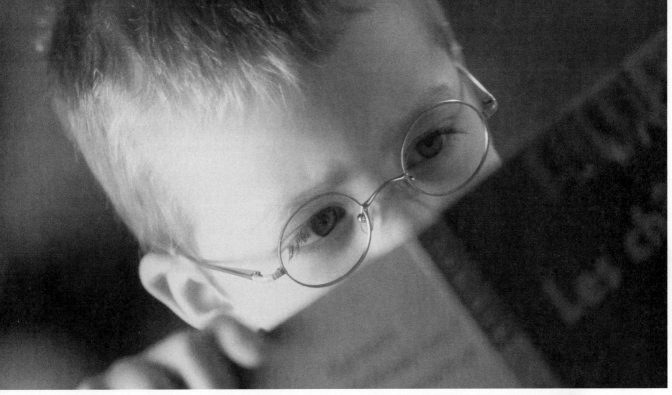

Early Reading: Strategies and Techniques

CHAPTER QUESTIONS

1. How do the three different models of reading explain how children read?

2. What stages do children go through as they learn to read?

3. What are some common reading problems that students with mild disabilities encounter?

4. What techniques should be taught to improve sight words, phonological awareness, word patterns, and syllabication skills for students with mild disabilities?

5. How can various reading skills be incorporated into a lesson to improve the reading skills of students with mild disabilities?

What do you think is the number one academic problem for students with mild disabilities, particularly students with LD?

If you guessed reading, you are correct. For students with learning disabilities, approximately 80 percent to 90 percent have problems with reading (Fletcher et al. 2007). Students with LD commonly have deficits in phonological processing skills, which are critical to acquiring beginning reading skills (Ackerman et al. 2001; Schatschneider et al. 2000).

This astonishingly high percentage of students who encounter reading problems means that teachers should have knowledge of powerful reading interventions to address students' problems on a daily basis. Furthermore, teachers should have knowledge of the responsiveness to intervention (RTI) approach to special education. We describe several interventions in this chapter; with careful monitoring, Chapter 6 could be used within RTI tiers, particularly Tier 2 and 3. Although we have discussed RTI in detail in Chapter 1, we would encourage special education teachers to review other resources such as the RTI Action Network (mentioned at the end of this chapter in the "Technology Resources for Improving Reading Skills" section). The RTI Action Network website serves as an excellent resource for teachers looking for addition information about RTI and associated tiered interventions. Finally, a number of professional organizations (such as CEC, IRA, and NCTE) require teacher education programs at universities to focus heavily on the "teaching of reading" as part of their program requirements for preservice teachers. With all of the emphasis on reading, it is critical for teachers to know how to teach reading and how to implement reading interventions for students with mild disabilities.

In this chapter, you will learn about early reading methods and strategies. The content of the chapter includes information about reading models, stages of reading, and reading techniques, strategies, and activities for students with mild disabilities. Although beginning reading problems are most common among preschool and elementary age students, you will find many of the techniques in this chapter useful with older students as well.

CASE 5.1   **What's Wrong with Latasha?**

Case Introduction

In this case, you will read about a student who has trouble with early reading skills. The case will begin with some background information and then move on to a discussion of her specific reading problems. As you read, you will see that her teacher has tried a number of different teaching techniques and yet Latasha is still falling farther behind.

At the end of the case, you will find case questions. These questions are meant to serve as points for reflection. Of course,

if you can answer them immediately, you should do so, but you may want to wait to answer them until you have read the portion of the chapter that pertains to the particular case question. Throughout the rest of the chapter, you will see the same questions. When you come to them again, try to answer them based upon the portion of the chapter that you just read.

Latasha is in first grade and has problems with reading. She also has been diagnosed with ADHD by her pediatrician.

Her mother, Cici, feels that she is doing fine in school, and really does not do much at home to assist her at reading. Cici also had problems with reading when she was a child, yet she feels that she outgrew these problems with age, despite still being a poor reader.

Latasha is still in the early stages of learning how to read, even though most of the children in her class have already become fluent readers. Latasha reads from a basal reader, but struggles to read even the easiest words unless she has memorized them as sight words. She has particular difficulty with novel words because of her lack of phonological awareness. She knows most (about 75 percent) of her letter sounds and can segment simple three- to four-letter words with success, but has difficulty if asked to blend those sounds back together and pronounce the word. In terms of comprehension, Latasha has great difficulty comprehending the short sentences that she reads, unless there are pictures in the book to aid her. She often spends so much time sounding out words that she does not remember what she has just read. As a result, she is a slow, laborious reader.

Her special education teacher, Mr. Coleman, has been working on State Standard 1.6 with Latasha. This standard states that "the student will apply phonetic principles to read and spell." In accordance with this standard, Latasha is to use phonetic principles to use short vowel sounds to decode and spell single-syllable words; blend beginning, middle, and ending sounds to recognize and read words; use word patterns to decode unfamiliar words; and read and spell common, high-frequency sight words.

When reading a recent story, Latasha made several errors or miscues. Prior to having the children read, Mr. Coleman reviewed the majority of the sight words that were found in the short story. Even with the review, Latasha still made several miscues. For example, when Latasha came across the word *spot*, she sounded out each letter sound but when she blended the sounds together, she said the word *stop*. On this day, she made other mistakes or miscues including pronouncing *word* for *very*, *sister* for *list*, *stop* for *lot*, *and* for *have* and *ready* for *every*.

On another day, Mr. Coleman was covering State Standard 1.6. This standard includes blending beginning, middle, and ending sounds to recognize and read words, and using word patterns to decode unfamiliar words. He decided to use a game called "Add Them or Lose Them" to cover this standard. In this game, students substitute an initial letter sound to form a new word (given *rat*, change the first letter to "s" and pronounce the new word: *sat*). This activity proved especially difficult for Latasha, as she made several errors substituting *v, n, p* to form new *at* words. In another activity, "Name That Letter," Latasha had mixed results. In this activity, when give a word, (for example, *fast*), students were to name the phoneme in the beginning, middle, or end. The teacher gave the word and asked students to repeat it and then asked either beginning, middle, or end, at which time students had to name the corresponding phoneme. Latasha was successful at naming the beginning phonemes about 90 percent of the time and end phonemes about 65 percent of the time; however, Latasha performed poorly when asked to name the middle phoneme (she was only able to name it correctly about 20 percent of the time).

Mr. Coleman is concerned; despite his best efforts, Latasha has fallen farther behind her classmates. Even though she is in the lowest reading group, she is still having the most difficulty.

CASE QUESTIONS

1. Latasha has difficulty with several of the most basic skills of reading. Are there particular skills Mr. Coleman should address first?
2. Latasha needs to improve her phonological awareness. What are some activities that will help her to recognize and name phonemes?

As you may gather from the case, Latasha's problems in early reading can prove to be a challenge to even the most skilled teacher, yet research shows that teachers can use techniques, strategies, and skills to help improve Latasha's reading problems. In this chapter, you will learn about methods and techniques for remediating reading problems like Latasha's.

Chapter Question
ALERT

In this section, you will find information that answers a Chapter Question:

1. How do the three different models of reading explain how children read?

Models of Reading

Reading models and theories (Chall and Stahl 1982) serve an important purpose in understanding the process of reading. They seek to explain how children learn how to read. Strategies and techniques are derived from models and, in turn, these models or theories help guide teachers as to how to teach students to read. As you read about each model, think back to when you learned to read and consider the role of each model in your own reading development. Special education teachers may use one model at a particular reading stage and then eventually shift to a different model at later stages. Some teachers may rely more heavily on one model (for example, using the top-down model to help students gain meaning of what they read), yet incorporate components of another model (using work-attack skills for unknown multisyllabic words) as the situation arises.

Bottom-Up Model

According to the **bottom-up model of reading,** young readers rely heavily on translating *print* to *letter sounds* to *meaning* as an approach to comprehending text. In other words, children must hear each letter sound (or each word) before they can gain meaning. During silent reading, readers translate words first to inner speech, before gaining meaning. This process of determining what sounds are present in a word is known as **decoding** (see Box 5.1 for a detailed listing of reading terms). In the bottom-up model, *attention* plays a major role in learning to read words. Skilled readers use decoding skills automatically (LaBerge and Samuels 1974). That way, readers shift attention from one aspect of reading to another. In some instances, readers rely heavily on decoding text to make sense of it and, at other times, automatic decoding enables students to focus on comprehension. Many believe that students must first be fluent and efficient in decoding skills to become proficient in comprehension. Moreover, these skills must become "automatic" before students can begin to focus the majority of their attention on the meaning of text.

Top-Down Model

Using the **top-down model** when teaching young students in the early stages of reading, teachers focus on a combination of decoding skills, sight words, and connected reading activities to gain meaning (such as reading sentence strips or forming sentences from known words). According to this model, students use background knowledge to generate hypotheses about what they are about to read shortly before reading or shortly after reading (Chall and Stahl 1982). This model assumes that students have prior knowledge about the topic. Moreover, research shows that prior knowledge plays a major role in comprehension (Pressley 2002). As information is processed (that is, as the student reads), the reader confirms, disconfirms, or refines earlier hypotheses or generates new ones. Many top-down theorists believe that a skilled reader goes directly from *print* to *meaning*, without transferring the information to *speech* (Chall and Stahl 1982). This model espouses that reading is very much an "active process," whereby the reader uses background knowledge, including personal experiences, to form or shape meaning while reading the text. According to this model, reading is not merely a collection of ideas that are organized into something that makes sense,

BOX 5.1

COMMON READING TERMS

- **Phonemes** refer to letter sounds. Each letter has one or more letter sounds.
- **Phonological awareness** refers to breaking down (segmenting) an unknown word into phonemes and then blending those sounds back together to pronounce the word.
- **Word-attack skills** refers to the ability to "attack" a word by identifying its phonemes and putting them together to form the word.
- **Segmenting** refers to breaking down a word into phonemes (for example, the word *dish* is segmented into the phonemes *d-i-sh*).
- **Blending** refers to combining phonemes to form a word (for example, the phonemes *t-a-p* combine to make the word *tap*).
- **Sight words** are sometimes referred to as high-frequency words, words that appear frequently in print and are likely to appear in published print such as basal stories.
- **Basal reading series** are a series of preplanned, sequentially organized books that contain short passages or stories. Typically, sight words are introduced a few at a time in each story, and new ones are added in each successive story, resulting in a cumulative effect as the stories become more complex.
- **Decoding skills** refers to breaking down unknown words into phonemes and syllables.
- **Structural analysis** refers to breaking down unknown words into prefixes and suffixes, and then breaking them into syllables. This process is more sophisticated than decoding.
- **Digraphs** refer to two letters that represent one phoneme.
  - **Vowel digraphs** refer to two letters that represent one phoneme (for example, *ai, ay, oa,* and *ee*). These are usually one of the phonemes in the digraph (you may remember from your schooling that the first letter does the talking, and the second letter does the walking).
  - **Consonant digraphs** refer to two letters that create a single phoneme or unit (for example, *ph, ch, sh, th,* and *wh*).
- **Diphthongs** refer to the vowel sound that cannot be represented by either sound, but forms a unique sound together, such as *au, aw, oi, oy,* and *ou*.
- **Consonant blends/clusters** refer to blends in which each letter can be pronounced by saying each letter sound (for example, *bl, str, cr, spl*).

but reading is a process that involves the reader constructing meaning and creating new meanings from text. In a sense, each new idea that readers come across in print transforms their knowledge of the topic.

To use this model, teachers should focus on activating students' background knowledge prior to, during, and after reading the story. This involves using activities that tap into their knowledge of the topic before reading the story (for example, using a KWL activity; see Chapter 6), previewing the text, and then discussing the previewed material and how it pertains to students' current knowledge about the topic. The gist is that activating the students' prior knowledge will help them to connect their ideas with newly learned information as they read. Next, students read the text, confirming or disconfirming prior statements that they made during the preview process. Finally, the teacher checks to see that students have an accurate meaning of the text by asking questions and probing students on what they read. Although top-down models seems to work well for skilled readers who intuitively incorporate decoding and other rudimentary skills into their reading repertoire, students with mild disabilities and lower-levels skills must be taught first or along with higher-level, top-down processing skills.

Interactive Model

As theorists began to examine the different models, it was clear that neither the bottom-up nor the top-down model sufficiently explained the entire reading process. As a result, the interactive model (Bos and Anders 1992; Chall and Stahl 1982) was developed. According to this model, theorists believe that information is derived from both kinds of processing (top-down and bottom-up), and is combined to determine the most likely interpretation of print. In other words, an interaction of these two models results in comprehension of text. At times, readers may use top-down processing, particularly with familiar material; yet, when readers encounter difficulty, they may switch to bottom-up processing to read the information slowly and methodically.

This interactive model means that if the purpose of a reading activity is to reinforce or practice word-attack or phonological skills, then teachers should de-emphasize comprehension and emphasize phonological skills as the child reads. On the other hand, if the purpose of a reading activity is comprehension, then the teacher should focus on comprehension strategies, such as asking students to pause periodically to check if they understood what they just read, paraphrase information, or identify main ideas or details. Teachers should be cognizant of teaching skills for monitoring comprehension as children read. Many of these skills could first be taught in isolation using explicit instruction (for example, practice finding the main idea), and then these skills could be practiced within the context of reading.

Stages of Reading

As children learn to read, they go through several stages (Chall 1983). Chall refers to six stages that describe how reading progresses from what Chall terms *pseudo-reading* in early readers to its most mature form in adults. In each stage, readers focus on different aspects of reading as they interact with printed material. In other words, they attack reading differently in each stage. Although they may revert to earlier stages with different types of reading materials, they essentially progress through each successive stage as reading becomes more complex, technical, and abstract.

Chapter Question
ALERT

In this section, you will find information that answers a Chapter Question:

2. What stages do children go through as they learn to read?

Stage 0: Pre-Reading (Birth to Age 6)

This stage covers the greatest period of time, from birth to Grade 1. In the pre-reading stage, students expand and master their use of language, particularly as it pertains to morphology (or word parts), semantics (understanding the meaning of words), and syntax (sentence structure or grammar).

As they begin to master their language, they also begin to understand various aspects of early reading. They begin to understand that words are composed of letters, and these letters comprise sounds. They also begin to understand that books are made up of words and that, in part, they can use visual cues (that is, pictures) in the book to tell a story.

During this stage, children rely heavily on contextual knowledge and information that is derived from pictures in the book to learn how to read. Children often pretend to read, or use **pseudo-reading,** as they tell the story in a book aloud to others. Watch young children read and, regardless of the words, they will look at the sequence of pictures and tell the story, frequently relying on memory of the story. This stage is very much considered by some to be an emergent stage of reading, whereby children begin to recognize letter names, print some letters, and perhaps even know a few words by heart. The child's description of the actions often mimics their own spoken language.

During this stage, the child begins to understand the process of reading. In other words, the child begins to realize that words are made up of sounds, and that when these sounds are segmented and blended together, they form words. This phonemic phase of reading development helps the child begin to recognize segmentation, blending, and rhyme. For students to be successful at this stage of learning, they need to be provided a print-rich environment, one that allows for experimentation with language and an opportunity to make connections between language and reading (Wolf 2007). A top-down approach to teaching reading is usually used during this stage as children begin to interact with print.

Stage 1: Initial Reading or Decoding Stage (Grades 1–2, Ages 6–7)

Students enter Stage 1 of reading when they are successful in the pre-reading stage and have progressed from pure reliance on picture cues and memory of the story line to reliance on phonological skills and recognition of sight words. In doing so, students can confidently read some words by sounding out the letters and eventually progress to the more complex decoding phase of a Stage 1 reader.

In this stage, students attempt to "crack the code." This means that students can no longer rely solely on memory or knowledge of certain words in the story; instead, they must learn phonological awareness skills and be able to apply these skills to read words. Instead of using pictures to make sense of the story, as was done in the previous stage, students must now search for words that make sense both in terms of what is occurring in the story and in terms of how well they match with the printed word.

During this stage, students rely heavily on (that is, are glued to) the printed word to pronounce words properly and focus attention on visual information. For some students, this can very much be a trial-and-error approach, relying on teacher feedback for confirmation of their phonic or sight-word skills to pronounce words. Even though students may have been able to pronounce words easily during the previous stage, they now sound out many of these words. Only through the realization that letters (both consonants and vowels) are made up of letter sounds do children fully progress through this stage. This "realization" has been described as "interiorizing of cognitive knowledge about reading"

(Chall 1983). For students in this stage, using those interiorized phonological skills is essential. Difficulty specifically with phonological memory can result in problems learning vocabulary in a first- and second language learner (Swanson, Howard, and Sáez 2006).

A bottom-up approach to teaching reading may be more applicable for this stage of reading development. Teachers need to teach phonological awareness and word-attack skills explicitly through modeling, providing practice with feedback, and allowing students to use the skills on their own. As students progress, their word-attack skills move from sounding out simple (monosyllabic) words to syllabication of longer words.

Stage 2: Confirmation, Fluency, and Ungluing from Print (Grades 2–3, Ages 7–8)

This stage involves the consolidation of word-attack skills learned in Stage 1 while at the same time moving away from this reliance on decoding skills. Continued teaching of decoding skills is an important activity that continues during this stage, even though students are becoming more fluent readers (Harris and Sipay 1990). Students who rely too heavily on decoding skills become "word callers," those who are still glued to text. To move successfully through this stage, students needs to leave the page and reflect on whether the words that are being read make sense in the context of the story line. Chall (1983) refers to this as being able to read "inside out" (that is, using phonological and decoding skills) while switching to an "outside in" mode of reading (that is, making sure the words make sense). For this to occur, students need to be confident in their decoding skills and must feel comfortable switching back and forth between reflecting for meaning and reflecting for proper pronunciation. To become fluent readers, students in this phase should be permitted to make mistakes, and the teacher should provide general rules for correcting such mistakes. Also, you should remember that automaticity of decoding skills is critical, because automatic decoding of words frees up working memory for comprehension.

During this stage, readers begin to develop comprehension skills and begin to become more concerned with the text "making sense," while at the same time becoming less reliant on it (unglued from it). These new phonological awareness and decoding skills enable students to become more fluent and expressive during reading. Because fluency requires practice, activities that permit practice, such as recreational reading (reading for pleasure) and repeated readings (reading the same text multiple times, to build comfort), will help students progress smoothly through this stage and onto Stage 3. Keep in mind that this stage is not necessarily for learning new information through reading, but to confirm what is known by practicing those skills that students have already acquired. Thus, stories with familiar content are typically used so that students can hone their word-attack and decoding skills while matching what they read to their knowledge of the topic. In this stage, readers must use all of their prior skills and strategies in an efficient and effective manner to gain new knowledge from what they read. Prior to getting there, however, teachers should provide students with multiple opportunities to read (that is, through structured repeated readings of stories or less structured "free" reading time), so that they can master skills while building confidence in reading at the same time. Once students can move efficiently between using context clues, sight words, word-attack skills, and making sense of the story, they are ready to move onto the next stage.

Stage 3: Reading for Learning the New—A First Step (Grades 4–8, Ages 9–13)

In earlier stages, students read to acquire rudimentary reading skills. During this stage, readers use previously learned reading skills to acquire new facts and concepts, and to gain an understanding of how things work (Harris and Sipay 1990). They develop strategies for attacking different types of text. Stage 3 is typically known as the "reading to learn" phase. At the same time, there is a shift in the purpose of reading activities. No longer is reading restricted to basal readers or storybooks, but now reading involves learning facts and concepts from textbooks and other expository text. Therefore teachers need to provide students with new strategies for reading this type of text.

During this stage, reading skills begin to focus on finding information in the chapter or book, learning new vocabulary, and approaching reading tasks in a strategic manner. Rather than reading sight words in isolation, vocabulary and word meanings now take top priority as students use these words on tests and in their writing. To acquire new information, students must relate new knowledge with prior knowledge, understand how the two relate, and then store that new information for later recall. Teachers may need to expand pre-reading activities so that students have sufficient background knowledge to acquire successfully new information that they read. Informational materials and fictional books are also introduced during this stage, and these materials require students to apply new comprehension monitoring strategies. Reading during this stage at times follows a top-down approach, as students begin to rely more on background knowledge about the topic to connect new knowledge with prior knowledge. At other times, reading follows a bottom-up approach, as students must stop periodically to read multisyllabic words and technical information (Chall 1983). Although some students may still be using decoding skills for new words, instruction in structural analysis will become more prominent as students begin to read multisyllabic vocabulary words, particularly those longer words containing affixes. In addition, as their working memory becomes more taxed with facts and bits of knowledge, students will need to rely on more efficient comprehension strategies.

What's more, children at risk for reading difficulties have greater difficulty performing short-term memory tasks in learning a second language than do others (Swanson, Sáez, and Gerber 2004). So, any strategies that allow them to search out, remember, and recall information will be useful. These strategies include various aspects of comprehension monitoring such as finding main ideas, details, and vocabulary, summarizing text, and drawing conclusions. At this stage, be aware that both native speakers and second language learners appear to exhibit the same types of reading difficulties across languages (Swanson, Sáez, and Gerber 2006). Although sophistication of vocabulary and idioms may differ, for example, core underlying reading processes like phonological processing skills are typically consistent. However, in their study of monolingual English-speaking children compared to bilingual Spanish-speaking children learning English, Swanson, Howard, and Sáez (2006) found that phonological processing problems in Spanish (but not in English) predicted limited growth in reading skills over three years; at the same time, difficulties in working memory for reading in both languages were found correlated with slow English-reading development.

Stage 4: Multiple Viewpoints— High School (Ages 14–18)

In Stage 4, students begin to read materials that are from another view or even multiple perspectives on topics and issues. This presents new challenges in reading textbooks and literature stories. Social studies, history, and even science textbooks begin to present information from multiple viewpoints. For example, students may learn about the Revolutionary War from the perspective of the merchant, the soldier, and the slave. These points of view, sometimes conflicting, present challenges for students and often go beyond factual conflicts, but may present moral and ethical issues that run counter to their own current views. They also learn more in-depth concepts and must deal with the layering of facts and concepts. Chall (1983) claims that students can acquire these more difficult concepts from multiple points of view because they previously learned "simplistic versions" of them. When students become successful with this type of critical comprehension, they have progressed from Stage 3 to Stage 4. Often, discussions and writing assignments help students sort out the details of multiple views and help them to accommodate this new knowledge more easily.

Stage 5: Construction and Reconstruction—A World View (College and Adult)

Chall (1983) claims that passage from Stage 4 to Stage 5 is perhaps the most difficult because moving forward depends upon "the reader's cognitive abilities, accumulation of knowledge, and motivation". In Stage 5, college students and other young adults rely heavily on prior knowledge and multiple comprehension strategies. Skilled readers in this stage not only have multiple strategies for reading (based upon the purpose for reading), but they have also developed the metacognitive skills necessary to determine when and where to apply each strategy. Inherent in their strategy development, these experienced students can also use strategies flexibly, depending upon the type of text and the purpose for reading or studying.

In Stage 5, students become selective in what they read and what they choose not to read. This selectivity depends upon the purpose of reading and determines the degree of detail needed while reading. Students use multiple comprehension strategies (for example, reading in-depth or skimming) to construct and reconstruct knowledge about the topic of interest.

Also during Stage 5, reading becomes more critical as students uses analysis, synthesis, and judgment to construct their own "truth" of the topic from multiple sources (or as Chall puts it, "from the 'truth' of others"). Students must not only feel confident about the topic, but they must feel a certain "entitlement" to use the knowledge of others to create new knowledge about the topic. Prior knowledge of a

⏩ ▶ ⏪

V I D E O   C A S E   C O N N E C T I O N S   B O X

Watch the Video Case entitled *Assessment in the Elementary Grades: Formal and Informal Literacy Assessment*. Listen to the instructions that teacher Christine Quinn gives to her students. Some are for formal assessments, and others are part of informal activities. For each instruction, name the basic reading skill you just read about that she is assessing in her students.

topic allows for a faster reading rate because knowledge has already been constructed about the topic, and comprehension occurs more easily from previously constructed schemata. As such, students may read at Stage 5 for selected topics (for example, those topics in which they have a special interest or specialization) because they have previously constructed schema for the topic; yet, for other topics, students may still read in Stage 4, or even Stage 3.

Common Reading Problems among Students with Mild Disabilities

Chapter Question
ALERT

In this section, you will find information that answers a Chapter Question:

3. What are some common reading problems that students with mild disabilities encounter?

When we look at how reading skills develop in students, we see that most children enter school with some pre-reading or prerequisite reading skills. Once in the school system, they often begin an intense immersion in the process of learning how to read. Teachers discuss initial letter sounds, sight words, and listening comprehension. Concurrently, students also learn other skills such as rhyming words, discriminating vowel sounds, pronouncing blends and clusters, and matching letter names with their sounds. Some students, particularly those with mild disabilities, experience difficulty in learning how to read. These problems range from beginning reading problems, such as phonological awareness, to later reading problems, such as problems with comprehension (which we will address in Chapter 6).

Basic Reading Skill Problems

Research has shown that reading is the primary academic area of difficulty for students with mild disabilities (Fletcher et al. 2007), and that an estimated 80 percent to 90 percent of students with learning disabilities are referred to special education because of reading problems (Kavale and Forness 2000; Welsch 2007). Mather (1992) states that students with reading or mild disabilities do not intuitively learn how to read and therefore, may require more explicit instruction in "letter-sound relationship"; without it, they do not learn how to "crack the code" of reading. According to some, students with mild disabilities fail to crack the code of reading because they have a specific deficit in the phonological language domain (Liberman, Shankweiler, and Liberman 1989). Similarly, researchers (Rack, Snowling, and Olson 1992) have proposed that these problems represent a **phonological deficit hypothesis** and that this deficit accounts for why students fail to acquire reading skills during their first few years of school. However, as you read the following sections, be mindful that it is important to assess reading difficulties as distinct from more general abilities with first language and English as a second language. In some cases, deficits in short-term memory may underlie observed working memory difficulties for bilingual children learning to read in their second language, although the same short-term memory deficits are not always found for both languages (Swanson et al. 2004).

Fluency and Comprehension Problems

Although a lack of phonological or **word-attack** skills has been linked to poor reading of words, the secondary effects of these skills deficits are exhibited in a student's poor comprehension of text. Because students with mild disabilities spend much of their intellectual resources (that is, attention and working memory) trying to pronounce words, they have few resources left for constructing meaning of text (Adams 1990). So, although phonological awareness is important for students to read individual words successfully, other factors may contribute to successful reading fluency and comprehension, namely recognizing orthographic patterns, rapid naming, and word-reading skills (Katzir et al. 2006). For students with disabilities, these are difficult skills to acquire. Specifically, students with mild disabilities have trouble recognizing words accurately and quickly (Rack, Snowling, and Olson 1992; Jenkins et al. 2003). Reading comprehension for these students is affected by weak word-attack and fluency skills. Yet, other students may have adequate word-attack skills, but still have poor reading fluency and comprehension (Wolf and Bowers 1999), because they lack fluency with reading words in context or they lack effective comprehension strategies in some cases.

In terms of specific comprehensions problems, students with mild disabilities may have difficulty with both word-level comprehension and sentence-level comprehension (Pressley 2002). Moreover, many students with disabilities have a great deal of difficulty making inferences in passages (Cain and Oakhill 1999), resulting in poor comprehension. For some students, poor working memory may interfere in their comprehension (Yuill, Oakhill, and Parkin 1989). For these students, learning novel vocabulary from context is a difficult task (Cain, Oakhill, and Lemmon 2004). For others, managing and coordinating cognitive and attentional resources becomes a problem. These problems, often referred to as metacognitive problems, may prevent students from understanding ambiguous vocabulary, drawing inferences, and processing redundant information in text (Meltzer and Krishnan 2007). Moreover, when reading becomes difficult, these students are less likely to shift strategies to use different, more effective comprehension strategies (Phillips 1988; Pressley 2002). As a matter of fact, this weakness in *cognitive flexibility* is often a trait of students with mild disabilities, particularly learning disabilities.

Teaching Reading Skills to Students with Mild Disabilities

Chapter Question

ALERT

In this section, you will find information that answers a Chapter Question:

4. What techniques should be taught to improve sight words, phonological awareness, words patterns, and syllabication skills for students with mild disabilities?

When teaching students early reading skills, the natural progression of skills (see Figure 5.1) would be from lower-level skills such as reading readiness activities (pre-reading skills), to phonological awareness, to syllabication, to word patterns and word attack, to more complex skills such as fluency, vocabulary, and reading comprehension. Despite these skills being listed as separate skills, there is overlap as they are taught (for example, when teaching children to pronounce words, we often ask them to comprehend short sentences that they read). In most cases, reading lessons comprise activities from a variety of these skill areas. In this chapter, we will discuss reading readiness activities, phonological awareness activities, syllabication, word patterns, and word-attack skills. Reading fluency, reading comprehension, and reading to understand text will be discussed in the next chapter.

FIGURE 5.1

Progression of Reading Skills

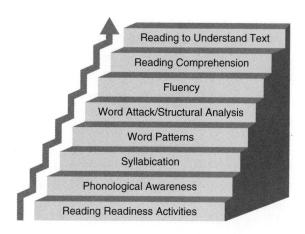

Early reading instruction includes teaching students a number of reading skills. For example, many children with mild disabilities benefit not only from phonics skills, but also benefit from *reading readiness* skills such as listening comprehension. Likewise, research has shown that good reading programs also incorporate other important early reading skills such as phonic skills, sight-word knowledge, and spelling patterns of sight words (Ehri 2003; Share and Stanovich 1995). In addition, the National Reading Panel (NRP) concluded that early reading should focus on the "big five" areas of reading: phonemic awareness, phonics, fluency, comprehension, and vocabulary (NRP 2000).

How these skills are taught is almost as important as *what* is taught. Research has shown that early reading instruction for students with mild disabilities should consist of explicit instruction (Pressley 2002; see Chapter 2 for a more detailed discussion on this topic). For example, using an explicit instructional method such as **direct instruction** in reading (Carnine et al. 2006), the teacher **models** the skill, uses **guided practice with feedback,** and uses **independent practice** to assess the effectiveness of the skills taught during the lesson. During instruction, teachers should provide immediate and frequent feedback on errors made while reading or during training of reading skills. In the following more explicit example of direct instruction, a teacher is working with a small group of students on the word *sit*.

- First, the teacher models for students. The teacher points to each letter in the word and says to students "Sssssiiit. Sit."
- Next, the teacher uses guided practice and asks all the students to say it with her. The teacher points to each letter in the word and says, "Everyone, say it with me, ssssiiit." Students and teacher say the word together. The teacher asks, "Class, what is the word?" Students respond together, "sit," as the teacher says it with them. The teacher provides feedback, "Great! Everyone read *sit* correctly."
- Finally, the teacher uses independent practice and asks one student at a time to say the word. The teacher points to the word and says, "Zane, what is the word?" Zane responds, "sit." The teacher provides feedback and says, "Zane, great job reading the word." The teacher asks another

student, "Kera what is the word?" Kera responds, "sat." The teacher provides feedback, saying, "No, Kera, the word is "sit." The teacher points to the word and says to Kera, "Sssssiiit. Sit." The teacher says to Kera, "This time, say it with me: 'ssssiiit, sit,'," as Kera and the teacher say the word together. The teacher says to Kera, "Your turn. What is the word?" Kera says, "sit." The teacher provides feedback by saying, "Terrific, you read the word *sit* correctly."

In addition to direct instruction, researchers (Ehri 2003) have shown that successful reading programs teach phonological skills "systematically." Ehri (2003) describes systematic phonics instruction as teaching *all* of the major grapheme-phoneme correspondences (in a clearly defined sequence). This includes short and long vowels, vowel and consonant digraphs, and blends when used as onsets (for example, such as the *c* in *cat*) or with rhymes (the *at* in *cat*). Furthermore, systematic phonological instruction incorporates plans for teaching all of the major letter-sound correspondences, rather than a casual phonics program that teaches phonics on an as-needed basis.

The following skills represent recommended reading skills (Reutzel and Cooter 2004), but are not meant to be all-inclusive. (Many of these skills, as well as others, will be described throughout this and the next chapter.)

Recommended Reading Skills
- Pre-reading skills
- Comprehension
- Phonological awareness
- Phonemic awareness
- Phonics
- Vocabulary
- Fluency
- Story structure
- Text structure
- Comprehension monitoring strategies
- Finding main ideas and details
- Making inferences
- Summarizing

THINK BACK TO THE FIRST CASE with Latasha . . .

1. What two specific skills would you try to remediate first with Latasha?

You could remediate a number of different skills with Latasha, particularly in the area of phonological awareness. These skills could include recognition of short vowel sounds; blending beginning, middle, and ending sounds; using word patterns to decode unfamiliar words; and reading and spelling common, high-frequency sight words.

METHODS AND STRATEGIES SPOTLIGHT

Data-Driven Teaching

Teaching should be data driven. The effectiveness of a student's learning ability for a particular skill determines *how* you teach (what teaching method you use), as shown by the student data that you gather. Whether special education teachers teach students how to read new words or teach phonological awareness (PA) skills, they need to keep track of student progress on a daily or every-other-day basis. Using student data should assist teachers in determining *how* to teach. Teachers can start by choosing one skill: number of times the child used PA to determine new words, percentage of words pronounced correctly, or number of words read correctly per minute in a story. Once a baseline or starting point has been established, either the teacher can graph the data or use curriculum-based measurement (C-BM) to determine the goal and aimline. C-BM involves assessing one child on one skill over time. C-BM typically assesses easy-to-measure skills such as percentage of sight words identified or words read correctly per minute, because these skills are part of the student's reading program, can be assessed as the student works on activities, and are easily measured. Please refer to the following graph.

FIGURE 5.2

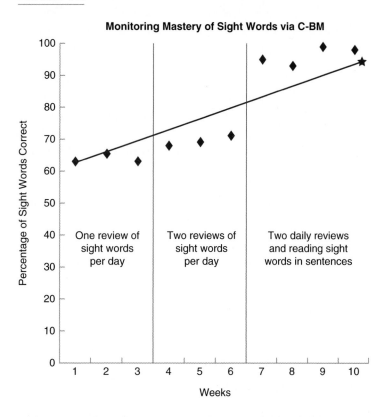

In this graph, the special education teacher is assessing the percentage of sight words pronounced correctly from flash cards once a week. First, the teacher needs to determine the student's current level (baseline point). Next, she decides upon a goal of where to expect the child to be after X number weeks. The goal can be determined by assessing nondisabled peers on the same skill, using charts that have been developed from experts, or determining where she wants the child to be X weeks later. In this case, the teacher has chosen 95 percent correct as the goal. Once this point is decided upon, she can connect the goal with the baseline point. This line is known as the aimline. Once she plots data, any data points above the aimline mean that the child will eventually achieve the goal. In other words, the technique or method that the teacher is using is working. If three or more data points are below the aimline, the technique/method is not working and, therefore, needs to be changed until the teacher finds a technique that will increase the child's data above the aimline. In the example given, notice how the teacher changed the technique until the child's data was above the aimline. Continue changing or adding on techniques or interventions until the child's data is consistently above the aimline.

Teaching Reading Readiness and Sight Words to Students with Mild Disabilities

Reading readiness activities represent those activities that prepare students for reading. Many of these activities are also referred to as *print awareness* activities. Print awareness activities are those tasks that help students understand the connection between print in written language or reading and using it as a form of communication. Many young children simply do not make the connection between the printed word and its meaning and, therefore, view reading and writing as very mysterious processes. Only over time do they begin to see the link that each letter has meaning (unique phonemes), particularly when blended together to form words. For children with disabilities, this process remains a frustrating mystery for many years until they too are able to unlock the "code of reading." Through using reading readiness activities, teachers can help students to see the link between "words" and "meaning." Many parents use reading readiness activities without ever knowing that they are building initial reading skills. For example, when a parent reads to a child and moves his finger from left to right (in the English language) while reading the words, he is in fact showing the child the directional aspect of reading.

Reading Readiness Activities

Reading readiness involves teaching students prerequisite skills for beginning reading. The following are a few skills:

Place names on seats, desks, or other objects. This shows children that words are used for a specific meaningful purpose.

Show pictures with brief titles. This activity represents one of the earliest reading comprehension activities, that words or phrases represent a picture.

Post simple reports/notices. Again, this is another activity that links words with actions or events. Simple reports could be daily weather reports or simple notes about the day's upcoming activities, such as a schedule that is written on the board.

Use predictable stories. From predictable stories, students learn that events are linked to one another and usually have a predictable outcome based upon a sequence of events. This activity serves as a precursor to reading comprehension.

Read decodable books These books use text that incorporates rhyme and frequently stories that contain words with similar spelling patterns. The sentences are usually short and contain many rhyming words, usually of the same pattern.

Read picture books. These are stories without words. These books link events to an outcome, and children can look at the pictures to create their own version of the story. These books serve as precursors to listening and reading comprehension.

Have adults read stories to children. When parents, teachers, or other adults read stories to young children and periodically ask questions, they are teaching children listening comprehension. This type of comprehension serves as a precursor for later reading comprehension.

Encourage children to label objects. As children begin to label objects, they also begin to realize the communicative function of print.

Use a language-experience approach. By writing out stories from students' experiences, teachers put their words and ideas into print. Often this experience creates memorable stories for students because they are drawn directly from their past experiences.

Sight-Word Approach

Using a sight-word or whole-word approach teaches children to learn and recognize words as a *whole*. This approach often incorporates the use of "high-frequency" word lists (see Table 5.1 for an abbreviated list and Appendix B on the book-specific website for a full list of sight words). Over the years, several lists have been developed and usually consist of frequent words in English that children would encounter in printed materials. These lists do not always match up, nor do they match up when ranking the importance of words. Some reading experts (Johns 1981) claim that 13 words (that is, *a, and, for, he, is, in, it, of, that, the, to, was, you*) account for over 25 percent of the words that children will encounter in printed materials; whereas, others (Fry, Fountoukidis, and Polk 1985) claim that 100 words account for over 50 percent of all words in print. (Teaching sight words will also be discussed in Chapter 6.)

Teaching Sight Words

Many teachers introduce these words in initial reading lessons, yet others wait until children have acquired some phonological skills before introducing children

TABLE 5.1 Sight Word Lists

Dolch Basic Sight Word Lists[1]			
the	at	do	big
to	him	can	went
and	with	could	are
Fry Sight Words - First Hundred Words[2]			
the	or	will	number
of	one	up	no
and	had	other	way
Functional and Survival Word List			
exit	hot	cold	open
closed	emergency	warning	caution
keep out	power	water	safety

[1]From "A Basic Sight Word Vocabulary" by E. Dolch, 1936, *Elementary School Journal*, February 1936, 456–60. Copyright © 1936 by The University of Chicago Press. Reprinted with permission.
[2]From *Reading Teacher* by Edward Fry. Copyright 1980 by International Reading Association. Reproduced with permission of International Reading Association in the format Textbook via Copyright Clearance Center.

to sight words. The main purpose of teaching sight words is to have children use them as they are beginning to read actual stories. Teachers commonly choose sight words from basal readers or beginning reading books so that students can experience "reading" and not become bored with reading-related activities such as phonemic awareness or phonics activities. Teachers usually transfer sight words from lists to index cards or use flash cards. Using index cards, teachers and students can either review sight words prior to reading words in text (for example, basal reading stories) or use the words as review after certain reading activities. When teaching sight words, teachers need to ensure that students know the words "on sight" (within three seconds); therefore, students need to memorize sight words.

When teaching sight words, keep in mind the following:

1. Use sight words during the initial stages of reading. Often teachers use these words to help students as they begin to read and then use them to supplement their vocabulary development as students become more advanced readers.
2. Decide which words will become sight words, and teach only a few words each week. Teachers can choose from multiple sources (for example, word lists, basal readers, or spelling words) to develop sight words for the week. When teaching sight words, students should be introduced to ten (or fewer) new words per week.
3. Present sight words before or after reading. Teachers should decide when and how often they will review sight words with students. Teachers can write sight words on index cards, and then students can store their sight words in an index box. Students can also refer to these words when writing essays or compositions.
4. Sight words should be known to mastery and "on sight" (within three seconds of presentation). Students who spend more than three seconds determining the correct pronunciation of the word are probably using phonics or word-attack skills.

One of the oldest, but still most frequently used word lists is the *Dolch Basic Sight Vocabulary* (see Table 5.1 for an abbreviated list). Originally developed in 1939, the Dolch Word Recognition Test (Dolch 1939) is a list of 220 words of increasing difficulty that are grouped by basal reading levels. This list has been revised over the years, but the original list still accounts for over 50 percent of words found in reading materials (Johns 1981). Finally, included in this chapter is a list of functional and survival words (Table 5.1 and Appendix B on the book-specific website). For students with more moderate to severe disabilities or older students who have not mastered reading, these words may be essential words to learn for life in the community and workplace.

Teaching Phonological Awareness to Students with Mild Disabilities

Phonological awareness is a broad term used to describe the manipulation of language skills that include, but are not limited to, segmenting of written words, blending of letter sounds, rhyming, alliteration, and also the manipulation of onsets/rhymes (Reutzel and Cooter 2004). *Phonemic awareness* is another term that is considered a subskill of phonological awareness (Reutzel and Cooter

2004). Phonemic awareness is the awareness that spoken words are made of phonemes and that these phonemes can be segmented into individual sounds. This also involves understanding that, if a student were given a word and asked to replace the first phoneme with another phoneme, she would form a new word (say the word *mop*, now take off the *mmmm* sound and replace it with *tttt*. What would the new word be?). **Phonics** refers to letter and sound correspondence. Phonics links the written symbol with phonemes.

Reutzel and Cooter (2004) suggest eight phonemic awareness skills that should be taught to students. These include the following:

- Phoneme isolation: teaching students to identify phonemes in words. *What sound does the word* cat *begin with?*
- Phoneme identity: discriminating phonemes in words that begin with the same phoneme. *Is the beginning sound the same in the words* hot *and* help?
- Phoneme categorizing: discriminating phonemes in words that begin with a different sound. *Which word begins with a different sound?* Tap, toe, sit?
- Phoneme blending: blending phonemes that are presented as separate phonemes. *What word does* C-A-T *make?*
- Phoneme segmentation: segmenting a word into individual phonemes. *What sounds are in the word* sssssiiitttt? *(sit).*
- Phoneme deletion: removing an initial phoneme and being able to pronounce the word. *If you take away the* S *sound from* STOP, *what word is left?*
- Phoneme addition: adding a phoneme and creating a new word. *If you add an* S *sound to the beginning of* CAT, *what would the new word be?*
- Phoneme substitution: changing one phoneme in a word. *If you change the* H *sound in* HAT *to* S *sound what would the new word be?*

When using these skills, present them in games and activities for students. Make them enjoyable and fun. Model a few examples first before asking students to try them. If students have a difficult time, exaggerate certain phonemes that you want students to focus on, as in the previous phoneme segmentation example. In some cases, teachers can use plastic letters to show students how spoken words are broken down into phonemes. Making oral language more concrete through the use of manipulatives often helps students better understand phonemic concepts.

Phonological Awareness Activities

Phonological awareness activities will vary in degree of difficulty for children and, as such, some children may find that some of the activities are easy whereas others are more difficult (see the following list for three activities). For example, rhymes and rhyming games may be easier for most children than a phoneme substitution activity. For first and second language learners, difficulty specifically with phonological memory can result in problems learning vocabulary (Swanson, Howard, and Sáez 2006). Chard and Dickson (1999) make some suggestions that might increase student success rates when teaching phonological awareness activities: model each activity so that students can see the skill being demonstrated; move from easier tasks to more complex tasks; consider using manipulatives (chips or blocks) to help represent sounds in words; move from larger units (words) to smaller units (phonemes); and start with continuous sounds

(s, m, f) that can be exaggerated (*sssssss*), rather than stop sounds (b, p, k). A signaling procedure (Carnine et al. 2006) can also be helpful for teaching students to focus on specific letter sounds in words. Using the signaling procedure, the teacher first points in front of the first letter of a target word (for example, *cat*). The teacher gets the student's attention with a prompt, such as "get ready." While still pointing in front of the first letter *c*, the teacher moves a finger under the *c*, pronounces the sound, and sweeps the finger in a loop to the next letter, *a*. Once a finger is under the letter *a*, the teacher pronounces the letter sound, and sweeps to the last letter. Once under the letter *t*, the teacher pronounces the letter sound and removes the finger from the word. Once students are able to use this procedure, they can take turns pronouncing the sounds of each letter in other words.

The following are phonemic awareness activities to assist young students:

- **Rhyme Time.** The purpose of this activity is to have children identify words that rhyme with the targeted word. For example, go around the room and ask children to think of a word that rhymes with *cat*. When you have exhausted the possible rhyming words, move on to another rhyming word. Another suggestion would be to use pictures and have children produce a rhyming word with the object in the picture. Once children can name rhyming words, move on to easy printed words. Tell the children the target word (for example, *hen*) while pointing out the rhyme part (*en*) of the word and having the children think of other words that have different onsets (*p –en* or *d –en*). Keep score of who gets the most rhyming words and award the winner a prize.

- **Clapping Words and Phonemes.** The purpose of this activity is to teach segmentation. At first, teach segmentation of words from sentences, move to segmenting syllables, and eventually move to segmenting phonemes from words. Begin by using words from familiar children's rhymes, and have them clap their hands for each word they hear. For example, "One for the mouse, one for the crow, one to rot, one to grow." After children master monosyllabic (one-syllable) words, move on to rhymes or songs with multi-syllabic words and have them clap out each syllable they hear. Finally, move on to clapping out the phonemes to simple words. The purpose of this game is to eventually teach segmentation of words into phonemes.

- **Rubber Band Man Blending.** The purpose of this game is to teach children to blend phonemes to pronounce words. Using their "slow motion" voice, children begin by exaggerating words in a sentence. Then ask them to repeat the sentence in their normal speed. Once they can do this, use pictures of objects that they can exaggerate the phonemes (*ffffannnnn*) to form the word. Finally, provide them with an exaggerated word, *sssssstarrrr*, and ask them to name the word.

Phonological Awareness Strategy

The phonological awareness strategy (Boyle and Seibert 1997) is used to teach students phonological awareness skills. The purpose of this strategy is not to teach initial letter sounds (that is, students should know most of their letter sounds), but rather to teach the next logical step—segmenting and blending.

VIDEO CASE CONNECTIONS BOX

Watch the Video Case entitled *Elementary Literacy Instruction: A Balanced Literacy Approach*. Observe Sandra Jenoski's students engage in word-study activities as she explains how the students "manipulate their words" by "building them and writing them." For each specific skill you observe her students practicing, name a way they could have drilled practice in the same skill.

Therefore, as a prerequisite step, students are required to know at least 80 percent of the initial letter sounds (phonemes) from a list of phonemes (consonant and short vowel sounds).

Because of the young age of students learning this strategy, it incorporates familiar keywords (that is, *stare, tell, open, put*) that they can easily understand. The phonological awareness strategy incorporates both segmenting and blending skills through the mnemonic STOP (see Box 5.2). The specific steps of the strategy were developed because: (1) previous studies demonstrated that segmenting and blending are two skills essential for pronouncing words (Rack, Snowling, and Olson 1992); (2) training students in one subskill (for example, segmenting) did not result in increases in other subskills (for example, blending) (O'Conner et al. 1992); (3) segmenting and blending must be taught together to assist students in pronouncing words (Torgesen, Morgan, and Davis 1992); and (4) phonological awareness training that explicitly linked phonological awareness skills with reading and taught specific strategies to implement those phonological awareness skills was proven to be more effective than a "skill-and-drill" approach (that is, teaching skills in isolation and out of context) (Cunningham 1980).

The first step, *stare*, cues students to look at each letter of the unknown word (that is, the first step of segmenting). In the second step, *tell*, students are asked to tell themselves each letter sound (the second step of segmenting). The third step, *open*, cues children to verbalize aloud the segmented sounds. The fourth step, *put*, cues students to blend letter sounds together to say the word.

Strategy instruction consists of introductory and mnemonic practice training, during which teachers instruct students on the components of the phonological awareness strategy. Initially, the teacher describes and models the strategy to students, and then they begin using the mnemonic STOP while the teacher provides feedback to them. Once students are proficient at using the strategy steps, they begin using the strategy with actual words. The initial phase involves

---

BOX 5.2

PHONOLOGICAL AWARENESS STRATEGY

The steps for the STOP strategy are as follows:

S Stare at the unknown word.

T Tell yourself each letter sound.

O Open your mouth and say each letter.

P Put the letters together to say the word.

using the strategy with ten monosyllabic words (three- to four-letter words that contain short vowel sounds) per training session. The teacher places each monosyllabic word on individual index cards. Use ten new words each subsequent session. During each session, use two or three words that are nonsense words that students pronounce using phonetic rules. Nonsense words should be used to ensure that students are applying the strategy steps and not just remembering the words as sight words. Once students master the strategy with monosyllabic words, introduce two-syllable multisyllabic words. These words follow similar phonetic rules as monosyllabic words. As with the monosyllabic word phase, include two to three multisyllabic nonsense words in each session.

The PHonological And Strategy Training Program (PHAST)

The PHAST program (Lovett, Lacerenza, and Bordern 2000) was developed to help students remediate their phonological skills and combines a number of phonological skills that we have previously mentioned. The five main components of the PHAST program are as follows:

- *Sounding Out Strategy* This strategy teaches children letter-sound correspondence and segmentation and blending of words (oral segmentation and blending at first, then print-based segmentation and blending of sounds). Initially, children say the segmented sounds slowly, from left to right, and then practice saying them fast.

- *Rhyming Strategy* This strategy teaches children to recognize words by analogy. Children are taught the rhyming rule: words with the same spelling pattern usually rhyme. Children are then taught to recognize rhyming pairs of words and are asked to generate their own rhyming words. A keyword is introduced (for example, *and*), and then students are introduced to words that contain the spelling pattern (for example, *hand, band, brand*, and so on). Students are next taught to use a keyword to pronounce unknown words (for example, *strand*), by recognizing the spelling pattern of the keyword (that is, *and*) to pronounce the unknown word.

- *Peeling-Off Strategy* This strategy teaches students to use their knowledge of affixes to peel off the prefix and suffix of an unknown multisyllabic word to get to the root word. Once students do this, they pronounce the root word, and then blend the affixes back with the root word to pronounce the entire word. Throughout the entire PHAST program, as many as 75 affixes are taught to students at a rate of about one to two per day. Students review their list of affixes in isolation and practice recognizing them in multisyllabic words. The "peeling-off" refers to students pulling off the affix (for example, *pre-* and *-tion*) at the beginning or end of an unknown word (for example, *presumption*) to try to pronounce the word.

- *Vowel Alert Strategy* In the vowel alert strategy, students are taught to try to pronounce the vowels in a word using different pronunciations.

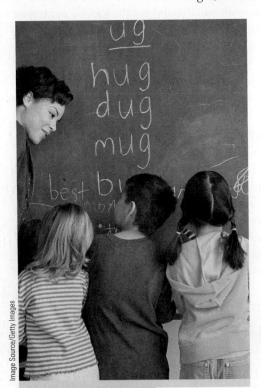

Learning word parts is an important skill in early reading.

For example, if two vowels are present such as in *tread*, the student is taught to pronounce the word with the *ea* sound as in *eat*. If that effort does not yield the correct pronunciation, students are taught to try a second sound as in the sound in *head*.

- *I SPY Strategy* Using this technique, students are taught to look for small, familiar parts of an unknown multisyllabic word. Specifically, children are taught to look for words within words, particularly in larger words such as compound words. For example, if students come across the word *daytime*, they are taught to "I Spy" *day* and then "I Spy" *time* to pronounce correctly the entire word, *daytime*.

Initially, each strategy is taught separately. After learning each, students are taught to use all of the strategies together to read unknown words. In this phase, called the *game plan*, students are taught to use four steps: *choose, use, check,* and *score/rechoose*. When students are given a word to decode (for example, *contender*), they first choose a strategy or strategies. For the example, the student might *choose* the peeling-off strategy and the rhyming strategy to pronounce the word. In the *use* step, students would peel off the *con* and *er* to get to the root word *tend*. Next the student would use the rhyming strategy to recognize the spelling pattern *end* of the keyword *bend*. Because students recognize *bend*, they pronounce *tend*. In the *check* step, students stop to think if they are using the strategy correctly and, if so, they put the parts back together to pronounce the word *contender*. Finally, during the *score/rechoose* step, if the students correctly pronounce the word, they *score* and congratulate themselves. If the strategies did not work, they go back to *choose* and begin again.

> **THINK BACK TO THE FIRST CASE** with Latasha . . .
>
> 2. *Name and describe a phonological awareness activity that you would use with Latasha.*
>
> A number of different phonological activities could be used with Latasha. For example, to assist Latasha with recognizing short vowel sounds, the teacher could use "Rhyming Word Bingo." Or, to assist Latasha with recognizing initial letter sounds, the teacher could use the activity "Clapping Words and Phonemes." Likewise, teachers could use the phonological awareness strategy or the PHonological And Strategy Training program (PHAST) to teach phonological skills such as segmenting, blending, rhyming, and other skills to students like Latasha.

Wilson Reading System

The Wilson Reading System is a commercial reading program that is used to teach students how to decode words fluently and accurately (Wilson 1996). The program was designed for students who are reading and/or spelling below grade level, including students who have poor auditory skills and ELL students. The program is based upon the principles of the Orton-Gillingham model and includes direct instruction and multisensory components (Yampolsky and Waters 2002). (For a more detailed description of the Wilson Reading System, see Wilson (1996), or see Ritchey and Goeke (2006) for more detailed description of Orton-Gillingham-based instruction.) In the Wilson Reading System, the lesson is broken down into ten parts that can be taught all in one session or can be broken into two sessions (for example, parts one through eight in session one and parts nine and ten in session two).

The ten parts to each lesson include:

1. Quick drill sound cards. The teacher shows students a sound card (that is, a letter), and the students say the letter name and corresponding sound.
2. Teach and review concepts for reading. The teacher makes words with sound cards (letters), and the student segments the words using a finger-tapping procedure and blending sounds. In more advanced lessons, syllable and suffix cards can be used.
3. Present word cards. Instead of creating words from sound cards, the teacher presents entire words on word cards, and the student reads words as fluently as possible.
4. Read word lists. The student reads words in a word list from the student reader, which contains short stories with easy-to-read words.
5. Conduct sentence reading. The student reads sentences in the Student Reader, silently at first and then aloud, and incorporates *scooping* of a few words at a time to improve fluency. Scooping involves breaking sentences into meaningful phrases in which students move (or scoop) their finger under a few words at a time as they read sentences (Reutzel and Cooter 2005).
6. Quick drill sounds. The teacher says a sound, and the student finds the sound card with the matching letter. This might also include having the student make letters on the table surface or in sand for tactile-kinesthetic support.
7. Review concepts for spelling. The student spells words from word cards using the finger-tapping procedure. In more advanced lessons when using multisyllabic words, the student names and spells affixes, syllables, and/or base words.
8. Complete written work. The teacher orally presents sounds (single words or sentences) that the student repeats, spells aloud, and writes in a composition book.
9. Read passages. The student silently reads a short passage, visualizes and retells the passage information, and then the student reads orally.
10. Check listening comprehension. The teacher reads a passage while the student visualizes story; the teacher asks questions to aid visualization, and the student retells the story.

Teaching Word Patterns and Syllabication to Students with Mild Disabilities

The ability to use word or spelling patterns in words as a decoding strategy is beneficial for children to decode unknown words (Ehri et al. 2001; White 2005). This technique, sometimes referred to as *analogy-based phonics* (White 2005), teaches children to decode an unknown word (for example, *clap*) by using a known word (for example, *nap*). When taught systematically as part of phonics instruction, children can use the technique to decode unknown words in isolation and in context, particularly when it is taught in context. In fact, research has found that reading by using analogy is easier for children with disabilities because it eliminates the need to blend segmented phonemes (Ehri and Robbins 1992; Walton, Walton, and Felton 2001).

Word Pattern Activities

Teaching students word patterns helps them break down polysyllabic words into recognizable parts. The following are two activities that help students become proficient at recognizing word parts:

- **Home Run Patterns.** The purpose of this activity is help students recognize patterns in words. Prior to the game, the teacher cuts out a small baseball bat from brown construction paper and cuts out small (2-inch by 2-inch) blank squares on white paper. On these white squares, the teacher writes one-letter consonants. The teacher also constructs baseballs (about 5 inches in circumference) from white paper with two-letter words (for example, from word groups such as *at, an, et, en, ot, on,* and so on) written on them. The game begins when the teacher places a baseball to the board and explains to students that the ball will change when they hit the ball with the bat. Prior to each hit, the teacher temporarily tapes a consonant square. As students make a hit, the teacher removes the consonant square and places it next to the ball to spell a new word (for example, using the bat with an *s* square taped to it, the teacher swings and hits the *at* ball to form the word *sat*). The teacher then removes the *s* square, adds a different consonant square to the bat, and then asks a student to hit the next one. Once the child hits the ball, by adding the square to the baseball, the child says the newly formed word. A variation of this would be to add consonant blends or clusters to the consonant squares (for example, *st* added to the baseball *op* would form the new word *stop*), so that students are now pronouncing more difficult words. This game is especially popular in spring when T-ball and baseball season begins.
- **Changing Words.** The purpose of this game is help children understand that changing one letter in a word changes the entire word and that recognizing patterns in word can help them pronounce unknown words. Begin by writing a short word on the board (for example, *pin*). Challenge the students to change the word by substituting only one letter in the word to create a new real word. For example, if we change the *i* in *pin* to *a*, the new word becomes *pan*. If we then change the *n* in *pan* to a *t*, the new word becomes *pat*. If we change the *p* to a *c*, the new word becomes *cat*. Once students run out of variations of new words, the teacher can suggest that students change two letters in the word (for example, *cat* can change to *that*). Encourage them to use consonant blends and clusters to make the game more challenging.

Syllabication of Words

Syllabication is considered an important skill for children to learn to read large (polysyllabic) words (Shefelbine, Lipscomb, and Hern 1989). In fact, poor readers often rely too heavily on segmentation and blending skills, as opposed to using syllabification structures (Bhattacharya 2006), leading to the incorrect pronunciation of polysyllabic words. The two skills that serve as a means for determining unknown words involve using context clues and syllabication strategies. When students use context, they are instructed to skip over the unknown word and try to determine the word based upon the context of the sentence and preceding sentence. When students use syllabication strategies, they try to break the word into recognizable "chunks" to pronounce the word. The assumption is that children have a store of words that they can use to match up with parts of the unknown word.

Several studies have been conducted in which students with and without mild disabilities were taught syllabication techniques to successfully read polysyllabic words (Bhattacharya and Ehri 2004; Cunningham 1980; White 2005).

Analogy Strategy

Cunningham (1980) suggested using a compare/contrast process (or analogy strategy) to help children determine unknown polysyllabic words. This technique is based on the premise that students can determine the unknown word by using similar known words. For example, when students come across an unknown word from their reading, they should ask, "Are there parts of the word that look like words that I already know?" If so, students should apply a known part of the word to the unknown word. For example, if the word *cantankerous* were used, students would look for parts of similar-sounding words within the unknown word. The child might see the familiar words, *cant, tank, er* and *us.* The belief is that children already have these known words in memory, and can find them using this compare/contrast process. If students do not have a store of known words, then the teacher would review or provide familiar words to help the child pronounce an unknown word. To practice this skill, Cunningham (1980) gave students a "mystery word" that consisted of the number of letters from the word (that is, the mystery word *resolution* was given as ten blanks), along with familiar words (*absolute, rebellion, and attention*). In this mystery word game, the teacher pronounced each word, gave its definition, and gave each in a sentence. The goal of the game was for students to determine which clue word contains the beginning, middle, or end part of the mystery word. Next, students were to guess the unknown word by using the familiar words (that is, the student would ask, "Does the mystery word end like *attention*?"). If yes, the teacher would fill in the end part of the mystery word (*-tion*), and the students would continue guessing (middle like *absolute (-solu-)* and beginning like *rebellion (re)*. After two weeks of training (or after solving 78 different mystery words), students were successful at increasing their decoding skills of unknown polysyllabic words.

Cunningham (1987) also suggests the following three games: "Mystery Word Match" (that is, compare/contrast that was previously described), "Word Construction and Demolition," and "Guess My Consonants." In the Word Construction and Demolition game, students begin with a root word, *nation*, and add affixes to build the word into a large polysyllabic word. For example, students add *-al* to create *national*, add *-ize* to create *nationalize*, add *inter-* to form *internationalize*, and finally add *-tion* to create *internationalization*. The purpose of this game is to help students understand that large polysyllabic words can be broken down (that is, by demolition) into smaller known words. In another game, students can be given a sentence that contains a mystery word with blank spaces (one space for each missing consonant) but with the vowels written in the correct location among the blanks. Next, students read the sentence and guess letters (one at a time) to determine the word.

Graphosyllabic Procedure

Bhattacharya and Ehri (2004) taught students a graphosyllabic procedure for determining unknown words. The following rules were used:

1. Every syllable has a vowel in it, and there is only one vowel sound per syllable.
2. Each letter can go with only one syllable. (In other words, you cannot use the same letter in two different syllables.)
3. The vowel sounds of the syllable should be as close as possible to the whole word (for example, *mustard* should be pronounced like *must-ard* or *mus-tard*, not like *muse-tard*).

The training consists of the teacher explaining and modeling the correct way to segment a word into syllables. In doing so, the teacher presents students with a model word (*finish*) on an index card, reads the whole word aloud, says the word in syllables (*fin-ish*), and raises one finger for each syllable. Next, the teacher tells students that the word has two syllables; she tells students to use their fingers to spell the letters for each syllable, and finally, blend the syllables together to say the whole word. Students then practice breaking down words into syllables while the teacher provides feedback. Several different ways of dividing words are considered acceptable (*finish* could be pronounced *fin-ish* or *fi-nish*). Many of the syllabication rules can be learned using the first-letter mnemonic CLOVER (Learning Disabilities Association of Minnesota, 2004).

- **Syllabication Rules for Pronouncing Polysyllabic Words**

  The following are syllabication rules for pronouncing polysyllabic words:

  1. **Check for affixes.** Check the unknown word for prefixes and suffixes. Remove any prefixes or suffixes that are present. In some cases, students should be formally taught affixes and their meanings.
  2. **Use the acronym CLOVER.** CLOVER is an acronym for the six major syllable types found in the English language. Use CLOVER to break the remaining word into syllables.
  3. **C Closed syllable.** A closed syllable has a short vowel sound and is followed by a single or double consonant (for example, *at, ex, un, ment, ness, black*). Keep double consonants together with vowel and divide off as a unit (for example, *ex/pect, dis/tress*).
  4. **L -le syllable.** An *le* syllable represents a consonant before *le* (for example, *ble, tle, dle, zle*). Divide off at beginning consonant along with *le* syllable (for example, *bot/tle, puz/zle, bat/tle*).
  5. **O Open syllable.** If an open syllable has a long vowel sound and ends in a vowel (*o, a, be, re, tri*), divide off after the vowel sound (for example, *mo/ment, ti/ger*).
  6. **V Vowel pair or double vowel.** For syllables with a vowel combination that makes a long vowel sound (*ai, ay, aw, oa, oo, oi, ou, ow, ee, ea, ie, ei, ue*), keep vowel pairs together, keep consonants before or after it, and divide off after the ending consonant (*train/er, con/geal, bea/gle*).

7. **E Vowel and consonant with silent *e*.** This syllable has a long vowel sound and the *e* at the end is silent. Divide off as one unit (for example, *re/mote, com/pete, des/pite, re/late*).

8. **R R-controlled.** This is a syllable containing an *r*-controlled vowel (for example, *ar, or, er, ir, ur, ear, our*). Keep vowel(s) and *r* together and divide off (for example, *chapt/er*).

Word Identification Strategy

The word identification strategy was developed by Lenz et al. (1984) and is meant to assist students in identifying unknown words. The key words are action words that prompt students to perform a specific step. An important part of the strategy training involves teaching students an extensive lists of affixes (prefixes and suffixes) and the meaning of each. Like other strategies from University of Kansas Center for Research on Learning, this follows the eight-stage training process (see Chapter 9).

The first-letter mnemonic **DISSECT** (see Box 5.3) should prompt students to dissect or cut words apart to read them. The first step, *discover*, prompts students to skip an unknown word, read the rest of the sentence, and then use the information to guess the unknown word. If students still have difficulty, they should proceed to the next step, *isolate*. In the *isolate* step, students should look at the first few letters to determine if they can identify a prefix. If a prefix is present, students draw a box around the prefix. If not and if the students still can't identify the word, they should go to the fourth step, *separate*. In the *separate* step, the students box off the suffix, if any. In next step, *say*, students should try to say the stem. The students should say all three parts (prefix, stem, and suffix), if recognized, together. If unable to pronounce the stem, the students should move to the *examine* step of the strategy. In this step, the students examine the stem using the "rules of twos and threes." If they can now read the stem using these rules, the students then combine the prefix, stem, and suffix together to pronounce the word. If, however,

---

BOX 5.3   **WORD IDENTIFICATION STRATEGY—DISSECT**

D Discover the context.

I Isolate the prefix.

S Separate the suffix.

S Say the stem.

E Examine the stem using the "Rules of Twos and Threes"

     Rule 1: If a stem begins with (a) a vowel, divide off the first two letters; or (b) a consonant, divide off the first three letters.

     Rule 2: If you can't make sense of the stem after using Rule 1, take off the first letter of the stem and then use Rule 1 again.

     Rule 3: When two different vowels are together, try making both of the vowel sounds (*diet*). If this does not work, try pronouncing them together using only one of the vowel sounds (*believe*).

C Check with someone.

T Try a dictionary.

| **CASE 5.2** | **Trouble with Casey** |

Case Introduction

Now that you have worked through the first case in this chapter, you should feel comfortable addressing issues in a second case. In this case, two teachers work together in an inclusion classroom to meet the needs of all the students, but, in particular, the learning needs of young Casey.

Karen Watson currently works as a first-grade teacher at Rosewood Elementary School in North Carolina. Karen has been working with Lucy Taylor, the special education inclusion teacher, in her classroom for only a month. Still fairly new to each other, they are both working out the "kinks" in the classroom. The inclusion classroom is a mix of general education first-grade students and six special education students.

After undergoing some educational testing last month, Casey Percy was identified as having ADHD under the OHI category. Casey's main academic difficulties continue to occur in reading; however, her inattention and hyperactivity also affect other academic areas. In reading, she has specific problems with phonological awareness. For example, Casey knows her initial letter sounds, but often forgets how to blend sounds together or confuses words with similar spellings (for example, *can* for *cat*). After her parents complained this year that she could not "sit still" and was "always bugging neighborhood children," along with teacher concerns, the school decided to move forward in testing Casey to see if she were eligible for special education services. Now Casey can receive special education services in the inclusion classroom, eligible under OHI.

Because Casey is in the lowest reading group, she has peers who have similar problems. This group typically works on early reading skills as they begin to learn to read. During a recent reading class, Casey seemed to be having an especially difficult time during the "Cap Game." In this game, students were working with "word groups." The word group that particular day was *at*. Students were given a cap (each contained a new consonant sound: *c, h, r, m,* and so on) and were to place it on the head to form a new word. Casey could pronounce the first combination (*cat*), but had a difficult time pronouncing new combinations. Despite that she knew each initial letter sound, she had difficulty blending them to pronounce the new words.

Later that day, as students left for home, Karen and Lucy met to recap the day and plan for the next day. Karen was the first to bring up Casey's difficulties and said, "Casey really had a rough time during reading. Do you think she'll ever catch on?" Lucy optimistically replied, "Let's hope." Next, the two teachers began brainstorming ideas to help Casey improve her phonological awareness skills. As the two sat down to co-plan lessons for the next day, they talked about how they could better integrate some of their ideas to help with Casey's reading problems.

CASE QUESTIONS

1. What early reading area would you target for remediation with Casey?
2. Name and describe two types of phonological awareness activities that you would use with Casey.

Chapter Question
ALERT

In this section, you will find information that answers a Chapter Question:

5. How can various reading skills be incorporated into a lesson to improve the reading skills of students with mild disabilities?

the students cannot pronounce the stem, they should *check* with someone. The students are taught to check with either the teacher or, if appropriate, another student. If no one is available, students should *try* a dictionary. In this final step, students look up the word and use the pronunciation guide to say the stem.

Putting It All Together: Incorporating Reading Skills into Lessons

As we have mentioned before, teaching students with mild disabilities to read involves teaching them multiple skills over time. For example, teaching sight words should be part of a larger reading lesson that might involve phonological awareness activities, reading in context activities, and listening comprehension

BOX 5.4

SAMPLE READING LESSONS

LESSON ONE:

- Sight words practice (10 minutes)
  - Students practice new sight words.
- Spelling sight words (5 minutes)
  - Using the same sight words, students practice spelling them while the teacher points out common patterns in them.
- Sight word games (10 minutes)
  - The teacher uses the sight words in a game format. For example, the teacher uses pairs of matching sight words in a memory game such as Concentration.
- Phonics activity (10 minutes)
  - The teacher teaches students common consonant and vowel combination in words by decoding and spelling the words.
- Oral reading (15 minutes)
  - Students spend about 15 minutes reading either a graded series trade book or basal reader. This activity is based upon the student's current sight word knowledge and phonological awareness level.

LESSON TWO:

- Sight word practice (10 minutes)
  - Students practice recently introduced sight words or review previously taught sight words.
- Spelling practice (5 minutes)
  - Students practice spelling sight words or other words that could be spelled phonetically.
- Silent and oral reading (20 minutes)
  - Students practice reading a passage silently and then read the same passage orally to improve their fluency and accuracy.
- Writing activity (15 minutes)
  - Students write sentences using sight words from current and previous practice sessions. The teacher monitors students for proper meaning of sentences, correct grammar, and correct spelling of words.

activities. Torgesen et al. (2001) developed an instructional reading program in which students with LD were introduced to a variety of reading activities, all within two 50-minute lessons (see Box 5.4). These students, between the ages of eight to ten years old, improved their reading skills; within one year following the training, 40 percent of them no longer needed special education services.

Basal Reading Series

Special education teachers regularly use basal readers or a basal reading series to teach children to read. Basal readers are books that contain short passages or stories that progressively become more difficult from the first few stories in each

TIPS FOR GENERALIZATION

Connecting Skills Together

Reading involves more than just a collection of phonics-based activities. Reading is a combination of skills that are built slowly over time. A combination of phonological awareness activities (learning the code), sight words, and connected reading activities (that is, using words in context) enable children to practice reading. Along with listening comprehension activities, such as teaching a child to answer questions to a story that the teacher reads to them, students will slowly learn to read simple stories. Early on in reading development, sight words are introduced and are often memorized, particularly during the first few lessons. Because sight words (sometimes referred to as "high-frequency" words) are seen in text repeatedly, students need exposure to them on a frequent basis. Essentially, basal readers are designed so that sight words are present in each story. Words from the first story repeat themselves in the next story (with a few more added), and words in successive stories are a reiteration of earlier learned words. Although the use of sight words is useful in learning how to read, students cannot learn all of the words needed to be a successful reader through sight words. Therefore, we teach phonological awareness skills so that students can segment (sound out) new words and blend those sounds together to pronounce the word. Segmenting skills also play a useful role in helping children determine vowel sounds for unfamiliar words. Rhyming also plays a supporting role as children sound out "vowel-sounding words" (rhyming words) and try to pick a match from long-term memory. Furthermore, using word patterns, children can match known words from prior knowledge with either matching words or word parts to decode unknown words.

The key to reading seems to be frequent exposure to reading skills, particularly those skills that can cross over or generalize from one activity to another. For example, if working on the phoneme *p* during a phonological awareness activity, teachers can use it in context in words as children learn sight words and as they read *p* words in a basal story. The more generalizing that can occur in class, the easier it will be for the child to use skills in a new context. Of courses, using drill-and-practice activities with immediate feedback will ensure that children master skills, and constant feedback will prevent students from practicing errors or learning miscues.

book to those at the end. The books are highly organized and typically arranged on levels that correspond with grade levels. Similar to basal readers, leveled books are written to follow a specific "leveling criteria" (for example, based upon number of words, sentence length, complexity, predictability, and so on), which results in a graduated level of increasingly more difficult stories from one level to the next.

Beginning teachers usually prefer basal readers because the teacher guides come with preplanned activities that correspond with each story and include pre-reading and post-reading activities. An advantage of using a basal reader is that new sight words (or vocabulary) are introduced in small increments in each story and, typically, the stories build on sight words learned in previous stories. Basal readers have been used in the United States since the 1860s, beginning with the McGuffey Readers. Over the years, others have included the once-popular Dick and Jane series. Despite the popularity of basal readers, some have criticized them as being too structured, focusing too much on teaching students isolated skills, rather than encouraging children to read for the simple joy and love of reading (Shannon 1993).

THINK BACK TO THE SECOND CASE with Casey . . .

1. What early reading area would you target for remediation with Casey?

Like Latasha, you could target a number of phonological skills for remediation with Casey that could include: segmenting letter sounds, rhyming words, or blending letter sounds.

2. Name and describe two types of phonological awareness activities that you would use with Casey.

As mentioned earlier in the chapter, any number of phonological awareness activities, such as segmenting, blending, or rhyming activities could benefit Casey, as well as any of the phonological awareness strategies.

Research Evidence

Phonological Awareness Strategy. This strategy was used with second and third grade students with either MMR or LD (Boyle and Seibert 1997). The results indicated that from pre- to posttest, these children increased the number of monosyllabic and multisyllabic words that they were able to pronounce, and increased the correct pronunciation of words used during generalization, nonsense words, and unknown words.

Word Identification Strategy. This strategy was used with seventh, eighth, and ninth grade students with learning disabilities (Lenz and Hughes 1990). The results from the study indicated that trained students were able to reduce the number of errors from baseline (range was 6.3 to 20.5 errors) to post-training (range was 0 to 6.4 errors). In addition, the average baseline score for the group's reading ability level materials was 39 percent and increased to 88 percent after training, while the baseline average score for students on grade-level materials was 39 percent and increased to 58 percent after training. Still, in another article Bremer, Clapper, and Deshler (2002) reported the results of two studies that were previously conducted. In the first study, ninth-grade students who were identified as struggling secondary readers were taught to use the word identification strategy. The results demonstrated that students showed greater gains when compared to a comparison group of students. In another study, sixth-grade students with low achievement who received the strategy improved from pre- to posttest scores on measures of decoding and comprehension.

Syllabication Techniques. According to Cunningham (1980), students who used the compare/contrast method improved their ability to pronounce words in isolation and in context more than those in a control group. In addition, students trained to use the compare/contrast method were also able to read polysyllabic words one week after testing. In the study completed by Bhattacharya and Ehri (2004), third-grade students with reading problems who were trained to use the graphosyllabic procedure outperformed students who were taught to read polysyllabic words as whole words; as well, they outperformed a control group of students on measures of segmenting words into syllables by counting and segmenting words by circling syllables.

CHAPTER SUMMARY

How students read can be explained by one of three models: top-down, bottom-up, or interactive. As students learn to read, they often use one or more of these models. Depending upon the difficulty of the text and the student's background knowledge of the topic, students may use different models at different times. As they learn to read, they progress through several stages, from initially understanding that spoken words are related to text, to learning *how* to read words, to later stages where they read to understand different viewpoints and read for the enjoyment of learning. Although most students transition smoothly through these stages, students with mild disabilities often encounter problems as they learn to read. Some students lack phonological awareness, while others lack reading fluency and/or comprehension strategies. Throughout this text, we have described not only reading skills that

should be taught to students, but also strategies and techniques that teachers can use to help students remediate skill deficits in reading. Finally, we have emphasized that teaching reading should be more than just teaching disparate skills. Instead, reading skills should be combined into literacy lessons that teach students components of several related skills (for example, sight words, phonics, fluency, comprehension). For example, an initial early reading lesson might involve teaching sight words for five minutes, having students practice in a "connected reading" activity for ten minutes, listening to a story read by the teacher and answering questions for ten minutes, and completing a worksheet on one initial letter sound for ten minutes. Only through a variety of skills and applications of skill combinations do students with mild disabilities learn how to read.

KEY TERMS

Basal Reading Series, 151

Blending, 151

Bottom-Up Model of Reading, 150

Consonant Blends/Clusters, 151

Consonant Diagraphs, 151

Decoding, 150

Decoding Skills, 151

Digraphs, 151

Diphthongs, 151

Phonemes, 151

Phonics, 165

Phonological Awareness, 151

Phonological Deficit Hypothesis, 157

Pseudo-Reading, 153

Segmenting, 151

Sight Words, 151

Structural Analysis, 151

Top-Down Model, 150

Vowel Diagraphs, 151

Word Attack, 157

APPLICATION ACTIVITIES

Using information from the chapter, complete the following activities that were designed to help you apply the knowledge that was presented in this chapter.

1. Visit a reading website like http://www .readwritethink.org (or other reading websites), and review an *early reading lesson plan*. Identify the early reading skills being taught. List two

other activities from this book that could be used to teach one of the skills described in the lesson.

2. Design a literacy lesson composed of different reading activities that will help children develop reading skills. Be sure to include lesson objectives and one or two state standards in your lesson. (See Appendix A on the book-specific website for a template.)

3. You are assigned a new first-grade student who has reading deficits in word attack. Describe some activities that you could use in your classroom to improve his word-attack skills.

4. Watch the Video Case entitled *Elementary Literacy Instruction: A Balanced Literacy Approach.* List each of the instructional techniques described in this chapter that you observe the teacher and students using.

TECHNOLOGY RESOURCES FOR IMPROVING READING SKILLS

Literally hundreds of different types of reading software programs are available for students, as well as different websites to help teachers better understand how to teach reading to students with and without disabilities. Of the software programs, each covers different reading skills or strategies. Special education teachers must match up student skill deficits with those software programs that best review that specific skill. The websites also provide different perspectives on teaching of reading, and most provide resources for dealing with struggling readers.

The following websites provide information about software or websites for early reading skills:

Leap into Phonics by Bright Start Inc.
www.leapintolearning.com

This software program teaches children to recognize letters and letter sounds through a slow, easy progression. It incorporates skill-and-drill activities to teach segmenting and blending skills to students.

3D Froggy Phonics by Ingenuity
www.ingenuityworks.com

This software teaches letters and letter sounds through a drill-and-practice process that is filled with fun games and activities. This program also has an assessment component that helps evaluate skill acquisition.

Let's Go Read! series by Edmark
www.learningcompany.com

The Let's Go Read! series incorporates both phonics and whole language activities to help children learn letters and letter sounds. In this program, students imitate and identify letter sounds, discriminate different letters, solve puzzles to form letter shapes, and identify letter sounds in words.

Word Munchers Deluxe by MECC
www.mecc.com

In this game, students must move a "muncher" to squares that contain the correct answer to questions posed. They must then "munch" the answer before being eaten by a Troggle. This game helps students practice skills in the following areas: grammar, phonics, vocabulary, and sentence structure.

RTI Action Network
www.rtinetwork.org

A program of the National Center for Learning Disabilities, this website provides excellent resources for learning about and implementing RTI in schools. It provides resources in the form of readings, such as a discussion of interventions for different tiers, RTI blogs and discussion boards, webinars, as well a wealth of other resources.

International Reading Association
www.reading.org

This professional organization provides materials and information to teachers and other educators who teach reading. It offers professional publications and web resources (such as lesson plans and parent resources), as well as a variety of other resources to help teach beginning readers, adolescents, and struggling readers.

LD OnLine
www.ldonline.org

This website is designed for parents and teachers of students with learning disabilities (LD). It provides great resources for helping children with disabilities improve their reading skills. The "In Depth" section of the website has an area dedicated to reading that includes articles, questions, and answers about addressing reading problems and recommended books.

International Dyslexia Association
www.interdys.org

This professional website is for educators, parents, and children. It provides resources for a wide variety of audiences and links to technology resources for most academic areas.

Reading Rockets
www.readingrockets.org

Reading Rockets is a national multimedia project offering information and resources on how young children learn to read and how to teach struggling readers. It provideds strategies, techniques, books, and other resources for both parents and teachers.

Visit the book-specific website at www.cengage.com/education/ boyle for a variety of study tools such as web links, tutorial quizzes, glossary/flash cards, bonus material not included in the text, and more.

The premium website offers access to additional materials, including the Video Cases. Go to www.cengage.com/login to register or purchase access.

Later Reading: Strategies and Techniques

6

CHAPTER QUESTIONS

1. What is reading fluency, and what are the components that make up fluency?

2. What is reading comprehension, and what are the different types of comprehension questions?

3. What fluency and comprehension problems do students with mild disabilities encounter in reading?

4. What strategies and techniques would be useful to improve the vocabulary skills of students with mild disabilities?

5. What strategies and techniques would be useful to improve the fluency skills of students with mild disabilities?

6. What strategies and techniques would be useful to improve the reading comprehension skills of students with mild disabilities?

How proficient are secondary level students with mild disabilities in the area of reading?

On average, students with mild disabilities can read only at the fourth-grade level when entering high school (Deshler and Schumaker 2006). Others have found that, compared to students' actual grade level, secondary students with disabilities are on average 3.6 years behind their grade level in reading, with 26 percent of those being five or more grade levels behind, and another 41 percent that are 3 to 4.9 grade levels behind in reading (Wagner et al. 2003). Moreover, the 2005 National Assessment of Educational Progress (NAEP) in reading indicated that among twelfth grade students with disabilities, 70 percent scored below the *basic level**, compared to only 24 percent of nondisabled students (Grigg, Donahue, and Dion 2007). Similar distributions were found for eighth grade students who took the 2007 NAEP, with 66 percent of the students with disabilities scoring below the basic-level reading (Lee, Grigg, and Donahue 2007). Thus, students with disabilities who have reading problems will more than likely have difficulty gaining information from textbooks and other school resources. At the secondary level, achievement of three to five years behind in reading is likely to hinder students' ability to access the general education curriculum and to tackle the increasingly complex academic content called for by most state standards tests (Wagner et al. 2003).

In Chapter 5, you learned about reading models, stages of reading, and reading techniques, strategies, and activities for addressing the early reading problems of students with mild disabilities. In this chapter, you will learn about later reading methods and strategies. This chapter is mainly about reading fluency and comprehension; yet, we will weave into this content information about various reading models to help you better understand how students learn to read. We will also discuss skills and strategies for addressing students with reading fluency and comprehension problems. Finally, we describe numerous reading interventions (for example, classwide peer tutoring); however, if searching for additional reading interventions, including commercial reading programs (for example, Reading Recovery), please access the What Works Clearinghouse website (http://ies.ed.gov/ncee/wwc).

Just as with Habib in the case 6.1, reading can be an exasperating experience for students with disabilities. Despite having general proficiency in the basic skills of reading, many students find reading a laborious process, and fluency and comprehension remain challenges for them. Because students with mild disabilities have processing and memory problems that interfere with learning, acquiring reading skills can often become a discouraging and frustrating experience. Further, even when English is not an elementary student's primary language, reading instruction in school typically begins with English phonics instruction (Reese et al. 2000; Swanson, Sáez, and Gerber 2006). Such children develop conversational proficiency in one language but begin to develop reading

---

*Of the three categories (basic, proficient, advanced), basic represented the lowest category of performance. Under the basic category, students should be able to identify and relate aspects of the text to overall meaning, make simple inferences, recognize interpretations, relate text ideas to their own personal experiences, and draw conclusions.

CASE 6.1   I Give Up!

Case Introduction

In this case, you will read about a student who has trouble with later reading skills. As you read the case, you will see that his teacher has tried a number of different teaching techniques, and yet Habib is still having problems.

At the end of the case, you will find case questions. These questions are meant to serve as points for reflection. Of course, if you can answer them immediately, you should do so, but you may want to wait to answer them until you have read the portion of the chapter that pertains to the particular case question. Throughout the rest of the chapter, you will see the same questions. As you see them, try to answer them based upon the portion of the chapter that you just read.

Habib is a third-grade student who was recently classified as having mild mental retardation. He was classified due to his low cognitive and achievement scores. The reading specialist and a member of his eligibility committee, Niki Gersten, has been working at his school, Poole Elementary, for several years. During her recent assessment, she found that Habib mainly had problems with fluency and comprehension. His fluency problems stem from the fact that Habib stumbles over many of the second and third grade-level words found in his literature reading series. He also has problems recalling facts and details from stories and cannot stay on task for long periods of time.

Two weeks after his eligibility determination, Niki began working with him. Niki has tried a number of different activities, including reviewing sight words prior to reading the story, having Habib spell his sight words, alternating between reading aloud to him and having him read aloud to her, and having Habib take the story home to read to his parents. Despite her best teaching efforts, Habib's current average reading rate is 57 words correct per minute (cwpm). This is well below the recommended reading rate of 79 cwpm for a third-grade student.

During a recent reading session, Niki had Habib read the story "Best Wishes, Ed," by James Stevenson (2003). The story is about a wayward penguin that floats off on an iceberg that has split in two as he sleeps. As Habib read the passage, he made numerous errors.

The passage went as follows:

"One night when Ed was asleep, he heard a loud noise, like ice cracking. Ed thought it was a dream. When he woke up, he saw that the island of ice was cracking in two. He was all alone on an island of his own. Ed's friends looked very little as his island floated away. Ed watched until he couldn't see them anymore."

As Habib was reading the passage, Niki recorded his miscues. Throughout the passage, Habib made several miscues including mistaking *nose* for *noise*, *creek* for *cracking*, *isand* for *island*, and *wake* for *watched*. He also skipped the word *until*, and did not seem to notice or self-correct. Upon finishing this passage, Niki asked Habib two questions. For the first question, she asked, "When Ed heard the ice cracking, what did he think was happening?" Habib answered that Ed seemed to be having a bad dream. Next, Niki asked, "When Ed's ice split, who else was with Ed as he drifted off?" Habib answered that his brother was with him when he floated off. Immediately, Niki told Habib that his answer was wrong and that Ed was alone when he floated away.

He then read the next passage:

"Then he walked all over the island. There was nobody on it at all. At last, he came to his own footprints again. Some birds flew over. Ed waved, but they did not wave back. 'I think I will be here the rest of my life,' Ed said. When the day was over, Ed wrote the words 'I GIVE UP' in the snow. Then he went to sleep."

During his reading, Niki again recorded errors. This time, Habib made fewer miscues. His miscues on this reading included mistaking *none* for *nobody*, *against* for *again*, and *wave* for *waved*. During this brief intermission, Niki again probed Habib with two questions. She asked him, "Was there anyone else on the island?" Habib answered. "No." When Niki probed further as to how he knew that nobody else was on the island, Habib responded, "It said there was nobody on it." The next question Niki asked was, "Why did Ed write the words, 'I GIVE UP' in the snow?" Habib answered that, "Ed was sleepy." Niki quickly restated her question to him, "Why did Ed give up?" Habib answered, "Because he was sleepy and wanted to go to sleep." (The answer Niki was looking for was that no one else was on the island, and Ed was tired of looking.) "Not really," said Niki, "Ed was tired of looking for everyone else and finally gave up."

continued

As Habib read the rest of the story, he made several more miscues and responded incorrectly to several of Niki's comprehension questions. With only two pages to go, Habib was at the end of his rope and was too exasperated to read anymore. Finally, he said to Niki, "I give up!" He soon followed with the statement, "Now, I know how Ed the penguin felt." Niki realized that, despite her best prodding and rewarding, she may have pushed Habib too far, and she felt badly. She gave him a sticker (of a penguin), told him he did a great job, and walked him back to his class.

CASE QUESTIONS

1. What skill area would you target to remediate for Habib in reading?
2. What other skills would you, as the teacher, address?
3. Name and describe one type of fluency activity that you would use with Habib.

proficiency in another. Although they may appear proficient at the basic skills of reading, fluent reading and comprehension can be more challenging. It is up to you, as their special education teacher, to help students develop effective reading skills so that reading can become an enjoyable activity.

Chapter Question
ALERT

In this section, you will find information that answers a Chapter Question:

1. What is reading fluency, and what are the components that make up fluency?

The Role of Fluency in Becoming a Skilled Reader

As illustrated in the case about Habib, fluency and comprehension go hand in hand in terms of reading difficulties. They are probably the most common reading problems for older students with disabilities. These two components are inextricably tied together when students read. Although it may be possible for a student to read fluently and lack comprehension, it is nearly impossible for a child who has fluency problems to have successful comprehension.

Fluency is not necessarily a skill that first comes to mind when teachers think about teaching reading skills. In fact, some (Allington 1983) have called fluency the "neglected goal" of reading programs. It has been only recently that reading fluency has gained attention as an important aspect in learning how to read. This newfound interest stems mainly from the findings of the National Reading Panel (2000) that identified fluency as one of the five essential areas in teaching children to read (the five areas being phonemic awareness, phonics, fluency, comprehension, and vocabulary). Prior to this report, other researches have known the importance of fluency in helping children to become proficient readers, yet little was done to include it in the daily staple of activities found in reading programs. For example, LaBerge and Samuel's (1974) seminal research discussed the role of automaticity in reading and posited that fluent readers are those children who have mastered decoding subskills at an automatic level. Because of their mastery of decoding skills, their attention during reading is free to focus on meaning and comprehension. Because of their mastery of word recognition, fluent readers can chunk information into larger units that aid them in comprehension.

Components of Reading Fluency

Being a fluent reader is more than just being able to read fast. In fact, when someone reads fluently, he or she does not necessarily speak quickly, but the words sound natural and language-like (Stahl 2006). With this in mind, consider the three components of **reading fluency:** accuracy, rate, and prosody (Hudson, Lane, and Pullen 2005).

- **Accuracy** As students read, they need to read accurately (or read the words correctly) and in a smooth motion to understand the text. For readers to read words accurately, they must have the prerequisite skills of phonological awareness, word knowledge, and word-attack skills.
- **Rate** When we think of reading fluency, *rate* is perhaps the most common term associated with it. Rate typically refers to automaticity when reading words, such as reading sight words (in isolation or in connected readings), and is often associated with the "speed" at which students can read these words. Reading at an appropriate rate also involves reading quickly and effortlessly (Rasinski 2003). Usually teachers measure rate based upon the number of correct words read per minute or the amount of time it takes to complete a story.
- **Prosody** This term refers to reading "with expression." The belief is that students who can read with expression understand the author's message and tone (Prescott-Griffin and Witherell 2004). When reading with prosody or expression, students break sentences into *phrases* and correctly use stress, intonation, and duration as they read each phrase (Schreiber 1991). Readers who break sentences down into phrases are able to gain a deeper understanding of the text, rather than just reading individual words in the text. These students can use larger phrases and are then able to focus their attention on the meaning of the text. Good readers use both textual cues, such as punctuation, as well as other cues, such as knowledge of phonological and morphological rules. These rules enable students to place the proper stress while reading multisyllabic words, proper intonation (that is, high or low pitch) when pronouncing words, and proper duration (that is, saying a word quickly or elongating its pronunciation) when speaking these words.

Fluency Development and Its Role in Chall's Early Stages

As you recall from the previous chapter, Chall (1983) refers to one of the first stages of reading as **Stage 1: Initial reading or decoding stage.** During this stage, students focus on breaking the code of reading through the acquisition of phonological skills and knowledge of sight words. At this stage, students are immersed in texts that have stories that use *narrative text*. Stories with narrative text are rich in dialogue and imagery. Next, children move through **Stage 2: Confirmation, fluency, and ungluing from print stage.** During this stage, children master their decoding skills and automaticity with text. As they learn to read words with automaticity, they also learn how to read using text features, such as punctuation and chunking of words into phrases (Kuhn and Stahl 2000). Using these prosodic features, children now move one step closer toward understanding the author's message and intent. Fluency now becomes the main focus of reading with children so that they can practice their word attack and gain meaning from the text. Somewhere in Stage 2 or Stage 3, children are introduced to *expository text*. In the next stage, **Stage 3: Reading for learning the new,** children become fully immersed in expository text. In reading expository stories, children now face a new challenge, as the structure of the text changes from narratives that dealt with plot, characters, and sequences of events to passages that deal with main ideas and details (Kuhn and Stahl 2000). Prior comprehension skills and newly developed ones become even more critical in this stage, as text becomes more difficult to understand and children are introduced to increasingly more difficult vocabulary from content-area textbooks.

Ehri's Phases of Development in Sight-Word Learning

Although Chall's stages describe reading in broad terms, Ehri's phases describe the skill of reading *sight words*. As students move from Stage 1 through Stage 2 of Chall's model, they go through a series of phases to learn words by sight (Ehri 1995, 1998; Pikulski and Chard 2005). According to Ehri (1995), students learn all words—irregularly spelled as well as easily decodable words—through a process of reading that occurs throughout phases of development. As children progress through these phases, they begin to learn words by making multiple connections based upon a word's spelling, pronunciation, and meaning. Eventually, the most skilled readers learn words by breaking them down into chunks of letters. Ehri believes that grapho-phoneme knowledge is essential in learning how to read and that, along with early phonological and word-attack skills, learning to spell words is also critical because the two are intertwined as children learn to read words quickly and accurately. Ehri's four phases are *pre-alphabetic, partial alphabetic, full alphabetic,* and *consolidated alphabetic,* and are illustrated in Figure 6.1.

The first phase that children go through is the **pre-alphabetic phase.** In this phase, beginners connect visual attributes of the word and its letters to pronunciations and the meaning of the word. Children may learn *pasta* because the *S* in the middle looks like a pasta noodle. These visual cues are learned early for children and, although helpful in this phase, become unreliable as children

FIGURE 6.1

Ehri's Phases of Sight-Word Learning

Pre-alphabetic Phase

bed

Child learns bed *because he thinks it looks like an actual bed.*

Partial Alphabetic Phase

Child learns boot *by pronouncing "b" and "t" and remembers this word because it begins with a "b" sound and ends in a "t" sound.*

Full Alphabetic Phase

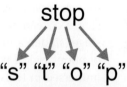

Child segments each sound and blends back together.

Consolidated Alphabetic Phase

Child uses knowledge of word parts.

Adapted from: Ehri, L. 1998. Grapheme-phoneme knowledge is essential for learning to read words in English. In *Word recognition in beginning Literacy,* ed. J. Metsala and L. Ehri, 18. Mahwah, NJ: Lawrence Erlbaum.

become exposed to other similarly spelled words. For most students, this first phase occurs through paired associates learning. As such, the cue is paired with the pronounced word and stored in long-term memory, rather than learning letters with their associated letter sounds.

In the next phase, the **partial alphabetic phase,** children begin to learn that certain letters are associated with letter sounds. In this phase, children begin to use phonological awareness skills to associate certain letters in the word to pronounce the word. When children first learn to read words, they often rely on the first and last letters of a word to pronounce it (Bowman and Treiman 2002). For example, as former teachers, we can remember children in this stage trying to pronounce the word *out.* They would open their mouths for the *o* sound and the *t* sound and then say the word *out.* They would use partial cues because they had not yet mastered all of the phonemes with graphemes. Although these students were well on their way toward developing phonological awareness, they often had difficulty with similarly spelled words.

Next, as children become more proficient with letters in words and their associated phonemes, they move into the **full alphabetic phase.** As children encounter familiar and new words, they are able to apply their phonological awareness skills to segment the word into letter sounds and blend these sounds back together to pronounce the word. In addition, children in this phase can now correctly discern between similarly spelled words. As children are able to read words as sight words, they can now alternate their attention between reading words on the page and constructing meaning from those words.

Finally, in the last phase, the **consolidated alphabetic phase,** children are able to pronounce words by recalling word parts or letter patterns. Typically, children learn word parts such as *ing, ion, est, ent,* or *able.* Children then use their knowledge of word parts when they encounter multisyllabic words in their reading. According to Ehri (1998), these letter patterns become part of the student's knowledge about reading and spelling. As such, spelling becomes part of the reading process. Accordingly, if children can spell words that they read, then it would make sense that these words would be stored rather strongly in memory and should improve their reading. As it turns out, research has confirmed that spelling instruction improves students' abilities to read and decode words (Uhry and Shepherd 1993).

Why Is Reading Fluency Important?

Fluency is important in learning to read for two main reasons. First, fluency is deeply intertwined with reading comprehension. For children to have the mental resources to comprehend the meaning of the text, they must be fluent readers. Fluent readers are able to switch their attention instantaneously back and forth from word recognition (or decoding) to understanding the meaning of the text being read. They not only have a store of sight words and efficient decoding skills, but they use comprehension monitoring strategies that help them to detect when the text does not make sense. Moreover, from a large-scale data analysis completed by the National Assessment of Educational Progress (NAEP) for reading, Pinnell and colleagues (1995) found a positive correlation between reading fluency and comprehension. Their work demonstrated that those students who rated higher on a fluency scale performed better on the NAEP reading assessment. Likewise, other researchers have found that fluency is highly correlated with reading comprehension (Deno 1985; Jenkins, Fuchs, et al. 2003a; Jenkins, Fuchs, et al. 2003b), and that interventions that increased fluency also increased reading comprehension (Kuhn and Stahl 2000).

Second, fluency helps readers understand the subtle or hidden meanings associated with an author's intent. Prosody enables readers to understand if the author is using irony or has stated things incorrectly in the text. A combination of background knowledge and prosody also probably helps students to fully understand an author's intent. Lack of fluency leaves little room for comprehension. In turn, this "inadequate capacity for comprehension robs reading of its inherent enjoyment because few resources are left for processing meaning, reflecting, becoming absorbed in a narrative, understanding humor, and using one's imagination" (Nathan and Stanovich 1991).

Understanding Reading Comprehension

Chapter Question
ALERT

In this section, you will find information that answers a Chapter Question:

2. What is reading comprehension, and what are the different types of comprehension questions?

Reading comprehension is the ability to understand what is read. Although other skills such as phonological awareness, phonics, fluency, and vocabulary are important skills to teach children, teachers should remember that the end goal of teaching children to read is comprehension. For readers, understanding text is a constructive process whereby readers use the text, prior knowledge of the topic, and comprehension skills and strategies to decode the text into meaningful units of connected knowledge. The keys to reading involve not only being able to say the word and know its meaning, but connecting it to prior knowledge throughout the process.

In reading, some view each unit of organized knowledge as a schema (plural is schemata) for a particular concept (Gunning 2000; Reutzel and Cooter 2005). A schema is defined as an "organized knowledge structure" (Gagne 1985), and can be thought of as a three-dimensional spiderweb. The topic is in the center of the web and is linked to features that characterize it. Schema theory attempts to explain how information is stored in long-term memory for different topics or concepts. For example, a simplified schema of the concept "fish" might look like the example in Figure 6.2. Each schema is linked to other schemata to form a complex of networks within one's long-term memory. When students read information, they are using prior knowledge of the topic to construct meaning. As the students read, they retrieve information from long-term memory into working memory. They then read and parse or chunk information that is read. This new information is then added to the retrieved schema to form newly reconstructed or elaborated schema that can be stored in long-term memory. This process occurs repeatedly until the students have completed the story (Gagne 1985). In doing so, students fill in new information from reading with existing information in the schema.

Types of Reading Comprehension Questions

In the last chapter, we discussed the different kinds of comprehension questions found in basal readers and textbooks. Authors use three main types of questions to check a student's comprehension of text (Applegate, Quinn, and Applegate 2002).

FIGURE 6.2

Schema of a Fish

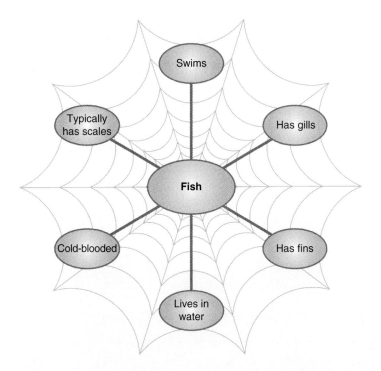

The first type is **textually explicit** or **literal comprehension** questions. A factual recall question is a type of textually explicit question. These types of questions are typically derived directly from the printed text on the page. For example, read the following sentences about a fictitious alien species:

> *Breggs raffled on the carbet squod.*
> *Breggs raffled loudly and quirked precociously.*

Now, answer the following questions.

1. Who raffled?
2. Where did Breggs raffle?
3. What did Breggs do?

Even though you knew nothing about this alien species, you were able to answer the questions by directly reading the text. These are known as textually explicit (or literal) questions. The answers can be found directly from the text or passage. The next type of comprehension question is **textually implicit** or **inferential.** With this type of question, your students are required to think and make conclusions about information that might not be readily evident from reading the passage or text. In other words, the students read "between the lines" to answer the questions. As you could guess, these questions are more difficult. Students find information to answer textually implicit questions by reading different parts of the story (textually derived) and then piecing together those parts to answer the question. Read the following excerpt:

> *Mr. Johnson opened his umbrella and decided to head home. The weather outside was beginning to turn ugly. His slow stroll turned into a run as the dark clouds opened up to dump their wet contents. The heavy wind banking off the tall buildings made the weather even*

worse. Even the sidewalks themselves took on a cascading effect. Finally, Mr. Johnson could barely see a few feet in front of him and had no choice but to hail a taxi.

Now, answer the following textually implicit questions:

1. What was the weather doing?
2. How was Mr. Johnson traveling before he caught a taxi?

Finally, the last type of question is **scriptally implicit.** This type of question requires students to use their script (or schema) of the topic to answer the question (Johnston 1997; Pearson and Johnson 1978). Using background and long-term memory of the topic, students must use this information to answer the question (Lipson and Wixson 1997; Pearson and Johnson 1978). In some cases, students may have to defend their responses by explaining how they derived their answers. Read the excerpt again and answer the following scriptally implicit questions:

1. What locality (for example, farm, home, city) was Mr. Johnson coming from?
2. Do you think Mr. Johnson got wet? Why or why not?
3. When Mr. Johnson began to run, what would other people on the same street be doing?

VIDEO CASE CONNECTIONS BOX

Watch the Video Case entitled *Reading Comprehension Strategies for Elementary Students: Questioning Techniques.* In the video, Ms. Page's students receive modeling and prompting to use oral language to express their reading comprehension. Identify whether each prompt is textually explicit, implicit, or scriptally implicit.

Other Elements of Reading Fluency and Comprehension

Not to be overlooked, other factors play a role in acquiring fluency and comprehension skills. These include prior knowledge of the topic, knowledge of text elements and text structure, language skills, "practice" with easy reading materials, and vocabulary development (Perfetti 1985).

As described by schema theory, prior background knowledge does make a difference in how students comprehend information. Students with prior background about a topic seem to attack the reading task differently and comprehend better than students who lack prior knowledge (McNamara and Kintsch 1996). The more background knowledge a student has about a topic, the more the student can connect with the ideas being read in the text. When key words or concepts are encountered, students are able to access this information from long-term memory and make connections to create "meaning" in working memory (Pardo 2004). Moreover, active processing during reading (via drawing on knowledge stored in long-term memory) seems to be critical in achieving high levels of comprehension (Gilabert, Martinez, and Vidal-Abarca 2005). This means that teachers should activate prior knowledge before reading, so that this knowledge is available for students to use for making connections with ideas from their reading. If students do not have adequate prior knowledge about a topic, it might be useful for teachers to build knowledge about an upcoming topic well beforehand; doing so immediately prior to reading may not help students to make "meaningful" connections (Gilabert, Martinez, and Vidal-Abarca 2005; McNamara and Kintsch 1996), because their new background knowledge will not have been adequately assimilated into long-term memory. Therefore, teachers should prepare days or weeks ahead of time by using informational books and having discussions on various topics (concepts). These planned-out, *knowledge-building sessions* will better prepare students to use new information and build a storehouse of knowledge about the concept.

Knowledge of text structures and elements of text are also useful for students to increase reading comprehension. With narrative text, knowledge of common **text elements** such as setting, characters, problem, solution, and outcome have been found to be useful to aid reading comprehension (Hall, Sabey, and McClellan 2005). In expository books, authors organize information using typical structural patterns called **text structure.** The following common text structures can be found in most expository text: description (or enumerative), problem/solution, comparison/contrast, cause/effect, and sequence (Hall, Sabey, and McClellan 2005; Pardo 2004). Pointing out these text structures before children read will enable them to organize the information during reading and, if accompanied by a visual organizer or framework, will enable students to understand the content of the passage better. The following are the common types of text structure:

- **Description** This type of text provides specific details about a topic, person, event, or idea.
- **Problem/solution** This type of text presents a problem, perhaps explains why it is a problem, and then offers possible solutions, usually settling on one solution as most appropriate.
- **Comparison/contrast** This type of text points out differences and similarities between two or more topics, including ideas, people, locations, or events. This text structure can be signaled by key words and phrases such as *like, as, still, although, yet, but, however,* and *on the other hand*.
- **Cause/effect** This type of text links events (effects) with their causes. Such text usually includes key words and phrases, called causal indicators to signal a cause-and-effect relationship structure. Some common causal indicators are *because, for, since, therefore, so, consequently, due to,* and *as a result*.
- **Sequencing** This type of text presents information in terms of a time or order sequence, such as the actions that led to an important historical event or the steps in a scientific process. This kind of structure most often includes signal words such as *first, second, last, earlier, later, now, then, next, after, during,* and *finally*.

Some experts (Perfetti and Marron 1995; Stahl 2006) also claim that language skills play a major role in the comprehension of text. Reading comprehension appears to be one subcomponent of language skills. In turn, language skills help

▶▶ ▶ ◀◀

V I D E O   C A S E   C O N N E C T I O N S   B O X

Watch the Video Case entitled *Metacognition: Helping Students Become Strategic Learners.* Teacher Julie Craven works first with a group of boys and then with a group of girls, coaxing their full expression by prompting them to consider the vocabulary they are reading or speaking. Suggest activities she could use to preview the same vocabulary prior to the students' reading.

students understand what they read. These language skills and experiences help frame our knowledge of a topic and help guide us as we read. Weaver (2002) suggests that, when we read, we use language skills and experiences, along with the syntactic and semantic cues in text, to help make sense of the text and to monitor comprehension. In fact, learning to read and write is highly correlated with oral language (Lipson and Wixson 1997).

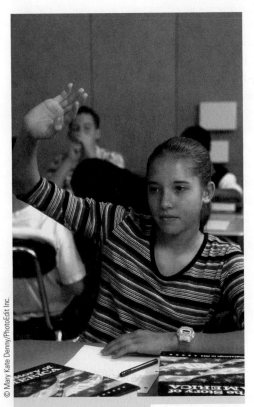

As students get older, they receive more information from textbooks.

Vocabulary represents another important area that relates to fluency and comprehension skills. Unfortunately, students with disabilities are at a real disadvantage when learning new vocabulary because they often lack strategies for learning words "in context," often do not engage in much independent reading (that is, where they would encounter new vocabulary words and be able to use them in new contexts) (Jitendra et al. 2004), and often lack background knowledge about the new vocabulary words. Therefore, before reading, teachers should consider spending time discussing and teaching vocabulary words, including finding what students already know about the vocabulary word or related words. In addition, having students learn vocabulary from text glossaries may not necessarily enable students to make meaningful connections that can be stored in long-term memory (Blachowicz and Fisher 2000). As such, teachers should use a variety of techniques to engage students when learning new vocabulary words.

Finally, practice makes perfect, or at least enables students with mild disabilities to become better readers. Reading a lot *does* matter (Adams 1990). Children need to read to practice the reading skills that they have learned. This may mean restricting students to certain books based upon individual reading levels, and showing children how to choose books based upon readability and text features. These steps will help students to have success and avoid frustration during reading. Highly effective teachers also find ways to maximize the amount of time their students have for easy reading by providing regular "blocks" of time when students can engage in independent silent reading or partner reading (Allington 2002). DEAR or "drop everything and read" time is one way to accomplish this in the school day.

Chapter Question

ALERT

In this section, you will find information that answers a Chapter Question:

3. What fluency and comprehension problems do students with mild disabilities encounter in reading?

Reading Fluency and Comprehension Difficulties in Students with Mild Disabilities

Research has shown that students with mild disabilities have numerous problems related to reading fluency and comprehension: they often (1) have slower reading rates—up to three times as slow when compared to their nondisabled peers (Jenkins et al. 2003a); (2) make more miscues (ibid.); (3) read in a slow, halting manner that impedes reading accuracy (Katzir et al. 2006); and (4) have a difficult time recognizing many words and acquiring word-reading proficiency

(Idol 1988; Jenkins et al. 2003a), making inferences in text (Cain and Oakhill 1999), and with general reading comprehension when compared to peers (Jenkins et al. 2003a).

Other research shows that these students perform poorly (when compared to peers) in reading rate and accuracy of words from a list and in context (Jenkins et al. 2003a). Many students with mild disabilities perform 1.5 to 2 grade levels or more below average on reading measures when compared to peers (Jenkins et al. 2003a), and, as time progresses, frequently fall farther behind as they struggle to keep up with their peers and as they encounter fewer grade-level words (Al Otaiba and Rivera 2006).

As mentioned earlier, these inefficient word recognition skills tax attentional resources and consume memory resources that are much needed for comprehension (Jenkins et al. 2003b). As a result, many students with mild disabilities have reading comprehension problems due to poor fluency, as well as due to other reading difficulties such as poor reading comprehension strategies. In one particular study, reading words in context (versus reading words in isolation) was the best predictor of comprehension (Jenkins et al. 2003b). It is surmised that when students read words in context, they are able to chunk words into meaningful phrases and are also able to use other cues from the context that assist them at reading (Jenkins et al. 2003a).

In addition to fluency problems, students with disabilities may also have problems with weak vocabularies, grammatical awareness, and background knowledge; poor retrieval strategies; and lack knowledge of text structure, all of which lead or contribute to poor comprehension (Venable 2003; Gersten et al. 2001). Other researchers claim that these students exhibit executive processing deficits and strategy deficits (Swanson 1999; Pressley 1991; Wong 1991) that contribute to or cause reading comprehension problems.

Finally, in terms of strategy knowledge, experts sum it up nicely when they point out that students with mild disabilities either do not have an appropriate reading strategy for a particular situation, may not know when to use the strategy (that is, lack metacognition of strategy use), or may not be willing to use a particular reading strategy even if they are taught it (Gersten et al. 2001). All three of these issues present challenges to teachers. However, teachers can take steps to ensure that students learn a strategy or technique, implement it with appropriate reading materials, generalize it to new settings and materials, and use it on a regular basis.

THINK BACK TO THE FIRST CASE with Habib . . .

1. What skill area would you target to remediate for Habib in reading?

Fluency would be one skill that you could target with Habib. More specifically, you could target fluency of words in context. You might want to also assess Habib's knowledge of words presented in a list. It would also be useful to assess his word-attack skills to determine whether he is using them appropriately.

2. *What other skills would you, as the teacher, address?*

Reading comprehension is another area that you could address. His fluency problems might be related to his comprehension problems. If so, you might want to target both fluency and reading comprehension.

Monitoring Reading Fluency and Comprehension

To know what kind of help your students need with fluency and comprehension, you need accurate information about their performance, not just your general impressions. Assessing fluency can be accomplished in any number of ways. Perhaps the most common is to select a starting point in a passage where you want your student to begin reading aloud and then time the student for one to three minutes. Count the number of words read correctly and divide by the total number of minutes read. This gives you the student's contextual reading rate in correct words per minute (cwpm). Complete this procedure a few times and average the cwpm rate. Of course, you should also note the reading level of the passage selected. (For an example, see the graph in the following Methods and Strategies Spotlight.)

METHODS AND STRATEGIES SPOTLIGHT

Using Curriculum-Based Measurement for Monitoring Reading Fluency

As we stress throughout this book, good teaching is data-driven. This means that you will determine how you teach (what teaching method you use) by the method's effectiveness for the target student, as shown by the student performance data that you gather. Recall that C-BM involves assessing one child on one skill over time. In the following case, this teacher chose to target correct words per minute (cwpm) because reading rate is highly correlated with reading comprehension. He set a goal cwpm based on the student's baseline performance and the expected rate for typical readers the student's age.

First, the teacher determined the student's current reading rate, which serves as the starting point or baseline (48 cwpm). Next, he determined a goal from the chart of oral fluency rates (Table 6.1) and from averaging reading rates from nondisabled peers (for example, 90 cwpm).

TABLE 6.1: Oral Fluency Rates of Words Read in Context

Grade	Correct Words Per Minute
1	25–50
2	50–90
3	70–110
4	95–125
5	110–140
6	125–150
7	130–160
8	135–170

Once the teacher decided upon 90 cwpm as the goal, he then connected the baseline point to the goal and drew in the aimline. Using different reading instructional methods, he determined that the student was not making adequate progress, so changes were needed in instruction. The "rule of thumb" is that a change in teaching methods/techniques should occur if data from three consecutive days fall below the aimline (Salvia and Hughes 1990), and should continue until the child's data is above the aimline.

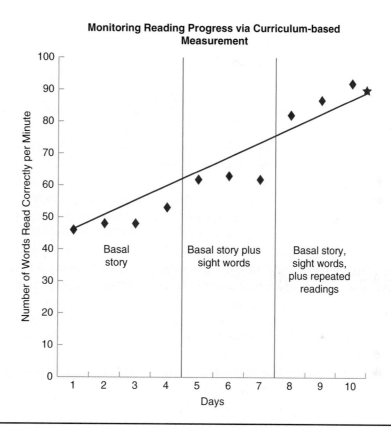

Monitoring Reading Progress via Curriculum-based Measurement

Because oral reading rates vary among sources, we developed a table (Table 6.1) that was derived from multiple sources (adapted from Hasbrouck and Tindal 1992; Hudson, Lane, and Pullen 2005; and Rasinski and Padak 2004). This table should serve as a guide to help teachers determine appropriate levels of fluency. Students who fall below the lower of the two numbers in a given range are probably experiencing problems with fluency and should receive assistance in improving their fluency. The middle or upper portions of each range (per grade level) can be used as goals for students to achieve (for example, 70-90 cwpm for a second grader).

Please keep in mind that this table represents an approximation of where children should be in terms of their reading fluency rates and, as with other fluency charts, should be used as a "guide." When using any fluency chart that illustrates a national norm group, always develop and incorporate local norms. In most cases, because your goal will be to integrate a child with mild disabilities into the general education's reading program, using students in the general education class as part of a local norm group makes sense. For special education teachers, this could mean choosing five to seven nondisabled students from general education (who are in the same grade as your target student) and then eliciting one- to three-minute reading samples from each of them. These general education students should be a representative sample of students from the class. Averaging the cwpm rates for this group of nondisabled students may give you a better "feel" for reading rates in your school and can be used in combination with Table 6.1 to determine the extent to which a child with disabilities has fluency problems. Although the use of these tables can guide you, others (Fuchs et al. 1993) recommend more moderate rates of improvement, based upon words per week increases (see Box 6.1).

Comprehension skills can also be targeted and charted using C-BM techniques. To assess comprehension, you could monitor percentage of correct answers to comprehension questions, percentage of correct paraphrases of paragraphs, or performance on cloze measures (Salvia and Hughes 1990). Whatever comprehension skill you monitor, be careful in selecting the reading passages and standardization of the measure that you use. For example, your student should consistently read passages of similar length and should slowly move up to higher readability level passages in an incremental fashion (for example, from third-grade readability level passages to fourth-grade readability level passages to fifth-grade readability, and so on). On each level, students should not advance to the next level until they have met a criterion for mastery (for example, 80 percent comprehension). Moreover, comprehension questions should remain constant in terms of the number and the type of questions (for example, textually explicit, textually implicit, and scriptally implicit).

Finally, an alternative way to assess reading fluency and other early reading skills is called Dynamics Indicators of Basic Early Literacy Skills (DIBELS). DIBELS are short (one-minute), standardized measures used to assess early reading skills (that is, initial sounds fluency, letter naming fluency, phoneme segmentation fluency, nonsense word fluency, oral reading fluency, and retell fluency) for students in kindergarten through sixth grade. These measures are meant to be used frequently to monitor the early reading performance of students throughout the school year. When students' scores are compared to

---

BOX 6.1

AVERAGE CWPM INCREASES PER WEEK

First Grade: 2–3 words per week increase

Second Grade: 2.5–3.5 words per week increase

Third Grade: 1–3 words per week increase

Fourth Grade: .85–1.5 words per week increase

benchmark goals, teachers can quickly determine if the student has a deficit, is at risk, or whether the skill is well established in the student's repertoire of early reading skills. (For more information about DIBELS, visit the University of Oregon's website at http://dibels.uoregon.edu/index.php.)

Deciding Upon Appropriate Reading Materials and Textbooks

When teachers choose texts for students with mild disabilities to read, care has to be taken not to exacerbate the students' current fluency and comprehension problems. In many cases, students have had embarrassing moments when reading aloud from books that were beyond their current readability level. Such experiences reinforce the idea that the student is a poor reader, and recurring failure further solidifies negative feelings toward reading. These experiences decrease the willingness to read and deflate motivation for future reading. Therefore, special education teachers should consider those texts that are interesting and well within the student's readability level, using readability formulas as a guide. For those texts that are especially challenging for students (for example, higher grade-level textbooks), teachers should provide students with plenty of supports such as teacher assistance during reading, cognitive or semantic organizers, digitized text, or recorded readings.

Other factors to consider in text selection include the *type* and *frequency* of words contained in them. To build fluency skills, students must have repeated exposure to reading the same or similar words. Less fluent readers spend most of their attentional resources on decoding or word attack, to the determent of comprehension. Thus, teachers should select texts at the students' current reading level and texts with features that promote fluency. Hiebert and Fisher (2005) identified key features in texts that promote fluency. These include a small number of rare words, a high percentage of the most frequently used words, and frequently repeated critical words (that is, those words that influence the meaning the most). These features are often cited as the critical factors in the success of repeated readings (Faulkner and Levy 1994). If a text has many different unique or rare words, students end up stopping to focus attention on each one; these present challenges because every rare word within a text, particularly those that show up only once, can require attention that may divert resources for comprehension. Conversely, books with high-frequency words—either sight words or words with phonetically similar patterns (for example, *cat, at, mat, rat*)—are easier for students to read and thus increase fluency. Finally, critical words are important vocabulary words that carry a great deal of meaning throughout sentences and paragraphs.

Determining Readability of Textbooks and Materials

When choosing materials for reading instruction or choosing textbooks for students to learn from, teachers should consider the interest of the passage, as well as the **readability level** of the passages. Determine readability levels of passages beforehand to ensure that the reading material does not frustrate students. Most formulas determine readability based upon a combination of frequency of multisyllabic words and sentence length. Usually, the result of using a readability formula is a quantifiable readability score based upon specific grade levels or ages. For example, the Fry Readability Graph (see Figure 6.3) determines

FIGURE 6.3

Fry Readability Graph

A. Select samples of 100 words. Choose the beginning, middle, and end of the passage, chapter, or book for your three 100-word samples.

B. Find the average number of sentences per 100-word passage (calculating to the nearest tenth).

C. Find the average number of syllables per 100-word sample.

D. Use the Fry Graph to determine the reading age, in years.

The curve represents normal texts for students. Points below the curve represent longer-than-average sentence lengths. Points above the curve represent text with a more difficult vocabulary (content-area textbooks).

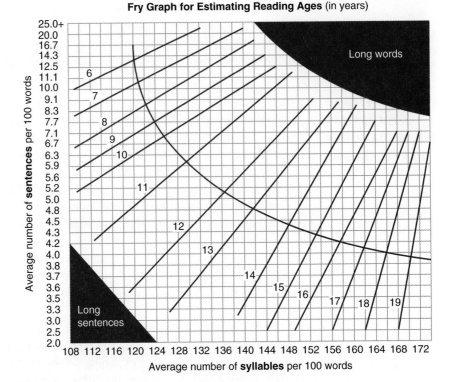

Fry Graph for Estimating Reading Ages (in years)

Reprinted with permission from Edward Fry, "A readability formula that saves time" (*Journal of Reading* 11:513–6. International Reading Association, 1968).

readability based upon the number of multisyllabic words (syllables per 100-word sample) and number of sentences per 100-word sample.

Strategies and Techniques for Improving Vocabulary

As we discussed previously, teaching vocabulary as pre- and post-reading activities is useful because students with disabilities have a difficult time understanding vocabulary they read in text, and this vocabulary aids fluency and comprehension. Prior to vocabulary instruction, teachers should consider the purpose of students' learning the vocabulary. If the purpose is to teach a new vocabulary word and its definition, then a direct instructional approach might work best. If the student already knows a definition for a vocabulary word and the purpose is now to teach multiple meanings, then a semantic approach, such as mapping, might be a better approach (Jitendra et al. 2004).

Whatever the purpose, teachers should try to tap into prior knowledge to help students make meaningful connections between new knowledge (vocabulary) and prior knowledge. Teachers should also keep in mind that children have different levels of "processing information," particularly for vocabulary. Stahl (1986) defines three levels of processing. The first level is *associative*. On this level of processing, students simply make association between a word and another word. This is a rather weak level of processing; if students do not use

Chapter Question
ALERT

In this section, you will find information that answers a Chapter Question:

4. What strategies and techniques would be useful to improve the vocabulary skills of *students with mild disabilities?*

the vocabulary frequently, they will soon forget the word. The second level is *comprehension*. During this level, children have a better understanding than on the first level, but still cannot generalize the word to new sentences. During this level, children understand the meaning and can use the word for activities such as fill in the blanks or categorizing. The final level is the deepest level of processing and is referred to as *generational*. During this level, children have mastery or ownership of the word and its meaning, and can now define the word in their own words. They can also use the word easily during writing activities and discussions. To attain this level, students must move from rote recall of the term, to using it in thinking and discourse. Through facilitating discussions, providing engaging vocabulary activities, and using multiple presentations of vocabulary words, teachers can bring their students to this deepest level of understanding. Other principles of vocabulary instruction include:

- Teaching a small number of vocabulary words at a time
- Using distributed practice to learn words
- Presenting new vocabulary in context, typically in simple sentences
- Matching the vocabulary taught with word meanings that are used in a story or textbook

For more information about research-based techniques used to teach vocabulary to students with disabilities, see Bryant et al. (2003) or Jitendra et al. (2004).

Word Maps A **word map** (Schwartz and Raphael 1985), similar to a semantic map (see Chapter 4), helps students to understand the meaning of vocabulary words. A word map provides students with a target vocabulary word and synonyms of it in the form of a visual display. Given a vocabulary word and using this map (see Figure 6.4), students ask three questions about the word: What is it? What is it like? What are some examples? Students answer these questions on the map and, if they cannot answer a question, they search for the remaining information from supporting materials (Schwartz and Raphael 1985).

FIGURE 6.4

Word Map for Vocabulary

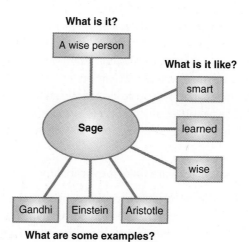

Teachers can create partial maps that students can work on prior to reading and then complete after reading. We feel that students should be allowed to fill in part or all of a map during the activity because this allows students to become actively engaged in the task. Furthermore, research supports this notion that students have better comprehension when they create their own maps, as opposed to when the teacher gives them a completed map (Boyle and Weishaar 1997). Not only are students actively engaged in the task, but they also physically link ideas together (main ideas with details) as they create a semantic map.

Keyword and Mnemonic Strategies

Keyword and mnemonic methods are effective techniques to help students learn abstract vocabulary words (Mastropieri, Scruggs, and Fulk 1990; Scruggs and Mastropieri 1990; Uberti, Scruggs, and Mastropieri 2003). Through making connections between new vocabulary and prior knowledge, students are better able to recall the vocabulary word, and the unfamiliar word becomes more meaningful and concrete.

To aid memory, the **keyword technique** links up a target vocabulary word with a similar sounding keyword. Many keyword techniques also use visual images to help students make more concrete connections between the vocabulary word and its definition. Researchers claim that, based upon reconstructive elaboration theory, the keyword method elaborates and reconstructs a vocabulary word, thereby making it more meaningful and concrete (Mastropieri, Scruggs, and Fulk 1990; Scruggs and Mastropieri 1990; Terrill, Scruggs, and Mastropieri 2004). The reconstructions described by Scruggs and Mastropieri (1990) are based on the principle that the more familiar, concrete, and well elaborated the information, the better it will be learned and remembered. This model employs three types of reconstructions that teachers can use separately or in combination.

The following are the three types of reconstruction:

1. **Acoustic reconstruction** links a vocabulary word with a similar sounding keyword (for example, *denominator–demons*).
2. **Symbolic reconstruction** links an abstract vocabulary word with a picture to make the information more memorable (for example, *insular* means *narrow-minded*; see Figure 6.5).
3. **Mimetic reconstruction** uses literal pictures for familiar, concrete information. For example, if students were studying simple machines in science and had to remember an example of the three classes of levers, a mimetic reconstruction of the levers might be illustrated as in Figure 6.6. To enhance memory, you could tell the children to visualize the fishing rod (class 2 lever) physically hooking the boy, picking him up from the seesaw (class 1 lever), and dropping him in the wheelbarrow (class 3 lever).

The following are three steps (Terrill, Scruggs, and Mastropieri 2004) for developing good keyword links for vocabulary words:

1. Develop a similar sounding word from the vocabulary word. For example, if we want to develop a good way to remember the word *dinoflagellate*, which means a type of plankton that propels through water in a whirling motion, a good

FIGURE 6.5

Symbolic Reconstruction

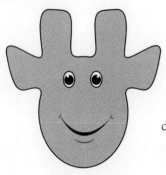

insular = narrow-minded

FIGURE 6.6

Mimetic Reconstruction:
Three Classes of Levers

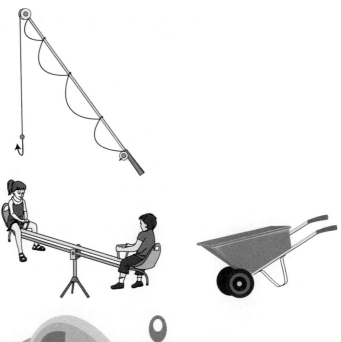

FIGURE 6.7

Keyword for Vocabulary

VIDEO CASE CONNECTIONS BOX

Watch the Video Case entitled *Elementary Literacy Instruction: A Balanced Literacy Approach*. Observe how Sandra Jenoski's students engage in word study activities as she explains how the students "manipulate their words" by "building them and writing them." Explain how this is an example of practicing specific vocabulary skills without drill.

keyword for *dinoflagellate* might be *dinosaur* (because it sounds like the vocabulary word).

2. Create a picture in which the keyword and the definition of the keyword are combined. The picture should be interactive, linking the keyword with the definition. For example, the picture could be a *dinosaur whirling through the waves*.

3. Students are then asked the meaning of dinoflagellate and are prompted to think of the keyword, what is happening in the picture, and the definition (see Figure 6.7).

Strategies and Techniques for Improving Fluency

Although teaching vocabulary has been shown to promote reading comprehension in students with LD (Bryant et al. 2003), building fluency is an even more influential skill that should be a consistent part of any reading program to improve comprehension, particularly for students with mild disabilities. Because of the link between fluency and comprehension, it is critical to teach students how to read fluently and then have them practice fluency skills using the following interventions.

Experts recommend that teachers should include the following in fluency programs: model good fluent reading, encourage fluency through phrasing, provide plenty of practice, and provide oral support for readers (Rasinski 2003).

- Modeling fluency is important because teachers can show students how to derive meaning from the text by matching the author's words with proper fluency. By reading aloud, teachers can model the detriments of reading too slow and too fast, and then demonstrate the benefits of reading at an appropriate pace.
- Meaning is often determined through phrases, not individual words. Phrasing involves chunking text into syntactic units while reading. Attending to punctuation is a useful guide to proper phrasing. Through repeated reading of a passage, students can begin to chunk text into appropriate phrases. Taking turns reading the same text also helps students to understand and use the phrasing of the text.
- Practice allows students to master those skills that they have already acquired. Opportunities to practice can occur through partner reading, repeated readings, or other activities.
- Finally, students with fluency problems need plenty of support during oral reading. This support can come in the form of a paired reading partner or through the use of recorded texts. Simultaneously hearing the text read while actually reading has increased both fluency and comprehension in students with disabilities.

Repeated Readings

Using **repeated readings** is a simple technique whereby teachers have students read one passage several times or until they reach a predetermined level of fluency. O'Shea, Sindelar, and O'Shea (1985) report that four readings appear to be the optimal amount because, by the fourth reading, children have reached maximum gains in reading speed, error reduction, and expression. Repeated readings have been used since the late 1970s (Samuels 1979), and have been proven effective for increasing fluency on passages that students read more than once and on new passages as well. Repeated readings have been shown to be successful when a teacher or another higher-level peer monitors a child's oral reading. In a review of repeated reading research, Therrien (2004) found that repeated readings were effective for increasing both fluency and comprehension. Moreover, repeated readings have transfer effects to new readings. In other words, increases in fluency and comprehension were found not only for the current passages that students were repeating, but for new passages as well. The

Chapter Question
ALERT

In this section, you will find information that answers a Chapter Question:

5. What strategies and techniques would be useful to improve the fluency skills of students with mild disabilities?

effects were more pronounced for those new passages that contained common words from the previous passage. Like any skill, it appears that practice makes perfect (or at least improves reading skills).

Repeated reading works best when the text is matched with the child's reading level. Some suggest that students practice repeated reading with easier texts that are below their readability level, and others suggest that repeated readings be used with more instructional level texts that are on the student's current reading level (85 to 90 percent word-recognition accuracy). You can determine which approach is most appropriate for individual students by monitoring their progress across repeated reading sessions. Remember the curriculum-based measurement (C-BM) rule of thumb: if you see no progress toward the goal after three lessons, it is time for a change in the intervention.

Teachers using repeated readings should prepare by allotting 15 to 30 minutes each day for them, using the same passage three to four times, and choosing short passages with reading levels that have been predetermined using a readability formula (Therrien 2004). If the passages are too difficult, students will struggle to read them and read too slowly. If passages are too easy, students may not be practicing newly learned sight words or vocabulary words.

Once students are ready to read, Rasinski (2003) recommends the following guidelines: use 50- to 500-word passages and have students orally read the passage until they reach a predetermined reading rate. The passages can come from a variety of sources including basal stories, newspapers, or textbooks. As discussed earlier, predetermined rates can be ascertained by using available reading rate charts, as well as past performance on C-BMs. Once students achieve the criteria, move on to a new passage that is as difficult or slightly more difficult as the last. Finally, be sure to track reading rates (as well as prosody) while the child is reading.

Paired Reading or Peer Tutoring

Paired Reading. Paired reading is another technique for improving fluency. Paired reading can be used with any two people, as long as one is a more proficient reader than the other. It can occur with a parent and child, teacher and child, or student and student. When using paired reading, the pairs find a comfortable area in the class, sit side by side and begin reading aloud together. Each paired reading session can last from 10 to 20 minutes and should take place daily or every other day. As with repeated reading, the materials that are used should be on the student's instructional reading level (85 percent to 90 percent word-recognition accuracy).

Paired reading also benefits proficient readers because it allows them to practice good reading skills too. As the pair begins to read together, they should match each other's reading rate, slowing for difficult parts and moving quickly through easy sections. During this activity, both students should read naturally, look at their own text while using a finger to follow along in the reading. Because the purpose of the activity is to increase fluency and comprehension a "word supply" method should be used when a student makes an error, whereby the more proficient reader supplies the correctly pronounced word for the other student's miscue. If a student becomes "stuck," the helping student should allow the other student two to three seconds to see if he or she can correctly pronounce the word or self-correct any miscues. Then, the helping student should supply the missing word or correct pronunciation. Using a "word supply" method, rather than phonetically sounding out the word, minimizes any interruptions in the student's comprehension.

As the student begins to feel more comfortable reading aloud, have the more proficient student eventually phase out supports by reading in a softer voice, eventually whispering, and then allowing the other reader to read independently. At the end of each session, provide oral or written comprehension questions for students to answer. Finally, if possible, try to keep track of miscues and reading rates by recording or charting the cwpm rate. Students can learn to perform the data collection by marking miscues in a print copy of the text while their partners read aloud.

Peer Tutoring. Peer tutoring is a technique that pairs students together for the purpose of tutoring each other as they read. In peer tutoring, students are matched up based upon reading ability, with a higher performing student matched with a lower performing student. Pairs then take turns reading orally to each other for about 5 to 15 minutes each (total reading time for the group is 10 to 30 minutes).

Fuchs and Fuchs (2005) developed three reading activities that occur during the peer-tutoring program called PALS (peer-assisted learning strategies). The three activities that are integrated into the 35-minute program are *partner reading*, *paragraph shrinking*, and *prediction relay*.

Every session begins with five minutes of *partner reading*. During this activity, the higher performing student reads first using a connected text. Once done, the other student rereads the same material. Each student then retells the events that occurred in the story for two minutes each.

Next, students read one paragraph at a time and then name the main idea in each paragraph. Once students decide the "who" and "what" of the paragraph, they report the main idea in statement of ten words or fewer. This activity is referred to as *paragraph shrinking* and lasts for five minutes, after which partners switch roles for an additional five minutes.

Finally, with the *prediction relay*, partners make predictions about what they will learn on the next half page. The lower performing reader reads the passage first to confirm or disconfirm their predictions and states the main idea. After completing this activity for five minutes, the partners switch roles.

PALS has been documented as effective for Hispanic bilingual students, because the program incorporates culturally responsive practices such as peer tutoring that resemble culturally traditional familial and social learning contexts (Calhoon et al. 2006; Saenz, Fuchs, and Fuchs 2005).

THINK BACK TO THE FIRST CASE   with Habib . . .

3. *Name and describe one type of fluency activity that you would use with Habib.*

You could use any or all of the previously mentioned fluency techniques: repeated readings, paired reading, or peer tutoring. Each accomplishes the goals of practice with modeling and feedback, using suitable level reading materials. Habib's teachers can observe to determine which he is more comfortable using, and they have flexibility in how to address his reading fluency as they teach in an inclusive classroom.

Strategies and Techniques for Improving Comprehension

Chapter Question
ALERT

In this section, you will find information that answers a Chapter Question:

6. What strategies and techniques would be useful to improve the reading comprehension skills of students with mild disabilities?

Reading comprehension represents another area of difficulty for students with mild disabilities. A number of factors contribute to difficulties in overall reading comprehension, such as lack of prior knowledge of the topic, difficulty making inferences, poor comprehension monitoring, and poor understanding of text structure (Cain and Oakhill 1999; Gersten et al. 2001; Pressley 1991; Wong 1991). A number of effective reading techniques and strategies have been identified as useful at improving reading comprehension for students with mild disabilities, particularly for students in secondary classes (Mastropieri and Scruggs 1997; Pressley 2002). More importantly, experts advocate that teachers should use explicit instruction to teach students comprehension strategies, and not just assume that students are already using comprehension-monitoring techniques when they read (Pressley 2002). The reading strategies and techniques presented in this book should be taught to students using explicit instruction.

Paraphrasing Strategy

The paraphrasing strategy (Schumaker, Denton, and Deshler 1984) is a reading comprehension strategy that asks students to find main ideas and details from each paragraph that is read and then to paraphrase orally that information. The purpose of the strategy is to help students become actively engaged in reading through searching for main ideas and details in paragraphs and then transforming that information through paraphrasing to make it personally meaningful. The three steps of the paraphrasing strategy are represented by the acronym RAP (see Box 6.2); students can remember that they need to "rap" or talk to themselves as they read for recall and comprehension.

Students use the strategy with short passages that are at least five paragraphs in length. For example, published reading materials such as *Timed Readings* are frequently used with this strategy. Similar to other strategies from University of Kansas Center for Research on Learning, this follows the eight-stage *Strategy Intervention Model* (SIM; Deshler et al. 1981). SIM is a model that promotes effective teaching and learning of critical content in schools through the use of strategies and other techniques.

The eight-stage SIM begins with the teacher pretesting the students to see if they qualify for the strategy. The results of the pretest are reviewed with the students to encourage them to make a commitment to learn the RAP strategy. If students need the paraphrasing strategy, the teachers describe the strategy for

---

BOX 6.2

PARAPHRASING STRATEGY

R Read a paragraph.

A Ask yourself, "What were the main idea and details in this paragraph?"

  Finding the main idea:

  1. Look in the first sentence of the paragraph.

  2. Look for repetitions of the same word or words in the whole paragraph.

P Put the main ideas and details in your own words.

them. Following the description of how and why the strategy works, teachers model using the strategy for the students. In this stage, teachers "think aloud" how they perform the strategy (for example, "Let's see, to find the main idea I know that I should look at what the first sentence is about . . .").

Next, students move on to verbal practice of the strategy steps. This practice involves naming the RAP mnemonic and stating what each letter stands for at an automatic level. Upon mastery of the steps of the strategy, students advance to controlled practice. In controlled practice, students begin reading passages that are on their current *reading ability level* and, upon reaching mastery (80 percent paraphrasing and 70 percent comprehension scores), progress on to *grade-level* passages in the advanced practice phase. They begin with controlled level passages so that they may initially concentrate on the RAP procedures; once comfortable with them, they move on to applying them with more challenging content.

Once students reach mastery in the grade-level phase, they take a posttest. Ideally, the posttest will be on the same passage they read at pretest to demonstrate their need to learn the strategy. The marked improvement in performance should be motivating to students. In the final stage of the SIM model, students proceed to the generalization phase. In the generalization phase, students are instructed on how to use the strategy with other materials and settings.

Throughout the strategy training, teachers keep a record of students' paraphrasing and comprehension scores as they silently read passages, but paraphrase each paragraph aloud. This explicit comprehension strategy, once mastered, enables students with weak comprehension skills to read below grade-level and at grade-level materials.

Story Map
A story map presents a basic framework for understanding important elements found in narrative stories. For students, general knowledge of these story elements such as setting, problem, goal, attempts, internal response, and resolution results in improved recall and comprehension (Gordon and Braun 1983). Because some students need a more concrete model of these story elements, researchers (Idol 1987; Idol and Croll 1987) developed a story map that contained these components (see Figure 6.8).

Using direct instruction procedures, students are taught to use story maps as they read narrative stories. Students should be matched to appropriate reading levels based upon their reading rates. Story maps are used with short reading passages (100-plus words). First, teachers model how to use the story map. During modeling, the teacher should familiarize students with the different components found in the story map. Next, the teacher should have the students read the passage and periodically stop at points where information needed to fill in the map is provided. At this point, students should write information directly onto the story map. Throughout this early training, the teacher should provide immediate feedback for errors. Upon completing each story, students should also answer comprehension questions of varying levels (textually implicit, textually explicit, and scriptally implicit). Throughout the training, students should be taught to rely less on the teacher and eventually be able to complete the map independently. As students reach a set level of mastery in comprehension, teachers should gradually phase out the use of the map while continuing to check comprehension.

FIGURE 6.8

Story Map Example

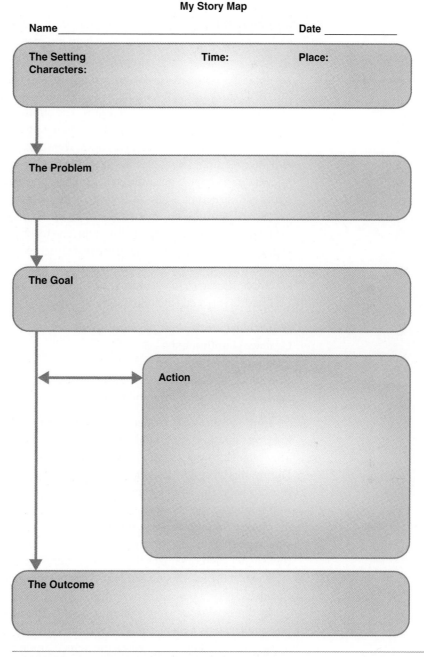

My Story Map

Name_____ Date _____

The Setting
Characters: Time: Place:

The Problem

The Goal

Action

The Outcome

Adapted from L. Idol, "Group story mapping: A comprehension strategy for both skilled and unskilled readers," (*Journal of Learning Disabilities* 20(1987):199).

Another version of a story map, developed by Boulineau et al. (2004), contains seven main areas for recording a narrative's story: setting/time, characters, problem, solution, outcome, reaction, and theme. These researchers used basal stories with the map and had students read portions of the story orally until they read the entire story. Prior to reading, students were taught each story element individually. Once they read the entire story, each student completed a story map.

Once students were able to complete maps with 90 percent accuracy, they were no longer instructed on story elements prior to reading. Instead, students read each passage and completed a story map independently.

POSSE Strategy

The POSSE strategy (Englert and Mariage 1990; 1991) was developed to enhance the reading comprehension skills of students with disabilities through reciprocal teaching and construction of maps. The strategy itself incorporates a variety of strategies that include predicting, organizing, searching, summarizing, and evaluating expository reading passages. The strategy can be used before, during, and after reading. Using POSSE, students predict ideas based upon background knowledge, organize predicted textual ideas and background knowledge based upon text structure, search/summarize by searching the text structure in the expository passage, summarize the main ideas, and evaluate their comprehension. As the students complete the steps, the teacher simultaneously constructs a cognitive map to display visually the text structure and organization of ideas. The POSSE training consists of two pre-reading strategies—predict and organize— and three strategies to use during reading—search, summarize, and evaluate.

The POSSE steps include the following:

Predict what ideas are in the story.
Organize your thoughts.
Search for structure.
Summarize the main idea in your own words.
Evaluate: compare, clarify, and predict.

In the *predict* step, students use cues from the book such as the title, headings, pictures, and the initial paragraph to predict what the story will be about. This brainstorming activity allows students to tap into their prior knowledge. During this step, the teacher guides students to relevant responses and records responses on the strategy sheet. Englert and Mariage (1990; 1991) recommend that teachers make a transparency and record responses on it.

During the *organize* step, the teacher directs students to choose ideas that are similar, so that they can be organized (see figure 6.9). Once the ideas are arranged, the teacher then organizes them into a cognitive map with the students.

Next, in the *search* step, students begin reading the passage as they search for the ideas to map out in the next step.

In the *summarize* step, students identify the main idea for a portion of the passage (such as a paragraph). This is done through group discussion and consensus. The teacher then records the agreed-upon main idea and places it in the circle of the cognitive map. The group leader—the teacher or student who has been assigned to lead the group—then takes the main idea and converts it into a question. As students answer this question, their responses become the details that the teacher records on the map. At the end of the passage, the students have now created a second cognitive map.

In the *evaluation* step, the students compare the two maps, clarify by asking questions about unknown vocabulary or unclear information, and predict what would be in the next section of the text. This starts the process all over again for the next chapter or passage.

FIGURE 6.9

POSSE Strategy Sheet

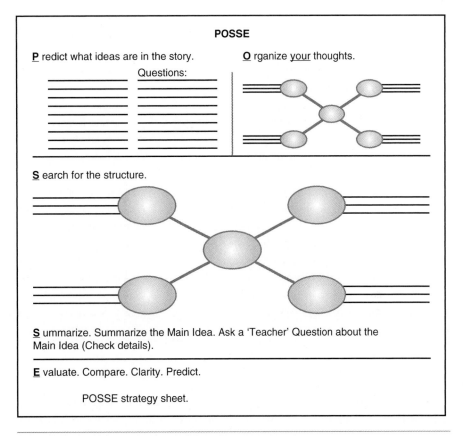

POSSE

P redict what ideas are in the story.   **O** rganize <u>your</u> thoughts.

Questions:

S earch for the structure.

S ummarize. Summarize the Main Idea. Ask a 'Teacher' Question about the Main Idea (Check details).

E valuate. Compare. Clarity. Predict.

POSSE strategy sheet.

Reprinted with permission from C. Englert and T. Mariage, "Making Students Partners in the Comprehension Process: Organizing the Reading 'POSSE'" (*Learning Disability Quarterly* 14(1991):123–138).

TIPS FOR GENERALIZATION

Effective Strategy Components

Training students to use a strategy, technique, or intervention requires explicit instruction. This means that teachers should set a clear goal when teaching the strategy and that students should master the strategy steps before actually using the strategy with materials. Adapting the eight-step instructional sequence described by Deshler et al. (1981), and using effective intervention components from Mastropieri, Scruggs, and Graetz (2003), we will describe the general steps for training students to use most techniques and strategies.

When teaching a strategy, teachers should use the steps of direct instruction (model, guided practice with immediate feedback, and independent practice) to show students exactly how to perform each step of the strategy. While performing these steps, teachers should use think-aloud techniques whereby they verbalize what is occurring in each step. When teachers verbalize their thoughts and actions, students can clearly see what is occurring during instruction. As students begin to understand the strategy steps being demonstrated, the teacher can slowly integrate them into the demonstration. As students become more involved in the strategy demonstration, they can begin to use the components with actual materials. As students use the strategy and materials, the teacher should be cognizant to give students immediate and corrective feedback to ensure that they are performing the strategy steps properly. If students are using a cognitive strategy, they should next practice the strategy steps until they can recite strategy steps to mastery.

Once students reach mastery on the strategy steps, they can begin using the strategy or technique with "easy" materials. The purpose of this portion of the training is to ensure that they can use the strategy steps properly, not necessarily reach mastery with content materials. Again, teachers should provide immediate and corrective feedback so that students can master the use of strategy steps with easy materials. Monitoring performance ensures that students successfully use the strategy or technique.

Next, students can begin using the strategy or technique with grade-level materials. Again, the teacher needs to monitor performance and provide feedback. Once students have mastered this step, they are ready for the last and perhaps most important step: generalization. Whenever teachers instruct students in a strategy or technique, one of the most important components of training is training for generalization. Although it is important for students to learn a strategy and demonstrate its effectiveness with the teacher, it is crucial that they can then use the strategy with new people and in new settings. In this last step, students think about how the strategy or technique can be applied to new settings or materials. This step may require students to modify the strategy or technique. In some cases, the teacher can begin to fade out materials (for example, teacher cues) so that students no longer rely on these supports. Once students can use the strategy or technique with new materials, they should be monitored periodically to ensure that they have properly integrated the strategy into their daily routine. These steps ensure that, from start to finish, students will be able to use successfully the strategy and techniques that you teach them.

Cognitive Mapping Strategy

The cognitive mapping strategy was developed to enable students with disabilities to independently map out information that they read from expository passages (Boyle 1996, Boyle and Weishaar 1997). Each passage used was approximately four hundred words long and contained about five to six paragraphs.

To teach the strategy, a teacher needs to model it for students while thinking aloud in each step. Next, the teacher should encourage students to use the strategy steps with the passage to create the map (that is, use guided practice). Finally, after providing students with feedback while they are reading the passage and creating a map, the teacher should check for accuracy of the content in the map. If students reach mastery of the content in the map and can use the strategy steps independently, they can now begin to use cognitive mapping independently (that is, independent practice). Initially, students read passages that are matched to their readability level. They then map out each readability-level passage. Once they complete these passages with mastery, they are given grade-level passages to map out.

The purpose of each step in the cognitive mapping strategy is to have students become actively engaged in reading by searching for pertinent information and creating a map of the information (see Box 6.3).

In the first step, *topic*, students are instructed to search for the topic, state where and how they find it, write it down, and circle it. Next, during the *read* step, students are instructed to read a paragraph. During this step, students read one paragraph silently. At the end of the paragraph, they move on to the *ask* step. During the *ask* step, students go back to the paragraph to find the main idea and three details, and write them down. Students then *verify* the main idea by circling it and linking its details to the main idea. In the next step, students

---

COGNITIVE MAPPING STRATEGY

T <u>W</u>rite down the <u>t</u>opic.

R <u>R</u>ead a paragraph.

A <u>A</u>sk for the main idea and three details, and write them down.

V <u>V</u>erify the main idea by circling it and linking its details.

E <u>E</u>valuate the next paragraph, and <u>a</u>sk and <u>v</u>erify again.

L When finished, <u>l</u>ink all circles.

---

are to *examine* the next paragraph, read it, and then *ask* and *verify* the main idea and details. The *read, ask,* and *verify* steps are repeated for each successive paragraph until the student comes to the end of the passage. Finally, after mapping out the last paragraph, students review the map, search for similar main ideas (in circles), and link up these main ideas. See Figure 6.10 for a map that was created by a student who used the TRAVEL strategy while reading a passage about the Statute of Liberty.

FIGURE 6.10

Student Map Using the
Cognitive Mapping Strategy

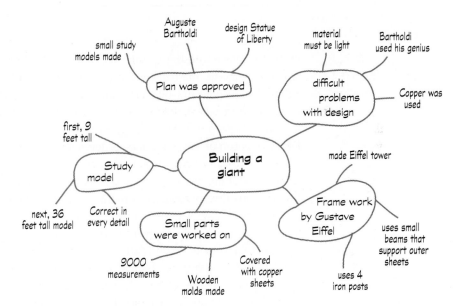

KWL The KWL strategy (Carr and Ogle 1987; Ogle 1986) consists of three components or steps to help students tap into prior knowledge, set a purpose for reading, and summarize what was read. The **K** step is what we **know**, the **W** step is what we **want** to know, and the **L** step is what we **learned**. Students list this information in chart form (see Box 6.4) and complete it pre-reading, during reading, and after reading.

During the pre-reading stage, children describe what they know about the topic. This stage involves a brainstorming session about ideas that they already know about the topic. The teacher should be very specific about the topic to be

---

BOX 6.4

KWL CHART ABOUT HURRICANE KATRINA

K: what we know	W: what we want to find out	L: what we learned and still need to learn
Fierce winds	What made the wind so powerful?	Strong winds near the eye Category 3 hurricane at landfall Winds were 125 mph
Heavy rain	Where did all the rain come from?	Warm water from the Gulf fueled it to a Category 5
Flooding	Why did it kill so many people?	Storm surge was 28 feet New Orleans is like a bowl
Loss of electricity and drinkable water	How did it form?	Circulating mass of air over Gulf's 80°F water
Destruction of buildings	Could we have stopped it?	No, too powerful
Left people stranded	How did they survive?	Rough time at first and then eventual evacuation

---

read (for example, information about monarch butterflies, not butterflies and moths) to delve into the specific schemata of students (Ogle 1986). As the students respond, the teacher records responses on the board or overhead. After students have finished responding with what they know about the topic (monarch butterflies), the teacher then leads them into categorizing the topics that are listed. Finally, the teacher records information in the "What We Know" column of the chart, and students do the same on their own charts.

Next, students develop questions about "What We Want To Know." The teacher and students discuss these questions and then all students record what they personally want to know from the passage on their charts. The purpose of having students write their own questions is so that all students can personally focus on their own goals for reading. After students finish reading the passage, they are told to write down what they learned from the reading in the "What We Learned . . ." column, as well as what they still need to learn. If the passage did not answer their questions, the teacher can provide new passages that students can read to find information that will answer their questions.

Research Evidence

Semantic Organizers, Cognitive Maps, and KWL. Semantic organizers have long been shown to be effective at increasing vocabulary and comprehension of students who use them. In studies by Bos and others (Bos and Anders 1987, 1990; Bos et al. 1989), students who used semantic maps outperformed students who learned vocabulary using a traditional approach (for example, dictionary approach). These researchers also demonstrated that, when students used semantic maps and organizers while they read, they increased recall of vocabulary and reading comprehension (Scanlon et al. 1992). Moreover, a recent synthesis of research on semantic organizers and cognitive

| CASE 6.2 | **Helping Junior Become a Better Reader** |

Case Introduction

Now that you have worked through the first case in this chapter, you should feel comfortable addressing issues in a second case. In this case, two teachers work together in an inclusion classroom to meet the needs of all the students, but in particular the learning needs of Junior.

Randolph (Junior) Wilson is a student in Jen Timson's eighth-grade class. Junior is considered at risk because of his poor word attack and comprehension skills. Jen and Karen Hopkins work side by side most of the morning. Karen is the special education teacher who collaborates with Jen during language arts (reading and writing) and social studies. Jen and Karen have been collaborating for about two years. On two days during the week, they have an opportunity to sit down and co-plan during their joint planning periods.

Junior has had a number of reading problems over the past two years but, with help from Karen and Jen, he has been able to avoid a referral to the self-contained class for students with LD. Through intense one-on-one from Karen, he has been able to remain with the eighth grade class for most of the year, despite his learning disability. During a recent literature lesson, students were reading the story, *The Cricket in Times Square,* by George Seldon. On this particular day, Jen noticed how poorly Junior was reading. He made 14 miscues in just one paragraph. He said *near* for *narrow*, *curse* for *curve*, *steam* for *streets*, *cardinal* for *cardboard*, *sheets* for *shells*, *bounty* for *beautiful*, *flow* for *flowers*, *grass* for *glass*, *win* for *wind*, *other* for *others*, *tinple* to *tinkle*, *hug* for *hung*, *bees* for *breeze*, and *cape* for *cage*. As he read, Karen and Jen began to hear some of the students giggling, but quickly warned those few students that their behavior would not be tolerated. Upon finishing his paragraph, Junior gave out an audible "whew." For Junior, reading is a daily struggle and often an embarrassing one. Even when he reads silently, Karen and Jen can tell that it is a similar struggle. During silent reading, Junior often has his hand raised, asking about the many unknown words that he encounters.

Naturally, his word-attack problems hinder his comprehension. But even when his teachers use word supply as he reads, Junior often knows the answer to either inferential or literal comprehension questions. Karen has kept a close eye on Junior and frequently notices that he appears "lost in space" as other students read or when one of his teachers reads part of a story aloud to the class. Junior's distractions seem to get worse as the day progresses. Jen has often complained that she has to "walk him through" his science lessons (which take place after lunch).

To counter his word-attack problems, Karen recently began reviewing sight words and vocabulary words with him prior to class. Junior hates these preview lessons because he hates reading. Initial results have been mixed. On some days, Junior makes fewer miscues, yet, on other days, Junior still makes many miscues.

Social studies also presents challenges for Junior and his teachers. Junior has difficulty reading the textbook chapters and answering questions. During independent seatwork, such as worksheets, Junior also has problems remaining on task and completing his work correctly. At home, his parents have also noticed problems. Junior has problems reading his textbooks and answering questions. His parents really struggle to keep him working and on task. For example, as soon as he gets home, he begins working on his homework. This works out fine when he doesn't have much homework but, on a typical day, it takes him three hours to complete his homework because it is so difficult for him.

CASE QUESTIONS

1. What specific skill would you try to remediate with Junior?
2. What other skill would you, as the teacher, address?
3. Name and describe one fluency technique and one comprehension technique or strategy that you would use with Junior.

maps (Kim et al. 2004) supported the use of these techniques as effective tools for increasing reading comprehension, pointing out the particularly large effect size (a statistical measure of effectiveness) of them on comprehension measures among students with mild disabilities. Similar positive results were found when students used the cognitive mapping strategy TRAVEL. Students who used this strategy to create their own maps while reading expository text outperformed control group students on both literal and inferential comprehension (Boyle 1996; Boyle and Weishaar 1997). Furthermore, Boyle and Weishaar (1997) found that students who created their own cognitive maps while reading performed better on inferential comprehension than students who were supplied with completed maps (expert-generated maps).

Finally, the KWL technique is based upon the schema model of reading, whereby students need to activate background knowledge to make new connections to information that they are learning and to fill in those slots in schema as they read (Gammill 2006). Research findings (Cantrell, Fusaro, and Dougherty 2000) support that students who were trained using KWL outperformed students who wrote summaries on a measure of reading comprehension.

Keyword and Mnemonic Strategies. The keyword or mnemonic strategy has been used in numerous studies to improve the vocabulary learning of students. Veit, Scruggs, and Mastropieri (1986) used it to improve the learning of dinosaur vocabulary for students with LD. In another study, Mastropieri, Scruggs, and Graetz (2003) found that students with LD who were taught to remember and recall vocabulary and facts about chemistry using the mnemonic strategy outperformed students in the traditional learning group.

Repeated Readings. Over 100 studies have been conducted on repeated readings since Samuels first introduced the strategy in 1979. The findings from studies have consistently shown that repeated readings lead to improvements in reading speed, word recognition, and comprehension (Samuels 2002). In addition, Dowhower (1989) summarized the findings from several studies and reported that, among students with reading problems, repeated readings resulted in decreased reading miscues, improved processing of text and retention of factual information, improved fluency, enhanced deeper questioning and insights, and improved recall of pertinent content from passages, such as main ideas and vocabulary.

Paired Reading and Peer Tutoring. Paired reading is another technique that has shown to be very effective at increasing fluency in students. Studies that examined paired reading and peer tutoring have shown benefits for both high-level students (tutors) and their tutees, particularly when students are carefully matched and progress is continuously monitored (Topping 2005). Mastropieri, Scruggs, and Graetz (2003) reported from their review of peer-tutoring research on reading that when compared to conventional teaching methods, peer-tutoring methods increased reading comprehension among students with disabilities.

Paraphrasing Strategy. The paraphrasing strategy has been shown to be effective at increasing reading comprehension among students with disabilities. Ellis and Graves (1990) reported that teaching the paraphrasing strategy was effective at increasing reading comprehension among 68 fifth through seventh grade students with disabilities. Similarly, Katims and Harris (1997) reported that the paraphrasing strategy was effective at increasing the reading comprehension for both middle school students with and without disabilities.

THINK BACK TO THE SECOND CASE with Junior . . .

1. What specific skill would you try to remediate with Junior?

A number of systematic approaches to teaching reading fluency would benefit Junior. Karen and Jen should review his specific reading strengths and weaknesses and then select from among possible reading strategies to find approaches that are successful for Junior. Because of his embarrassment, they should select activities he can do away from his peers, or when matched with peers with whom he is comfortable.

2. What other skill would you, as the teacher, would address?

Junior's other reading problem is with comprehension of the story.

3. Name and describe one of fluency technique and one comprehension technique or strategy that you would use with Junior.

For fluency, teachers could use repeated readings or paired reading. For comprehension, teachers could use a number of different strategies or techniques that include RAP, POSSE, TRAVEL, or story maps.

CHAPTER SUMMARY

As we have shown, fluency is a critical skill for students with mild disabilities to learn if they are ever to become skilled readers. Fluent readers not only read words accurately and with a sufficient speed to gain meaning, but they are able to use prosody to chunk information into larger units that aid them in comprehension. When reading fluently (that is, with expression), students break sentences into phrases and correctly use stress, intonation, and duration as they read each phrase (Schreiber 1991). In doing so, they break down sentences into phrases that allow them to gain a deeper understanding of the text than when just reading individual words in the text. This deeper understanding aids students in answering not only lower-level comprehension questions (such as textually explicit or literal questions), but perhaps more importantly, higher-level questions (textually implicit and scriptally implicit questions).

Unfortunately, because students with mild disabilities have problems with fluency and comprehension, they constantly struggle to understand what they read. The good news, however, is that these students can improve their fluency and comprehension by learning instructional techniques and strategies. Like nondisabled students, students with disabilities can improve their reading skills and use them more effectively and efficiently through practice. Teachers can assist students in learning reading skills by giving them immediate feedback while they learn the skill and monitor their progress on a frequent basis via curriculum-based measures. Teachers should also be certain that reading materials are matched to the students' reading levels by using readability measures. If the materials are too difficult for a particular student's reading level, then teachers should either teach students strategies and techniques that could help compensate for the difference or modify the material so that the students can comprehend what they are reading. Some of these techniques or strategies, such as word maps and mnemonic techniques, can help students better understand vocabulary, and others, such as repeated readings or peer tutoring, can help improve students' fluency. Finally, because students with disabilities do not effectively monitor their comprehension when they read, teachers should instruct students in how to use comprehension strategies.

As with Habib in the first case and Junior in the second case, reading can be a painful and traumatic experience for your students. It is up to you to help your students. Think back to the last time you read a good book. Do you remember how it felt to get through some of the more exciting chapters or how it felt to read a book that was so good that you just couldn't put it down? Do you remember how good it felt to finish it? Maybe you felt a sense of accomplishment?

Every time you work on reading skills with students with disabilities, don't just think about helping the child to complete the task; instead, think that one day these students could feel the same sense of accomplishment upon completing an article or book, if you are willing to assist them through the reading process. The reading skills that you teach today may become their life skills of tomorrow. Students with disabilities need to learn how to read as part of the schooling process, but reading is much more than that.

KEY TERMS

Acoustic Reconstruction, 202

Consolidated Alphabetic Phase, 189

Full Alphabetic Phase, 189

Inferential Question, 191

Keyword Technique, 202

Literal Comprehension
    Questions, 191

Partial Alphabetic Phase, 189

Pre-Alphabetic Phase, 188

Readability Level, 199

Reading Fluency, 187

Repeated Readings, 204

Scriptally Implicit, 192

Symbolic Reconstruction, 202

Text Elements, 193

Text Structure, 193

Textually Explicit Question, 191

Textually Implicit Question, 191

Word Map, 201

APPLICATION ACTIVITIES

Using information from the chapter, complete the following activities that were designed to help you apply knowledge that was presented in this chapter.

1. Design a reading lesson comprised of different activities that will help readers to develop fluency and comprehension skills. Be sure to include lesson objectives and one or two state standards in your lesson.

2. Use a textbook from a middle or high school classroom. Review the questions at the end of the chapter and determine what they are (that is, textually explicit, textually implicit, or scriptally implicit).

3. Use the TRAVEL strategy to summarize any one major section of this chapter (for example, Strategies and Techniques for Improving Vocabulary). Next, create a story map for the case about Habib. List similarities and differences in the way the content of these expository and narrative comprehension summaries differ.

TECHNOLOGY RESOURCES FOR IMPROVING READING SKILLS

Educational Software Programs for Reading

There are many different types of software programs and websites on reading skills for students. Of the software programs, each covers different reading skills or strategies. Special education teachers should match up student skill deficits with those software programs. Websites also provide different perspectives on teaching reading, and most provide resources for dealing with struggling readers. The following are some reading programs and websites that could increase reading skills:

Reader Rabbit's Interactive Reading Journey by the Learning Company.
www.learningcompany.com

In this program, children are exposed to 30 stories that progress from easy, single-sentence, stories in the beginning to more difficult, multiple-paragraph passages in later stories.

Building Reading Skills by Failure Free Reading
www.buildingreadingskillsonline.com

This is a reading program for older, at-risk students and adults (from fourth grade on) with reading skills as low as 2.5. Building Reading Skills covers reading skills such as vocabulary, fluency, and comprehension. All responses are recorded and reported for tracking student progress.

Read Naturally
www.readnaturally.com

Provides reading passages and educational software from kindergarten through adult levels that is designed to improve students' fluency. It includes stories on CD that students read along with and a quiz to assess their comprehension.

Read Write and Think
www.readwritethink.org

This website provides teachers with resources for teaching reading to children that include lesson plans, reading standards, web resources, and student materials.

National Institute for Literacy
www.nifl.gov

This government-sponsored website provides a variety of resources for teachers and parents, ranging from free reports about research-based reading techniques to online discussion websites.

Florida Center for Reading Practice
www.fcrr.org

This website disseminates information about research-based practices on reading, reading growth, reading assessment, and reading instruction for children in preschool through 12th grade.

Visit the book-specific website at www.cengage.com/education/ boyle for a variety of study tools such as web links, tutorial quizzes, glossary/flash cards, bonus material not included in the text, and more.

The premium website offers access to additional materials, including the Video Cases. Go to www.cengage.com/login to register or purchase access.

Written Language: Strategies and Techniques

CHAPTER QUESTIONS

1. What is the process approach to writing?

2. What problems do students with mild disabilities encounter in written language?

3. How do you teach handwriting skills to students with mild disabilities?

4. How do you teach spelling skills and strategies to students with mild disabilities?

5. How do you teach writing techniques and strategies to students with mild disabilities?

221

Do you think most regular education students are good at writing essays?

If you answered *yes*, you might want to reconsider your answer. When students in Grades 4, 8, and 12 from across the nation were asked to write essays as part of the National Assessment of Educational Progress (NAEP) for writing in 2002, only 34 percent passed at or above the *proficient* level (U.S. Department of Education 2003). While students scored higher compared to students who participated in the 1998 version, the scores of students in these three grades remain low in terms of the percentage passing at the proficient level (that is, the proficient level was the desired goal of those administering the test) (ibid.).

Do you think students with disabilities did much better?

As you probably guessed, students with disabilities who took the NAEP writing assessment performed worse on this measure when compared to national peers. For students with disabilities (that is, defined as those students with an IEP) in Grades 4, 8, and 12, only 6 percent passed at or above the proficient level (U.S. Department of Education 2003). Even more astonishing, 43 percent of fourth-grade students with a disability scored *below* the "basic" level in writing; 53 percent of eighth-grade students scored *below* basic; and 70 percent of twelfth-grade students scored *below* basic level. As reflected by NAEP tests, written language is an area in which all students, especially students with disabilities, need to develop better skills. The NAEP writing assessment scores were derived from students' writing of three types of essays: narrative, informative, and persuasive.

In this chapter, you will learn in detail how to teach handwriting, spelling, and composing skills to students with mild disabilities. We present information about the Hayes-Flower model that addresses writing as a process, the stages of writing, and writing difficulties of students with mild disabilities. We begin the chapter by discussing the case of Xavier's writing problems.

Have you ever had a bad writing experience? Think about writing papers for classes. Perhaps you know students who have experienced some days that were similar to Xavier's. Writing can be a frustrating experience for students with disabilities. Often, they lack adequate prerequisite skills to be able to compose paragraphs and essays. Or, if they have the skills, they may lack writing strategies for planning and composing. As you read this chapter, you will learn how writing develops and how you, as a teacher, can facilitate students' writing in the classroom.

The Process of Written Language

Chapter Question
ALERT
In this section, you will find information that answers a Chapter Question:

1. What is the process approach to writing?

There are three main components to written language: **handwriting, spelling, and composing. Handwriting** involves teaching children how to write manuscript and cursive letters. **Spelling** involves teaching students how to spell words from a list or spelling book. **Composing** involves teaching students how to write sentences, paragraphs, and essays. The process approach to writing addresses all three in an integrated way. After we explain the process approach, we will identify common problems with writing for students with mild disabilities.

CASE 7.1   NBA Dreams Come Crashing Down

Case Introduction

In this case, you will read about a student named Xavier who has trouble with writing. As you read the case, you will see how he actually writes an essay. Think about how you could help him if you were his teacher.

At the end of the case, you will find case questions. These questions are meant to serve as points for reflection. Of course, if you can answer them immediately, you should do so, but you may want to wait to answer them until you have read the portion of the chapter that pertains to the particular case question. Throughout the rest of the chapter, you will see the same questions. As you see them, try to answer them based upon the portion of the chapter that you just read.

Xavier Marcus Howell was writing a paper on what he wants to do with his life after high school for his eleventh-grade English class. The only thing that Xavier wanted in life was to become an NBA star, like Ron Artest. As he looked up at the poster of Ron Artest on his bedroom wall, he thought how great it would be to play like him and live his rich lifestyle with his seven-million-dollar salary.

It was now 11:00 p.m., as Xavier began working on his paper that was due at 8:00 a.m. in English class the next day. As Xavier began his paper, he wrote about how cool it would be to jump, dunk, and block passes like the NBA stars. As he struggled to write the words, he counted each of them in an attempt to keep track of the paper's minimum length requirement of 300 words. As he continued to write, he slowly began to get angry because he wasn't very good at writing assignments and had grown to hate them. He performed poorly on writing assignments, and his teachers often remarked that his lack of effort resulted in his poor grades.

It was now midnight, and Xavier had about 100 words written. Here is what he wrote:

Ron Artest is be a man for plays basketball like a wild rocket. Jumping like a wild roket that goed off. My man Ron jumped. Stufted other playrs. Jumped and stuffed the ball through net. I play like him on fire. Hot on fire and smoking. Go to the NBA for me I will. I would like to be tough and pack the other guys. I got hops when I shoot my rock. My boys complane that I be camped out at the paint. I just be shooting rocks from downtown. Jumpin and shootin like the D is on crack.

Xavier was first identified as having LD in fifth-grade. More recently, he was also diagnosed as having an emotional disturbance (ED) because of inappropriate classroom behaviors and a suspected underlying emotional problem of depression.

By 1 a.m., Xavier was able to add only the following sentences:

That is what I want to do cause I shoots good. When I do make it to NBA I will give money to my family who need it. I will buy a big ol house and a nice car.

Unable to write any more, he soon fell asleep only to be awakened by his alarm early the next morning.

The next day he turned in what he had written to his English teacher, Mr. Maiquel Saurez, who graded it and turned it back to him later that day. On Xavier's paper, Mr. Saurez wrote, "Xavier, your paper was too short and contained too many errors. Please proofread it and turn it back in tomorrow. Grade = 'D'."

That night, Xavier again added a few more sentences and proofread his paper, but missed many of his grammatical and mechanical errors. He was able to add a few more lines:

When I hit it I will come back to my hood to help my boys. I will teach how I jump. I will teach how I stuff. Everyone will be happy cause I give them somethin. I dno't know what else to say.

Again he handed in his paper, but this time Mr. Saurez decided to have a writing conference to help Xavier improve his paper. Together they worked on both his grammatical and mechanical errors, but Xavier's ideation was still poor.

CASE QUESTIONS

1. What aspects of Xavier's approach to writing his essay may indicate that he is not likely to produce a quality essay?
2. What specific writing skill of Xavier's would you try to remediate first?
3. Name and describe two types of writing activities or techniques that Xavier could use prior to handing in his paper to improve the quality of his writing.

Product Versus Process

For many years, writing was viewed simply as a product whereby writers would transcribe their thoughts onto paper to create end products such as essays or papers. Using this **product approach,** the product would be proofread, corrected, and turned in to the teacher for a grade. This product approach placed a great deal of pressure on students to produce a "perfect draft" that would allow them to meet the length requirements of the assignment and move on to the next paper. As students worked on papers using this product approach, they often placed excessive pressure on themselves and, as a result, "blocked" when it came to putting ideas down on paper. As you can see, the product approach is often a poor way to approach writing assignments.

Employing this product approach, students would often use weak writing strategies as they wrote. According to Flower (1985), this approach commonly includes the following weak strategies: *trial-and-error, perfect draft strategy, words looking for ideas,* and *waiting for inspiration.*

Trial-and-Error Strategy. Students who write using trial and error are trying out different combinations of words and phrases with the hope that one combination will result in an acceptable form. When using trial and error, students are often so busy juggling different sentences and phrases that they lose track of previous attempts and end up writing previously rejected versions. Using this trial-and-error method, students work slowly and produce products that contain minimal ideas and content.

Perfect Draft Strategy. Using the perfect draft strategy, students write their papers from start to finish in one slow laborious process. Using this weak strategy, students strive to perfect each sentence before moving on to the next one. Usually, students use this strategy with introductory sentences or paragraphs as they try to produce the perfect beginning paragraph to a paper. As you can guess, this strategy may lead to writer's block during the beginning stages of writing and, in turn, may lead to procrastination on future writing projects.

Words Looking for Ideas Strategy. In some cases, students may use certain words that they hope will trigger ideas as they write the paper. Typically, students may rely upon transition words (for example, *first, second, third,* or *next, now, soon*) to trigger ideas about the topic. Although the use of transition words to bridge ideas is a good tool, using these words by themselves to trigger ideas is an unreliable procedure.

Waiting for Inspiration Strategy. Some students may simply wait until the "writing mood" strikes and then begin a paper or continue their work on a writing project. Although effective for some students, it may be a risky procedure to use and may cause unwarranted stress as deadlines approach. For many students, the deadline itself is the inspiration or motivation to begin the writing project; however, it may also increase stress levels and actually lead to writer's block.

More recent views of writing have led to a **process approach** to writing that ultimately results in a better product (this will be discussed later in this chapter). The Hayes-Flower model of writing (Hayes and Flower 1980) strongly influenced this shift in thinking in the academic field. When students use a process approach, the quality of their products, completed essays, or compositions, is typically much improved.

Hayes-Flower Model

The original Hayes-Flower writing model (ibid.) is perhaps the most popular model used to describe how writing occurs within a cognitive framework (please review cognitive theories in Chapter 3). Since its inception in 1980, its designers have reworked it. The new model (see Figure 7.1) differs from their old model in several aspects; most noticeably, the new model (1) has a heavier emphasis on working memory, (2) incorporates visual-spatial and linguistic components, (3) includes motivation and affect as factors that influence writing, (4) rearranges text interpretation (formerly called revision), (5) has reflection replacing planning, and (6) subsumes translation under text production.

In the new model, the two major components are the task environment and the individual. The task environment refers to outside influences on the students' writing. The social environment is one component of the task environment that refers to social aspects of writing such as the audience and collaborators. Hayes (1996) believes that writing is purely a social activity. He views writing as a form of communication with others in our social environment. For example, when

FIGURE 7.1

Modified Hayes-Flower New Writing Model

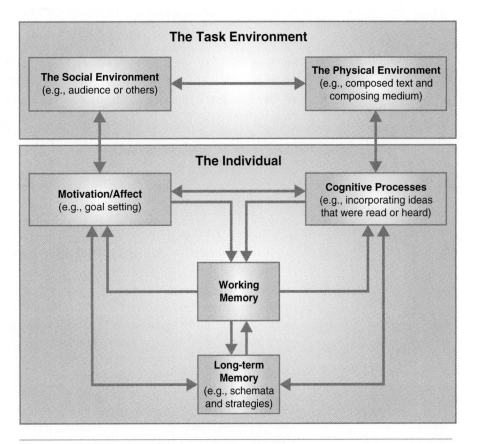

Adapted from J. Hayes, "A New Framework for Understanding Cognition and Affect in Writing" in *The Science of Writing*, ed. C. M. Levy and S. Ransdell (Mahwah, NJ: Lawrence Erlbaum, 1996, 4).

students write, they need to consider the intended receiver of their message, or the audience. Students write differently based upon whether their audience is the teacher, who will assign a grade for a formal writing assignment, or friends, who are looking for more information and are less concerned about the "formality" of the information. In addition, if a student works with another student or collaborator on a written assignment (for example, a research paper), the collaborator will influence how and what is written. Peers influence the writer and, in turn, the peers are influenced by what the writer has written.

The task environment also includes the physical environment, which refers to the text that has already been written and its effects on changing the direction of future writing. Also included under this physical environment domain are the composing medium and its influence on writing. Within the past decade, this component has taken on added importance, as much of our writing is now completed with the assistance of computers. With the help of computer software, students can write papers, compose emails, or develop other media products such as websites, text messages, and other forms of communication. According to Hayes (1996), computers have drastically changed the way that students plan and write compositions when compared to paper-and-pencil compositions. For example, word processing programs have allowed students to revise text more easily through "cut-and-paste," spell-check, and grammar options. Computers have aided countless students with disabilities who otherwise would struggle to spell words or edit papers because of their writing disabilities.

The individual component looks at how different factors within the writer influence the final product. Central to the individual is working memory. Within the Hayes-Flower model, motivation, cognitive processes, and long-term memory all have two-way interactions with working memory. Despite working memory's limited capacity to hold information, it plays a central role and is the engine that drives the production of ideas into words and words onto paper. As writers begin to formulate ideas, they often sketch or map them out on paper. For example, Xavier retrieves information from long-term memory about his favorite basketball players and uses it in working memory as he tries to formulate sentences for these ideas. This process relies heavily on both visual-spatial and phonological memory components of working memory. Visuospatial memory processes both visual and spatial information which is used in the initial planning process. Later, as the writer verbalizes (or uses inner speech) and translates these ideas into sentences, semantic memory works to generate ideas, and phonological memory works by looping ideas into appropriate phrases, clauses, and sentences (Hayes 1996; Kellogg 1996). Throughout this process, the writer draws ideas from long-term memory and transfers these ideas to working memory. Xavier demonstrates this process as he writes more ideas, from long-term memory via working memory, on his paper.

Motivation represents another important domain that certainly plays a role in student writing. Students who are highly motivated often set goals and achieve them. They also use strategies or design activities that lead to achieving their goals, with the end result being production of high-quality papers (Graham and Harris 1996). Cognitive processes in writing involve incorporating information into the planning or transformation stages of writing. This information can come from reading, listening, or reviewing graphic information (for example, illustrations, charts, graphs). Problem solving and inference making are also included in these processes. Through reflection, as students read, they are able to use information in existing schemata to form new schemata; then through text production, they transcribe these ideas/concepts on paper or through spoken language.

Planning, Translating, and Reviewing

According to the Hayes-Flower model, as students compose essays or papers, three main processes occur in writing: **planning, translating,** and **reviewing.** Writing is viewed as a recursive process whereby students write, revise, and edit at multiple stages during their writing. In the Hayes-Flower model, planning is the process that is dedicated to generating ideas, organizing ideas, and setting goals. As students begin to plan, they may map out ideas and build upon them, they set one or more goals (that is, a specific number of words or points written), and, eventually, they organize those ideas. During the next process, translating, students take ideas and translate them into sentences and paragraphs.

Berninger et al. (1995) have further defined two specific subcomponents during this translating process: text generation and transcription. In their research, they noticed that most younger students could use text generation to translate ideas into oral language, but found that only a small number were able to use transcription of these oral ideas into written text (graphic symbols). In addition, these researchers also saw that students not only organize ideas during the previous process, planning, but they often change the organization and revision of ideas as they write during the translating process ibid. As a result, a second reorganization step may occur as students draft ideas, and a preliminary revising step may occur during the translating step.

Finally in reviewing, students evaluate and revise their writing. The purpose of the reviewing stage is to improve the quality of the text that they wrote during the translating process (Hayes and Flower 1980). During this process, students detect weaknesses in writing conventions, determine the accuracy of the written text based upon their "intent," and determine if they have met their writing goals. These actions occur through various activities such as revising the text by moving large chunks of text to appropriate sections; clarifying meaning in certain parts of text; and revising the text by looking for grammatical errors, incorrect words, and missing content. Hayes and Flower (1980) point out that any editing that occurs earlier may interfere in other processes. This is an important point to remember.

THINK BACK TO THE FIRST CASE with Xavier . . .

1. *What aspects of Xavier's approach to writing his essay may indicate that he is not likely to produce a quality essay?*

Based upon the Hayes-Flower model, Xavier either omits or does not spend enough time in the planning, translating, and reviewing stages. For example, spending more time planning out his ideas would help him so that, once he is in the translating phase, he could elaborate more on his ideas that were planned out. He could also spend more time in the reviewing phase by revising and editing his paper more often.

Chapter Question
ALERT

In this section, you will find information that answers a Chapter Question:

2. What problems do students with mild disabilities encounter in written language?

Problems with the Writing Skills of Students with Mild Disabilities

As shown by Xavier (from Case 7.1) and the NAEP scores reported in the chapter's opening paragraph, learning to write is a difficult process for students with disabilities. It involves more than simply translating inner thoughts or conversations into written words. A developing writer must master lower-level spelling and grammar skills while at the same time using higher-level processing skills to plan out thoughts and ideas on paper. Unfortunately, when students with mild disabilities compose, they devote little attention to higher-order processes and often rely on weak lower-levels skills to get them through the writing process.

Students with disabilities have writing problems that range from lower-order mechanical problems to higher-order strategic problems (Wong 1997). Moreover, their lower-level problems often consume cognitive resources that could be used for higher-level metacognitive skills such as the recognition of ambiguities in essays ibid. Students with mild disabilities make both qualitative and quantitative errors in their written products; that is, their compositions are shorter than their peers', and they have more problems with coherence in paragraphs (Chalk, Hagan-Burke, and Burke 2005; Nodine, Barenbaum, and Newcomer 1985).

In terms of the different stages of writing, students with mild disabilities experience difficulty at all stages of the writing process (Lewis et al. 1998). Their problems generally include low levels of productivity; weak mechanical skills, and difficulty in planning; generating, organizing, revising, and editing (Graham et al. 1991; Lewis et al. 1998; Mayes, Calhoun, and Lane 2005).

Some students experience difficulty in the initial stages of writing, such as planning. Research shows that students with disabilities do very little advanced planning and do not use effective strategies even when prompted to during the planning stage (Ellis and Colvert 1996; MacArthur and Graham 1987). In terms of generating ideas during this stage, students with mild disabilities have difficulty writing multiple statements for a familiar topic, even though they have much more information about the topic in their memory (Englert and Raphael 1988). Also during the planning stage, students have a difficult time categorizing ideas into sets of related ideas and ordering them into a coherent overall presentation (Englert and Raphael 1988). Essays are more likely to be personal accounts by the student, rather than including a developed story line or story schema (Nodine, Barenbaum, and Newcomer 1985).

During the drafting process, many students with mild disabilities use a "retrieve-and-write" approach that results in a paper that is full of personal accounts and devoid of relevant and related ideas (Troia and Graham 2002). These students also have little understanding of the structure of paragraphs (Englert et al. 1988) and use a plan-as-they-write approach in which they use preceding ideas to generate new ideas, regardless of the relevance of the new ideas (Troia and Graham 2002). This approach often results in an essay in which students ramble on and on about whatever ideas come to mind. In one study, students with LD had greater difficulty generating compositions that could be classified as stories when compared to nondisabled peers, and their stories were inordinately short and lacked coherence (Nodine, Barenbaum, and Newcomer 1985). Graham and Harris (1993) have theorized that students with mild disabilities have writing problems because they have difficulty transcribing ideas into words, limited knowledge of the writing process, and they fail to use effective writing strategies; instead they rely upon less effective strategies that hinder their progress during the writing process. Other production errors include more mechanical errors (spelling, punctuation, and capitalization errors), errors with word usage, and less legible handwriting (Graham and Weintraub 1996; Moran 1981).

Students with disabilities have additional problems during revising and editing stages. Typically, students with mild disabilities often fail to monitor their own writing and detect errors made during or after writing (Ellis and Colvert 1996). They have a poor concept of revision, whereby they view it as correcting spelling errors, and they use limited strategies for revisions (MacArthur, Schwartz, and Graham 1991). As a result, students with mild disabilities are often more dependent on external resources, such as the teacher, to help them monitor the completeness and correctness of their writing (Englert and Raphael 1988). Even when given time to revise and edit essays, students with mild disabilities make only surface changes (for example, changes in conventions—free from mechanical errors and sentence fluency—for carefully constructed sentences), rather than deeper structural changes (changing ideas, supporting them with details, and reorganizing ideas) (Crawford, Helwig, and Tindal 2004).

Finally, students with disabilities have many problems in terms of writing different types of essays (persuasive, comparative, and so on). They have difficulty using genre-specific knowledge to frame their writing of a particular type of composition, and have a difficult time monitoring the quality of text and regulating their writing (Graham et al. 1992). It could be that students lack knowledge of text structure, which hinders their proper construction of essays and compositions (Englert and Mariage 1991). For example, in one study (Gleason 1999), students with LD had trouble with persuasive writing and instead wrote essays in a narrative style, using unsupported or nonexistent evidence; in some cases, they presented an argument that agreed with the other side.

Across the stages of the writing process, students with mild disabilities often have problems with legible handwriting and producing neat products (for example, writing on a straight line, staying within margins, cleanly erasing), which can impede effective communication to their readers and even to themselves as they try to read what they wrote. As you can see, students with disabilities have problems that

VIDEO CASE CONNECTIONS BOX

Watch the Video Case entitled *Elementary Writing Instruction: Process Writing*. Literacy coordinator Patricia Donahue discusses how she and classroom teachers watch for trends in students' writing to identify skills on which to focus instruction. Listen to the three stories written by children that are read in the video. Although the child authors in this video have not been identified as having mild disabilities, identify evidence the teachers would find of the common problems for students with disabilities presented in this section of the chapter.

cut across many areas of writing, from problems with handwriting and spelling to problems composing and editing essays and papers. Next, we look at ways that teachers can remediate problems in these areas.

Chapter Question

ALERT

In this section, you will find information that answers a Chapter Question:

3. How do you teach handwriting skills to students with mild disabilities?

Teaching Handwriting Skills to Students with Mild Disabilities

Handwriting represents an important skill for students with mild disabilities because it is one means of communicating with others. Students use handwriting skills to express ideas, record important information, and share their own ideas and feelings. Students spend up to an estimated 50 percent of each day on writing tasks (for example, note taking, writing stories or summaries, answering questions) (Amundson and Weil 1996; Tseng and Cermak 1993), and, for many students, handwriting can be a challenge (Rosenblum, Weiss, and Parush 2004). One study found that, among children with LD, 30 percent to 40 percent had handwriting difficulties, and these rates are often higher for students with more severe types of mild disabilities (Cratty 1994). Interestingly, certain letters are particularly difficult for students to write. One study (Graham, Berninger, and Weintraub 1998) found that about half of the handwriting errors (that is, omissions, miscues, and illegible writing) for children in grades one through three could be accounted for by the following six letters: *q, j, z, u, n,* and *k.* It appears that these letters are either the most difficult to recall or the most difficult to produce.

The importance of how handwriting skills fit in with later composition skills cannot be overlooked. When students have to attend to lower-level writing skills as they transcribe their ideas onto paper, they are often diverting resources from high-level cognitive processing to do so. As we have discussed, these higher-level skills are essential during planning, content generation, and other aspects of the composing and writing process (Graham and Harris 1992). Mastery of handwriting skills allows students to become fluent writers who can shift their attention away from transcribing words and letters to expressing their thoughts and ideas. The reason students learn handwriting skills in the first place is to be able to convey messages to others in written form (stories, answers, ideas, feelings, and so on). However, if their messages are to be read and understood, they must be legible. Legible handwriting may not seem like an important aspect as children grow older, but these skills are used on an every day basis. For example, studies have shown that students with disabilities often have a difficult time reading their own recorded notes from class lectures because the notes were not legible (Suritsky 1992). As you can guess, this often leads to trouble as students begin to review or study their notes from class. Moreover, students who have a difficult time with handwriting (that is, students with disabilities) often place too much emphasis on lower-level skills, and this results in shorter essays and compositions that habitually lack coherence and ideation (Isaacson 1989). Therefore, it is essential that teachers provide formal instruction in handwriting early on as part of the students' daily or every-other-day routine so that students can eventually become fluent writers.

Handwriting as Part of the Curriculum

When teaching handwriting, teachers should coach skills within a model of direct instruction. Direct instruction is particularly appropriate when teachers want students to replicate specific skills. First, teachers should model for students how to write letters and numbers. Not only should teachers show children how to produce letters on the board, an overhead, or a whiteboard—commonly referred to as **far-point copying**—but students also need an example or model on their desk that they can refer to as they write the letters—**near-point copying.** Teachers can also visit each child's desk to model how to make the letter, showing each student where to begin and the direction that lines should go to form the letter correctly. Next, as students begin practicing letters, the teacher should circulate around the room and provide guided practice with feedback to catch errors immediately, before students have a chance to practice errors. As teachers will tell you, once students practice a skill incorrectly, particularly in the area of motor skills such as handwriting, correcting it later becomes extremely difficult. Moreover, students should be given specific feedback so that they know which parts of the letter were formed correctly and which parts were formed incorrectly. Once a teacher catches a student making an error, the teacher should model the skill correctly; the student should practice the corrected skill multiple times while the teacher looks on and provides feedback, and then the student should practice the skill on his or her own.

During this early stage of handwriting, teachers should use visual cues on students' papers to describe and model where to begin and which direction to go when forming the letter (see Figure 7.2). Providing visual cues, such as starting points and arrows, along with writing the letter from memory, was found to be a very effective handwriting technique among young, at-risk students (Berninger 2003). In one study, Berninger and her associates (Berninger et al. 1997) taught students to examine carefully numbered arrows in a model of a letter, cover it with an index card, and then write it from memory. In terms of growth rate, students who used the visual cues plus memory technique performed better than those using other treatments (for example, motor, visual cues alone, copy). Over time, these cues should be faded as the students become more fluent at producing letters. Typically, students move from tracing over fully formed letters, to tracing over partially formed letters, to copying letters on lined paper. Ideally, good handwriting skills will be mastered at an early age, but older students with poor handwriting can correct bad handwriting habits and can also benefit from these same techniques, even though they may not be appealing to students (Graham 1999).

Some experts have used **backward chaining** with students to expedite their training of certain skills, particularly motor skills (Smith 1999) and complex community skills (McDonnell and Laughlin 1989). Backward chaining involves breaking down a skill into substeps. In the first step, the teacher completes all but the last step of the process; the student must complete only the *last* portion

FIGURE 7.2

Letter Formation with Cues

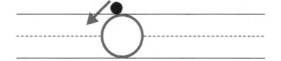

FIGURE 7.3

Example of Backward
Chaining

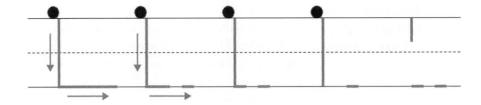

of the task. Next, the student completes the *last two* portions and so on until the student completes the entire portion. In Figure 7.3, the letter *L* is provided for the student to trace. First, the student simply traces all of it. Next, the student traces three-quarters of the letter and must complete the last quarter independently. As the example illustrates, the student completes longer sections of the last portion of the letter. Unlike forward chaining, in which the student would be given the beginning or entire portion in dashes, backward chaining involves giving the student the last portion in dashes to complete with subsequent letters in which the child must complete longer and longer portions.

Finally, once students have mastered the skill, they should practice it independently for the teacher to assess. Previously learned letters should also be practiced periodically to make sure that students can recall these skills and produce them correctly when needed. This type of maintenance is needed to ensure that students will be able to recall and reproduce all of the letters of the alphabet.

Typically during handwriting activities, teachers use commercial writing programs such as the Zaner-Bloser program (see Figure 7.4) or others. These two programs provide models and samples of the correct formation of letters and numbers. Even though teachers use commercial programs, they may want to incorporate or modify some material to provide additional cues or practice for students with disabilities. As with any subject to be taught, teachers need to allocate time to teach it. This may involve listing it on the class schedule or writing it in lesson plan notebooks. When allocating time for handwriting, it is important that sessions be distributed throughout the day and week for students to practice their skills. This is known as **distributed practice** (Kame'enui et al. 2002). Rather than assign page after page of letters to practice in one large block of time, present basic skills (particularly those that require memory or drill, such as handwriting) in short (that is, 10- to 15-minute), distributed lessons and practice throughout the day and week along with previously mastered letter skills. Also, remember that these lessons should incorporate some fun activities such as writing letters on the chalkboard in chalk or, if letters are already written in chalk, dipping a paintbrush in water and tracing over them so that no chalk lines appear when the letter is completed. Teachers could also incorporate other media and drawing instruments, such as using a paintbrush to write letters on paper; writing letters in sand, clay, or other media; or using permanent markers to trace over letters on laminated sheets (aerosol hairspray will clean the laminated sheets). Graham (1999) points out several other important aspects of handwriting that include incorporating spelling words into handwriting, using traditional manuscript letters (that is, there is a lack of evidence that using a special style of manuscript

FIGURE 7.4

Zaner-Bloser Handwriting

Manuscript Alphabet

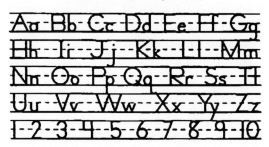

Cursive Alphabet

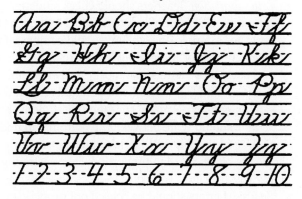

Manuscript/cursive card by the Zaner-Bloser Company
(Columbus, OH).

such as D'Nealian benefits students), knowing the names of the letters in the alphabet, and paying close attention to student errors. In particular, among lowercase letters, eight letters (*q, z, g, u, n, k, j,* and *y,* in that order) were the most difficult for first-grade students to produce legibly (Graham, Weintraub, and Berninger 2001). This information is important because it can help teachers develop a sequence for teaching lowercase letters, can point out those particular letters that may need additional time or teacher attention, and can help the teacher monitor student progress in handwriting skills (Graham, Berninger, and Weintraub 1998).

Initially, the focus of teaching handwriting should be quality over quantity. Students should first learn how to write letters properly, both upper- and lowercase, and then they can work at improving the speed or rate at which they write them. In addition, some in the field of education have advocated that students should be taught letters based upon groups of associated letters. For example, they might begin practicing capitol letters from the "circle" group (that is, *O, C, Q,* and *G*) and eventually move to the "line" group of letters (that is, *L, I, T, F, H, E*). Next, the students might move on to the group of manuscript uppercase letters that have "lines and circles" (that is, *D, P, B,* and *R*). Following this group, students might next work on the "slanted line" letters (*V, X, Y, N, M, W, K, A,* and *Z*) and then "hook" letters (*J, U,* and *S*). Finally, students should be taught handwriting in meaningful contexts. Children (or older students correcting bad habits) should be shown that the payoff for their hard work is that good handwriting skills eventually lead to creating messages, whether they are short notes to mom or dad or other small meaningful phrases or sentences that convey the student's thoughts or feelings.

When providing feedback on students' handwriting, teachers should focus on the following aspects of writing letters: pencil grip, letter formation, letter size and proportion, spacing, alignment, and line quality (Hackney 1993).

- *Pencil grip.* Students should hold a pencil in their hands with a reasonable grip, not too tight that cramping occurs and not too loose that the line quality is too light. As a rule of thumb, teachers should be able to pull the pencil easily out of the students' hands while they are writing.

- *Letter formation.* Teachers should check students' letters, looking for proper formation when compared to a model letter. If a student is practicing a letter *C*, for example, the student should compare it to the model after writing each letter. After completing the entire page, the student should go back and circle those letters that most closely resemble the model.

- *Letter size and proportion.* Letters should remain the same proportion and not increase or decrease. For example, students practicing lowercase manuscript *e* should write between the bottom and middle line on lined handwriting paper. Letters that do not fall between these two lines are either too big or too small in proportion. Demonstrating how certain letters fall between the lines will help students understand letter size and proportion.

- *Spacing.* Letters should be spaced out properly on the student's paper, as determined by the teacher. The main concern is that the student uses a consistent amount of spacing between each letter.

- *Alignment.* Alignment refers to how letters are presented on the page in relation to the lines. For example, for properly aligned letters (manuscript uppercase letters), each should fall between the two lines with its top touching the upper line and the bottom of the letter resting on the lower line.

- *Line quality.* Line quality refers to the thickness or thinness of the line of each letter or number. Aside from the aesthetic aspect, if a students' grip and pressure produce a thick line quality, it could cause the student's hand to cramp or quickly fatigue.

Manuscript Versus Cursive Handwriting

Manuscript handwriting is an important skill for students to learn because most children and adults use manuscript handwriting as part of their daily life, and manuscript letters form the basis of the text that we read. Traditionally, manuscript has been taught before cursive handwriting and is thought to be an easier form of handwriting for children to learn and produce. Cursive handwriting is typified by the use of letters that are connected by flowing strokes. Some experts claim that cursive handwriting is easier for children with mild disabilities because students have to see the entire word before writing it down, as opposed to manuscript that uses a letter-by-letter approach. Yet, for some students with disabilities, cursive handwriting remains a struggle all of their lives, or at least until they are no longer required to write in cursive.

Teachers often debate whether to teach cursive handwriting, especially for students with writing or motor difficulties. When deciding whether to teach cursive handwriting to a particular student, teachers should consider the form of writing that the student's peers use, as well as the form the student's teachers use. If peers use cursive in notes or other written products, you may want to teach this form because it may serve as the primary form of communication between the student and her or his peers. If teachers decide not to teach cursive handwriting to students, they should consider teaching them to read cursive handwriting, at the very least, because this may be the form that other teachers or peers use in class notes, written directions, or everyday communication. On a final note, research has shown no difference in the speed and legibility among students (in grades 4 through 9) who used manuscript versus cursive handwriting. Moreover, students with mild disabilities who used a combination of both manuscript and cursive often had the fastest and most legible handwriting (Graham, Berninger, and Weintraub 1998).

Transitional Handwriting

When transitioning from manuscript to cursive handwriting, Mann, Suiter, and McClung (1992) recommend using a transitional writing technique (see Figure 7.5). This technique uses students' prior knowledge about the formation of manuscript letters to assist them in the formation of cursive letters. Using this technique, students move from writing words in manuscript to writing manuscript letters in words (using connecting lines) to writing words in cursive.

Using this technique, students trace over words that are in manuscript. These words typically slant slightly to the right so that they resemble cursive letters. Next, students trace over the letters that are connected, using dots. Finally, students trace over words that are written in cursive. For more difficult letters, teachers should use more cues (for example, dots) for students to trace and follow. Initially, teachers should use those letters that easily connect, without adding extra lines or humps, such as those shown in the example. Certain cursive letters (that is, *b, e, f, k, r, s,* and *z*) must be taught separately, because they do not closely resemble their manuscript counterparts. Also, certain letters (for example, *m* and *n*) will require extra spacing for the added humps that are used when these letters are written in cursive (Mann, Suiter, and McClung 1992). Eventually, teachers should phase out the use of cues.

FIGURE 7.5

Transitional Handwriting

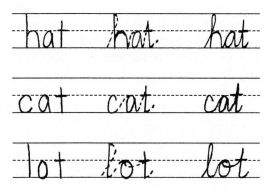

Chapter Question
ALERT

In this section, you will find information that answers a Chapter Question:

4. How do you teach spelling skills and strategies to students with mild disabilities?

Spelling Skills and Strategies for Students with Mild Disabilities

Spelling can be a challenging task for even the most proficient students. We personally know professors who rely on the spell-checker that is built into their word-processing program to help them write and edit articles, books, or simple emails. Spelling involves knowledge of countless rules, word structure, and irregularly spelled words. Of course, it does not help that many letters (or graphemes) have more than one phoneme associated with them (see Chapter 4 for more details about these terms). This lack of one-to-one correspondence can create difficulties even for typically achieving students, let alone students with disabilities. Spelling is a complex memory, visual, and, sometimes, verbal process. First, students must search their memories to recall target words to be spelled. If the search is unsuccessful, students may try to segment or use phonological awareness to try to spell the word verbally. If this step proves unsuccessful or if the spelled word is still not recognized, students might consult a teacher, another student, or, usually as a last resort, the dictionary to determine the correct spelling.

Spelling problems begin in elementary school and often worsen as students progress to higher grades where words become longer and more complex (Dixon 1991). Studies have found that students with disabilities typically misspelled two to four times as many words as their nondisabled peers, resulting in 10 percent to 20 percent misspelled words in writing (Deno, Marston, and Mirkin 1982; MacArthur and Graham 1987). Not only do these misspellings cause problems when students spell vocabulary words, but spelling difficulties slow down the writing process and interfere in the transcription and flow of putting ideas onto paper. Moreover, as we have mentioned in earlier chapters, improved spelling is often linked to improved reading (Ehri 2003).

Over the years, a number of techniques have been developed that were proven to be effective at augmenting the spelling performance of students with mild disabilities. In typical classrooms, students may be given between 15 and 20 words per week to study. In most of those classrooms, teachers use commercially prepared materials that often advocate a study-test method whereby students are given their spelling words on Monday and are tested on Friday (Brown 1990; Fulk and Stormont-Spurgin 1995). One of the problems with this approach is that students often postpone studying until the night before the test and using this traditional approach, particularly for students with disabilities, may not be the most effective method of preparation (Murphy, Hern, and Williams 1990). Instead, teachers should use research-based spelling techniques that advocate changes in the way students with disabilities prepare for spelling tests.

Before we discuss specific instructional techniques, we review general principles that have improved students' spelling performance. Gordon, Vaughn, and Schumm (1993) and Brown (1990) have suggested several changes that could be incorporated into spelling instruction to improve student performance. They recommend the following:

- *Assess unit size.* Reduce the number of words that students study. Instead of 12 words for the week, teachers could introduce three words per day. Overloading with too many words may lower performance.

- *Consider distributed practice.* Students should study daily or twice daily in short sessions (10 to 15 minutes per day).
- *Provide immediate feedback.* Students should be given immediate feedback for words that are misspelled.
- *Review response format.* When studying, students should write their responses on paper to simulate the format of the spelling test. If teachers use a different format, they should match their practice to the actual administration and response format used in the classroom.
- *Develop spelling lists.* Some experts (Graham 1999; Graham, Harris, and Loynachan 1994) have advocated developing spelling lists from several sources that include commonly misspelled words from students' writing assignments; vocabulary or important words from students' academic areas (for example, reading, science, social studies); words that students plan to use in compositions (or future writing assignments); and words that follow similar, but different, patterns, such as *see* and *sea*, so that students can compare patterns and learn the correct spelling of each word.
- *Teach for transfer.* Teach students to transfer words to writing and reading activities in other classes (Gettinger, Bryant, and Fayne 1982).
- *Use computer-assisted instruction (CAI).* A variety of software programs are on the market that aid students in practicing spelling and make spelling an entertaining activity.

Study Techniques for Spelling

The spelling techniques presented in this chapter incorporate a variety of methods, and students may favor them over traditional study techniques. They all incorporate a critical element in spelling study techniques: immediate feedback and correction of misspelled words. Providing students with immediate feedback of misspelled words, followed with extended practice in which students practice the correct word several times, which regularly results in improved performance. All of the following techniques have been used with students with disabilities and were proven effective in research studies.

Classwide Peer Tutoring. Classwide peer tutoring (CWPT) is a technique that has been shown to be effective at increasing the number of correctly spelled words for students with mild disabilities (Burks 2004; Mortweet et al. 1999). During CWPT, students are assigned in pairs to be either the tutor or tutee for 10 minutes, and then they switch with one another for an additional 10 minutes (for 20 minutes total). Each pair is given a list of spelling words, paper on which to write their spelling words, and a sheet to keep track of points earned. The tutors begin by reading the spelling words, one at a time, to the tutees who write the words. As tutees write each word, they also say the letters aloud. The tutors award the tutees two points for each correctly spelled word. If a word is misspelled, tutors tell the tutees how to spell the word correctly and the tutees practice spelling the word correctly three times while saying the letters aloud. If the tutees spell the word correctly three times, the tutors award one point. If the tutees still spell the word incorrectly, the tutors do not award any points. The tutors continue through the list of words and repeat them as necessary, until the timer sounds to end the first 10-minute session. Once the timer sounds, the students switch roles so that the tutees are now the tutors and the tutors are now the tutees.

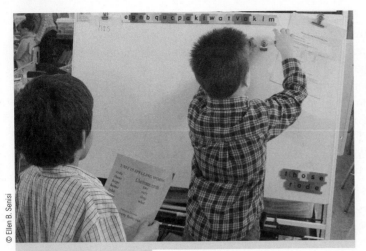

Peer tutors working on spelling together.

They proceed for 10 minutes, spelling words from the same list. After the second 10-minute session ends, the teacher collects materials and students report on the total number of points. The pair with the most points is rewarded with a prize or special privilege (for example, five minutes extra library time, lining up first). Throughout the tutoring, the teacher circulates around the room and awards bonus points for students who are working correctly and cooperatively.

Analogy Technique. Using the analogy strategy in a study (Englert, Hiebert, and Stewart 1985), students were taught to spell new words using familiar spelling patterns from known words, and outperformed students in a control group who used a traditional spelling study method. Using words that rhymed and were spelled the same as the last part of the word, students were taught to use known words that rhymed with an unknown word, to spell the unknown word. First, students were taught to spell common words (for example, *hot, bat, rake*), referred to as spelling bank words. These spelling bank words rhymed with missed words from a pretest (for example, *rot, mat, snake*). During this portion of the training, students spelled the spelling bank words aloud while looking at the written version. Next, students wrote each word from memory three times. In doing so, students had to write the word correctly twice from memory and then a third time after a one-minute delay. Once students could correctly spell these common words, they moved on to the transfer phase. In that phase, students were presented with practice transfer words. These transfer words were a set of four unknown words that rhymed with common words (for example, *cot, dot, got, not*). Once students were presented with a transfer word, they would perform the following three steps:

1. They found the printed spelling bank word that rhymed with the orally presented word.
2. They identified the portion of the word that rhymed and was spelled alike.
3. They spelled the new word using the rhyming part from the spelling bank word.

Once students could successfully practice these skills with a set of words, they moved on to the final training phase. In this phase, students read a list of words from the previous transfer phase and were asked to write/spell these words from memory. If they could not, they were to follow the three steps from the previous phase.

Spelling Package. The spelling package (Frank et al. 1987) involved a variety of practice and study skills to help students spell a set of ten words that were numbered on index cards one to ten. Five of the ten words were words that the students could already correctly spell. Students who were trained to use this spelling package improved their spelling of unknown words. During training, students followed a **five-step procedure** for spelling their set of words.

Step 1. Students opened their envelopes and arranged their cards in order from one to ten.
Step 2. Students traced over the word on the first card with a pencil until they felt that they could spell the word. Once they stated they could spell the word, the card was removed from sight and the student wrote the word from memory.
Step 3. Students checked their spelling by comparing the spelled word with the word from the card. If correct, students drew a star or happy face next to it. If incorrect, they would draw a line through it, and erase the misspelled word. Next, the student was to copy the word from the card and write it an additional four times.
Step 4. Once students correctly spelled the word, they were tested on it by spelling the word from memory. Steps two through four were repeated until all ten words were spelled.
Step 5. In this step, students marked on their spelling chart the correct number of words spelled (that is, self-graphing) for that particular day (during step 4).

Other researchers (Murphy, Hern, Williams, 1990) have used a similar technique called a **copy, cover, and compare approach** with special education students to improve their performance on lists of 14 to 18 words. Using this approach, students would (1) check the spelling of the word by saying the word aloud while looking closely at the letters, (2) copy the word from the list, (3) cover the word with a card and write the word from memory, and (4) compare the second spelling of the word against the word list to check its accuracy.

Five-Step Word-Study Strategy. Graham and Freeman (1986) developed a kinesthetic method for students with mild disabilities to use for studying spelling words. Students who used this strategy in the study spelled more words correctly than students who used their conventional study procedure. Using the five-step strategy, students participated in a 20-minute training session during which the strategy was taught using direct instructional procedures. The five-step strategy consisted of the following:

1. Say the word.
2. Write and say the word.
3. Check the word.
4. Trace and say the word.
5. Write the word from memory and check.

Initially, the teacher modeled the strategy to students. Next, students practiced the strategy with several words while receiving assistance and feedback from the teacher. Finally, the students had to demonstrate proficiency of the strategy by using it correctly with two consecutive words before being permitted to use it in the study session.

Visual Imagery. Berninger et al. (1995) used a visual imagery (or orthographic imaging) method to help students imagine words and practice spelling them for a test. Using this procedure, students were to complete the following directions:

1. Look at the spelling word and say its name.
2. Close your eyes and imagine the word in your mind's eye.
3. Name the letters from left to right with your inside voice.
4. Open your eyes and write the word.
5. Compare your spelling to the correctly spelled word.
6. Repeat the above steps if the word is misspelled.

This method is similar to a visual imagery method that Sears and Johnson (1986) developed to improve spelling among elementary students. Using this procedure, the teacher introduced a spelling word on a transparency and then asked students to use visual imagery to remember the word. This involved (1) seeing the image in your mind, (2) imagining the word displayed on a large outdoor screen, (3) imagining each letter being pasted on the screen to spell the word, and (4) imagining nailing each letter into place with fantasy nails.

Teaching Writing Techniques and Strategies to Students with Mild Disabilities

Chapter Question
ALERT

In this section, you will find information that answers a Chapter Question:

5. How do you teach writing techniques and strategies to students with mild disabilities?

In a 2003 article, Jean Schumaker and Donald Deshler asked the question, "Can students with LD become competent writers?" Given the data that we have for students with disabilities, researchers have shown that they have many obstacles to overcome to gain competence in writing. In an earlier portion of this chapter, we discussed these problems in detail. Despite these challenges, research has consistently shown that, once students are taught strategies and techniques, they can improve their writing performance, in some cases to the point where their performance is comparable to nondisabled peers (McNaughton, Hughes, and Clark 1994).

Before we discuss specific strategies for improving composing skills, we discuss some common principles for teaching writing skills. Graham and Harris (1988) have recommended several principles that should serve as a framework for writing programs for students with disabilities. These principles, many of which reflect practical ideas, will enhance any teacher's writing program and are drawn from research. First, allocate time for writing. It has been reported that students spend very little time working on composing skills in the classroom. As always in education, if you plan to teach skills, you must first allocate time to it. This means writing out schedules that block or dedicate time to composing. Composing, particularly drafting, is a skill that requires **massed practice,** large blocks of time (for example, 45 minutes or more), because it involves getting ideas down on paper and relating ideas back to the main topic or theme. Once students start writing, it is difficult to stop and then start again. Graham and Harris recommend that at least four times per week should be dedicated to writing, along with teaching writing skills.

Second, good writing programs should expose students to a broad range of meaningful writing tasks. The sources for deciding different writing tasks can be determined from end-of-the-year tests (for example, essays on different genre), state standards, content areas that classes demand (for example, report writing), goals for writing (for example, journal writing may best accomplish this goal), social/recreational purposes (for example, personal letters, letters of complaint), or functional reasons (for example, applications). Whenever possible, writing activities should serve a meaningful purpose. If students are practicing forming letters, teachers should make the activity meaningful by having students write sentences with words that have that particular letter in them.

Third, integrate writing with other academic subjects. General instruction in reading and oral language does little to improve a student's writing skills; however, specific targeted writing-related skills can influence writing skills. For example, an oral discussion about a topic prior to writing can influence the student's planning and development of the topic during writing. To influence the effects of writing in other subject areas, students must be taught task-specific skills or strategies (for example, a strategy for responding to specific types of essay questions, or a strategy for writing a research report).

Fourth, automatize lower-level skills or disregard lower skills until the latter stages of writing. Adopting this principle has several benefits. One, just as fluency is an important skill for comprehension during reading, automatizing of lower-level writing skills, such as mechanics, is an important precursor of higher-level skills during writing. For example, mastery of mechanics prevents cognitive overload during the drafting stage of writing (Graham and Harris 1988). Students should practice these lower-level skills to mastery so that putting ideas onto paper is an automatic process. Two, even if students lack some of these lower-level skills, they can still use higher-level processes by bypassing them. For example, instructing them not to pay attention to mechanics while writing will often result in higher quality compositions. In fact, when the physical requirements of mechanics are removed (for example, by using dictation), students with mild disabilities composed better stories (MacArthur and Graham 1987).

Fifth, expose students to different types of genre for writing. Many students with disabilities lack knowledge of story genre for writing and often use narrative or story genre when assignments require other types of genre (for example, persuasive or comparison/contrast) (Gleason 1999). For example, NAEP writing tests require students to produce three different types of essays: narrative, informative, and persuasive. Narrative essays should be imaginative, creative, and speculative, allowing students to express thoughts and emotions. When writing informative essays, students must analyze information and report in essay form about what they learned from it. Lastly, persuasive tasks require students to make an argument for a certain perspective or against an opposing perspective.

Sixth, help students develop goals for improving their written products. Because students with disabilities seldom use goals during the planning stage, teachers need to assist in goal planning and, eventually, teach students to plan for goals during the early stages of writing. Writing conferences or peer evaluations might help students to identify and set goals. Several studies have shown that students who set goals improve their monitoring of those goal areas and reach those goals in their writing. Such goals can include increasing amount and type of vocabulary used, better use of transitional words in paragraphs, and greater variety of sentence types such as compound and complex versus simple.

The seventh and perhaps most important principle of good writing instruction involves using a **process approach** as a framework for writing. We discuss this framework in detail later. All of the principles previously mentioned should be integrated into any writing program for students with mild disabilities.

METHODS AND STRATEGIES SPOTLIGHT

Computer-Assisted Writing

In terms of using computers in the classroom, the following statement best sums up what teachers should remember about technology and writing: "The computer is not a magical writing tool that will transform the way in which exceptional students write; neither is it a writing curriculum or an instructional method" (MacArthur 1988). MacArthur goes on to write that, despite these statements, computers are "powerful" and "flexible" tools for use in the writing process. Like other technologies and CAI, computers can assist students in learning, but can never fully teach students all of the aspects of writing. When we look at the components of the process approach to writing, computers can readily assist students in the planning stage through the use of brainstorming software such as Inspiration©, assist students in the drafting stage through the use of word-processing programs such as Microsoft Word©, assist students in the revising stage through the use of "cut-and-paste" functions, assist students in the editing stage through the use of spelling and grammar checking programs, and assist students in the sharing and publishing stage through word-writing programs or print publication programs such as Microsoft Publisher©.

Despite all of these wonderful options, students must still generate ideas, organize those ideas in a determined order, write the ideas down on paper (or enter them in the computer), and revise and edit those ideas so that sentences are meaningful and paragraphs/essays are coherent and meet their writing goals.

The research is mixed as to the effectiveness of word processing on the written products of students with disabilities (MacArthur 1988); however, studies do seem to indicate that the effectiveness of word-processing programs depends upon how the teacher chooses to use them during writing activities (Rubin and Bruce 1985). Computers can aid students in several areas: editing the paper, producing a polished product, providing a motivating medium, and providing access to Internet resources and other assistive software (Cramer 2004, MacArthur 1988). Obviously, the editing capability of spelling and grammar programs is appealing to students who may have problems with proofreading skills. However, spelling and grammar checkers may not detect missing words, incorrect but similarly spelled words, sentence meaning as determined by the writer, choice of punctuation, and other variables that only proofreading by humans can detect.

Computers can, however, print out a relatively smudge-free finished product, one that is ready to be displayed or published. Motivation is still another advantage; students are often very motivated to use the computer to write essays and compositions over drafting with paper and pencil. The last advantage of computers is that they allow students to access other Internet resources for research and technology for assistance in writing. Using computer technology and software, students can use speech-to-text programs to produce a written product and readers that read text aloud to assist students in proofreading.

Computers offer students an active tool for writing; however, technology can also frustrate students if they lack the skills to use the technology. Part of using technology properly involves learning how to use it, how it can help, and even how it cannot assist. For teachers, this may involve teaching students keyboarding skills and how to use software programs and peripherals (for example, printer, touch screens, external memory drives). In addition, teachers should remember that computers can assist teaching, but are not meant to be the teacher. Teachers should integrate computers into their writing programs so that the technology becomes an integral part of writing and not the writing program itself.

An Instructional Framework for Teaching Writing Skills

Derived from the Hayes-Flower model, the following instructional framework evolved to become one of the most commonly used frameworks in today's classrooms (Bisaillon and Clerc 1999; Bos 1988). This process approach (Graham and Perin 2007; De la Paz and Graham 2002; Graves 1983) consists of the following five stages: planning, drafting, revising, editing, and sharing/publishing. Often, teachers break these stages into distinct activities so that students essentially work on one distinct stage at a time. This is an important point because students with disabilities may become overwhelmed or confused working on more than one stage at a time.

Planning. During the planning stage, students map out ideas and organize them. This stage involves selecting topics, choosing goals for writing, identifying audience, brainstorming ideas related to the topic, and organizing ideas into a framework for drafting (Bos 1988). In some cases, the teacher helps students through these components and, in other cases, students work independently. Teachers often incorporate cognitive maps or other visual displays to help students structure and expand on ideas. Inspiration© and similar software can also be used to help students arrange ideas and expand on details of the composition. Although this stage may not seem essential to writing, MacArthur and Graham (1987) have shown that students who spend time planning prior to writing produce higher-quality written products. In addition, sufficient planning time seems to help with ideation of student essays. Ideation refers to how students develop and express their ideas in a clear and understandable fashion.

VIDEO CASE CONNECTIONS BOX

Watch the Video Case entitled, *Including Students with High Incidence Disabilities: Strategies for Success.* Listen to teacher Martha Cleveland explain how she guides students with nonverbal learning disabilities to recall and organize information in order to facilitate oral and other forms of language expression. Observing the student-drawn and computer graphics cognitive maps, list ways the two types of organizers likely differ in how they would help the featured student write his essay.

Drafting. This stage consists of putting previously generated ideas into written sentences. During this phase, students work to craft sentences and paragraphs by juggling various versions of them from brainstormed ideas. Just as decoding problems can interfere with reading comprehension, spelling errors and handwriting problems may interfere in the writing process (see Suritsky and Hughes 1996). Recall that working memory is limited in its capacity to hold information;

therefore, if ideas are not written down quickly enough in rough draft form, they may be lost forever. Students who lack prerequisites, such as an understanding of sentence or paragraph structure, may also have difficulty during the drafting stage because they may have to recall the rules and procedures for sentence formation, using precious resources needed for ideation. For other students, using a weak strategic approach to writing may interfere in effective drafting of ideas.

Revising. Revising usually involves proofreading a writing product for meaning. While reading, students check to see whether the written draft makes sense on a micro level (sentences and paragraphs) and macro level (does the paper as a whole make sense and does it fit the intent?). Revising may involve moving chunks of text around to improve the transition between sentences and develop coherence of the paper as a whole (Lipson and Wixson 1997). In other cases, revising might be as simple as filling in missing words. Finally, revising provides students with an opportunity to check to see if their papers meet their goals.

Editing. Editing primarily involves proofreading for grammatical and mechanical errors in the paper. Grammar refers to the system of rules by which words are arranged into meaningful units. Some rules are implicit and we may not be able to state them, but we know when they have been violated. Other rules are explicit, such as subject-verb agreement, and are taught to students as a tool to check their writing during proofreading.

In terms of mechanics, most teachers focus their attention on basics of mechanics such as spelling, punctuation, and capitalization. Punctuation, specifically commas and periods, has been identified as the most frequent problem for elementary school students (Porter 1974).

Sharing and Publishing. This last stage is sometimes omitted from the writing process, but we feel that it should always be part of it. We feel that, if students spend the time to produce a written product, then it should be shared with others. Sharing can be as simple as posting a report (for example, weather report) with young children, or more involved such as having students read poems or other works aloud to the class. In some cases, the writing product can be posted on the bulletin board, read to the class, read to parents, compiled into a collection of works that is bound together, posted in the class newsletter, or posted on the class website. In some cases, teachers could model written products to show students how they wrote during the different stages of writing from drafting ideas to the final, polished product.

THINK BACK TO THE FIRST CASE with Xavier . . .

2. What specific writing skill of Xavier's would you try to remediate first?

Xavier has quite a few problems in his writing. Perhaps the two biggest areas for improvement are writing complete sentences and proofreading. Although there are others, these two areas provide a good place to begin.

Strategies for Composing Sentences, Paragraphs, and Essays, and Monitoring Errors

Because writing is much more than just the mechanical aspects that have been addressed thus far in this chapter, we now address more complex tasks of writing as communication, composing, and error monitoring. As you will see, many of the writing strategies featured in this section incorporate one or more of the five stages of the process approach framework into their steps. As you teach writing skills to students, consider carefully how you can structure writing programs so that students participate in each stage of writing or use strategies that will cover each stage. With effective teaching, students will internalize the process approach to writing and begin to view writing as a recursive process rather than as a perfunctory task that results in a written product that meets the required assignment.

Sentence Writing Strategy. The sentence writing strategy (Schumaker and Sheldon 1985; see Box 7.1) was developed to assist students in writing a variety of sentence types. Ellis and Colvert (1996) provide an adaptation of this strategy, as well as additional examples of the different types of sentences that students create with the strategy. Because most students with disabilities rely on simple sentences for the majority of essays and compositions, the sentence writing strategy enables them to produce not only simple sentences, but also compound, complex, and compound-complex sentences (Deshler and Schumaker 2006). This variety is not meant to make their writing more complicated, but is meant to help them express their ideas more fully and to make the written product more readable.

Using the steps of the PENS strategy, students pick a formula (see Box 7.2) and explore (that is, choose) words (subjects and verbs) that fit the formula. In the next step, note, students write down the sentence from the formula that they chose. In the last step, search and check, students examine the sentence to make sure that it is a complete sentence, identify the subject(s) and verb(s), determine whether the sentence has proper capitalization and punctuation, and read it to determine whether it makes sense.

BOX 7.1

SENTENCE WRITING STRATEGY—PENS STRATEGY

P Pick a formula.
E Explore words to fit the formula.
N Note the words.
S Search and check.

BOX 7.2

FORMULAS AND SAMPLE SIMPLE SENTENCES

S = subject and V = verb
S V = Tom ran home.
SS V = Tom and Judy walked home together.
S VV = Haja ran and kicked the ball.
SS VV = Yogi and Sevin ate three pizzas and drank soda.

BOX 7.3

FORMULAS AND SAMPLE COMPOUND SENTENCES[1]

S V = Tom ran home and he ate dinner.

SS V = Tom and Judy walked home together, *so* they could talk to each other.

S VV = Haja ran and kicked the ball, *but* it was caught by Tucker.

SS VV = Yogi and Sevin ate three pizzas and drank soda; they were still hungry.

---

[1]*And, so, or, for, nor, yet,* and *but* are coordinating conjunctions and are used with punctuation separating independent clauses. The sentence formulas use subject(s), verb(s), and a semicolon (with no coordinating conjunction).

Applying the PENS strategy to actual sentences, students first learn how to use the four formulas with simple sentences, next with compound sentences, then with complex sentences, and finally, with compound-complex sentences (Ellis and Colvert 1996). Once students can successfully create the four types of simple sentences, they move on to compound sentences. As shown in Box 7.3, students create compound sentences by using a comma and a coordinating conjunction such as *and*, *so*, or *but* with two independent clauses. Variations of these sentences are created using one or two subjects and verbs from the formulas.

Once students master compound sentences using the PENS strategy, they move on to complex sentences and compound-complex sentences.

In some cases, prior to using the PENS strategy, students may need to be taught prerequisite sentence writing skills such as identification of subjects and verbs, use of proper punctuation, and rules for capitalization. Frequently, students need much practice to master these different types of sentences. Initially, they are taught first to identify a particular type of sentence before they are asked to create and write their own (Ellis and Colvert 1996).

PLEASE Paragraph-Writing Strategy. The PLEASE strategy (Welch 1992) was developed by addressing writing deficits that students with disabilities frequently made. This strategy incorporates components of the process approach into a strategy format using the mnemonic, PLEASE. In other words, students learn to write all of the parts of a paragraph using the planning, composing, and revising components of the process approach. Each step is meant to elicit a specific action associated with writing. The steps are illustrated in Box 7.4.

In the first step, pick, students are taught to pick a topic and decide their audience. Once students have chosen the topic, purpose, and audience, they continue in this step by choosing the proper format (for example, enumerative, compare/contrast, cause/effect) to use to write the paragraph. In the list step, they are taught techniques to generate and list ideas about the topic. Generating ideas can include asking various questions about the topic and then answering them, as well as listing or mapping out ideas (Kytle 1970). These ideas include

> ### BOX 7.4   PLEASE PARAGRAPH-WRITING STRATEGY
>
> P <u>P</u>ick a topic.
> L <u>L</u>ist your ideas about the topic.
> E <u>E</u>valuate your list.
> A <u>A</u>ctivate the paragraph with a topic sentence.
> S <u>S</u>upply supporting sentences.
> E <u>E</u>nd with a concluding sentence.
>   AND
> <u>E</u>valuate your work.

topic ideas and related (that is, supporting) ideas. In the next step, students are taught to evaluate their list in terms of completeness, organization, and sequencing of ideas that will be used to generate supporting sentences. In the next step, students are taught to activate the paragraph with a topic sentence. During this stage, students are also taught how to write a short declarative topic sentence. In the fifth step, students are instructed on how to supply supporting sentences for their topic. During this step, students generate supporting sentences from their list of ideas. Over time, students are taught to enhance ideas by generating clarifying or expanding sentences. Finally, in the last step, students are taught to end with a concluding sentence and evaluate their work using the COPS strategy (See the Error Monitoring Strategy later in this chapter).

The training for this strategy took place over 20 weeks with 30-minute sessions occurring three times per week. The training incorporated video presentations that consisted of seven steps: stated learning objectives, lead-in activities, focused viewing activities, segmented viewing activities, post-viewing discussion, follow-through activities, and evaluation (Welch 1992). These presentations demonstrated to students what each step entailed and how to use it.

THINK BACK TO THE FIRST CASE) with Xavier . . .

3. *Name and describe two types of writing activities or techniques that Xavier could use prior to handing in his paper to improve the quality of his writing.*

To assist Xavier in writing complete sentences that contain at least a noun and verb, his teacher could use the sentence writing strategy. Using this strategy would enable Xavier to write sentences that contain both nouns and verbs. A second strategy is the PLEASE paragraph writing strategy. This strategy would enable Xavier to use a process approach to writing that should improve his writing. This strategy also contains the COPS proofreading strategy (discussed further in this chapter) that would teach Xavier to proofread his paper by looking at specific aspects (for example, capitalization, punctuation, and spelling) prior to handing it in.

BOX 7.5

TREE MNEMONIC FOR AN ARGUMENTATIVE ESSAY

T Topic: note the *topic* sentence.

R Reasons: note the *reasons*.

E Examine: *examine* your reasons (will the reader buy them?).

E Ending: note an *ending*.

Self-Instructional Strategy for Essays. Graham and Harris (1989) developed a strategy that was designed to assist students with mild disabilities with generation, framing, and planning during writing. Specifically, this strategy sought to improve argumentative essays. An example of an argumentative essay prompt is, "Do you think children should be allowed to have their own pets?" The general framework for the arguments consists of a premise, reasons and data to support the premise, and a conclusion. The premise represents the student's statement of belief (for example, "I think I should be allowed to own a dog."). Reasons are explanations as to why the student believes in this premise (for example, "If I owned a dog, I would take care of it every day by feeding it and walking it."). The conclusion is a closing statement that ties everything together (for example, "Because I would love and care for my dog, I think I should be allowed to own one."). In addition, elaborations are encouraged and count toward the student's final score if they are sentences that expand on the premise, reasons, or conclusion.

Prior to strategy training, students are taught about the components of a good argumentative essay through the mnemonic TREE (see Box 7.5). The mnemonic and its prompts correspond to the components of a good argumentative essay.

Using this mnemonic, students have to generate ideas about the topic, support for the topic (that is, reasons), and a conclusion. As Graham and Harris (1992) explain, in the topic step, students had to think about the topic (for example, "Do you think children should give some toys to children who do not have them?") and generate a written statement that supports their belief (for example, "I believe that children should give some toys to other children."). Next, students need to generate reasons that support their premise statement. During this stage, students should try to generate at least three to four reasons to support their premise (for example, "It would be nice, it would make them happy, and we should share what we have with those who have less than we do"). Next, during the examine stage, students should examine those reasons to determine if the reader would believe them. Students should cross out those that are unbelievable and generate other more reasonable ones. Finally, during the last stage, ending, students should come up with a good ending statement (for example, "Because of the following reasons, I think kids should share their toys with others.").

During the actual strategy training, students were taught the following three-step strategy for writing good essays: think, plan, and write:

1. *Think:* Who will read this? And why am I writing this?
2. *Plan:* Plan what to say using TREE (determine topic sentence, note reasons, examine reasons, and note ending).
3. *Write:* Write and say more.

The strategy steps require students to generate ideas and reasons for writing the essay, evaluate ideas based upon the potential readers of their essay, generate notes about their essay during planning, and continue generating notes and ideas as they write the essay. Throughout the training, instructors model for students and use "think-aloud" techniques to facilitate strategy instruction and demonstration. Following modeling, students are required to practice the three-step strategy and mnemonic TREE until mastery. The main purpose of the strategy is for students to spend increased time on the planning stages (that is, think and plan) and draft (that is, write) sentences from their ideas only after they thoroughly develop their ideas.

CASE 7.2	**Crayon Colors**

Case Introduction

Now that you have worked through the first case in this chapter, you should feel comfortable addressing issues in a second case. In this case, Awar and Henry work in a collaborative classroom for science, math, and possibly language arts. Myles's eighth-grade teacher is working on Standard 8.7 that deals with writing skill. This standard states the following:

> *8.7 The student will write in a variety of forms, including narrative, expository, persuasive, and informational. Use prewriting strategies, organize details, use specific vocabulary and information, revise writing for word choice, sentence variety, and transitions among paragraphs, and use available technology.*

Read the case and see if you can suggest skills to target for remediation and techniques or activities to help remediate the targeted writing skills.

"All right class, listen up!" Mrs. Awar Hall said to her eighth-grade students in language arts. She continued, "This is the famous 'Creative Writing Crayon Paper' that you've heard so much about. Your creative writing assignment will be to choose a color of crayon that you want to be and describe why you would be that color of crayon." The students who had been sitting quietly in their seats until now began cracking jokes about different colors. "Mrs. Hall. What did the blueberry ask the sick banana?" Terry yelled out. "I don't know," said Mrs. Hall. "How are you peeling today?" replied Terry. Randi next yelled out, "Did you hear about the girl who wanted to color her hair?" Mrs. Hall couldn't resist and said, "No." "She wanted to, but she couldn't find a blonde crayon," Randi quipped back. With that, the class began to laugh and become noisy.

Realizing that she was about to lose control, Mrs. Hall began to settle them down. "Alright, now. Settle down, settle down, settle down," she repeated to them. She handed out the assignment directions and told students that it would be due in two weeks. As she whisked by Myles Faircloth, placing an assignment sheet on his desk, she noticed that he had a very despondent look on his face. "Myles, what's wrong?" she said to him. "Nothing," he responded in a flat, less-than-enthusiastic voice. As she continued down the aisle handing out the assignment sheets, Mrs. Hall remembered that Myles had a difficult time with writing. Because this was his first assignment, she suspected that he might

continued

need a lot of help. Even though they were only six weeks into the new school year, Myles had already exhibited problems with spelling and writing that concerned Mrs. Hall, but she knew that Henry Brown, the special education teacher, was assisting him. Despite her concerns, she was certain he would be fine because of Mr. Brown's support.

Myles had been identified as having mild mental disabilities about two years ago when he first entered Mapleview Middle School. The committee found that Myles had problems in written language, specifically composing, spelling, and handwriting. Myles had always been a hard worker since coming to Mapleview from Parkview Catholic School. Although he had been held back a year in second grade at Parkview, Myles continued to struggle to maintain a minimal grade point average to pass from grade to grade. "Would this be the year that they moved him permanently to the self-contained special education class?" Mrs. Hall thought. It was not that she wanted him moved, but she felt that she did not have the "special skills" necessary to teach him. Mrs. Hall really liked Myles, but she had 24 other students to attend to and could not work one on one with him to complete this assignment as she had done in the past.

Later that day, Mrs. Hall caught up with Mr. Brown to alert him of the language arts writing assignment. "I know we have collab (that is, collaborative teaching) math and science, but you may want to try to work collab language arts into your schedule," she remarked to Mr. Brown. After giving her a blank look, he said, "OK. I'll see what I can do." Mr. Brown had his schedule set for the year; however, once again, he had to rearrange it so that he could assist his three special education students in Mrs. Hall's class. Mr. Brown knew that, if he did not fit collab language arts into his schedule, Myles and the two others would end up getting poor grades or failing the class.

Myles dreaded this assignment. He hated writing in no uncertain terms and already began thinking that he was going to fail the assignment. When he brought the assignment paper home for his parents to sign, they too dreaded another writing assignment; however, they knew that, if he could begin early enough, he might have a fighting chance at passing it. Despite the best efforts of both Myles and his parents, they waited to begin working on it until the weekend before it was due. Their five-day business trip to Japan had distracted them from his school assignments. Now, with it due in 24 hours, Myles sat down and began working on the assignment.

As Myles sat down to write a rough draft, he started with, "If I were a crayon. . . ." After several minutes, he became distracted with his dog, and his mother prompted him to get back to work. In the next hour, Myles struggled to write down several sentences, most of which were poorly written and riddled with spelling errors. Myles decided that he wanted to be the color fuchsia. After a while, his mother came in the room to check on him and told him to finish up upon seeing his lack of progress. She decided to help him by giving him some sentences. "Here, write this down," she said to him. "I want to be fuchsia because it is the color of plums, my favorite food. I want to be fuchsia because my favorite shirt is that color. OK, now clean up and get ready for dinner," she continued. As Myles scribbled down those lines, he again made spelling and grammatical errors. After his mother called him again a few minutes later, he squeezed his paper into its folder, placed the folder in his backpack, and zipped it up ready for school the next day.

When Myles handed in his paper, Mrs. Hall just looked at it in amazement. He had erasure marks on it from where he had made corrections, and his paper had various folds in it after being removed from his stuffed folder in his backpack. As Mrs. Hall tried to straighten the corners, she thought that the paper would earn one of the lowest grades in the class, and now she was in a quandary. Here is what she read:

If I Were A Crayon
By: Myles Faircloth

If I were a crayn I'd be fuchsia. I would be this color cause is it my favorites. This color is a mix of pirple and blue. These colors got mix up one day and made fuschia. It can hide at nite and not seen by other color crayens. Use yellow crayen to lite my way at nite. Protect me would be color gray crayen. I want to be fuchsia because it is the color of plums, my favorite food. I want to be fuscsia because my favorite shirt is that color. Fushie it is!

"Wow," Mrs. Hall exclaimed. She thought to herself, "Should I give him time to revise it before I grade it? Or, should I just grade it along with the rest of the class?"

CASE QUESTIONS

1. What are two other writing skills that you, as the teacher, would address?
2. Name and describe two types of writing activities/strategies that you would use with Myles.

TABLE 7.1: The Essay Planning Strategy

Planning Strategy: STOP	Instructions for Each Planning Step:
1. Suspend judgment	Consider each side before taking a position. Brainstorm ideas for and against the topic. When you can't think of more ideas, see the first three cue cards: (a) Did I list ideas for each side? If not, do this now; (b) Can I think of anything else? Try to write more ideas; and (c) Another point I haven't considered yet is . . .
2. Take a side	Read your ideas, decide which side you believe in, or which side can be used to make the strongest argument. Place a "+" on the side that shows your position.
3. Organize ideas	Choose ideas that are strong and decide how to organize them for writing. To help you do this, see the next three cue cards; (a) Put a star next to the ideas you want to use. Choose at least (__) ideas; (b) Choose at least (__) argument(s) to refute: and (c) Number your ideas in the order you will use them.
4. Plan more as you write	Continue to plan as you write. Use all four essay parts (see the last cue card if you can't remember **DARE**): **D**evelop your topic sentence **A**dd supporting ideas **R**eject at least one argument for the other side **E**nd with a conclusion

Note. In the third step, "**O**rganize ideas," goals to choose the number of supporting ideas and arguments are adjusted for each writer, based on initial writing ability. Remind students that their primary goal is to be convincing, so they may include more (or even less) items as they write.

Reprinted with permission from S. De La Paz, "Strategy instruction in planning: Teaching students with learning and writing disabilities to compose persuasive and expository essays" *(Learning Disability Quarterly* 20(1997):227–248).

The Essay Planning Strategy. Through a refinement of the self-instructional strategy, De La Paz (1997) developed an essay planning strategy that assisted students in examining an issue from multiple perspectives before taking a side. This essay planning strategy incorporates the two mnemonic prompts STOP and DARE (see Table 7.1).

In the first session of teaching this strategy, the teacher discusses with students the purpose of the strategy and how it helps during the planning stages of writing. This discussion should include the benefits of the strategy and the goal of learning to write better essays. After obtaining a commitment to learn, describe the strategy steps and inform students that the STOP strategy is meant to have them stop, reflect, and plan before writing. Review all of the steps. Following the review, model all of the steps to STOP for the students. Students will slowly become involved in this demonstration and contribute ideas and formulate sentences during the writing portion. Once this session ends, have students work together to practice collaboratively the steps to write essays. Finally, once students have successfully used the strategy with feedback, they begin working independently. During collaborative and independent practice, students will rehearse the strategy and have to recall to mastery.

When using the essay strategy, the first step, suspend, cues students to consider each side of the argument before taking a position on the topic. The students brainstorm ideas for each side and record them on paper. During the second step, take, students evaluate the merit of both sides, choose a position for the topic, and record it on paper. The next step, organize, cues students to choose the strongest ideas from their paper and choose ideas that could be refuted. During this process, the students indicate which ideas they will use with a star, make sure that they have ideas for both sides of the argument starred, and number the ideas in the order that they will be presented. The last stage, plan, cues students to write down ideas and reminds them to make changes as needed. Also, during this step, students are prompted to use the DARE strategy to develop their topic sentence, add supporting details, reject at least one argument for the other side, and end with a conclusion.

The Error Monitoring Strategy. The purpose of the error monitoring strategy is to teach students to detect and correct errors in written products (Deshler and Schumaker 2006; Schumaker, Nolan, and Deshler 1985). The strategy stresses the importance of proofreading written products before handing them in. The error monitoring strategy uses the mnemonic WRITER and incorporates the COPS acronym within the strategy (see Box 7.6).

In the first step of the strategy, write, students are told that they should write on every other line of the paper when writing a rough draft of a composition or essay. Writing on every other line allows students to write corrections on the blank lines of the paper. Once the paper is written, students move on to the next step, to read the paper for meaning. While reading, students should check each sentence to make sure it relates to the paragraph topic and that the wording is correct. In the third step, interrogate, students review their paper, sentence by sentence, using the following COPS questions:

- Have I capitalized the first word and proper nouns?
- Have I made any overall errors (in handwriting, margins, neatness, or spacing)?
- Have I used punctuation correctly (periods, commas, and semicolons)?
- Do the words look like they're spelled right? Can I sound them out or should I use a dictionary? (Schumaker et al. 1982).

Beginning with the first sentence, students ask all of the COPS questions and then move on to the second sentence and ask all of the COPS questions, and so on until they finish all of the sentences in the paper.

In the next step, students take their papers to someone if they have questions (or are unsure) about aspects of it or if they just want someone to double-check it. Once students are fairly certain that they have caught mistakes, they move on to

---

BOX 7.6

ERROR MONITORING STRATEGY

W Write on every other line.
R Read the paper for meaning.
I Interrogate yourself using the COPS questions.
T Take your paper to someone for help.
E Execute a final copy.
R Reread your paper.

the execute step. In this step, students write the final copy on a new piece of paper (or they make corrections on a computer and print out a final copy). In the final step, students reread their paper a final time before handing it in.

THINK BACK TO THE SECOND CASE with Myles . . .

1. *What are two other writing skills that you, as the teacher, would address?*

Myles has problems with planning his writing and proofreading for errors (particularly spelling). You might want to begin with planning and brainstorming for writing and discuss what to do during the prewriting stage.

2. *Name and describe two types of writing activities/strategies that you would use with Myles.*

Myles could benefit from using a planning strategy (perhaps the self-instructional strategy for writing by Graham and Harris (1989)). You could also try using the error monitoring strategy to help Myles improve his proofreading skills.

Research Evidence   The following strategies are supported by research.

Sentence Writing Strategy. In one study, students who were taught the sentence writing strategy improved their performance on measures of sentence type and grammatically correct sentences. Before training, students exhibited mostly incomplete sentences and simple sentences; after training, students exhibited

---

TIPS FOR GENERALIZATION

Explicit Instruction

Writing strategies, like other strategies, should be taught using explicit instruction. As you read the description of several writing strategies, you probably noticed that teachers used direct instruction steps. In most of the interventions, teachers modeled the strategy while thinking aloud and, over time, involved students in the strategy training (that is, while providing feedback). As students become involved in strategy demonstrations, they can begin to use the steps to help create sentences or paragraphs. Once students are shown all of the steps, they should be permitted to use the strategy or parts of the strategy with easy material. For example, if students are using the PENS strategy, the teacher may want to first have them identify one type of sentence (for example, compound). Next, students would finish partially completed compound sentences and, eventually, students would create

their own compound sentences (Ellis and Colvert 1996).

This type of instruction introduces sentence construction in incremental steps as the teacher provides feedback on student performance. In other cases, if providing think sheets or organizers, teachers might consider fading out these sheets as students reach mastery on certain aspects of writing. Furthermore, because we want students to generalize this strategy to new settings, material, and people, teachers should consider ways to fade out cues and prompts so that these techniques could be used in general education classes. As always, student progress should be monitored to determine that they have internalized the strategy steps and are properly using the strategy in new settings. Teachers can check students' strategy use by asking them which parts of the strategy they used with a specific composition and for some evidence of its use.

more sophisticated and complete sentences. Their sentences were more varied and included compound, complex, and compound-complex sentences (Deshler and Schumaker 2006; Ellis and Colvert 1996).

PLEASE Paragraph Writing Strategy. Students with mild disabilities were trained to use the PLEASE strategy over 20 weeks. Student essays were scored based upon each containing a topic sentence, a minimum of three supporting sentences, and a concluding sentence. In addition, the sentences had to be grammatically correct, functional, as well as related to the topic, and the concluding sentence had to be accurate. Results from the study (Welch 1992) indicated that trained students not only improved their performance from pre- to posttest, but also outperformed a comparison group.

Self-Instructional Strategy for Essays. Students with mild disabilities were trained to use the self-instructional strategy to improve their planning time and quality of essays. Results from the study (Graham and Harris 1989) showed that students who were trained increased the total number of functional elements (premise, reasons, conclusions, and elaborations) for essays (from 7 percent to 82 percent), exhibited higher coherence scores, increased prewriting time, and exhibited higher holistic scores on their essays.

Essay Planning Strategy. After training in the strategy, all students improved their essays by increasing the number of functional elements, increasing essay length, and increasing quality rating of essays. In addition, students exhibited essays that were highly coherent throughout the training. Equally important, students maintained these improvements after the training ended.

Error Monitoring Strategy. Students with mild disabilities who were trained to use the error monitoring strategy were able to improve their detection and correction of errors (Schumaker et al. 1982). Results from the study showed that, prior to training, no students were able to detect more than 25 percent of the errors; after training, they were able to detect more than 90 percent of the errors. In other studies (Deshler and Schumaker 2006; Shannon and Polloway 1993), students with disabilities who used the COPS acronym improved in their ability to detect errors.

CHAPTER SUMMARY

Xavier (from Case 7.1) presented some challenges much like the students with mild disabilities that we find in today's classes. Despite the many obstacles that students face, instruction in writing strategies and techniques can improve their skills and written products. The main approach that teachers can take is to help students understand that writing is a process, not a product. Using the steps of the process approach allows students to spend more time planning and organizing their writing, as well as spending time drafting, revising, and editing their work. The research has shown that students with disabilities have difficulties with writing that include low levels of productivity; weak mechanical skills; and difficulty in planning, generating, organizing, revising, and editing (Graham et al. 1991; Lewis et al. 1998). These students also have difficulty monitoring their writing (Crawford, Helwig, and Tindal 2004; Ellis and Colvert 1996; MacArthur, Schwartz, and Graham 1991). Despite these problems, the research has also shown that, once they learn specific handwriting, spelling, or composition/essay strategies, these students can improve their writing, in some cases as well as nondisabled students (McNaughton, Hughes, and Clark 1994). Likewise, once they receive explicit instruction in handwriting, these students can improve their legibility. As in other areas of instruction, when teaching students with mild disabilities, it is often best to model the skill, use guided practice with feedback, and finish by having students use independent practice to demonstrate that they have mastered the skill.

KEY TERMS

Backward Chaining, 231

Composing, 222

Copy, Cover, and Compare
    Approach, 239

Distributed Practice, 232

Far-Point Copying, 231

Handwriting, 222

Massed Practice, 240

Near-Point Copying, 231

Planning, 227

Process Approach, 224

Product Approach, 224

Reviewing, 227

Spelling, 222

Translating, 227

APPLICATION ACTIVITIES

Using information from the chapter, complete the following activities that designed to help you apply the knowledge from this chapter.

1. Drawing on your knowledge of reading instructional practices (Chapters 5 and 6), identify activities that will help students develop writing skills.
2. You are assigned a new eleventh-grade student who has problems with spelling. What activities or strategies could you teach her to improve her spelling skills?
3. Take one of the strategies/techniques that was presented in this chapter and use it to write an essay or story. Next, write a description of how you applied it and how you would use it with students with disabilities.

TECHNOLOGY RESOURCES FOR IMPROVING WRITING SKILLS

Educational Software Programs for Writing

Many different types of software programs and websites are available for improving the written language skills of students with disabilities. Each software program covers different skills or teaches specific strategies. Special education teachers should match student skill deficits with those software programs. Teachers may need to teach prerequisite skills prior to allowing students to work independently on the software program. The websites listed can serve as resources on the topic of writing or, in some cases, can serve as a source of activities to help students improve their written language skills.

Inspiration© and Kidspiration by Inspiration

These two software programs are designed to help students develop and organize their ideas through the creation of diagrams or maps. Many types of maps and diagrams can be created with the programs, including concept maps, idea maps, webs, and storyboards.

Secret Writer's Society by Panasonic Interactive

This program attempts to teach students the basic skills needed for good writing. Students complete six training levels that will prepare them to tackle a variety of writing assignments. The program uses animated characters to walk students through different steps in writing. Students can also create writing samples or messages, and can use and keep a writing diary.

The Write Connections

This program by Children's Choice focuses on teaching students handwriting. Tucker the Tiger walks students through different handwriting lessons. Using dot-to-dot letters, students learn how to form upper- and lowercase letters. A special "Print" option allows teachers to print out worksheets for students to practice specific letters and numbers.

Spelling Blasters by Knowledge Adventure

This software offers activities that have students recognize misspelled words, fill in missing letters of words, use context clues to complete sentences, and recognize common spelling patterns. This game also provides students with activities that involve proofreading and editing misspelled words. The software contains more than 1,700 words and is organized into 140 spelling lists.

Read Write and Think
www.readwritethink.org

This website for teaching reading and writing to students provides teachers with resources that include lesson plans, reading standards, web resources, and student materials.

Writing Tips and Lesson Plans
www.kimskorner4teachertalk.com

This reading and writing website provides lesson plans for a variety of areas in written language including grammar, parts of speech, and tips for teaching writing.

Guide to Grammar and Writing
http://grammar.ccc.commnet.edu/grammar

This website provides teachers with a variety of terms, definitions, and examples for written skills. The website also provides advice and tips for writers, as well as interactive quizzes on parts of speech, grammar, punctuation, spelling, and a variety of other areas.

Visit the book-specific website at www.cengage.com/education/boyle for a variety of study tools such as web links, tutorial quizzes, glossary/flash cards, bonus material not included in the text, and more.

The premium website offers access to additional materials, including the Video Cases. Go to www.cengage.com/login to register or purchase access.

Math: Strategies and Techniques

CHAPTER QUESTIONS

1. What knowledge and skills are essential for learning all forms of mathematics, and how can they be taught to students with mild disabilities?

2. What are the challenges that problem solving and advanced levels of mathematics pose for students with mild disabilities, and what are effective instructional responses?

3. What are essential features of effective mathematics curricula?

We often think of math as quite different from reading and writing, but can you think of some ways that they are similar?

How your students learn mathematics is similar to how they learn to read and write. It involves mastering "pre-" math concepts (for example, number sense). They have a number of basic skills to learn, as well as a variety of processes that range from simple to complex. Students must receive explicit instruction in—and practice with—a variety of basic concepts and operations. They also need guidance in thinking about and performing mathematical procedures. Yet, although the learning processes for mathematics, reading, and writing mirror one another, the underlying difficulties that some students have with learning mathematics are often of a different nature from those for reading and writing (Jordan, Hanich, and Kaplan 2003; Robinson, Menchetti, and Torgesen 2002).

Chapter Question
ALERT

In this section you will find information that answers a Chapter Question:

1. What knowledge and skills are essential for learning all forms of mathematics, and how can they be taught to students with mild disabilities?

Developing a Foundation in Mathematics

Just as humans naturally observe language and begin to develop language systems in infancy, we also observe and begin to make use of mathematics in infancy. That is, we learn the foundational concepts and skills of mathematics in much the same way we learn language for communication. Parents, toys, television, and daily experiences all help developing children to recognize mathematical concepts such as proportion, time, linearity, and additive properties. For example, *take two more bites, you may pick out the next story we read,* and *oh, that's just a tiny boo-boo* all convey mathematical concepts to children.

Once children arrive at school, effective instruction helps their mathematical literacy to grow. When students have difficulty with mathematics in school, a common cause is a limited foundation in mathematical literacy. Sometimes, however, ineffective mathematics instruction is part of the explanation for mathematics difficulties. Math instruction is not always matched to how individual students need to learn (for example, students' prior knowledge is not assessed and procedures are taught globally instead of delineating major and minor steps) and students do not always receive sufficient guided practice to master mathematics (Bottge 2001). In addition, mathematics involves complex language; a single term can represent an entire mathematical concept (for example, *solve, estimate*), which can be uniquely challenging for English language learners (ELLs) with mild disabilities (Freeman and Crawford 2008; Garrison, Amaral, and Ponce 2006).

Each of the mild disabilities may be a cause of mathematics difficulties. To be "literate" in mathematics requires learning a variety of mathematical processes (for example, for problem solving, geometry, and algebra) and how to apply them. Students who struggle with higher-level mathematics typically have difficulty with basic mathematics skills as well (Maccini and Hughes 1997). An estimated 4.6 percent to 6.5 percent of school age students actually have a "mathematics disability" (sources cited in Seethaler and Fuchs 2006). Mathematics difficulties problematic enough to constitute "mathematics disabilities" should be evident by third grade (Fuchs et al. 2008).

| **CASE 8.1** | **Rodney's Mathematical Abilities** |

Case Introduction

In this case, you will read about a student who has trouble with mathematics skills. As you read the case, you will see that he appears to know a variety of basic math concepts and skills; he just does not seem to use them consistently—inside or outside of school.

At the end of the case, you will find case questions. These questions are meant to serve as points for reflection. Of course, if you can answer them immediately, you should do so, but you may want to wait to answer them until you have read the portion of the chapter that pertains to the particular case question. Throughout the rest of the chapter, you will see the same questions repeated. As you see them, try to answer them based upon the portion of the chapter that you just read.

Rodney is a sixth-grader who studies math in Ms. Abbott's resource room. This is the first year Rodney has been scheduled for the resource room since he was identified for special education in third grade. Previously, he received his special education for mathematics in the general education classroom, occasionally going to the resource room with Ms. Abbott for intensive one-on-one review. Math is the only academic area addressed on Rodney's IEP. According to his performance on the Key Math Diagnostic Arithmetic Tests-Revised/Normative Update at the end of fifth grade, he was performing at 2.7 grade level for basic concepts, 2.1 for operations, and 1.7 for applications.

In the resource room with Ms. Abbott, Rodney routinely drills the basic math facts for addition, subtraction, multiplication, and division. He and Ms. Abbott also do a variety of activities where he must show that he understands how to perform the basic operations. Every three days he attempts timed drills for one of the four types of math facts. Rodney is making steady progress in mastering performance of the facts for single-digit calculations. He has reached approximately 70 percent accuracy in timed drills, and he has steadily increased the number of problems he attempts as well. He has less than 40 percent accuracy rates for two-digit addition and subtraction, however, and has not begun to address multi-digit multiplication and division. Rodney has persistent difficulty with explaining the basic mathematical operations, even for the single- and two-digit operations he performs well.

When he wrote **2 + 4 = 6**, Ms. Abbott asked him to now write it the "tall" way. He wrote the following:

After Ms. Abbott probed him with several questions, he explained that the four belongs on top because "it is bigger than the two."

In another problem, he wrote the following:

Ms. Abbott asked him to explain what it said. He replied, "You get three."

Ms. Abbott then asked him to explain how he got the answer. Just as he had done when solving the problem, he held up nine fingers and counted down as he lowered each finger; forgetting to lower his thumb, he produced three fingers and said, "see, three."

Despite a 70 percent accuracy rate for one-digit addition, he wrote **16** when recently given the following problem:

When asked to explain how he got the answer, he could not.

Then when asked to try again while speaking out his process, he said, "Four plus two is six [writing **6**], and two plus one is" [writing **3**].

Rodney's Math Outside of School

When Rodney boards the public bus to go to school, he flashes his student pass to pay the discounted rate of 60¢ per trip. Students must pay with exact change because bus drivers do not make change. Because Rodney is not sure of how to make 60¢ in any combination other than two quarters and one dime, he often pays with a dollar bill to avoid confusion.

Each day when Rodney gets home, he gets his key from Mrs. Davis who lives across the hall. Once in the apartment, Rodney finds a note with the chores that he has to complete before his mother gets home from work. On days when his chore is laundry, he first has to sort the dirty

continued

clothes by type. Then, based on how many loads he observes that he has, he needs to take the correct amount of money from the cookie jar down to the building's laundry room. There he loads the washer, fills the detergent cup to one of the lines his mother has marked for him ("small load," "big load"), and then tries to load enough coins to start the machine. He can never remember how much a load costs, and the sticker on the machine is long gone, but remembering what combinations of coins make the right amount is even harder. Rodney's strategy is to load the washing machine cartridge with a combination of coins and push it in, trying different combinations until it doesn't pop back out. The drawback is that the coins will be accepted if he overpays, but this approach works for him. Fortunately, the dryers have a different type of cartridge, with an exact size slot to lay the coins into for each coin that he needs. He finds that easy.

Rodney doesn't have to wait in the laundry room for the washing and drying to be finished but he typically does. Although he can tell time, he can never seem to figure out when to go back downstairs to get things out of the dryer, and his mother yells at him if she comes home and finds she has to retrieve the laundry.

CASE QUESTIONS

1. What do the examples of Rodney's in-school and out-of-school mathematics performance reveal about his mathematical strengths and weaknesses?
2. What types of activities will help Rodney to think about why and how basic math operations work?
3. Will Rodney be able to learn the types of mathematics other sixth-graders study if he is still working to master basic computation facts?

Mathematics Difficulties for Students with Mild Disabilities

Observations of Rodney's mathematical performances in and out of school are good indications of the mathematical literacy and computation skills he has acquired. From sorting the laundry, determining the number of loads, and pouring the right amount of detergent per load, we can note that he is able to classify, recognize relative proportions, and, probably, estimate. From his schoolwork, we can see that he knows how to add and how to subtract single digits at least. Noting how he lines up addends, operation signs, and sums, he has not mastered lining up numerals in an equation by place value; however, these examples do not make clear whether he appreciates the concept of place value. Likewise, he has confused rules for setting up equations (always putting the larger number on top in addition) and is at least inconsistent in following the rules for solving equations (subtracting the tens place digits in two-digit addition and failing to apply skills of estimation when reviewing his calculations). It also appears that, although Rodney is able to perform basic calculations correctly on worksheets, he may not be able to perform the same skills so well in everyday contexts. In addition, Rodney is not able to perform addition and subtraction with money, despite the fact that he recognizes different coins and bills. Also important to note is that, despite using certain amounts of money on a routine basis, he has no memory for how to "make" those amounts from the coins available to him. Although Rodney can tell time, he cannot calculate the ending of a set period of time using a clock (for example, how long the dryer cycle runs).

Rodney's performance in and out of school is representative of the mathematics difficulties that many students with mild disabilities encounter in their lives. They are literate in some, but not all of the concepts we would expect. Based upon their age and grade, they can perform certain operations with moderate proficiency at least, but routinely make errors and have little understanding of what they are doing (Bryant, Bryant, and Hammill 2000). Teachers sometimes characterize these students as "careless," when, in truth, they have only partially mastered certain concepts and skills before the teacher moved on in instruction without supporting the development of those basics. Ms. Abbott is pleased that Rodney has begun to make steady progress with his skills since beginning in her resource room this year, but she knows that they must aggressively address his basic skills needs.

Foundational Concepts and Skills. Children learn concepts such as sets, one-to-one correspondence, and number names and values through instruction, games, and daily experiences. These foundational concepts are essential to comprehending the mathematical concepts and skills addressed in math instruction from elementary through high school. Because ELL and minority students may be less familiar with foundational concepts and skills (Andrews and Slate 2002; Garrison, Amaral, and Ponce 2006), they may benefit from being directly taught the new vocabulary prior to learning the mathematics concept or skill that is the focus of the day's lesson (for example, learning to say "one, two, three, four, five" before beginning instruction in counting to five) (Miller and Hudson 2006). Just as phonemic and phonological awareness are essential "pre-" skills for reading (review Chapter 5), foundational concepts of **number sense** are essential pre-skills of mathematics (Gersten and Chard 1999).

Inadequate learning of number sense pre-skills is readily evident in children who have difficulty learning to count or perform simple addition (Geary 2004; Robinson, Menchetti, and Torgesen 2002). Often, children who have not adequately mastered the pre-skills nonetheless make progress in performing basic math skills. These are students like Rodney, who cannot perform those skills consistently and who have limited knowledge of what math operations mean. However, students from diverse backgrounds, including poverty, are more likely to be steered into less demanding secondary school courses if they do not master basic literacy and numeracy in the early grades (Thomas-Presswood and Presswood 2008). Most minority students have consistently achieved below their peers in mathematics (Kloosterman and Lester 2004; Perie, Grigg, and Dion 2005).

The National Council of Teachers of Mathematics (NCTM) (2000) has identified standards in ten areas of mathematics that should be addressed across mathematics curricula (see Table 8.1). Among the basic numeracy knowledge

TABLE 8.1: NCTM's Ten Areas of Mathematics Standards

Content Standards	Process Standards
Numbers and operations	Problem solving
Algebra	Reasoning and proof
Geometry	Communication
Measurement	Connections
Data analysis and probability	Representations

Reprinted with permission from National Council of Teachers of Mathematics, *Principles and Standards for School Mathematics* (Reston, VA: National Council of Teachers of Mathematics, 2000).

and skills identified in the ten areas are: understanding and applying one-to-one correspondence, number, grade-level appropriate vocabulary, relationships, and counting. When students of any age have difficulty with these concepts and skills, they require intervention that addresses them directly. The appropriateness of interventions you use to address basic number sense will vary based on the developmental age of the students and the types of mathematical skills they have already begun to address.

One-to-one correspondence is one of the very first math concepts students should learn (reflected in the NCTM's Numbers and Operations Standard) because it is essential for much of mathematical understanding. It simply means recognizing that units have numerical values. In the lower grades, students can participate in activities in which they distribute objects, one per peer in a group, for example. Older students can perform sorting and matching tasks that require one-to-one correspondence, including for values greater than one. You can assign them to add five drops to each of three test tubes or identify how many problems are in each section of a workbook page.

Closely related to one-to-one correspondence is the **vocabulary for numbers.** Memorizing the names of various digits can be helpful for developing number sense, but is insufficient by itself (Gersten and Chard 1999). Students should be encouraged to name numbers, both for sets of objects and for their written forms. Likewise, to master vocabulary for numbers when shown or told a number, students should be able to count it off on a number line, count out objects, or make hash marks to represent that number. **Vocabulary for relational concepts** should also be developed. Teachers can instruct their students to name and demonstrate which sets are the same and different, as well as which sets or numbers are greater than or less than others. Students just beginning to form basic number sense will need some work on each of these concepts and skills in isolation. Students who have progressed further in their mathematics learning, like Rodney, can benefit from addressing multiple numeracy skills at once. They can, for example, sort objects by type (for example, protons, electrons, and ions in science), count and record how many are in each set, and estimate or compute how many must be added to certain sets to make each equal in proportion.

THINK BACK TO THE CASE about Rodney . . .

1. *What do the examples of Rodney's in-school and out-of-school mathematics performance reveal about his mathematical strengths and weaknesses?*

Rodney is likely a student who demonstrated proficiency in one-to-one correspondence and vocabulary for numbers, but has only began to develop relational concepts. His prior math instruction did not sufficiently address his understanding of the vocabulary he could apply by speaking and writing, however. This would partially explain why he is generally able to add single digits on a worksheet but cannot add coins whose values he recognizes or count forward on a clock.

To truly understand the proportional relationships among numbers, students need to understand the relative values they represent. For example, a student might readily note that both 5,876 and 5,786 are greater than 90, but not be able to identify which of the four-digit numbers is greater than the other. To determine which of those four-digit numbers is greater, students need to master foundational concepts of place value. **Place value** identifies the value of each digit in a number. Before students appreciate place value, they may not recognize that the number 10 is a combination of the numbers 1 and 0, nor may they grasp why the 1 and 0 must be written in that order. Further, when students work on performing mathematical calculations, they need to understand place value so they can set up a problem correctly (note in Case 8.1 that Rodney did not make consistent use of place value columns when writing addition problems or their sums). Failure to use place value appropriately in calculations can indicate that students do not sufficiently appreciate the meaning of place values, and that they perform calculations more as rote operations than as thought out for what they represent.

Students can learn the meaning of place value by discussing what the digits in a number represent. They can be asked what the digit *2* represents when written as "2" versus when written in "20," for example. Initially, students should attend to place value for two-digit numbers. The basic concept of place value is less confused when students focus only on ones and tens places, both because students are likely to be familiar with the amounts represented by up to two-digit numbers, and because focusing on those two establishes the value of the tens place. Understanding units of tens will in turn be useful for appreciating the hundreds, thousands, and so on place values.

Understanding **classification** will prove useful for students as they learn to comprehend the meaning of the tens place. When students classify, they group objects by like properties. Students' initial attempts at classification can consist of grouping objects by colors or shapes; then they can group sets of objects or written numbers themselves. Students can progress to sorting objects into groups of tens to represent the concept of ten being the accumulation of ten ones. By seeing demonstrations, practicing with manipulatives, and writing numbers in the ones and tens places, students can come to appreciate the value of multiples of ten and its written form. (See the following Methods and Strategies Spotlight for useful activities about teaching number sense and place value at different grade levels.)

METHODS AND STRATEGIES SPOTLIGHT

Activities for Learning Place Values and Related Number Sense Skills at the Lower and Upper Grade Levels

Activities for Number Sense

Regardless of age or grade level, students need to develop number sense if they are going to understand and perform a variety of mathematical functions as basic as counting or as advanced as the theoretical mathematics of calculus.

Lower Grades

Practice saying the names of numbers

Speak the names of numbers printed in numeric form

Count objects to 10

Write the numbers 1 to 10 in order (in numeric form)

Organize objects by size

Point to print numbers when heard aloud

Identify which of two sets of objects contains more objects

Write numbers (in numeric form)

Match the written (script) form of numbers to their numeric forms

Although students at upper grade levels who still need to develop number sense would benefit from many of the same activities used in lower grades, they are not likely to be willing to engage in such "childish" activities. Also, they will benefit from exercises in number sense that are directly related to the more advanced types of mathematics they are exposed to in the upper grades.

Upper Grades

Count $1 bills into piles to exchange for $5 and $10 bills (or use pennies and other coins)

Follow directions that involve counting units (for example, 1 egg in recipes, add 3 drops in lab procedures, walk 10 paces and turn right in a scavenger hunt)

Number the main points represented in an outline for writing a paper

Organize assignments from the lowest to the highest grade earned

Compare sets for numbers of components and then overall size

Sort piles of materials into equal numbered sets

Activities for Place Value

Lower Grades

Use graph paper to line up digits in the ones and tens places

Sort sets of objects by whether they represent numbers filling the ones place or tens plus ones places

Upper Grades

Rename a numeral as high as possible by successively adding one more 0 to the ones place

Marking a decimal point, shade squares of graph paper to represent whole numbers and their decimal fractions

Maintain a checkbook or account ledger

Convert piles of ten objects into sets of ones; repeat with piles of 100 objects into sets of tens

Line up numeric representations of money amounts or weights of objects (in decimal units) by decimal points

At least three additional pre-skills are prerequisite to learning computation. Like the other pre-skills, students may ultimately master them by moving on to computation, but learning computation will be greatly eased if the student is already comfortable in these pre-skills. **Counting** is a vital skill for computation. Students should be comfortable with counting to at least 10 or 20 before they will be ready for addition. Younger students will enjoy many counting games, and older students are more interested in counting out cards, or parts and objects related to an academic activity. Once students are fluid in counting to at least 10, they should practice "counting by." **Counting by** twos, fives, and tens (for example, 10...20...30...40...) is particularly useful for calculation operations. Students who learn to count by twos, fives, and tens relatively easily would benefit from learning to "count by" for all of the digits between 1 and 10, for the same reason that this will facilitate operations during calculations. Students who have difficulty mastering the counting by strategy can be expected also to have difficulty when they begin practicing calculating, but waiting until they first master the counting by technique may delay needed practice in calculations, and beginning calculations practice can provide another avenue for practicing the counting by technique.

When students are comfortable with counting and counting by 2, 5, and 10, they should learn to **count backwards.** A countdown or challenge to write numbers in descending order can provide practice in this skill, which will be useful when estimation or subtraction is involved in a calculation. As with counting up, students may first master **counting down** from 10 and then might attempt it from 20 or even higher numbers. Ideally, they will master counting down from 100.

Basic Computation Concepts and Skills. **Computation** includes addition, subtraction, multiplication, and division. Initially, each of these forms of equations is taught in isolation, and, typically, in the sequence named, as this order is considered to be easiest to most difficult for comprehending and mastering. Instruction for each should begin with single-digit problems. Once students have begun to master the procedure, they will be ready to progress to two-digit and other multi-digit examples (that is, progress to **algorithmic computation**), which can involve operations from the preceding calculation type for borrowing, reducing, and estimating. So, for example, students attempting $5\overline{)15}$ can count up by fives to estimate an answer, and then use multiplication (5×3) and subtraction ($15 - 15$) to check the answer.

Effective mathematics instruction also progresses from **concrete** concepts and skills to **semi-concrete** and, eventually, **abstract** representations (NCTM 1991; Witzel, Riccomini, and Schneider 2008). So, you should move students from using strictly manipulatives to represent a calculation, to drawing the problem or representing it with hash marks, to eventually only representing the problem by writing numerals or performing the calculation in their heads. This instructional sequence should be applied to each of the various mathematical concepts and skills students learn. Math is sometimes said to become increasingly abstract as students progress to higher grade levels; even for abstract/higher level mathematics, the progression from concrete to abstract phases of learning should be used, especially for students with mild disabilities who are less likely to grasp concepts that are initially presented solely in abstract form.

A first skill of learning computation is learning the vocabulary of computation, which may be taught as a pre-skill. The **vocabulary of computation** includes the terms *add, subtract, multiply,* and *divide.* It also includes terminology for the outcomes of those operations: *sum, difference, product,* and *quotient,* respectively. Furthermore, students must learn to read the following symbols: $+, -, \times, \div,$ and $=$. Students should practice associating the vocabulary for the operations and corresponding outcomes, in both oral and written forms. They can be asked to do matching exercises when the terms and symbols are randomly ordered in adjacent columns. You can also have them read aloud an equation such as

$5 + 6 =$ ___. Being comfortable with the vocabulary of computation will enable your students to concentrate on the numerical task of computation, without second guessing what the task is asking (Lee and Herner-Patnode 2007).

THINK BACK TO THE CASE about Rodney . . .

2. *What types of activities will help Rodney to think about why and how basic math operations work?*

In the sections that follow you will read about specific instructional practices that should help Rodney to master the four types of computation. The previously named activities will help prepare Rodney for success in those upcoming lessons. He should practice the foundational concepts and skills of mathematics by a combination of games, drill and practice, and opportunities to speak and write about them. He will benefit most if he receives intensive instruction in the foundations (Fuchs et al. 2008; Maccini, Mulcahy, and Wilson 2007; also see Chapter 2).

Addition

Having developed familiarity with counting, students can learn that addition is counting by set amounts. In the concrete phase of learning, students will benefit from demonstrations and practice attempts using manipulatives. They will be able to see that four chips plus three chips, added together, equals seven chips. Students should practice narrating the process themselves, using sets of manipulatives they have counted and then counting the sum when the two are added together. Using a number line is also helpful to make the addition process apparent. Students can use their "counting up" skill to move from the first digit of the equation to the sum by counting up the equivalent of the second digit.

For initial practice, have students perform calculations that are easy for them to get correct. Although counting on fingers slows the process of adding, allow students to use their fingers or some form of manipulative during initial attempts to help make the abstract process concrete. As they begin to comprehend the addition process, discourage finger counting and have them count up from memory instead. Eventually, discourage counting up and similar practices in favor of more automatic recall of addition facts.

When students progress to solving written addition problems and writing their own, they should practice writing them both horizontally and vertically so that they appreciate how to read and perform computations in both formats. To help students develop initial proficiency in counting, encourage them always to start from the larger of the two addends, regardless of whether it appears first or on top. As stated, multiple-digit addition should be practiced once students become comfortable with single-digit problems. Because carrying and renaming are more complex skills, begin practice in multi-digit addition only with addends that do not require carrying, including to an additional place value in the sum (for example, 14 + 93 would not be appropriate).

Students benefit from learning the commutative properties of addition and subtraction. Understanding commutative properties enables them to rearrange the problem from the order in which it is presented to one that is more efficient to solve and, therefore, less likely to result in error. A student presented with 2 + 8 should know that solving it as 8 + 2 when using counting up will be easier and quicker, for example.

Subtraction

Subtraction will make more sense to a student who is already familiar with addition. The same logical practice sequences of solving sample problems of the concept with manipulatives, simple to more challenging practice problems, and single-digit before multi-digit equations apply. To practice subtraction, begin with subtracting a smaller whole number from a larger one; encourage students to count down digit by digit from the larger number. In Case 8.1, Ms. Abbott might encourage Rodney to say "seven take away three means seven, six, five, four; seven take away three is four." Just as with addition, students can use manipulatives, fingers, or a number line during initial attempts at subtraction. If the students learned that in addition they may elect to begin from the larger addend no matter its position in the equation (the commutative property), you will need to overtly explain to them why that same practice does not apply to subtraction.

Students should practice solving addition problems by converting them to subtraction, and likewise for learning subtraction problems. Ms. Abbott could ask Rodney to fill in the blanks on the following exercise:

$$3 + 4 = \underline{\quad} \quad 7 - 4 = \underline{\quad}$$
$$7 - 3 = \underline{\quad}$$

$$8 - 2 = \underline{\quad} \quad 6 + 2 = \underline{\quad}$$
$$8 - 6 = \underline{\quad}$$

Multiplication

Although addition and subtraction may be somewhat intuitive concepts to students, multiplication is less likely to be so. To understand the purpose and function of multiplication, students need overt examples to grasp the concept behind it. Note that to say, "it is a faster way to do addition" is technically true, but this is not particularly useful for explaining what it means to multiply. To grasp the concept of multiplication, students can rely on their skills of counting. They can again use sets of manipulatives, this time to represent multiplying. A student could lay out three sets of four chips to represent 3×4; by adding the total number of chips, the student can see that she or he has represented three, four times, and that $3 \times 4 = 12$. Although any type of easy-to-sort manipulatives may be used, students might particularly benefit from practicing with base 10 blocks (see Figure 8.1). As they graduate to multiple-digit problems, students will find the blocks' representation of place values useful.

Counting by can also benefit students in learning to multiply, just as it is useful for learning addition and subtraction. Using counting by, students can learn to count efficiently by multiplicands to solve calculations. They will learn that 3×3 is 3...6...9, for example. If students have not mastered the counting by technique, performing the same task will be more involved, requiring counting 1, 2, 3...4, 5, 6...7, 8, 9, while holding the highest digit from each set of three (3 and 6) in working memory and counting up by three more.

FIGURE 8.1

Base 10 Blocks and Fraction
Blocks

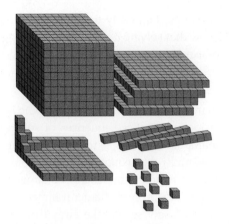

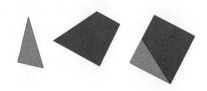

Fraction blocks are cutouts of fractional
portions of *pattern blocks*. They may be laid
atop the pattern blocks to demonstrate how
much ½, ⅔, etc., of a shape is.

Base 10 blocks include individual blocks,
rods equivalent in length to 10 blocks, and
squares equivalent to 10 rods.

As part of learning math facts, students may find it easier to learn certain
patterns. **Patterns** for multiplying by twos, fives, nines, and square numbers may
be easier for students to recall than memorizing all possible multiplication facts
(Chambers 1996; see also Woodward 2006). Those patterns will in turn be useful
in solving multiplication problems that are close to the memorized fact.

Another useful approach to multiplication, which relies on knowing patterns,
is **derived facts** (Woodward 2006). By using well-rehearsed facts, and relying on
number sense skills, students can readily derive the product for a multiplication calculation. If, for example, a student is asked to solve 7×8, the student
can recognize that she or he already knows that 7×7 is 49 and that by adding
one more 7, the total becomes 56. The derived facts students can use depend on
(a) which multiplication facts they have committed to memory, (b) recognizing
that a known fact is close to the one called for, and (c) not turning the problem
into a more complex algorithm (for example, $7 \times 10 = 70, \ldots -7, \ldots -7$), although
$[7 \times 10] - [7 \times 2]$ is a simple subtraction problem for some students).

Woodward (2006) notes that many students can perform a procedure similar to derived facts. By recognizing the value of a multiplicand, a student may
perform a **"split-add"** to simplify the problem. So, for example, 6×4 could be
recognized to be the same as $6 \times 2 + 6 \times 2$.

The purpose of practices such as split-add and derived facts is to simplify
the mental calculations involved in determining the product. Although grasping
the concept of multiplication is necessary for students to understand the operation, and memorizing facts speeds their processing, multiplying is generally a
more complex task than either addition or subtraction. Thus, students learning
multiplication should benefit from learning a variety of approaches so that they
may use the most expedient one for a given task, or even integrate them (for
example, to solve 4×7, a student could first recognize that 4×6 is personally
easier because he is more familiar with counting by with even numbers, and
then separate the problem into $(2 \times 6) + (2 \times 6)$, and, finally, add 4).

Just as they learned for addition, students should learn that the commutative and associative properties apply to multiplication. Then they will come

to appreciate that 3×6 and 6×3 will yield the same product. This will be useful to students who know how to multiply by threes more readily than by sixes. Likewise, learning that the numbers in a string of multiplication tasks can be regrouped can facilitate making a problem easier to solve. For example, $(3 \times 5) \times 8$ can become $3 \times (5 \times 8)$.

Division

Similar to learning multiplication, students need to learn the concept of division. That is, they need to realize that to divide is to partition a quantity into sets. They also need to consider why they would want to do that. You can ask them to think of objects or sets they might wish to break into portions and ask them to explain why. Having established the concept of division and its utility, they should also be cognizant of how it relates to other operations they know about.

Memorizing simple division facts, including the consequences of dividing a number by zero, one, or itself, will help students to develop efficient division practices. Likewise, learning that dividing a number by two will result in a product that is one-half of the dividend will be helpful to students who have a firm command of number sense and also are efficient at multiplication.

Do not neglect to use manipulatives when teaching division. Concrete representations of the operation will be helpful to students appreciating what they are actually doing. Using base 10 blocks, individual objects, or other manipulatives, students should perform the division task (for example, divide a set of 14 chips into two piles by putting equal numbers in each pile) and be able to narrate what they are doing. They should also learn to use manipulatives to represent written problems that are presented to them. With mastery of concrete representations and good number sense, they will be able to graduate to performing calculations written out in numerals.

For many students, division is complicated by the fact that problems are organized differently than are the columnar addition, subtraction, and multiplication problems that they are used to. They will need to learn to read the four following problems, for example, as the same:

$$7\overline{)14} \qquad \frac{14}{7} \qquad 14/7 \qquad 14 \div 7$$

The first of the four examples represents division problems in a format that may be most useful to students beginning to understand the concept and operations involved. They can easily see that the divisor "goes into" the dividend; the layout of the problem also facilitates writing a quotient in the correct place and aligning numbers in multistep division equations. Because some students have spatial or graphomotor difficulties with aligning numbers they write, or simply do not fully grasp the importance of place value, using graph paper or drawing their own place value columns on a sheet of paper before beginning can be useful. Students can also turn lined writing paper sideways for this purpose. Then, they can readily observe the appropriate place to print each numeral in the problem as they show their work and answer.

Students who know that **distributive properties** apply to division calculations can simplify a problem such as $(6 + 12) \div 3$ into $(6 \div 3) + (12 \div 3)$. So, you can see that skills such as utilizing number patterns and the counting by technique that students learned for other forms of calculations will serve them for learning division as well.

Learning that division is the inverse of multiplication may be useful for students curious to understand the operation they are performing. However, learning that division and multiplication are inverse operations will also provide students with options for solving both types of equations. By applying the inverse operation, students can check their work on division problems (for example, use 7 × 3 to check whether the answer 14 ÷ 7 = **3** is correct). It is important to remember that students who understand the inverse nature of the two operations will be more facile at using multiplication and division to check their work on the other problem type than will students who know only by rote that they can perform the inverse function as a check. They are less likely to be able to "diagnose" any errors they detect.

METHODS AND STRATEGIES SPOTLIGHT

A Strategy for Systematically Teaching Math Facts

Curriculum-Based Measurement for Mathematics Learning

Curriculum-based measurement (C-BM) (Deno 2003a; 2003b) is particularly well suited to the teaching of basic facts. Using C-BM, teachers identify which specific facts (or fact skills) students are proficient at and which they need to study more. There are five basic steps to employing C-BM. Addition with renaming is used in this example, but C-BM could be used with either more basic or more advanced mathematics.

STEP 1: Prepare Materials

Teachers should identify the specific skill students are to learn (for example, addition with renaming in the tens column). Considering the sequence of prerequisite skills the students either should have mastered or have minimal proficiency in, determine if they are ready for the present lesson (following the procedures of Step 2 is one way to determine this).

Prepare a series of practice tests containing problems of equal difficulty, long enough that no student could complete all problems accurately within one minute (longer time intervals may be used).

STEP 2: Teach Lesson

Using effective mathematics teaching practices, provide students with opportunities to comprehend what is being represented by renaming, and to practice calculations requiring renaming in the tens column. Do not include problems that do not require renaming in the tens column or that extend to the hundreds column (that is, do not require adding more than 1 to 8, 2 to 7, and so on; and do not use problems that yield a three-digit sum). Once students have mastered renaming in the tens place, they may graduate to renaming that extends to the hundreds column.

STEP 3: Administer a Progress Probe

As often as every three days or once a week, have students complete a practice test prepared in Step 1. Inform the students that they are being graded on the number of correctly added problems and that they should attempt to complete accurately as many as they can within one minute, but that they will lose points for all attempted problems they do not complete correctly.

STEP 4: Score and Graph Individual Test Performance

For each student, tally the number of problems attempted and the number correct. Plot the two data points on a bar or line graph that will be shared with the students (students can learn to plot the data points themselves). Over time, connect the data points for problems attempted with a dashed line, and connect the data points for problems correctly solved with a solid line.

Students and teachers can use the graph to observe learning progress. By drawing a goal line indicating the targeted level of proficiency (for example, 80 percent, 100 percent), students and teachers can observe how efficiently students are progressing toward a targeted outcome.

STEP 5: Use the Data to Inform Instruction

Using the plotted data points, teachers may consider whether students' levels of progress and rates of progress are satisfactory, or whether instructional practices should be changed.

For more on C-BM, review Chapter 2.

Memorizing Calculation Facts. Rodney's mathematical performances in Case 8.1 indicate that he makes computation errors and is not clear on the processes of various computation operations. He could reduce his error rate and improve his comprehension of the processes if he were to memorize computation facts. It may seem counterintuitive to have students recall calculation outcomes from rote memory, but it frees students to think in more engaged ways about problems (Gersten and Chard 1999; Woodward 2006). It also reduces instances of random error due to calculation mistakes that even proficient calculators make from time to time (Woodward 2006). Students who know from memory that $3 + 7 = 10$ do not have to count up, count by threes and add one, or stop to consider whether 3 or 7 is the greater number. By committing the addition facts to memory, students can instantly recognize that the sum is 10. Although rate of performance is less critical than accuracy, it does matter to correct performance.

Memorizing calculation facts can be a challenging task for students. There are 400 calculation facts for the digits 1 through 10, 100 each for addition, subtraction, multiplication, and division. Students should not begin learning calculation procedures by memorizing facts. Memorization for automatic recall can result in students failing to develop conceptual understanding of mathematics problems if they are not also provided opportunities to think about the operations they are performing (Isaacs and Carroll 1999; Sherin and Fuson 2005). Once students develop conceptual understanding of the procedures, however, fluent performance depends on facts memorization.

Students with mild disabilities are particularly likely to engage in inefficient calculation practices, rather than to memorize and automatically recall math facts (Hanich et al. 2001; Koscinski and Gast 1993). Inattention to task and the particulars of a problem contribute to students' difficulty in developing skills for algorithmic computation and story problem solving (Fuchs et al. 2005). Memory storage and retrieval difficulties may prevent some students from developing automatic fact retrieval. Inefficiency or lack of automaticity with math facts results in mathematics being a more cumbersome process and increases the probability for error in calculating (Woodward 2006). Through regular practice or drills, students with mild disabilities can learn to recall math facts automatically. Throughout math drills, it is important to remember that quality of the drill matters as much as the skill being taught. (See the Tips for Generalization for tips on teaching facts memorization to students with mild disabilities.)

TIPS FOR GENERALIZATION

Calculation Facts Memorization for Students with Attention or Memory Difficulties

In the process of memorizing a set of facts, students should drill on a number of sample facts (10 to 20 for younger students; 20 to 40 for older students; or based on an individual student's fatigue rate). The following are factors to keep in mind when using fact drills:

- Fact drills should be begun once students begin to develop proficiency in performing the basic operation.

  If they drill on facts before they begin to understand the operation (for example, single-digit multiplication) and the fact set being drilled (for example, × 5), they will learn the facts as a rote process with limited understanding for how to apply the operations they are performing mechanically.

- Students with mild disabilities effectively recall math facts when they are drilled at frequent and intensive intervals (Burns 2005).

  When drilling students on facts, the drills should be conducted as often as daily, or even twice a day (for instance, at the beginning and ending of a lesson).

  Student drills should include a high enough number of problems for students to observe and ingrain the processes.

  The exact number of problems students should drill in one sitting should be enough so that students consistently perform the tasks correctly (for example, accurately multiplying by five on 80 percent of the problems, or better yet, both to 80 percent and at least five times consecutively). Whatever the correct performance rate you set (percent correct, accurate consecutive performances), students should demonstrate it on at least three consecutive timed drills before you presume the skill is "mastered." Even then, periodically revisiting the skill with another drill practice is appropriate.

- Just as basic math facts and concepts do not need to be mastered in a rigid order, practice drills do not have to be achieved to mastery in a strict order either. All students, including those with mild disabilities, benefit from distributed practice (Kame'enui et al. 2002).

  In distributed practice, students practice subsets of like problems within the same drill. For example, they may practice two to three different fact families (for example, × 1, × 5, × 10) within the drill.

  If fact drills occur at frequent intervals, the like problems may be distributed across the drills that are close together in time.

- Because many students with mild disabilities are "inactive learners" (Torgesen 1982), you should not presume that mastery of fact drills alone will result in proficiency at applying those facts to other mathematics tasks.

  A combination of facts drill and instruction in mathematical strategies is more likely to result in the successful application of facts to more complex operations for students with mild disabilities (Woodward 2006) than is either alone.

  Although fact drills are part of an effective instructional practice, students with mild disabilities will benefit from a balance of mathematics instruction that also addresses strategic application of those facts to simple calculations, problem solving, and more advanced mathematics.

Using a Calculator. The working memory and short-term memory capacity of some students with mild disabilities (Swanson and Beebe-Frankenberger 2004; Zentall 2007), as well as the attention difficulties some experience (Fuchs et al. 2005), can make performing mathematical operations difficult. These students often face difficulties with memorizing facts and keeping track of content as they perform calculations on paper or in their head. They may need to drill routinely on the basic facts to retain them in memory, whereas others will get sufficient practice by progressing to applying the facts in other forms of mathematical learning. Students for whom fact memorization is challenging will benefit from routine, lifelong math drills (as well as from mastering such skills as the counting by technique). However, because that is unrealistic for many students, they should be taught how to use a calculator.

Learning to perform mathematical operations on a calculator should be viewed as a compensatory skill. Using a calculator can be facilitative for students for whom memory or attention is a persistent block in practicing calculations or performing more advanced mathematics. They may always have to rely on a calculator to perform some of those operations. Others who develop mathematics proficiency in part by using a calculator will not always need to rely on one. For them, it is a useful learning tool, just like manipulatives or drawing.

These students must still learn number sense pre-skills to understand what buttons to push when performing the operation and determining its outcome. Calculator use does not reveal the concept or procedural steps, as does using manipulatives or writing out problems, so calculators are not particularly effective for introducing mathematical procedures. However, in an instance when a student is being introduced to a new operation (for example, division) without first attaining proficiency in other needed forms of calculation (for example, subtraction), using a calculator to perform steps within the equation would be helpful.

Perhaps because the virtues of using calculators for basic math are often debated (Maccini and Gagnon 2006; Thurlow et al. 2005), calculators are sometimes not introduced until students exhibit persistent difficulty with operations. With the availability of low-cost calculators, and as a standard tool found on many types of technologies, most people should learn how to operate them anyway. As a general rule, students should begin to learn to use calculators by the middle school/junior high school years. Rules will then need to be established as to when your students are permitted to use their calculators. In the case of students for whom using a calculator may be an appropriate accommodation during standardized testing, using the calculator to learn and practice the same types of operations that will be on the test is essential (see Thurlow, Elliott, and Ysseldyke 1998).

Skills That Build Upon Numeracy and Calculation

Among the concepts and skills requiring facility at calculation are fractions and decimals, using money, and measurement, including telling time. Students use each of these skills frequently in daily living and may not recognize them as mathematics. Number sense is needed to comprehend each and is reinforced by the learning of each (Gersten and Chard 1999; Seethaler & Fuchs, 2006).

Fractions. Young children first become aware of the concept of fractions as they learn about proportions and parts of wholes. Parents may tell them that they must eat "three more bites" of a vegetable they dislike, which helps them recognize that the pile of vegetables on their plate is composed of parts (in essence, a set). Likewise, sharing a cookie requires dividing it. Learning that the numeric unit represented by a whole number is composed of other whole numbers (for example, 10 is a set of ten 1s or two 5s) enhances the concept of relations among whole numbers and their number value. Thus, activities that develop number sense (estimation, mental calculation, approximation, and generally thinking with and about numbers; Gersten and Chard 1999) and computation skills are also introductory to the concept of fractions. Just as students learn numbers and their values, they must learn fractions and their values (for example, recognizing that when a sibling does not break a cookie exactly in half, it does not result in getting "the smaller half" but rather "less than half"[1]). You can teach this to your students in some of the same ways that you taught whole number values. Your students may, for example, divide manipulatives into fractions such as ½ and ⅓ (for example, divide a set of Popsicle sticks, use Cuisenaire rods to construct ½ of a base 10 block next to it). Learning the concept of fractions and how to manipulate them in mathematical problems in turn helps students to master related mathematical areas such as proportion, ratio, and probability.

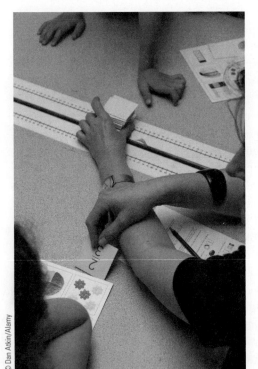

Following the sequence of concrete to semi-concrete to abstract representation can help students grasp mathematical concepts beyond the basic operations.

© Dan Atkin/Alamy

Fractions can be particularly difficult for students with mild disabilities because of their abstract nature. Even in the case of students who grasp the concept of fractions as parts of a whole, being able to manipulate fractions mathematically can still be abstract. In fact, many students who are successful in mastering number sense and calculation first exhibit signs of mathematical difficulties when beginning to learn about fractions (see Hecht, Vagi, and Torgesen 2007). Middle school students with LD benefit from learning to represent and solve fraction problems using manipulatives; in fact, learning with manipulatives improves their ability to recognize and solve fraction problems embedded in story problems as well (Butler et al. 2003). Fraction blocks can also be used to depict various fractions (see Figure 8.1). Like much of mathematics learning, students should learn about gradually more complex fraction concepts and operations in a progression from simple to complex. That is, simple fractions and operations using them should be familiar to students before they progress to mixed fractions (for example, ½ before 1½ and ³⁄₂).

Decimals. Decimals may make more intuitive sense to students than fractions do. Certainly performing calculations with decimals will be more familiar to students who can comfortably perform calculations with whole numbers. The

---

[1]Although the dictionary definition of *half* means only approximately equal proportion between two parts of a whole (Merriam-Webster 1991), the mathematical concept is 50 percent.

appreciation of place value is critical to comprehending decimals. Decimal place values can be taught and practiced in the same way that whole number place values are taught. Students should learn to pay particular attention to the alignment of decimal points when writing calculations.

Other Basic Skills for Mathematical Operations and Daily Living

Being able to perform the basic operations of addition, subtraction, multiplication, and division are essential forms of mathematical literacy. They are used in daily functioning and are integral to a variety of more complex mathematical operations for problem solving, algebra, geometry, calculus, and the like. However, a variety of other basic mathematical concepts and skills must be mastered for both daily living and more complex mathematics as well. Measuring, telling time, and recognizing shapes are examples of these other types of mathematics. Just as is the case for the basic operations of computation, children should begin to learn the essential pre-skills and concepts for these other skills prior to elementary school.

Estimating. To **estimate** is to approximate an outcome to a problem. Students use estimation skills when they make an "educated guess" about an answer. However, an estimate is not an out-and-out wild guess. An estimate comes close to ("approximates") the actual outcome. Estimating speeds mathematics performance, and is indispensable in checking one's own work. Estimation is commonly used in daily life, to approximate distance, time, and costs. Estimation can be used before or after performing a calculation or other operation as well. To do estimation, students must have fluency in numeracy and place value. Abilities to calculate and estimate rely on one another, and students' performance abilities for the two skills tend to be similar (Dowker 2003; Seethaler and Fuchs 2006). Students who have difficulty with mathematical calculations are commonly found to have difficulty estimating, regardless of whether they have been identified as having a mathematics-related disability (Jordan and Hanich 2003; Montague and van Garderen 2003).

A simple approach to estimation is rounding. Students can **round up** or **round down** numbers to convert them to numbers that they are good at counting by. So, 13 can be rounded down to 10. In the case of having to multiply 13×7, for example, students can use rounding down to convert the problem to 10×7. Then they can (a) know the correct sum is greater than 70, or (b) calculate $(10 \times 7) + (3 \times 7)$. When rounding for a calculation, students can round (up or down) to **compatible numbers.** Compatible numbers are numbers that are easy for students to calculate, so they depend on which numbers the students are good at counting by. In the example just provided, 10 and 7 are compatible numbers.

Students can use a variety of approaches for estimating the outcomes of calculation. When a student encounters a multi-digit calculation (for example, $5{,}363 + 4{,}295$), she or he can estimate the answer using **front-end estimation.** To do front-end estimation, the student needs to observe the numerals on the "front," or that are leftmost. So, in this example, the student observes that the 5 and the 4 must be added, and also that the digits are in the thousands

⏩ ▶ ⏪

VIDEO CASE CONNECTIONS BOX

⟶─────────────────────────────●──────────

Watch the Video Case entitled *Bilingual Education*. Teachers Sarah Bartels-Marrero and Sheila Donelan used estimation and prediction as part of lessons to build bilingual language skills. Based on what you have read so far in this chapter, write a paragraph explaining how their activities also help students learn mathematics vocabulary and concepts for calculating.

place. Now the student knows that the correct sum will be in the nine thousands. To be more accurate, the student may wish to front-end estimate the two front digits; now the student can see that the correct answer will begin *9,5_ _*. As you have likely observed in this example, the student must be aware that carrying over from adding the lower place value digits may cause the value of the thousands place (9) to increase. Note that, if the problem were 5,763 + 4,895, front-end estimating for two digits would yield a more accurate estimation of the sum.

The Sequencing of Math Concepts and Skills

As suggested earlier in the chapter, although there is a clearly established sequence for teaching math concepts and skills that build off one another, those concepts and skills do not need to be taught and mastered exclusively in a lock-step order. In fact, appreciation for the relevancy of certain concepts and skills can be enhanced by linking them to other aspects of mathematics. The same is true for students developing the ability to apply them. Still, students should achieve a comfort level for understanding and using the numeracy pre-skills before they can be expected to have success in basic operations (Gersten and Chard 1999). In turn, addition, subtraction, multiplication, and division are best *introduced* in that sequence, as (a) they each rely on pre-skills emphasized in the procedures of the preceding calculation form, and (b) the operations for each are incorporated into the successive skills (Seethaler and Fuchs 2006).

THINK BACK TO THE CASE about Rodney . . .

3. *Will Rodney be able to learn the types of mathematics other sixth-graders study if he is still working to master basic computation facts?*

The answer is *yes*. Rodney's teachers will have to follow the logical sequence for introducing and practicing concepts and skills. However, working on other skills of mathematics such as measurement and using money, and proceeding to learn about operations with fractions and decimals can all interact to reinforce conceptual understanding and skill proficiency for the variety of basic math topics he still needs to master.

The approaches to calculation described in this chapter by no means exhaust the lists of procedures that teachers can employ to help students learn to add, subtract, multiply, or divide. Students can become confused by learning a variety of procedures, especially if they do not comprehend the relationships among them. Furthermore, too much emphasis on drill and accurate skill performance can result in students who can perform operations but have little understanding

TABLE 8.2: The "Big Ideas" That Can Anchor Math Instruction

• Place value • Associative property • Rate of composition or decomposition	• Expanded notation • Distributive property	• Commutative property • Equivalence

Source: Reprinted with permission from M. K. Harniss, D. W. Carnine, J. Silbert, and R. C. Dixon *"Effective Strategies for Teaching Mathematics."* In *Effective Teaching Strategies that Accommodate Diverse Learners,* ed. M. D. Coyne, E. J. Kame'enui, and D. W. Carnine, 3rd ed. (Upper Saddle River, NJ: Pearson Prentice Hall, 2007).

of what they are doing. For these reasons, Harniss et al. (2007) advocate teaching the myriad concepts and skills of numeracy and the four basic calculations by centering instruction on "big ideas." The **big ideas** of mathematics are the concepts that make major or foundational mathematical operations meaningful. Equivalence, for example, is a big idea that is essential for appreciating what many mathematical procedures indicate. Understanding the big idea of equivalence means understanding that the information on the left and right sides of the equal sign are the same (Harniss et al. 2007). Students who do not understand equivalence may fail to appreciate why $(5 + 2) - 3 = (equals)$ 4, for example. Without understanding equivalence, students will have difficulty solving the task outside of a drill sheet, will have an insufficient knowledge basis for estimating, and will not appreciate what more complex mathematical tasks such as problem solving and advanced algorithms ask of them. Harniss et al. (2007) have proposed seven big ideas related to performing basic calculations (see Table 8.2).

As Harniss et al. suggest, the rationale for using the variety of mathematical procedures that students practice to learn for even a single operation will be more meaningful if they understand the big ideas behind them.

Problem Solving and Advanced Mathematics

Chapter Question
ALERT

In this section, you will find information that answers a Chapter Question:

2. What are the challenges that problem solving and advanced levels of mathematics pose for students with mild disabilities, and what are effective instructional responses?

The NCTM (2000) Principles and Standards for School Mathematics calls for an increased emphasis on conceptual understanding and problem-solving skills in mathematics curricula. Students with mild disabilities who have difficulties learning computation or other basic skills have sometimes been denied instruction in problem solving or more advanced forms of mathematics (Woodward and Montague 2002; Schoenfeld 2002). (No Child Left Behind [2001] expectations for all students to work toward the same high standards are intended to curtail such inequities in curriculum. Mathematics educators and scholars refer to this as the "equity principle" [Woodward and Brown 2006].) Students may have been denied participation because they had yet to master pre-skills or computation (see Wilson and Sindelar 1991), or educators may have considered higher-level mathematics to be unobtainable or simply unnecessary for them. Of course, students with mild disabilities can and should perform problem solving and other higher forms of mathematics. It is also true that many students with mild disabilities do participate in studying math at higher levels, and, although those who continually struggle may need more work on lower-level skills, they also need instruction in higher mathematics.

Problem Solving

Problem solving could describe what is done in many types of mathematics. The geometer solves for angles and missing sides, and algebraic and quadratic problems are solved; even those who are measuring, telling time, or comparing properties of two entities are "solving for" the answer to their question. Typically, however, **problem solving** is used in mathematics to refer to tasks that have calculations imbedded in them, mostly in the form of story problems. Students with math-related disabilities often have difficulty with problem-solving tasks (Jitendra, DiPipi, and Perron-Jones 2002; Montague and Applegate 1993). Sometimes their problems are an extension of more basic difficulties with calculation, and sometimes they are due to the particular challenges problem solving poses. Parmar, Cawley, and Frazita (1996) found that the problem-solving proficiencies of third- through eighth-graders with LD decreased as they progressed from addition, to subtraction, then multiplication and, ultimately, division problems. For some students with mild disabilities, their difficulties with learning to solve math problems stem from an early math curriculum steeped exclusively in facts and calculations; these students are not prepared for the novelty of mathematics applied to problems (Giordano 1990).

Story problems (also commonly referred to as word problems) can present a math problem to solve as simple as single-digit addition, yet strike the student with a mild disability as far more complex. Thus, consider a student who is given the following problem:

$$\begin{array}{r} 4 \\ +2 \\ \hline \end{array}$$

The student may be ready to respond correctly but may not recognize the problem when asked the following question:

> "Manny already had four earrings; today he got two more. Now how many earrings does Manny have?"

Problem solving requires recognizing the mathematical problem and solving it, relating the outcome or solution (in this example, a sum) to the context of the problem (that is, the sum is six but the answer is "six earrings"). Consider slightly modifying the story problem for Manny and his earrings:

> "Manny already had four eyebrow piercings; today he got two lip piercings. Now how many face piercings does Manny have?"

The calculation is still $4 + 2$, but the unit for the outcome, face piercings, requires the student to translate "eyebrow" and "lip piercings" into "face piercings." Further, the question requires the presumption that Manny has no other piercings on his face, but only indirectly implies this in its wording. Thus, in addition to recognizing that the question is asking for $4 + 2$ and a sum expressed in units of face piercings, the student must convert two distinct forms of piercings into a common category, or set (face). It also requires the student to search for and determine whether any other piercings must be accounted for (and to consider if either "eyebrow" or "lip" does not qualify). It would be a more challenging conundrum if the question had included Manny's ear piercings. In addition to recognizing and solving the addition problem, processing all of this information requires suspending information in working memory while reviewing the task. For many students with mild disabilities, attending to all of these factors and organizing the necessary information is overwhelming.

In addition to lacking sufficient prerequisite skills for computation operations, students with mild disabilities may find at least four other factors that can cause story problems to be uniquely difficult: motivation, mathematical and other literacy (for example, reading), confounded story problems, and complex math tasks. The first of the four factors is **motivation.** Instead of recognizing its relevancy to everyday life and academics, some perceive mathematics as a "school" task that they are required to suffer through to receive their diplomas. Some abstractly assume it "builds their minds" (Scanlon and Mellard 2002). Many students with disabilities are unmotivated to practice and learn math because of the confusion they experience during lessons and their unrewarding high failure rates. The poor mathematics learning of students with mild disabilities can lead to low motivation and generally low school performance (Mercer and Miller 1992). Likewise, culturally and linguistically diverse students can be more motivated by mathematics when the tasks seem more relevant to them. A change as simple as switching the focus of a story problem from hot dogs to tacos can make the problem seem more relevant to Latino students (Cartledge, Gardner, and Ford 2009), for example.

As noted, to address motivational learning factors, students with disabilities should receive explicit instruction on the purposes and utility of learning the specific mathematics practices they are studying. Although becoming prepared for math (and other) courses at higher grade levels may be motivating for some students, more practical motivations such as enhanced daily functioning should be emphasized as well. Likewise, because some math lessons can focus on micro aspects of larger operations (for example, drills on reducing fractions), using lesson advance organizers can remind the students of the relationship of any one lesson to the overall mathematics curriculum and can help them to appreciate the purpose of the individual lesson (Bulgren and Lenz 1996; see Chapter 2 also). Mathematics can also be more motivating to individual students when culturally relevant problems and materials are used, such as exploring "the numeracy system from different cultural perspectives [and] games from different cultures" (Thomas-Presswood and Presswood 2008).

Motivational practices such as reward systems for lesson participation and progress in skills can also be effective (even improved performance still at a failing level can be a form of success). (Review the previous Methods and Strategies Spotlight, and Chapter 2, for tips on using curriculum-based measurement in mathematics, which has been documented as motivating to students with mild disabilities across grade levels.) In a study comparing the impact on women's and men's spatial reasoning task performance, being told positive attributes enhanced performance for both genders (Wraga et al. 2006). In addition, students who learn to think of positive affirmations before beginning a task can improve and sustain their motivation during a lesson (Morgan and Sideridis 2006).

Story problems such as that in the previous Manny example are sometimes daunting to students, not because of the mathematical operation they ask students to solve, but because of the **embedded literacy tasks** involved in discerning the operation. Students who have learned mathematics vocabulary such as "plus" and "minus," and print symbols such as "+" and "−" have not necessarily learned how to recognize when those operations are called for if none of the familiar vocabulary or symbols is used in the story problem (as in the problem about Manny). **Mathematical literacy** in such situations requires that the word problem include the skill of inferring implied operations and answer units. This also involves the skill of recognizing a problem type when it appears in an unfamiliar format (Fuchs et al. 2004). Remember the principle of beginning skill instruction with tasks that are relatively easy when students are new to navigating story problems, and begin with ones that incorporate familiar math vocabulary. For example, consider the following:

> "Manny already had four earrings; today he added two more. Add Manny's two new earrings to the four he already had to tell how many earrings Manny has now. Total = ___earrings___ "

In this example, the student's primary challenge is to discern the math question. For initial story problem practice, ask students only to write the math calculation instead of solving for the outcome.

Research Evidence

Recognizing Cue Words to Comprehend and Solve Story Problems. Research evidence indicates that when students are taught to recognize **cue words** for mathematical operations, they are better able to identify the calculation asked of them (Verschaffel and de Corte 1997). They may engage in drills of math vocabulary or other activities that emphasize recognizing and using cue words. *Add, plus,* and *sum* are all cue words, but students should also learn the meanings of "all told," "how many," "together," and "combined". However, when students with disabilities learn to search for cue words, they often make calculation errors (Nesher and Teubal 1975). This may be because they do not carefully focus on what the problem is asking of them (Willoughby 1990). Therefore, instruction in cue words should focus on students learning to recognize various mathematical words and symbols and knowing their meanings, but it should not be offered as a short cut to discerning problems. Various researchers (for example, Jitendra 2002; Miller and Mercer 1993; Montague and Bos 1986; Woodward 2006) have documented that students with mild disabilities also need strategies to help them understand the mathematical questions and operations the problem requires.

Of course, in addition to mathematical literacy, students need to have appropriate levels of **reading literacy** to comprehend the story problem they are given. As is discussed in Chapters 5 and 6, students need to be able to recognize and recall most of the vocabulary they encounter in a passage, as well as have strategies for decoding and comprehending when confronted by unfamiliar vocabulary, complex sentence structures, or conceptually dense verbiage. Students who are still developing their mathematical literacy and are also confronted with taxing reading literacy demands are given a far greater learning challenge than their peers face. English language learners have demonstrated greater math proficiency when taught in their native language (Harry and Klingner 2006).

Reading story problems can, nonetheless, be looked upon as an efficient approach to providing students with practice at both mathematics and reading. In such cases, reading instruction and mathematics instruction should be coordinated so that they support one another. However, when the instructional task is to teach students how to respond to a story problem, the required reading literacy should be on their reading level so that extraneous reading challenges do not confound learning the skill of understanding story problems. For this reason, be prepared to guide students with reading tasks posed by story problems.

Confounded story problems—those that include extraneous or confusing content—can compound students' mathematical and reading literacy difficulties. Some story problems can include so much narrative that the portion relating to the task is difficult to discern. Anecdotal information that makes for a more interesting story but that is not relevant to the mathematical question can needlessly distract students. The story problems concerning Manny's piercings could be an example of a distracting problem. Students used to encountering more staid problem topics, such as a trip to the market, might find the Manny examples more engaging but might also be overly distracted by the scenario. In the case of extraneous content, avoiding story problems with such excessive or diverting content is appropriate. Confusing content is a more realistic aspect of everyday problems students must learn how to address. Students must carefully consider confusing content to determine whether it is part of the mathematical question. Problems may present quantities of objects to be added, and the students need to discern which is part of the math problem (for example, whether ear piercings would qualify as face piercings). As well, an aspect of the question may obscure what operation is called for (for example, "Manny used to have six studs in his left ear and five in his right, but he has since let some of the holes close up in each. So today, Manny already has four earrings . . ."). Again, as is the case for dealing with mathematical and reading literacy, avoid confounding initial practice in story problems with confusing content. Supported practice can gradually build to working on confusing stories.

Finally, complex math tasks are part of the fourth category of factors that can make story problems uniquely difficult for students with mild disabilities. Often, solving story problems requires more than identifying and solving for a simple calculation. The same is true for other advanced levels of mathematics. Multiple calculations can be involved, and more than one approach may be possible to solve the task. **Complex math tasks** require students to perform multiple operations to arrive at a solution. Students are expected to read and comprehend the problem in the ways previously described while they identify the order of multiple operations and perform them, keeping track of their solution in process.

The following is an example of a complex story problem:

Dahlia and Malka live next door to each other. Their mothers sent them to the market together to buy food for each of their family's meals for the day. Because it was Dahlia's birthday, her mother gave her extra money to buy herself a treat. At the market, the girls found boxes of tomatoes by the dozen, which was more than either family needed. So they decided to pay half the cost each and divide up the box when they got home. Malka bought a container of chickpeas so her grandmother could make hummus, but Dahlia knew that her family didn't need any. At the next stall they visited, Malka bought a ripe melon for her four family members to share; Dahlia bought two because her family is larger than Malka's. Each girl bought small white fish they thought would be good for the main meal; Dahlia bought six for her family. They then pooled their money to buy a large bag of dates that their mothers could divide up. Using the rest of the money their mothers gave them, they bought a stack of ten pita breads to divide up, one per member of each household. Before they left the market, Dahlia used her birthday money to buy herself a pomegranate and four candied figs, one of which she gave to Malka.

> **Not counting the bag of dates, how many individual food items did Dahlia buy for her family?**

When written out as mathematical operations, the problem appears as:

$(12/2) + 2 + 6 + (10-4) =$

A student who is adept at each of the required mathematical operations and who could readily identify any of the steps in a simple story problem faces a number of challenges to finding the solution to this problem.

CASE 8.2 Is Felice Benefiting from Effective Math Instruction?

Case Introduction

Now that you have worked through the first case in this chapter, you should feel comfortable addressing issues in a second case. You are going to read about the challenges Felice has in learning to apply calculations in geometry class. You will also read about the approach to teaching that Mr. Truffaut, her geometry teacher, uses for the whole class. As you read the case, ask yourself whether Felice might be inadequately prepared to learn geometry problem solving. Also ask yourself whether Mr. Truffaut's teaching sufficiently supports students' understanding and skill at geometry problem solving. These are the same questions Andrea, a special education teacher who is asked to consult, is considering.

As a special educator and member of her school's Child Study Team (CST), Andrea was asked to observe Martin Truffaut's ninth-grade geometry class. Their school has begun to experiment with the responsiveness to intervention (RTI) approach to investigating learning difficulties, which could possibly result in learning disabilities identification (see Chapter 2). Mr. Truffaut had asked for help with a girl named Felice.

Mr. Truffaut explained to the team members that he had observed Felice routinely make simple calculation errors and have difficulty recalling the correct order of steps for what should now be simple algorithms. He realized this as he investigated why Felice was having persistent difficulty mastering new mathematical operations, which most of her classmates had mastered readily.

Using the RTI model, Andrea's first task was to observe whether Mr. Truffaut was providing effective instruction to Felice and her classmates. In a pre-observation meeting, Mr. Truffaut explained that he taught geometry skills in a three-stage process: first, on Mondays, he modeled them by narrating the steps as he performed problems on the overhead projector (for example, finding the circumference of a circle). In the second stage, he provided scaffolded support of student practice by circulating around the classroom while students completed ten practice problems that first day, ten more for homework, and twenty more in class on Tuesday. Finally, in the third stage, he had students apply their developing knowledge to solve story problems and other "real-world" math tasks of appropriate difficulty on Wednesday. He gave more story problems for homework that third night.

Mr. Truffaut also explained to Andrea that he was following the sequence of the ninth-grade geometry textbook. In the book, each new skill is introduced with an engaging story example, and the operation is illustrated with graphics. Next, the book walks students through the steps of the operation one step at a time, showing geometric drawings translated into numeric problems, and then numerals being reduced, renamed, and so on, step by step. Then there are several small sets of progressively more difficult problem examples for the students to complete. As homework to reinforce the first day of his instruction (Monday), students read the textbook introduction and do the first ten problems from the book's practice sets.

In response to Felice's problems, Mr. Truffaut has her practice drills of the basic calculation facts for ones, fives, tens, and zeroes (for example, +1, −1, ×1, ÷1). She does this for homework every Tuesday night instead of the regular class assignment—Mr. Truffaut reasons that she "is better off" doing the drills than attempting the new operations for the week without him present to scaffold her work. She repeats the drill every Thursday night; the other students do not have math homework on Thursday nights.

Although Andrea knew that her first RTI tasks included documenting the quality of instruction that was going on, she couldn't help but also observe how the teenagers in the room were benefiting from the instruction they were receiving. Following two weeks of occasional observations, she observed that many of them did not seem to grasp the purpose of the operations they were learning or why the steps of the operations progressed as they did. She also noted that most students steadily increased in percent of problems they performed correctly across the week. In fact, by Friday, most students achieved above 75 percent accuracy on the practice activities Mr. Truffaut assigned.

Based on the four times Andrea sat with Felice in class and asked Felice to explain how she was solving the problems, Andrea was able to corroborate Mr. Truffaut's observation that Felice could not reliably perform basic calculations, and that she had difficulty remembering the steps of the operations she was supposed to be learning, in addition to not understanding the purpose of the operations. All of those factors contributed to the problems Felice was having with Mr. Truffaut's instruction.

Andrea was prepared to suggest some instructional adaptations Mr. Truffaut could use to address Felice's needs. She was uneasy about the fact that, although she observed Mr. Truffaut's practices to be generally effective, she also had a few suggestions on how he could improve his teaching for all of his students.

CASE QUESTIONS

1. How could Andrea help Mr. Truffaut determine whether Felice was benefiting from effective mathematics instruction?
2. Was Mr. Truffaut's approach to teaching both concepts and skills truly focused on students developing proficiency in both areas?
3. What specific instructional practices would benefit Felice and her classmates more?

Responding to the Challenges of Problem Solving and Advanced Mathematics

Consistent with NCTM's 2002 revisions to its math teaching standards, Mr. Truffaut was teaching basic skills as well as focusing on conceptual understanding and application of skills to problem solving. Andrea had noticed that, although a number of students in the class were developing proficiency in both basic skills and in problem solving, many did not have conceptual understanding of what they were doing. Felice was having difficulty with all three aspects of the lesson. Teachers of mathematics need to appreciate the spectrum of learning demands involved in learning to solve problems, and they need to know how to support students in that complex learning process. Unfortunately, many secondary school math teachers are unlikely to use instructional practices particularly appropriate for students with mild disabilities. In addition, their special educator counterparts frequently lack sufficient knowledge and skills in secondary level mathematics (Maccini and Gagnon 2006). Two important practices that are commonly neglected are controlling the difficulty level of tasks students attempt and attending to the conceptual foundations of mathematics (Fuchs et al. 2008). The following approaches are effective for any teacher wishing to help students with problem solving and other advanced mathematics (see Foegen 2008).

Task Analysis. A starting point for effective instruction is for teachers to understand what knowledge and skills a task demands of students. Once teachers determine this, they can match that with a student's knowledge and skills. Both types of information are determined through task analysis. The following Methods and Strategies Spotlight presents explanations for these two main areas for task analysis: lesson expectations and student learning.

METHODS AND STRATEGIES SPOTLIGHT

Task Analysis of the Learner and the Lesson

Task analysis is a useful approach to analyzing both what a lesson demands and how a student learns. It is particularly amenable to math instruction because math, from basic facts to advanced problem solving, involves hierarchies of knowledge and skills.

Using **task analysis for a lesson**, teachers identify prerequisite knowledge and skills, as well as corequisite knowledge and skills, required to accomplish the lesson goal (what is to be learned). Teachers then determine the level of detail by which the topic must be broken out to address the corequisite content (for example, teaching multi-step calculations is typically broken out by each individual step of the operation). Mr. Truffaut does not appear to have used an analysis of Felice's learning needs when he planned his whole class lesson.

To understand how students approach a learning task, **task analysis of student learning** can be performed. By means such as observations, student think-alouds, interviews, or performance probes, teachers can ascertain what a student knows and does when attempting a task. When Andrea sat with Felice, she completed task analyses of Felice's learning to understand why Felice was having difficulty with Mr. Truffaut's lessons.

Both regular and special education elementary teachers are stronger at identifying errors in students' subtraction calculations, both common and unconventional errors, than they are at identifying appropriate instructional responses (Riccomini 2005). This seems to indicate that teachers are unsure of what processing difficulties students have in completing an operation, as opposed to having a generalized misunderstanding of how to teach subtraction concepts and processes. In fact, only 17 percent of their instructional responses included attending to nonobservable student performances such as sustained attention to task or self-checking. Because of the teachers' incomplete task analyses, instruction is devoted to practice of skills that either carry little meaning to students or that are not the specific skills or concepts that are difficult for the students.

THINK BACK TO THE CASE about Felice . . .

1. *How could Andrea help Mr. Truffaut determine whether Felice was benefiting from effective mathematics instruction?*

By using task analysis of student learning, Andrea and Mr. Truffaut could observe for patterns in Felice's mathematical abilities. This could involve reviewing her work samples and, ideally, would include having Felice narrate problem solving for them as well.

When researchers used task analyses for subtraction with regrouping errors for eighth-graders with LD (Woodward and Howard 1994), they discovered that most of the students had systematic error patterns. The patterns reflected mis-understandings of both mathematical concepts and basic computational proce-dures. With this information teachers can reteach background knowledge and skills instead of merely increasing drills of subtraction with regrouping.

Teachers have been found to focus reteaching almost exclusively on basic facts instruction, neglecting other aspects of process, including comprehension and the variety of approaches possible for addressing the task (see Riccomini 2005). Reteaching basics without helping students to understand their connec-tion to the more advanced concepts and operations they are learning can result in improved rote performance of the basics, but continued limited understand-ing of both the basics and the more advanced mathematics.

Strategies and Techniques for Improving Problem Solving

When students have difficulty with mathematics tasks, the difficulty may be in their ability to (a) analyze the task (for example, determine the question and identify the operations to perform), (b) perform the basic operations accurately (in correct sequence, without simple errors), and (c) manage the process. That is, they may lack strategic ability to perform the collective tasks involved. In one study, third-graders with LD who learned story problem-solving procedures using a direct instruction strategy learned more in a nine-day period than did those who learned the same procedures but in a nonstrategic format (Wilson and Sindelar 1991).

Students can apply a simple arithmetic strategy to solve a variety of math-ematics tasks, simple or complex. They can follow the mnemonic DRAW to remember the process.

Discover the sign.
Read the problem.
Answer, or draw and check.
Write the answer. (Miller and Mercer 1991a; 1991b)

This strategy is for math problems written out in numeric form. Students begin by looking at the problem and isolating the sign for the appropriate operation. Then, they can read the problem, already knowing what operation is required. Performing this step requires students to be literate in the signs for arithmetic operations (for example, $+$, $-$, $\times$, $\div$, $=$). Already having identified the opera-tion, students can attend more fully to the number values involved when read-ing the problem. In the third step, students answer the question if able to do so. If not able to, then they draw a graphic representation of the problem. If the problem is part of a story problem, students can draw the pertinent information from the story (for example, Dahlia and Malka splitting a stack of pita breads). Some students will draw pictorial images (for example, the stack of pitas) instead of the pattern or relationships among the objects (the divided pitas), however. They must practice depicting the problem before drawing will be helpful to them (Edens and Potter 2007). Alternatively, students can draw each numeral as a set of dots (unless large numbers are involved, which would make this procedure too cumbersome), or they could use graph paper and shade in the appropriate number of squares for each number. If students cannot immediately answer the question, it is reasonable to presume that they have a higher potential to make errors. Therefore, students who draw the problem to understand and answer it should always check their work, by such procedures as estimating or redoing the entire calculation. Finally, students should be sure to write down the answer to the problem. In the case of story problems, students should remember to write down the units as well (for example, "6 pitas").

Students who have mastered DRAW may benefit from proceeding to learn the FAST DRAW strategy (Miller 1996). Because the DRAW strategy is appropriate for problems presented in their numeric forms, many students will need a strategy to help them "translate" a story problem into its numeric representation. Students can perform the FAST steps to ascertain the numeric problem, and then follow with the DRAW steps when they need them.

F̲ind what you're solving for.
A̲sk yourself, "What are the parts of the problem?"
S̲et up the numbers.
T̲ie down the sign. (Miller 1996)

Even the DRAW and FAST DRAW strategies presume students' facility with the processes of problem solving. The SOLVE strategy (Miller and Mercer 1993) gives more guidance on the overall process to follow. In this strategy students learn the following:

S̲ee the sign.
O̲bserve and answer; continue if you cannot answer.
L̲ook and draw.
V̲erify your answer.
E̲nter your answer. (Miller and Mercer 1993)

By adding the verify step, Miller and Mercer remind students to use practices such as estimation to check the accuracy of their work; in other words, they learn that math problem solving involves more than rote performance of steps.

As already noted, some students' difficulties with solving story problems relates to their inability to comprehend the story scenario and the embedded problem. Montague and Bos (1986) offer a strategy designed to guide students who have difficulty conceptualizing the problem. The verbal problem-solving strategy guides students through verbally stating the problem and the appropriate solution process. This strategy acknowledges that, for many students with mild disabilities, poor language skills interfere with efficient cognitive processes (Montague and Bos 1990). The steps of the strategy are as follows:

Read the problem aloud.
Paraphrase the problem aloud.
Visualize the information.
State the problem aloud.
Hypothesize and think the problem through aloud.
Estimate the answer.
Calculate and label the answer.
Self-check by using self-questioning to ask if the answer makes sense.
    (Montague and Bos 1986)

You might presume that these problem-solving strategies overlap in their purpose and design, and that any one is as suitable as another. Careful review of the procedure steps for each will reveal subtle differences in the problem-solving processes they address, however. Conducting a task analysis of an individual student's math learning strengths and needs should indicate the strategy that might be most appropriate.

General Approaches to Math Instruction

Two general instructional approaches have been documented as particularly effective for teaching mathematics to students with mild disabilities, and have been presented in other chapters of this book. The following applications of PALS and Direction Instruction (DI) to mathematics teaching are highlighted.

PALS. The PALS (peer-assisted learning strategies) peer-tutoring approach was developed based upon Greenwood, Carta, and Maheady's (1991) classwide peer tutoring (CWPT) model. Both approaches are rooted in curriculum-based measurement (C-BM). The primary difference between PALS and CWPT is that PALS prescribes instructional procedures related specifically to, in this case, mathematics (see Chapter 6 for a description of PALS for reading comprehension). The CWPT procedures involve more generally effective teaching practices (see Greenwood, Delquadri, and Carta [1999] for CWPT instructional materials). Math PALS has been found effective in increasing the quality and amount of computation that students with mild disabilities are able to perform at both the elementary (Fuchs et al. 1994) and secondary levels (Calhoon and Fuchs 2003).

In Math PALS, students are assigned to tutor-tutee pairs based on ability level or specific math topics they need to address (Calhoon and Fuchs 2003; Fuchs and Fuchs 2001). After rank-ordering the ability levels of all students in the class, the teacher then divides the roster in half, assigning the highest member of each list as peers, the second highest to each other, and so on. Following training of the students in PALS procedures, the tutors use scripted lessons to prompt tutees on mathematical calculations. The tutors model and then fade out prompting of procedures for the tutees. When the tutees perform the task correctly, tutors circle the correct response; otherwise, the tutors prompt the tutees to correct a mistake or even to work through the problem again. The scripts and preplanned lesson content help the tutors to provide only accurate feedback. Your job is to circulate around the room to ensure pairs are working appropriately. After a set period of time, the tutors and tutees switch roles and repeat the activities. Setting personal learning goals and graphing progress may be as motivational for secondary level students participating in Math PALS as are team competitions and rewards for lower grade students (Calhoon and Fuchs 2003).

Direct Instruction. Direct Instruction is a specific approach to teaching (Stein, Silbert, and Carnine 1997; see also Chapter 2). There is also a published mathematics curriculum named "Direct Instruction: Corrective Mathematics" (Engelmann and Steely 2002). Research evidence indicates that students with mild disabilities benefit more from DI mathematics instruction than from discovery-oriented approaches (Kroesbergen and Van Luit 2003). The DI approach includes carefully sequenced instruction that is based on task analysis. It calls for systematically checking on students' prior knowledge and reteaching as necessary. **Reteaching** begins with a variety of forms of feedback that include prompting students to try again, telling students the correct response, and reminding students of a strategy for determining the response (Gersten 1992). Check on and improve skills and concepts that students should master before advancing in the sequence of mathematics instruction, as need be.

DI also calls for explicit teaching of generalizable strategies (Stein, Silbert, and Carnine 1997). **Explicit instruction** means teaching information overtly in a teacher-directed lesson incorporating some of the principles of DI (review Chapter 2). Accordingly, in DI mathematics curricula (for example, *Connecting Math Concepts*, Englemann, Carnine, Englemann, and Kelly 2002; *Direct Instruction: Corrective Mathematics*, Engelmann and Steely 2002), concepts and skills are taught in a logical sequence. Using the concept of "big ideas," students learn mathematical procedures to mastery.

THINK BACK TO THE CASE about Felice . . .

3. What specific instructional practices would benefit Felice and her classmates more?

Mr. Truffaut should consider using curricular approaches such as PALS and Direct Instruction. Both he and Ms. Abbott could attend to students as they systematically practice all aspects of the operations they are learning, from conceptual understanding through application to story problems and abstract tasks.

Advanced Mathematics

In addition to representing the application of mathematics to daily living, story problem solving can be useful to prepare students for the tasks required in advanced levels of mathematics. Advanced mathematics in high schools can include geometry, pre-algebra and calculus, trigonometry and statistics, as well as related courses such as physics. Approximately 25 states require meeting algebra standards for earning a high school diploma (Dounay 2007).

Advanced mathematics call on many skills of basic math and problem solving. Students need to recognize the math question and then transform and reduce an algebraic equation, for example. They must come up with an approach to setting up the problem and solving it, as opposed to discerning the problem, as is typically the task with basic math story problems.

Algebra is a "gateway to abstract thought" (Witzel, Mercer, and Miller 2003). It requires students to be able to think abstractly, not just to translate abstract concepts into concrete representations. Still, teaching the skills of algebra should follow the sequence of concrete, to semi-concrete, to abstract instruction and practice (Witzel, Riccomini, and Schneider 2008). When adolescents with LD were taught to solve geometry problems by using manipulatives to represent the problems, they quickly learned the procedures to the point of mastery (Cass et al. 2003). (See Cass et al. for a brief summary of research on teaching mathematics procedures to students with LD by using manipulatives.) In multiple measures across periods as long as five to six weeks following the instruction to use manipulatives, students were found to have retained the skills they developed.

Attempts to represent abstract problems in concrete forms can be inconsistent with the task some advanced math problems pose (Witzel, Mercer, and

Miller 2003). In another experimental study, sixth- and seventh-graders with LD or who were "at risk" successfully learned algebraic concepts and operations when their math teachers represented the problem with manipulatives, followed by the students learning symbols to depict the problems in semi-concrete forms, and then writing them in numeric form. (Cass et al. [2003] have questioned whether the semi-concrete stage is truly necessary, however.)

Mathematics Curricula

Chapter Question
ALERT

In this section you will find information that answers a Chapter Question:

3. What are essential features of effective mathematics curricula?

As noted previously, expectations that mathematics instruction address conceptual understanding and application, in addition to skills proficiency, are consistent with efforts to ensure that students with disabilities participate in and benefit from advanced mathematics instruction. Replacing "general" or lower-track mathematics classes with inclusive college preparatory math classes has resulted in marginally improved math achievement for students with mild disabilities, but they continue to perform below their peers and levels expected in those classes (Gamoran and Weinstein 1998; Bottge 2001). Further, increases in the challenging standards in those classrooms have not resulted in the positive learning outcomes that more explicit mathematical instruction provides (Woodward and Brown 2006). Sadly, the math difficulties many students with mild disabilities typically exhibited 20 years ago are still commonly observed (Bryant, Bryant, and Hammill 2000). Current traditional mathematics curricula are at least partially responsible (Cawley et al. 2001).

Perhaps more so than for any of the other basic skills areas, mathematics instruction at all levels needs to include systematic instruction in specific skills, coordination of the order in which they are taught, and review of prior knowledge and skills (Harniss et al. 2007). For this reason, following professionally developed curricula is especially appropriate for mathematics instruction. That is to say, in addition to using generally effective mathematics instructional practices, mathematics teachers should follow a curriculum in which lessons and units follow a careful sequence. In fact, many school districts adopt mathematics curricula that span several grade levels with this purpose in mind. There is still room for good teachers to use their own effective teaching skills with such curricula.

THINK BACK TO THE CASE about Felice . . .

2. Was Mr. Truffaut's approach to teaching both concepts and skills truly focused on students developing proficiency in both areas?

Although Mr. Truffaut was using effective instructional practices, some students had persistent difficulties with certain aspects of Mr. Truffaut's lessons. Andrea's task analyses of Felice's problem-solving processes revealed that Felice had difficulty with some of the foundational concepts and skills of the four basic operations. Andrea also noted that several students had difficulties with both discerning and solving the algorithms. Felice and the other students needed instruction that also provided practice and support in prerequisite foundational skills. Thus, despite using scientifically based instructional practices, Mr. Truffaut was not meeting the learning needs of some of his students.

The primary source of math curricula has been textbooks (Miller and Mercer 1997). However, rigidly progressing through a textbook may not always suffice for a comprehensive curriculum, especially in the case of students with mild disabilities. Analyses of published math textbooks have indicated that they are overly focused on rote learning of computation skills and tend to have low-quality instructional features (Carnine, Jitendra, and Silbert 1997; Jitendra, Salmento, and Haydt 1999; see also Wilson and Sindelar 1991). Further, math textbooks can "overwhelm" students by presenting too many concepts, with little or no coordination of the concepts presented (Stein, Carnine, and Dixon 1998; Miller and Mercer 1997). Witzel et al. (2003) noted that the sequences of lessons in popular algebra textbooks may not be tested.

Critical Elements of Effective Math Curricula

The focus of math instruction for students with math-related disabilities should include a focus on detecting errors and reteaching those skills and concepts (Riccomini 2005). However, that instruction alone will not necessarily result in students who are strategic in their ability to apply the skills they have mastered (for example, Calhoon and Fuchs 2003).

As noted previously, Harniss et al. (2007) advocate building mathematics instruction around the "big ideas" behind major mathematical operations. Stressing the importance of mastering both mathematical concepts and procedures, they suggest that a focus on the big ideas will help students appreciate what they are learning. Harniss et al. advocate for drill of mathematical procedures and regular review, as well.

Timed drills improve automaticity for students with LD (Burns 2005). However, drills in basic math facts can result in facts mastery but not improved ability to apply the skill for problem solving (see Gersten and Chard 1999). Likewise, a disproportionate emphasis on strategy instruction for facts does not always lead to automaticity (Tournaki 2003). For these reasons, an integration of skill mastery and strategic application seems most appropriate (Ginsburg 1997). Students with disabilities benefit from a combination of timed practice drills and strategies for learning facts, more so than from either alone (Woodward 2006). Because ELL and minority students may have less proficiency in foundational concepts and skills, they will benefit from mathematics curricula that include a variety of practice opportunities (Cartledge, Gardner, and Ford 2009).

Harniss et al. (2007) advocate the teaching of "conspicuous strategies," or those that have wide applicability. They note that some strategies are so specific that they can only work for a specific operation; others can be so broad that they seem to be "little more than a broad set of guidelines", their fit to a given task hard to discern. A conspicuous strategy is one that is applicable to a variety of mathematically related tasks.

Fuchs et al. (2008) have recommended "seven principles of intensive intervention" (see Table 8.3).

These principles, which have been addressed throughout this chapter, should be incorporated into any mathematics curriculum or general approach to instruction.

TABLE 8.3: Seven Principles of Intensive Intervention

✓ Ongoing progress monitoring ✓ Drill and practice ✓ Instructional explicitness	✓ Instructional design to minimize learning challenge ✓ Cumulative review	✓ Systematic motivation to promote self-regulation and encourage students to work hard ✓ Conceptual foundation

Reprinted with permission from L. S. Fuchs, D. Fuchs, S. R. Powell, P. M. Seethaler, P. T. Cirino, and J. M. Fletcher, "Intensive intervention for students with mathematics disabilities: Seven principles of effective practice" (*Learning Disability Quarterly*, 2008).

CHAPTER SUMMARY

Students with mild disabilities can present a variety of difficulties with learning mathematics. Similar to problems with reading for some students with disabilities, insufficient understanding of foundational concepts (for example, number sense) may be the root cause of their mathematics difficulties. Students with "math disabilities" and their peers benefit from instruction that sequences from concrete, to semiconcrete, to abstract, for all levels of mathematics. Despite difficulties with foundational concepts and skills, students may progress to learn the basic calculation facts, and then more advanced level mathematics. However, careful examination of students' knowledge and skills—typically performed via task analysis—often reveals that their learning "progress" is mostly rote, and that they do not comprehend the operations they are performing.

In some cases, the mathematics difficulties that students with mild disabilities face relate to the challenges of more advanced mathematics. These students benefit from instruction that is considerate of their learning needs (for example, explicit instruction). They also benefit from mathematics instruction that routinely incorporates review of necessary prior knowledge and skills. With supportive instruction that guides students to apply their prior mathematics learning to new tasks, those with mild disabilities can learn more advanced mathematics at the same time that they develop their foundational mathematics knowledge and skills.

KEY TERMS

APPLICATION ACTIVITIES

Using information from the chapter, complete the following activities that were designed to help you apply knowledge that was presented in this chapter.

1. Perform a task analysis on yourself (or, if you are working with a student studying mathematics, you might ask that student). Explain a sample problem that is easy for you to solve at the concrete, semi-concrete, and abstract levels. Then repeat the activity with a problem type that is more challenging. Note whether you exhibit the same levels of understanding and skill between the two problems.

2. Locate the example of a math practice drill on which a student performed poorly (for example, less than 60 percent accuracy) found on this book's website. Perform a task analysis for the skill being drilled. Then note whether you can determine whether there is a pattern to the student's errors.

3. Review the DRAW/FAST DRAW and Math PALS strategies. By comparing the skills these strategies emphasize to the NCTM (2000) Mathematics Standards, decide whether or not they satisfy the concept of "conspicuous strategies" that Harniss et al. (2007) advocate teaching.

4. To help you summarize what you have read in this chapter, list one or more instructional activities described per each of the seven recommended principles for mathematics instruction (Fuchs et al. 2008).
- *Ongoing progress monitoring*
- *Instructional design to minimize learning challenge*
- *Systematic motivation to promote self-regulation and encourage students to work hard*
- *Drill and practice*
- *Cumulative review*
- *Conceptual foundation*
- *Instructional explicitness*

TECHNOLOGY RESOURCES FOR IMPROVING MATH SKILLS

Numerous websites and software programs are available for teachers interested in teaching students math or teaching students with mathematics-related disabilities. The following list provides a sample of choices from those that provide research articles, materials, and software:

National Council of Teachers of Mathematics
http://nctm.org/

The NCTM includes links to their Principles and Standards for mathematics teaching. Other useful information on this professional organization's website includes information for teachers, parents,

and administrators. Professional development materials and opportunities are also provided.

LD OnLine
www.ldonline.org

This popular website for teachers, families, and students with disabilities includes information on mathematics teaching and learning.

Dyscalculia.org
www.dyscalculiaforum.com/news.php

This website provides scholarly discussions of mathematics-related learning difficulties sometimes referred to as "dyscalculia." Useful instructional tips and materials are also available.

NLD

www.nld-bprourke.ca/index.html

The website of Byron Rourke, PhD, one of North America's leading proponents of the nonverbal learning disabilities (NLD) designation, provides scholarly papers and a question-and-answer section on the concept of NLD.

Math Missions: The Race to Spectacle City Arcade by Scholastic Inc.

This math program is for students in grades K-2 and provides students with practice in basic math skills (for example, counting, sorting, measuring) through 12 different activities such as counting candy, sorting toys, or constructing a skyscraper.

Timez Attack by Big Brainz

This software provides students with a review of multiplication facts through a high-tech video game. Teachers can decide which math facts they want students to learn ahead of time and then let students play the game. The program also keeps track of student progress as they play the game, recording the number of questions attempted and answered correctly.

Math Blasters: Master the Basics by Knowledge Adventure Inc.

This traditional math software program provides students with drill and practice of math skills through a game format. This program, for students ages 6 through 12 years old, covers addition, subtraction, multiplication, addition, fact families, problem solving, equivalents, and mental math.

Mathematics Deluxe by MathSoft Inc.

This program provides help for older students (ages 14 and up) in different math areas. It comes with practice problems and solutions in areas of pre-algebra, algebra, geometry, calculus, statistics, and business math. Students can use lessons and problems, online tests and games, online homework help and tutorials, an equation solver, a graphing calculator, and a unit converter.

Visit the book-specific website at www.cengage.com/education/ boyle for a variety of study tools such as web links, tutorial quizzes, glossary/flash cards, bonus material not included in the text, and more.

The premium website offers access to additional materials, including the Video Cases. Go to www.cengage.com/login to register or purchase access.

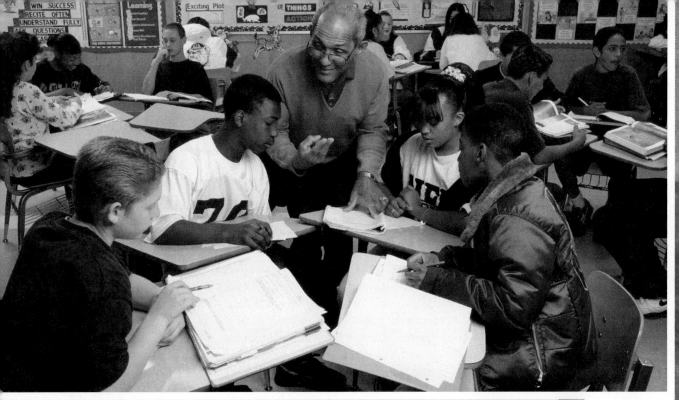

Teaching in the Content Areas: Strategies and Techniques

9

CHAPTER QUESTIONS

1. What are some practical teaching practices that can be used in inclusive content classes to benefit students with mild disabilities?

2. Because students with mild disabilities need help with basic skills as well as with content, are there instructional practices to guide both types of learning at once?

3. What types of skills are needed for success in inclusive content-area classrooms?

4. What are instructional accommodations and how are they provided?

Do you think that students with mild disabilities should participate in the regular curriculum and are prepared to do so?

Nearly half of school-age students with LD spend at least 80 percent of their school day in regular education classrooms.[1] However, the percentage of time they spend in regular education drops across the secondary school years (U.S. Department of Education 2004). From elementary to secondary level, the curriculum continuously shifts from an emphasis on learning the skills for learning to applying those skills for learning. In this chapter, we discuss methods to help students with mild disabilities participate in and keep up with the regular curriculum, even when they continue to need help with basic skills. When students with disabilities are in the regular education content-area classroom, their education is the joint responsibility of the classroom teacher and a special educator.

Special education policy requires that all students are provided access to the regular curriculum and are held to the same high standards (NCLB 2001; IDEA 2004). **Access to the regular curriculum** means providing students with disabilities opportunities to meet the same educational standards to which all other students are held (Hitchcock et al. 2002). In this chapter, you will learn about the challenges that students with mild disabilities typically face in the content-area curriculum and classroom (for example, English, foreign language, geography, health, mathematics, science), and the corresponding instructional challenges for teachers. You will learn about methods you can use to teach content and needed skills simultaneously to those students. You will also learn about how to organize instruction in ways that maximize access so that you meet the needs of all learners in the class. In short, you will learn that it is possible to meet the needs of an academically diverse class without sacrificing either your content or the students.

CASE 9.1 Ramona's Biology Class

Case Introduction

As you read the following case, ask yourself how students with disabilities resemble other students in a typical class. Do the tasks that they find challenging also represent challenges to other learners? Also think about their teacher, Ramona. Ask yourself how she can best respond to the tension between her students' learning needs and the expectations for content she will cover. Are there assumptions about how a content-area class should be conducted that need to be considered as well?

At the end of the case, you will find case questions. These questions are meant to serve as points for reflection. Of course, if you can answer them immediately, you should do so, but you may want to wait to answer them until you have read the portion of the chapter that pertains to the particular case question. Throughout the rest of the chapter, you will see the same questions. When you come to them again, try to answer them based upon the portion of the chapter that you just read.

Ramona is a ninth-grade biology teacher who is expected to complete topics and activities featured in all 18 chapters

[1]Just under 30 percent of those with emotional/behavioral disorders spend that much time in the regular education environment, but approximately 50 percent spend more than 40 percent of their school day in regular education environments. Statistics for those with mild mental retardation and attention deficit/hyperactivity disorder are not readily calculated, because their categories of disabilities are not separated in the U.S. DOE report.

of the textbook by the end of the year. Her class of 23 includes nine students who read and write below grade level, some significantly; five students are enrolled in special education and have IEPs to address difficulties with basic literacy skills, comprehension, or attention; one other student with a disability in the class is currently performing and achieving on grade level thanks to receiving appropriate accommodations specified on her 504 Plan. Although the students often do labs and occasional outdoor activities, most class days involve lecture and discussion that Ramona leads, followed by independent or small-group seatwork. The students usually do their weekly reading assignment for homework. They take a quiz each time they finish a chapter and the class activities associated with it.

Ramona is not sure how to meet the learning needs of her multiple learners at once. When she leads lecture-discussions, several seem to have difficulty following along and taking notes. Those with reading difficulties find the textbook very challenging, but in different ways from one another. Also, Ramona has noticed that certain students are consistently among those who do poorly on the quizzes, including four of those with IEPs.

Three of Ramona's Students

Luis finds reading the textbook difficult. Directions on handouts and quizzes are almost as hard for him. His IEP states that he reads best at a sixth-grade level; much of the vocabulary he encounters is well above that level, and the sentence structure of the ninth-grade biology textbook is very complex. In addition to reading difficulties, Luis is a very poor speller. Ramona has noticed that he has a hard time learning to spell the weekly vocabulary. He does a little better at remembering the definitions of the words. Ramona thinks that if it weren't for his literacy difficulties, Luis would be "one of the smarter students in the class."

Tara has a working memory deficit and some troubles with retrieval, resulting in difficulty memorizing information or steps of a procedure. Tara's memory difficulty is a problem, not just when Ramona asks the class to memorize new vocabulary for the chapter quiz, but also for remembering facts and concepts that are basic to understanding information that comes next in class. Tara's

difficulties with retrieval mean that she cannot instantly recall the information she has committed to memory. Sometimes she looks as if she knows the answer but "just can't get it out."

Rocco has difficulty paying attention, but, although Ramona is aware that Rocco has ADHD-inattentive, she seldom notices when he stops paying attention. He is very easily distracted, so she has assigned him a seat in the front of the class, where his classmates cannot distract him and where he can't see out the window into the hallway. However, Rocco still stops paying attention to the lesson or what he is reading when something triggers a distraction. For example, during a lesson on how the heart pumps, he didn't even realize that he had stopped listening and instead started to recall a movie that grossed him out when the vampire pulled a pumping heart out of a victim's chest. Ramona's movements or loud voice often call him back to the lesson, but he is never sure of what he has missed.

Ramona has been doing her best to meet the needs of all of her students, including Luis, Tara, and Rocco. By planning carefully and getting support from veteran teachers and her special education colleagues, including guidance from IEPs. Ramona has had some successes; however, she still worries that these three students in particular are not fully benefiting from her class. Ramona is worried that the class is going to get conceptually more difficult as they move from studying anatomy and physiology aspects of biology to cell functioning and DNA.

CASE QUESTIONS

1. What are some ways that Ramona can continue to use a lecture-discussion format but make the information more clear to Tara and her classmates?
2. How can Ramona provide the class with cues as to what information is critical and how to remember it, while also helping Tara and Rocco keep track when they get behind or distracted?
3. How can the students become involved in checking their own knowledge and comprehension during a lesson?

Ramona is a good teacher; she always knew she would teach a diversity of students, including students with differences in interests and abilities for biology. Still, she should have assistance to make sure that she does the best job she can do and that her students all receive the education planned for them. The days of teachers being "locked" in their rooms without any contact with other adults until the end of the school day are behind us (Tickle 2005; also see Goodlad 1984).

Special educators play varied roles in the content-area classroom. It is rare for the special educator to serve as *the* regular education classroom teacher, especially in the case of content-area classrooms. More typically, the special educator collaborates with or supports the general educator in the regular classroom. In limited instances the special educator may provide students with mild disabilities with curriculum parallel to that of the regular education classroom. Of course, sometimes the student with a mild disability will go to the special educator in a learning center or resource room. In the particular case of content-area teaching, the special educator must balance responsibilities for academic skill instruction and content instruction (Deshler, Schumaker, Lenz et al. 2001; Rhia and Mather 1995). Because the roles of the regular education content-area teacher and special educator are intertwined, we address you as a teacher of content in this chapter.

Facilitating Student Learning in Content Areas

Chapter Question
ALERT

In this section you will find information that answers a Chapter Question:

1. What are some practical teaching practices that can be used in inclusive content classes to benefit students with mild disabilities?

Students who do not understand content may not have prerequisite knowledge and/or may not have desired academic skills, such as Ramona's student Luis from Case 9.1. Those students need to be taught the prerequisite content and either the necessary skills or how to learn the lesson without primary reliance on those skills.

Problems with learning are rarely entirely due to a student's cognitive limitations. In some instances, students do not understand because they do not know what they are supposed to be learning (the purpose of the lesson). Other times, students do not understand what is expected of them as a participant in the lesson (for example, when to take notes, or the need to estimate or theorize a solution versus find one) (Bulgren et al. 2002). The cause of these problems is that teachers have not clearly communicated what is expected of the learner. These students would have benefited from the teacher devoting a few minutes of class time to explain why the lesson mattered and what its goal and process would be.

Cultural and linguistic factors also influence how well students benefit from a lesson. Students of color account for approximately 40 percent of the nation's school population, and 22 percent of those students have disabilities (National Center for Educational Statistics 2002). Furthermore, there is a continuing increase in the percentage of students in America who may be considered as English language learners (ELL); in some instances English is not the primary language in their home. In contrast to these statistics, only 14 percent of public school educators are culturally and/or linguistically diverse (National Collaborative on Diversity in the Teaching Force 2004). The percentage of students who are both ELL and have a disability is difficult to calculate; however, schools report having difficulty distinguishing between ELL status and learning disabilities (Wagner, Francis, and Morris 2005). They also claim inadequate services to support the needs of students who do have the combination (Zehler et al. 2003). In addition to language differences, ethnicity and social class can lead to lower expectations that, in turn, lead to teachers' differential treatment of students (Ishii-Jordan 2000). Diverse students benefit from instruction that is responsive to their culture. For example, Black and African American students benefit from culturally responsive teaching practices, including encouraging high academic performance and promoting students' cultural identities (Neal et al. 2003).

Lessons should not only be respectful of individual differences, they should address the act of learning in ways that are helpful to the students present. Think of the difference between the prompts to "take notes" and "take notes that include enough detail for you to explain the process when you write your unit reports." Likewise, the content might be too confusing for students to comprehend. For example, think of the barriers to comprehension that your class textbook poses (see Box 9.1). Most lessons pose similar problems.

BOX 9.1

PROBLEMS THAT TEXTBOOKS POSE FOR STUDENTS WITH MILD DISABILITIES

- Novel vocabulary
- Lack of transitions
- Assumed prior knowledge
- Few/unhelpful features
- Complex language
- Poor organization

Teaching is never just the presentation of information. Teaching is the process of facilitating students in learning. Sadly, an oft-heard complaint from content-area teachers is that "these kids were not properly prepared to be in my class." The implication is that content-area teachers do not have time to devote to teaching academic skills or reviewing what they presume should be prior knowledge. The reality is that students need guidance with the academic skills of reading, writing term papers, tracking data, formulating interesting questions, taking tests, and so on, and not simply because some lower grade teacher did not adequately prepare them. Traditional content class instruction can be enhanced to meet the needs of the learners present.

Effective Lecturing

Even though lecturing is more commonly used in the upper grades, elementary grade-level teachers should not skip this section thinking it does not pertain to them, as they occasionally use lecturing to teach content-area material. Even a ten-minute talk to a second-grade class is as much a lecture as is a 40-minute talk to a tenth-grade class.

Most teachers use a variety of lesson formats in their classrooms, often using those varied formats within a single lesson or class period. In addition to lecturing, teachers may have students participate in classwide discussions, group activities, problem-solving tasks, reading activities, projects, independent investigations, peer tutoring, and more. Students stay alert and motivated when they receive varied forms of instruction. Certain principles of effective lecturing can be applied to almost any teaching format. Among these principles teachers should know how to use are the following:

- Orient all learners to the lesson topic(s) and goal(s).
- Use effective presentation skills.
- Engage learners in the learning process.
- Check for understanding.

Each of these is addressed in the following sections on teaching content.

Perhaps the first principle should be *don't lecture*. If you are not an effective lecturer, it is a misconception to think that lecturing is an effective approach. Granted, some lecturing can be an efficient mode of communication, and students should learn to attend even when they do not wish to. Also, other forms of teaching are not always more appropriate than lecturing, but the truth remains that lecturing is not a very effective form of communication if no one is listening.

The following principles of effective lecturing help make the material more engaging. These principles are related to a tried-and-true maxim of teaching: *Tell them what you are going to teach, teach them, and then tell them what you taught them.*

Orienting. The very first step of lecturing, or any other form of teaching, is to get the students' attention, so that you can "tell them what you are going to teach." Lenz (in Bulgren and Lenz 1996; Lenz et al. 1995) suggests that you start with a "grabber." A **grabber** is anything that provokes your students to (a) attend to and think about the topic, and (b) think about the topic in ways you want them to think. A grabber might be in the form of a riddle; it might be a popular song that relates to the topic; it might be an unusual fact that will stun, gross out, or titillate your class; or maybe when the bell rings you appear in a costume relevant to the topic. Because the purpose of your grabber is to grab the students' attention to the topic, you do not want merely to get their attention (for example, scratching your fingernails across the board); be sure your grabber is relevant to the content.

The second important quality of a grabber is that it provokes students to think about the topic in ways you want them to. If you want students to think about why a topic is important (for example, what happens when a DNA chain mutates, why study revolutions), make sure your grabber reflects this approach to the topic, instead of simply having them memorize content.

Once you have your students' attention, your next challenge will be to keep it. To help your students follow your lecture, give them an advance organizer (Allsopp 1999; Ausubel, Novak, and Hanesian 1968; Lenz et al. 1993) that tells them what you are going to teach them. Think of an **advance organizer** as a "map" to the points you are going to address in your lecture. If Ramona tells her biology students that she is going to teach them about "the DNA structure of chromosomes, how it is replicated, and, finally, how DNA mutations occur," they will know more than that she is going to say something about DNA; they now know the three main points she will make and the probable order of information. This preview will enhance their ability to follow the lesson (Lenz, Alley, and Schumaker 1987; Lenz, Ellis, and Scanlon 1996). An even more effective advance organizer explains how the different topics of the lesson are related (for example, we are going to discuss mutations after learning how new DNA strands are created because . . .”). Now the students will know what they will be studying, and they will not have to wait until the lesson is over to know why. They will have a much better sense of what they are listening to and why, especially if your advance organizer also tells them what you expect of them (for example, take notes, participate by asking questions) and what else you have planned for the class period (after I explain the process to you, you are going to read a little more about it, then each of you will draw a “cartoon” depicting how a normal DNA sequence mutates in the case of Down syndrome). Students should have a sense of where the lesson is going if they are going to remain attentive and get anything out of it. Simply telling students information about the lesson at the start of the class constitutes an advance organizer, but it may not be effective if students cannot recall it. You can make ready reference to it and students can independently review it when it is written down. To this end, you might write the day’s advance organizer on a corner of the board. Lenz, Alley, and Schumaker (1987) validated the Lesson Organizer Routine in inclusive classrooms, which includes a graphic organizer of the key lesson content and critical questions for students to keep in mind (review Chapter 2).

THINK BACK TO THE CASE with Ramona and her students . . .

1. *What are some ways that Ramona can continue to use a lecture-discussion format but make the information more clear to Tara and her classmates?*

2. *How can Ramona provide the class with cues as to what information is critical and how to remember it, while also helping Tara and Rocco keep track when they get behind or distracted?*

By receiving information about the lesson “up front” with an advance organizer, Tara and Rocco have been better prepared to know what they should be thinking about. Tara will be able to make more connections to familiar information, and Rocco will have a better sense of where they are in a lesson and how information connects when he finds he needs to refocus on the lecture. Depending on how explicit Ramona’s advance organizer is, Tara and Rocco will know what topics will be covered during the lesson, why they are important to learn, and what the expectations are for them.

Either as part of or following your grabber and advance organizer, provide students with some **key questions.** These questions suggest what the students should be thinking about during the lesson. A good key question is not so literal that students merely have to listen during the lecture for the correct answer (Lenz et al. 1993). Instead, a key question provokes synthesis of lecture information and the listener’s own knowledge. Good key questions are open-ended and higher order. Tips on posing effective questions include (1) *focusing on essential content,* (2) *clearly relating them to lesson activities,* (3) *relating lesson topics to larger unit topics,* (4) *exploring conceptual relationships,* (5) *using questions that can help to monitor student progress (including student self-assessment),*

> ## TIPS FOR GENERALIZATION
>
> ### Keeping Advance Organizers Handy
>
> Although students will find the information in an advance organizer helpful, they should not expend effort to memorize it. They will appreciate being able to review the advance organizer periodically to remind themselves of unique vocabulary, the learning objectives, and what is still ahead. Tara and Rocco from Case 9.1 can also use it like a "program" to remind them of where they are in sequence of the lesson. In fact, Ramona would do well to reference the advance organizer periodically as she moves the class between the major topics and activities. Some ways to remind students of the content presented in an advance organizer include:
>
> - Have students keep a personal copy on their desktops.
> - Have students keep a copy as a section organizer in their binders.
> - Write it in outline form on a corner of the board where it can be easily consulted.
> - Begin each class with a one-minute review of the advance organizer, pointing out where the class is today.
>
> The Lesson Organizer Routine (Lenz, Alley, and Schumaker 1987) is a ready source of a tangible advance organizer.

(6) *motivating students, and* (7) *even letting students generate some questions* (Taymans and Lynch 2004). A key question does not have to be limited to your immediate lecture; it could relate to an entire unit.

Grabbing your students' attention, providing orientation via an advance organizer, and supplying them with a few key questions can all be done in under five minutes. These activities are investments well worth the short amount of time they take.

Presenting Effectively. Once you orient students to the lesson, you must keep them engaged and teach in ways that facilitate their access to the curriculum. There is more to teaching than being a persuasive communicator; nonetheless, a few public speaking tips can be useful. The first is to **provide clarity.** If you have ever read a challenging textbook, you have undoubtedly gone back and reread a difficult sentence or paragraph. Many students who listen to lectures wish they could play back the lecture.

There are no formulaic steps to ensure clarity; rather, think about what information is likely to make sense to all of your students. If something will not be clear (for example, "nondisjunction when chromosomes split can result in trisomy 21"), present the material in a way that makes it clear. This process can be as simple as presenting information in an order that is logical to your students. For example, think about which you should teach first, the DNA structure of trisomy 21, the functions of DNA that compose chromosomes, or how chromosomes replicate. To help you determine the best order, think about how each option matters to learning the other concepts.

Also, be sure to explain terms or concepts that may not be clear to the students, even when you think those concepts should be prior knowledge (for example, "Remember, we said *replicate* means to reproduce or make a copy of itself, and chromosomes do this by splitting in half"). Just because you taught new information in yesterday's lesson or even five minutes ago does not mean that your students are ready to use it to learn further information (thus, try "Remember, *replicate* means to reproduce or make a copy of itself, and chromosomes do this by splitting in half. The most common way chromosome replication may form the mutation trisomy 21 is when a fertilized egg receives an extra 21st chromosome because one parent donated it"). You can also use repetition to reinforce information (for example, "An extra 21st chromosome results in trisomy 21. And as we just said, *trisomy 21* means 'three pairs of the 21st chromosome instead of the usual two'"). You can also ask students to do the repeating (for example, "Who can tell us what we said *trisomy* means? Look to see what your notes say, or think about the first part of the word, *tri.*").

To aid clarity, effective lecturers often use **visuals** or other props when speaking. These can enhance the presentation of information. Effective visuals can serve as backdrops to your presentation; they might list key points you are going to make, supply definitions for important terms, display processes, or depict the organization of information (Boyle and Yeager 1997). You may keep a visual up for the duration of your lecture. Students can hear you explain a point and see an example of it. When teachers use technologies such as PowerPoint and SMART Boards (see Chapter 11), students may receive copies of the material presented to the class. If you have students with vision impairments, you may need to use tactile materials or you can provide individual copies (see the section on "Accommodations" in this chapter).

If you want students to attend to your visual, you should wait to display it until the appropriate time, lest they be distracted by it while you are talking. A student like Rocco could easily lose focus on the class while inspecting a visual; for such students, you may need to monitor them periodically to see if you need to prompt them to pass the visual along or make a connection back to what you are discussing. In the case of a visual on the board, stand near it so that students do not have to divide their attention between you and it. Also, if your visual is complex (for example, a map or chart), you can help focus your students by pointing to the relevant areas.

Visuals can enhance your lecture, but they can also detract from it. Inappropriate visuals or inappropriate presentation of them, such as described in the preceding paragraph, can confuse students. To enhance your lecture, visuals must be consistent with what you say or demonstrate. Contradictory spoken and displayed terminology can confound students, even when the terminologies are synonyms (for example, reproduce and replicate).

Another way to provide clarity in your lecture is to incorporate cueing. When you use **cueing,** you signal to your students what to pay attention to (Bond 2007). Berry (1999) has identified three important forms of cueing: *mannerisms*, *organizational*, and *emphasis*. The three forms often overlap.

Mannerism cues include counting off key points by holding up your fingers, and gesturing by pounding your fist or signaling thumbs up or thumbs down, for example.

Organizational cues include counting, stating, "the most important thing for you to know is . . .," or stating, "what these three features have in common is. . . ." A cue is organizational as long as it somehow indicates how information is related (organized), be it linear, hierarchical, contrasting, or proportional, for example.

Finally, *emphasis cues* signal relevance by highlighting a point. For emphasis you might repeat a point, say "listen carefully to this," and then have a dramatic pause or write a term on the board and underline it. Cueing your students to the importance or relevance of information ensures that they know both that it is important, and how it is important.

In studies of intervention instruction, Carnine and others (Carnine and Carnine 2004; Gleason, Carnine, and Vala 1991) have found that the **pacing** of instruction and **student response rate** impact student learning. Although those studies were of timing between prompts and student response during highly structured Direct Instruction lessons (Stein, Carnine, and Dixon 1998), the same point is important to keep in mind when lecturing. An effective lecture must be presented at an efficient pace. Going too slowly by belaboring points or meandering off onto side topics is distracting and confusing. By the same token, presenting too rapidly and jumbling multiple facts or concepts into a sentence or two without elaboration or cueing can overwhelm listeners. A helpful gauge of whether your pacing is appropriate is to observe what students are doing. If they are taking notes at breakneck speed and rarely have time to look up at you, they are too busy trying to keep up to really pay attention. In contrast, if you are just talking endlessly, you may note that your students are not necessarily being provoked to think, which they would be if you asked a question or otherwise cued them to think actively.

METHODS AND STRATEGIES SPOTLIGHT

Tracking Students' Learning

In a crowded classroom, continuously keeping track of whether all students are paying attention, routinely participating, and learning can be difficult. Many teachers try to estimate how well these things are happening as they conduct their lessons. What these classroom teachers often do is judge whether about half of the class is having success (Scanlon, Schumaker, and Deshler 1994). If so, they continue with the lesson. Although this may seem to be a good way to estimate, it still leaves the other half of the class. Those who are not "getting it" are likely to regularly be in that half.

Teachers have an alternative way to estimate how well a lesson is going that accounts for the range of learners present. Before you begin a lesson, try to think of a student representative of those likely to do well in the lesson, a second student representative of those likely to perform in the average range for the particular lesson, and a student representative of those likely to have difficulty with the lesson; also think of students who have unique learning demands, such as needed accommodations. You can use the mnemonic HALO (Bulgren and Lenz 1996; Kissam and Lenz 1994) to remind you:

H <u>H</u>igh achievers
A <u>A</u>verage achievers
L <u>L</u>ow achievers
O <u>O</u>ther needs

Granted, these students only approximate their peers in how well you predict they will do, but they do reflect a cross section of your class. During your lesson, if you observe how well these student representatives are doing, you will have a better sense of how all of your students are doing.

Even those students who are engaged with your lecture will benefit from periodic **lecture pauses.** If you think of your lecture as divided up into a series of key points, you should plan to pause before beginning succeeding key points. Students will be able to review their notes and repair them if need be. Let students know that you are pausing and why; you might say, "Take a moment to go over your notes and make sure everything is clear before we go on." Better yet, say, "Be sure that you have all three mutations that result in Down syndrome explained in your notes." Lecture pauses are also helpful as you explain an important fact or concept; students should have a moment to "digest" what you just said before moving on, not just enough time to get it in their notes.

You may also capitalize on lecture pauses as a chance to guide student reflection. If students do not have any questions for you and seem to be comfortable with their notes, you may want to ask them one of the key questions or simply quiz them on important information that they should have received from your lecture thus far. Remember that recall is not the only goal of a lesson; you might choose to ask students an application, synthesis, or reflection question instead. A short pause can also provide students with a "cognitive break" before forging ahead with the lecture. Finally, a lecture pause can also be a good time to remind students where you are in the advance organizer.

THINK BACK TO THE CASE about Ramona and her students . . .

3. *How can the students become involved in checking their own knowledge and comprehension during a lesson?*

Lecture pauses provide students with a chance to reflect. Guiding their reflection ensures the likeliness of the lesson being a useful experience. Read on to learn ways that you can prompt students to be reflective as they attend to the lecture-discussion, including as they take notes.

Keeping Students Engaged. Another approach to keeping your students oriented to your lecture is to **interact** with them. Attentive listening by itself is a very low level of interacting; listening and just taking notes is somewhat higher. For students with mild disabilities, attending can be difficult. If your students can ask questions, answer questions, figure something out, share opinions, and perhaps even contribute lecture content while you lecture, they will be far more engaged.

As just noted, teachers have myriad ways to make lectures interactive. You can ask students questions such as, "Based on what I just told you, what would happen if . . . ?," or "What else would you like to know about how chromosomes replicate?" Your questions could serve as prompts to relate new information for already familiar concepts, such as, "Does this remind you of anything else we have learned in this class?" The essential component of an interactive lecture (actually a dialogue) is that multiple participants are sharing information through discussion, in the form of ideas or questions (Bos and Anders 1992).

Students might respond to you or to contributions from others, or they might test a theory out loud. A quick technique to do this is Turn to Your Partner (Johnson, Johnson, and Holubec 1993). In Turn to Your Partner, students are instructed to turn to someone sitting next to them and repeat information, explain a point, or ask a question.

Students can also be kept engaged in a lecture by being responsible for **taking notes.** There are a variety of approaches to note taking. (See Chapter 10 for a full discussion of note-taking techniques and how to support them.) As previously discussed, taking notes while the teacher lectures is a low level of interactive engagement by itself. Although note taking is not a substitute for more interactive lecture practices, variations on note taking can help it to be more interactive. One such example involves guided notes. In guided notes, students are given some form of an outline or template for note taking (see Figure 10.7), which the student is responsible for completing. By using guided notes, students are cued to what is important and assisted in taking notes that are complete by the teacher's standards. When students with mild disabilities have difficulty taking notes (for example, those with MR may not have the skills to take notes independently, and those with ADHD may be distracted and miss vital content), peer scribes can provide them with copies of the class notes. To maintain confidentiality about students' disabilities, sometimes the scribes do not know to which classmate(s) their notes are going. Also, when teaching using technology such as a computer projection or a SMART Board, provide copies of the lesson materials directly to the students.

Checking for Understanding. By now you realize that checking for understanding is important for a successful lecture. It is better to find out whether your presentation is effective during the actual lecture than at the end of a unit. Some of the previously mentioned practices incorporate asking your students about their comprehension. This is certainly a valuable and straightforward way to check for understanding. To **check for understanding,** you can "quiz" your students by asking questions, or you can generically ask them about their understanding.

Teachers have a variety of ways to check for understanding within a lecture. As we already noted, you may ask students to demonstrate what they have learned during lecture pauses. This technique can be used to determine the quality of their notes and well as to check on their comprehension. Calling on just one or two students to respond can be a good way to keep students on their toes, especially if they think they *might* be called on next. This method is not especially effective for knowing how the overall class is doing. So, you might consider calling on HALO students to better sense how various students are doing. By using response devices, you can efficiently check on how all individual students are doing during a lesson. Students may simply respond using a show of hands, a low-tech response "device" to inform you as to whether they think some statement you made is correct or not. They can use response cards, which may be jumbo index cards or slates, to write one- or two-word responses to questions you ask (for example, "write which has a positive charge, a proton or a neutron."). You can quickly see who has the concept right when they hold up their cards. You can also use prewritten response cards; distribute cards reading "proton," "electron," "neutron," for example, or "yes" and "no," which students then hold up at the appropriate times. Using handheld keypads, more commonly known as "clickers," students can press a button to respond to your yes-no or multiple-choice questions. Using a computer to which the clickers are linked, you can immediately see which students answered the question correctly. One apparent benefit of clickers over either response cards or hand raising is anonymity. A study of college students found greater percentages responded to instructor questions using clicker technology (Stowell and Nelson 2007). The study also recorded more "honest" answers, as students were not able to delay their responses until they could first see how their classmates responded.

One additional way to check for understanding is embedded in the process of providing **informative feedback.** In this process, teachers not only check for understanding but reinforce or correct it as need be. Long ago, behavioral theorists confirmed that humans are more likely to remember things for which they are reinforced (for example, praise for knowing) (Snowman and Biehler 2006). More recently, learning theorists have added that information on the accuracy of performance, including when, why, and how to perform a task or use certain information, also improves learning (Borkowski 1992).

A critical quality of informative feedback is that it is not just feedback. If a teacher were to say "good job" or "that's not right," chances are that students would not leave either situation with a clear understanding of what the correct response was and why. What was missing was the informative part; simply adding "because. . . ." to either of those examples of feedback would upgrade them to informative feedback. Informative feedback provides students with useful information for maintaining, enhancing, or correcting performance (Kline, Schumaker, and Deshler 1991). Thus, the informative piece must have that quality. It should help students know what was right, why it was right, or what was wrong and why that was; it should discuss the process that students need to follow to be correct in the future.

Teachers can ask students if they know if information is correct and why. They can also ask students to paraphrase the informative portion of the feedback. If they cannot paraphrase the information, they do not understand it very well.

Informative feedback is useful to students because it provides them with a gauge of accuracy. Individual students can participate in charting their performance by (a) keeping track of feedback on a particular skill (for example, vocabulary words learned per week) and (b) providing their own informative feedback (that is, evaluating their own performance). Figure 9.1 provides an example of Luis's graph of vocabulary words learned for each biology chapter. The lines connected by boxes indicate the number of words spelled correctly (spell-c) and incorrectly (spell-i) each week, and the lines connected by dots indicate the

FIGURE 9.1

Luis's Vocabulary Quiz
Performance Graph

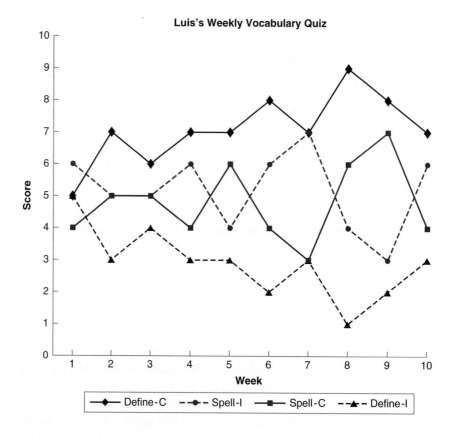

number of words defined correctly (define-c) and incorrectly (define-i). With this data, Luis and his teacher can note whether particular studying efforts are having the desired effect and indicating progress. Simply charting his weekly total test score would not be as useful. Reading Figure 9.1, Luis can note that he is doing well on learning word meanings but needs more work on spelling. Without this type of data, Luis could be optimistic and believe he is doing great in vocabulary because he scores so high on the definition parts of the test, or he could be pessimistic because he has the spelling data to prove that he "is no good at learning vocabulary."

Concluding the Lecture. Finally, although many of us use some form of advanced organizers in our teaching, we often neglect to extend a similar courtesy to our students at the end of lectures or lessons. A **post organizer** serves to summarize the key points of a lecture (tell them what you taught them), reminds listeners of how the topic related to things they already knew about, and predicts future uses of the information (Lenz, Ellis, and Scanlon 1996). This informational organizer helps students to reflect on the just-completed lesson, and to match what they learned with what you intended for them to learn. So you might conclude your lecture by stating what your topic was ("I told you three important things about DNA . . ."), why it matters ("In addition to the fact that you will need to know this for our next test, you need to understand how chromosomes are structured and how mutations in that structure can cause disabilities as part of understanding where disabilities come from and why"), and predict future lessons ("After we finish studying DNA, we are going to study how the human embryo blastula develops into a fetus, and we will continue to discuss how disabilities develop, so we will see how your DNA sequence determines things like your eye color, how many toes you have, and whether you might have a disability"). Ideally, when you provide a post organizer, you will recall your advance organizer.

PASS and SCREAM

As previously stated, the principles of effective lecturing can be applied to most forms of teaching. Regardless of the instructional approach, an effective teacher embeds the principles in a broader process of teaching, one that begins with good planning. Remembering the mnemonics PASS and SCREAM can help you remember the overall process (Mastropieri and Scruggs 2002).

As explained in Chapter 2, a lesson actually begins in a preplanning phase, during which you consider the content and skill standards for the lesson topic, individual students' IEPs, resources, and your own skills (Schumm et al. 1995). In this systematic way to think about effectively teaching an academically diverse class, the first step is to *Prioritize objectives.* This step reminds you to plan taking into account the varied skills required to complete an activity and determine how to help students with disabilities who must complete them, as well as to eliminate others that are unnecessary. The second step is to *Adapt instruction, materials, or the environment,* which is a reminder to be prepared to provide students with individually appropriate accommodations as needed (see Chapter 2 for a definition of accommodations plus procedures for determining and using them effectively). The third step of PASS reminds you to *use Systematic instruction* by incorporating the SCREAM variables. Finally, the fourth step, implement *Systematic evaluation procedures,* encourages you to conduct ongoing evaluations of individual students' progress toward the lesson goal(s) (ibid.), and reminds you to observe carefully your practices and student learning to be fully informed on how effective your lessons are and whether you may need to adjust your plans and teaching practices (for example, use the curriculum-based measurement [C-BM] procedures outlined in Chapter 2 and other chapters).

The SCREAM variables remind you to incorporate certain principles of effective instruction into your lesson. These principles include structure, clarity, redundancy, enthusiasm, appropriate pace, and maximized engagement (Mastropieri and Scruggs 2002). Although SCREAM is a useful mnemonic, we encourage you to incorporate all of the principles of effective lecturing whenever you can.

Read on to learn about a set of content teaching procedures that are based in effective special education practices and that have been found effective for the diversity of learners in content-area classrooms.

Helping Students Make Sense of Lesson Content

In any classroom, on any given day, there will be variation in how students learning the same content or skill come to understand it. The challenge for teachers is to communicate clearly the critical content of a lesson to an academically diverse room of learners. If students fail to appreciate key concepts fully or their

Chapter Question
ALERT

In this section you will find information that answers a Chapter Question:

2. Because students with mild disabilities need help with basic skills as well as with content, are there instructional practices to guide both types of learning at once?

relationships to bigger ideas (for example, the lesson or unit topic), the lesson will not be a success for them. Although effective lecturing is essential for clear communication of important concepts, students also need assistance in thinking about the concepts, so that they may comprehend them.

Because our materials and lessons are not always as clear as they could be, and our students vary in their preparedness to learn, teachers need to know how to:

- Relate current lessons to past and future lessons
- Differentiate learning goals from learning activities
- Guide students to engage actively in considering new concepts
- Guide students to comprehend individual concepts
- Guide students to form relationships among concepts
- Ask questions that prompt clarification and in-depth learning

Content Enhancement

As the name suggests, content enhancement is an approach for enhancing the presentation of critical content in a lesson. Take a moment to review Box 9.1, which lists examples of the faults of many textbooks. If you think about your own experiences in the classroom, the examples parallel faults of many classroom lessons. Using content enhancement, teachers anticipate that all learners will not find certain concepts to be sufficiently clear and use specific practices to clarify those concepts as part of the lesson (other content enhancement routines are focused on supporting student work completion). Content enhancement routines, therefore, provide access to the curriculum (*IDEA* 2004) for an academically diverse group of students.

Content enhancement incorporates the following four instructional conditions:

1. Both group and individual needs are valued and met.
2. The integrity of the content is maintained.
3. Critical features of the content are selected and transformed in a way that promotes learning for all students.
4. Instruction is carried out in a partnership with students. (Lenz, Deshler, and Kissam 2004)

Content enhancement instructional approaches incorporate instructional routines, devices, and procedures (Bulgren et al., forthcoming). The teacher leads the class through a routine and uses a visual device to help students organize the information. The *routines* involve some classroom teacher and student behaviors common to all content enhancement approaches and others specific to the one being used. The *visual device* is some type of a graphic organizer that visually depicts the organization or relationship among concepts the students are studying. It also helps to cue cognitive actions, such as comparing or relating concepts. The completed device can be saved as a permanent record of the information learned during the content enhancement lesson. Finally, all content enhancement routines include *procedures* to (a) inform the students about using the routines and devices, (b) explicitly teach content, (c) orchestrate student interaction, and (d) co-construct learning (Bulgren et al., forthcoming). Although initially confusing in the language of content enhancement, the combination of behaviors engaged in and the visual device used is collectively referred to as a "content enhancement routine"

(Deshler and Bulgren 1997). Read on to learn how to use a content enhancement routine specifically designed to help students explore key concepts.

The Concept Mastery Routine. The Concept Mastery Routine was developed by Bulgren, Schumaker, and Deshler (1993), who are three of the scholars who initially developed content enhancement. Instead of stopping the lesson to go over a difficult concept or relegating it to a weekly vocabulary word list and hoping more complex learning ensues, the class uses the Concept Mastery Routine to study the concept in relation to other content in the lesson. Using the routine, students develop an understanding of the meaning of the concept at the same time they learn how it relates to other important information (Bulgren and Scanlon 1997/1998). An instructional device called the concept diagram (see Figure 9.2) is used to guide the routine.

Each step of the routine is cued by following the circled numbers on the diagram. In place of following the numbers, students can instead learn the mnemonic CONCEPT, which cues each of the seven steps.

FIGURE 9.2

Concept Diagram for *Revolution*

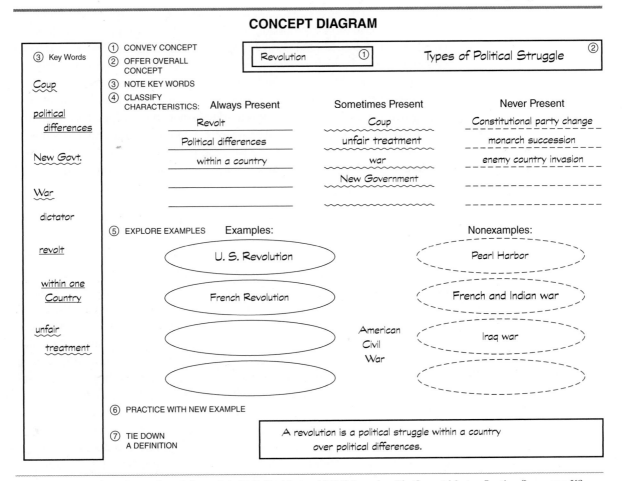

Source of concept diagram template: Bulgren, J. A., D. D. Deshler, and J. B. Schumaker. *The Concept Mastery Routine*. (Lawrence, KS: Edge Enterprises, Inc., 1993).

In **step 1, convey the concept,** the teacher identifies the concept to be explored by the class and writes it in the box numbered 1 (revolution). Alternatively, the teacher could name several representative conflicts and ask students to identify what the concept is. The teacher may explain why this concept is centrally important or may state expectations for students to learn it. The teacher should have a copy of a blank concept diagram projected on an overhead projector, or somehow posted in the classroom in such a way that all can see it. Ideally, the students will each have a blank diagram to fill in as they participate in the lesson.

In **step 2, offer overall concept,** the teacher explains (or elicits from the students) the overall concept to which the target concept is related. In Figure 9.2, revolution is going to be studied as part of a larger lesson or unit on types of political change.

Having established the topic of the content enhancement lesson and its relevance, the class now participates in **step 3, note key words.** Using either brainstorming or a series of prompts that the teacher has prepared based on what students should already know, the teacher and students generate a list of terms and concepts that the students hypothesize are relevant to understanding the concept. Although traditional brainstorming involves posting ideas without discussing them, here the teacher may prefer to have students explain why they consider their contribution appropriate, and the class should get involved in deciding whether or not each should be included on the key word list. This type of conversation allows students to interact with each other and the content in order to learn. The key word list should be limited to approximately ten concepts, whenever possible (Bulgren, Deshler, and Schumaker 1993). As will be seen in the following two steps, content of the list is used to explore the concept. This is another reason to stray from the traditional brainstorm practice of posting all that comes to mind without considering it critically (see also Troia, Graham, and Harris 1999).

Step 4, classify characteristics, is the step in which the thoughts developed in steps 1 to 3 begin to be put to use to determine the qualities of the target concept (revolution). Beginning with the contents of the key words list, students are asked to list characteristics of the concept that are *always present, sometimes present*, or *never present*. The discussion will almost certainly provoke the students and teacher to come up with additional information to be included on the diagram. Precisely how these activities are done is at the discretion of the teacher, but the class should develop a set of routines across multiple instances of using the Concept Mastery Routine so that they become highly familiar with the expectations for their participation. Students could convene in small groups at this point or hold a spirited classwide discussion (Bulgren, Deshler, and Schumaker 1993), for example. Although the teacher leads the students through the routine, it should be clear that the teacher does not simply present the content to the learners; in content enhancement, the learners are actively engaged in reflecting on what they know and making predictions that are investigated, all of this necessarily involves making rich connections among concepts familiar and new.

Following step 4, students progress to **step 5, explore examples,** as a test of the characteristics they have classified. Students should list multiple examples of the concept that satisfy the various conditions of *always present, sometimes present*, and *never present*. Also, list nonexamples because students who have not mastered the content can better comprehend the limits of a concept and its examples when they can identify instances that might reasonably be mistaken for an example (Prater 1993; Scanlon 2002). This is a true test of students' ability to comprehend the concept being diagrammed. One of the many options in how to complete the CONCEPT steps is for the teacher to provide the examples and nonexamples prior to steps 1 to 4 and guide the students to determine that content inductively (Bulgren, Deshler, and Schumaker 1993).

For **step 6, practice with a new example.** This step requires teachers to be prepared with an item not discussed in the routine thus far, which may be an example or a nonexample. This new item can be written in the "proving ground" or space on the diagram between the examples and nonexamples bubbles. The students are then challenged to determine whether or not it is an example of the concept. For example, the teacher could write "The Northern Ireland 'Troubles'" in Figure 9.2. Using practice examples becomes a test of both the accuracy of the concept diagram and of the students' learning. Of course, at any time the students realize they need to refine the content on some section of the diagram, they should be able to discuss it and do so.

Finally, students define the concept in **step 7, tie down a definition.** The definition should name the concept and incorporate all of the *always present* characteristics. Using the Concept Mastery Routine, students will have thoroughly investigated the concept in question and considered related important information. This particular content enhancement routine can be used to begin a lesson, as a central learning activity of a lesson, or as a way to summarize and evaluate learning.

Other Content Enhancement Routines. Several other content enhancement routines are available, some of which are intended to help teachers in their planning and to share that planning with their students (review Chapter 2 for the purposes and benefits of sharing planning with students). Others are designed to help students explore and apply key concepts of a lesson. Content enhancement routines can be categorized into four domains. In the first, routines for planning and leading learning help teachers to identify critical content and activities at the course, unit, and lesson levels (for example, Lenz et al. 1995; Lenz et al. 1998). They include routines and graphic devices to help students understand connections among lessons and to keep track of learning goals and assignments (review Figure 2.8 for an example). The second domain includes routines for exploring text, topics, and details; these guide students and their teachers through processes for clarifying concepts that are confusing and abstract. For example, the Framing Routine (Ellis 1998) guides students to transform abstract main ideas into concrete representations; the Survey Routine (Deshler, Schumaker, and McKnight 1997) helps students to navigate texts that are dense and confusing. The third domain consists of routines for teaching concepts, including the Concept Mastery Routine and Concept Comparison Routine, which guide students through a process of identifying critical similarities and differences between concepts (for example, opposing political parties, protons and electrons). Finally, fourth domain comprises routines for increasing performance. These include the Quality Assignment Routine (Rademacher et al. 1998) featured in Chapter 10, as well as the Recall Enhancement Routine (Schumaker et al. 1998), which helps students to recall critical lesson content; its validated benefits include significantly improved performances on class tests. These various content enhancement routines are especially beneficial because they are easily integrated into the inclusive classroom environment (Bulgren 2006; see also Little and Hahs-Vaughn 2007).

Research Evidence   *Content Enhancement.* Bulgren and her colleagues have researched the effectiveness of various content enhancement routines (Bulgren and Lenz 1996) and

---

CASE 9.2   **Students with Comprehension Difficulties**

Case Introduction

Now that you have worked through the first case in this chapter, you should feel comfortable addressing issues in a second case. In Case 9.1, you considered effective instructional practices for the content-area classroom (aka the "inclusion classroom"). Those practices were discussed in relation to lecture-discussion instructional activities, but, as stated, they can be appropriate practices for any of the myriad of ways a teacher might lead a lesson. In this case, you are introduced to another teacher, a special educator named Alok. He is particularly concerned with how to facilitate his students in reading challenging texts. As you read the case, think about the ways Alok's challenges resemble those Ramona claimed.

Alok is co-teaching U.S. history with Selma Bean. So that their students can take historical perspectives, they have them read original documents in addition to using the district-adopted textbook. They plan to have the students rely heavily on original documents, to help them understand both the unfolding causes of the American Revolution and the sentiments of colonists and others at that time. Alok and Selma want students to develop their own theories of cause, which they will then compare to those presented in the textbook. Although the students don't know it yet, Alok and Selma plan to use this same approach a little later in the school year, when they turn their attention to the Civil War.

Two Students

Alok and Selma co-teach following the alternative teaching approach, where one teacher works with the large class and the other works intently with a few who have particular learning needs (see Chapter 13). Luis is one of Alok's students. Luis has many of the same problems that he has in Ramona's biology class. He reads below grade level, but the history text

is written at grade level. The original documents are sometimes even more challenging for him, as some are written in outdated language styles, and others were written for certain audiences that do not include current-day ninth-grade students. These texts are even less considerate than the textbook in helping readers to think about their main ideas and how they relate to other topics in the lesson or unit.

Selma wondered if they should excuse Luis from all of the activities involving the original documents. Alok proposed the alternative teaching approach instead, as a way he could work directly with Luis and a few others intensively supporting their reading.

Tara, who is also a student in Alok's group, seems to have particular difficulty with the lecture-discussion portions of class. Although she is seldom off task, Alok and Selma feel she almost never understands what the class is talking about. Alok has stopped asking Tara questions in front of the group, because Tara is embarrassed to reveal how confused she is. Tara records very little information in her notebook, even though Selma has started using cueing and lecture pauses as parts of her lectures. Alok finds that he needs to go over everything with Tara in detail after Selma's whole class lectures. Selma finds teaching Tara unrewarding because she has so little success, and Alok sometimes feels that way too, because Tara is never able to articulate what she needs help understanding.

CASE QUESTIONS

1. How can Alok facilitate Luis and other students in comprehending often-challenging original documents?
2. What are some accommodations that Alok could try with Luis instead of excluding him from certain lessons or sending him to the learning center?
3. How can Alok and Selma determine effective accommodations for Tara?

Learning in the content-areas requires the integration of a range of skills that are not commonly taught in higher grade levels, including reading, note taking, and organizing.

Chapter Question
ALERT

In this section you will find information that answers a Chapter Question:

3. What types of skills are needed for success in inclusive content-area classrooms?

found them to be effective for students with and without mild disabilities, as well as usable by their teachers. In an overview of published research on "procedural facilitators," Baker, Gersten, and Scanlon (2002) reported that content enhancement routines and related instructional interventions were effective when they included graphic or mnemonic supports for performing cognitive processes and were taught in an instructionally supportive routine.

In the case of the Concept Mastery Routine, Bulgren et al. (1993) report that secondary students with and without LD performed better on tests, and at comparable rates to one another in inclusive social studies and science classes. The students' enhanced performance was likely due to their improved quantity and quality of note taking during the routine. Finally, Bulgren et al. report that teachers improved in their cueing of critical content.

Student Skills Commonly Required for Content-Area Learning

A student's full participation and learning in a classroom takes a variety of skills. In two separate studies (Scanlon 2003; Scanlon, Schumaker, and Deshler 1994), middle school teachers from a variety of content-area and special education classrooms collectively identified the skills students need to be successful in content classes. The teachers identified a range of skills, including traditional academic skills involved in reading, writing, and comprehension, and skills for participating in a classroom that incorporates a variety of learning activities (see Table 9.1 and Figure 9.3). Some skills needed for success in the content-area classroom are unique to content learning, and some are even specific to particular content areas.

In all grade levels, all students, regardless of disability, can stand to improve upon their learning skills; however, for students such as Luis and Tara, improvement is essential for their success. Typically, students with special needs are among those who must develop more proficient skills if they are to be successful in the classroom. Without sufficient study skills, students can have difficulty accessing the curriculum. The following are challenges common for students and teachers in content-area teaching and learning.

Reading   Reading is an essential academic skill for most content-area classes (Goodlad 1984; Woodward and Elliot 1990; also see Fisher and Ivey 2005); reading is also

TABLE 9.1: Study Skills Needed as Identified by Middle School Social Studies Teachers

Strategy Requirements of Social Studies Curricula			

Study groups
Social skills
 	
Organization
Put items in order
Have a plan—"This is
    how I'm going to . . .
 	
Probing questions
 	
Formulating opinions
	Excellence in homework
	Completion of homework
	
	Read to understand
	Explain in own words
	Pick out most significant
	    characteristics
	Differentiate irrelevant
	Give examples
	Application
	
	Transforming content
	Forming relationships
		Memorize—then apply
		Writing versus memory
		Know the terminology
		
		Understand and use key
		    vocabulary
		
		Notetaking
		Draw it!
		Graph it
		Visually depict information
		Timeline
		Sequencing events
		Think chronologically
			Evaluating
			
			Identify problem and offer solution
			Think ahead of now
			Consider other possibilities
			
			Express themselves
			Vocalize freely
			
			Processing lots of information
			Gather information about issues
			Be able to retrieve information
			Use maps correctly—gather
			    information

Source: D. Scanlon, J. B. Schumaker, and D. D. Deshler. Collaborative Dialogues Between Teachers and Researchers to Create Educational Interventions: A Case Study. (*Journal of Educational and Psychological Consultation* 5(1994):69–76).

the most common skill difficulty for students with mild disabilities, such as learning disabilities (Lyon and Moats 1997; Snow, Burns, and Griffin 1998).

Classrooms involve a lot of reading. They have posters and bulletin boards, chalkboards, computer programs, schedules, handouts, tests, classmates' notes, handheld PDAs, and original documents, in addition to textbooks. From first grade to twelfth grade, students are expected to decode and comprehend these many forms of text.

Content-area reading requires that students recognize and comprehend grade-level appropriate, and sometimes content-specific, vocabulary (for example,

FIGURE 9.3

Study Skills Needed as Identified by Middle School Team Teachers

Skills/Strategies Students of All Ability Levels Need to Master to Have Success in MY Class			
Organization Structure long-term projects Time management Follow structured format for notebook Reading comprehension Reading and following directions How to ask for and seek help	_____ Self control _____ Peer assessment Portfolio system Connections to prior knowledge _____ Number skills Vocabulary Number sense	_____ Outlining Logical sequences Time sequences Topic identification Writing/communication/ evaluation	Preferential seating Independent note taking Studying for tests Group dynamic skills Listening How to use a "tool" Responsibility for personal / school material _____ Summarizing

Source: D. Scanlon. Learning Strategies Expected in Content-Area Inclusion. (*Developmental Disabilities Bulletin* 31(2003):11–41).

gigabyte, trilobite, dilute, passage, plot—notice how these five words share a structural or semantic feature with the preceding and/or following word, are not all key vocabulary in the same disciplines, and sometimes have different connotations by discipline) and phrases (for example, "the measure of man" [sic], "estimate the earth's rotation in rpm," "plot the reaction"). Students need to read in sophisticated ways to acquire information and make connections between new and known information. Thus, content-area students must be able to perform reading skills that include the following:

Basic reading skills (review Chapters 5 and 6)
Vocabulary and concept recognition
Main ideas and key content identification
Main ideas and key content comprehension
Author's perspective interpretation
Other content connections

Review Chapter 6 on Later Reading: Strategies and Techniques, as it contains many useful practices to teach necessary reading skills for the content classroom. The following are a variety of practices that can be used in conjunction with those techniques. The following practices differ from those in Chapter 6 in that these not only support good reading practices but are equally focused on learning the content of readings, which is your primary but not exclusive responsibility in content-area teaching.

Begin with Pre-Reading. We are generally more successful readers when we know something about what we are about to read (Palincsar and Duke, 2004). (You benefit from the chapter introductions and orienting questions in this book.) Before reading, tell your students a little about the topic about which they are going to read. Even better is to also ask them to discuss what they already know about the topic (see the KWL technique in Chapter 6). If the material has chapter questions or a chapter summary, reading those before the main text can also be helpful.

Students should also thumb through the reading to gauge how long it is, and whether they will need to attend to any graphics. If you anticipate difficult vocabulary or concepts, be sure to preview them with the students, so that the terms will not be a hindrance when encountered in reading. This preview should include seeing the word in print, hearing how it is properly pronounced, and establishing what it means (Proctor et al., forthcoming). Helping your students know why the term is important will be all the better for their reading comprehension.

VIDEO CASE CONNECTIONS BOX

Watch the Video Case entitled *Reading in the Content Areas: An Interdisciplinary Unit on the 1920s*. Teachers Tanya Earls-Milner and Laura Mosman and their students discuss a graphic device that they use to help them categorize interdisciplinary information relevant to a novel they have read (*The Great Gatsby*). Think of how the same graphic could have been used as a pre-reading activity. List the teaching steps you could use with your students to fill in the graphic prior to reading (Note: You do not need to be familiar with *The Great Gatsby* or events of the 1920s in America to complete this activity).

Use Partnered Reading. Round-robin reading, where students in a circle take turns reading paragraphs aloud, is generally not an effective approach for any member of the group (Gill 2002; Wolf 1998). Variations where two partners are matched on reading ability can actually be more productive. The two can read and ask each other questions as they go. Asking two poor readers to help each other with a difficult text may seem illogical, but it can work if they know some ways to problem-solve their poor reading and to ask for help when needed. Matching a weaker reader with a stronger reader is a more typical practice (see paired reading in Chapter 6). This approach requires that the text not be so challenging for one that the other has to do all of the work, and it requires that both readers know how to seek and provide the help they can. Reciprocal teaching (Palincsar and Brown 1984) and classwide peer tutoring (Fulk and King 2001; Mortweet et al. 1999) are two established approaches to ensuring that reading partners of unequal ability are able to support each other in reading. Even "inactive" students like Tara in Case 9.2 can learn to use these approaches, because students are cued on questions to ask and skills to use.

Motivate the Reader. Students benefit from having a purpose for reading. The best purpose is motivation to learn. Do what you can to get your students to want to read the assigned material. Previewing the chapter can help to get some students interested; discussions of the chapter topic or why it is important to be studied may be motivating to others. To give the students a purpose for reading, you can provide them with questions (or they can generate their own as part of pre-reading) or guided notes (see Chapter 10). Looking for information can help readers to stay focused and comprehend (Dimino et al. 1990).

Find an Alternative. Students should learn to read and should be supported in reading as a part of your class. On occasion, it may be more practical, however, to find an alternative to reading. Could you show a video or use a demonstration instead? Why not use a content enhancement routine in place of a challenging reading to introduce new concepts? Could students do some kind of a project to learn the same information? Maybe you will need to present material with supplemental information. You may be able to find an alternative version of the text that uses simplified vocabulary and sentence structure, or that incorporates helpful graphics. Perhaps the students could listen to the text instead of reading it themselves; struggling readers can read more fluently and comprehend more when they read along with a text that is read aloud (Smolkin and Donovan 2003; see Chapter 6 also for more about this). In addition to recorded books, you can use interactive technologies, including devices that "read" print text aloud (for example, Kurzweil 3000, Readingpen®. See Chapter 11 for other text-to-speech programs.).

Select the Best Text. Whenever you have a choice among texts, select the one that has useful reading features. These features include guiding questions, a chapter introduction and/or summary, margin notes, highlighted vocabulary, graphics that support the written text, plenty of white space on a page, and features such as appendices, glossaries, and reference lists. See Crawford and Carnine (2000),

Dzaldov and Peterson (2005), and Stein et al. (2001) for guidelines on qualities of texts.

As stated, these good reading practices can be used to help students like Luis, Tara, and their classmates to read and learn necessary content. A teacher who was to implement a responsiveness to intervention (RTI) model in Alok and Selma's classroom could use many of these practices as part of the tiers of intensified reading instruction (review Chapter 1).

THINK BACK TO THE CASE) about Alok's U.S. history class . . .

1. *How can Alok facilitate Luis and other students in comprehending often-challenging original documents?*

Many of the reading comprehension practices presented in Chapter 6 can be used in Alok and Selma's classroom. Alok can also use the practices just described in this section in his regular education classroom. His students can use some of these practices together, regardless of their individual reading abilities.

Using the Reading Process to Integrate Reading Skill Development and Content Learning

There is more to reading than finishing a text in a timely manner and answering some recall questions correctly. Good reading begins with pre-reading activities that orient readers toward the topic, providing a chance to think about the topic and prepare for what is ahead. The act of reading the text itself involves reading with a purpose, by such means as having an interest or seeking specific information.

Good readers also think carefully about main ideas and which information is important; this is in addition to considering how their prior knowledge relates to what is being presented in the text.

Following reading, good readers reflect on what they have read, thinking carefully about whether their opinions about main ideas, important details, and connections to prior knowledge are accurate, and whether pre-reading questions were sufficiently answered now that the reading is complete.

Because the complete reading process actually has a number of steps, students may benefit from an organized strategy to help them complete each stage of the reading process successfully (Boyle 1996).

Interactive Semantic Mapping. Many students who have difficulties with reading do not have difficulties only in basic skills (for example, recognizing words in print) or in higher-order skills of reading (for example, imposing organization on complex information), but they have strengths and weaknesses in both types of skills. The interactive semantic mapping (ISM) strategy (Bos and Anders 1992; Scanlon et al. 1992) provides guidance in performing the range of basic to higher-order skills involved in the content-area reading process. The strategy can be used as either an instructional routine or as a reading strategy that small groups of readers perform (see the following Methods and Strategies Spotlight).

The ISM strategy begins with thinking about the topic to be read and previewing the text. Good readers do both of these things. Thus, **step 1, activate prior knowledge,** is the process in which students focus on the topic and think about what they already know or would like to know. To perform this step, the students need to be told only the topic of the reading; they read the title of the chapter or text, but no further. They then brainstorm a list of information they consider important about the topic. For example, Alok's students might generate the list of concepts in Figure 9.4. In this process, the students are both activating prior knowledge and generating vocabulary and concepts they are likely to encounter when reading. Recognizing and remembering that content will enhance their ability to get through and comprehend the text. Creating the brainstorm list as a group activity will help students remember or discover vocabulary and concepts they would not have generated in isolation. Debate and complementary discussion should also arise as students work together to create their list.

FIGURE 9.4

Brainstorm List for "Causes of the American Revolution" and Classroom Dialogue for Creating the List

> **Causes of the American Revolution Brainstorm List**
> colonies
> oppression
> slavery
> cultural differences
> representation
> taxation
> armies
> minutemen
> Declaration of Independence

The following is the dialogue Alok and his students had to develop their brainstorm list:

Alok:	Let's begin by brainstorming what we already know about the causes of the American Revolution. Who can tell us something we should know to understand the causes?
Thomas:	Well, you should know we weren't even a country yet.
Rachel:	Yes we were, we were British.
Luis:	But it was a revolution because we weren't really British; they were oppressing us and stuff.
Alok:	OK, so what is important to know about what caused the revolution?
Thomas:	Put that we were a colony.

(*Alok writes* colonies.)

Luis:	No, I think it was that they were making us work for them without paying us and kicking us out of our homes and things like that.
Alok:	We will have to look into exactly what things the British were doing, but what's a good word to describe the kinds of things you are describing?
Luis:	They were oppressing the colonists.

(*Alok writes* oppression.)

Tara:	Also there was slavery, and people wanted an end to that.
Lee:	Only some people, mostly those living in the north. Other people owned slaves.
Thomas:	No, you're thinking of the Civil War; that comes later.
Aaron:	There wasn't any slavery because the United States didn't exist until after the war.
Rachel:	Yes, Thomas Jefferson had slaves and he helped start the revolution.
Luis:	So put slavery down.
Alok:	OK, we are not all in agreement about whether there was slavery or if it was a cause for the revolution, but I'll add it to our brainstorm because we think it might be a cause.

(*Alok writes* slavery.)

Luis:	It's a kind of oppression.
Rachel:	Also there were differences between how the slaves and the colonists lived...and between the Americans and the British who ran things.
Alok:	Could I put down *cultures?*
Rachel:	How about cultural differences?

(*Alok writes* cultural differences.)

Lee:	Thomas Jefferson wrote in the Declaration of Independents that they had taxation without representation.
Luis:	That's good, write *representation.*

(*Alok writes* representation.)

Lee:	Yeah, but it's just as important that they had too much taxation, so write that too.

(*Alok writes* taxation.)

Alok:	What other kinds of causes might there be?
Lee:	I saw in that movie, *The Patriot,* that the British army took things without paying for them, burned peoples' homes, and stuff like that.
Luis:	We already have that; they did oppression.
Lee:	No but it's important, remember they were the redcoats!
Alok:	I think you are making a good point; what is important that we don't already have on our list?
Lee:	That they had an army here and we were supposed to be their citizens.
Rachel:	No, we were only their colony.
Alok:	OK, let's just focus on Lee's main point for a minute.
Luis:	But our side had an army too...it was a war!
Alok:	How about I put down *armies?*
Lee:	You should put *minutemen* because that's what our side was called.

(*Alok writes* armies *and* minutemen.)

Alok:	Let's go back to what Lee told us Thomas Jefferson wrote, because I think it is important; but Lee, I have to correct the name you gave it just a little bit.

(*Alok writes* Declaration of Independence.)

Alok:	Why do you suppose it was called that?

FIGURE 9.5

Clue List for "Causes of the United States Revolution"

Causes of the U.S. Revolution
Clue List
oppression
George III
patronage
Crispus Attucks
Stamp Act
Tea Party
Redcoats
Impressment
Quartering Act

Note: Clue list source from L. C. Mason, W. J. Jacobs, and R. P. Ludlum, *History of the United States, volume 1: Beginnings to 1877* (Boston, MA: McDougal Littell, 1997).

After the students have brainstormed, they **develop a clue list** in **step 2.** This is a list of "clues" as to what is important to know about the topic. For this step, the students skim the text looking for vocabulary and concepts that seem to be relevant (see Figure 9.5). They will have to learn that skimming involves reading the title and headings, looking at graphics and reading their captions, looking for vocabulary or text that is bolded, italicized, offset, and so on, and considering any margin notes or chapter questions.

In this process, the students will find some of the content already named on their brainstorm list. They will also encounter vocabulary or concepts that they cannot yet decide whether or not to have importance. Trying to decide information's relevance is a source for more discussion that gets the students using vocabulary and concepts relevant to the reading, and generating questions they will want to resolve by reading. The clue list content can be added directly onto the brainstorm list, or it can be kept separate as Alok's students have done in Figures 9.4 and 9.5.

Not only does this second step help the students preview more vocabulary and concepts and make links to prior knowledge, it provides them with a sense of how long the reading is and how it is organized. Knowing the layout of the text is valuable to following the author's organization of the content, as well as for predicting a strategic time to take a break.

In **step 3, predict relationships,** the students generate a semantic map, which predicts the relationships among the vocabulary and concepts from their lists. This is the central purpose of the strategy, to help students comprehend how the important content of the reading is related. Understanding the relationships among content is essential to comprehending the big ideas in the text; it is also essential to recalling vocabulary and concepts. To perform this step, the students must discuss which content from their lists is important for understanding the topic they will read about, and predict how that content related. A good prompt to help students predict relationships is to ask "Which items on our list have an especial lot to do with each other, so that we can put them in a group by themselves?" The discussion must include an explanation of *why* they go together. For example, Alok's students might put together "no representation," "taxation,"

FIGURE 9.6

Semantic Map for Causes of
American Revolution

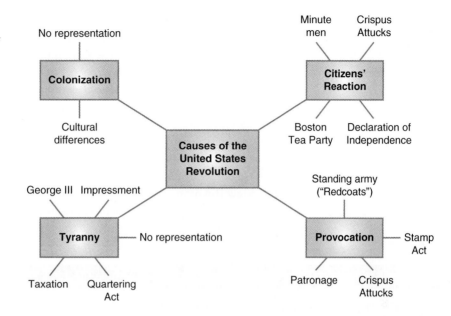

and "Quartering Act," and justify this by saying "These are all examples of how the British oppressed the colonists."

A semantic map has three levels of content (see Figure 9.6). The superordinate level concept (that is, the one that is most encompassing ordinally) states what the content of the entire semantic map is about. Depending on how explicit the text's title is, that may be what is written on the map for the superordinate concept (that is, the map's title), or the students might instead generate a more meaningful title. The lowest of the three levels are the subordinate level concepts. These are the various terms and concepts that must be understood and related if the overall concept of the reading (for example, causes of the Civil War, great twentieth-century authors) is to be meaningful. The subordinate concepts are organized by coordinate level concepts (the middle level of content), which serve to explain the relationship among those particular subordinate concepts that are especially connected. This "coordinating information" is the information that most often is not explicitly stated in a text (Lipson and Wixson 1997), and thus only skilled readers infer this information and fully comprehend the reading. The ISM strategy provides all readers a chance to infer this level of organization. When the students explain why a group of subordinate concepts go together on their map, they will be generating the coordinate concept.

Through step 3 of the ISM strategy, students have looked at the book but have not begun to read it. Now they are ready to do so. Their prior knowledge has been activated; they have previewed the text and its content, and now have purposes for reading. In **step 4, read to confirm,** students read the text. While reading, they seek to confirm the relationships they have predicted on their semantic map. They are also likely going to read for information that will resolve debates they began when contemplating content on their brainstorm and clue lists.

Students may read using whatever good reading process you like. They may read silently, with a partner, or listening as you read aloud; they might be told to read straight through, to stop each time they find an update for their semantic map, or to stop and discuss when they get to each major heading. You may also remind them to take notes, or maybe underline or highlight. However, when they finish reading, they should know that they will need to work as a group to review and update their semantic map based on what they found. Because you likely have other specific purposes for their reading, you should reveal these as well (for example, "This reading is part of our unit on understanding the lives of proponents of nonviolent revolution," or "You will be quizzed on the functions of mitochondria in cell reproduction.").

Once students have read the text, they work to revise their semantic map in **step 5, review the map.** At this stage they should add, delete, or move content on their map based on what they learned from reading. This is also the time to answer any questions generated in any of the previous steps of the strategy.

METHODS AND STRATEGIES SPOTLIGHT

When Is It A Strategy or A Routine?

A strategy is a process that cues specific cognitive activities, such as the steps or procedures of the ISM strategy. Students can perform most strategies alone. A small group or whole class could perform a strategy collaboratively, however. Routines are teacher-led activities designed to enhance the presentation of content. Routines typically include visual devices such as the concept diagram. When a teacher leads a group of students through the steps of a strategy, it may become a routine. Routines are not all as easily transformed into strategies, however. For this to happen, the embedded cues for cognitive processing that the teacher provides when leading a routine would have to be made overt and transferred to the student, perhaps using a mnemonic cueing device (for example, CONCEPT).

Accommodations

Chapter Question

ALERT

In this section you will find information that answers a Chapter Question:

4. What are instructional accommodations and how are they provided?

Students with disabilities should only receive a different curriculum than other students when it is unrealistic for them to benefit from the regular education curriculum (*IDEA* 2004). This does not mean that the only choices are full participation in the general curriculum with no individualization versus participation in some wholly separate curriculum. Students should receive accommodations that enable them to participate in the regular curriculum. The United States Department of Education explicitly endorses the use of accommodations (see Box 9.2). Providing accommodations is a primary way of ensuring access to the content-area curriculum for students with mild disabilities.

Some students have such poor test-taking, essay writing, or interpersonal communication skills that a teacher may assume they do not know the content, when in reality they would have little difficulty learning and performing with accommodations. Students who are slow to formulate answers may appear to be struggling to come up with the answer. The reason they are struggling may only be the pressure of time, however. Unless a fast response is necessary for accuracy (for example, capping a chemical reaction in chemistry lab, doing a timed math

BOX 9.2

U.S. DEPARTMENT OF EDUCATION OFFICE OF SPECIAL EDUCATION PROGRAMS ENDORSEMENTS OF ACCOMMODATION PRACTICES

Children with disabilities are included in general state and district-wide assessment programs, with appropriate accommodations, where necessary
—*Individuals with Disabilities Education Improvement Act* 2004 [Sec. 612 (a) (16) (A)]

Teachers ensure that students work toward grade-level content standards by using a range of instructional strategies based on the varied strengths and needs of students. Providing accommodations during instruction and assessments may also promote equal access to grade-level content.
—*Accommodations Manual: How to Select, Administer, and Evaluate Use of Accommodations for Instruction and Assessment of Students with Disabilities.* 2nd ed. (Thompson et al. 2005; www.ed.gov/about/offices/list/osers/index .htmlwww.ed.gov/about/offices/list/osers/index.html).

drill), allowing a longer response time or a more comfortable response format will allow students to show their abilities. This is an example of an accommodation. Other examples include being allowed to use a dictionary or not being graded on spelling, being provided guided notes, and reading an alternative version of the required text. Accommodations are appropriate whenever they are "reasonable" (*IDEA* 2004; *NCLB* 2001, as cited in Thompson et al. 2005); that is to say, they must not be too cumbersome to provide, the student should be able to make use of them, and they must not substantially alter the content of the lesson or methods the teacher or student uses (Thompson et al. 2005).

Defining Accommodations

Terminology in the education profession can be a bit like the Wild West at times; we make up the rules as we go along. The terms *accommodations, adaptations, alterations,* and *modifications* have been used inconsistently, leaving educators confused. We will adhere to the definitions that most closely align with the 2004 Reauthorization of the IDEA (our source, Thompson et al. 2005, is posted as a downloadable PDF on the U.S. Department of Education, Office of Special Education and Rehabilitative Services website in a "Toolkit on Teaching and Assessing Students with Disabilities"). Hence, the following are the currently used terms and their meanings:

Accommodation This is a minor change in how content or material is presented to the student and/or how the student participates in the lesson. An accommodation level change does not significantly alter the method of learning or learning outcomes; that is, students are held to the same expectations as others but meet those expectations in alternate ways.

Modification This is a significant change in how content or material is presented to students and/or in how the students participate in the lesson. Although not an entirely different curriculum, modification has students learn similar content or the same content but with different expectations for learning compared to others. Sometimes modifications are so extensive that the students learn a

parallel curriculum, which means they study the same content-area curriculum but learn significantly different content or skills (for example, a high school student studying the history of cartography and its relation to predicting revolutions whose goal is instead to learn how to follow the class schedule through the school building).

To add to the terminology confusion, **accommodation** is used as the label to name the overall category of practices that include accommodations and modifications (as well as the more outdated terms *adaptations*, and *alterations* when they appear), just as we are using the term in both capacities in this book. What's more, many of the effective teaching practices presented in this book can function as accommodations or modifications. Remember, accommodations are minor changes and modifications are major changes, and in either case they are provided specifically to meet the needs of individual students. Even when you elect to apply the accommodation to the whole class (for example, use guided notes, provide in-class assignment directions orally and in writing), it is still an accommodation because you are doing it to meet the needs of a particular student(s). At this point, you would probably like definitions to help you distinguish "minor" and "significant" changes; that distinction is a subjective judgment, however. There are always going to be examples that cause experts to disagree, but think of *minor* changes as altering performance (the teacher's or the student's) and *significant* changes as altering expectations.

Providing Accommodations

To provide accommodations, teachers need to do the following:

- Be familiar with the concepts of "accommodation" and "modification."
- Know a variety of possible accommodations.
- Collaborate with other educators and the student to identify suitable accommodations.
- Adjust classroom instruction so that one or more students can participate via accommodations.
- Evaluate the effectiveness of accommodations, including the learning that results.

The list of possible accommodations is as endless as is the imagination. However, they may be thought of as falling into one of the following four categories:

- **Presentation accommodations** allow students to access information in ways that do not require them to read standard print visually. These alternate modes of access are auditory, multisensory, tactile, and visual.
- **Response accommodations** allow students to complete activities, assignments, and assessments in different ways or to solve or organize problems using some type of assistive device or organizer.
- **Setting accommodations** change the location in which a test or assignment is given or the conditions of the assessment setting.
- **Timing and scheduling accommodations** increase the allowable length of time to complete an assessment or assignment and perhaps change the way the time is organized. (Thompson et al. 2005)

See Table 9.2 for a sample list of possible accommodations.

TABLE 9.2: Examples of Accommodations for Students

Adjustable lighting	Advance organizers
Checklist for assignments	Color code keys on computer or calculator
Computer with speech recognition	Duplicate set of texts at home
Background noise elimination	Extra time
Fidget objects	Guided notes
Manipulatives	Pen or pencil grip
Texts rewritten	Rocking chair
Study carrel	Visual cues
Writing templates	Written copy of oral directions

THINK BACK TO THE CASE with Alok and Luis . . .

2. *What are some accommodations that Alok could try with Luis instead of excluding him from certain lessons or sending him to the learning center?*

As already noted, the list of possible accommodations is as long as your imagination. In this chapter, you have read about a variety of instructional activities to support struggling readers in the content-area classroom. Alok and Selma could use many of those practices or features of them as accommodations for Luis. They are already using a setting accommodation by having Luis work in a small group with Alok. They might also try a presentation accommodation such as transcribing the original documents into easily readable fonts, and even updating the language if that won't violate the lesson.

An IEP should inform all concerned parties as to which accommodations are appropriate for an individual student. The test of an accommodation's appropriateness should consider three factors: maintaining lesson integrity, student appropriateness, and manageability. To **maintain lesson integrity,** an accommodation cannot significantly alter the learning standard (content) or method of performance, and a modification can do those things but must remain true to the lesson topic. The learning standard is relatively easily judged: if the accommodation results in lower proficiency than should be acceptable for a student studying the topic, then the accommodation may not be appropriate. The catch is that proficiency is related to what is necessary for the student to learn the lesson, not for simply how you would like the student to do so. Take the first of two examples: Luis from the two cases in this chapter reads significantly below grade level, so whenever there is a reading assignment he either listens to the book on tape or reads a text presenting the same information but written at a lower reading level. When the class is reading the original text of documents supporting the American Revolution (for example, *Common Sense*, the *Declaration of Independence*), Luis finds their complex language too challenging to read, so he reads modernized and simplified versions of the same text. He is fully able to participate in the lesson and learn about the principle positions espoused in each document. His accommodations have enabled him to participate in the lesson and to be held to the same learning standards as others. On the other hand, if the goal of the lesson were to learn how to read the original source documents and independently determine their principle positions, Luis should not read modernized and simplified versions of the texts; he could still listen to recordings of them, however. This accommodation would cross the line to becoming a modification only if the lesson goal included reading the original documents in print format only.

As a second example, consider Tara, from the two cases, who has trouble with working memory. Whenever a task involves memorizing information, she has tremendous difficulty and often fails. Her memory deficits also tend to cause her to take longer to recall and perform steps of a skill she has learned (for example, the steps involved in multiplication that includes carrying), although she can usually perform the skills given an occasional prompt and enough time. In Tara's math class, the teacher gives a speed quiz every Friday. Students earn points for both the percentage of problems correct and the percentage attempted. The math teacher acknowledges that speed is a desirable skill for solving equations, but not an essential one, so Tara is allowed to complete the same quiz as everyone else, but she takes it untimed. Because the scoring system for the quiz incorporates the number of problems attempted, the teacher must also alter how Tara's quiz is graded. Thus, to be accommodated on speed quizzes in math class, Tara must be allowed to be quizzed only on the essential skill of solving problems and not be held to evaluation standards that are inconsistent with her accommodation (in this example the accomodation would unfairly advantage Tara).

As you can judge from the examples of Luis and Tara, **student appropriateness** means that the accommodations provided match what the student needs and from which the student can benefit. Luis has difficulties with the visual process of reading; if he had a more general comprehension problem, recording grade-level books on tape may not be an appropriate accommodation for him. Simply put, to be appropriate, an accommodation should be matched to what the student can do.

Finally, **manageability** means that providing the accommodation does not unduly tax the student, classmates, teacher, or environment. If an accommodation requires a student to use a heavy piece of equipment that cannot be transported into the chemistry lab, for example, other accommodations should be tried before modifying the one student's chemistry curriculum to exclude labs. An accommodation is manageable as long as it does not impede the lesson. Most charges of accommodations not being manageable can be overcome by thinking creatively about how to provide the accommodation. A paraprofessional or peer tutor may need to assist the student with an accommodation (for example, a student needs to verbalize the steps of a procedure to someone in order to perform them), the student may need to be trained in using the accommodation before it is employed in the classroom (for example, Luis operating a tape recorder, or a student who is allowed to use a template for planning content of writing assignments), or the classroom configuration may need to be permanently altered so that using the accommodation does not disrupt the routine (for example, for a student who must sit in the front row or move to a study carrel in order to read without distractions). When a particular accommodation truly is unmanageable, an alternative accommodation can be found in most cases.

Selecting Accommodations

Here again, decisions about accommodations require intuition instead of matching to some checklist. Possible accommodations should be suggested on an IEP. Thus, the list of possible accommodations should be considerate of your curriculum and classroom routines. In some cases, students have very few recommended accommodations. This may be because the student cannot benefit from a great variety of accommodations; although, as we noted above, creative thinking almost always results in devising more accommodations that are appropriate. More often, you will able to select from a menu of appropriate accommodations, depending on the task and the student's needs in that particular situation (for example, Luis may be accommodated some days by working in a small group where the other students read aloud to him, but on other occasions he may need to use a modified text or book on tape). The student should be a helpful resource in selecting the accommodation to use and when to use it. Asking students which accommodation they think best to use helps you to make an informed decision; at the same time, it helps the students to exercise control of their own learning skills. To build facility with accommodations, the student should use the same repertoire whenever possible, instead of using an endless array of different ones.

Evaluating Accommodations

Students and teachers both might have favorite accommodations, but these may not always be the ones that best fulfill the purposes of accommodations. Just as with any instructional practice or student performance, an accommodation should be evaluated to make certain it has its desired effects. After providing accommodations, if a student does not seem to benefit from a particular lesson, the teacher should look into whether the accommodation is being using correctly, whether the accommodation truly matches the task, and whether the accommodation is effective for meeting the performance/learning goal (having satisfied the first two conditions). As always, evaluation should not just occur when the lesson is over; observe the accommodation in practice to assess how it is going. If it is not going well, perhaps there are ways to "troubleshoot" its use; otherwise, you can determine how to transition into an alternate accommodation in the hopes of saving the lesson. The observations that you and the students make about accommodations in practice can be used to update the list of suggested accommodations supplied to you and future teachers via the IEP.

(THINK BACK TO THE CASE) about Alok's U.S. history class . . .

3. How can Alok and Selma determine effective accommodations for Tara?

Tara might be a good source of information as to what accommodations might be effective for her. If Alok and Selma cannot come up with effective ideas on their own or in collaboration with Tara, they could consult other teachers, including the building's Teacher Assistance Team (review Chapter 2). Importantly, they should keep data on how well the accommodations they try work. Accepting that it will take some time for any accommodation they try to become a comfortable routine for Tara, they can plot her skill at employing the accommodation as well as her learning gains following C-BM charting procedures (review Chapter 2).

CHAPTER SUMMARY

Academic diversity is present no matter how homogeneous a classroom seems. Students with disabilities are full-fledged members of the classroom, regardless of whether they are held to different curricular standards and may require accommodations or other adjustments in a lesson. Teaching and learning in the content classroom are shared responsibilities. Teachers must attend to their learners and not unquestioningly to their content; students must use appropriate learning skills and work with their teachers to learn those skills.

In planning and teaching a lesson, teachers must be mindful of the students who are present. They can use a variety of effective lecturing techniques to ensure effective communication of information for learning. Teachers who incorporate these practices into their teaching are being thoughtful about their content and about how their students are receiving it. Content enhancement routines can be used

to further bridge teaching and learning processes; using these routines, teachers coach students to attend to critical concepts.

Students can become active in the learning process by being supported in learning and applying good practices in the classroom. Research evidence indicates that students benefit from learning how to learn as part of content lessons in ways they do not when they first learn skills in isolation (Scanlon, Deshler, and Schumaker 1996). Students should be informed as to the importance of attending to how to learn. Teachers should remember that even students in the upper grades still need to learn how to learn, not just to be reminded to use skills they may not have fully mastered. Students who are actively engaged in content learning can participate in initiating, monitoring, evaluating, and improving their own learning performance.

KEY TERMS

Access to the Curriculum, 296
Accommodation, 325
Advance Organizer, 300
Check for Understanding, 306
Cueing, 303
Grabber, 300
Informative Feedback, 307

Interact, 305
Key Questions, 301
Lecture Pauses, 305
Lesson Integrity, 327
Manageability, 328
Modification, 325
Pacing, 304

Parallel Curriculum, 326
Post Organizer, 308
Provide Clarity, 302
Student Appropriateness, 328
Student Response Rate, 304
Taking Notes, 306
Visuals, 303

APPLICATION ACTIVITIES

Using information from the chapter, complete the following activities that were designed to help you apply knowledge that was presented in this chapter.

1. If you have ever created a lesson plan, write notations into it "scripting" your role and your

students' roles for each component of effective lecturing.

2. Develop both a concept diagram and a semantic map for the content from one lesson or reading you recently completed.

3. Together with a content-area teacher colleague, discuss (a) a lesson plan from the general educator's content class, and (b) the learning needs of a student with a mild disability in that class (hint: you should consult the student's IEP). Then separate and each devise lists of at least four accommodations (or modifications if more appropriate) for the student and the lesson. Compare lists and discuss your opinions as to what constitutes an accommodation versus a modification.

TECHNOLOGY RESOURCES FOR IMPROVING CONTENT-AREA TEACHING

Numerous websites are available for teachers interested in teaching children to read or teaching children with reading problems. The following list provides a sample of choices in websites from those that provide research articles and materials to those that are informative.

University of Kansas Center for Research on Learning
www.ku-crl.org

This website has a variety of information on research-validated learning strategies and content-enhancement routines. The site includes descriptions of a variety of strategies and routines, reprints of research and practice articles, and information on professional development, as well as discussion areas.

Office of Special Education and Rehabilitative Services
www.ed.gov/about/offices/list/osers/index.html

This portion of the U.S. Department of Education's Office website includes information and links related to special education regulations and practices. Downloadable sample materials are included. Search for the "Tool Kit on Teaching and Assessing Students with Disabilities" (April 2006).

Inspiration©
www.inspiration.com

Inspiration and Kidspiration by Inspiration© are two software programs that are designed to help students develop and organize their ideas through the creation of diagrams or maps. Many types of maps and diagrams can be created with the programs, including concept maps, idea maps, webs, and storyboards.

Eduscapes
http://eduscapes.com/tap/topic73.htm

This website provides teachers with a variety of visual organizers and serves as a resource on how to use organizers.

Visit the book-specific website at www.cengage.com/education/boyle for a variety of study tools such as web links, tutorial quizzes, glossary/flash cards, bonus material not included in the text, and more.

The premium website offers access to additional materials, including the Video Cases. Go to www.cengage.com/login to register or purchase access.

© Lisa Pines/Photonica/Getty Images

Organization and Study Skills: Strategies and Techniques

10

CHAPTER QUESTIONS

1. What types of organizational skills are required of students with mild disabilities throughout the school day?

2. How can students with mild disabilities learn to follow schedules, and even to plan them?

3. What factors other than content knowledge contribute to students' successful completion of assignments?

4. How can students learn to be efficient note takers?

5. What factors contribute to a fair testing situation for students with mild disabilities, and how can they perform on tests to reflect most accurately what they know?

What ways of being organized are difficult for you? What study skills do you need to improve? How do those needs for improvement affect you as a learner? Most students need help with organization and with learning the skills for learning. They need to learn how to have the right materials on hand, plan and perform learning tasks, manage time, and coordinate all that is expected of them. In this chapter, you will learn about the organizational needs of students with mild disabilities and how you can teach needed skills. Organization and study skills can be particularly challenging for students with attention difficulties and memory impairments, which are common for those with mild disabilities. They often need explicit teacher cueing to use appropriate skills. Organization and good study skills are essential to academic success. In addition to learning how to teach students to be organized and use good study skills, you will learn ways to integrate organization into *your* assignments, tests, and classroom routines.

The Organizational Needs of Students

One key to successful functioning is organization. Without organization, students do not remember schedules or find materials they need, and lack of organization may prevent students from performing tasks efficiently. Although organizing is a central trait of cognitive processing for encoding, recalling, and expressing information (Snowman and Biehler 2006), having organizational skills is not automatic. For many students, organization skills must be taught.

Students of all ages and ability levels need to learn skills for organizing. The specific skills they need to learn depend on both the organization skills they already have and the demands of the classroom. You can be relatively confident, however, that they will all need to learn to set, read, maintain, and follow schedules, complete assignments, and study and take tests—all of which rely on aspects of organization. Students with mild disabilities have the compound effect of having life experiences (for example, missing periods of school due to emotional or behavioral disorders [EBD]) and cognitive processing deficits that make organization particularly challenging.

Chapter Question
ALERT

In this section you will find information that answers a Chapter Question:

1. What types of organizational skills are required of students with mild disabilities throughout the school day?

| CASE 10.1 | **A School Day in the Life of Jeremy** |

Case Introduction

As you read the following case about Jeremy, you may recognize many of your students; you may even recognize yourself. Maybe you won't see all of the forms of disorganization that Jeremy must contend with in a single individual, but you will see some familiar traits. As you read, ask yourself why Jeremy persists in some of these forms of disorganization. Also ask yourself what the consequences may be.

At the end of the case, you will find case questions. These questions are meant to serve as points for reflection. Of course,

if you can answer them immediately, you should do so, but you may want to wait to answer them until you have read the portion of the chapter that pertains to the particular case question. Throughout the rest of the chapter, you will see the same questions. As you see them, try to answer them based upon the portion of the chapter that you just read.

In many regards, Jeremy is an average teenager. He would rather stay in bed than go to school in the morning, and his constant nodding off in first period is proof that he has trouble waking up. He has good academic days and not-so-good days when he seems distracted and disgruntled. Sometimes his work is good, and sometimes it is sloppy in both appearance and quality. Sometimes he's late or he simply fails to do his work, and his explanation for this is usually "I forgot." Although these are characteristics of many teens, they are more constant and more difficult for Jeremy to manage because of his ADHD-inattentive.

This past Thursday, Jeremy got out of bed late, ran downstairs, skipped breakfast, and hurriedly filled his backpack with his books and papers until it was overflowing. Once at school, he held up the first period math teacher while he dug his homework out of his backpack and scribbled his name on it before handing it in. Seeing his incomplete science lab observation sheet from Tuesday, he quickly filled it in so it would be ready to attach to the report they would be finishing today. Between becoming distracted in class, jotting down his lab "observations," and nodding off once or twice, Jeremy's attempts at multitasking did not work out very well.

He grabbed the wrong notebook from his locker for period two, but only because he couldn't find the right one. (According to Jeremy's logic, he could either transfer the notes later, or just remember to use both notebooks when he studied for that class.) Second, third, and fourth periods all went well, except that he neglected to copy the assignment off of the board in period three, and his notes from period four were disorganized and missing some vital content.

After lunch, he met with his study skills tutor for period five; she was teaching him how to sort out when to reduce when converting combined whole numbers and fractions. He couldn't seem to remember the rule. He arrived at his next class, science lab, late, because he had forgotten the order of his schedule for the week, something he does periodically. When he got to science lab, he didn't follow the directions quite right, in part because he didn't understand everything and in part because he wasn't paying attention. Rather than ask for help, he simply completed the week's lab report in the same reckless fashion that he had filled in his observation sheet earlier.

For homework, Jeremy needs three out of the fours sets of books and notebooks that he hastily shoved into his backpack before running for the bus. When and if he remembers to do his civics homework tonight, he will discover that he grabbed the wrong notebook. To top things off, he almost missed the bus. Once on the bus, he discovered that he neglected to bring home one other notebook he needs. In this case, it was due to his poor attention in period three English class, because he didn't realize that students were assigned to make a timeline of events in the play they are reading. Also, he won't realize that he should have read a chapter and written a summary of it until Monday morning, the day it is due.

Once home, he surfed the Internet for about an hour while instant messaging friends and got in trouble for not peeling some potatoes, as described in the note to him on the kitchen counter. After dinner, Jeremy denied having much homework, which was half a lie, so that he could watch more television, and half what he thought was the truth, because he didn't fully know about several of his assignments. The missing assignments included remembering to study for the weekly math quiz, which his teacher had decided not to remind him about today in class.

CASE QUESTIONS

1. What types of organizational skills are expected of students at different levels of schooling?
2. What can students like Jeremy do to remind them of their schedules?
3. How can Jeremy both keep track of his assignments and have a plan for completing them on time?

For students like Jeremy, the first problem of the day is getting to school. Teens are notorious for their poor sleep habits. Many stay up as late as they can at night, and most have a problem with getting out of bed in the morning. Medical research findings indicate that teens typically need 9.2 hours of sleep per night, and even those who get that amount can still expect bouts of tiredness throughout the day (Wolfson and Carskadon 1998). Rapid physical development during puberty is a key factor in their routine state of exhaustion (Carskadon, Vieira, and Acebo 1993; Wolfson and Carskadon 1998). Others have suggested that the fast-paced life of today's teen, which includes multiple demands on time and overscheduling, may also be factors contributing to their daily fatigue (see Carskadon, Vieira, and Acebo 1993; Crowley, Acebo, and Carskadon 2007; also see Fuligni and Hardway, 2006).

Organization in the Early Years

As toddlers develop cognitively, they gain memory skills that help them to recall things like names, events, and places. They also begin to learn concepts such as order (for example, by learning about proportions, numbers, and sequences) and classification (for example, by naming and grouping like objects). These rudimentary concepts and skills are the cognitive foundations for learning how to be organized. Most toddlers also begin to learn about and participate in daily routines. For example, many come to expect that their mornings begin with being dressed and whisked out of the home to go to day care, and they more or less know what is expected of them at meal times.

Despite their preschool backgrounds, children entering elementary school typically still have a lot to learn about organization, schedules, and routines. To learn about them, particularly in the lower elementary grades, they practice lining up, sitting silently, putting crayons where they belong, and only using them at designated times. The teacher creates the organizational schemes and teaches the students how to conform to them. The students need coaching and practice to learn them; organization skills are a central tenet of the elementary school curriculum, as much so as basic literacy skills.

THINK BACK TO THE CASE) about Jeremy . . .

1. What types of organizational skills are expected of students at different levels of schooling?

As students progress through the elementary grades, they learn more advanced organization skills. They are also increasingly expected to take responsibility. Whereas a first grade teacher might tell students when to stop working on an assignment, for example, a third grade teacher might announce "watch the clock, you have only three minutes left." Customarily, elementary teachers expect that students graduating to middle or junior high school should be ready to take the initiative at employing a variety of organizational skills to be successful students. They are right.

The Organizational Skills Teachers Expect of Students

In the United States, the elementary school curriculum gradually changes from a focus on learning basic skills to a focus on applying the skills to learn content. Typically, a major shift occurs in fourth grade, away from basic skills and toward acquiring content knowledge (Reid and Lienemann 2006). However, in this era of standards and accountability, that shift may be occurring at lower grades.

By junior high or middle school, those who are unable to perform skills for learning face major challenges in keeping up with the curriculum. In 1994, Scanlon, Schumaker, and Deshler asked middle school general education teachers to identify the priority academic areas in which their inclusive classroom students need to study learning strategies. As is seen in Table 10.1, the teachers named a variety of areas that almost all require organization. Although "organizing" is only explicitly named in one of the areas, "creating visual devices," "note taking," and "creating relationships," each require students to organize information. A similar study (McMullen, Shippen, and Dangel 2007) also found that middle school teachers expect students with mild disabilities to possess organizational skills. According to that study, the top skills that students with learning disabilities should have include turning in homework, starting working

TABLE 10.1: Teachers' Strategic Requirements of Middle School Social Studies Students

Strategy Requirements of Social Studies Curricula			

Study groups
Social skills
 	
Organization
Put items in order
Have a plan—"This is
    how I'm going to . . .
 	
Probing questions
 	
Formulating opinions
	Excellence in homework
	Completion of homework
	
	Read to understand
	Explain in own words
	Pick out most significant
	    characteristics
	Differentiate irrelevant
	Give examples
	Application
	
	Transforming content
	Forming relationships
		Memorize—then apply
		Writing versus memory
		Know the terminology
		
		Understand and use key
		    vocabulary
		
		Notetaking
		Draw it!
		Graph it
		Visually depict information
		Timeline
		Sequencing events
		Think chronologically
			Evaluating
			
			Identify problem and offer solution
			Think ahead of now
			Consider other possibilities
			
			Express themselves
			Vocalize freely
			
			Processing lots of information
			Gather information about issues
			Be able to retrieve information
			Use maps correctly—gather
			    information

Source: Scanlon, D., Schumaker, J.B., & Deshler, D.D. (1994). Collaborative dialogues between teachers and researchers to create educational interventions: A case study. *Journal of Educational and Psychological Consultation, 5,* 69–76.

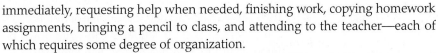

immediately, requesting help when needed, finishing work, copying homework assignments, bringing a pencil to class, and attending to the teacher—each of which requires some degree of organization.

In addition to acquiring and using organization skills in school, students need to manage their time and energies to ensure a proper balance between their in-school and out-of-school activities. Students with mild disabilities, like Jeremy in Case 10.1, are often frustrated by their constant disorganization. Obiakor (2007) states that students with disabilities from minority groups often lack motivation to improve their organization skills, because of the history of sociocultural problems they face. He suggests that it is particularly important to provide them with structured opportunities to succeed, along with affirming feedback.

Student Schedules

A student's schedule involves much more than just getting from class to class. It includes knowing due dates and prioritizing tasks; moreover, it also involves updating schedules as events are added, completed, or changed. A well-planned schedule not only tells the outcome (for example, where to go next, what is due today), it tells the student how to achieve it. Students who truly comprehend their schedules know to bring books for period two along to period one to forego unnecessary trips to their lockers. A student who has a ten-page paper due should have a plan for doing the research, writing sections of the draft, and proofing that does not include pulling an all-nighter.

Teaching Students about Schedules. Students with organization and memory difficulties cannot be told a schedule once and be expected to remember it. Whenever a new schedule is instituted, you and the students should go over it together. Begin by making sure the students can read and understand a printed copy of

Chapter Question
ALERT

In this section you will find information that answers a Chapter Question:

2. How can students with mild disabilities learn to follow schedules, and even to plan them?

ule should be pasted inside the cover of a binder or inside each and every subject notebook the student uses. Students who routinely use a notebook computer or some form of PDA throughout the school day might store their schedule in those locations for quick consulting. A wallet-sized card might make more sense for some. You and the student should experiment with options to find out which ones the student will actually use and find beneficial.

Students with mild disabilities who use some type of planner have much higher success at following schedules than students who do not (Flores, Schloss, and Alpers 1995; Rademacher, Schumaker, and Deshler 1996). Two useful forms of planners are desk blotter calendars and book-style calendars (students can experiment to determine whether weekly or monthly planners work better for them, as well as whether pocket-size or notebook-size is more functional). Using a planner or calendar, students can write down both the due dates and critical interim "production deadlines." See Figure 10.1 for an example. In Figure 10.1, Jeremy has drawn lines so that he has a visual reminder on a daily basis of what he should be working on. He has also noted dates by which he should complete certain tasks, so that he can keep on task.

THINK BACK TO THE CASE about Jeremy . . .

2. What can students like Jeremy do to remind them of their schedules?

Some students carry a designated **assignment notebook** with them. All assignments for the day are written in this one notebook. This is much the same as carrying a calendar all day. Even though a student may have a separate notebook for each class, the assignment notebook is a unique book in which only assignments are written. Each page can be marked with the day's date. The advantage of using a notebook for this purpose is that detailed information can be recorded into the book (for example, all of the details provided on the procedure to follow and what kind of content is expected). Also, each teacher can sign the assignment notebook at the end of class to ensure that the assignment has been recorded correctly. A parent could be asked to sign the notebook each evening, which is a way to inform parents that the student has homework and encourages monitoring of work habits at home.

A student such as Jeremy has a high probability of losing his calendar or assignment notebook. So, although a planner that fits in his backpack seems ideal, all of the moving around it will do poses a risk for losing it. A desk blotter is stationary and big. Although things might get piled on top of it, Jeremy will always know where it is if he

FIGURE 10.1 Jeremy's Production Deadline Calendar

SUNDAY	MONDAY	TUESDAY	WEDNESDAY	THURSDAY	FRIDAY	SATURDAY
1	2	3	4	5	6	7
Work	Work	Study Vocab.	Eng.–Vocab. quiz	Study	Math quiz	Work
		Work	Finish lab report	Math HW due	Civics HW due	
			Work	Science lab due		
8	9	10	11	12	13	14
	Draft outline	Study–Vocab.	Eng.–Vocab. quiz	Study	Math quiz	Work
		Draft Outline	Begin essay	Finish & proof		
		Begin essay	Finish essay	Proof essay	Eng.–essay due	
				Work		
15	16	17	18	19	20	21
	Work	Study Vocab.	Eng.–Vocab. quiz	Study	Math quiz	Work
		Work	Finish Lab Rep.	Span. Translate play	Span–proof	
			Work	Science lab due	translation	
22	23	24	25	26	27	28
Work	Span. Rehearse	Study Vocab.	Eng. Vocab. quiz		Math–no quiz!	
Span. rehearse	lines	Spanish play		Work	Study civics	
lines		Work				
29	30	31				
Review civics	Civics–exam	Study Vocab.	Eng.–Vocab. quiz			
	Work	Work				

339

has a dedicated workspace at home. Students who are homeless or from low-income families may not have a dedicated workspace at home or reliable storage space for a blotter or other resources, so relying on the portable assignment notebook might be more appropriate for them. The bigger problem for Jeremy is that he now needs a system for recording all assignments and bringing them home to add onto the desk calendar. He will still need to get into the habit of carrying an assignment notebook to all of his classes. If Jeremy can afford a PDA, he will have the capacity to enter assignments as he receives them. Information entered into certain PDAs can then be synced with a computer hard drive or some other electronic storage system. Students who bring notebook computers to class will have a centralized system for organizing assignments and most of their materials as well. Some students may use computer software to create schedules on the computer, and even rely on the computer to help them determine efficient pathways to meeting production deadlines.

Although you might think these details of organization are minor, they are the intricacies that keep many students from becoming organized. In addition to having the right tools of organization, students must know how to use them properly.

METHODS AND STRATEGIES SPOTLIGHT

Selecting the Right Type of Organizer

Having the right tools is essential to being organized. Students who bring a flashy notebook that has no pockets for collecting handouts could be in trouble if a teacher frequently supplies handouts. Likewise, in classes where teachers expect notes to be turned in for checking and then placed back in a notebook for future reference, a three ring binder would work much better than spiral-bound notebooks.

Some teachers consider the choice of notebooks and other materials to be so important that they communicate to parents over the summer what types of materials students should acquire for the coming school year (Scanlon 2003). Unless their choices are dictated, students will have to experiment to find out which system of notebooks works best for them. The following are some factors to consider when determining what type of notebook is appropriate for your students:

- The advantage of a three-ring binder is that materials may be easily added or removed; however, students must learn to place things where they belong for the binders to be effective.
- Individual subject notebooks might be more practical for some students. If each notebook is clearly labeled by subject area, the students can easily grab what they need.
- The best of both worlds might be individual subject notebooks that are three-hole punched so that they can be stored in a three-ring binder. Students will need to develop a routine of returning removed notebooks to the binder collection as soon as possible.
- For other students, a laptop computer is the most efficient way to take and keep notes, as well as to keep assignments and related materials. Students will need to develop an organized system of folders and files, so they can reliably store and locate needed content. (Using search functions may not always work if students cannot remember key words in a file name.)

Managing Schedules. Students rarely get to set their own schedules for due dates. Consequently, their good intentions to study hard for tomorrow's vocabulary quiz might be thwarted by an unexpected homework assignment in another class and the sudden realization that a project has to be completed for yet another class. So, even students who plan production deadlines need to be able to manage their schedules. Managing a schedule means that they need to be able to set a schedule, read and comprehend their own schedule, coordinate production deadlines, and revise their plans as new activities are added and deadlines are missed.

VIDEO CASE CONNECTIONS BOX

Watch the Video Case entitled, *Classroom Management: Best Practices.* Teacher Sandra Jenoski discusses the process she uses over a series of weeks to teach her students about classroom routines and expectations. Using the same process she uses, restate her explanation for how she could teach students to manage their own schedules.

THINK BACK TO THE CASE about Jeremy . . .

3. *How can Jeremy both keep track of his assignments and have a plan for completing them on time?*

Using a planner notebook or desk blotter calendar, Jeremy should begin by writing down the due date. He should next carefully consider the intermediary tasks that need to be accomplished to complete the assignment (Hughes et al. 2002). Does it involve library or Internet research? Does a draft have to be handed in? Having determined what must be done to accomplish the task, he should carefully think about how long it will take to do each intermediary task and the logical order in which to do them. All of this can then be marked on a production timeline right in the planner or calendar. On Jeremy's production timeline in Figure 10.1, he did not get his draft essay outline done on time because he fell asleep watching his favorite TV show on Monday, so he moved his intermediary tasks forward a day. He still has a plan to complete the assignment on time, but he is now going to have to work longer and harder on the days remaining to make it all work.

The management plan has to suit the needs of the planner, not just impose deadlines. Jeremy enjoys his friends and tries to socialize with them whenever he can. He also has an after-school job. That job is at a fast-food restaurant, and the schedule changes from week to week. So if Jeremy is going to be successful at managing his school schedule, he is going to have to plan for his out-of-school life too. If he keeps one calendar for his school assignments, he will be wise to keep his social and job schedule on that same calendar. This way he will be sure to work around his social schedule as much as possible.

As his teacher, you will need to teach Jeremy how to plan and modify his schedule. Start by making a list with Jeremy of every assignment that he knows he has coming up. Organize that list by due dates. Then for each assignment, one at a time, discuss what production deadlines it will entail. A disorganized student like Jeremy is likely to find this to be a novel question; you will have to guide him to think about what goes into writing an essay or preparing for a quiz. Then show Jeremy how to plot his production deadlines so that he will complete the assignment on time. Be sure to do this in pencil, because you will next plot Jeremy's second assignment, then third, and so on. In this process, he will see that he has to adjust production deadlines based on other assignments. With the experience of matching his draft production schedule to reality, he will be able to realize that he needs to plan well in advance.

Chapter Question
ALERT

In this section you will find information that answers a Chapter Question:

3. What factors other than content knowledge contribute to students' successful completion of assignments?

Completing Assignments

Assignments matter. They are major factors in determining grades, particularly at the secondary levels (Munk and Bursuck 2001; Polloway, Epstein, Bursuck, Roderique et al. 1994; Putnam, Deshler, and Schumaker 1993). Of course, they are an important component of the learning process too. When a student has difficulty completing an assignment, often both the teacher and the student contribute to the problem. How you give an assignment, including how you explain it, may be the problem on your side. How the students receive the assignment and how they approach doing it are the problems on the students' side.

CASE 10.2

Teaching In Better Ways for Students to Demonstrate Their Learning

Case Introduction

Now that you have worked through the first case in this chapter, you should feel comfortable addressing issues in a second case. You are going to read about how a special educator named Berta Strauss and her inclusive classroom co-teacher improved their students' performances on assignments, including homework and tests. They taught the students specific skills, but they also adopted some new practices for themselves to facilitate their students' performance.

Berta Strauss is a middle school special education teacher who co-teaches a few periods a day. She is pleased with the learning her students are doing in their general education classrooms. After being frustrated last year by the fact that her students were not demonstrating their learning on typical classroom assignments and tests in health class, she and her co-teacher set a "self-improvement" summer goal of learning how to get their students to perform better on those tasks. They learned that, in addition to teaching the

students specific skills, they would have to change some of their own practices as well.

Things are going much better this year, for both the special education and regular education students. To begin with, the two teachers have been much more thoughtful about the assignments they give their students. In the past, they sometimes used assignments that came with commercially prepared curriculum materials, even though they weren't teaching from those materials; other times, they made up assignments at the last minute. They still rely on prepared assignments, and occasionally come up with an assignment in haste, but they have improved at relating the assignments to the lessons they teach and at considering their students' potential to complete the assignments successfully. One of the things they realized over the summer was that they were treating assignments like tests, instead of extensions of the lesson. In fact, in the past, they sometimes planned assignments by saying "let's see if they can. . . ." Now they think critically about why they want to give assignments.

The two teachers also realized that the ways they gave assignments in the past were often inadequate. Often, assignments were hurriedly shouted out as the students began to pack up in anticipation of the bell ringing. Berta barely had time to ask her special education students if they knew the assignment and what they needed to do. Because time was tight, she had to take their word for their answer.

The students with disabilities were worse than their classmates at both completing assignments and doing quality work; however, the regular education middle schoolers were not consistently strong at these skills either. Berta took responsibility for teaching the whole class to record assignments and check what they had written down for accuracy and comprehension before leaving class. This year, completion rates and quality have improved greatly.

Berta has noted that, although her special education students are better at the skills of receiving and completing homework, they still have difficulties with applying content that she is sure they comprehended in class. She is beginning to examine the quality of notes they take during class. She has come to realize that they have trouble discerning what information to write down and, consequently, try to write so much that they can't get it all in their notes and keep up with the class. She is wondering if she and her co-teacher could more clearly cue them as to what to record, without actually saying "now write...."

CASE QUESTIONS

1. How can teachers, and their students, be sure that students are clear on their assignments?
2. Why might students with disabilities who are clear on an assignment nonetheless have difficulty completing it successfully?
3. Although all middle school students have to learn how to take notes, what particular difficulties will Berta likely observe for students with mild disabilities?

How to Assign Logically, how you present an assignment has a lot to do with how well your students know what is expected of them, and with how they respond. Making assignments clear and meaningful can enhance the rates at which students with disabilities attempt, complete, and succeed at them.

You may be surprised by how often your students assume the reason for getting an assignment is merely that you are trying to keep them busy. Even when they realize that an assignment is a form of practice or an extension of a lesson, they may have no appreciation for what they are supposed to learn from it (Lenz et al. 1993; Rademacher, Schumaker, and Deshler 1996). In Chapter 9, we addressed the importance of using advance organizers to give students an indication of what is expected of them in a lesson and why. The same principle applies here; when students know why they are asked to do an assignment and what is expected of them, they find doing a good job easier.

Giving Assignments. Rademacher and her colleagues (Rademacher, Schumaker, and Deshler 1996) reviewed the professional literature on giving assignments to identify effective practices. They then involved more than 270 middle school students with and without mild disabilities and 22 of their general education teachers in identifying the practices they believed to be effective. Next, they tested the effectiveness of the practices on students attempting, completing, and succeeding on assignments. They also researched how satisfied the students and teachers were. The subset of students and their teachers who participated in

TABLE 10.2: Student and Teacher Ranking of Assignment-Giving Behaviors

Explanation Factors	Teachers			LD Students			NLD Students		
	M	*SD*	GR	*M*	*SD*	GR	*M*	*SD*	GR
Give Clear Directions	6.58	.79	1	6.41	1.01	1	6.31	1.15	1
State Purpose/Completion Benefits	6.32	.84	2	5.73	1.29	7*	5.61	1.08	6
Provide Models/Examples	6.34	.84	3	5.85	1.28	5	5.57	1.38	5
Consider Time Factors	6.51	.89	4	6.18	1.29	3	6.11	1.27	3
State Quality Work Criteria	6.04	1.02	5	5.78	1.49	9	5.85	1.20	9
Provide Social Interaction Direction	5.78	1.15	6	5.90	1.20	7*	5.40	1.29	8
Provide Student Choice	5.73	1.18	7	6.11	1.15	2	6.18	.93	2
Encourage Creative Expression	5.75	1.04	8	5.70	1.38	6	5.83	1.18	7
Name Available Resources	5.93	1.02	9	5.89	1.10	4	5.68	1.48	4

Note. M = Mean rating, *SD* = Standard deviation; GR = Group rank according to respondent votes; LD = students with learning disabilities; NLD = non-learning disabled students.

*These explanation factors were tied with regard to group ranking.

Source: J. A. Rademacher, J. B. Schumaker, and D. D. Deshler. Development and Validation of a Classroom Assignment Routine for Inclusive Settings. (*Learning Disability Quarterly* 19) 1996):163–78).

that follow-up research identified nine assignment-giving behaviors as important. Interestingly, all three groups (students with and without mild disabilities, and their teachers) concurred that all nine are important, with mostly minor variations in their priority rankings. See Table 10.2 to compare the relative rankings by the three different groups.

Based on their research, Rademacher, Schumaker, and Deshler (1996) developed a routine that teachers may follow to be sure they are effective in giving assignments. Teachers can use the mnemonic device ASSIGN to remember the routine. Each step cues an important quality assignment-giving activity. According to Rademacher, Schumaker, and Deshler, to give an assignment effectively, you should:

> **A**ctivate the assignment completion process by completing the lesson and alerting students to use their 'REACT' steps [provided further in this text]; **S**tate clear directions that were created [during planning]; **S**top (that is, pause 15 to 30 seconds) for students to use their REACT steps; **I**nvestigate student understanding by asking students specific questions about the assignment information; **G**uarantee work time in class for beginning the assignment, and offer help as needed; **N**ote the due date, expectations for students to do quality work, and assistance for anyone who needs it outside of class. (172)

Inclusive middle school students and teachers validated these steps as the teachers used the routine in their classrooms.

In the following section, we describe a quality assignment in terms of how the teacher produces it. First, however, we consider the product of assignment giving, which is the student receiving the assignment.

Students Receiving Assignments. When you give an assignment, you should have fairly clear ideas of how you expect the students to complete it and the content and appearance of their finished product. Your students' conceptions of the finished product can easily differ from what you think it should be. You should consider the homework product as a starting point before you explain the assignment to the students, followed by how they will follow instructions, and culminating with the creation they hand in and their use of the feedback you provide. Also, consider what a good time frame would be for completing the assignment and the resources that students should use (or not use).

Students need to learn how to receive an assignment, as well as how to plan to and actually complete it. This is as essential a school skill as learning to follow schedules.

Rademacher, Schumaker, and Deshler (1996) validated the five REACT steps that students should follow to ensure they receive and perform assignments correctly:

> **R**ecord the assignment as the teacher gives verbal directions; **E**xamine the requirements and choices offered by the teacher; **A**sk questions to better understand the directions; **C**reate a written goal for improving or matching performance on a similar assignment that may have been completed in the past; **T**arget a time to begin, finish, and evaluate the assignment for quality before turning it in to the teacher. (172)

THINK BACK TO THE CASE about Berta and her co-teacher . . .

1. How can teachers, and their students, be sure that students are clear on their assignments?

It will help you to consider what a student must go through to be a successful assignment recipient. You can (a) make sure your assignment-giving strategy is responsive to the process students should follow, and (b) troubleshoot when students struggle to master the process. As the REACT steps indicate, the first thing students should do when receiving an assignment is to be sure to record it, and to then immediately check to make sure they have fully and accurately recorded and understand what they should do.

The first REACT step indicates that assignments should be given orally. You may increase the clarity of your presentation if you also write the assignment on the board. This way, students will have plenty of time to copy it down. You can also point to parts of the assignment as you discuss them, even underlining parts for emphasis or numbering the steps or components. Also, you can hand out an assignment with the directions printed on it. This can be a way to ensure that students who have difficulty recording information get the correct assignment in the first place. Still, Rademacher, Schumaker, and Deshler (1996) are correct, you should provide oral instructions even if you also provide a print version. By speaking the directions you can offer emphasis and state the same point in multiple phrasings, which may help.

Questioning your students to make sure they understand the assignment (including its purpose) is a good idea. Your students should also learn to question themselves, though. When you give an assignment, require your students to record it, and then require them to check the assignment to make sure they understand it. The following are five easy ways to have students check their assignment notes:

Ask students to . . .

1. Explain the assignment to a partner;
2. Check a partner's assignment notebook;
3. List the steps they follow to complete the task;
4. State what they are supposed to get out of the assignment;
5. Explain why the particular assignment should contribute to #4.

The Nature of Effective Assignments. Rademacher, Schumaker, and Deshler (1996) also asked their middle school students and teachers to identify the characteristics of "quality assignments." The following 12 characteristics were identified:

- **Clear, well-organized directions** ensure that students will know how to do the work.
- **An understood purpose** ensures students will understand how completing the work will benefit their learning.
- **A set of product evaluation criteria** ensures students will know how their finished work will be judged.
- An **optimal challenge** ensures students will not become bored or frustrated.
- **Personal relevance factors** relate assignment completion to the social, learning, behavioral, and cultural characteristics of students' lives.
- **Assignment completion feedback** lets students know what they did correctly and what they need to do to improve their work.
- **Format variety** will differ from the traditional worksheet format.
- **Available resource lists** necessary for doing the work must be provided.
- **Creative expression opportunities** allow students to use their imagination in some way.
- **Interpersonal or social actions** allow students the opportunities to work with others.
- **Completion time considerations** include giving students time to work in class.
- **Student choices** allow for options within the dimensions of the assignment itself and how it is to be completed. (Rademacher, Schumaker, and Deshler 1996, 167–168)

Interestingly, the students with and without disabilities did not differ meaningfully from each other in terms of how they ranked the 12 they considered most important, but they did differ from their teachers. Teachers ranked "student choice" lowest, but students ranked it highest. However, all three of the groups ranked "clear, well-organized directions" among the very highest (first or second). See Table 10.3 to compare the groups' rankings.

Homework: A Particular Type of Assignment

All students, including those with disabilities, have more homework than ever before (Jakulski and Mastropieri 2004). Expectations for doing homework also increase in frequency and complexity as students advance in grade levels (ibid.;

TABLE 10.3: Characteristics of Effective Assignments

Assignment Characteristics	Teachers			LD Students			NLD Students		
	M	*SD*	GR	*M*	*SD*	GR	*M*	*SD*	GR
Clear, Well-Organized Directions	6.69	0.55	1	6.65	0.72	1	6.66	0.70	2
Understood Purpose	6.11	0.87	2	6.34	0.99	9	5.93	1.32	8
Product Evaluation Criteria	6.21	0.98	3	5.80	1.48	11	5.81	1.27	10*
Optimal Challenge	5.94	0.79	4*	5.66	1.64	8	6.04	1.13	6
Personal Relevance Factors	5.85	0.94	4*	4.87	1.59	10	4.79	1.49	12
Assignment Completion Feedback	6.30	0.93	6*	6.10	1.12	12	6.20	1.03	10*
Format Variety	5.59	1.37	6*	5.73	1.37	7	5.77	1.19	7
Available Resource Lists	5.90	1.04	8	5.97	1.37	5	6.01	1.19	9
Creative Expression Opportunities	5.59	1.20	9	5.68	1.16	4	5.83	1.08	4*
Interpersonal/Social Interactions	5.65	1.17	10	5.47	1.37	3	5.55	1.31	3
Completion Time Considerations	5.62	1.06	11	6.17	1.33	6	6.50	0.85	4*
Student Choices	4.90	1.39	12	6.17	1.01	2	6.17	1.10	1

Note. M = Mean rating, SD = Standard deviation; GR = Group rank according to respondent votes; LD = students with learning disabilities; NLD = non-learning disabled students.

*These characteristics were tied with regard to group ranking.

Source: J. A. Rademacher, J. B. Schumaker, and D. D. Deshler. Development and Validation of a Classroom Assignment Routine for Inclusive Settings. (*Learning Disability Quarterly* 19(1996):163–78).

Polloway, Epstein, Bursuck, Jayanthi, and Cumblad 1994; Polloway, Foley, and Epstein 1992). In fact, in 1993, Epstein et al. found that students could expect an average of eight hours of homework per week by the time they reach the secondary level.

Homework is a useful teaching and learning activity when it is rightly used. When students do homework, they can develop skills and apply information that they have been learning; depending on the nature of the homework assignment, they may discover new things. Homework is a way for students to learn responsibility for meeting expectations, it requires personal accountability—as students must have some degree of self-discipline to take it home and complete it, and it helps students learn that learning is not merely something they do during school hours (Jakulski and Mastropieri 2004). As early as elementary school, students who receive homework assignments begin to develop their work habits.

Homework and Students with Mild Disabilities. When used properly, homework can be a way to equalize learning opportunities among those with and without disabilities, and to extend the amount of time a student with a disability devotes to studying a particular skill or concept (O'Melia and Rosenberg 1994). However, students with disabilities typically do not manage the homework process well when it involves skills affected by their disabilities (Kerr and Nelson 2002; Hughes et al. 2002; Salend and Gajria 1995).

THINK BACK TO THE CASE about Berta and her co-teacher . . .

2. *Why might students with disabilities who are clear on an assignment nonetheless have difficulty completing it successfully?*

The problems that students with LD or EBD have with homework range from correctly receiving the assignment all the way to remembering to turn in completed work (Epstein et al. 1993). Polloway, Foley, and Epstein (1992) reported that students with LD have difficulties with homework success because they are likely not to bring home the appropriate materials. Even when they do take the appropriate materials home, some of the problems they exhibit in school are the same ones that inhibit homework performance. Trouble with reading, concentration, or remembering the steps to a calculation all go home with the student. Other problems due to a disability that may be managed during the school day can be a greater problem at home. For example, a student who has a highly structured school routine due to distractibility may not have the same kinds of structure and monitoring available at home. Also, students may not have needed supports at home. Some students come from households where English is not commonly spoken. Some parents may not have the academic skills necessary to help their child with homework, or at least not be confident that they do; this is more likely to be the case in low-income households (Kohn 2006). Even parents who try to participate in their child's homework may not know the routines effectively to help their child with difficult readings or to remember how to organize an essay answer.

Different Purposes for Homework. The different types of homework assignments relate to what kind of learning experience homework is intended to be. The following are the major types of homework and their purposes.

Homework can be a form of *preparation*. That is, if students need some background information or experience before you launch a new lesson, you might be able to have them acquire it via homework. You might have them review or look at new information that is easily comprehended and that will be checked at the beginning of the new lesson. By completing homework for preparation, they should be ready to begin the lesson that will follow. Because students with mild disabilities may have difficulty with homework, you should be ready to address the learning needs of those who did not do the assignment or who had trouble with it.

Homework as preparation could also be a form of a *grabber* (review Chapter 9; Lenz et al. 1993). You can grab students' attention at the start of a lesson with some stunt or challenge that provokes them to start thinking about the topic. To grab their interests via homework, you might give an assignment that previews a topic that you will begin studying tomorrow (for example, you can ask students to come prepared with first impressions or questions to share), or you might give some exciting or fun assignment, such as a puzzle to solve that motivates them.

Homework can be *practice*. This type of homework extends the amount of time available to a teacher and students for practice. Being taught how to parse a sentence, multiply fractions, or evaluate the moral underpinnings of a government policy is not going to be very effective if students are not able to try their skills. Homework as practice can provide that opportunity to apply (practice) what was just studied. Indeed, because homework is removed from the teaching episode, it is a chance for students to recall skills and content instead of only performing them immediately after they are introduced in class. As long as your students have had enough instruction to practice with some degree of accuracy and success, homework can be a good way to ensure they get the practice they need.

Homework is also a way to *extend a lesson*. When students learn the basics of a new skill or information, they can be sent home with the task of figuring out the rest of it. Of course, this use of homework will require that you prepare them to be able to do that task, and that you check on the results, with the intention of correcting mistakes. So homework that extends a lesson may have an element of practice, but this type of homework allows students the opportunity to learn more original content. That extension makes it different from only practicing what they have begun to learn.

Slightly different from extending a lesson is *completing a lesson*. The school day rarely goes exactly as planned. For any number of reasons, lessons do not always end before the bell rings. If you were able to get far enough into the lesson that students should know how to complete it with success, the students can finish activities at home. You can then start your next lesson exactly as you have planned.

Homework is also a way to *connect parents to what is going on during the school day*. Parents can be asked to check that students bring home and complete their assignments, if that is a problem for a student. Also, parents can be asked to help with their child's work. This is a great way to show parents what you are teaching and for them to have direct insights into their child's learning strengths and weaknesses. It is also a great way for students to receive immediate feedback as they practice. In addition, you can spend less time in parent-teacher conferences just bringing parents up to speed on what their child is studying. Be aware, however, that parents and families in some cultural traditions consider it their role to stay out of what the teacher and their child are studying (Salas et al. 2005).

Just about the worst form of homework is that assigned so students can *learn original information* on their own. Not that we do not value students becoming independent learners or that we assume they are never up to the task, but some direction and checking are in order when something new is being learned. Students need to know how to learn on their own; however, in school, we tell, demonstrate, describe, model, monitor, provide feedback, reinforce, and regulate complexity, among many other teaching activities. We do these things because we know that this is how students learn effectively. (Teaching research and problem-solving skills, as well as encouraging students to follow their interests to learn more about topics that motivate them, are more productive ways to teach independent learning.)

Research Evidence   *Effective Homework for All Students.* In light of the unique challenges homework can present for students with disabilities, success may depend on the type of homework assigned. The most effective form may be practice homework. Cooper and Nye (1994) found that students with disabilities were more successful with homework when it was intended to reinforce learning established in the classroom. Thus, extension and completion homework could also be successful for this population, but most likely in cases where the basic knowledge and skills required have been well learned during the in-school portion of the lesson. According to Cooper and Nye, two other important factors for homework success are that (a) assignments are brief, because tedium and frustration are less likely to set in otherwise; and (b) the assignment is more likely to be focused on only one or a few topics and supported by parents who communicate effectively that homework is valued (that is, they show it is important but do not turn it into a punishment) and who can provide some supervision that includes academic help and feedback.

Epstein et al. (1993) suggest that homework should also be relevant to students with disabilities. If they understand why they are given a particular assignment, it is more likely to be valued. In this same regard, the academic expectation is also more likely to make sense to them. Effectiveness in giving homework assignments is not much different from giving assignments effectively in the classroom.

Learning from Your Students' Homework. Bryan and Sullivan-Burstein (1997) suggest that you treat homework performance as a form of data (also see Rademacher, Schumaker, and Deshler 1996). How homework is done, how well it is done, and the consequences of homework can all be tracked; this data can inform you on just how effective your homework-giving practices are, in addition to your students' homework completion practices. Bryan and Sullivan-Burstein suggest that you start with yourself, by assessing how well your estimates of time and effort required for homework match your students' reality. To begin, they suggest that you make notes about how long you expect completing a particular assignment will take for your students. Then ask your students to write on a corner of the page how long they actually took. Your findings could tell you whether your estimates are on or off, as well as whether individual students are uniquely over- or underchallenged by certain assignments. Bryan and Sullivan-Burstein also suggest asking students to make a note of how easy or difficult an assignment is; you can give them a rating scale so that they all answer in the same format.

They also suggest that students graph their own homework performance. As in Figure 10.2, students can graph rates of turning in assignments on time, turning them in but late, and not completing them. The graph can be used to

FIGURE 10.2

Jeremy's Math Homework Completion Graph

	Week 1					Week 2					Week 3				
	M	**T**	**W**	**Th**	**F**	**M**	**T**	**W**	**Th**	**F**	**M**	**T**	**W**	**Th**	**F**
Complete		■		■						■		■		■	■
Incomplete	■		■								■		■		
Not Done					■			■							

discuss their homework skills and habits with them, to communicate to parents about homework performance, or as the basis for rewards used as incentives to improve performance (Trammel, Schloss, and Alper 1994).

Doing the Homework. Because students can have difficulty with getting homework done, the skill of doing homework should be taught and valued. To help make it meaningful, you can set homework contracts with your students. Students can agree that they will meet some kind of performance standard for homework assignments, based on amount completed over time or timeliness. Some teachers allow students to cash in points for a "homework-free night." The contract's standards for amount, timeliness, or quality should reflect homework success skills that are important to build. The standards for satisfying contracts can be gradually increased. Eventually, students need to learn to manage their own homework processes (Hughes et al. 2002).

Once you get students to bring assignments home and know what they are supposed to do, you still have to get your students to do them. One form of help is to have parents sign homework assignment sheets (or initial individual assignments) as proof that they saw the assignment; even better is if parents sign the sheets after their child explains the homework to them. Keep in mind that homework is not just about the discipline to sit down and do the work, but also about the students' ability to complete the assignment correctly. Parents may not always be able to help with assignments. As an effective alternative, establish **homework buddies.** These are students who are assigned to be available to each other at homework time. If they live in the same housing community or can connect by phone or Internet, they can be ready resources if one of them has a question. Just as is the case with cooperative learning groups, these students must be able to work well together. Buddies need to establish a common time during which they can be contacted if help is needed.

O'Melia and Rosenberg (1994) have suggested that students form **cooperative homework teams** (CHT). These teams should be formed following some of the same principles as used to create homework buddies; members of the team should know how to help each other when they have questions about an

VIDEO CASE CONNECTIONS BOX

Watch the Video Case entitled *Classroom Management: Best Practices*. Teacher Ilene Miller talks about the importance of matching students who will work together in a group; however, she does not state what her criteria are. Make a list of factors you would use to match students who become homework buddies or CHT members. (Hint: some of your list should come from the previous section.)

Note taking is an essential skill. Students must learn effective note-taking skills, which can be cued by a teacher as part of the lesson.

Corbis RF/Jupiter Images

assignment. Each buddy has to understand how to articulate a need for help. Thus, cooperative homework team members need to be taught the skills of peer tutoring to be effective (see Chapter 2). In the CHT model, team members begin by turning in their work to the team's "checker." That individual is responsible for grading the work based on a scoring guide that the teacher provides; specific errors should be marked (as opposed to simply marking the item as incorrect). Team members can then help each other to correct their errors, a process that might take up to ten minutes of class time. (The checker can be responsible for checking and marking the corrected work, but with a different color ink, which would be helpful for a busy teacher.) Next, the assignments are turned in to the teacher, who can see how well students performed both before and after the team cooperatively assisted one another. The CHT students in O'Melia and Rosenberg's (1994) study improved in both the amount of homework completed and overall accuracy of their work.

Note Taking

Chapter Question
ALERT

In this section you will find information that answers a Chapter Question:

4. How can students learn to be efficient note takers?

There is an expectation that students with mild disabilities in the general education classroom will be able to access, learn, and master information from the general education curriculum. In the general education classroom, the majority of content-area information is presented in a lecture format, and most of the material on tests comes directly from classroom lectures (Moran 1980; Putnam, Deshler, and Schumaker 1993; Ward-Lonergan, Liles, and Anderson 1998). To succeed, students must be able to attend to the lecture, use selective listening skills, decide which lecture points are worthy of recording, and record those points using an efficient note-taking technique whereby they can simultaneously record notes and listen to the lecture. The importance of listening and note-taking skills in these classes cannot be overstated. In Putnam, Deshler, and Schumaker's (1993) investigation of regular classroom demands, teachers reported that "their lectures were the major source of information [upon] which test questions were based" (340); they also noted that almost half of a student's grade is derived from performance on tests in secondary content classes (see also Polloway et al. 1994). Even when classrooms are not dominated by lecture formats, students are still expected to take notes during classwide discussions, group work, and in-class independent work. In some of these contexts, teachers use less cueing to guide the note-taking process.

THINK BACK TO THE CASE) **about Berta and her co-teacher . . .**

3. *Although all middle school students have to learn how to take notes, what particular difficulties will Berta likely observe for students with mild disabilities?*

Unfortunately, students with mild disabilities exhibit a number of listening and attending deficits that interfere with their ability to learn information from lectures (for example, Ward-Lonergan, Liles, and Anderson 1998) and other instructional

activities. They may allocate attention to irrelevant parts of tasks rather than focusing on the most important parts, for example. They may also have information-processing problems that interfere with their ability to receive information and/or "translate" it into notes (Ward-Lonergan, Liles, and Anderson 1998).

Researchers have consistently documented written language deficits in students with LD, from basic writing skills such as spelling, punctuation, and legible writing (Hughes and Smith 1990; Poteet 1979) to more complex skills such as detection of writing errors and planning for writing (Ellis and Colvert 1996; Englert et al. 2007; Graham and Harris 1993). Not only do spelling and handwriting deficits interfere with the act of note taking, but difficulties with these rudimentary skills also create later also problems when students review and study their incomplete and illegible notes for tests. Their incomplete notes can be difficult to decipher and comprehend.

In addition to written language deficits, students with LD exhibit deficits in specific note-taking skills. Suritsky (1992) observed that students with LD often take notes in a verbatim fashion, despite the fact that this word-by-word method of recording notes is the least effective and most detrimental to learning content information. Those students reported that they had difficulty deciding what information was the most important to record, as well as difficulty maintaining attention to the lecturer. Hughes and Suritsky (1994) confirmed students' self-reports; for example, when compared to nondisabled peers, students with LD produced fewer units of recorded information (that is, more incomplete notes), even when given explicit instructor cues of important information to record. Missing cued information and recording incomplete notes have immediate repercussions not only with understanding lecture information, but also with later recalling information for tests.

Appropriate Notes

The skill of taking notes begins with being prepared to take notes, and with attending and knowing what information to include or exclude from notes. Notes must be organized and transcribed in a format that will prove useful to students who wish to use them. Specific skills of note taking include deciding what is important to note; efficiently telegraphing the information while continuing to monitor the lecture, discussion, and so on; organizing the content of the notes; reviewing and modifying the notes; and studying the notes.

Teaching Note-Taking Skills

Students' note-taking activities encompass the before, during, and after phases of a lesson. Different note-taking strategies emphasize the different phases.

Strategic note taking (Boyle 1996; Boyle and Weishaar 2001) was developed based on the premise that students with learning problems are passive learners during note taking. Therefore, teachers can give students written "cues" on note-taking paper to prompt them to use metacognitive skills during lectures (that is, organize information and combine new with prior knowledge), thereby increasing active engagement (see Figure 10.3). In the first portion of strategic note taking, students quickly identify the lecture topic and relate the topic to their own prior knowledge, before the lecture begins. By identifying a relationship to prior knowledge, the students make the information more meaningful. In the next step, students cluster three to seven main points with details as they are presented in a

FIGURE 10.3

Abbreviated Strategic Note-Taking Form

Fill in this portion before the lecture begins.

Page 1

What is today's topic? *Human cell parts & functions*

Describe what you know about the topic.

odd shapes, has nucleus, contains genes

As the instructor lectures, use these pages to take notes on the lecture.

Today's topic ? *Nucleus functions*

Name three to seven main points with details of today's topic as they are being discussed.

Store genes on chromosomes

Organize genes into chromosomes to allow cell division

Produce messenger ribonucleic acid (mRNA) that code for proteins

Organizes DNA uncoiling, to replicate key genes

Summary - Quickly describe how the ideas are related.

Important for cell division. Stores genes on chromosomes and ensures replication during division.

New Vocabulary or Terms: MRNA, uncoiling, replication

— —

Page 2

Name three to seven <u>new</u> main points with details as they are being discussed.

New Vocabulary or Terms:

Summary - Quickly describe how the ideas are related.

— —

Page X

Name three to seven <u>new</u> main points with details as they are being discussed.

New Vocabulary or Terms:

Summary - Quickly describe how the ideas are related.

— —

Last Page

At End of Lecture

Write five main points of the lecture and describe each point.

Source: Reprinted with permission from J. R. Boyle, "Learning from Lectures: The Implications of Note-Taking for Students with Learning Disabilities. (*Learning Disabilities: A Multidisciplinary Journal* 14(2006):91–7.

lecture. Categorizing ideas is helpful to aiding memory of information (Snowman and Biehler 2006). At the bottom of each page, students are asked to summarize lecture information, again, to assist in encoding the information. The steps of naming three to seven new main points and summarizing immediately after naming the points are repeated until the lecture ends. The last step, completed at the end of the lesson, involves writing five main points and describing each. This step is intended to serve as a quick review of the lecture. Strategic note taking is more effective than conventional note taking for students with mild disabilities in terms of the number of notes recorded, immediate recall, long-term recall, and comprehension of content (Boyle 1996; Boyle and Weishaar 2001).

Guided notes are "a skeleton outline that lists main points of a verbal presentation and provides designated spaces for students to complete as the speaker

FIGURE 10.4

Student Copy of Guided
Notes

Comparison of Mars and Earth

I. Similarities: Mars and Earth

   A.

   B.

II. Differences: Mars and Earth

   A. Mars

   B. Earth

III. Effects of an atmosphere on planets

   A.

   B.

   C.

   D.

Adapted from B. Lazarus, B., Guided notes, review, and achievement of secondary students with learning disabilities in mainstream content courses (*Education and Treatment of Children* 14(1991):112–27.

elaborates on each main idea" (Lazarus 1991). To construct guided notes, pull out the main points from your lecture notes prior to a lesson. List those main points on prepared notepaper with space left for the student to fill in details during the lecture (see Figure 10.4).

Using guided notes offers the advantage of giving students an outline listing and structuring the main ideas. These main ideas serve as anchors to which to connect related ideas. Guided notes can also be developed using lecture slides from presentation software such as PowerPoint. In doing so, teachers can leave the slide blank, using only the slide title, or use the slide title plus the main points associated with it (Austin, Lee, and Carr 2004). Teachers can then provide students with handouts of the slides, or students can simply use the structure from the slides to record their own notes.

Research Evidence

Guided Notes. Research indicates that students who are trained to use guided notes record more notes than with conventional note taking and earn higher scores on tests and quizzes (Austin, Lee, and Carr 2004; Lazarus 1991; Sweeney et al. 1999). Lazarus (1991) also found greater gains when students with mild disabilities in content classes use guided notes in conjunction with a review period.

Columnar format is a student-directed technique useful for organizing written materials (for example, textbook information). Information is visually organized according to the type of information to be recorded. According to Saski, Swicegood, and Carter (1983), the columnar format uses two to four columns to assist note taking. One way to use the columnar format is to divide a sheet of paper into three sections or columns (see Figure 10.5). The first column is about five inches wide and labeled "Basic Ideas." The second column is about two inches wide and labeled "Background Information." The third column is about one inch wide and labeled "Questions." Also at the top of the page is a line for "Topic Sentence." The teacher might complete the topic sentence for the lecture or direct students to copy the topic sentence from the board. During the lecture, students complete the first section and write down any important facts that

FIGURE 10.5

Columnar Notes

Topic Sentence

Basic Ideas	Background Information	Questions

might be needed for future study. After the lecture, students complete the "Background Information," where they note anything of interest or areas in which the student has prior knowledge. This section guides students to make connections between the new information and prior knowledge, thereby increasing comprehension. In the last column, students indicate questions or information that is not clear. The columnar format is effective at increasing comprehension when used by students as they read passages (Horton, Lovitt, and Christensen 1991).

Teachers can use a continuum of approaches before, during, or after a lesson to increase the number and quality of notes students record. Some other easy, unobtrusive practices teachers can use on a daily basis include providing better cues, using a pause procedure, and allowing students time to review notes.

Lecture Cueing. Lecture cuing involves calling attention to important lecture points. Three efficient types of lecture cues are mannerism, organizational, and emphasis cues (Berry 1999). **Mannerism cues** signal students via gestures that information is important. Saying "there are three important things to remember" while holding up one, two, and then three fingers as you note each is an example. Gesturing or pounding a fist for emphasis or pointing to important information are also mannerism cues. **Organizational cues** are given for points in a cluster of related information. For example, the cue, "there are six components to a plant cell," informs students to record the category "components of a plant cell" and at least six points about a plant cell. **Emphasis cues** on the other hand are meant to call attention to a critical lecture point. For example, the cue "it is important to remember that . . ." serves to call attention to a point that may later show up on a test. Writing notes on the board serves as another type of cue that increases the probability that students will record the information. Research has shown that students record up to 88 percent of lecture information when lecture points are written on the board (Locke 1977).

The Pause Procedure. Another guide to good note taking, the pause procedure, was first investigated as a promising practice with college students in the 1970s and '80s (Rowe 1976; Rowe 1980). Later, Ruhl and others (Ruhl, Hughes, and Schloss 1987; Ruhl, Hughes, and Gagar 1990; Ruhl and Suritsky 1995) began to assess its effects with students with mild disabilities and found that it benefited both short- and long-term recall of lecture information. The **pause procedure** requires a two-minute discussion (pause) at least three times during each lecture. During the two-minute pause, students may pair up to review or discuss notes and/or lecture content since the last pause. When the two minutes have ended, the teacher may ask questions related to the notes before moving on to new material. The pauses are placed at random intervals or at logical breaks in the lecture content (for example, before beginning a new topic). Results from a number of studies indicate that students with disabilities who use the pause procedure perform significantly better compared to students not using the procedure, in terms of immediate and long-term free recall and total information recorded in notes (Ruhl, Hughes, and Schloss 1987; Ruhl, Hughes, and Gagar 1990; Ruhl and Suritsky 1995).

Review Time. Finally, **review time** is an important skill for all students, especially students with disabilities. Having students review their notes has proven quite beneficial for increasing recall on tests (Lazarus 1991). A "brief review" can allow students to make corrections to notes, fill in gaps in notes, and/or elaborate on them (Lazarus 1991; Suritsky and Hughes 1996). Reviewing notes serves an important function because students tend to focus on the highest level of information in a lecture during note taking (Kiewra et al. 1991), leaving little time for filling in the details. Moreover, in reviews of note-taking research (Hartley 1983; Kiewra 1985), students who reviewed their notes had higher achievement on performance tests than those who were not permitted to review notes. Many review procedures are built into note-taking techniques or strategies, such as the pause procedure. Lazarus (1991) found that, when students were instructed to review their guided notes six times (that is, read them from top to bottom) and subsequently place a check mark in each of six boxes provided on the notes page, they improved more than when just using guided notes alone.

Test Taking

As already suggested in this chapter, students with mild disabilities perform many academic skills poorly (for example, following schedules, doing homework, taking notes) until they are taught how to do them correctly. Test taking is

Chapter Question **ALERT**
In this section you will find information that answers a Chapter Question:

5. What factors contribute to a fair testing situation for students with mild disabilities, and how can they perform on tests to reflect most accurately what they know?

like any other academic skill; students with mild disabilities often lack effective test-taking skills (Scruggs and Mastropieri 1992). Students who lack sufficient test-taking skills need to learn and practice them.

Many times students perform poorly on tests because they do not prepare adequately. This may be because either they did not study, or they did not know how to study appropriately. In addition, the actual taking of a test requires performing specific skills that influence the outcome. Those skills range from time management to deduction to accurate expression. Inefficient test-taking skills are a major factor in poor test performance for students with mild disabilities (Hughes 1996). Successful test-taking skills encompass preparing for the test; comprehending the test instructions and purpose; self-monitoring test performance; expressing oneself clearly; and assessing test performance.

Not having mastered the content sufficiently to pass a test is also a factor in test performance, but in this section we are focusing on the skills of test taking and giving.

The Testing Continuum

Testing is ideally thought of as a continuum of activities (see Table 10.4). First, both the students and the teacher prepare for the test. Then there is the testing itself. The test(s) you use, how you administer it, and how the student approaches taking the test all impact the testing experience. Important also is what happens

TABLE 10.4: The Testing Continuum of Activities

Teacher's Role	Student's Role
Preparing for the Test	
1. Decide if you need to give a test. 2. Determine how you wish to test. 3a. Ask what is a fair testing situation. 3b. Consider test-taking skills. 4. Prepare a fair test. 5. Prepare the student.	A. Prepare for the test.
Giving/Taking the Test	
6. Make sure the setting is appropriate. 7. Establish a routine for taking tests. 8. Plan for a stress-free test. 9. Administer the test correctly. 10. Be respectful of accommodations. 11. Take notes during the test.	B. Start by preparing to take the test. C. Use common sense. D. Check your work.
Assessing Performance on Tests	
12. Use test results as instructional data. 13. Provide feedback.	E. Learn from the test.

after the test; this includes how the test results are interpreted, how they are used, and what type of benefits the student reaps.

Preparing for the Test. Why test students at all? One obvious reason is to determine what they have learned. A second reason is to "encourage" them to study. Also, tests are often required as one contributing source to report card grading. NCLB regulations call for periodic testing of students in various areas, which is often "high stakes" as a condition for promotion and matriculation. Additionally, the NCLB requirements for curriculum standards include an expectation to assess student-learning outcomes (see also Kohn 2002). The tests may also be used to evaluate teachers' performances (Birman et al. 2007–2008; Schoen and Fusarelli 2008). No matter what your reasons are for testing, you should plan to capitalize on the situation by thinking about the productive use you can make of the test. The testing continuum begins with preparing to test.

The Teacher Prepares to Test

1. Decide if you actually need to give a test. This is the first step in the testing continuum. Again, common reasons for testing include finding out what students have retained, how students respond when directly questioned, or how students apply information instead of being directly questioned, and having data to calculate a term grade and report as part of progress monitoring requirements (review Chapter 2). Once you have determined that you want to (a) see what your students know or can do, (b) figure out how they compare to one another, or (c) encourage them to study, you *may* have your reason for testing. Ask yourself if you really need to test to accomplish this goal. You could construct *portfolios* with the students that document what you want to know. More informal than portfolio construction, you could *sample* the students' work periodically; that is, you could examine the students' performance of a skill (or application of knowledge) from in-class or homework assignments every so often (see the following Tips for Generalization).

2. Determine how you wish to test your students. This is the second step of the testing continuum. Do you require a demonstration, or could they just tell you how to do a task? Under what conditions would they make their demonstration—individually, under time constraints, with a resource guide available, being told what the product should look like, one time or several times, all at once or in parts, while narrating the how and why of the process, on identical or successively more difficult examples? Answering such questions relates to the original question: *Why do you want to test?*

3a. Ask what is a fair testing situation for your students. Once you know what you would like to do, you will ask yourself what you should do in step three. For example, take a math teacher who wants to test problem-solving skills by giving several word problems. The teacher is not going to get very accurate results from students for whom reading is a challenge, even if they are skilled problem solvers. Unless a skill (for example, reading) is integral to the task, teachers are not accurately assessing their students' knowledge

TIPS FOR GENERALIZATION

Alternatives to Tests for Data Collection

Portfolio This is a collection of students' work samples that demonstrates their skills. Typically collected over time, portfolios show how students perform the skills (or apply the knowledge) in question in a variety of contexts. When added to over time, portfolios can also trace students' progress in learning. Some portfolios only contain positive examples of the students' work. Students can actively participate in selecting materials for the portfolio and may even submit their own commentaries on their contributions. In addition to contributing to grading, portfolios can be used by students to observe their own learning progress and to set goals. Further, portfolios can be shared with parents and be a useful data source in the IEP development process. Portfolios may be a folder or a box, depending on the format of work samples being collected, or they may be electronic.

Sampling Teachers may periodically collect the students' work to see how they are performing skills (or applying knowledge) in question. Sampling may help to monitor the learning process, or to ensure the students are maintaining skill proficiency over time. Whenever teachers believe they need updates on how students are doing, they can sample a current piece of work where the skill should have been applied. When using sampling, teachers should be careful the work collected is from a representative task. Further, teachers should bear in mind that a single sample may not be representative of students' true abilities. Depending on the nature of the task, teachers might sample by having students periodically repeat a specific task (for example, a drill sheet in math or a response to the same essay topic in social studies). (Review the discussions of curriculum-based measurement [C-BM] in Chapters 2 and 5 for a more systematic and formalized approach to sampling.)

or skill when test performance is incumbent upon such other skills. So, test for what you want to find out. A simple way to do this is to assess the same knowledge or skills in multiple formats. At a minimum, it is a good idea to have more than one "make-it-or-break-it" test item to evaluate what students know. This principle should be remembered when constructing end-of-unit, end-of-quarter/semester tests or final exams with which you are trying to test students on a high volume of content.

3b. Test taking is a skill too. Student skill in what is actually being tested is just one of two aspects of fair testing. Different test formats require different test skills. Answering questions via filling in the blanks is different from answering multiple-choice questions, and both are different from matching. Distinguishing the right choice from three or four others (multiple choice) or from provided clues (fill in the blank, matching) is different from recalling without cues or prompts. All of these variations are different again from application questions such as asking for a narrative explanation or watching a student apply knowledge or skill in a real-life context. In addition to the differences in cognitive demands, prolonged sitting and writing is different from actively demonstrating. Note that the question here is not, "how would you like to test your students?" Rather, it is for what forms of testing are they prepared?

The Teacher Prepares the Test

Now you are prepared to advance to the task of preparing a fair test. Some tests simply do not test what they are purported to or whether students can apply that knowledge; for example, asking, "why did South Africa end its apartheid policy?" is not a good way to find out if students know "why so many South Africans wanted an end to the apartheid policy." Construction of individual test items might be the problem, or it might be the entire testing format.

4. Prepare a fair test. Step four in the continuum is a seemingly obvious one. Although steps 3a and 3b also address the fairness of a test, there is more to it; you have to construct one that actually is fair. A fair test satisfies certain psychometric properties. If a test does not, it cannot be a fair test, no matter how well you have matched it to your student's skills and knowledge.

There are two central concepts to test fairness: reliability and validity. These terms are often heard in relation to formal and standardized tests, but the principles of reliability and validity can and should be applied in all test construction. To be **reliable** means simply that a test can be relied upon to measure what it is intended to. The most common way to think of reliability is to question whether the test would yield the same results if given twice. If not, excepting a reasonable margin of error, the test cannot be relied upon. (This is known as **test-retest reliability.**) You can assess tests for reliability dependent on all students in your class or for individual students. If you are new at test construction, you might actually observe how reliable a test is by administering the same test twice (say, with one day off between administrations and without any additional content teaching in between). You can also assess reliability by giving an exam to a subset of your students as a pilot test and asking them afterward what they thought various items asked them. Although this will not tell you whether they would consistently answer the same way, it does provide insight into why they responded as they did.

Sometimes the whole test is not problematic, but rather just a few of the test items are. This can have to do with **item reliability.** If you give a test to a whole class and a sizable portion have a problem with an item, this may indicate that the item is not very reliable. The beauty of giving a test with multiple items that assess the same or related information is that you can compare performance across items to see if the students' performance is more a function of an item than of what they actually know.

It is important to test consistently and *accurately* for what you are measuring. **Validity** means that a test is valid, or accurate, for what it is purported to measure. For example, if a test of fraction skills presents all of the fractions in decimal form but the students learned them in the traditional numerator/denominator format, the test will not be a valid test of whether your students have learned what you taught them. A more clear violation of validity would be to test a skill at reducing fractions by presenting fractions greater than 1 with a whole number (for example, 1 7/10) as an assessment of whether students know how to convert unreduced fractions (for example, 17/10).

5. Prepare the student. Elliott (1994) proposed a continuum of "low to high" testing skills. Pointing to a correct choice might be a low-level skill, whereas

synthesizing information in order to apply it would be a high-level skill. Such continuums can be useful when planning how sophisticated to make a test, but teachers should always take into account the unique needs of students when estimating test complexity. For a student with limited arm mobility, pointing to a correct answer could be a difficult task. The inappropriateness of such a testing demand is obvious, and you surely would come up with an alternate format. Not all testing challenges are as obvious, however. For students with attention difficulties or other cognitive disabilities, tasks such as discerning between alternatives on multiple-choice questions might outweigh the possible benefit of having to recognize the correct answer versus, say, recall it without any clue. Such unique testing needs are individual; they are not uniformly tied to a specific disability. When a particular testing format is important to your content, or to a high-stakes exam, and a student is not skilled at that format, teaching those test-taking skills is imperative.

We continue to address what teachers must do before addressing a student's role, but you will learn about how students should prepare for a test as well when you read ahead. We hope that you are getting the picture that testing is not something that you do separate from the lesson. Even testing mandated by others (for example, tests to assess adequate yearly progress required for NCLB compliance) should be linked somehow to what you teach and how you have prepared your students to succeed (Thurlow and Thompson 2003).

Giving the Test. Just as preparing for an appropriate testing experience is important, so is actually having an appropriate test. Many factors contribute to testing being fair and accurate. You can probably recall experiences when something prevented you from showing all you know on a test. Obvious distractions include a work crew using a jackhammer right outside the classroom window. Many other factors are not so readily apparent but can have an equal impact on the testing experience.

6. Make sure the setting is appropriate. Before you begin the test, thinking of the needs of your students with special needs can be a good way to help you prepare the environment. If some students are going to require extra attention from you, they should be seated in a place where they are easily accessible to you. Using noticeable accommodations during a test might be cause for students to take it in a different location or at a separate time. Those using common accommodations in the general classroom may be seated together so that the teacher can easily administer the common accommodation, so they or their classmates are not distracted by having alternative formats or procedures, or to minimize students standing out as different.

You can prevent disruptions from outside the classroom by coordinating with other teachers, posting a "no interruptions sign," and closing the door. Ensure the lighting is bright enough for reading. If students are going to need reference materials, make sure they are out and accessible in ways that will not disturb classmates. Likewise, if students need to look at information posted on the board, be sure that all are able to see.

7. Establish a routine for taking tests. Also, remind students of the routine. Make certain the setting and students are prepared before you distribute the test. Remind students to read directions (see ahead to Student Test-Taking Skills). To minimize disruptions, tell students who have questions to raise their hands instead of coming to you. Tell students how long they have for the test, and experiment with individual students to determine if periodically prompting them on how much time is left is helpful or anxiety provoking. Options for appropriate routines are nearly endless and depend a good bit on your unique students and setting. As these examples make clear, you must consider the factors that could influence test performance and minimize their potential to interfere.

8. Plan for a stress-free test. If you know students have a major project due soon, this is not a good time for them to focus on your test. Unless completing the test within an allotted time is necessary (think of the concept of test validity), plan for what will happen with students who need extra time, and let students know that plan in advance.

As noted, you should experiment with your student to find appropriate testing formats prior to actually giving tests. That information will be useful for identifying accommodations on an IEP as well. Taking a practice test or at least being exposed to the test format and item style in advance can be helpful in anticipating the test (Hughes 1996).

You can alleviate a lot of test anxiety by instructing students to skip one or two of the questions of their choosing. Students with disabilities will benefit from this practice in particular, as they know that they can skip items that are unique challenges to them.

Students with mild disabilities benefit from making a positive affirmation before they begin a test (Barron et al. 2006).

9. Administer the test correctly. Suffering through a standardized test can involve practices like listening to the teacher dryly reading instructions word for word from an administration booklet, and everyone starting exactly when the second hand reaches the hour. Although these might be anxiety-provoking practices, they are important to standardized tests' reliability. Be sure that everyone has everything they need (and has put away what they should not have, so taking it away later does not become a disruption).

It is very important to be sure that everyone understands the directions. You might ask students to paraphrase the directions back to you, or at least ask if anyone has any questions about what is expected. You should check in with your students with special needs as soon as the test begins. A common characteristic of students with mild disabilities is to act before planning (Harris, Reid, and Graham 2004), thus they may need to be reminded to review all components of the directions or to think about and make notes about what they know before responding. Observe to be sure that they are actually doing behaviors consistent with following the directions correctly; you might even quietly ask those students to paraphrase the expectations to you.

10. Be respectful of test accommodations. This means being sure that you allow accommodations (see Chapter 9) and monitor their proper usage. Students with disabilities are entitled to test accommodations in order to have an equal testing opportunity (Thurlow and Thompson 2003). The most effective test accommodations are those that are consistent with accommodations provided during instruction (Thurlow and Thompson 2003). The time to discern what accommodations are needed is not at the beginning of the test (for example, "Leon, do you need to use your calculator today?"). You should know in advance what accommodations may be used and be sure that the student (a) knows how to use them, and (b) expects to use them or at least decide on the spot whether they are needed. Preparing the environment includes making sure materials are on hand for possibly needed accommodations.

11. Take note of circumstances during testing. You are already aware that you should be vigilant during testing to see if you can prompt or otherwise assist students. You should also watch to see how well your test is working. Make note of circumstances during testing that may have been disruptive. Notice if students have confusion about one of the test items, if needed materials are late in arriving, and so on. Also, pay attention to individuals. Note particular cases of nerves. Watch to see if students with ADHD are particularly distracted or if others appear frustrated or just need a lot of time to perform one part of the test. That information can be considered during scoring and can be useful for teaching students to improve their test-taking skills for the future.

Assessing Performance on Tests. When you are scoring a test, be sure to consider the data you collected during test taking. Take into consideration whether a test was fair for individual students. Also check to see if a particular item was problematic for multiple students; if so, you may need to make amends by adjusting your scoring.

12. Use the test results as instructional data. This next-to-final step of the teacher's side of the testing continuum applies to both teachers and students. Students know why they took the test: because you made them. You need to remember the pedagogic reason why you gave the test (steps 1 and 2). Use the results as intended. Alter your upcoming lesson plans accordingly and be sure to reteach anything that was not learned well. Also make note of the testing and learning needs of individual students. Students should make good use of the test results too—but, in order for them to do that, you must provide feedback.

13. Provide feedback. The final score is what everyone wants to know, but there is much more that they should know. Be sure to explain to students why each answer is right or wrong. Simply identifying whether a response was right or wrong is *consequated feedback*. Students will benefit more from *differentiated* or *informative feedback*, which also helps them to understand

why responses were correct or incorrect. (Review Chapter 1 for descriptions of different formats for feedback.)

Student Test-Taking Skills. Just as teachers have a continuum of actions for preparing, administering, and evaluating testing, students also have a continuum for actions related to the three phases of preparation, test taking, and review.

A. Students prepare for the test. As already stated, students need to know in advance what they will be tested on and when, including what is expected of them to do well. They should also know the format of the test in advance, so they can prepare accordingly. Being able to define vocabulary or major concepts is different from explaining or demonstrating their application, for example. With advance information, students can coordinate a study plan.

Earlier in this chapter, we addressed student organizational skills important for remembering to study in a timely fashion and for approaching assignments and homework for success. Much of that information also applies to preparing for tests.

In addition to having a good study plan, a useful way for students to prepare for a variety of testing scenarios is for them to *assess their test-taking skills.* They should not wait until an important test is coming up to assess their skills; rather, they should do it immediately, so that they are prepared when testing situations arise. You may need to direct them on this task. Indeed, it may not even occur to them that varied skills are called for depending on test format. One simple way for students with a few years of schooling experience to assess their compatibility with different test formats is to reflect carefully on previous test performances. Old test banks (from the teachers' files, from published curricular materials no longer used, or found in the back of a textbook) can be used to try out test-taking skills; to provide an accurate indication of test-taking abilities, these test banks should test information on which the student is reasonably informed. That way, the students can focus on what was difficult or not about the testing format. From there, you and the students can work together on learning the appropriate skills for particular testing formats.

The most helpful test-taking skills are those that help students to understand what the test is asking and to respond effectively, not tips that help the test taker to "out-strategize" the test writer. Take the example of multiple-choice test items. Many students learn sometime in their careers that the most commonly correct answer is C (or is it B?), and that "all of the above" and "none of the above" are never the right answer unless only one or two items on the whole test feature them, in which case they are always the right answer. Also, students are sometimes told to look for response options that are grammatically inconsistent with the stem (the multiple-choice question) and to rule those out as foils (options that are incorrect) that the teacher probably came up with in a hurry (Hughes, Salvia, and Bott 1991). Although these can, in fact, be useful tips, they are not skills that will help students demonstrate what they know in most testing situations. It would be far more useful for students to learn to eliminate the least probable choices and weigh the probability of what remains, for example

(Hughes 1996). At least they are attending to the content of the test instead of trying to guess their way to success.

FIRST-Letter Mnemonic Strategy

Of course, an important aspect of test preparation is studying and remembering necessary content. Students can use the FIRST-letter mnemonic strategy (Nagel, Schumaker, and Deshler 1986) to remember and recall lists of information for tests. Even when a test calls for application of information (instead of strictly recalling information to fill in a blank, for example), this recall strategy can be useful. The strategy consists of two parts: FIRST and LISTS (see Box 10.1). The FIRST steps are followed to create a memorable cue word (for example, forming a word that prompts recall, by drawing on keywords from a selected list). The purpose of the cue word is the same as when students are taught to remember the Great Lakes by using the familiar mnemonic device HOMES (that is, Huron, Ontario, Michigan, Erie, and Superior). The LISTS steps are then used to create study cards, by selecting lists of word from instructional materials and making them memorable by creating a FIRST device (Hughes 1996).

Students are first taught to create a mnemonic by following the FIRST steps. In step number one, *Form a word*, they write down the first letter of words from a list they need to be able to recall (for example, names of the Great Lakes). They use capital letters and write the letters horizontally (for example, HOMES for the Great Lakes) to create a "real" word or memorable nonsense word. If students cannot form a word using the F step, they then use the second step, *Insert a letter(s)*, to insert lowercase letters (one or two at the most), to try to form a word. For example, a student who realizes the names of the plants spell MVEMJSUN, would try inserting letters such as MoViEM _ _ _ _. If unsuccessful, the student is taught to *Rearrange the letters* to form a word (for example, SUN _ _ _ _ _). If still unsuccessful at forming a memorable mnemonic, the student will *Shape a sentence* to form a memorable sentence. For example, in certain cases, students cannot change the order of the words (for example, for the order of the planets) and must try to form a sentence. In this case, the student might form the sentence, *My Very Educated Mother Just Served Us Noodles* (Mercury, Venus, Earth,

---

BOX 10.1

FIRST-LETTER MNEMONIC STRATEGY

F <u>F</u>orm a word.

I <u>I</u>nsert a letter(s).

R <u>R</u>earrange the letters.

S <u>S</u>hape a sentence.

T <u>T</u>ry combinations.

L <u>L</u>ook for clues.

I <u>I</u>nvestigate the items.

S <u>S</u>elect a mnemonic device using FIRST.

T <u>T</u>ransfer information to a card.

S <u>S</u>elf-test.

Mars, Jupiter, Saturn, Uranus, and Neptune). Finally, if still unsuccessful with the list of words, the student could <u>T</u>ry combinations of the F, I, R, and S steps (for example, *MoViEs of Mars v. Jupiter play on SUNdays*).

In the next stage, LISTS, students are taught to locate information that could be used to create lists from school materials (for example, notes or textbooks), write those lists down on paper, use FIRST to create a mnemonic device, then transfer this to cards, and then review the cards.

So, in the <u>L</u>ook for clues step, students look for different types of clues (word clues, importance clues, and other clues) that might indicate some part of the material that should be used to create a list. For example, they might look for "word clues" such as *there are six parts to a cell* (first, second, third . . .) or *there are four types of cells*. "Importance clues" refer to study guide questions or information the teacher says to study for an upcoming test. "Other clues" are highlighted, bolded, or italicized words, or illustrations that are labeled.

Once students have identified a list in the L step, they must create a heading that is concise yet accurate for the items that will be placed in the list. In the *Investigate the items* step, students write down a short, yet related list of items as they relate to the heading.

Next, students *Select a mnemonic device using FIRST;* they choose one or more of the steps for the list and form a mnemonic.

After they form a mnemonic (a word, sentence, or combination of the two), students <u>T</u>ransfer the information to a card. On one side of an index card, they write down the heading (for example, Great Lakes); on the other side, they write the mnemonic word using capital letters (for example, HOMES) in the upper left-hand corner and the items in the center of the card (that is, Huron, Ontario, Michigan, Erie, and Superior).

Finally, students <u>S</u>elf-test by looking at the heading and trying to remember the mnemonic and the items for that mnemonic, quizzing themselves until they no longer have to flip the card over to remind themselves of the terms.

Students who used the first-letter mnemonic strategy improved test scores by 30 points on average (Hughes 1996). Deshler and Schumaker (2006), reporting the results of Nagel's study, indicated that students with average baseline scores of 53 percent on ability-level tests and 51 percent on grade-level tests improved to averages of 95 percent on ability-level tests and 85 percent on grade-level tests after using this strategy.

Students Taking the Test

Just as students can employ many skills to study for a test, they can learn a variety of test-taking skills in advance and employ them during a test. Hughes and his colleagues have conducted a number of investigations of testing demands and the test-taking skills of students with disabilities. They have also published a useful learning strategy aptly titled *The Test Taking Strategy* (Hughes et al. 1988), but better known to many special education students by its mnemonic steps: PIRATES (see Figure 10.6).

B. Start the test by preparing to take it. The test-taking strategy begins at the beginning. Students with disabilities such as LD or ADHD are often easily spotted

TIPS FOR GENERALIZATION

Three Activities to Promote Improved Test-Taking Skills

Administer practice tests. Give a practice test to familiarize students with the format of an upcoming test and to provide practice on responding to the types of test items you will be including on the test. You can discuss together the demands of the test, instead of the content covered on it.

Prompt positive self-attributions. Positive thinking can help students to perform better on homework assignments or tests (Barron et al. 2006). Teach students to identify a positive attribute that will be helpful to success on homework assignments (for example, I know who to call if I find I need help) or tests (for example, I know how to eliminate unlikely foils on tests).

Teach the ANSWER strategy for essay test responses. The following ANSWER strategy (Hughes 1996; Hughes, Schumaker, and Deshler 2005) is a six-step procedure for efficiently and effectively responding to essay test questions:

A **Analyze the situation** (scrutinize what the question is asking and estimate the time needed to respond).
N **Notice requirements.**
S **Set up an outline.**
W **Work in details.**
E **Engineer your answer** (plan and follow your plan).
R **Review your work.**

FIGURE 10.6

Major Steps of the Test-Taking Strategy

Step 1: **P**repare to succeed.
    *P*ut your name and PIRATES on the test.
    *A*llot time and order to sections.
    *S*ay affirmations.
    *S*tart within 2 minutes.

Step 2: **I**nspect the instructions.
    *R*ead instructions carefully.
    *U*nderline what to do and where to respond.
    *N*otice special requirements.

Step 3: **R**ead, remember, reduce.

Step 4: **A**nswer or abandon.

Step 5: **T**urn back.

Step 6: **E**stimate.
    *A*void absolutes.
    *C*hoose the longest or most detailed choice.
    *E*liminate similar choices.

Step 7: **S**urvey.

Reprinted with permission from C. Hughes, "Memory and Test-Taking Strategies." In *Teaching Adolescents with Learning Disabilities*, ed. D. D. Deshler, E. S. Ellis, and B. K. Lenz, 2nd ed. (Denver: Love Publishing, 1996, Figure 5.15, 25).

BOX 10.2

EXAMPLES OF MARKED-UP TEST DIRECTIONS AND ITEMS

(Circle) the best answer to each question.

Convert the fraction 21/3 into a (whole number.)

(List) three causes of the Industrial Revolution.

(State) whether a virus is living or not, and (explain) your answer.

in a testing situation because they are the first ones to start writing or filling in answer bubbles (for example, Harris, Reid, and Graham 2004). Although their initiative may seem impressive, it is actually a problem. The other students are remembering to (a) write their names, (b) check the instructions, (c) preview the entire test, (d) establish a plan for completing the entire test within the allotted time, and (e) think about their responses before making them.

Performing these preliminary steps can guide students to avoid test-taking problems down the line. Students with disabilities often have a particular need to check the instructions carefully, as well as each question before they answer it. They should get in the habit of underlining the question and circling the expected response format (see Box 10.2). This simple action will force students to attend to what the question is actually asking of them. Also, it will make reviewing the test before handing it in easier (see step D, "Check Their Work").

C. Use common sense. Although we advocate teaching skills for effective study-ing along with skills for understanding and completing tests over tips for out-strategizing the test writer, Hughes (1996) suggests that using common sense *in addition* to other good test-taking skills can make the difference in the final grade a student earns. He found tips such as ruling out grammatically incor-rect foils to be effective for students with mild disabilities. Remember, how-ever, following tips alone is not likely to result in good test performance, so students need to be cautioned explicitly not to overly rely upon them.

Students can use common sense when answering questions, though. Hughes, Salvia, and Bott (1991) reviewed 100 teacher-made and published tests to identify clues that students with disabilities can use to determine effectively how to answer items correctly. They found that 75 percent of the tests included one or more clues. The most frequent clue was found on items that presented response options (for exam-ple, for multiple choice): they found that the longest option was usually the correct choice. Behind that, they found that questions (stems) grammatically cued the answer (for example, "The horse's favorite fruit is an: (a) apple, (b) banana, (c) kumquat).

Students should also reduce their options to those that are the most rea-sonable, and this skill is not limited to forced choice test items; they should be willing to let go of answers that they brainstorm for open-ended questions but begin to realize are not quite right. Also, if they are just not sure about an answer, they should move on and come back (Hughes 1996). Moving on will ensure that they complete as much of the test as they can first; they might get lucky and find a hint to the correct answer somewhere else in the test.

D. Check their work. Students often work on a test until the bell rings, and even work on it as they slowly approach the teacher's desk to turn it in. Instead, they should check their work before turning in the test. Certainly they want to be sure that their name is on the test and that they have attempted to answer all of the questions they were expected to (the PIRATES steps encourage them to do these things at the start of the test so they are not neglected). They should also glance at their responses. If they marked up the directions and individual questions to indicate how they should respond, this will help speed the checking process. As they read over their answers, they might be tempted to self-doubt. A good skill to learn is to review answers objectively. Are they responding to the question asked? Are the answers reasonable? Are they complete? Students should learn that, if so, they should not change their answers unless absolutely certain they now know what the correct answer is (this is different from only being sure "I must be wrong") (Hughes 1996).

E. Learn from the test. Finally, just like their teachers, students should learn from the test once it is returned. Students should review their responses, especially those that were wrong, to see if they now understand the information on which they were tested. Careful reviewing the test takes time. Ideally, the students will read over each item and revisit what is appropriate/inappropriate about various response options. Reviewing will cause students to reengage content actively. With these actions, testing can be part of the learning process.

Research Evidence

Do Test-Taking Skills Make a Difference? A history of research has indicated that students with mild disabilities tend to have poorer test-taking skills than their peers (see Hughes 1996 for a discussion). Among the test-taking skills found to be problematic for these students are comprehending the task, time management, and clear expression. Of course, academic skill deficits such as reading and numeracy difficulties are also deterrents to good test performance. Most useful test-taking skills that can be taught to students are not tricks such as discerning the correct multiple-choice option by analyzing the grammar of the item; rather, they are methods to work efficiently and effectively. Hughes (1996) reports that students with LD who are taught the PIRATES mnemonic experience an average of 10 percent improved performance on tests. That is easily a change of a whole letter grade on most tests. Other researchers have reported similar positive gains for students with disabilities learning test-taking skills (see Hughes 1996).

CHAPTER SUMMARY

Successful participation in school requires organization. As students progress through grade levels, they are increasingly expected to be responsible for their own organization. Getting to the right class on time and having the appropriate materials can be a challenge for students with mild disabilities, because the nature of their disabilities includes difficulties relating and organizing information, attending to details, and remembering, among other challenges to organization.

To be organized effectively, students need to learn systems for organization. They can learn how to keep schedules for their in-school and out-of-school daily routines; they can also learn to keep track of assignments, by establishing routines for using assignment notebooks or other systems that might include electronic devices. Likewise, they can learn to create production schedules, so that they can manage all that is expected of them. As we presented in this chapter, teachers can also employ specific practices to create appropriate assignments and give them in ways that are effective.

Homework is a particular type of assignment. Most appropriately, it is given to extend or reinforce what was taught in a lesson. Students need to be prepared for completing homework; they need skills that range from writing down the assignment and bringing the materials home, to having a schedule for completing it.

Beginning no later than the middle/junior high school years, the skills of note taking are essential to classroom learning. Students can learn specific procedures for taking notes efficiently. These procedures are consistent with those teachers can use to cue students effectively about information that they should include in their notes. Just as is the case with note taking, students can learn skills for efficient test taking. Those skills begin with preparing for being tested and extend through making good use of test results. Following a testing continuum, we have outlined the stages teachers should use in deciding to test and determining the nature of a test, as well as how to teach their students to be effective test takers, to administer tests, and make the findings educational. In the various topics presented in this chapter, we have identified how critical organization is to success in school; we have also identified effective practices for teachers and their students with mild disabilities.

KEY TERMS

Assignment Notebook, 338
Columnar Format, 355
Cooperative Homework Teams, 351
Emphasis Cues, 357
Guided Notes, 354

Item Reliability, 361
Homework Buddies, 351
Mannerism Cues, 356
Organizational Cues, 356
Pause Procedure, 357

Review Time, 357
Test-Retest Reliability, 361
Validity, 361

APPLICATION ACTIVITIES

Using information from the chapter, complete the following activities that were designed to help you apply knowledge that was presented in this chapter.

1. Develop a production deadline for an assignment that you have to complete. Then add your other assignments, activities, and responsibilities to the schedule and note how realistic your production plan was, in consideration of all the other things you wish to accomplish.

2. Using a lesson plan you have created (or use the sample from the book-specific website), make a set of notes that would match an ideal set of notes you would like your students to take for the lesson. Translate the notes into at least two of the different forms of note taking described in this chapter.

3. Using the notes from Application Activity #2, modify your lesson plan from Application Activity #2 to include cueing your students and instructing them in the note-taking process.

4. Along with a classmate, construct several items to test what a reader should have learned from this chapter. Instead of answering one another's test, present an analysis of why you do or do not believe each item is part of a fair test.

TECHNOLOGY RESOURCES FOR TEACHING ORGANIZATION AND STUDY SKILLS

Numerous technology resources are available for teachers interested in teaching students organizational skills. The following list provides a sample of websites that provide research articles and materials.

The Faculty Room
www.washington.edu/doit/Faculty/Strategies/Academic/Testtaking

This website provides teachers with strategies for accommodating students with disabilities on tests. It offers accommodations for different types of disabilities.

LD OnLine
http://ldonline.org

LD OnLine provides a variety of resources for both parents and teachers of students who lack organization skills. Many of the articles discuss organization,

study skills, and accommodations for students with learning disabilities.

How-to-Study
www.how-to-study.com

How-to-Study.com is a website that provides tips to students on various topics that include preparing to study, procrastinating, setting goals, and listing skills, to name a few.

Study Guides and Strategies
www.studygs.net

Study guides and strategies is another website that provides tips on preparing to learn, learning, and studying, as well as a variety of other topics. For example, under the studying heading, there are tips for effective study habits, concentrating, and memorizing. Moreover, the memorizing link discusses how to use mnemonic and first-letter mnemonic strategies for studying.

Visit the book-specific website at www.cengage.com/education/boyle for a variety of study tools such as web links, tutorial quizzes, glossary/flash cards, bonus material not included in the text, and more.

The premium website offers access to additional materials, including the Video Cases. Go to www.cengage.com/login to register or purchase access.

Technology and Teaching

11

CHAPTER QUESTIONS

1. What technology skills are important for students?

2. What are some different types of technology that students can use to access text for reading and to produce written products?

3. What are some ways that teachers can use technology to improve their own teaching and time management?

What are the implications of technology growth in the past decade?
The Internet is the fastest-growing tool of communication ever. It took radio broadcasters 38 years to reach an audience of 50 million; television, 13 years; and the Internet, just 4 years (Learningpartnership.org). The number of Internet users has grown tremendously over the short time it has been in existence. In 1995, there were an estimated 20 million users. In 2000, the number jumped to 400 million users. In 2008, there were an estimated 1.4 billion Internet users (Internet World Stats 2008). Today, technology is an integral part of our lives. From laptops to cell phones to palm devices, we find it difficult to separate ourselves from our technology. What does this growth in technology mean for students? According to the U.S. Department of Labor (2000), nearly 75 percent of tomorrow's jobs will require the use of computers or other forms of technology. This prediction means that educators must keep up with the latest technology. Teachers need to know how to support their students in their technology use because even teachers who consider themselves to be members of the digital age can have trouble keeping up with the technologies that their students take for granted.

In this chapter, you will learn about technology skills for students with mild disabilities. We will present information about technology standards, technology for students to use in the classroom, and technology for teachers to use to teach students with disabilities.

CASE 11.1   Writing Pains

Case Introduction

In this case, you will read about two teachers who co-teach tenth-grade English and encounter problems with a student. Think about the problems that the student exhibits with writing, and think about how you could use technology with this student to improve her written compositions.

At the end of the case, you will find case questions. These questions are meant to serve as points for reflection. Of course, if you can answer them immediately, you should do so, but you may want to wait to answer them until you have read the portion of this chapter that pertains to the particular case question. Throughout the rest of the chapter, you will see the same questions. As you see them, try to answer them based upon that portion of the chapter that you just read.

Cecilia's assignment for the weekend was to write an essay about an influential person in her life and why that person is influential. Now in tenth grade, she is expected to turn in an essay that contains at least 1,000 words and is void of mechanical errors such as punctuation and spelling. The other requirement is that it should not contain any incomplete

sentences (that is, fragments). Cecilia's teacher added this last requirement because her students this year are having problems forming complete sentences in their writing.

Cecilia sat down on the couch in her living room and began writing her essay in her notebook. Her paper looked like this:

My favorit person is Shakira. Shakira was born in Columbia and wanted sign when young. She would sing all the time. Even go kicked out of school quior because her singing was loud. Her voice drowneded out others who were singing. Best song ever is Underneaf Your Clothes. She is also good at dacing and her videos are cool to see. Great albus also Oral Fixation and Off the Record. Can't wait to get het new album Oral Fixation.

Cecilia knew that this English paper would not be an easy paper to write. She hated to write and was doing poorly in Mrs. Lilia Mena's English class. Mrs. Mena has taught English for the past five years at Estefon High School. She has been co-teaching with the special education teacher, Nancy Barton, for the past three years. Cecilia is one of Mrs. Barton's students and was diagnosed with learning disabilities (LD) in seventh grade. Cecilia's most problematic areas are reading and, this year, English.

Estefon High School is located in a poor section of Los Angeles (LA). It was once a prominent school in the 1970s; however, as more people moved out of that portion of the city, housing prices and city revenue declined. Because of the lack of revenue and maintenance, the school has become run-down, and many of the classrooms are in poor shape. Teachers often lack resources such as books and paper to teach students. The students themselves come from poor housing developments, and the majority is on the school's free-lunch program. Despite these conditions, the school does have a well-stocked computer lab, and teachers often have at least one computer in their classroom. Thanks to the benevolence of local Los Angeles native Calesto Ferazzi, who owns a chain of famous restaurants, this school has plenty of technology resources.

Cecilia turned in what she wrote to her teacher, Mrs. Mena. As Mrs. Mena went through students' papers, she came across Cecilia's and began to mark it up. She was surprised with the poor quality of her paper and decided to ask Mrs. Barton about it. "Nancy, weren't you working with Cecilia on her English paper this week?" asked Mrs. Mena.

"Lilia, I asked her to work on it at home and then I would take a look at it before she handed it in," responded Nancy. "I even offered to let her use the computers in your class, but she said didn't need to use them," Nancy elaborated.

"It seems that she needs to use a word-processing program to help her hand in a legible paper and one that is much better than this one," said Lilia, handing Nancy Cecilia's paper. "Cecilia also complained that she types too slowly to use a computer for composing her paper," Lilia added.

Nancy looked at the paper and shook her head at the poor quality of writing. "We really need to do something to help her write better. What do you think we should do?" asked Nancy. "Many of these problems are mentioned in her IEP," remarked Nancy.

Nancy and Lilia then sat down and reviewed Cecilia's writing goals for the year. Among the goals were writing longer papers (at least 1,000 words), writing in complete sentences, and using better organization in essays and compositions. With these goals in mind, Nancy and Lilia developed a plan to teach her these skills, which included teaching her a composition strategy and teaching her to use a word-processing program to compose essays.

CASE QUESTIONS

1. What technology skill or skills would you remediate with Cecilia?
2. What are two types of technology or software that you could use to assist Cecilia's writing?

Cecilia's lack of technology skills affected her writing. Although technology alone will not help Celia's writing skills, Cecilia can improve her writing skills when technology is combined with teaching her writing skills and strategies. The first step for teachers is determining where to begin at teaching technology skills to students. A good starting point would be to examine technology standards and then determine which skills students need.

Technology Standards and Universal Design for Learning

Chapter Question
ALERT

In this section you will find information that answers a Chapter Question:

1. What technology skills are important for students?

Technology skills are important for all students, but just what skills should be taught? The International Society for Technology in Education (ISTE) (2007) has established technology foundations (standards) for students (see Table 11.1). These broad standards simply provide a framework for states to develop specific technology skills for students. Many states have taken these standards and further refined them as specific skills (for example, proficiency at using a word-processing program) and as general skills (for example, using content-specific

TABLE 11.1: Technology Foundation Standards for Students

Basic Operations and Concepts

- Students demonstrate a sound understanding of the nature and operation of technology systems.
- Students are proficient in the use of technology.

Social, Ethical, and Human Issues

- Students understand the ethical, cultural, and societal issues related to technology.
- Students practice responsible use of technology systems, information, and software.
- Students develop positive attitudes toward technology uses that support lifelong learning, collaboration, personal pursuits, and productivity.

Technology Productivity Tools

- Students use technology tools to enhance learning, increase productivity, and promote creativity.
- Students use productivity tools to collaborate in constructing technology-enhanced models, prepare publications, and produce other creative works.

Technology Communications Tools

- Students use telecommunications to collaborate, publish, and interact with peers, experts, and other audiences.
- Students use a variety of media and formats to communicate information and ideas effectively to multiple audiences.

Technology Research Tools

- Students use technology to locate, evaluate, and collect information from a variety of sources.
- Students use technology tools to process data and report results.
- Students evaluate and select new information resources and technological innovations based on the appropriateness for specific tasks.

Technology Problem-Solving and Decision-Making Tools

- Students use technology resources for solving problems and making informed decisions.
- Students employ technology in the development of strategies for solving problems in the real world.

Source: ISTE NETS website (www.iste.org/NETS/).

tools, software, and simulations to support learning and research) (Burke 2001). In some cases, the technology standards have been incorporated within state standards, as in Virginia, yet in other states, such as Texas, the standards are integrated directly in the curriculum. Teachers should check their own state and school division standards and curricula to find specific technology standards or specific technology skills that students should be taught across different grade levels.

In terms of technology on the state level, Illinois for example has developed matrices that span preschool to twelfth grade and that describe those specific skills for each ISTE standard. In the Illinois technology standards, ISTE Technology Foundation Standards are subsumed under larger skills categories (that is, skills, social issues, productivity, and Internet); however, specific skills are described in detail. We have included *some* examples in each area, along with the ISTE standard to give you a better understanding of specific technology skills that are related to each standard. For example, in the area of *basic operations and concepts,* some of the specific skills include using input devices (that is, keyboard, mouse, and remote control), using multimedia resources, opening and quitting applications, and *keyboard skills.*

In the area of *social, ethical, and human issues,* some of the specific skills include following rules for technology use, working cooperatively and collaboratively with others when using technology, and following personal safety practices on the Internet (not typing personal information).

In the area of *technology productivity tools,* specifically *technology tools,* example skills include opening and saving text, printing text, inserting and editing text, and using a spell-checker and thesaurus. Also under productivity tools, another area identified, *multimedia* skills, includes viewing or using a linear slide show, creating a linear slide show (using *KidPix, PowerPoint, iMovie, iPhoto*), and taking digital images.

The area of *technology research tools* includes using grade-level appropriate search engines, evaluating sites and information for validity and accuracy, and copying and pasting text or images from Internet and multimedia sources.

Finally, the area of *technology communications tools* includes using and understanding appropriate use policy, using sites that are bookmarked, and launching a browser and navigating.

For a more detailed listing of all of the skills for Illinois, please see the following website: (www.springfield.k12.il.us/admintech/techskills). Again, teachers should check their own state and school division technology standards and curriculum to see specific technology skills that students should be taught in their schools across different grade levels.

Technology's Role in Universal Design

Technology used within a **universal design for learning (UDL)** framework can provide a powerful tool that allows students with mild disabilities to access general education curriculum. Using UDL with the general education curriculum means that students can access materials more easily and teachers can teach and assess students more effectively. For many students with disabilities, accessing the general education curriculum through traditional means has proven to be a challenge. Without accommodations and modifications, and specially designed instruction for most, students with mild disabilities typically have difficulty accessing reading materials (for example, basal readers, worksheets, and textbooks) because a disability prevents processing and remembering text information. Their disabilities not only prevent them from accessing text materials effectively, but the implications carry over to classroom learning and affect academic achievement. For example, students who cannot learn efficiently from printed text truly lack access and participation in the general education curriculum (Hitchcock et al. 2002). To help with access problems, teachers can present text information digitally; text containing vocabulary terms hyperlinked to definitions and examples are particularly effective for helping students comprehend the information (Higgins and Boone 1990; Higgins, Boone, and Lovitt 1996).

Teachers who do not take advantage of technology are limiting their teaching in terms of pedagogy used and assessment of learning. Teaching effectively is often a matter of using good pedagogy. UDL approaches that incorporate technology allow teachers to be more flexible in their teaching. The use of technology allows teachers to highlight critical features and provide multiple examples more easily than they could through traditional lecturing methods (Hitchcock et. al 2002). For example, using PowerPoint with accompanying notes, teachers can present complex topics in a more manageable way. Because of space restrictions, the PowerPoint slides often limit how much content teachers can type in per slide, with teachers usually presenting three to six lecture points per slide. This chunking of information helps students learn content in "parts" and benefits student comprehension of lecture content (Stephenson, Brown, and Griffin 2008).

Like pedagogy, teachers can use technology to monitor student progress and embed technology within learning activities so that teachers do not have to administer a separate assessment of information that students have just learned (Hitchcock et. al 2002). For example, digital books contain stories that have questions embedded with them. After students read a portion of a story, the program would ask students a question, check for accuracy, and then prompt the students to return to that portion of the story from which the question was drawn. *Thinking Reader* (Scholastic; Tom Snyder Productions) is a research-based reading program that presents students with a story that contains hyperlinks for vocabulary, as well as other prompts and supports (for example, use of a reading strategy, such as predicting, summarizing, and clarifying). Periodically, students are given a quick comprehension check through the text to assess comprehension. Moreover, teachers can monitor student performance through a reading log that keeps track of students' responses (for example, strategy use or performance on reading quizzes).

As you will see, teachers can incorporate technology into a variety of lessons and activities to assist students with disabilities prior to learning, during learning, and following learning. Many of these technologies incorporate the principles of UDL by allowing for multiple means of representation of information to students, expression and action by students, and engagement for students with disabilities.

THINK BACK TO THE CASE) about Cecilia's writing skills . . .

1. *What technology skill or skills would you remediate with Cecilia?*

Cecilia should be working on improving her computing skills with word processors. In particular, she should be taught how to use all of the functions of a word-processing program such as cut-and-paste functions for revising and spelling and grammar checks for editing. These functions should help her improve the quality of her papers and, over time, her teacher can help her with other aspects of writing such as planning and drafting.

Technology and Learning

Chapter Question
ALERT

In this section you will find information that answers a Chapter Question:

2. What are some different types of technology that students can use to access text for reading and to produce written products?

The development and use of technology for people with disabilities is not new. The history of technology and disabilities goes back to the invention of the telephone by Alexander Graham Bell (note: others have also been credited with this invention) in 1876. His earlier experiences, working with his mother who was deaf led to his interest in acoustics, and later experiences training teachers who worked with deaf people, strongly influencing his life's work. Today, technological inventions have helped countless individuals with disabilities by improving the quality of their lives. Those inventions range from assistive and augmentative technology to different types of technology that teachers use to improve their own teaching.

Assistive technology devices serve to improve the communication skills of students with disabilities. More specifically, they are "a wide variety of technology applications designed to help students with disabilities learn, communicate, and otherwise function more independently by bypassing their disabilities" (Friend and Bursuck 1996). Many of these technologies include augmentative or alternative communication devices, as well as assistive technology.

Assistive Technology for Accessing the Curriculum

Certain types of technology were developed to allow students with disabilities better access to the curriculum. These devices do this by allowing students to hear written words, to write from their own words, or to learn from simulations of events. In other words, technology allows students with disabilities to circumvent their disability so that they can successfully complete classroom tasks, thereby allowing them greater access to the curriculum. Keep in mind, that although such technological devices help students gain greater access to the curriculum, teachers must also balance these technologies with their usefulness and accessibility once students complete school and move on to the work world or post-secondary education. For example, although a handheld spell-checker is helpful for students in school, it may be more of a hindrance than help in the workplace. Math teachers in the 1970s sought this same balance when handheld calculators became widely available. Then, as now, they had to decide how much skills and knowledge to teach students before introducing them to this new technology.

VIDEO CASE CONNECTIONS BOX

Watch the Video Case entitled *Assistive Technology in the Inclusive Classroom: Best Practice*s. Watch how Jamie uses both high-tech and low-tech devices to augment her limited verbalization skills. Add more examples (stated in this chapter) to teacher Tony Byers' discussion of the benefits of technology for enabling Jamie to engage in traditional oral language communications.

Text-To-Speech. A number of technologies have been developed that translate text on a screen or scanned text into speech. Many of these **text-to-speech (TTS) programs** are meant for students to use as read-aloud or read-along programs. These programs use either synthesized speech or digitized speech. Essentially, theses programs convert text to phonemes and then convert the phonemes into synthesized speech.

The two biggest factors for determining the usefulness of TTS programs are *intelligibility* and *naturalness* of the speech. Intelligibility refers to the correct pronunciation of words, and naturalness refers to the tone, rhythm, pitch, and intonation of words, as well as proper chunking of clauses and phrases. Many TTS programs offer options for students, such as highlighting text as it is read, allowing the reading rate to be adjusted, choosing from different voices, altering the background and highlight colors, and saving the TTS file as an MP3 or wave file that can be transferred to digital recorders (Hecker and Engstrom 2005). A number of different TTS programs are available, a few of which include *Browsealoud, TextAloud, HELP Read, ReadPlease!, AspireREADER 4.0,* and *Kurzweil 3000.* These programs work to read electronic documents, including documents that have been scanned into files. Some programs are free, and others are available at a cost for the user. Those that are available at a cost often have more options.

Despite the usefulness of TTS programs, they should be carefully considered for use with students with disabilities, because students might not benefit from the use of this type of technology; they may become passive learners as the software reads aloud the words. If the computer simply reads text from a screen and the student is not actively involved by reading the text on the screen and comprehending the information, it is questionable whether such a program should be used. In fact, research has shown that, when students with disabilities read the text and simultaneously listened to it being read, the results were inconclusive (Davis, Caro, and Carnine 2006) or contradictory (Leong 1995; Strangman and Hall 2003). However, when students interacted with the text by periodically stopping to answer comprehension questions or discuss them with a partner, students' comprehension was much improved (Kim et al. 2006; Torgesen, Dahlem, and Greenstein 1987). In addition, technical aspects may make TTS usage a frustrating experience for students. For example, the voice may be robotic and difficult to understand or the program may read the text too quickly or slowly. Teachers should always assist students when using these programs until students can adjust the programs according to their needs and use them fluently. Moreover, when TTS programs are used with reading, teachers should ensure that students are actively engaged in reading the electronic text, asking or answering questions, or using comprehension strategies.

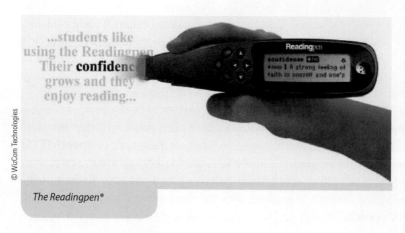

...students like using the Readingpen. Their **confidence** grows and they enjoy reading...

The Readingpen®

A *Readingpen* (see Photo 11.1) is a handheld device that optically scans text and translates it into speech. The Readingpen not only converts the text to speech, but displays the meaning of the word on its screen, shows syllabication, and spells the word. The Readingpen is meant to be a compensatory device to help individuals with reading disabilities bypass their deficits by hearing the printed text and thereby comprehending the text (Higgins and Raskind 2005).

Hypertext is another alternative for students who have difficulty understanding vocabulary used in text. Hypertext, sometimes referred to as hypermedia, allows students to access additional text, data, graphics, or audio bites as they read electronic text. By clicking embedded links, students can hear the pronunciation of the word, read the definition of it, read background information about the concept, see a picture of the word, or be prompted with a strategy (Strangman and Hall 2003). The interactive features of using hypertext with electronic text allow students to elaborate on their knowledge of the word or concept.

Several studies (Higgins and Boone 1990; Higgins, Boone, and Lovitt 1996; Horton, Boone, and Lovitt 1990; MacArthur and Haynes 1995) have examined the use of hypertext and hypermedia to allow students with LD to interact with passages in a nonlinear fashion. Rather than read from start to finish, using hypertext study guides, students were encouraged to access hypertext links when they needed assistance. The hypertext was linked to strategies, definitions, or graphics that supplemented the student's reading. Results from these studies showed that hypertext and hypermedia study guides were more effective than traditional learning for students with LD. Despite these positive results, others (Davis, Caro, and Carnine 2006; Strangman and Hall 2003) have cautioned that, although hypertext and hypermedia electronic text shows potential for students with mild disabilities, more research is needed.

Electronic books, commonly known as *e-books,* are electronic texts that are available on CD-ROM, other special disks, or can be downloaded from the Internet. Typically, e-books include enhancements such as hypertext (for example, for word definitions), illustrations, or animation that complement the text itself (Holum and Gahala 2001). Some e-books are embedded with speech software so that students can either listen to the story as they read along with it (sometimes referred to as talking books). Advantages of using e-books are that they support and coach students as they read, provide accurate pronunciations of unknown words, increase motivation to read, aid comprehension of text, and improve decoding skills (Holum and Gahala 2001). Despite these advantages, the current research is mixed as to whether talking books are any better than traditional print storybooks (Strangman and Hall 2003), particularly for students with disabilities. What is known is that, like other forms of multimedia and technology, students must be trained to use e-books, to access the hypertext and other components of the book (pronunciation clues and other supports). For students with disabilities, this training requires explicit instruction with feedback. Teachers should model aspects of e-books that might be useful to the students. For example, when modeling using e-books, teachers should stop when they come to a hypertext link for a vocabulary word and click the link to see what information it describes (for example, pronunciation and definition). When finished, teachers should reread the sentence that contained the link and check for comprehension.

Assistive Technology for Writing Tasks

Word processors have dramatically changed the way we write. They have helped poor writers to become good writers, and good writers to become better. Word processors and their built-in tools have encouraged otherwise hesitant writers to sit down at the computer and not have to worry about spelling or grammar.

Other features such as "cut-and-paste" have greatly helped with the revision process, and spelling and grammar checkers have helped shorten the stages of writing. Even the use of electronic files have helped with transferring them to publishers so that student newspapers can come out in print faster. Although these advances have been good for writing and composing, in the end, students still need to be instructed in writing skills and still need to be given strategies and specific directions on how to use computers to get the most out of their writing. Moreover, despite these advances, students with disabilities can still benefit from other advances in technology to compensate for processing and motor problems when writing. Some of these advances include: **speech-to-text** programs, brainstorming programs, idea organizers, word predictors, spell-checkers that use phonetic rules, and homonym checkers.

Using the process approach to writing (that is, brainstorm, draft, revise, edit, and publish; review Chapter 6), there are software programs for every stage in the process. In the initial stage of writing, several programs are available that help students brainstorm and map out ideas for their writing project. *Kidspiration, Inspiration,* and *Draft:Builder* are software programs that are available for students to map out ideas and organize those ideas prior to writing. Using these programs, students are able to arrange ideas as they think of them in interrelated maps or outlines that help with organizing prior to the drafting stage. In many cases, students can transform an organizer into an outline and check their choice of words using a dictionary (with word meanings) and thesaurus.

Just as software for translating text to speech is available, voice recognition software that translates speech to written text is also available. Often used during the drafting stage of writing, these programs can fairly accurately transcribe the user's spoken words into text. Although it may not make students better writers in terms of organization or mechanics, it may allow them to turn more ideas into text. Most voice-recognition programs require some training to interpret words correctly from the owner's voice. For students with disabilities, this requirement is no different; however, once trained, students with disabilities can use it fairly accurately (MacArthur and Cavalier 2004). Using this type of software has other potential issues: some programs confuse homonyms (for example, Chile, chili, or chilly), and others have problems with extraneous background noise commonly found in classrooms. Regional and ethnic accents, as well as speech impediments, can also be challenging for some software programs to "hear." However, for students with writing problems who have strong oral composing skills and clear articulation, the programs might be a viable alternative to typing words into a word processor.

Prominent speech-recognition programs that enable students to use their voice to write on the computer are *Dragon NaturallySpeaking* or *ViaVoice* (for PCs) and *iListen* (for Mac). These programs allow students to dictate words directly into the computer and convert them to text. Other programs, such as word predictors, spell-checkers, and writing assistance programs, can help students as they compose stories. For example, *WordQ* (see Figure 11.1) is a software program that predicts words for students to use. It is used along with standard word processors. It suggests the spelling of words based upon the word that the student is currently typing, and it also makes predictions (in the form of suggestions) about which word

FIGURE 11.1

WordQ

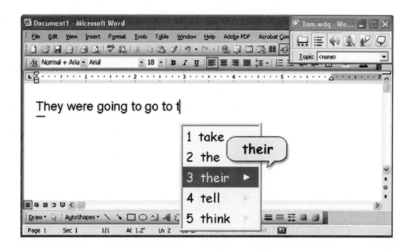

might come next in a sentence. In addition, students can use the "read" function to have the software read back what they have just written, similar to other TTS software. Some students enjoy using this function during the editing and revising stages of writing because hearing text read aloud allows them to catch errors or other compositional features they would like to revise. *Co:Writer* incorporates a linguistic word-prediction function, along with TTS options and flexible spelling dictionaries. Other writing software programs that assist students as they write include *Write:OutLoud* and *WriteAway*. These programs work by providing TTS options so that students can hear what they are writing, and they include spell-checkers, homonym checkers, and other tools to assist students as they write. Some of these programs will say and spell words so students can hear them being spelled if the spell-checker does not provide the correct suggestion. Finally, during the last stage of the writing process—publishing—students can save their work as a TTS MP3 file or as a podcast they can listen to, or they can use publishing software such as *PageMaker* to save the document as an unchangeable file.

A number of studies have examined the use of technology on the written language skills of students with disabilities. Overall, word processors appear to be beneficial to students with disabilities in terms of quality of written products and fluency of writing (Graham and MacArthur 1988; MacArthur et al. 1990). In addition, studies indicate that the use of spell-checkers (Graham and MacArthur 1988; Hetzroni and Shrieber 2004) and speech synthesizers reduce the number of spelling errors students with disabilities make in papers (Raskind and Higgins 1995). With respect to whether word processors can be credited with helping students produce written products that are longer or contain more words, the results from studies appear to be mixed (Hetzroni and Shrieber 2004). Some researchers indicate that students who use word processors do produce longer documents (Bangert-Drowns 1993). MacArthur and Cavalier (2004) found that students with LD who used speech-to-text software (that is, dictating into speech-recognition software) via a word processor produced better quality essays than students who only wrote them. Finally, word processors are helpful at organizing and structuring written products for students with disabilities (Hetzroni and Shrieber 2004).

(**THINK BACK TO THE CASE**) about Cecilia's writing skills . . .

2. *What are two types of technology or software that you could use to assist Cecilia's writing?*

As described in this section, a number of software programs could assist Cecilia with her written language skills. For example, *Write:OutLoud* offers TTS functions for students who have problems typing text quickly. In addition, this program offers the Franklin spell-checker that suggests words as well as displays and speaks words and definitions, a homonym checker that searches the document for homonyms, and teacher editing tools (for example, marking up text) that could assist Cecilia as she writes. Another program that could help Cecilia is *WordQ*. This program can be used with any word-processing program (for example, *Microsoft Word*) that the student already uses. This program works by predicting words that the student may want to write and displays a list of words for the student to choose. When finished writing the sentence, Cecilia could use the playback function to have the software program read it back to her so that she could hear if she made any mistakes in what she wrote.

METHODS AND STRATEGIES SPOTLIGHT

Technology Solutions to Student Learning Problems

Thompson et al. (2004) examined how different technologies could address specific academic problems for students with disabilities and developed a list for those problems. The following is an abridged and updated list of the technologies that aid specific academic issues, based upon their work:

Students with Reading Problems

Problems reading assigned books or textbooks

Bookshare

www.bookshare.org

This organization provides digital books for people with disabilities. Users need proof of disability and a subscription to download thousands of books and textbooks.

Recording for the Blind and Dyslexic

www.rfbd.org

This organization provides educational books such as textbooks on CDs and other digital files for students in a variety of subject areas from grade 4 through postgraduate.

Text-to-speech software (for example, Kurzweil)

This software is for use with downloaded readable materials or scanned material. The newest version, the Kurzweil 3000 USB, is available on a flash drive so that, when students are working at a different computer, they can gain immediate access to the program without having to install it on the computer.

Websites that offer public domain books and other materials for downloading:

Project Gutenberg

www.promo.net/pg
This site offers many different types of downloadable materials that are not copyright protected (that is, pre-1923; see the website for more details).

Caveat Lector

www.hicom.net/~oedipus/etext.html
This site offers many high school level topics that are accessible through speech synthesizers and text-based browsers.

Internet Public Library Youth Division

www.ipl.org
This is the Internet public library website and it contains books, magazines, and newspapers.

Students with Writing Problems

Problems with motor skills or legibility of writing

Portable keyboards such as AlphaSmart

Speech synthesizers (for example, *Dragon NaturallySpeaking*) can translate speech to text.
Writing assistance programs (for example, *WriteAway*) give verbal feedback as students write.
Digital recorders can record digital files. These files can then be transferred to text using speech synthesizers. For example, lectures can be translated to text using this combination of digital recorder with a speech synthesizer.

Problems with "word find" or other types of word-processing disorders

Word-prediction programs (for example, *WordQ* or *Co:Writer*) can suggest alternatives to a typed word or suggest the next word.

Problems organizing ideas

Brainstorming and organizing software (for example, *Inspiration, Kidspiration,* or *Draft:Builder*) can help students organize and order ideas prior to writing.

Students with Mathematics Problems

Difficulties with math problems

Solving math problem programs (IntelliTools MathPad and MathPad Plus) are programs that allow students to solve math problems directly on the computer. Teachers can enter problems and track how well students perform on the problems. The program also verbalizes the numbers as students solve the problem.

CASE 11.2

Textbook Problems

Case Introduction

Now that you have worked through the first case in this chapter, you should feel comfortable addressing issues in a second case.

Ruby is currently a junior at Howell Senior High School. Ruby's homeroom teacher is Larry Kingman. Mr. Kingman teaches sections of a class in current events for most of the morning and history in the afternoons. Mr. Kingman has worked at Howell for 15 years and has only recently begun collaborating with the new special education teacher, Suzie Wetzman. In the class on current events, students discuss everyday news events. Mr. Kingman requires his students to read stories from the newspaper and *Newsweek* magazine prior to coming to class. Class discussion then centers around current news events from these materials. Because a presidential election is coming up in a few months, most of their discussions have been about candidates and their views.

For Ruby, learning has been tough. Since having been assigned the label "emotionally disturbed" (ED) in third grade, she has always been in classes for students with disabilities, and she has struggled to learn new content and knowledge. Her emotional problems, anxiety and depression with resultant behavioral problems, have interfered with her learning. Despite these problems, her high aptitude has kept her academically competitive in mainstream classes (in her younger days) and inclusion classes, more recently. Although she does have serious emotional problems, many of her teachers believe that she also has a learning disability, particularly in the area of reading. To complicate matters, her psychotropic medications often leave her tired, further complicating her learning problems. Now in eleventh grade, Ruby struggles with many of her reading assignments.

Ruby's problems in the current events class stem from her difficulty on her reading assignments, particularly in reading articles that use vocabulary above her head. She often becomes frustrated and then either quits reading the materials or becomes angry and behaves inappropriately. Similarly, she also has problems reading her chemistry book. Her poor completion of reading assignments often puts her in jeopardy of failing classes. Her teachers have tried to help compensate for her reading problems by having another student in the class read to her; however, they know that this is not the best solution.

During one recent co-planning session, Mr. Kingman and Mrs. Wetzman discussed Ruby's problems. Mrs. Wetzman mentioned her problems and offered to brainstorm with Mr. Kingman.

"Hey Larry," she starts, "Ruby really needs some help with her reading assignments. What would you think about sending home some scripted notes of the articles?"

Larry, hesitant about taking on more work, responds, "Well Suzie, last time we tried modifying her assignments, she really didn't take advantage of it."

"Yes but," Suzie continues, "she needs to pass as many courses as possible if she has any hopes of going to Ben Franklin Community College."

Larry remains quiet because he feels that he has given Ruby enough chances. Then he speaks, "If you want to develop these 'scripted notes,' then go ahead. But this year I am already overwhelmed with the increased documentation that I have to do for the SFS (Standards For Success) and the new lesson plans that old man Varina (the new principal) has us doing."

Suzie did not quite get the support that she wanted from Larry, but even half-hearted support was better than none she thought. "OK. I understand," she replied. "Well, do you think there may be something that we could do to use technology to help her?" Suzie went on.

"Well, we are supposed to be getting new computers in a few weeks and funds to purchase software," Larry replied.

CASE QUESTIONS

1. Describe one technology skill that Ruby needs to be taught.
2. What are two types of technology or software that you could use to assist Ruby's reading problems?
3. Name and describe a reading technique or strategy that you could teach to Ruby to improve the quality of her reading as she uses technology.

Technology to Enhance Teaching and Management Skills

Chapter Question

ALERT

In this section you will find information that answers a Chapter Question:

3. What are some ways that teachers can use technology to improve their own teaching and time management?

Teachers can use different types of technology to enhance their teaching of students with and without disabilities. PowerPoint presentations, newsletters, websites, whiteboards, digital video, electronic IEPs, and electronic grade books all can add to a teacher's repertoire of skills and lead to enhanced presentation, communication, and management. These software tools and technology allow teachers to present information in an enhanced and motivational format and allow them to manage day-to-day paperwork issues such as writing up IEPs and keeping track of grades.

PowerPoint. PowerPoint is a software tool for presenting information in a slide show format. PowerPoint uses text, charts, graphs, sound effects, and video to present new information to students. Whether in a classroom lesson or a parent meeting, PowerPoint allows you to make a powerful impression on your audience, using both visual and auditory formats. When used along with handouts of a presentation, PowerPoint-enhanced lessons represent a form of universal design that benefits everyone in the classroom. Handouts of the slides can serve as guided notes for students and assist in their learning. When handouts are presented as "partial notes," student have a guide for being engaged in the lecture. Because information is typically presented in a category with three to six points per slide, students are presented with small chunks of information that aids learning (Stephenson, Brown, and Griffin 2008). Finally, when presented with handouts, students have a permanent product to use to study for tests and quizzes.

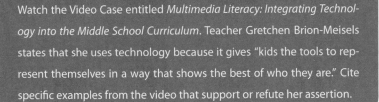

VIDEO CASE CONNECTIONS BOX

Watch the Video Case entitled *Multimedia Literacy: Integrating Technology into the Middle School Curriculum.* Teacher Gretchen Brion-Meisels states that she uses technology because it gives "kids the tools to represent themselves in a way that shows the best of who they are." Cite specific examples from the video that support or refute her assertion.

Teachers are directed to the following websites to learn more information about creating PowerPoint presentations for students:

- PowerPoint basic steps for beginners (*The Basics of PowerPoint* by Amy Gaimaro) http://www.techlearning.com/article/2144
- PowerPoint course http://office.microsoft.com/en-us/training/HA102184981033.aspx

In addition, please see Table 13.3 in Chapter 13 for tips on creating effective PowerPoint and hypermedia presentations.

Classroom Website. Another form of technology to enhance teachers' communication is the development and use of a classroom website. A classroom website serves many purposes. It is a great way to keep the lines of communication open between teachers and parents. Classroom websites provide parents with news and activities in their child's classroom. Teachers can link parents to the curriculum that is being used in the class. For example, if students are learning about

TIPS FOR GENERALIZATION

Effective Electronic Presentations

The follow tips will help teachers make electronic presentations for the classroom:

- Focus on content. Do not forget that the purpose of a presentation is to present content.
- Limit the amount of each slide to three to six points.
- Keep each point brief (distill a sentence into one to three key words). During the lecture, elaborate on each point.

- Use a consistent format in your presentation; jumping from one color or texture to another is distracting.
- Limit sound, graphics, and animation; although these are fun to use, they may be distracting to the learner.
- Before using your presentation, preview it, check for errors (particularly spelling errors), and practice with it.
- Be sure students can read the slides from the back of the room.

the American Revolution, teachers can post links to other revolutionary websites that they are using and parents can see directly the information that their children are learning. The website can contain information about long-term projects or units. For example, the fifth-grade class might be doing a project on how caterpillars grow into butterflies. On the website, parents, students, and the teacher can keep track of the changes over time. Another option is that the website can serve as the weekly newsletter for parents. Often, teachers spend time during the day catching up on classroom news; for some teachers, the time can be spent inputting information into the website. Links can also lead to other school websites such as those of the PTA, the principal, the district, or other teachers who interact with the class (for example, physical education and art).

When students are sick or miss school, classroom websites are a good way for them to find out what happened in the classroom. The website can serve as a place for teachers to post homework assignments and other important activities such as field trips, so that parents can make sure that they and their child have not missed anything. Permission forms and other forms can also be posted on the website in case students lose them on the way home from school.

Classroom websites also allow grandparents and other relatives a chance to keep up on students despite the distance between them. Classroom websites give students opportunities to work, to read, and post writings from their classes. In many cases, a website can serve as the publishing stage of the writing process.

Today, most schools offer teachers some type of professional development pertaining to website development and maintenance. In some cases, the technology specialist gives each class a template to use to fill in information from their class, and helps teachers with maintenance. Microsoft's *Publisher* or *FrontPage* programs offer teachers templates with links that can be turned into web pages by simply changing the text and graphics. Most classroom websites are kept fairly simple and uncluttered. Links are an easy way to keep it uncluttered. Teachers are cautioned, however, that classroom websites are public spaces, even when password protected, and students' identities and personal information should not be posted to them. This warning extends to not using streaming videos or still pictures that capture students' images or voices.

Interactive Whiteboard. An interactive whiteboard is an electronic presentation device that interfaces with a computer. It is useful in many of the same situations as is a chalkboard, creating a space that multiple people can see, refer to, or interact with, and on which one can write and erase. The teacher can use a special pen or highlighter to write and add information to the board. The digital images displayed on the board (for example, lesson notes) can then be captured by a computer, printed out, and distributed to the class. The teacher can also control software from the board by simply using a finger as a mouse to click buttons. Similarly, a whiteboard on a computer class website can be used during a computerized teleconference–a speaking or chat (typed text) session when students are in remote locations. If used in this way, everyone can see what is being written on the whiteboard. Typically, the teacher controls what is written on the whiteboard; however, students can also write on the whiteboard area that everyone participating in the chat or voice teleconference session sees.

According to Bell (2002), an interactive whiteboard has many useful functions for teachers that include the following:

- Whether used to demonstrate software or to point out important features, the electronic whiteboard is great in allowing live demonstrations.
- A whiteboard allows teachers to present in color and to highlight important information.
- Classrooms that have only one computer can utilize the whiteboard so that multiple students can access technology.
- The large whiteboard area allows students, particularly those with motor disabilities, to run programs easily by tapping on the board rather than using a mouse.
- A computerized whiteboard can be used with other digital devices such as cameras or video players to display objects (for example, a cell) that can then be labeled on the board.

Whiteboards are good for lessons in which you would like to distribute copies of what is written or drawn on the board.

Digital Video. Although analog video has been around for years, it has been used mostly to support classroom learning and is often limited in its format. Digital video, on the other hand, has the potential for interactivity and integration (Thornhill, Asensio, and Young 2002). Digital video can be manipulated by slowing its pace, fast-forwarding to specific scenes, or showing sections in short segments (Okolo 2006). Likewise, digital video can be integrated and directly linked to the content of the lessons or PowerPoint presentations. Digital video can include DVDs, CD-ROM, or streaming video clips from websites. Various organizations and government entities provide video clips that can be downloaded, some for a small fee (for example, Discovery Channel website) or others for free (for example, National Oceanic and Atmospheric Administration [NOAA]). In content-area instruction, integrating clips into content lessons is particularly useful to break up large sections of lecture content. For example, if a teacher is presenting science content about atmospheric conditions and the formation of hurricanes, the teacher could easily download a clip from NOAA's National Hurricane Center that shows a radar loop of Hurricane Katrina or a NASA image of Hurricane Wilma.

Okolo (2006) offers the following tips for teachers using digital video clips in content-area instruction:

- Show the video in short segments that focus on key concepts.
- Help students to integrate the video with other sources on information (for example, textbook or lecture notes).
- Encourage note taking during the video so that students can recall key points.
- If the concept is important, view the video clip more than once. Multiple viewings of a video will allow students to learn it well and record it accurately in their notes.
- After viewing the video clip, discuss it to help students understand it.
- Pause the video clip at points and ask students to make predictions (for example, What will happen when the hurricane moves from water to land?).
- Pause and have students examine certain features of the video clip.

Electronic IEPs. Teachers have known for some time that preparing handwritten IEPs can be a very time-consuming process, and research has documented this fact (Price and Goodwin 1980). In addition to being time-intensive, writing an IEP requires knowledge of pedagogy, school curricula, and state standards (Wilson, Michaels, and Margolis 2005) that teachers will have to research prior to writing or have available while writing the document. Teachers must also know how various components pertain to the development of the IEP (for example, regarding the IDEA: how progress of objectives will be monitored; state and local laws: accommodations permitted for state tests; and school district policy: extent of participation in district-wide tests). Moreover, because teachers are taught to write goals, objectives, and other components differently, written IEPs may lack conformity and standardization (Margolis and Free 2001).

One solution to address many of the shortcomings of handwritten IEPs is to ask teachers to produce electronic IEPs. Electronic IEPs allow for conformity and standardization because the computer programs require teachers to write standard components and often have uniform goal and objective statements, which can be slightly modified to individualize each student's needs, but result in similar appearance in terms of goals, objectives, and other IEP components. Although electronic IEPs may not address all of the problems associated with handwritten IEPs, they should meet the need for efficiency and consistency, be able to be personalized for each child, and allow for the integration of IEPs into databases that can be used for state and federal reports (Margolis and Free 2001).

According to Margolis and Free (2001), there are three main types of IEP technology: *stand-alone systems, distributed network systems,* and *centralized network systems.* Using *stand-alone systems,* teachers write IEPs on their own computers that are not networked to other computers or databases. The IEP software typically has a selection of statements (for goals, objectives, modifications, aids, and services), required fields for all IEPs, options to modify statements, and other options to help create professional IEPs. Using this type of software, teachers can prepare IEPs on a computer, make changes as needed, and then print out a finished copy upon completion of the IEP meeting.

Teachers using *distributed network systems* also prepare IEPs on their own computer; however, these computers are networked together and are connected via a secure connection to a central server that contains student information, as well as IEP templates. Using this system, teachers can easily access previous IEPs and student information to prepare or update IEPs. Despite the convenience, schools may require that teachers go through training to transfer content appropriately and maintain confidentiality standards.

Finally, the third type of system is a *centralized network*. In this system, teachers typically have to travel to one or more central locations to work on the IEPs or have to submit coded forms that are fed into the system. When all of the information has been filled out via coded sheets, the information is entered and the IEP is printed. We used this type of system several years ago when we were teachers developing IEPs for our own students. Of course, the downside of using such a system is lack of convenience and additional forms to fill out.

Some of the IEP software programs that are available include *IEP Anywhere* by Smart Solutions Inc., *Encore IEP* software by Spectrum K12 School Solutions, *SEAS—Special Education Management Systems* by Computer Automation Systems Inc., and *IEP Team Software* by Teachers' Pet Productions.

Electronic Gradebooks. As technology becomes more accessible, teachers often take the lead in using different types of management tools, such as electronic gradebooks. Electronic gradebooks provide ease and expediency when recording scores and keeping running totals of students' grades. In addition, electronic gradebooks can weigh categories, average, and print out students' scores in an easily readable format at a moment's notice (Vockell and Fiore 1993). These reports can then be presented to principals, parents, or other teachers who request progress reports for a student with mild disabilities. Vockell and Fiore (1993) point out several other time-saving features that electronic gradebooks have over traditional gradebooks, including their ability to alphabetize class lists, produce progress reports, display distributions, and perform other analyses (for example, calculating means and standard deviations, and item analysis). In fact, in one study (Tetreault 2005) that examined the use of electronic gradebooks by teachers, the author reported that the four biggest uses were (1) tracking student attendance, (2) monitoring student grades on individual assignments and tests, (3) calculating students' cumulative grades, and (4) producing progress reports. Despite the convenience of using these types of gradebooks, teachers should always double-check the accuracy of information that has been entered into gradebooks because it is easy to transpose or omit numbers when entering scores and grades. Some examples of electronic gradebooks include *Pinnacle Gradebook* by Excelsior Software, *iRespond Gradebook* by iRespond, *ClassMate Gradebook* by ClassMate Software, and *E-Z Grader Gradebook* by E-Z Grader Company. (Shareware versions of gradebooks are available that include *Gradekeeper* and *Gradebook 3.0*.)

THINK BACK TO THE CASE about Ruby . . .

1. *Describe one technology skill that Ruby needs to be taught.*

2. *What are two types of technology or software that you could use to assist Ruby's reading problems?*

Taking these questions one at a time, Ruby should be taught how to access textbooks using a text-to-speech program such as Kurzweil. To use this technology, the text has to first be scanned into a usable format (for example, Microsoft Word, portable document file—pdf). The program works with most scanned files, as well as electronic files. Therefore, one of the first skills that Ruby could learn would be how to use a scanner. Next, Ruby should be taught how to use the Kurzweil software program to read scanned files.

Ruby could also learn to use a reading aid such as the *Readingpen*. Using the *Readingpen*, Ruby would simply scans printed text that it would read aloud. This may help students such as Ruby with unknown vocabulary or possibly with reading comprehension.

Research Evidence

We have described a variety of technology resources in this chapter. Their utility for teaching students with mild disabilities has been carefully researched. The following are examples of findings from such research on specific devices and software:

Reading Pens. Students who used reading pens while silently reading passages outperformed students who silently read passages without any assistance on reading comprehension questions (Higgins and Raskind 2005). In addition, students who used reading pens required very little assistance and created few distractions.

Speech-to-Text Software. Using speech recognition software to dictate compositions offers promise for students with mild disabilities. MacArthur and Cavalier (2004) have shown that, for the most part, students with mild disabilities can be taught to use speech-recognition software accurately. Moreover, students who used speech-recognition software, via dictation to a computer, composed essays of better quality and with fewer spelling errors than handwritten essays (MacArthur and Cavalier 2004).

Word-Prediction Software. Word-prediction software programs have been shown to increase the accuracy of words spelled in journals among students with mild disabilities. MacArthur (1998) compared student performance when students used a word processor during the baseline phase to the their performance using a word processor with word-prediction software and speech synthesis during the treatment phase. He found the students with mild disabilities were able to increase legibility of words and correctly spelled words in dialogue journals. A similar study found that, when students with physical disabilities used a word-prediction software, they improved not only their spelling accuracy and legibility, but also improved their writing quality on ten-minute writing samples (Mirenda, Turoldo, and McAvoy 2006).

> **THINK BACK TO THE CASE** about Ruby . . .
>
> 3. *Name and describe a reading technique or strategy that you could teach to Ruby to improve the quality of her reading as she uses technology.*
>
> In terms of using a strategy with technology, it seems reasonable that Ruby could be taught to integrate the paraphrasing strategy (review Chapter 7) with either of the technologies described. Of course, her teacher would have to provide explicit instruction in how to integrate the strategy while using the technology.

CHAPTER SUMMARY

Remember that "technology does not obviate the need for work on the part of the learner. It is not yet possible to download knowledge and experience directly into the brain. To understand something we must engage with it..." (Finnis 2004, 2). Students with disabilities must be taught how to use technology, just as with other learning tasks, and teachers still have to determine which skills to teach to students with mild disabilities.

Although teachers may use a number of different technologies in the classroom, ISTE standards serve as a framework for determining the areas in which students need technology. Students with mild disabilities should be able to master the use of technology (for example, a computer), productivity tools such as a word processor, presentation software such as PowerPoint, communication tools such as email, and research tools such as the Internet to find materials. Likewise, students with mild disabilities can be taught to use a variety of software programs to improve their written essays or compositions, reading comprehension and fluency,

and understanding of concepts in content areas. We have reviewed a number of technologies that could be used in each of these areas. In addition, teachers can incorporate different technologies into lessons, depending upon the skill or content being taught. If teaching content, PowerPoint and whiteboards are useful technologies to help students record notes, and teachers can copy their notes directly from a PowerPoint presentation or whiteboards and distribute those to students.

Finally, teachers should use explicit training with feedback to ensure that students can access and efficiently use all of the components of software or hardware. A software program is only as good as the student's knowledge about how to use it. A software program serves no good if students are unsure how to use it accurately. Just as we need practice to become better at using new devices (for example, a GPS mapping system or cell phone), students also need explicit instruction and practice to be able to use new devices and technologies effectively and efficiently.

KEY TERMS

APPLICATION ACTIVITIES

Using information from the chapter, complete the following activities that were designed to help you apply the knowledge that was presented in this chapter.

1. Visit a website that offers assistive technology and view a demo, or find out more about one specific product and describe how it can assist students with mild disabilities.

2. Visit www.cast.org and read about how technology can improve the lives of students with disabilities.

3. Create a PowerPoint lesson for a content area you will one day be responsible for teaching that can be used to teach students in an inclusive classroom.

TECHNOLOGY RESOURCES FOR IMPROVING STUDENT LEARNING

The following are websites for technology products:

AlphaSmart®
www.alphasmart.com/products/index.html

ApireREADER
www.cast.org/products/ereader/index.html

BIGmack®
www.acciinc.com/Html/bigmack.htm

Browsealoud
www.browsealoud.com

ClassMate Gradebook
http://classmategrading.com

Co:Writer
www.donjohnston.com

Draft:Builder
www.donjohnston.com

Dragon NaturallySpeaking
www.advancedspeech.com/index.htm

Encore IEP
www.spectrumk12.com

E-Z Grader Gradebook
www.ezgrader.com

FrontPage
http://office.microsoft.com/en-us/frontpage/FX100743231033.aspx

Help Read™
www.pixi.com/~reader1/allbrowser

IEP Anywhere
www.iepsoftware.com

iListen
www.macspeech.com

Inspiration
www.inspiration.com

iRespond Gradebook
www.irespond.com

Kidspiration
www.inspiration.com

Kurzweil
www.kurzweiledu.com

Optimist II™
www.acciinc.com/Html/optimist.htm

Partner/Two™
www.acciinc.com/Html/PartnerTwo.htm

PageMaker®
www.adobe.com/products/pagemaker

Pinnacle Gradebook
www.excelsiorsoftware.com

PowerPoint
http://office.microsoft.com/en-us/powerpoint/default.aspx

Publisher
http://office.microsoft.com/en-us/publisher/default.aspx

ReadPlease!®
www.readplease.com

SEAS
www.computerautomation.com

Tech/Speak™
www.acciinc.com/Html/techspeak.htm

TextAloud
www.nextup.com

Thinking Reader
www.tomsnyder.com

ViaVoice
www-306.ibm.com/software/voice/viavoice

WriteAway
www.freewebs.com/write-away

Write:OutLoud
www.donjohnston.com

WordQ
www.wordq.com

Visit the book-specific website at www.cengage.com/education/boyle for a variety of study tools such as web links, tutorial quizzes, glossary/flash cards, bonus material not included in the text, and more.

The premium website offers access to additional materials, including the Video Cases. Go to www.cengage.com/login to register or purchase access.

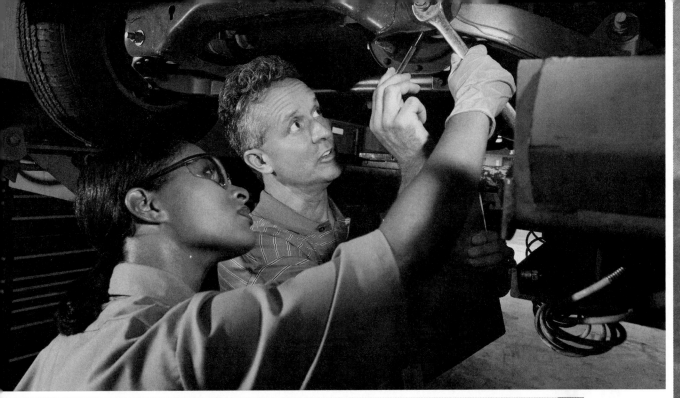

Transitions

12

CHAPTER QUESTIONS

1. Why should there be a transition initiative for students in special education?

2. Transition is supposed to be a "results-oriented" process. What types of results should transition initiatives call for, and why are they the focus?

3. What demands do various post-school settings put on students with mild disabilities, and how should those demands be taken into account when planning for successful transitions?

4. What is the appropriate process for transition planning, and what role should students play in preparing for their own transitions?

5. What skills should students develop to participate in their transition planning, as well as for continued success following the time of transition?

Do you think that special education is effective for students with mild disabilities? When you answer that question, what is your definition of "effective"?

The number of students with mild disabilities who receive an appropriate education has increased dramatically since passage of the nation's landmark special education law (Public Law 94-142, now known as the *Individuals with Disabilities Education Act*). The many research-proven teaching and learning practices you are learning about in this textbook have certainly made a difference in special education students' knowledge and skills. Some believe that the effectiveness of education is ultimately measured by students' lives once they leave school (Kliebard 1992). If using that standard, the effectiveness of special education is mixed. In spite of successes *in* school, some students with mild disabilities still *leave* school underprepared for their lives ahead.

Chapter Question

ALERT

In this section, you will find information that answers a Chapter Question:

1. Why should there be a transition initiative for students in special education?

The Need for Transition Planning

In 1984, the then-director of the U.S. Office of Special Education and Rehabilitative Services (OSERS), Madeline Will, criticized special education as a dead end for too many students with disabilities. She charged that special education resulted in post-school outcomes that were not much better than before nationwide special education had begun (Will 1984; 1986).

Coinciding with Will's 1986 publication of her criticisms of special education, *Educating Children with Special Needs: A Shared Responsibility* (Will 1986), special education began an initiative to clarify elements of successful transition for students with disabilities. The focus of the transition initiative was initially on preparing special education students to enter the world of work, but it has since been expanded to address their full participation in society and their personal well-being. The history of academic, social, and economic underachievement by those with disabilities makes it clear that special education must attend to post-school and post-special education outcomes.

CASE 12.1

The Challenge of Planning for the Most Appropriate Options

Case Introduction

As you read the following case, ask yourself what options are appropriate for Adam at the end of ninth grade; also consider what his needs are likely to be if he stays in school through twelfth grade, and what supports he might need after that.

At the end of the case, you will find case questions. These questions are meant to serve as points for reflection. Of course, if you can answer them immediately, you should do so, but

you may want to wait to answer them until you have read the portion of the chapter that pertains to a particular case question. Throughout the rest of the chapter, you will see the same questions. When you come to them again, try to answer them based upon that portion of the chapter that you just read.

Adam's ninth-grade year at Monroe High School was quickly coming to an end. Mary Alice had been looking forward to his IEP meeting. As the high school director of special education services, she had participated in his eighth-grade IEP meeting when he was preparing to come up from the Sumner Middle School. This year, she had a high level of direct involvement with Adam and his family, due to several incidents of inappropriate behaviors by Adam. Adam was one of Mary Alice's favorite students, and she often thought that students such as he made her enjoy special education work so much.

Adam came to Monroe High with a thick special education file. The year he entered elementary school, he was permanently placed to live with his aunt's family, after suffering an early childhood of neglect and sexual abuse. Mary Alice could never get a clear answer from Adam's aunt or caseworker as to where Adam's mother is or how involved she is in his life. All she knows about the father is that "he is no longer on the scene," but that he attempted to contact Adam once or twice but never followed through. She knows that Adam's life with his aunt is not ideal; his aunt had taken him in out of a sense of obligation. She sometimes commented in front of him that she is glad to model the importance of family for him even though he poses a burden on her family. Adam had told Mary Alice that his aunt routinely favored his two younger cousins, whom she referred to as her "real children."

Because of his diagnosed EBD, Adam has been receiving counseling services. He also has yearly IEP goals related to social skills and academics. He has two friends with whom he spends time, but they often argue, and Mary Alice doubts they would be friends if each had someone else with whom to spend time. Adam generally gets along well with other students while sitting next to them in class; however, most students seem to avoid interacting with him. Mary Alice presumes this is due to his sullen and sometimes aggressive behavior. It is common knowledge in the school that Adam has attempted suicide at least once.

Adam's last IEP meeting was a challenge, with much of the time spent discussing his behaviors and recent incidents that occurred in middle school and at home; almost no time was spent discussing his academic needs that result from his comorbid EBD and LD or how to help him successfully move to the high school.

Mary Alice looked forward to this meeting because in scheduling it everyone talked about the importance of developing "really clear" IEPs for Adam's final years of schooling. Mary Alice even sent all parties an advanced agenda: 15 minutes to discuss academic goals, 15 minutes to discuss behavior and counseling goals, 15 minutes to discuss other family goals or concerns, and 15 minutes to identify transition plans. She thought that this order of topics would ensure that all important topics would be discussed before the session could be derailed by focusing on some recent incident.

Despite her planning, Mary Alice wasn't prepared when, at the start of the meeting, the school counselor stated that he was afraid Adam was feeling "lost" at the large high school and that he would be better off attending a smaller vocational program. He suggested that the smaller vocational school would be more conducive to Adam making progress on his social skills. Adam's aunt immediately endorsed the transfer as a good idea. Despite Mary Alice's best attempts to discuss Adam's academic and behavior goals before contemplating a change in placement, the conversation never recovered. The rest of the meeting was spent discussing what Adam could do by attending the vocational school. Adam wasn't present at the meeting, but his aunt was sure that he would like the switch.

Mary Alice felt as if she had lost a fight. Everyone else in the room was satisfied with virtually repeating academic goals from this year's IEP; instead of developing a transition plan, they agreed that Adam simply needed to transfer to the vocational program, and that they would have a better idea of transition needs based on how the year went.

CASE QUESTIONS

1. When in the course of Adam's schooling should discussion of his transition needs have begun?
2. What evidence may indicate a student, such as Adam, needs a transition plan?
3. What post-school options should a transition plan address?

The discussion of Adam's transition needs did not go well, nor did his IEP meeting in general (review Chapter 1). Transition planning is done within the IEP planning process and should progress from a discussion of interests, strengths, and needs, to identifying goals and steps to meet those goals. Even if moving to the vocational school was the right decision, the IEP/transition meeting did not go well. Participants focused too much on reacting to Adam's behaviors. By beginning with a focus on why the high school may not be appropriate for Adam, participants negated careful discussion of what transition goals should be addressed and how best to address them. Without that information, it is hard to know if Adam would be better off in a vocational curriculum. Further, the focus was only on Adam's short-term transition. The discussion also should have addressed post-high school options for Adam, how those options should be explored, and what experiences he should begin to have to be ready for leaving school.

Trends in Post-School Outcomes

Students with mild disabilities are a diverse group. Many of them are academically and socially successful in school and generally have positive lives. Likewise, as a benefit of special education, the majority of students go on to fulfilling adult lives, which may include employment, further education, and successful transitioning through stages of adult living (see, for example, *Federal Outlook for Exceptional Children* [CEC 2007]; Hamill 2003; Lee and Jackson 2001). However, the statistics indicate that individuals with disabilities are more likely to have a diminished quality of life upon leaving school, when compared as a population to their nondisabled peers (Wagner and Blackorby 1996; Phelps and Hanley-Maxwell 1997; Wagner et al. 2006; see also Jenkins et al. 2006; Rusch and Loomis 2005). They can have diminished experiences and achievements in the areas of education, employment, and daily living.

Education. Students with mild disabilities are more likely than their general education peers to leave school without graduating. This likelihood includes dropping out (Edgar 2005; Scanlon and Mellard 2002) and abruptly leaving by expulsion or entering a correctional system (Baltodano, Harris, and Rutherford 2005; Quinn et al. 2005). Students of color or from low-income families and communities are also more likely to leave school before completion (see Murray and Naranjo 2008). Even those who do complete school by traditional standards are more likely to complete lower track curricular options or meet minimal standards for passing (Skinner and Lindstrom 2003), which leaves fewer post-school options available to them.

Once out of school, students with mild disabilities are also less likely than their peers to participate in the range of postsecondary education options, which include adult basic education, correctional education, vocational training, and community college or baccalaureate and graduate programs (Wagner and Blackorby 1996; Murray et al. 2000; Stodden and Dowrick 2000).

When students with disabilities do enter postsecondary education, they are more likely to leave the program without completing it, whether it is an adult basic education or college program (Horn, Peter, and Rooney 2002; Milsom and Hartley 2005). In fact, within ten years after graduating from high school, the majority of nondisabled adults will have graduated from either community or four-year college, while the majority of those with LD will not have (Mellard and Lancaster 2003), and those with EBD and MMR are even less likely to have attended and graduated from postsecondary education (Wagner and Blackorby 1996). Among the two biggest hurdles that postsecondary students with mild disabilities experience are not being prepared for the academic demands of their new setting (Lowery-Corkran 2006) and not being equipped to deal with the demands of daily living (for example, lacking transportation, family and social relationships, organization) (Troiano 2003; see also Mull, Sitlington, and Alper 2001).

Employment. The employment trend upon leaving high school for young adults with mild disabilities has steadily improved; however, those with mild disabilities continue to be unemployed and underemployed up to three years after leaving high school (Frank and Singleton 2000). Employment trends for females with mild disabilities are worse than for their male counterparts, both for holding employment and earning comparable wages (Wagner and Blackorby 1996). Although young adults with mild disabilities have been found to earn more than their peers without disabilities in the initial years after leaving secondary school, the probable explanation is that fewer students with LD are entering college and instead enter the workforce. Beginning the fifth year after leaving high school, those without disabilities begin to earn more, and the gap between the two populations only widens (Goldstein, Murray, and Edgar 1998; also see Madaus 2006). Those adults with disabilities who do complete postsecondary education also typically earn more than adults with disabilities who do not (Dickinson and Verbeek 2002; Madaus 2006).

Daily living. Reports on daily living for young adults and adults with mild disabilities indicate limited independence and social satisfaction (Barkley et al. 2006; Coutinho, Oswald, and Best 2006; see also Gresham and MacMillan 1997). As young adults with mild disabilities they more commonly continue to remain single and live with their parents (Lindstrom and Benz 2002). They also tend to have fewer friends or close relationships (Elksnin and Elksnin 2001; Stacy 2001). Often, they lack the social competence to use social skills effectively in varied contexts (Gresham, Sugai, and Horner 2001), such as in interacting appropriately with peers versus adults or in academic or work situations where tasks must be completed efficiently. As Hill and Coufal (2005) report, communication disorders are often associated with general social difficulties, particularly when they are linked with emotional and behavioral disorders that often occur.

The diminished quality of life that many students with mild disabilities experience upon leaving school is well documented. The directions they go upon school leaving are pivotal. You may have observed that we have used the labels *young adult* and *adult;* the **young adult** years (approximately age at school leaving to twenty-three years old) are often studied as gateway years into adulthood. The young adult years are often crucial predictors of one's future quality of life (Arbona 2000; Kenny et al. 2007). (The adult years begin when the young adult initiates a period of stability, although most do not achieve stability at the outset of that period.) Despite these problems, students with disabilities can lead successful, independent young adult and adult lives if given proper support.

The Concept of Transition

Since the 1990 reauthorization of the special education law, the IDEA, **transition** has been defined as being about preparation for leaving school. However, the importance of transition was stated prior to that version of the law. It was

▼

Chapter Question
ALERT

In this section you will find information that answers a Chapter Question:

2. Transition is supposed to be a "results-oriented" process. What types of results should transition initiatives call for, and why are they the focus?

first identified in the 1983 Education of the Handicapped Amendments (Public Law 98-199), which addressed the need for coordinated education, training, and related services to prepare students for post-school experiences, with employment as the ultimate goal.

The 1990 reauthorization was the first version of the IDEA to require that transition planning and services be provided as needed; it included the requirement that transition goals and objectives be written. **Transition planning** is the process of identifying and addressing the needs of a special education student associated with successfully moving to post-school experiences. The IDEA requires that **individualized transition plans (ITPs)** be developed by members of the IEP team and other appropriate parties, who are the transition team (see the section titled Transition Planning in this chapter).

THINK BACK TO THE CASE about Adam . . .

1. *When in the course of Adam's schooling should discussion of his transition needs have begun?*

When Adam was still in eighth grade, there was reason to be concerned about his transition to high school. The IEP team should have developed transition goals and a plan for him while he was still in eighth grade. The IDEA 2004 Regulations call for teams to develop transition plans as soon as they anticipate the student will have a transition need. Therefore, had the team members anticipated a need for transition support even earlier than eighth grade, they should have begun preparing for the transition then.

If Adam is likely to need counseling or personal living supports after high school, the team should begin planning for that. Likewise, it is time to plan for Adam's post-high school goals for employment or education. If the team members anticipate that he will have difficulty finding success in those new settings, they should begin planning for his transition. These are decisions Adam and his IEP team members should make. Without a doubt, the team members should have been more thoughtful in discussing Adam's transition to the vocational school, beginning with identifying his interests, strengths, and needs.

Expanding the Transition Focus Beyond Employment

Critics of the original transition initiative argued that the emphasis on transition to work was too narrow a goal (see especially Halpern 1985). They suggested that other aspects of adulthood and well-being need to be equally valued to successfully achieve post-school outcomes (Halpern et al. 1995). **Well-being** refers to physical and mental health, including one's personal satisfaction with life. Halpern (1985; 1993) noted that, in addition to employment, those leaving school need to be secure in three domains—*physical and material well-being, performance of adult roles,* and *personal fulfillment*—for a satisfactory **quality of life** (see Box 12.1). Halpern's three domains respond directly to the shortcomings of special education outcomes that Will and others (for example, Gartner and Lipsky 1987; Lipsky 2005) have identified over the years.

> **BOX 12.1**
>
> ## HALPERN'S QUALITY OF LIFE DOMAINS
>
> ### PHYSICAL AND MATERIAL WELL-BEING
>
> Physical and mental health
> Food, clothing, and lodging
> Financial security
> Safety from harm
>
> ### PERFORMANCE OF ADULT ROLES
>
> Mobility and community access
> Vocation, career, employment
> Leisure and recreation
> Personal relationships and social networks
> Educational attainment
> Spiritual fulfillment
> Citizenship (for example, voting)
> Social responsibility (for example, doesn't break laws)
>
> ### PERSONAL FULFILLMENT
>
> Happiness
> Satisfaction
> Sense of general well-being
>
> *Source:* Reprinted from A. Halpern, "Quality of Life as a Conceptual Framework for Evaluating Transition Outcomes (*Exceptional Children* 59 (1993):486–98).

THINK BACK TO THE CASE about Adam . . .

2. What evidence may indicate a student, such as Adam, needs a transition plan?

In reviewing evidence that a student will need any type of transition planning, educators should take into account whether the student has the functional skills for academic tasks and other demands associated with the quality of life domains. Likewise, the team members should consider whether the student has realistic goals or any goals at all. As need be, transition planning can focus on helping the student to determine personal goals. When the team members consider what is required to succeed at a particular goal, they can next consider whether the student will need support to be prepared to succeed.

Relying on population statistics about students with mild disabilities is a dangerous way to make plans about transition. Although it is useful to know that students with EBD, like Adam, are among the most likely to drop out of school (Cobb et al. 2006) and have difficulty holding jobs (Wagner and Cameto 2004), educators must first look for evidence that the student is at risk for such experiences before presuming that transition efforts should focus on preventing certain scenarios.

Current IDEA Requirements for Transition Planning and Services

The IDEA Regulations state that "transition services means a coordinated set of activities" (§ 300.43(a), 46762) to improve both academic and functional achievement of a student, with the intent of facilitating transition to post-school activities. Those post-school activities include the following:

- Postsecondary education,
- Vocational education,
- Integrated employment (including supported employment),
- Continuing and adult education,
- Adult services,
- Independent living, or
- Community participation. (§ 300.43(a)(1), 46762).

Therefore, transition planning and services must address the areas of *postsecondary training and/or education, employment*, and *independent living or community participation*. In the following section, we describe the transition demands related to different settings in each of those three areas, but first we consider the demands associated with exiting special and/or secondary education.

Note that the IDEA Regulations plainly state that transition services need to address a student's academic and functional *achievement*. That phrasing not only supports the NCLB and IDEA emphases on achievement as school outcomes, but also indicates that transition service is not merely about identifying the student's next "placement" upon leaving school. Transition is also about preparing for the student to succeed in that placement.

The IDEA (2004) identifies transition as part of a "results-oriented process" (§ 300.43(a (1), 46762). If a high school graduate enters a new job, for example, but soon finds that she or he lacks critical entry-level skills or the ability to self-advocate as an adult with a disability, that placement may soon be a failure. It is too late for the former student to return to the school for further assistance, because transition services end when the student leaves special education (for example, by graduating or completing school, dropping out, or no longer being identified as needing/benefiting from special education). (There are limited due process rights that may allow a return to school when appropriate special education had not been provided; however, that is a legal recourse that is rarely enjoined.) Effective transition planning, however,

© vario images GmbH & Co.KG/Alamy

The transition planning and implementation process must be responsive to the student's goals and personal profile. Standardized transition practices cannot meet the needs of unique individuals.

Chapter Question
ALERT

In this section you will find information that answers a Chapter Question:

3. What demands do various post-school settings put on students with mild disabilities, and how should those demands be taken into account when planning for successful transitions?

involves anticipating the demands that different settings and contexts will place upon transitioning students, and preparing them to successfully meet the demands.

Addressing the Demands of Various Transition Settings

Upon leaving secondary education, students with disabilities may not realize that, unlike in primary and secondary education, they must be "otherwise qualified" to gain access to most post-school placements (see Americans with Disabilities Act 1990; Section 504 of the Rehabilitation Act of 1973). This is quite different from K-12 education, where the emphasis is on determining how to make the education accessible to the student. As we will explain further in this chapter, students must learn to self-advocate for their rights.

Exiting Special Education

Some students exit special education while still enrolled in school, because they no longer require special education services to benefit from their education. They may receive related services in accordance with Section 504, if needed. In making that decision, the IEP team must address whether a student may, nonetheless, have disability-related needs for a supported transition beyond high school (see Mull and Sitlington 2003). Keeping a student enrolled in special education with an education plan solely to address transition goals is appropriate (see the section called "Transition Planning" in this chapter). No longer requiring special education does not usually mean that the disability has ceased to exist. When students leave the familiar environment of secondary school, they may immediately be confronted by situations they are not ready to navigate, due to their disability. For example, a former student with an emotional disturbance may not be able to adjust to the changes in daily routine, or someone with ADHD may not have learned self-regulation strategies that are feasible on the job. Such students could have benefited from transition services to prepare them for post-school circumstances.

Dropping Out, Transferring, Removal, and Expulsion

Some students leave school without the benefit of having completed their education. Prematurely leaving school, via dropping out, temporary removal, or expulsion are almost always detrimental. They are all also more likely to occur for students with disabilities (Scanlon and Mellard 2002) and result in a number of problems.

Dropping out. A number of intractable factors such as race/ethnicity, sex, and socioeconomic class increase a student's risk for dropping out (Horn, Peter, and Rooney 2002; Murray and Naranjo 2008). Having a disability is also an intractable risk factor for dropping out of school.

Other factors, such as school attachment, academic success, and positive attitudes toward school are also related to dropping out; these can be adjusted (Dunn, Chambers, and Rabren 2004; Eisenman 2007; Scanlon and Mellard 2002).

Four areas of adjustable factors that have been found to contribute to drop-out prevention are (a) academic success, (b) students believing that adults in the school care about them, (c) support for immediate and pressing personal concerns, and (d) an appreciation of the relation between schooling and personal goals (McPartland 1994). The most effective interventions will address the constellation of factors that may contribute to dropping out, and not just one or two in isolation (see Eisenman 2007). Thus, IEP teams concerned that a student is at risk for dropping out should plan to address these four areas to prevent the student from dropping out (see the section titled "Transition Planning" in this chapter).

Effective interventions to prevent dropping out of school not only seek to prevent it but also to promote the student staying in school (Eisenman 2007). Such interventions address the student's relationship with the school. Unfortunately, many students with disabilities do not feel as though they are valued members of their school community (Cameto 2005).

Transferring Out of Public Education. For various reasons, students and their families may elect to transfer from public education to private or parochial education. Possible reasons include dissatisfaction with public education, desiring a more competitive school (for example, for postsecondary admissions or potential to play sports), religious reasons, family changes, or seeking a school that specializes in services for students with special needs. As Hardy (2004) has reported, the phenomenon of "white flight" occurs when white students and others from middle- and upper-class families leave public education at the secondary level (see Kahlenberg 2001 for a historical perspective). It occurs most commonly in urban school systems (Hardy 2004; Orfield et al. 2004). Consequences of white flight include lessened community investment in the schools and students who remain, and less academic diversity (for example, Murray and Naranjo 2008). That lessened diversity results in increased proportions of students with special needs remaining.

Families of students who are considering transferring out of schools should be informed that nonpublic schools are not bound to provide the services afforded by the IDEA. Even private special education schools that **"tuition in"** students from public special education (that is, the public school pays the students' tuition so that they may receive IEP-mandated special education in the private school) are not bound to comply with the IDEA for students who are not tuitioned in.

Later in this chapter you will read about preparing students for transitions by developing their self-determination and self-advocacy skills. Students preparing to transfer to another school should be prepared with these types of transition skills too, even when the new school is perceived as "better" or "more supportive."

Temporary Removal. There are ways in which students may leave school on a temporary basis. Some students may be removed from schooling, either voluntarily or involuntarily, for reasons such as substance abuse, mental or physical health interventions, or pregnancy. Students may also be temporarily suspended from school for disciplinary reasons. The conditions of removal in such cases are often case-specific, and laws related to them can vary by state as well as by individual case circumstances. Unless the cause for removal is related to a disability, such as a student with LD who placed others at risk due to impulsive decision making or a student with an emotional disturbance who posed a threat to others, students are not protected by the IDEA from being removed from school. IDEA Regulations stipulate that special education students involuntarily removed from school must continue to receive IDEA services; however, the students may be removed to an alternative setting to receive those services.

The length of time the student is removed can vary. Even when short-term, removal represents a transition. Whenever possible, IEP and transition teams should anticipate such transitions as plausible events (for example, teams can often be aware of whether a student with EBD is at risk for needing placement full-time out of school) and plan for successful transitions. The student should know what circumstances could cause the removal, what the alternate placement will be like, and whether education and transition curricula and services will follow the student.

Depending upon where the student is removed to, full services realistically may not be able to follow. Although the law requires that special education and related services be continued, specialized equipment, trained professionals, and the like simply may not be readily matched. The transition team needs to participate in determining whether or not transition services can be provided in the alternative context. Of course, the team also needs to evaluate whether and how transition plans and services will need to be altered for a student returning to school from an alternative setting.

Incarceration. Some adolescents may leave school due to entering corrections. Their change in status may be abrupt. As with the risk factors for dropping out, some of the risk factors for delinquency and detention are social whereas others are more personal. At least some of the social factors correlated with juvenile delinquency are fairly common; they include broken families, parent incarceration, poverty, substance use and trafficking, and limited education success (Zabel and Nigro 1999). Males, as well as youths from certain racial and ethnic minority groups, are more likely to be found as delinquent and juvenile offenders (Coutinho, Oswald, and Best 2006; Ochoa and Eckes 2005). Among youth with mild disabilities, those with EBD are the most likely to be incarcerated (Quinn et al. 2005). Their risk factors for arrest include extended placement in residential or day treatment facilities, young age at initial admission to corrections systems, and prior adjudication (Davis 2001). Researchers found that urban youth with mild disabilities were less likely than others to identify ways to get out of situations to avoid sanctions such as arrest (Pearl and Bryan 1994). Although the circumstances by which adolescents can become involved with the law are too many for a team to address systematically, the team can be made aware of academic, disciplinary, home, and social behaviors linked to delinquency. They can then target teaching the student alternative or preventive skills, including problem-solving skills for when the students find themselves in a situation that could lead to arrest.

Expulsion. In the case of expulsion, students are permanently removed from education in a particular setting. Depending on the circumstances of the expulsion, the students may be eligible to enroll in a different school or district. For the purposes of IDEA-related services, however, although expulsion can mean the students have otherwise exited public education, IEP and ITP rights and services may continue. Nonetheless, the ITP team should carefully anticipate whether a student is at risk for expulsion. Just as in instances of temporary removal, the team should both work to prevent the expulsion by teaching the student positive skills and help the student prepare for life following expulsion. The student may not be able to access in-school services once the expulsion is finalized. At-risk students should understand their rights, responsibilities, and options for entering another school system. They should also have an idea of alternative options to pursue once out of the school system (for example, employment, GED preparation), and procedures to activate them.

The GED Alternative. The General Educational Development (GED) diploma is an option for those who leave school early and do not return to complete their degree. The higher levels of sustained employment and marginally higher average income resulting from obtaining a GED indicate its advantage over entering adulthood with no secondary degree or equivalent (Childtrendsdatabank 2007; Reder 1995). An estimated two-thirds of students who leave school early obtain a high school diploma or GED within eight years of exiting school (Hurst, Kelly, and Princiotta 2004). Some high school dropouts may quit school assuming the GED is an easy alternative to enduring more years in school. However, the GED exam is normed so that one-quarter of high school graduates fail it (Mellard and Lancaster 2003). That means it is not an easy option for most who leave high school early. Many young adults and adults take up to eight years or more to study for and pass their GED exam (Hurst, Kelly, and Princiotta 2004). In the 1990s, only slightly more than one-third of those who took the GED completed all sections of the exam and passed (GED Testing Services 2002). Moreover, young adults with learning difficulties had even lower passing rates (Dynarski and Gleason 2002).

Those considering the GED option should be informed that they must first drop out of school, that the exam is not easy to pass, that they will typically earn less that high school graduates over their lifetimes, and that those who go on to earn a GED earn only marginally more than other dropouts and still typically earn less than high school graduates (Tyler 2002; see also Day and Newburger 2002). Transition preparation could include attempting practice exams, as well as teaching study and test-taking skills.

The World of Work

Transition planning should include consideration of work goals, even for students who plan on postsecondary education, military enlistment, or some other option prior to entering the world of work full-time. Part of the challenge of identifying work goals and setting transition plans for students is that they have so many options for employment. Many adolescents are not prepared to identify their career preferences.

Educators concerned for a student's transition to the world of work have limited resources for identifying potential work or career options. They also have limited resources for planning coursework and experiences to prepare the student for those options. In part, that is because the realities of the workplace are rarely treated in the professional literature on transition (Gerber et al. 2004). Further, studies of young adults with mild disabilities in the workplace seldom address much beyond their initial transition (ibid.).

Lindstrom and Benz (2002) identified three phases of career development: *unsettled, exploratory,* and *settled*. Adolescents are often limited in their knowledge of career options; being asked what career they would like to prepare for can result in no reply or a forced choice that is based on limited information, at best. Those adolescents would be beginning in Lindstrom and Benz's *unsettled* phase. To help adolescents identify promising work directions, their interests, capabilities (including potential to develop capabilities via training or education), and potential for opportunities (for example, ways that postsecondary tuition can be afforded) should be considered. The many students who do not yet know what they would like to do can still specify information related to what they would enjoy, be good at, and realistically could accomplish in work. From there, work options can be *explored*. Based on the results of exploration, workers can enter into the *settled* phase by becoming stable in a work routine and find work fitting within a positive quality of life (although entering the settled phase does not ensure the worker will stay settled).

> **VIDEO CASE CONNECTIONS BOX**
>
> Watch the Video Case entitled *Motivating Student Learners: Curriculum Based on Real Life*. Listen to math teacher Kelly Hammond-Franklin discuss ways that she makes mathematics curriculum relevant to her students' lives. Make a list of all the skills of the world of work that she is teaching her students. Note that these are all skills they will need when they eventually transition.

RIASEC Theory. Holland (1985; 1997) proposed a taxonomy for both personality types and work environments. Although the purpose of his model is to facilitate matching an individual's personality to different work places or occupations, it can be useful to help adolescents think about aspects of the world of work that may be important to them. You can engage them in conversations about work and lifestyle interests, as well as about activities they enjoy. Most are able to describe some attributes of work and other contexts that they consider important (for example, they may wish to work with their hands, not sit behind a desk, be creative, make a middle-class income, positively impact the environment, be spiritually fulfilling), if not choose a specific occupation.

Holland's taxonomy, also know at the **RIASEC theory,** identifies six work-related types of personalities and work environments. The six types are Realistic, Investigative, Artistic, Social, Enterprising, and Conventional (see Figure 12.1). According to Holland's theory, the closer an individual's personality type and a work environment match, the better the fit for work will be. Holland's taxonomy has been independently validated and widely promoted as a helpful tool (for example, Fritzche, McIntire, and Yost 2002; O*NET OnLine).

Disabilities in the Workplace. Identifying potential work directions is merely the first step in preparing for transition into the world of work. In addition to

FIGURE 12.1

A Hexagonal Model for Defining the Psychological Resemblances Among Types and Environments and Their Interactions

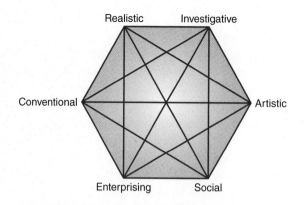

Source: Reprinted with permission from J. L. Holland, *Making of Vocational Choices: A Theory of Vocational Personalities and Work Environments.* 2nd ed. (Englewood Cliffs, NJ: Prentice Hall, 1997).

possessing job-seeking skills such as searching for and applying for work, and the necessary skills for holding a job (for example, personal conduct, technical skills), people with disabilities must also employ appropriate skills related to managing potential influences of their disability. Most adults do not disclose their mild disabilities at the initial job interview, for fear of it harming their prospect of being hired (Gerber et al. 2004). Most do not request accommodations in the job interview process either, even when those accommodations may be needed as part of the interview (Gerber et al. 2004). Gerber et al. (2004) offered the example of a job applicant who claimed he did not need accommodations during the job interview, "because I could bring [the paperwork] home, and my mom will help me" (287). Once on the job, most adults with disabilities do not request accommodations either. This is often due to fear of embarrassment or retribution, including being fired (Gerber et al. 2004). Thus, transition planning for many students needs to include preparing them to know their disability rights and to self-advocate.

The Military   Students leaving high school may seek to join the military for a variety of reasons, such as patriotism, scholarship (for example, via ROTC), skill training, a military career, desire for structure or security, or a perceived lack of other options. Several of these reasons are directly related to the experiences and needs of those with mild disabilities. The decision to join the military involves weighing a variety of factors, which may pose a challenge for those with mild disabilities. Because of the commitment involved, it is particularly important to help adolescents make informed choices. A common misperception among teens is that they can easily resign if they regret enlisting (see Ayers 2006). Those seeking to enlist to receive preparation for nonmilitary careers may need to be reminded that they may be "called up" during times of military conflict. In addition, undocumented immigrants should be informed that they are not eligible for military service, despite the fact that males are required to register with selective services, and that speeded pathways to citizenship available via enlistment are not open to them (National Immigration Law Center 2004). Likewise, gay, lesbian, and questioning youth need to be prepared to make informed choices about participating in the "Don't Ask, Don't Tell" policy, by which they must disavow their sexual orientation or risk being discharged (Belkin and Bateman 2003).

To be considered eligible for military service, Department of Defense (DoD) standards must be met for "age, citizenship, education, aptitude, physical fitness, dependency status, [and] moral character" (DoD Instruction 1304.26). Operational standards are periodically adjusted, but have recently included that individuals must also have graduated high school. Aptitude is assessed using the Armed Forces Qualification Test (AFQT), which is a composite of arithmetic reasoning, math knowledge, paragraph comprehension, and word knowledge subtests from the Armed Service Vocational Aptitude Battery (ASVAB). The tests are multiple choice and timed, with no accommodations permitted. All three of those factors reflect testing challenges for people with mild disabilities. Interested students should know that rights and protections under Section 504 of the Rehabilitation Act are not available to military personnel, beginning with entrance requirements (although they are available to civilian employees).

Additional standards may prevent students with mild disabilities from entering the military. Those identified as having chronic academic skills difficulties or "perceptual defects secondary to organic or functional mental disorders that interfere with work or school after age 12" may be rejected for military service (DoD Directive 6130.3). So, a learning disability, for example, does not immediately exclude a student from eligibility, but the degree to which it impacts an individual's functioning may. Those with ADHD can be excluded from military service if they have taken medication for their condition within the past year or have "significant" hyperactive or impulsive behaviors, as judged by a military examiner (Jaksa n.d.) (other daily medications, such as for asthma or diabetes, are also cause for disqualification). Records of any treatment for ADHD within the past three years must be provided to a medical examiner (Jaksa n.d.) (also see National Research Center on AD/HD 2008). Those with EBD or other mild disabilities might also be excluded if their "personality or behavior disorders" (DoD Directive 6130.3) result in character that is considered inadaptable to military life; examples include antisocial attitudes or behaviors, multiple interactions with the legal system, immaturity, and instability (Latham and Latham n.d.). Mental retardation as a primary disability is also a cause for exclusion (DoD Instruction 1332.38).

Based on the fact that military enrollment depends on meeting academic standards that may be challenging for those with mild disabilities, and that certain disabling conditions may be cause for exclusion regardless, those considering a transition into the military are advised to do the following:

- Talk to a knowledgeable recruiter and apply anyway.
- Be completely honest and open about your medical and educational background (being disqualified from service now is better than being discharged or even prosecuted for providing false information later).
- If you are disqualified initially on medical grounds, ask how you can apply for a waiver. (www.help4adhd.org)

Postsecondary Education Options

A significant factor in earnings is whether or not a person attends some form of postsecondary education. For example, young adults with LD who attend postsecondary education have earned significantly more than their counterparts who do not (Wagner and Blackorby 1996).

Despite the facts that most high school students with mild disabilities have been directed toward vocational education more often than four-year colleges (Janiga and Costenbader 2002), and that mild disability labels have the effect of disproportionately reducing opportunities based on race, class, and sex (Reid and Knight 2006), students with mild disabilities are participating in postsecondary education in increasingly larger percentages (see Hart et al. 2004). Indeed, the percentage of young adults with mild mental retardation enrolled in community college is increasing. Often these students are "dual enrolled" in secondary and postsecondary education, which means they take some life-skills oriented instruction in the postsecondary setting before completing high school (ibid.). Part of the reason for the increase is transition planning (Skinner and Lindstrom 2003). The varied postsecondary education options place different demands on students, beginning with admissions and extending through accessing services, to the academic and social expectations upon the student.

Adult Basic Education. Estimates of the percent of participants in adult basic education who have disabilities have ranged from 50 percent to 80 percent (Wagner 1991). Adult basic education (ABE) tends to be more learner-centered and individually paced than K-12 education (Beder and Medina 2001). Thus, in adult basic education placements, enrollees with disabilities (some adult education agencies avoid the label *student* because older adult participants may take exception to it) can expect to spend a significant portion of their time working alone and progressing at their own pace (Mellard et al. 2005; Smith and Hofer 2003).

The curricular focus in ABE programs is almost exclusively on basic skills (for example, reading, writing, mathematics) (Mellard et al. 2005). Adults enrolled in ABE programs should, therefore, be prepared to work intently on some of the same skills by which they were challenged in their K-12 education (Zoino-Jeannetti 2006). Some ABE programs also offer services in job preparation and academic skills preparation for transitioning into community college.

Admission to adult basic education placements typically depends solely on making application. However, potential enrollees have to know the program exists and that they may be eligible to participate. As K-12 students, those individuals may not have realized that the *child find* requirements of the IDEA and established special education programs in some ways relieved them and their parents of responsibilities to seek out services. No such provision exists for Section 504 or the Americans with Disabilities Act (ADA), and there is tremendous variation in how community adult education programs advertise themselves. The individuals must have the skills of contacting the agency and providing necessary documentation for enrollment (which may include documentation of high school completion status, proof of residency, and health and insurance information). Depending on whether a program has rolling admissions or set periods when enrollment may begin, the adult will also have to coordinate the schedule of the program with other life activities; a person may need to juggle immediate work and leisure opportunities with an enrollment schedule that will not commence for three to four more weeks or longer. Although seemingly minor, this can prove a significant challenge for individuals with poor organizational skills and limited skills of self-advocacy. Once enrolled, adults in adult basic education tend to have highly sporadic participation rates for just such reasons, in addition to lacking commitment to the program (Scanlon and Mellard 2002).

Although one adult education option for those who did not complete secondary school is the GED, those who attend ABE programs may earn a certificate of completion or diploma that is useful to show to prospective employers or when applying to further postsecondary education options.

Participation in adult education can require particular fortitude. Transition preparation for entrance into ABE programs should also address students' clarification of their goals and understanding of what ABE will require, so that they will be more prepared to participate and continue if they feel overwhelmed by the demands.

Two- and Four-Year Colleges. Students with a variety of "learning, cognitive and intellectual disabilities" are increasingly participating in postsecondary education, including college (Hart et al. 2004). In 2000, 40 percent of freshmen college students disclosing a disability identified themselves as having an LD (Henderson 2001; see also Harbour 2004). Overall, students with disabilities represent approximately 6 percent of four-year college enrollees (Newman 2005).

College programs are sometimes linked to high schools, so students may enroll in postsecondary education while still enrolled in (and served and protected by) special education (Hart et al. 2004). When deemed appropriate by an IEP or ITP team, the young adult between the ages of 18 and 21 may receive transition supports in the postsecondary setting while still technically enrolled in secondary education. In those cases, however, the student cannot be simultaneously considered as a degree-seeking college student (Grigal, Dwyre, and Davis 2006). Enabling students to participate in college settings as part of transition services greatly expands their prospects for successful transition in all of the quality of life areas (ibid.).

Young adults who enter two-year and four-year college settings will find the demands on them as students quite different from most high school experiences. College students are expected to assume responsibility for keeping up with academic expectations, such as budgeting their time, taking notes, and seeking accommodation resources (Lowery-Corkran 2006). According to disability service providers on postsecondary campuses, successful college students with LD are motivated, academically prepared for college, and self-advocates (Hicks-Coolick and Kurtz 1997); the same can be assumed for successful students with other mild disabilities. ITP teams need to be sure that students planning to transition to college or another postsecondary education option are motivated and prepared for the learning routines expected in college.

The application to college presents the first challenge for young adults with mild disabilities. Those potential students must select a school that will be an appropriate match for their academic goals and abilities, which requires research and inquiry skills. In addition, the potential applicants will have to be aware of their disabilities and how they might impact enrollment at that college. The potential students with a disability should research what services will be [available to them (National Joint Committee on Learning Disabilities [NJCLD], 2007). Remember, although the students would be correct to assume that Section 504 and the ADA provide them with certain rights and protections, they would still be wise consumers to investigate an institution's capacity to provide needed services (NJCLD, forthcoming).

Skinner and Schenck (1992) reported that some young adults with disabilities attempt their first year in college without disclosing their disability or seeking any accommodations or support services. They are exploring whether or not they can "go it on their own." Before beginning college, students should be aware that this decision must be made carefully, as how successful students are in their first year can be critical for the quality of continued participation. In some cases, students may not seek appropriate services because of a lack of awareness; many special education students who transition to postsecondary institutions do not even know the label for the disability they have (Madaus et al. 2006).

Skinner and Lindstrom (2003) identified the following as influential to college success for students with mild disabilities:

Knowledge of the nature of their disability,
Awareness of degree of impairment,
Knowledge of compensatory strategies,
Ability to proactively manage a disability (for example, self-advocate),
Available emotional and academic support,
Motivation, and
Willingness to persevere when conditions are adverse.

Disability services coordinators at 74 postsecondary institutions reported in a survey that they were least satisfied with how prepared students with LD were to engage in self-advocacy (Janiga and Costenbader 2002). On top of those skills, as college students, they will also need to be able to balance college life with other aspects of daily living (for example, living in a community, working, being a parent or other family member). In the book *Faking It*, Christopher Lee (Lee and Jackson 1992) chronicled his experiences of going through college first unaware, and then trying to conceal and compensate for a mild disability.

Despite the increasing participation of students with mild disabilities in postsecondary education, transition preparation for postsecondary options remains limited. Cummings, Maddux, and Casey (2000) report six problems that persist in transition planning: (1) inadequate transition planning, (2) inconsistencies between secondary and postsecondary curriculum requirements, (3) failure to coordinate activities between schools and postsecondary institutions or community agencies, (4) inadequate transition services, (5) beginning transition planning too late, and (6) transition initiatives that do not begin early in the K-12 years. In a published research study, Hitchings, Retish, and Horvath (2005) noted that only four of more than 100 IEPs they reviewed included transition planning for postsecondary education. They also reported that almost half of the tenth graders with IEPs who expressed interests in postsecondary education did not express the same desire three years later. Transition planning should serve to support students in maintaining their education goals.

Skinner and Lindstrom (2003) suggest the following important strategies for preparing high school students to have successful transitions to college:

- Teach students about their disability and personally effective compensatory strategies and accommodations.
- Teach students to self-advocate.
- Teach students about legal rights and responsibilities, including those that pertain in secondary as well as postsecondary education.
- Help students select postsecondary schools wisely.
- Work with students and parents to develop a timeline for preparation for college.
- Encourage students to self-identify and seek appropriate assistance during their freshman year.
- Teach students how to organize for learning and living.
- Facilitate a support network—family, social, professionals, and educators.
- Assist students in obtaining a comprehensive psychoeducational evaluation in high school.
- Encourage participation in postsecondary preparation programs.

Making Assistive Technology Work in Postsecondary Transitions. According to Todis (1996; cited in Mull and Sitlington 2003), college students with LD abandon almost one-third of assistive technology devices, for reasons ranging from difficulties with equipment operation and a mismatch between the technology and required tasks, to students not wishing to be burdened or embarrassed by the equipment. In a 1998 study, the majority of college students receiving assistive technologies received ones that did not match their needs. Those students reported typically not having participated in a review of their technology needs (Roessler and Kirk 1998).

In a review of the literature, Mull and Sitlington (2003) identified the following five categories of problems for students with LD using assistive technology accommodations in postsecondary settings:

1. The use of assistive technology in the role of "cognitive prosthesis" (Cavalier, Ferretti, and Okolo 1994) versus "cognitive partner" (Chandler, Czerlinzky, and Wheman 1993; Day and Edwards 1996; Margolis and Michaels 1994; Raskind 1994);
2. The availability and high cost of assistive technology;
3. Abandonment by students of purchased assistive technology devices;
4. Training needs related to the use of technology and assistive devices; and
5. Eligibility questions.

(Like a body part prosthesis, a "cognitive prosthesis" stands in for a cognitive skill that is absent or does not operate as desired, such as any device that reads a text aloud to a student with reading difficulties.)

Mull and Sitlington (2003) offer the following four suggestions for effectively planning to meet assistive technology needs in the transition placement:

1. Financial resources should be identified for securing and operating the technology device in the transition setting, so that a plan incorporating technology can be realized and enacted. Also, arrangement to ensure the

technology is in place should be made before the student arrives at the postsecondary site.

2. Technology should be selected based on (a) the student's needs and (b) the demands of the transition setting. Thus, the student and representatives of the secondary and postsecondary settings should be involved in the selection process.
3. The technology should be accessed prior to transition so the student can become familiar with it.
4. Decisions about removing students from secondary special education should be made with consideration of the impact on future transition needs, including the denial of accommodations to individuals without documented needs.

Documentation Needs. Students with mild disabilities should have up-to-date psychoeducational evaluations, so that planning for transition needs is accurate. IEP and ITP teams may need to be reminded of this, as they are not required to complete a three-year reevaluation for those graduating with a regular diploma or aging out of special education services. Further, the teams should realize that secondary school evaluations are sometimes limited to documenting academic weaknesses and not cognitive processing needs (for example, memory or auditory recall) (Madaus and Shaw 2006; Mull, Sitlington, and Alper 2001; Skinner and Lindstrom 2003). Postsecondary institutions may not accept outdated information, and information focused on documenting weaknesses will not adequately inform institutions about appropriate accommodations. Gormley et al. (2005) found that only four states provided guidelines for what documentation postsecondary institutions must require for a learning disability. In most cases, individual institutions may set their own requirements for what they will expect. They found that a number of institutions not only identify the types of assessments that must be performed but name actual tests that must be used. Without institution-specific acceptable documentation, disability-related services may be denied. Gormley et al. also found that postsecondary institutions may require use of tests normed on adult populations instead of school-aged populations.

The IDEA (2004) requires that the IEP/ITP team provide a **summary of performance (SOP)** statement for students who do not receive a reevaluation prior to exiting secondary education. The SOP document must include a summary of the students' academic achievement and functional performance, as well as state recommendations on how to support the students in meeting their postsecondary goals. The National Transition Assessment Summit (NTAS)—a coalition of professional organizations concerned for effective transition practices—notes that the document should include sufficient documentation to establish a student's eligibility for accommodations in postsecondary settings, as well as useful information for appropriately determining accommodations in those settings. The NTAS further notes that the SOP is most useful when linked to the IEP process and when the student actively participates in its development. Kochar-Bryant and Izzo (2006) have proposed a template for an SOP form and Madaus et al. (2006) have recommended the nature of content to include on that template (see Box 12.2).

BOX 12.2

RECOMMENDED CONTENT FOR A SUMMARY OF PERFORMANCE (SOP) REPORT: FOR STUDENTS WITH MILD DISABILITIES

PART 1　　DEMOGRAPHIC INFORMATION

To establish the student's history as a person with a disability and eligibility for services:

State the student's primary disability.

State the date of initial diagnosis.

List formal and informal assessment methods conducted with the student.

Include all that clearly contribute to identifying the student's disability and functional strengths and needs.

Attach only the most recent formal and informal assessment reports.

PART 2　　STUDENT'S POSTSECONDARY GOALS

Restate the student's postsecondary transition goals from the IEP form.

PART 3　　SUMMARY OF PERFORMANCE

The Summary of Performance section is divided into three sections; Present Level of Performance and EAMAT information should be provided in each of the three sections.

Tips on the Types of Information to Include:

Present Level of Performance

- *Do not just list scores or reference an "attached report."*
- *Be sure content corresponds to student's postsecondary transition goals **(Part 2)**.*
- *Include strategies and skills the student knows and uses.*
- *List gaps between student's knowledge/skills near secondary school exiting and targeted postsecondary path.*

Essential Accommodations/Modifications and Assistive Technology (EAMAT)

- *List accommodations and modifications currently used by the student in secondary school.*
- *Accommodations recommended on an IEP but not actually used may not need to be included.*
- *State the rationale for why particular accommodations are needed, particularly for standardized testing.*

ACADEMIC CONTENT AREAS

(Reading, mathematics, written language, and learning skills)

Provide specific and objective information.

Provide information based on formal and informal measurement sources.

Use multiple sources of assessment data to fully represent the student.

continued

Provide indicators of the student's strengths and needs.

Use age-level appropriate data.

List recommendations based on what student currently needs/will need in future (consult transition goal).

Provide essential supports for student to access information or help, and share information.

Provide information separately for each academic content area.

COGNITIVE AREAS
(GENERAL ABILITY AND PROBLEM SOLVING, ATTENTION AND EXECUTIVE FUNCTION, AND COMMUNICATION)

Do not include information for cognitive areas that are not areas of need.

It is imperative to provide a range of information instead of a single score.

State sources of information, include a cautionary statement for subject information.

FUNCTIONAL AREAS
(SOCIAL SKILLS AND BEHAVIOR, INDEPENDENT LIVING, ENVIRONMENTAL ACCESS/MOBILITY, SELF-DETERMINATION AND SELF-ADVOCACY, AND CAREER/VOCATIONAL/ TRANSITION)

State information based on current functional skills and the context of intended transitions.

Provide data collected near the end of the student's high school experience.

Include both adaptive and problematic behaviors.

You may include anecdotal information.

Provide a summary of student's interests regarding career/vocation/transition.

Include results of functional or career/vocational assessments.

Provide key content of an individualized behavior intervention plan.

Provide results of assistive technology needs and usage assessments.

Note: Content in italics is adapted from Madaus et al. (2006). Nonitalicized content represents section headers of an SOP form proposed by Kochar-Bryant and Izzo (2006).

For additional suggestions on developing useful SOPs, see Association on Higher Education and Disability (AHEAD) (2008).

In light of the experiences of students with mild disabilities in postsecondary education, Mull, Sitlington, and Alper (2001) suggest that while still in high school, students determine which accommodations they will likely need in their postsecondary setting and that they determine how to arrange for them; in addition, their teachers need to provide them with practice and experiences in the demands of postsecondary education. Students may also need to become familiar with assistive technologies prior to entering postsecondary settings. The following is a list of resources that students with mild disabilities may need in college settings:

Preferential registration
Counseling
Accommodations
Assistive technology
Notification of rights and responsibilities
Daily living (including social skills, personal safety) and academic skills
Organizational skills

Independent Living and Community Participation

Many adolescents have unrealistic expectations for independent living. They may not grasp the costs associated with daily living or the responsibilities and expectations upon them when they live autonomously. Based on a review of research on transition to young adult and adult status, Sitlington (1996) reported that adolescents with LD have been found less successful than their peers in the areas of maintaining a home (for example, managing bills, preparing meals, cleaning, and maintenance), community involvement (for example, socializing, participating in recreational activities, not getting in trouble with the law), and personal and social relationships (for example, having friends, not feeling lonely or awkward).

Halpern's quality of life model can be useful for thinking about preparing for the many dimensions of independent living. Physical and material well-being, performance of adult roles, and personal fulfillment are all essential to independence. The IDEA expectations for education and transition plans to address functional performance concern independent living needs. Thus, special education and transition curriculums should include addressing such skills as counting money and making change, performing personal health care and hygiene, and developing transportation skills such as learning to navigate public transportation (for example, reading schedules, problem solving missed connections) or to drive a car. As Sitlington noted in 1996, "the abundant data on the learning characteristics of these individuals also point to the need for systematic instruction in the basic concepts of maintaining a home, participating appropriately in the community, and experiencing satisfactory personal and social relationships" (see also Sitlington and Frank 1999).

Independent living does not necessarily mean that young adults with disabilities will live self-sufficiently outside of their parents' homes. Indeed, that standard for independence has been characterized as a white European American value (for example, Tang 1995) and as inconsistent with economic realities of lower- and middle-class America in the twenty-first century (for example, see Sarkisian, Gerena, and Gerstel 2007). In some cultures, communal living—remaining in the family home until marriage or caring for elders—is valued over living on one's own. In such instances, independent living refers to having personal responsibilities and contributing to the household. Nonetheless, in a study of Apache Native Americans who had left school, Ramasamy, Duffy, and Camp (2000) found that those with learning disabilities were less likely to live independently. Therefore, even across cultures, preparation for independent living may be a more pressing need for students with mild disabilities.

THINK BACK TO THE CASE   **about Adam . . .**

3.   *What post-school options should a transition plan address?*

A transition plan should be comprehensive, but it does not have to target activities for every aspect of a student's life. The needs identified and the goals and plans to address those needs should focus on the quality of life domains that the team anticipates will be problematic for the student. As with academic and functional performance IEP goals, ITP goals should focus on priorities. Accordingly, an ITP may address goals and plans related to further education, employment, self-care, and independent living, as appropriate.

Chapter Question
ALERT

In this section, you will find information that answers a Chapter Question:

4.   What is the appropriate process for transition planning, and what role should students play in preparing for their own transitions?

Transition Planning

According to the IDEA (2004), transition planning should begin no later than the IEP year in which the student turns 16. Ideally, transition planning will begin as early as the elementary school years, where students begin to become aware of options for adulthood and pathways for accomplishing them (Blalock et al. 2003; see also Madaus and Shaw 2006). Transition planning should be done in a collaborative process with the student (IDEA 2004), taking into account the student's interests and preferences. Also, to facilitate positive outcomes, transition goals should be based on the student's strengths. Despite the logic of planning for transition and including the student in that process, fewer than 10 percent of college students with LD recall meetings while in high school to discuss their transition plans (Hitchings et al.1998).

The IEP team is responsible for anticipating if a student will have transition needs, as well as for developing and implementing the transition plan. Just as an IEP document is developed in a team process, so is an individualized transition plan, or ITP. Also, as is the case with an IEP, progress toward stated goals must be monitored, and the plan must be updated at least annually.

The Transition Planning Team

The members of the IEP team (special educator, general educator[s] administrator, parent, student, appropriate others [review Chapter 1]) are also members of the ITP team, because transition planning is done in concert with planning and providing a special education. The IDEA stipulates that the ITP team should invite the participation of representatives of other service agencies when they are relevant to the student's transition needs (for example, counselors, related service providers, representatives of agencies to which the student will transition, such as an employer, a job coach, residential specialist, postsecondary institution accommodations manager).

Members of agencies and institutions not affiliated with public school districts cannot be compelled by the IDEA to participate in the transition planning process. Nonetheless, every effort should be made to involve them. In most instances, representatives will participate because it falls within their professional mission (for example, recruitment offices, community mental health agencies, supported employment programs), and they too will profit from a successful transition.

Although some representatives may not be willing or able to participate in ITP team meetings, they can still provide valuable input to the team.

Teams may not always be able to identify specific agencies or institutions for a given student's transition interests. For example, students who know they want to enter immediately into the world of work may not yet be certain of what type of work is desired. Students who want to enter a particular trade may not yet be sure of the level of skill they are most interested in pursuing, and team members may not know if immediate job entry, additional vocational training, community college, or baccalaureate education is most appropriate. In such cases, knowledgeable professionals can inform the team as to the nature of the different options, what the additional options may be, and requirements for obtaining the different options. They can also identify other representatives of the team they should consider contacting. In many school systems, those responsibilities fall to a transition specialist, or a career counselor or guidance counselor.

The professional accreditation standards for school counselors (Council for Accreditation of Counseling and Related Educational Programs 2009) state that school counselors should be prepared to facilitate education transitions. However, research studies have found that approximately one-third of counselors do not participate in transition planning for students with disabilities (see Milsom and Hartley 2005). Given that high school counselors are often involved in advising high school students about college admissions criteria and strategies, their involvement in a coordinated transition effort is needed. Further, in many high schools, counselors serve as institutional liaisons with test companies that administer college entrance exams.

Standards for Educators Participating in Transition Planning. The Division on Career Development and Transition (DCDT) of the Council for Exceptional Children (2000) has recommended a number of skills and actions secondary level special educators need to be able to perform in the transition process. The skills and actions span planning, instruction, and service responsibilities. The DCDT has organized them into five categories originally proposed by Kohler (1998).

Within the first category, *student-focused planning*, educators should be able to identify students' goals and needed accommodations, identify measurable transition goals, and develop the students' abilities to participate in transition planning and activities, among other actions.

In the second category, the *student development* area, educators should teach self-determination skills, independent living and family living skills, and use mentors to facilitate student learning, for example.

As part of the third category, *Interagency Collaboration*, educators should interact effectively with community service providers and collaborate with general and vocational educators as needed.

In the *family involvement* category, educators should provide information to families about transition services and facilitate parents' attendance and participation in the transition planning process.

Within the last category, *program structures and policies*, secondary educators should be prepared to develop outcome-based curricula and provide flexible program and curricular options, among other skills.

The Council for Exceptional Children (CEC) has also identified a number of knowledge and skill standards for special education transition specialists. Many school districts employ **transition specialists,** who have specific responsibilities for coordinating transition efforts. Those individuals would serve as members of an ITP team. The standards that the CEC has identified for them reflect practices that should be the responsibility of other team members in districts that do not have designated transition specialists. Thus, they are not common core standards for all special educators, but the secondary special educator would be wise to be informed of them and skilled in as many as possible. As with other special educator standards identified by the CEC (see inside cover of this textbook), there are transition specialist knowledge and skill expectations in all ten standards areas (see CEC, forthcoming, or visit www.cec.sped.org for lists of the standards and corresponding knowledge and skills).

METHODS AND STRATEGIES SPOTLIGHT

Community Mapping

The NJCLD (forthcoming) has offered recommendations on how secondary school personnel can facilitate documentation of disability and accommodation needs for an exiting student (for example, content for the SOP document). Among its recommendations, educators should create lists of community resources through which psychological and education evaluations are available to families. Secondary educators also need to know of other district and community resources that may be useful during the transition preparation process, in addition to being aware of resources that may be needed by a young adult and family once the student has exited special education. Tindle et al. (2005) suggest that educators engage in "community mapping" to develop lists of such resources.

The intention of community mapping is to create either a geographical or abstract "map" of resources within a targeted region (the "community"). "When educators engage in community mapping, they explore such things as resources, housing, businesses, social-service providers, recreational facilities, religious institutions, neighborhood history, and public opinion about local issues" (Tindle et al. 2005).

Ideally, educators create a community map in a collaborative process. The process followed depends on the type of community map being developed.

- In the case of **geographical mapping,** the team members disperse within the target region, talking to community members and agency representatives, as well as collecting photographs and artifacts from the sites they visit to create a concrete map.
- In **abstract mapping,** the team members use resources such as the telephone and Internet to gather information on the community.

The information gathered from either approach is then assembled into a resource that team members may use for transition planning and preparation.

Students can also become involved in community mapping, following an initial mapping process by the educators (Tindle et al. 2005). In the community mapping process, participants may take on specific roles of participants; they interact in an approach known as contextualized teaching and learning (see Tindle et al. 2005 for more information).

The ITP   The transition plan is typically developed as part of the IEP meeting. However, the IEP/ITP team may meet separately for the two functions; they should not, however, think of the two programs as unrelated. Although, technically, those individuals who serve on the IEP/ITP teams solely for transition purposes are not needed for IEP development, their input into the IEP is appropriate to ensure coordination and integration of the two initiatives. When IEP team members are considering which high school English courses are most appropriate for a student with particularly low literacy skills, for example, they may need the input of a college representative to tell them which courses are more appropriate if the student will be seeking college admission.

Just as the IEP and ITP meetings may be consolidated into a single meeting, so may the IEP and ITP documents be one and the same. Although the IDEA requires that a transition plan be recorded and updated annually, the law does not specify that a separate document be drafted. Indeed, because transition goals and activities should be enacted in concert with the student's academic education, it makes sense to plan, document, and act on both types of information in a unified process. If for no other reason, the goals and activities for education and transition should not contradict one another. Proper ITPs include statements of need, profiles of a student's relevant strengths and weaknesses, annual goals, and service delivery plans for addressing those goals—all categories of information that can also be found on an IEP form. Nonetheless, some school districts do have distinct transition plans. In those cases, the IEP/ITP team has the responsibility of making sure the two plans are integrated.

In addition to the common problem of transition not being addressed in students' IEP processes, research findings indicate that teams are often not creating ITPs when they should be (for example, Cummings, Maddux, and Casey 2000; Hitchings, Retish, and Horvath 2005; Trainor 2005). Even when plans are created, there is a tendency to not follow them (Trainor 2005). Thus, the transition initiative is sorely neglected in many students' special education.

CASE 12.2	**Things are Not Always as They Appear: Matching Transition to the Student**

Case Introduction

Now that you have worked through the first case in this chapter, you should feel comfortable addressing issues in a second case. You are going to read about two high school students who have identified their career interests, although some of the adults who work with them have misgivings about those goals. As you read the case, ask yourself how sustainable goals can be identified for high schoolers, and consider how students might be involved in that process.

Ricardo and Tamara, best friends for years, are in the tenth grade. Ricardo hopes that he will go to college and study to become a journalist after completing high school. Tamara hopes to become an auto mechanic. Neither looks forward to being separated, but each wants to pursue their goals.

Tamara has helped out in her uncle's garage over the years, and she hangs out there when she's not helping out. She loves to fix things, all the more so if she can get greasy while doing it. When they were younger, children in the

continued

neighborhood knew to come to her if they needed a bicycle fixed. Now she is obsessed with fixing cars. She can be quite handy for other types of fix-it jobs as well; for example, she rehung Ricardo's locker door when it got smashed in.

Ricardo is not quite so clear as to why he wants to become a journalist. The best explanation he can give, even to himself, is that he wants to be able to express his ideas, and journalism seems like a good career for doing that. He likes the idea of writing a regular newspaper or magazine column. He hasn't taken advantage of any journalism-related clubs at school though.

Ricardo has a learning disability that affects his reading and writing abilities. He struggles to read and to write, and his literacy performances are barely passable for grade level. In addition to struggling with basic skills of reading and writing, he also has difficulty with organization of information and recall. Consequently, his reading comprehension is low, as is his ability to effectively communicate what he knows.

Tamara has been diagnosed as having ADHD-impulsive. She is very quick to act on her impulses. Her uncle constantly has to shout "stop" to prevent her from doing something to a car in his garage before she knows if it is the right thing to do. In school, her academics suffer because of her impulsivity. She performs terribly on exams and often blurts out answers or opinions in class before they are fully formed.

Ms. Stewart, a civics teacher, is sure that it is more than Tamara's ADHD that causes her to speak out so often in civics class. She finds Tamara to be impassioned about rights and opportunities for those she considers marginalized in society. Although not particularly well informed, in part because she seems seldom to complete assigned readings, Tamara argues for what she believes with fervor. Ms. Stewart thinks Tamara should go to a liberal arts college, where she hopes Tamara will embrace her social justice interests and leave mechanics for a hobby.

Ms. French, a guidance counselor, likewise thinks that Ricardo is not being thoughtful about his interests when he says he wants to become a journalist. He seems defeated about his own literacy skills, so she cannot understand what drives this interest. He doesn't seem to be able to defend it beyond saying it would be something he is sure he would like to do.

CASE QUESTIONS

1. What types of activities should Ricardo be engaged in to help him determine the validity of his interests in journalism?

2. Because Tamara seems to be passionate about both mechanics and social justice, how can she explore if either interest represents a career, hobby, or community participation goal for her?

3. Because some of the adults on Tamara's IEP team believe auto mechanics would make a better hobby than career choice for Tamara, how can she appropriately express her interests in mechanics to her team?

Chapter Question
ALERT

In this section, you will find information that answers a Chapter Question:

5. What skills should students develop to participate in their transition planning, as well as for continued success following the time of transition?

Transition Practices

Mellard and Lancaster (2003) summarize research on transition to cite the following as best practices in transition preparation:

- Individualized transition planning and plans
- Parent involvement in transition planning
- Interagency collaboration
- Social skills training
- Vocational training
- Paid work experience during school

Unfortunately, parents and agency representatives are not consistently invited to transition planning meetings and individualized plans are not routinely based on student interests, preferences, and needs (Williams and O'Leary 2001, cited in Mellard and Lancaster 2003).

Before students become engaged in activities such as vocational training, work experiences, or selecting electives intended to facilitate a transition, the goals behind such activities should be clearly articulated. Those goals should emanate from the student's strengths and interests.

Identifying Transition Goals and Plans

The process for identifying a student's transition goals and plans is essentially no different than that for identifying academic and functional performance goals and plans. With the student's and family's interests as well as the student's strengths and needs in mind, the team collaborates to identify annual goals that are obtainable. Of course, those annual goals must contribute toward realizing an ultimate transition goal. Thus, the team members should not limit themselves simply to planning for where a student will transition to next. They should also consider why the student will go there (for example, does a student entering the military plan to become a career soldier or move on to something else after one term of enlistment? Would Ricardo or Tamara be better off in a technical college or an institution with a wider range of major options?). Transition goal planning should take into account the students' goals and needs in relation to each of the quality of life domains. Furthermore, the students must be actively involved in the planning process.

Self-Determination

Self-determination is the process of taking lead of one's own life by setting personal goals and making decisions about one's own quality of life. Therefore, **self-determination** is one's ability to set goals, make choices, and self-assess, as well as to act on those abilities by problem-solving and self-advocating (Eisenman 2007; Trainor 2005). Certainly others may give input into that process, but self-determined individuals have primary control (Wehmeyer 1996). Self-determined individuals know, for example, what living arrangement they want, what type of occupation and lifestyle is desired, and what pathways are involved in getting there (for example, Kenny et al. 2007). Having positive self-determination skills is essential to setting realistic goals and succeeding (Eisenman 2007). There are positive correlations between self-determination skills and both employment and adult living outcomes for youths with disabilities (Gerber, Ginsberg, and Reiff 1992; Wehmeyer and Schwartz 1997; see also Halpern et al. 1995).

In light of the importance of self-determination, promoting it has become an important special education practice, endorsed as an integral part of transition preparation (for example, Carter et al. 2006; Skinner and Lindstrom 2003; Trainor 2005; Wehmeyer 2007), and required since the 1999 IDEA Regulations.

Teaching Skills of Self-Determination. At any life stage, knowing what you want to accomplish in the quality of life domains and having the needed dispositions to be successful can be a challenge. This assessment poses a particular challenge to the many high school students who do not know what career they want to embark upon to start their adult lives. Even when they do know, or think that they do, they still need to understand their own strengths and needs in relation to attaining that goal, in addition to having realistic self-dispositions for success.

"Teaching self-determination skills can be an effective prevention activity aimed at reducing students' involvement in risky behaviors and tipping the scales toward their persistence in school" (Eisenman 2007). The many young adults with mild disabilities who have diminished qualities of life upon exiting high school (Sitlington and Frank 1999; Scanlon and Mellard 2002) would likely benefit from improved skills of self-determination. For example, students with mild disabilities who drop out often understand the negative consequences associated with dropping out, but do so anyway (Bounds and Gould 2000; Kortering, Braziel, and Tompkins 2002). They would benefit from self-determination interventions that instill in them the foresight and wherewithal to commit to remaining in school.

Trainor (2005) found evidence that only two of fifteen high school students she studied had participated in any preconference strategies to engage them or identify their transition preferences. Interviews with those students revealed that they typically did not know what steps to follow to realize their goals. What's more, Trainor observed that the students were rarely addressed once in the ITP meetings, even when their goals for the future were being discussed.

Factors that positively influence the effectiveness of self-determination programs for students with mild disabilities include the following:

- Using curricula for teaching self-determination,
- Teaching for and coaching students' participation in their education planning (for example, the IEP/ITP process), and
- Student practice in choice and decision making outside of instructional contexts (Karvonen et al. 2004).

Making choices and self-advocacy are the skills most often targeted in self-determination interventions for students with mild disabilities (Algozzine et al. 2001). Multi-component interventions are not common (Eisenman 2007), although they clearly are needed.

THINK BACK TO THE CASE about Ricardo and Tamara . . .

1. *What types of activities should Ricardo be engaged in to help him determine the validity of his interests in journalism?*

It is perfectly plausible that Ricardo is sincerely interested in becoming a correspondent, and that, despite his current literacy skills deficits, he could go on to be successful in that line of work. However, the adults responsible for planning for his transition needs doubt his thoughtfulness.

Ricardo could complete a career interest inventory to help him consider whether he is truly interested in journalism. Additionally, he could participate in setting goals for learning about his avowed profession. To meet those goals, he could also begin to engage in activities that will teach him about journalism. His team could encourage him to join one of the journalism clubs in his high school, such as the student newspaper; he might be steered toward English electives that would require journalistic writing. The ITP team could also arrange for Ricardo to visit with a journalist or to do an internship or after-school job with a local newspaper. Any of these activities should result from the team carefully considering the types of experiences Ricardo should have to form fuller insights about his career choice. The team should not neglect to help Ricardo explore other career options as well.

Despite the established importance of developing students' self-determination skills, few validated self-determination curriculums exist (Algozzine et al. 2001; Carter et al. 2006). Based on those curriculums that have been studied, we are able to identify important components of effective practices. Effective self-determination interventions include the following three components:

- Goal setting,
- Setting and acting on plans, and
- Goal and plan modification (Wehmeyer et al. 2000).

Wehmeyer (2007) has identified the following ten "guidelines" for promoting students' self-determination skills that are consistent with the three components:

- Model problem solving for your students.
- Tell students you believe they are capable of making things happen in their lives.
- Emphasize students' strengths and uniqueness.
- Create a learning community that promotes risk taking.
- Promote choice making.
- Empower students to make decisions and set goals.
- Teach self-determination skills.
- Encourage self-directed learning.
- Involve peers without disabilities to provide social and academic support.
- Use technology to support self-direction.

The guidelines identify steps special and general educators can take to promote self-determination within the general education classroom and curriculum. As Wehmeyer notes, self-determination skills can be taught in isolation, yet students' ability to apply them should be enhanced by experiencing them within the curriculum.

As Wehmeyer (2007) notes, most states' curriculum standards include problem-solving skills. In addition, content-area teachers have identified problem solving as an essential skill for comprehending content and for participating in classroom learning routines (Bulgren et al. 2006). Still, many students are not taught procedures to follow for effective problem solving. Generic steps of problem solving include "(1) identifying and defining the problem, (2) listing possible solutions, (3) identifying the impact of each solution, (4) making a judgment about a preferred solution, and (5) evaluating the efficacy of the judgment" (Wehmeyer 2007). Skills such as problem solving are learned in part by the steps of the process being explicitly taught, as well as by teacher and peer modeling, but are also learned through application (review Chapter 2 for more on these instructional techniques). Classroom learning communities are one effective venue for promoting problem-solving skills. When a classroom or a cooperative group becomes a learning community, students work together in a respectful way, guiding and relying on one another. In a learning community, students are able to take risks, explore decision options, apply their strengths, and receive support and encouragement from others. Self-determined learners are, by definition, learners who are responsible for planning, executing, and evaluating their own decisions, but that does not mean they need to perform those skills in isolation.

Effective promotion of self-determination includes adults (for example, teachers and parents) ceding control and responsibility over to students for goal setting and success (Wiest et al. 2001). Adults need to guide students in possessing and using the skills necessary for success, as well as in recognizing their own proactive abilities. In addition to gaining a stronger sense of self, students who develop self-determination skills will actually commit positive actions such as self-advocacy, which will have a direct, positive impact on their transition success.

Research Evidence

Self-Determination Training Makes a Difference. Although self-determination is not necessarily a new concept, the expectation to teach self-determination as part of special education is fairly new. Consequently, as has been noted, self-determination is seldom addressed in secondary students' IEPs or ITPs (Karvonen et al. 2004). Consequently, although the field recognizes the importance of self-determination, educators are less certain as to how to teach for it (Wehmeyer, Agran, and Hughes 2000). Teachers are not helped by the fact that "little research exists that attempts to determine the conditions that either support, or are barriers to, implementing strategies to promote SD skills" (Karvonen et al. 2004). As Carnine (2000) reminds us, most teaching practices lack sufficient research to validate their effectiveness. Further, Carter and colleagues (Carter et al. 2006) found that students with EBD are rarely included in existing studies on teaching self-determination.

Although our knowledge base is limited, Browder et al. (2001) have researched the professional literature to provide a "map" of reliable resources that do exist. They organized their review of nearly 800 publications and materials into two "paths"; one guides educators to learn more about the concept of self-determination, and the other informs on ideas for instruction and environmental support in education settings. This helpful publication includes (a) references to additional research reports and a variety of the published resources reviewed, as well as (b) tips for educators on how to interpret both the literature review findings and the original sources reviewed.

The **self-determined learning model of instruction** (SDLMI) (Wehmeyer et al. 2000) is a curriculum used to teach students with mild disabilities to change inopportune experiences as part of effecting positive self-determined outcomes. The model was designed in recognition that students may be able to set goals and work toward them but that environmental factors (for example, others' attitudes, policies, the availability of opportunities) may prevent full attainment of desired outcomes (see Wehmeyer et al. 2000; Kenny et al. 2007).

The SDLMI curriculum involves a three-phase problem-solving sequence. At each phase, students are guided in identifying and solving problems. In the first phase, the students must determine what their goals are (see Box 12.4). Determination of the goal leads to the second phase, developing a plan to accomplish the goal (see Box 12.4). Based on the plan developed, which includes recognizing potential barriers and planning to act on the plan, the students take stock of what was learned in attempting to accomplish the goal and make appropriate adjustments to the plan; all of this occurs in phase three (see Box 12.4). Thus, students must set goals, set and follow plans related to those goals, and adjust actions based on evaluation of progress within each of the three phases of the self-determination curriculum. Although the student questions in each phase are written in the first person, the teacher guides the students through the process. The teacher will introduce the

BOX 12.4

THE THREE-PHASE PROBLEM-SOLVING SEQUENCE OF THE SDLMI CURRICULUM

INSTRUCTIONAL PHASE I FOR SELF-DETERMINED LEARNING MODEL INSTRUCTION

Set a Goal
Problem for Student to Solve: What is my Goal?

Student Question 1: What do I want to learn?

Teacher Objectives

- Enable students to indentify specific strengths and instructional needs.
- Enable students to communicate preferences, interests, beliefs, and values.
- Teach students to prioritize needs.

Student Question 2: What do I know about it now?

Teacher Objectives

- Enable students to identify their current status in relation to the instructional need.
- Assist students to gather information about opportunities and barriers in their environments.

Student Question 3: What must change for me to learn what I don't know?

Teacher Objectives

- Enable students to decide if action will be focused toward capacity building, modifying the environment, or both.
- Support students to choose a need to address from prioritized list.

Student Question 4: What can I do to make this happen?

Teacher Objectives

- Teach students to state a goal and identify criteria for achieving goal.

Note: Educational supports include: (a) student self-assessment of interests, abilities, and instructional needs; (b) awareness training; (c) choice-making instruction; (d) problem-solving instruction; (e) decision-making instruction; and (f) goal-setting instruction.

INSTRUCTIONAL PHASE 2 FOR SELF-DETERMINED LEARNING MODEL OF INSTRUCTION

Take Action
Problem for Student to Solve: What is my Plan?

Student Question 5: What can I do to learn what I don't know?

Teacher Objectives

- Enable student to self-evaluate current status and self-identified goal status.

Student Question 6: What could keep me from taking action?

Teacher Objectives

- Enable student to determine plan of action to bridge gap between self-evaluated current status and self-identified goal status.

continued

Student Question 7: What can I do to remove these barriers?
Teacher Objectives

- Collaborate with students to identify most appropriate instructional strategies.
- Teach student needed student-directed learning strategies.
- Support student to implement student-directed learning strategies.
- Provide mutually agreed upon teacher-directed instruction.

Student Question 8: When will I take action?
Teacher Objectives

- Enable student to determine schedule for action plan.
- Enable student to implement action plan.
- Enable student to self-monitor progress.

Note: Educational supports include: (a) self-scheduling; (b) self-instruction; (c) antecedent cue regulation; (d) choice-making instruction; (e) goal-attainment strategies; (f) problem-solving instruction; (g) decision-making instruction; (h) self-advocacy instruction; (i) assertiveness training; (j) communication skills training; and (k) self-monitoring.

INSTRUCTIONAL PHASE 3 FOR SELF-DETERMINED LEARNING MODEL OF INSTRUCTION

Adjust Goal or Plan
Problem for Student to Solve: What have I Learned?

Student Question 9: What actions have I taken?
Teacher Objectives

- Enable student to self-evaluate progress toward goal achievement.

Student Question 10: What barriers have been removed?
Teacher Objectives

- Collaborate with student to compare progress with desired outcomes.

Student Question 11: What has changed about what I don't know?
Teacher Objectives

- Support student to reevaluate goal if progress is insufficient.
- Assist student to decide if goal remains the same or changes.
- Collaborate with student to identify if action plan is adequate or inadequate given revised or retained goal.
- Assist student to change action plan if necessary.

Student Question 12: Do I know what I want to know?
Teacher Objectives

- Enable students to decide if progress is adequate, inadequate, or if goal has been achieved.

Note: Educational supports include: (a) self-evaluation strategies; (b) choice-making instruction; (c) problem-solving instruction; (d) decision-making instruction; (e) goal-setting instruction; (f) self-reinforcement strategies; (g) self-monitoring strategies; and (h) self-recording strategies.

students to each of the questions and may paraphrase them in some instances. The teacher objectives (see Box 12.4) guide the teacher in helping the students to understand and respond to each of the student questions. Across all phases, the teacher guides the students, gradually ceding control of the process to the students (that is, scaffolding) (Palmer and Wehmeyer 1998; Wehmeyer et al. 1998).

Because employment is a central aspect of adult living, many transition and self-determination curricula address it. However, career development curriculums are often developed based on the aspirations (for example, independent living, career oriented) of middle-class European Americans (Rojewski 2002). For that reason, career guidance that prioritizes career advancement over family and community focuses narrowly on attaining high income; guidance that reifies middle-class values may clash with the quality of life aspirations of students from cultures other than middle-class European American. Responding to cultural differences relates to how transition and self-advocacy curriculums are delivered as well. African American and Hispanic American male students, for example, are more likely to problem-solve and discuss imminent academic concerns (for example, attendance) when talking about transition at home (Trainor 2005). Therefore, effective transition planning for traditional African American and Latino students in particular should directly involve the family.

Vocational aptitude tests are sometimes used to help adolescents discern possible career tracks. The tests range from those that ask students their opinions to those that assess ability in specific skills associated with various occupations. The Carl D. Perkins Vocational and Applied Technology Education Act of 1990 (and its 1998 Amendments) includes the requirement that students enrolled in vocational education take vocational aptitude tests to discern their vocational education needs and likelihood for successful completion of the program. Although vocational aptitude tests are not required for other students enrolled in special education or general education, they can be useful for those populations as well. For examples of vocational aptitude tests (including ability and interest measures), visit the Career Exploration Tools section of the O*NET website (www.onetcenter.org/tools.html).

Regardless of the predictive qualities of vocational aptitude tests, events can happen in students' lives after taking the tests that may alter their interests and goals. For this reason, students and transition team members need to remember that results of aptitude tests do not constitute a foregone conclusion for the students' future directions. In many instances, new opportunities and interests that arise should be explored.

THINK BACK TO THE CASE about **Ricardo and Tamara . . .**

2. *Because Tamara seems to be passionate about both mechanics and social justice, how can she explore if either interest represents a career, hobby, or community participation goal for her?*

There is evidence from Tamara's experiences that she has thought out her career interests more than has Ricardo. Although her civics teacher, Ms. Stewart, has identified

continued

another area that Tamara might wish to explore, the team should be careful to encourage Tamara to consider various options instead of dictating a direction for her. Certainly a career inventory might be helpful to Tamara and her team. Tamara can also apply problem-solving skills to discern the nature of her interests. Following a procedure such as SDLMI, Tamara can challenge herself by questioning why she wants to be a mechanic and what her life will be like if she becomes one. Within that process, she can, with assistance from her team, identify exploratory/preparatory experiences she should have and set plans to both have those experiences and evaluate what she learns from them.

Self-Advocacy

As the expectation for students to be self-determinate about their goals reflects, the students play critical roles in effective transitions. Typically, by the young adult years, students with mild disabilities assume primary responsibility for transition-related activities. For that reason, students must learn how to self-advocate.

Self-advocacy builds from self-determination. By using **self-advocacy,** students express and work toward their own goals. Self-advocating includes both expressing and negotiating for one's own interests, needs, and rights (Van Reusen et al. 2002). Self-advocacy activities may be as simple as selecting classes, arranging one's own accommodations, or naming a career path.

Students who are able to self-advocate have self-awareness, self-acceptance, awareness of their rights and resources, assertiveness, and problem-solving skills (Hicks-Coolick and Kurtz 1997). They "become self-advocates when they (a) demonstrate an understanding of their disability; are aware of their legal rights; and (c) can competently and tactfully communicate their rights and needs to those in positions of authority" (Skinner 1998, as cited in Skinner and Lindstrom 2003).

Furthermore, they must be aware of effective accommodations and strategies (Skinner and Lindstrom 2003; see also Milsom and Hartley 2005). To be effective self-advocates, they must know how to actually secure the services to which they are entitled (Milsom and Hartley 2005). However, as Madaus and Shaw (2006) found, many postsecondary students with mild disabilities are not aware of their own disabilities and needs. Also, people with LD have been found reluctant to self-disclose their learning disability status and needs in the workplace for multiple reasons, but principally due to a lack of knowledge about their own disabilities (Price, Gerber, and Shessel 2002). The self-esteem and social skill difficulties of people with disabilities can also cause them problems with attempting to self-advocate (Skinner and Lindstrom 2003).

VIDEO CASE CONNECTIONS BOX

Watch the Video Case entitled *Social and Emotional Development: Understanding Adolescents*. Identify instances of guidance counselor Shaina Martinez modeling or coaching her students' self-determination and self-advocacy skills for appropriate behavior.

THINK BACK TO THE CASE about **Ricardo and Tamara . . .**

3. *Because some of the adults on Tamara's IEP team believe auto mechanics would make a better hobby than career choice for Tamara, how can she appropriately express her interests in mechanics to her team?*

Beginning with planning, Tamara can carefully reflect on her interests in mechanics. Tamara should be able to articulate not only her interests in auto mechanics, but a clear understanding of the work and lifestyle options for a mechanic, as well as an appreciation of how one becomes a mechanic and how prepared she is to succeed in that process. By constructively sharing that information with her team, Tamara can collaborate with them to determine if and how to pursue her interest.

Teaching Self-Advocacy Skills. Schreiner (2007) suggests that self-advocacy goals be written into IEP/ITPs; she recommends, for example, that the annual goals include that "the student will describe the nature of his/her special education program services . . . the student will access appropriate helpers and resources to address challenges presented by the disability" (302–3). Writing the goals into the IEP/ITP is a way to ensure they get addressed, she suggests.

Van Reusen et al. (2002) have validated a strategy for students to identify their own goals and advocate for them. The Self-Advocacy Strategy can be applied to participation in IEP/ITP development and in transition settings such as the workplace, living environment, or postsecondary institutions. The following mnemonic device I PLAN (Elksnin and Elksnin 1996; Van Reusen et al. 2002) reminds students of the steps of the process.

Inventory strengths, weaknesses, goals, and learning choices.
Provide your inventory information.
Listen and respond.
Ask questions.
Name your goals.

The *inventory* step takes place prior to an IEP/ITP meeting or other situation that calls for students to self-advocate. In that step, the students identify their goals, needs, and desires that are appropriate to communicate in the upcoming meeting. For the sake of an IEP/ITP meeting, the areas addressed should span the quality of life domains (Halpern 1993). In a meeting related to securing college or workplace accommodations, students should be prepared to focus on just the priority goals and needs for success in those contexts. To inventory goals, needs, and desires, students should consider (a) strengths, (b) areas to improve or learn, (c) goals, options, and preferences for (d) learning and (e) accommodations.

Once students have created an inventory, the content needs to be communicated effectively. Following the I PLAN steps, students share their goals, and so on, with others. Van Reusen et al. note that each step of the I PLAN strategy calls for specific skills that must be learned and practiced with an educator familiar with both the I PLAN strategy and the planning/transition situation in which the students will make use of the strategy.

METHODS AND STRATEGIES SPOTLIGHT

Using Ear Buds to Guide Students' Self-Advocacy in the Transition Planning Process

Preparing students to participate in transition planning meetings is essential, but does not guarantee they will participate successfully when the time comes. Discussing the meeting in advance and preparing for specific scenarios are helpful preparation activities that are commonly used (for example, Test and Neale 2004; Van Reusen et al. 2002). Goodman and Duffy (2007) have studied an effective approach to coaching a student *during* the transition meeting.

Using bug-in-ear (BIE) technology (Goodman and Duffy 2007), a student can receive telecommunicated prompts from a coach observing the actual transition meeting. The student wears an earbud and the coach speaks into a radio transmitter. Because the student is using a personal listening device and the coach communicates via microphone (possibly a cell phone) outside of the meeting group, their interactions are not observed by other members of the team. The coach's role is to prompt the student, not to provide the student with specific content. So, if a student has difficulty naming goals, the coach might prompt "read the rest of your goals" or "tell them about the job exploration you want to do this summer."

Using BIE technology does not replace preparation activities. Students should still identify their strengths, needs, and goals in advance of the meeting, as well as discuss the format of the meeting and even rehearse (Test and Neale 2004; Van Reusen et al. 2002). Advance preparation reduces student anxiety during the meeting. When that preparation includes practice using BIE procedures, student anxiety during the actual meeting is further reduced, as the student feels supported and knows how to make use of the coaches' prompts during actual meetings (Goodman and Duffy 2007).

CHAPTER SUMMARY

Transition initiatives were developed in response to the limited successes that students with disabilities have had upon leaving school. Although, overall, the quality of school outcomes has improved for students with mild disabilities since the beginning of the transition initiative in the mid-1980s, many still make unsatisfactory accomplishments once out. In education and employment sectors, those with disabilities are underrepresented and less accomplished when they do participate. In their personal lives as young adults and adults, many report limited independence and personal satisfaction.

The transition initiative was initially focused almost exclusively on employment as an outcome. Although this is an important adult outcome, other aspects of well-being are also necessary to leading a good quality of life (Halpern 1985). Areas such as health, having and meeting personal goals, and being satisfied with one's own circumstances are also important. For these reasons, the concept of transition has been expanded to consider both the paths to successful employment and other dimensions of living.

Consistent with this expanded view, transition teams must be aware of the contexts into which a student might transition. That awareness includes anticipating the knowledge and skills the student will have to have to select that destination and to thrive in that context. Preparing for the world of work versus postsecondary education, for example, requires different preparation experiences. One of the most challenging transition preparation activities is identifying appropriate goals for students.

Setting goals and plans for transition, as well as acting on those plans, continues to be neglected in special education practice. Individualized education program planning teams have responsibility for determining if students will need help with transitions. The ITP they develop is much like an IEP, only

focused on transition. Beginning with an awareness of the demands of various post-school options and of the students' interests, the IEP/ITP team needs to work with the students to plan experiences that will result in the students having successful transitions. The entire process should be "results-oriented" (*IDEA* 2004).

Transition success is not limited to the students making it into whatever institution or circumstances come next; rather, it includes the students thriving. Students are enabled when they have the self-determination skills to think carefully about their own interests and the self-advocacy skills necessary to ensure their disability-related needs are met.

KEY TERMS

Individualized Transition
    Plan (ITP), 402
Quality of Life, 402
Self-Advocacy, 432

Self-Determination, 425
Summary of Performance (SOP), 416
Transition, 401
Transition Planning, 402

Transition Specialists, 422
Tuition In, 406
Young Adult, 401
Well-Being, 402

APPLICATION ACTIVITIES

Using information from the chapter, complete the following activities that were designed to help you apply knowledge that was presented in this chapter.

1. Locate an IEP form as well as a sample individualized transition plan (ITP) (samples are available on the book-specific website). Determine where on the IEP form to record the content called for on the ITP. Based on this activity, think critically about whether transition planning can be satisfactorily addressed with or without a separate ITP form.

2. Make a list of reasons you intend to become an educator. Also list your strengths that will contribute to your success as (a) a student

learning to become a teacher and (b) as a new teacher. Next, complete a vocational aptitude test (for example, visit O*NET) and reflect on how the findings relate to your interest in becoming an educator.

3. Review the CEC knowledge and skill standards for transition specialists. Think critically about how well prepared you are to satisfy each for the students in the cases from this chapter (Adam, Tamara, and Ricardo).

4. Meet with a special education student preparing to transition either to a different educational setting or out of school. Talk with that student about his or her concerns and goals.

TECHNOLOGY FOR TRANSITION PLANNING AND PREPARATION

Numerous websites are available for teachers interested in transition. The following list provides a sample of websites that provide research articles and materials.

National Center for Secondary Education Transitions

www.ncset.org

This website provides a variety of useful resources for educators, students, and families. A wide variety of published "briefs" inform on many facets of transition. Regional resources can also be located via the website.

O*NET Resource Center

www.onetcenter.org

The O*NET website is sponsored by the U.S. Department of Labor. On the expansive website, you can find information about an extensive array of occupational options. Information includes profiles of needed skills and competencies for various occupations.

You may also wish to read the following:
C. A. Mull and P. L. Sitlington, "The Role of Technology in the Transition to Postsecondary Education of Students with Learning Disabilities" (*The Journal of Special Education* 37(2003):26–32.

Visit the book-specific website at www.cengage.com/education/ boyle for a variety of study tools such as web links, tutorial quizzes, glossary/flash cards, bonus material not included in the text, and more.

The premium website offers access to additional materials, including the Video Cases. Go to www.cengage.com/login to register or purchase access.

Collaboration and Co-Teaching to Enhance Instruction

13

CHAPTER QUESTIONS

1. What are the defining characteristics of effective collaboration?

2. What skills are needed for effective collaboration and co-teaching?

3. What are the roles and responsibilities of collaborators and co-teachers?

4. What can teachers do to design effective collaborative classrooms?

5. What can teachers do to teach effectively in collaborative or co-taught classrooms?

How do educators collaborate, and why do they do it?

Collaboration involves two people working together to achieve a common goal. It can include a variety of educators and parents. In the case of co-teaching, collaboration usually involves teachers who are working together to instruct students with disabilities in a regular education setting. Typically, the setting is an inclusion classroom and, more than likely, the classroom is composed of regular education and special education students with mild disabilities. Collaboration involves more than just getting together and starting to work together. It involves learning about collaboration, as well as learning specific skills to collaborate and co-plan effectively. As teachers become more comfortable working together and learning about collaboration, they become more effective teachers. Furthermore, through training and development, they can begin to teach more diverse groups of students.

According to a study by the National Center on Educational Restructuring and Inclusion (NCERI 1995), the collaborative or co-teaching model was the most frequently cited model used by schools with inclusive programs throughout the United States. In addition, NCERI (1995) data reveal positive student outcomes on academic, social, and behavior measures for students with disabilities who participated in inclusive programs. Moreover, the report indicated positive "behavioral and social outcomes" for nondisabled students, as well and no negative effects on academic skills for those students. These inclusive programs are successful due to the teachers who develop collaborative partnerships with each other, and particularly due to their efforts to make adaptations in the classroom so that *all* students benefit from instruction. In this chapter, you will learn about collaboration and co-teaching, components of effective collaboration, and different models of co-teaching.

CASE 13.1   # We've Come a Long Way Baby!

Case Introduction

In this case, you will read how two teachers work together to co-plan and co-teach. As you will see, it took time to develop a collaborative relationship and time for their collaborative skills to grow. At the end of the case, you will find case questions. These questions are meant to serve as points for reflection. Of course, if you can answer them immediately, you should do so, but you may want to wait to answer them until you have read the portion of the chapter that pertains to the particular case question. Throughout the rest of the chapter, you will see the same questions. As you see them, try to answer them.

As Jubia Maha stood in the front of the class of 26 students at Jefferson High School, she thought about how things had changed since she first started collaborating with

Richard Wilson, the tenth-grade biology teacher, four years ago. At that time, she was relegated to grading papers and occasionally helping students with assignments.

When she first began working with Richard, she was miserable. It wasn't until she sat down and began talking to him about collaboration that things changed dramatically. Even more critical was the fact that Richard became open to developing and learning about collaboration. They even attended a few professional development workshops together to learn more about collaboration and to improve their skills.

It took some time, but slowly Richard turned over more and more responsibility to Jubia. For some teachers, it is a matter of building trust with one another to fuel a collaborative partnership. For others, it is a territorial issue, to allow a stranger (that is, the collaborative teacher) to enter your class and teach "your" students. The attitudes of both

Richard and Jubia slowly changed over time. The students in their class are now affectionately referred to as "our students" and Richard goes out of his way to help all students, especially those with mild disabilities, to understand his lectures and content. Likewise, Jubia has learned to teach large groups of students and has had to brush up on her biology. It was a learning experience for both of them.

Today Jubia finished her portion of the lecture on bacteria and traded places with Richard, who began to teach the next section of the lecture on viruses. As Jubia walked around the room and monitored students, her mind drifted back to her college days as she remembered Professor Sarson's descriptions of collaborative classrooms. He would describe the harmony of two co-teachers working hand in hand to teach all students in the class. It sounded so nice when he described it.

"It wasn't easy, but we've come a long way baby," she thought to herself, referring to the long transformation from "helper" to "colleague."

As Jubia walked around the room, she monitored students' notes and headed off potential behavior problems.

"Mr. Wilson," she said, "when you mentioned that compound, RNA stood for what?"

Mr. Wilson knew that Jubia's question was a cue to him that he went too quickly describing RNA. "Ribonucleic acid," Mr. Wilson replied as he spelled the words on the board.

Immediately, students began writing it down in their notes, including one student Jubia prompted by pointing to his notebook. After a short pause, Mr. Wilson began describing how a virus attacks a host cell and takes over to make more virus particles. Periodically throughout his lecture, Jubia added facts such as, "viruses cannot multiply on their own; they need a host," and that "some viruses (for example, West Nile virus) can be spread through a carrier (for example, a mosquito)."

Similarly, Richard also added to her comments, describing which organisms can serve as hosts. It was soon time for a comparison and contrast activity.

Now it was Jubia's turn as she switched with Richard and took over at the chalkboard. Jubia loved using visual organizers to help students learn. She handed out a Venn diagram to students in the class, with the circles already traced in.

"OK," she asked, "what are the unique traits of bacteria?" as she created a Venn diagram on the board. Students looked through their notes and began to yell out answers.

"Whoa, slow down and raise your hand," Mr. Wilson said. "OK, Henry, name one trait," he followed up, as he helped Henry find the answer in his notes. When Henry gave his response, Mr. Wilson looked around the room and moved to those students who were recording the information on the wrong part on the Venn diagram. As he corrected them, he began to think about how much fun it was to work side by side with another teacher. At the same time, Jubia wrote Henry's contribution on her Venn diagram.

For Richard Wilson, this was indeed a new experience. He was a veteran teacher at Jefferson High School, with 20 years teaching experience. He taught a number of science classes, including tenth-grade chemistry. He taught the same way for years and resisted changing just because his school was "going inclusion." He was, in his opinion, the content guy who was responsible for making sure that his students learned the content well enough to pass the state standards test. Of those who took his end-of-the-year science tests, he had an 88 percent pass rate, one of the best passing rates in the school.

"My how things have changed," he thought to himself. His passing rate is even better now that he is co-teaching.

During their planning time, both Jubia and Richard discussed their students' potential learning problems and the upcoming content for the lesson. Both recorded numerous notes about who would teach each part of the lesson and the duties of the other person, originally referred to as the "drifter." Now, however, they speak of "lead" and "support" roles, and Richard even reviews IEPs with Jubia to keep current on each student's learning and behavior problems.

As the day's planning session came to a close, Richard and Jubia both remarked how much they enjoyed co-teaching together. As Jubia left the room, Richard said, "Hey, now that we are co-teaching, I never want to go back to teaching alone."

With that, Jubia just smiled and nodded her head in agreement. As she walked down the hall, she got goose bumps just thinking about what a great friendship she has developed with Richard and how much fun she is having as a co-teacher.

CASE QUESTIONS

1. Why does this collaborative teaching pair work so well?
2. With increased pressure to pass state standards tests, should regular education teachers be solely responsible for teaching all of the content? Why or why not?
3. What are the advantages of co-teaching compared to traditional teaching?

As you can see from the case, good co-teaching does not just happen overnight. It takes time and work to make a solid and long-lasting collaborative partnership. Gately and Gately (2001) believe that co-teaching is a developmental process and that teachers go through three distinct stages.

In the *beginning stage,* teachers are often cautious in their professional exchanges with one another. Their communication is limited and superficial, and their interactions are guarded. Some teachers have an especially difficult time developing social relationships with their colleagues. The first year is often the most difficult and challenging, filled with trials and tribulations as teachers test one another's limits as well as find each other's comfort zones.

Over time, teachers move to the second stage, the *compromising stage.* During this stage, teachers are open in their communication and are more supportive of their partners. A sense of give-and-take develops as teachers learn to trust one another more. Teachers in this stage will give up a favored duty or responsibility, but may expect something in return.

Finally, in the third stage, the *collaborating stage,* teachers openly communicate and interact with one another. Teachers are comfortable working with each other and develop a rapport that makes them a team. During this stage, teachers are truly concerned about how to improve their collaborative skills because they know that any improvement made in their teaching will ultimately benefit students.

As you will learn in this chapter, great co-teachers are more than just effective communicators. Great co-teaching involves getting to know the teacher next door, the one you thought you already knew. To get to that point, "co-teachers need to establish a rapport in the classroom so that kids feel that both teachers are equal" (Magiera et al. 2005). In classrooms with great teams, it is difficult to discern who is the special education teacher and who is the regular education teacher. Rapport is more than just knowledge of the content, effective communication, and well-developed support skills. As you will see in the remainder of this chapter, the whole is greater that the sum of its parts in terms of co-teaching.

The Changing Classroom: Effective Collaboration and Co-Teaching

Collaboration occurs on many levels in today's schools and can occur among different professionals. Teachers can collaborate with parents, administrators, specialists (such as a speech pathologist or physical therapist), or other teachers. Teacher-teacher collaboration is perhaps the most common type of collaboration that occurs in schools. In special education, the most common pairing is a special education teacher collaborating with a regular education teacher. These teachers commonly collaborate in content-area classes (for example, science, social studies, history, English) to teach students with and without disabilities. Throughout this chapter, we will use *collaborative teaching* and *co-teaching* as synonymous terms.

Collaboration in its "true" sense means two teachers working together to plan and teach students with and without disabilities in an inclusion or collaborative setting. Friend and Cook (1992) view collaboration as "a style for direct interaction between at least two coequal parties voluntarily engaged in

Chapter Question
ALERT

In this section, you will find information that answers a Chapter Question:

1. What are the defining characteristics of effective collaboration?

shared decision making as they work toward a common goal." It is referred to as a style because individuals can collaborate to varying degrees. For example, some teachers may choose to be more accommodating, whereas others may be more direct when interacting with others. Moreover, collaboration is a "shared process," whereby both educators are viewed as coequals valued for their expertise, and both support the learning of all students in the class. In collaborative classes, both teachers share the responsibility and care for all of the students in the class. No longer do teachers view the students as "your" students versus "my" students; rather they view the students as a collective "ours," and they share and accept the responsibility for their successes and failures in the classroom. Successful collaboration results when two teachers value each other and communicate effectively with one another to meet their students' needs.

For some teachers, collaboration means having minimal interactions with students in a co-taught class. For others, collaboration means becoming fully involved while teaching content in academic classes. Collaboration requires teachers to work together and to share. Friend and Cook (2000) point out the following six defining characteristics of effective collaboration:

- Collaboration is voluntary.
- Collaboration requires parity among participants.
- Collaboration is based upon mutual goals.
- Collaboration depends on shared responsibility for participation and decision making.
- Individuals who collaborate share their resources.
- Individuals who collaborate share accountability.

Collaboration is voluntary. Collaboration works best when two teachers volunteer to collaborate. Like some school initiatives, mandating that teachers collaborate rarely works. Typically, teachers who have worked together in some capacity in the past are more amenable to collaborating than teachers who have never worked together. In most cases, teachers form a natural pairing and both look forward to working together. Teachers who have already developed a bond and established communication and collaborative working skills often make an ideal pair to begin collaboration Gately and Gately (2001). Despite these teachers having an established working relationship, principals and other administrators should support them to ensure their continuing relationship, as well as to encourage new pairs of teachers to collaborate. Support from administrators and others can come in many forms. For example, principals might offer incentives such as smaller class sizes for beginning collaborators, flexible scheduling so that collaborators can meet frequently, opportunities to attend professional development workshops, opportunities to decide upon class makeup, and the like. Incentives and other supports can often prompt other teachers to begin establishing a collaborative relationship with other educators.

Collaboration requires parity among participants. Simply put, **parity** involves viewing your colleagues as equals. Parity is likely to develop when both teachers have respect for one another's skills as teachers. According to Friend and Cook (2000), if one teacher views the other teacher as lacking in expertise, parity is unlikely to develop. Respect is a key component to keeping the relationship working and viable over the years.

Collaboration is based upon mutual goals. Collaboration works best when two teachers have the same shared goals. For collaborative pairs, this means having open discussions about goals and expectations for their impending work together. When using mutually agreed-upon goals, two teachers can work together to accomplish them. Although the pair may not agree with all of the goals, Friend and Cook (2000) point out they need only to agree upon one goal to make the collaborative relationship work.

Collaboration depends on shared responsibility for participation and decision making. Shared participation and decision making are key components of effective collaboration. We often hear from co-teachers that their participation is limited and that they are omitted from the decision-making process. When teachers have not been trained to collaborate or when one of the teachers makes all of the decisions, the other teacher may harbor resentment or may refuse to fully accept ownership of all of the students in the class. Those teachers may still be grateful to be collaborating, but simply wish for a greater role in the collaborative partnership. For some teachers, this does not necessarily mean an equal division of labor between the pair (Friend and Cook 2000). For instance, some teachers may be happy serving in a support role for the pair. One teacher may lecture in the front of the room while the other teacher records notes on the board, asks questions, and monitors student note taking.

Individuals who collaborate share accountability for outcomes. As previously mentioned, not only do co-teachers share participation, but they also share accountability for outcomes. Working as a pair or group, the members work toward a common goal and share the responsibility for reaching that goal. It is a group effort to assist the students, and all members of the group work toward that end.

Finally, *individuals who collaborate share resources.* Teaching resources fall into three general categories: teaching materials, classroom space, and knowledge or skills. Teaching materials include all of those materials used in the classroom, from books and worksheets to quizzes and tests to computers and electronics. Classroom space is another shared resource. We have known collaborative teachers who push a cart from classroom to classroom because they do not have a classroom or any place to store their teaching materials. These "nomadic" teachers work with different teachers and move to each new classroom ready to co-teach the next group of students. Teachers with fixed classrooms should share space so that these co-teachers can store their materials and have a place to call home.

VIDEO CASE CONNECTIONS BOX

Watch the Video Case entitled *Teaching as a Profession: Collaboration with Colleagues*. As you listen to teachers discuss the process and benefits of collaborating, followed by observing a collaborative team meeting, identify at least one instance of each of Friend and Cook's (2000) six defining characteristics of effective collaboration.

Teachers also share knowledge and skills for teaching students with disabilities. In collaborative contexts, teachers will share what they learned from books, classes, or professional development activities with others. These skills and techniques are viewed as public property, void of any one person's ownership, and are meant to be shared and used by all.

THINK BACK TO THE CASE about Mr. Wilson and Mrs. Maha . . .

1. *Why does this collaborative teaching pair work so well?*

The co-teaching of Jubia and Richard contains many of the six defining characteristics of effective collaboration previously listed. For them, collaboration is very much a voluntary process that each enjoys. You can see that the partnership has parity, and each teacher has respect for the other. You can also see that they share responsibility when working with all of the students (that is, those with and without disabilities) and they share decision making (for example, Richard reads IEPs and the teachers plan lessons together).

Chapter Question

ALERT

In this section you will find information that answers a Chapter Question:

2. What skills are needed for effective collaboration and co-teaching?

Skills Needed for Effective Collaboration and Co-Teaching

For teachers to work together effectively, they must possess or acquire skills that allow them to communicate clearly to their partners and that enable them to provide support to one another throughout their working relationship. Some individuals already possess these skills and are effective communicators in their own right. However, some individuals lack the appropriate communication and support skills and may benefit from professional development activities to enhance their skills. Four key skills are important for effective collaboration: (1) communication skills, (2) support skills, (3) problem-solving skills, and (4) co-planning skills.

Communication Skills

Teachers need effective communication skills to be productive and to develop healthy working relationships with colleagues. Those communication skills involve understanding both verbal and nonverbal communication, as well as effective listening. According to Friend and Cook (2000), effective communication involves active listening as well as interpersonal communication skills or verbal communication skills.

Active Listening Skills. Active listening means that the person listening is engaged in the conversation and trying to understand what is being said. Effective listeners typically use nonverbal cues, body movements, vocal cues, posture, and verbal cues to communicate with and understand the person who is speaking. Active listeners lean forward slightly toward the speaker, maintain eye contact with the speaker, and use verbal and nonverbal cues to communicate their attention and involvement in the conversation. All of these ingredients are necessary to be a good listener.

Nonverbal Listening Cues

Miller (2005) reports that 93 percent of communication comes through facial expressions and vocal intonations. For collaborators, this means that paying attention to nonverbal cues is essential for understanding the message. Nonverbal cues can express feelings that are too upsetting to state and are usually a more accurate indication of the true intent of the message (Miller 2005). Nonverbal cues include body language, vocal cues, and encouragers.

Body Language

Body language includes body posture, gestures, and facial expressions that serve as cues to inform us about underlying messages that accompany verbal messages. We often use body language to add meaning to our spoken messages. The gestures and facial expressions show the speaker that the listener is attending to the conversation and doing his best to understand what is being said. Although body language by itself has no exact meaning, it can confirm or reject the spoken words when paired with vocal language. Hence, when communicating, teachers should be cognizant of students' body posture, gestures, and facial expressions to fully understand messages and detect any mixed signals by following up with questions or summarizing information to confirm the accuracy of the message.

Vocal Listening Cues

Vocal cues are another important component of active listening. Vocal cues help the listener detect the emotion behind the spoken message. Vocal cues are provided in the pitch, tone, and volume of the spoken word. People tend to speak in a louder tone when upset; when excited, people tend to speak in a higher pitch and louder tone; when depressed, people tend to speak in a lower and quieter tone. All of these cues can help us understand the message and help others understand our message to them. Another cue called encouragers, can come in the form of nonverbal encouragements, such as nodding or smiling, or can be verbal encouragers, such as "OK," "Yeah," "Go on," or "Right."

THINK BACK TO THE CASE **about Mr. Wilson and Mrs. Maha . . .**

2. *With increased pressure to pass state standards tests, should regular education teachers be solely responsible for teaching all of the content? Why or why not?*

Although the regular education teacher is the specialist in terms of content, special educators have some content expertise; over time, they can come to know the content nearly as well as the regular education teacher. Ultimately, however, co-teachers are effective in guiding their students to learn the content, regardless of how well both teachers know the content. Therefore, both co-teachers can teach the content sufficiently for students to pass state tests.

Verbal Communication Skills. When listening to others speak or when communicating with others, it is important to be accurate in your understanding of their message and, likewise, it is important for you to try to send an accurate message. When listening to someone describing a problem, you have to be in tune to the feelings and message to ensure that you understand the problem from the speaker's perspective. Remember that you are both working toward a solution from a "shared" perspective. For example, if you ask a child to clean up his room, he may pick up toys and put them in a pile, but he may leave clothing on the floor. From the child's perspective, he has "cleaned up," yet the room still needs to be "cleaned" from your perspective. For two people to understand the solution from a shared perspective, both must do their best to make sure the message is clear and explicit and, when necessary, use questions to clarify any discrepancies. Likewise, when co-teachers make a statement about teaching, both should use questions and summary statements to ensure that each has the same or a similar perspective about the problem.

Communication and Co-Teaching

Two teachers, Akrid Samoney and David Masterpond, were talking about the English class they co-teach during their common planning time. They were trying to clarify problems that occur in English class so that they could target them for corrective action.

In college, David was an English major. He loves to teach this subject and expects his students to have the same love of English. Akrid is the special education teacher who collaborates with him. Over the past few weeks, students in his class have become more talkative, to the point where David has to stop class and wait for them to be quiet. Whenever David lectures, a small, chatty group of students in the back of the room talks. During a recent co-planning meeting, David repeatedly complained that they had to "change the atmosphere in the room." Akrid was uncertain about what David wanted to accomplish, so he tried clarifying David's statements.

"Akrid, what a rough group of eighth-graders we've got this year," David blurted out at the start of the meeting. "Those boys are really immature," he continued. Akrid sat quietly and let David talk. "I think we should really try to 'sit on them' so they grow up this year," David continued.

Akrid asked, "What do mean 'sit on them'?"

"You know, try to cut down on some of these immature behaviors," replied David.

"You mean all of the jokes and pranks they do while in class?" Akrid asked.

"No, I mean all of the talking that they do while we teach," David said, trying to clarify.

"Oh, talking, yeah, they are a loud class," replied Akrid. Akrid then asked, "When does their talking bother you? Before you begin to lecture? Or, towards the end of class?"

David then explained, "The talking that gets to me occurs when I am trying to teach them new concepts. You know, after class begins when they are taking notes and before they begin working in groups."

"So you want them to be quiet when you are lecturing, but other times are OK?" Akrid summarized.

"Yeah, I guess, their talking really gets to me in the middle of class time during my lectures," David concurred.

As you can see in this example, Akrid has to ask quite a few questions to clarify the problem that David wants to address, and Akrid uses a summarizing statement at the end to make certain that he understood the problem. Now that the problem has been identified, thanks to effective communication skills, both co-teachers can target it for corrective action.

Co-teaching has a number of advantages for students, including lower student/teacher ratio, immediate available support, exposure to varied teaching styles, and access to help for *all* students. Likewise, co-teaching has numerous advantages for teachers, including shared skills and materials, exposure to varied teaching models, increased knowledge about teaching, mutual support for one another, and greater job satisfaction (Bradley and Switlick 1997; Scruggs, Mastropieri, and McDuffie 2007), just to name a few.

THINK BACK TO THE CASE) about Mr. Wilson and Mrs. Maha . . .

3.   *What are the advantages of co-teaching compared to traditional teaching?*

Co-teaching has a number of advantages for students that include lower student/teacher ratio, immediate available support, exposure to varied teaching styles, and access to help for *all* students. Likewise, co-teaching has numerous advantages for teachers that include shared skills and materials, exposure to varied teaching models, increased knowledge about teaching, mutual support for one another, and greater job satisfaction (Bradley and Switlick 1997), just to name a few.

Support Skills

Along with verbal communication and active listening skills, support skills also play an important role in collaboration. **Support skills** are verbal and nonverbal forms of communication to show your partner that you understand the problem and any feelings associated with the problem. Supports skills are important because, along with effective listening and verbal communication skills, they aid in the development of bonds between teachers. These support skills are often the "glue" that holds the co-teaching team together. Support skills include the feedback that you provide to others.

Friend and Cook (2000) have suggested that feedback should be descriptive, specific, and concise. Moreover, it should be directed toward changeable behavior, and you should always check for agreement and understanding. Descriptive feedback refers to proving feedback in an objective, nonjudgmental form. In doing so, the observer should describe a specific event in descriptive terms and in a concise form. Rather than chat on and on about an event, describe it, check to make sure the individual understood your statements, and then move on to another area or discuss some possible solutions to the problem. When discussing solutions to problems, they should be feasible and based upon behavior that the individual can change. These guidelines allow statements to become more "objective," more about the action and less about the person.

Types of Feedback Statements. There are three main types of feedback statements: positive feedback, constructive feedback, and supportive feedback. Positive feedback statements are those in which a teacher describes affirmative actions that the person has completed. Any meetings that involve providing feedback to teachers should always incorporate positive and constructive statements. These positive statements should address actions that can be shaped over time into more appropriate target behaviors. For example, "I noticed that you were assisting Nathan with his worksheet this afternoon. You did a wonderful job giving him feedback on his answers." Again, the statement is descriptive and reflects observable behavior while providing positive reinforcement for the actions.

Constructive feedback includes statements that provide the individual with suggestions for changing actions or behavior. Constructive feedback, like the other types of feedback, should be objective and descriptive. It should describe observed events or actions and should provide recommendations for modifying those actions. According to experts, "feedback that is immediate, specific, positive, and constructive holds the most promise for bringing about change in teacher behavior" (Scheeler, Ruhl, and McAfee 2004).

Akrid and David were discussing a student who repeatedly failed to return homework. Akrid was asking David about it. "You asked what you could have done differently with Tim," said Akrid. He continued, "When I walked into the room this afternoon, I saw you speaking loudly to him for not having his homework completed. Is that what happened?"

"Yeah, that's exactly what happened," David replied.

"You do a great job communicating with students in our class, but your angry tone with Tim only told him that you were upset with him, not how to change his behaviors. I think we need to develop a plan to address his return rate of completed homework," Akrid remarked.

David agreed and the teachers began to develop a list of possible solutions to address the problem.

Co-teaching works best when both teachers have a chance to share the stage.

Nicholas Prior/Taxi/Getty Images

Supportive feedback is another type of feedback that you could provide to colleagues. Supportive feedback lets the individual know that you relate to the feelings or emotions that the person feels about an incident. In the above example, Akrid could have let David know that he empathized with David's frustration; that would help prevent David from interpreting his comments as criticism. These statements also let the individuals know how much you appreciate their support. Statements of support might include, "I agree with your idea and will help to implement it" or "I think you handled that situation well." Of course, the most effective feedback is feedback that has been solicited. Individuals who ask for assistance or advice are more likely to take your advice.

Problem-Solving Skills

Problem-solving skills are another important component of effective collaboration. Problem-solving skills can be used to help solve behavior and academic issues of students or they can be used to address issues with instruction or classroom management. When problem solving, consider not only what the student can do differently, but also what the teacher(s) can do differently to help remediate the problem.

Problem solving can be approached from many different perspectives. Perhaps one of the best approaches is Knackendoffel's (2005) collaborative problem-solving approach. This particular approach uses a worksheet that incorporates 13 steps. When using this approach, teachers record information at the different steps. The following are Knackendoffel's 13 steps for problem solving:

1. *Define the problem.* The problem must be clearly defined so that all parties have a clear understanding of it. Problems that are not clearly defined will result in solutions that are not appropriate. When defining a problem, state it in observable and measurable terms that all parties can agree on.

2. *Gather specific information about the problem.* This step refers to identifying factors that are related to the problem and determining the extent to which the problem affects other areas of the student's life. Teachers also should consider other factors that may be contributing to the problem. For example, if a student is constantly failing tests, is it because the student did not study or is it because the student did not learn the information when initially presented? Or, are other factors possibly interfering with the student's performance. Also, consider the extent to which the problem is affecting other areas of the student's life. Perhaps failing a class will result in the student becoming ineligible to play sports. Gathering as much information as possible about the problem will result in a greater understanding of the problem.

3. *Explain the problem-solving process.* Explain to all parties that the problem-solving process involves keeping an open mind when generating possible solutions (that is, alternative solutions), and refraining from making judgments about possible solutions until all of the solutions are examined.

4. *Identify alternative solutions.* When generating possible solutions, all parties should consider all solutions that are generated. Writing a list of each of them is a good way to ensure each is actually considered.

5. *Summarize solutions.* When finished writing down the solutions, summarize all of them and make one final check for other possible solutions before moving on to the next step.

6. *Analyze possible consequences.* With each alternative solution, discuss the impact of each on the student and others. Discuss the benefits and other consequences of each alternative solution.

7. *Rate each solution.* After discussing the solutions one at a time, rate each solution or vote on each solution. Use a rating scale to determine how each person feels about the solutions. For example, "best," "better," and "fair" might be useful categories used to describe the alternative solutions. You could then vote on each based upon one of the three categories. Remember, in this step, you are rating *each* solution, not ranking them one versus another.

8. *Select the best solution.* After rating solutions, it is now time to determine the best solution or solutions. Choose the best solution based upon how participants rated them. If more than one solution is appropriate, chose two or even three solutions.

9. *Determine satisfaction with the chosen solution.* Once the best solution or solutions are selected, determine how others feel about implementing it. If no solution seems appropriate, return to generating new alternative solutions.

10. *State support for the decision.* Express your support for the chosen solution even if it is not the ideal solution. Discuss how the solution will benefit the student.

11. *Develop an action plan.* Once the solution or solutions are chosen, develop an action plan. This action plan should include the person responsible for each task, when each task will begin, and when each task will be completed.

12. *Develop a monitoring system and specific criteria.* Determine how and when the solution(s) will be monitored and determine criteria for success. Establishing criteria for success helps all parties involved to determine whether the goal has been met based upon their expectations.

13. *Schedule the next appointment.* Finally, conclude the problem-solving session by recording a date for the next meeting. Setting the next meeting date increases the likelihood that it will occur and places accountability on those responsible for implementing the plan.

Using Problem Solving. Using Knackendoffel's approach, let's walk through an example of what Akrid and David did during a recent problem-solving session. The main problem is Roberta Johnson's behavior during class. She is a loud student who constantly disrupts the class by talking and making inappropriate comments. Her teachers define the problem: Roberta speaks at inappropriate times and frequently has inappropriate conversations with other students during class lectures. During the gather specific information about the problem step, Akrid and David discuss how Roberta's constant talking and interruptions disrupt the class and result in the teacher lecturing her about her talking or putting her in the hallway until she can quiet down. In addition, she is earning C and D grades in English and is at risk of having to repeat the class if she fails. During the next series of steps (explain the problem-solving process, summarize solutions, analyze solutions, and rate solutions), both teachers begin generating possible solutions while withholding judgment about them until all solutions are generated and summarized. The following is their list of alternative solutions:

1. Cue Roberta so that she will remain quiet during class lectures by using a nonverbal cue. David demonstrated this by placing his finger to his own pursed lips.

2. When Roberta is sitting quietly listening to the lecture, she could receive verbal reinforcement from her teachers for sitting quietly.

3. Roberta should be taught how to self-monitor her talking. She could be given a chart on which she could record how often she is quiet and how often she talks.

4. Roberta's seat could be moved to the front of the room away from her friends.

5. Roberta could be given time to talk to friends at the beginning and end of class.
6. Every time Roberta talks excessively or disrupts class, she could be kept after school to work on additional English worksheets.
7. Using a group contingency periodically throughout class, the teacher could move a marble from one jar to another if the class is quiet. Once the 30 marbles have been moved from one jar to the other jar, the class would earn a popcorn party, 15 minutes of free time on Friday afternoon with popcorn and juice.
8. Each time Roberta is disruptive, a note could be sent home to her parents.

Next, Akrid and David reviewed and analyzed their solutions by discussing them and then finally voting on a rating for each. In the select the best solution step, David and Akrid chose to combine several solutions that included using a cuing system, verbally reinforcing her for being quiet, teaching her to self-monitor, and using the group contingency. The decision to choose these solutions came about through a discussion of satisfaction and support for these solutions and how each might show the most promise for success.

Next, the co-teachers developed an action plan. In the action plan, each teacher was responsible for carrying out one or more steps; they decided to begin the action plan the next week. Prior to beginning it, Akrid would teach Roberta how to self-monitor and David would review with the class how the group contingency program would work. Both teachers agreed that the criteria should be that Roberta should sit quietly for 90 percent of the time in class. In terms of monitoring, Akrid agreed to record the frequency and duration of her talking on a daily basis. Both teachers then scheduled a formal meeting in two weeks to discuss progress on Roberta's behaviors.

VIDEO CASE CONNECTIONS BOX

In the Video Case entitled *Students with Special Needs: The Referral and Evaluation Process*, a team of teachers collaborates on the pre-referral process to help fourth-grade teacher Mike Costello. To appreciate how collaboration can be incorporated into a teacher's routine, listen to the ways the team collaborates with Mike to problem-solve how to help his struggling student.

Co-Planning Skills

Co-planning is just as important as co-teaching. A well-planned lesson may not always guarantee a well-taught lesson, but it certainly increases the chances that the lesson will go well. Conversely, having no plan is an invitation for disaster. Therefore, it is important to have a plan that is developed by all who will teach the lesson and that has been well thought out ahead of time. During co-planning, establish a routine and, initially, use a written guide to structure co-planning time (see Table 13.1). The written guide should cover the previous lesson, should break down the new lesson into sections that can be discussed, and should include an area for assigning who will be responsible for carrying out that portion of the lesson. Each portion should be assigned based upon each teacher's skills or expertise as well as students' needs. A guide or lesson plan is needed so that both teachers are clear about their roles and responsibility during teaching.

TABLE 13.1: Co-Planning Guide and Lesson Plan

Evaluation of Previous Lesson Which portion of the lesson went well? Which portion of the lesson went poorly? Which content should be reviewed or retaught? Which activity could be used to review content that is being retaught? Are there parts of co-teaching that could be improved (that is, introduction, preview, transitions, review, preparation/distribution of materials, monitoring of students, feedback to students, and so on)?
Lesson Considerations What cognitive supports could be used in the lesson to ensure that all students learn the content? What accommodations do students with disabilities need? What effective teaching methods or supports are used in the lesson to enhance learning? What classroom management components are needed for the lesson?
New Lesson Format: **Advanced Organizer or Review of Previous Content or Skills** What will you say/do? Who does this? How long? Partner-teacher does what?
Introduction to New Content or Skills What? Who? How long? Partner-teacher does what?
Guided Practice of Content or Skills Through Activities **Activity 1** What? Who? How long? Partner-teacher does what? **Activity 2** What? Who? How long? Partner-teacher does what? **Activity 3** What? Who? How long? Partner-teacher does what?
Assessment of Learning What? Who? How long? Partner-teacher does what?
Summary or Review What? Who? How long? Partner-teacher does what?
Filler, Enrichment, or Follow-Up Activity What? Who? How long? Partner-teacher does what?

In middle or high school math classes, the special education teacher might be responsible for the warm-up portion of the class. In the warm-up, the teacher reviews problems that were previously taught and ensures that students understand previous material before moving on to new material. The regular education teacher might then take over for teaching new content while the special education teacher walks around and monitors students, checking for correctness of work and understanding of new information. Each of these areas should be worked out ahead of time and assigned to the teacher responsible for that portion.

Establishing a routine ahead of time prevents teachers from having downtime during their co-planning periods. Routines are especially important for novice teachers or new co-teachers. Routines ensure that all people know what they are responsible for during planning and what materials are needed. For example, an effective co-planning routine might involve meeting in the same room every time to plan out the next day's lesson, having all of the necessary materials that will be used during planning (for example, the textbook, the teacher's guide, paper, pencils, ancillary materials related to the lesson, the teacher's gradebook, students' work, master copies of handouts), having the school secretary hold all calls during your meeting time, having a method for recording the lesson plan (for example, one person is a scribe to record notes and you switch the next time you meet), following a set procedure (see Table 13.1), and ending within a reasonable amount of time. Again, the purpose of a routine is to minimize downtime and make the meeting flow smoothly. Planning time is such an important part of co-teaching for teams that protecting it is often a *number one* concern (Dieker 2001).

The actual co-planning guide and lesson plan can serve as a record of agreed-upon components and roles. The first portion of it serves to review the previous lesson. If planning takes place in the afternoon, an evaluation of the lesson that was taught that day would be recorded in this portion. The purpose of this section, the evaluation of previous lesson, is to learn from what did and did not work and then make the appropriate changes. Be sure that you base your decisions on data from the previous lesson. If students did not adequately learn a new concept or skill, to what extent did they not learn it? Is it based upon test or quiz results, or is it based upon oral questions? Similarly, if students mastered content or skills, how do you know they reached mastery? Did all or a small majority of students reach mastery? High-achieving students can frequently master content and skills despite the teacher's lack of skills at teaching it. Many of these students are self-motivated learners capable of learning on their own. Because you are teaching a diverse group of learners, consider whether other students (for example, average, low-achieving, and students with disabilities) reached mastery of specific skills or content (see the HALO procedure in Chapter 9). For some students, reviewing or even reteaching of content or skills may be needed for them to progress on to the next skill level.

The lesson considerations portion serves to remind teachers about cognitive supports (for example, guided notes, cognitive maps and organizers, outlines, mnemonics, study guides) that could be used to help students record better notes and remember the content of lectures. This section also prompts teachers to identify and include effective teaching methods (for example, differentiated instruction, direct instruction, discovery learning, mnemonics techniques, pause procedure) or supports that they could use to deliver content to students. The accommodations question serves to remind teachers to consider appropriate accommodations for students with disabilities (see Chapters 2 and 9 for a more detailed discussion of accommodations).

The classroom management component serves to remind teachers that different management components might be needed when using different co-teaching models. For example, if using station teaching, teachers might provide additional reinforcers (such as stickers, tokens, points) for students who are quiet, transition quietly, cooperate while working in groups, and follow directions.

The last portion of the co-planning guide and lesson plan, new lesson format, is the actual lesson plan. This portion could be modified depending upon the lesson, but be sure to use the following components: advanced organizer, introduction, guided practice activities, assessment of learning (for example, independent practice), and summary of lesson.

Roles and Responsibilities of Collaborators and Co-Teachers

Chapter Question
ALERT

In this section you will find information that answers a Chapter Question:

3. What are the roles and responsibilities of collaborators and co-teachers?

Generally, teachers negotiate and work out the roles and responsibilities of co-teaching as they begin teaching together. It is important that teachers discuss these duties to prevent any conflict between them and to prevent any misunderstanding about roles and responsibilities. To share duties, teachers must come to an understanding as to what duties each teacher is responsible for completing. Table 13.2 and Table 13.3 present typical duties

TABLE 13.2: Co-Teaching Roles and Responsibilities: Nonteaching Duties

Part I Directions: Choose a collaborative or co-taught class and list your current roles and responsibilities in this class. Each co-teacher completes a separate list. When complete, compare with your co-teacher. Of the duties listed, describe who will be responsible for completing them and which will be shared.

Part I. What are my *current* (non-teaching) responsibilities? List them under each category and briefly describe or provide an example. Use a number scale to describe how frequently you complete the task. Use 1 = rarely, 2 = occasionally, and 3 = often.

1. Taking attendance
2. Checking homework
3. Establishing a daily routine
4. Establishing classroom rules
5. Enforcing classroom rules
6. Developing or monitoring behavior management plans
7. Grading papers
8. Reporting grades
9. Completing teacher referrals
10. Writing IEPs
11. Communicating with parents
12. Other: list and describe

TABLE 13.3: Co-Teaching Roles and Responsibilities: Teaching

> **Part II Directions:** Choose a collaborative or co-taught class and list your current roles and responsibilities in the class. Each co-teacher completes a separate list. When complete, compare with your co-teacher. Of the duties listed, describe who will be responsible for completing them and which will be shared.
>
> **Part II.** What are my *current* (teaching) responsibilities? List them under each category and briefly describe or provide an example. Use a number scale to describe how frequently you complete the task. Use 1 = rarely, 2 = occasionally, and 3 = often.
>
> 1. Deciding upon content to teach
> 2. Lesson planning
> 3. Researching and selecting instructional material
> 4. Implementing instructional strategies
> 5. Working with small groups
> 6. Working with large groups
> 7. Modifying assignments
> 8. Assisting students with learning problems
> 9. Coordinating IEP goals with the curriculum
> 10. Monitoring daily performance
> 11. Preparing materials for lessons
> 12. Other: list and describe

and responsibilities of teachers. Both teachers can rate the items on the lists and then compare them against their partner's list. Through compromise and consensus building, they can decide which duties each will be solely responsible for completing, which duties each is willing to let the other complete, and which should be shared.

To achieve more positive outcomes for students, establish a more pleasant work environment, and increase the chances of pairs working together longer, teachers should go beyond merely knowing the roles and responsibilities of each collaborator (Thousand, Villa, and Nevin 2006). By doing so, they will get to know each other better in terms of their co-teacher's skills, personality, goals, and communications skills. Although the co-teaching roles and responsibilities tables help teachers the next shared activity, the Working Together Survey (see Table 13.4), allows teachers to know each other better in terms of communication, feedback, teaching support, and pet peeves.

▼

Chapter Question
ALERT

In this section, you will find information that answers a Chapter Question:

4. What can teachers do to design effective collaborative classrooms?

Designing Effective Collaborative Classrooms

Collaborative classes are often structured differently from typical regular education classrooms. With the introduction of students with disabilities and a second teacher, changes occur in the way students are taught and how the class is organized. These changes should be carefully and purposefully made to enhance the learning environment and create a community of learners.

TABLE 13.4: Working Together Survey

Directions: Choose a collaborative or co-taught class. Both co-teachers complete this list and then compare it with their co-teacher.

Communication and Feedback:

1. When is the best time of day to communicate with me?

    Are some times (such as morning) better than others?

2. How should others communicate with me?

    I prefer to be contacted in person? By e-mail? Through notes?

3. Where should we meet to discuss problems?

4. We all make mistakes. If I make a mistake when teaching, how would I like my co-teacher to address it? Slip me a note? Tell me immediately by pointing it out? Let me know after class or at a break?

Teaching:

1. What co-teaching model do/would I prefer using (for example, station teaching, interactive teaching, parallel teaching, alternative teaching, or other)?

2. What role or roles would I prefer to fulfill during our collaborative teaching?

3. What are the written rules of the class? What are the unwritten rules of the class?

4. What type of groupings would I prefer during which activities? Whole class during lectures? Small group? Peer tutoring? Cooperative learning groups? Independent seatwork? Other groupings?

5. How would I prefer to address behavioral problems, such as a disruptive student or excessive talking? Academic problems, such as a student who does not understand the concept being taught? Noise levels, particularly when the class becomes loud?

Pet Peeves: Please list any pet peeves that you might want to share, such as classroom organization, noise levels, interruptions, and so on.

When finished, share with your co-teacher!

Balancing the Number of Students in Collaborative Classrooms

When introducing new students with mild disabilities into collaborative classrooms, teachers should carefully seek a balance in the number of students with and without disabilities. As a general rule, the maximum number of students with mild disabilities should not exceed one-third of the total students in a heterogeneous inclusive or collaborative class (Klamm 1990; Roberts 1996). With one-third of students having mild disabilities, the remaining two-thirds should include average, below-average, above-average, and gifted students, resulting in a heterogeneous classroom. Likewise, Walther-Thomas et al. (2000) have recommended that balanced classes consist of approximately 10 percent to 20 percent of students with mild disabilities, 10 percent to 20 percent of high-performing students, and about 60 percent to 70 percent of average students. These authors also caution that the number of students with mild disabilities in the class should be reduced when they require extensive support. Care should be taken that a collaborative classroom does not become the automatic placement for students just because they have been identified as having a disability. Overloading the classroom with students with disabilities defeats the purpose of appropriate placement and results in a frustrating experience for students and teachers.

Grouping of Students

Within a collaborative classroom, students are typically grouped differently during instruction. The two most common groupings are the formation of cooperative learning groups and peer-tutoring pairs.

Cooperative Learning Groups. Cooperative learning consists of organizing students into heterogeneous groups of four to five students. Within each group, students are responsible for achieving both an individual and group goal (Putnam 1993; Slavin 1990). Individual accountability ensures that everyone works. Teachers can take a number of steps to ensure that individual and group accountability occurs within the cooperative groups. Teachers can have students identify an individual goal and then provide a reward, such as a separate grade, for achieving each goal. Additionally, the teacher can assign a group goal and then reward the entire group when group members achieve the goal. Before beginning cooperative learning activities, it will be useful to teach students cooperative working skills. Teachers should identify several cooperative skills that they would like students to use and teach these skills to students. These skills could include contributing ideas, accepting the ideas of others, sharing information or resources, assisting others, taking turns, and complimenting others' contributions. The specific skills will vary depending upon the skills that students already have in their repertoire and how well they use those skills in context. If you find that students lack skills, those skills should be taught by describing the skill, explaining its importance, demonstrating the skill, and having the students role-play the skills, while you provide feedback. In some cases, you can ask students to use the skill at home or in other social situations and then report about its use. (Review Chapter 2 for a detailed description of cooperative learning procedures, including cooperative skills.) Finally, teachers need to reinforce students' use of the skills once students are working in cooperative learning groups.

Classwide Peer Tutoring. Classwide peer tutoring (CWPT) is another grouping method to help students learn from one another. Using CWPT (Greenwood, Delquadri, and Carta 1997), students in the class are paired up, assigned roles as tutor or tutee, given a task, and then spend a specified amount of time practicing the task (usually 10 minutes). After the time has expired, the students switch roles and again practice the task. CWPT has been used to teach in a variety of subject areas including spelling, reading sight words, oral reading, vocabulary, and math (Burks 2004; Hughes and Fredrick 2006; Greenwood et al. 2001; Greenwood, Delquadri, and Carta 1997; review also Chapter 2 for a detailed description of CWPT procedures).

The main steps to CWPT are to distribute the materials to students (for example if using spelling, the teacher would provide the tutor with a spelling word list and points sheet, and the tutee would get a blank sheet to record words read by the tutor), students work for 10 minutes, and then switch roles. For example, the tutor begins reading spelling words one at a time to the tutee. The tutee writes down the word as the tutor looks, checking to make sure each word is spelled correctly. If the tutee spells the word correctly, the tutor awards two points. If the tutee does not spell the word correctly, the tutee practices spelling the word correctly three times while the tutor looks on, making sure it is accurate. If the tutee correctly spells the word three times, the tutor awards one point. This continues for 10 minutes, at which time the students switch roles. The group with the most points at the end of the 20-minute session is awarded a prize.

Structuring of Rules and Routines

Within collaborative classrooms, it is important to create and maintain a structure and organization that maximizes engaged time and minimizes downtime. Teachers can accomplish this with classroom rules and routines that specify the expectations of the teacher and procedures for initiating and concluding activities. Following rules and routines becomes an expectation of all students as they get older.

Classroom Rules, Written and Unwritten. Prior to beginning the school year, teachers should discuss the classroom rules, both written (for example, raise your hand and wait to be called on) and unwritten rules (for example, speak nicely and treat others with respect). They should also discuss whether to post the rules and when they will review them with students. In addition, both teachers should discuss the positive consequences for students who follow the rules. What are the rewards for following the rules? How often will rewards be given to students and by whom? Both teachers should also discuss the consequences for students who break the class rules. How will they handle student outbursts and other disruptive behavior? Finally, teachers should mention the unwritten rules for classroom behavior to students. These unwritten rules might include following teacher directions, completing your own work (no cheating), or speaking in a pleasant tone to others. Discussing these rules early can alleviate later problems.

Classroom Routines. In some classes, established routines can be as important as class rules. Routines serve to minimize disruptions and downtime and give the class a sense of organization. Routines can be used for a variety of tasks such as entering the classroom, turning in completed work, beginning the lesson, recording notes during the lecture, or completing activities after the lesson. Once routines are established and students are using them regularly, the class often can run smoothly with fewer interruptions. Teaching students about routines often requires teachers either to list or describe the steps and have students practice the steps while the teacher monitors and provides feedback.

Implementing Supports During Instruction

After careful planning, teachers need to employ supports (see Table 13.5) for students to benefit fully from instruction in the regular education or inclusive classroom. Typically, the regular education teacher thinks "globally" in terms of teaching content to the entire class, whereas the special education teacher thinks "individually" to ensure that accommodations and adaptations are made and supports are in place so that students with disabilities can benefit from the instruction (Scruggs, Mastropieri, and McDuffie 2007). These supports assist student learning by highlighting important points and organizing content. In some cases, key content is pointed out and is linked with supporting information, such as with a cognitive map. Instructional supports come in many different shapes and sizes and they serve to enhance instruction (they have been discussed in every chapter of this textbook). They can be anything from mnemonic devices to

TABLE 13.5: Examples of Instructional Supports in Academic Areas

Skill or Content	Presentation Mode	Instructional Support
Math		
Double-digit addition with carry over	Visual via overhead	DRAW strategy transparency
Science		
Order of the planets	Visual	First-letter mnemonic: *My Very Eccentric Mother Just Sent Us Neckties*
Social Studies		
Comparison of Chief Powhatan and John Smith	Verbal	Venn diagram
Written Language		
Written composition	Verbal	Cognitive map

help students remember important vocabulary, strategies to help students solve math problems, or concept maps to help students organize and structure science content. Although these devices may seem common sense, students should be taught how to use them and provided with feedback for their proper use.

CASE 13.2   **When Is Enough "Enough"?**

Case Introduction

Now that you have worked through the first case in this chapter, you should feel comfortable addressing issues in a second case. In this case, you will see how two teachers work together, even as students' grades begin to slide lower despite the high level of support the special education teacher provides.

Frank Dupree was recently awarded the Deer Park Teacher of the Year Award. Working with high school students at Deer Park, Frank teaches students with mild to moderate mental retardation. Frank has done his best to make sure that his students are prepared to live independent, self-sufficient lives. Frank was credited as being one of the first teachers in the state to get his students clerk jobs within the State Department of Health and Welfare. Such clerk jobs mean good pay and full health care coverage. Students in these jobs run errands, file and copy paperwork, and deliver interoffice mail. Recently, a similar opportunity opened up at the State Department of Game and Fisheries.

Through Frank's persuasion and persistence, state officials agreed to a trial run of the integrated employment program. Over the years, the program has grown from 2 to 32 young adults. With such a high success rate, Frank is constantly searching for other state departments to expand the job opportunities for his students. Most of Frank's students have him as their teacher for the four or more years they are at the high school. Frank combines functional skills with their academic skills. He also integrates prevocational and vocational skills into their education. As they prepare to begin a new job, Frank and coworkers coach them with on-the-job training.

Frank is a strong believer that all students should learn both academic skills (that is, those related to state standards testing) and functional skills (that is, those skills that prepare them for daily living). Not all of his students are capable of the workload; those who need an entire functional curriculum are transferred to Elaine Rabin's class. In her class, students learn functional skills and are often graduated with a certificate of completion, as opposed to a diploma. Frank likes to integrate his students into inclusion classes that pertain to the student's potential employment.

Frank teaches in two inclusion classes, literature and biology. In each, Frank switches roles from that of teaching to that of support. Frank especially looks forward to working with Elizabeth Johnson, the new biology teacher. Biology is one subject that students will need if they expect to work for the State Department of Game and Fisheries. For Frank, his idea was simple: provide the same content, and yet provide lots of visuals, organizers, guided notes, modified readings, and reteaching, as well as modified assignments. Of course, this means a lot of work for Frank, but he is willing to work overtime and weekends to make inclusion work in his school. The prior biology teacher resisted having Frank's students integrated into his class; however, Elizabeth is new and willing to try it.

As the school year began, Frank did his best to keep up with the demands of transferring the curriculum into an easily understood form for his students. The students involved in the biology class were Qaadira Sharpe, Torry Naskel, and Butto Nimby. These students were categorized with mild mental retardation and had IQ scores of 66, 69, and 70, respectively. As the school year began, Frank was able to help these students keep up with the class, but slowly, he began to realize that his students did not fully understand some concepts and their grades were beginning to reflect this fact. In the meantime, Elizabeth also saw how difficult it was for Frank to help his students keep up in the class, but she was simply following the state standards' pacing chart. As she examined the grades from the class, she saw that, with the exception of Frank's students, all of the other students were able to maintain at least a C average or better, further reinforcing her belief that her pacing and teaching were appropriate for her class. She felt that, with some minor tweaking, she could improve the borderline grades of those nondisabled students who were experiencing some difficulty. Yet, two things bothered her with Frank's approach to integrating the students with MR and his approach toward co-teaching. One, she felt that Frank was "spoon-feeding" these students and that it was neither fair nor realistic to continue doing this. Two, Frank's constant interruptions, to "reteach" small portions or to "re-explain" certain concepts often interrupted her flow in teaching and slowed her pace. This slower pace often resulted in her using Fridays as what she called, "catch-up" days.

Before long, Elizabeth began to feel that she had to express her concerns to Frank. Recently, she spoke with him after class. "Frank, could we chat for a few minutes?"

Frank replied, "Sure," not knowing what to expect. Before long, Frank was into a full conversation with Elizabeth, who was trying to convince him that it was unrealistic to expect his students to progress much further in the class because eventually they would not pass the end-of-year standards test, which counted for 80 percent of their final grade.

"Frank," said Elizabeth, "they currently have a C or D average and I really don't think they will make it."

Ever optimistic, Frank responded, "I feel that I can help them make it and that their grades will improve over time."

Elizabeth shook her head and left the room. She knew that the content would become much more difficult over time and that even her own nondisabled students would have difficulty understanding the content.

CASE QUESTIONS

1. What practices related to collaboration and co-teaching could you suggest to help Frank and Elizabeth instruct students more effectively?
2. Is it realistic to expect these students to learn and understand the content in biology?
3. What supports and modifications could Frank use to assist his students' learning?

METHODS AND STRATEGIES SPOTLIGHT

Universal Design in the Content-Area Classroom

Universal design refers to designing products and environments that are "usable by the largest group of people possible without the need for additional modifications beyond those incorporated into the original design" (Nolet and McLaughlin 2005). Universal design for learning (UDL) is a type of support that benefits everyone in the classroom, rather than just a select few students. Some refer to it as a "design-for-all" approach; UDL helps students with disabilities learn, but also benefits nondisabled students. An example of an environment universal design is a curb cut (Rose and Meyer 2002). A "curb cut" allows people who use wheelchairs to cross the street easily and travel up to the sidewalk. Not only does this benefit a person who uses a wheelchair, but also aids young people on bicycles and mothers pushing strollers. In the classroom, teachers frequently use learning supports that are based upon universal design. For example, a teacher might create guided notes that outline the lecture, with the intent to give them to students with disabilities. However, all students can benefit from well-designed guided notes, not only students with disabilities. Teachers can use or create supports based upon the universal design principle. Another example might be where teachers use a text-to-speech program that reads the text to students. Again, students with reading disabilities benefit along with others who wish to use such a program.

Typically, there are three main components of UDL. If used properly, UDL allows for one or more of the following: multiple means of representation, multiple means of expression, and multiple means of engagement (Rose and Meyer 2002). Multiple means of representation refers to information that is presented in more than one format. For example, the use of guided notes allows students both to hear and see the important points of a lecture. Multiple means of expression refers to allowing students to use alternative communication and expression to demonstrate their knowledge of a topic. Rather than complete a classroom test that requires students to write responses to essay questions, students might be able to demonstrate their knowledge by explaining it or completing a research project in which they apply those same skills that are being tested. Lastly, multiple means of engagement refers to allowing students choices about how to learn specific content. In some cases, students can read the information from a website. In other cases, students can hear the information from a text-to-speech program. Still in other cases, the students can learn content from a teacher and then use that information in an activity to apply what they have learned.

Rose and Meyer (2002) suggest four methods to improve learning though UDL, (1) providing multiple examples, (2) highlighting critical features, (3) providing multiple media and formats, and (4) supporting background knowledge.

When teachers provide multiple examples, students can see critical features and recognize patterns of a concept. For example, using digital media such as a website to learn about the animals in a desert biome, students can open hyperlinks as they read the text to see pictures, illustrations, or examples of the animals found in the biome.

Teachers can also help students learn important concepts by highlighting critical features of them. In some cases, teachers can present a simplified version and allow students to highlight the features. In other cases, teachers will want to point out or use written cues to help students see the critical parts of the concept they are learning. For example, if students are reading a math word problem, the teacher might underline or highlight critical cue words and numbers.

Using multiple media and formats is another method that teachers can use to help students understand concepts. Multiple media and formats allow students to learn about a concept through multiple senses (for example, using pictures as examples with text and hearing it described).

The fourth method is checking background knowledge and providing multiple means of representation for students who need more background knowledge. Teachers can easily check background knowledge either by asking questions pertaining to what students know about the topic or by completing the first step of a KWL chart: What do I know about the topic? (review Chapter 6 for KWL procedures).

Chapter Question
ALERT

In this section you will find information that answers a Chapter Question:

5. What can teachers do to teach effectively in collaborative or co-taught classrooms?

Teaching Effectively in Collaborative and Co-Taught Classrooms

Effective teaching is effective whether one teacher or several teachers teach the class. Effective teaching follows six basic principles.

One, students need to be engaged at high levels of learning to be productive (for example, they learn a lot of knowledge, then demonstrate on tests or practice skills such as writing letters or math facts until they become proficient at them). Dieker (2001) found in a study that active learning was a common component of all of the co-teaching teams that she observed. Rather than just having students read about information, students could be involved in active learning activities such as making predictions ahead of time, periodically stopping to ask questions, and summarizing when finished.

Two, in order to have students reach high levels of active engagement during learning, they must participate in learning activities that are motivational, rewarding, or interesting. Mastropieri et al. (2005) identified the teacher's ability to motivate students as a key factor in effective co-teaching teams that they observed.

Three, teachers need to use effective, research-based techniques and methods to increase student achievement. The reason teachers use research-based techniques is because they know that these techniques have worked in the past and they should work in the class now, as opposed to the uncertainty that comes with untested techniques. Other studies support the use of effective instructional techniques to teach students and to make instruction explicit for those having learning problems (for example, Brownell et al. 2006; Mastropieri et al. 2005).

Related to this, four, teachers should have high expectations for all students. In one study, Dieker (2001) found that teachers in all of the co-teaching teams that she observed had high expectations for both behavior and academic performance of *all* of the students, including students with disabilities.

Five, teachers constantly need to monitor student behavior to prevent potential disruptions in learning (that is, ensure that students are not off task), to ensure that students are practicing skills correctly (that is, not practicing errors), and to provide the teachers themselves with feedback about their own teaching. If students are off task, teachers may have to modify their teaching during the lesson. Studies have shown that teachers not only need to create a positive learning environment for students (Dieker 2001), but they need behavior and classroom management skills to manage student behavior (Brownell et al. 2006; Mastropieri et al. 2005).

Six, all teachers should be knowledgeable of the curriculum so that they can present information in a clear and coherent manner, know which skill to present next in a sequence, and pace themselves throughout the year to be able to cover the entire content for that particular grade level. Not only is it important for the regular education teachers to know the curriculum well, but it is important for the special education teachers as well (Brownell et al. 2006; Mastropieri et al. 2005). In addition, they should know the content well enough so that they can move quickly through certain portions of the curriculum and be able to spend extra time helping students understand and learn other key portions of the curriculum. For teachers, this means breaking down content for the year into units of time and then ensuring proper coverage of content on a daily, weekly, and

TIPS FOR GENERALIZATION

Co-Teaching: Modifications and Adaptations

Curricular issues always present a challenge in a co-taught class (Cook and Friend 1995), particularly when students with disabilities are being asked to perform tasks and learn concepts that are difficult (Deshler and Schumaker 2006). Few, if any, modifications or accommodations are needed for students in co-taught classes where the content or skills match their needs. However, in classes where the content demands are great or the gap between what students know and what they need to know is wide, teachers will need to provide accommodations and/or modifications. Early on in elementary school the gap may be small; however, over time, this gap is likely to widen if students are not provided with sufficient academic supports (Deshler and Schumaker 2006).

Switlick (1997) recommends that teachers consider the FLOW acronym during the planning process to help determine the viability of a modification and likelihood of implementing it in the general education setting (as we acknowledged in Chapter 9, terminology to name accommodations and modifications has gone through a number of changes. The terms *modification* and *adaptation* as used by Switlick mean the same practices that are now more commonly known as accommodations and modifications [as defined in Chapter 9], respectively):

- F <u>F</u>it into the classroom environment
- L <u>L</u>end themselves to meeting the individual student's needs
- O <u>O</u>ptimize understanding for each student
- W <u>W</u>ork well with the activity planned for the lesson

To assist in student learning, teachers can implement a variety of modifications and adaptations during the delivery of instruction, as students learn, and when students demonstrate their knowledge of skills learned. Switlick (1997) has suggested the following ideas:

Modifications or adaptations in the delivery of instruction:

- Use multiple presentations of content or skills.
- Use consistent format during presentations.
- Review key points frequently.
- Use color coding to match materials or concepts.
- Highlight sections of the text.
- Use manipulatives, pictures, or real-life examples to emphasize a concept.
- Use oral and written directions.
- Reduce written requirements.

Modifications and adaptations as students learn:

- Use consistent daily routines and list daily schedule.
- Provide samples of finished product.
- Provide time to transition and get organized.
- List materials needed for the lesson.
- Inform students of how much time is given to complete an activity.
- Provide organizers or guided notes outlining key concepts of a lesson.
- Provide step-by-step directions for completing assignments.

Modifications or adaptations for student demonstration of knowledge or skills:

- Reduce the size of the assignment.
- Allow more time to complete assignments.
- Allow the students to demonstrate their knowledge in an alternate form (for example, student presents oral book report rather than written one).
- Provide teacher or peer support as the student completes an assignment.
- Provide students with a checklist to use prior to handing in assignment.
- Provide students with a grading rubric.

Source: Adapted from D. Switlick, "Curricular Modifications and Accommodations." In *Teaching Students in Inclusive Settings: From Theory to Practice*, ed. D. Bradley, M. King-Sears, and D. Tessler-Switlick, 225–51. (Boston: Allyn & Bacon, 1997).

quarterly basis. Now that the "how" and the "what" of teaching are covered, we will review different co-teaching models that can be used to coordinate teaching between two teachers.

Co-Teaching Models

The main models of co-teaching that we will discuss in detail include **station teaching, interactive teaching, alternative teaching,** and **parallel teaching** (see Figure 13.1) (Cook and Friend 1995; Friend and Bursuck 2006; Walther-Thomas et al. 2000). Each model can be used with different content. Depending upon the purpose of a lesson, one model might work better than others. For example, parallel teaching might be used when teachers want to review content before a test. On the other hand, alternative teaching might be used if a portion of the class has missed content and the purpose is to catch those students up with the rest of the class.

Station Teaching. Using station teaching, depending upon the size of the class, teachers set up three to five stations around the room and students move in groups from one station to another after a designated period of time (10 to 15 minutes). As you could guess, station teaching requires quite a bit of preparation on the part of the teachers. Prior to the lesson, teachers have to prepare each station with the appropriate materials and make sure that the directions are clear. If directions

FIGURE 13.1

Co-Teaching Models

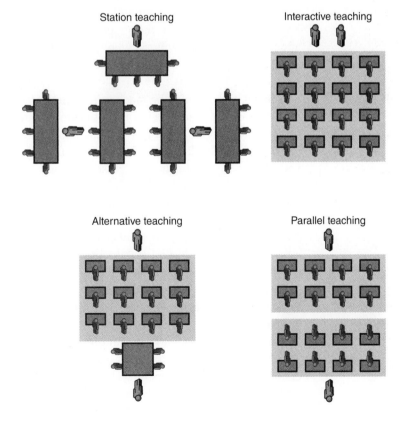

are not clear or if expectations for student behavior are not explicit, students may become sidetracked trying to figure out what to do or may end up using materials in an inappropriate manner. In station teaching, teachers have to monitor the noise level and behaviors.

When used in collaborative classrooms, each teacher will work at a station where teaching or direct supervision is required; at the remaining stations, students are expected to work independently. For example, if students were studying the parts of a plant, you would set up five stations. One station would contain a short video that shows how plants grow from a seed into a mature plant; one station would contain a puzzle or activity that students have to complete to demonstrate the life cycle of a plant over the four seasons; one station would take place at the computer where students play a virtual reality game by adding the proper amounts of sunlight, water, and fertilizer to make the plant grow; a teacher would explain and discuss how photosynthesis works at one station, and another teacher would teach students about functions of a plant cell at yet another station (for example, cell wall, nucleus, vacuoles, and chloroplasts).

Interactive Teaching. With interactive teaching, one teacher assumes the lead, teaching in front of the class while the other teacher supports by monitoring student learning. After a short period of time, the teachers switch roles. In effective co-taught classes, teachers work efficiently so that it becomes a symbiotic relationship. Each teacher has multiple opportunities to serve in both the teaching and supportive modes. In the support role, teachers are engaged in the lesson and ask questions or rephrase when they see students having difficulty understanding a concept. The support teachers also supervise practice and monitor behaviors.

For example, while one teacher is discussing how light refracts through a convex lens, the other teacher is monitoring students' notes and checking for understanding. Occasionally, when the support teachers see a student having difficulty, they would stop and ask questions to the lead teacher such as, "Did you say the light refracts as it passes through the lens? You also mentioned that *refracts* means to bend, is that correct?" The support teacher uses questions in this fashion, rather than drawing attention to a student who is having difficulty understanding the concept. Shortly after convex and concave lenses are explained, the support teacher becomes the lead teacher and walks the class through a lab in which students project images into different types of lenses to see the effects of each. The same teacher then continues to explain how light changes when it comes from air and enters water. This teacher explains to students how light refracts in water at a different angle than when it is in the air.

The support teacher now now monitors students' notes to ensure their accuracy. Although interactive teaching can be an enjoyable way to teach, both teachers have to know the content well and have to plan ahead of time to ensure smooth transitions between their teaching. Teachers should be careful not to get stuck performing the same limited tasks because they might be viewed as less than equals in students' eyes. For example, if one teacher is the one who handles disruptive behavior, students may be more likely to behave inappropriately on a day when that teacher is absent. If one teacher is the one who teaches the content, then students are more likely to turn to that one for their questions. The point is that both teachers should share the different roles, roles that are both burdensome and rewarding.

Alternative Teaching. Alternative teaching involves creating a small group of students and then teaching them in one section of the room, usually a corner or table in the back of the class. While one teacher works with the small group, the other teacher instructs the rest of the class. The purpose of the grouping is for reteaching concepts, providing enrichment activities, helping students who were absent to catch up, or addressing special problems that students may be having (for example, students who are talkative or disruptive, who need prerequisite content, or who need extra assistance taking notes). Using this model, teachers will alternate roles on a regular basis so that they do not become cast as the person who always works with small groups (the implication being that the particular teacher cannot handle large groups or only works with a certain type of student).

Likewise, the group should be heterogeneous and not include the same students every time, lest the small group take on the appearance of students who have behavior and academic problems. All students should be given opportunities to participate in both large and small groups. For example, if a student with a mild disability is having difficulty understanding the concept of a recessive gene, that student might be paired up with a high achiever who understands the concept well, and then both could be given practice activities in a small group. In this way, both the teacher and high achiever could explain the concept to help the student with mild disabilities understand it. The purpose of the alternative teaching configuration is still met; because the students with the highest needs have been distributed between the two teachers, they will be able to receive the levels of attention they need.

Parallel Teaching. Parallel teaching involves dividing the class in half and having each instructor teach students the same content. Each group of students is heterogeneous (that is, consisting of high, average, and low achievers). This configuration provides a good format for students who are reluctant to respond in larger groups or for those times when teachers want more interaction with students. As such, it would be an appropriate format to use when teaching difficult concepts, when students need a lot of practice with skills, or when teachers want to make sure that all students have mastered a set of content or skills. Parallel teaching does require careful planning so that both teachers cover the same content, and it requires both teachers to maintain an adequate pace to ensure covering all of the designated content by the end of class. Of course, two instructors teaching in the same classroom may be more distracting and may create higher levels of noise. Some teachers may need some time to acclimate to this format, particularly teachers who are unsure of their teaching and classroom management skills.

> **THINK BACK TO THE CASE** with Frank and Elizabeth . . .
>
> 1. *What practices related to collaboration and co-teaching could you suggest to help them instruct students more effectively?*
>
> Alternative or parallel teaching might be two options for these teachers. Using alternative teaching, Frank could take a small group of students to a section of the classroom and reteach portions of the lesson. Using parallel teaching, Frank and Elizabeth could split the class in half and each could teach the same lesson.

Other Approaches to Co-Teaching Models

The previous four models of co-teaching represent the primary different configurations possible for co-teaching. Many other variations can be used with one or more of the four models. These approaches include speak and chart, speak and comment, one teach and one observe, and one teach and one assist. As you read about these four approaches, you will note many similarities and slight differences among them.

Using speak and chart (Garmston 1997), the lead teacher presents content, and the support teacher (that is, the scribe) records notes on a flip chart, overhead transparency, or PowerPoint slide. As the information is recorded and projected on the screen or board, students record it in their own notes. Using this approach, the support teacher remains silent and simply records notes.

A second approach is called speak and comment. Garmston (1997) reports that speak and comment requires the lead teacher to direct the discussion and make decisions about when to end the discussion and when to move on to new content. The support teacher adds comments, gives examples, or elicits a question about the topic for the class. The purpose of the support teacher's comments and questions is to keep the conversation lively and engaged. When using either of these methods, co-teachers should feel free to monitor and intervene in discussions and should develop signals for switching from lead to support teacher. Some of these signals may include verbal intonation, purposeful pauses, physical proximity, or eye contact.

A third approach, one teach and one observe, is used when one teacher instructs and the other teacher observes a student(s) to see how the student responds to instruction, behavior during instruction or intervention, or how well the teacher interacts with students (for example, does the teacher ask questions to all the students or just a select few? Does the teacher use sufficient wait-time after asking questions?) (Friend and Bursuck 2006). Through these systematic observations, teachers can accurately improve their own teaching behavior or carefully monitor changes in student behavior.

A fourth approach is one teach and one assist. Using this approach, one teacher instructs students and leads students through the lesson while the other teacher assists students who have questions or need additional assistance. Typically, the lead teacher is teaching content while the other teacher circulates around the room making sure that students are recording notes, are on task and paying attention, and are exhibiting appropriate classroom behaviors.

As can be the case for other approaches, this last approach can be problematic when the regular education teacher is doing the actual "teaching" and the special education teacher ends up assisting the teacher or is delegated to nonteaching tasks (for example, grading papers, monitoring student behavior, or preparing materials for the lesson). The biggest complaint voiced by special education teachers in ineffective co-taught classes is that they are often "stuck" doing similar nonteaching tasks and often feel like a teaching assistant as a result. Of course, with better communication between teachers and the willingness of both teachers to share the teaching role, they can usually resolve many of these problems.

THINK BACK TO THE CASE with Frank and Elizabeth . . .

2. Is it realistic to expect these students to learn and understand the content in biology?

Because the IEP guides the skills and content that students learn, students' mastery of biology content should be guided by the goals and objectives from their IEPs. How realistic it is for these students to learn the content may depend upon how well the content is taught and the supports available to them. In some cases, the content may have to be modified; however, much of this depends upon the teacher(s). Comparing past performance on similar content may help them determine how students will do learning the content.

Research Evidence: Collaboration and Co-Teaching

Numerous studies and reviews (for example, Dieker and Murawski 2003; Weiss 2004; Weiss and Brigham 2000) indicate that co-teaching has positive effects on student achievement and social skills. For example, researchers (Rea, McLaughlin, and Walther-Thomas 2002) who compared outcomes for students with LD in co-taught inclusive classes versus pull-out programs found that students with LD in inclusive classes (a) achieved higher course grades (that is, in language arts, sciences, mathematics, and social studies), (b) achieved higher scores on the language and mathematics subtests of the Iowa Test of Basic Skills, (c) had comparable scores on state proficiency tests, (d) had comparable low rates of in-school and out-of-school suspensions and, (e) attended more days of school than students with LD in pull-out programs. More recently and perhaps the most comprehensive analysis on co-teaching research, Scruggs, Mastropieri, and McDuffie (2007) found several similar overall benefits of co-teaching. Their metasynthesis found that co-teaching benefited teachers (both regular education and special education), students with disabilities, as well as students without disabilities. Highlights of their findings include the following:

- Regular education teachers reported that co-teaching with special education teachers led to their own improved professional development.
- Both regular education and special education teachers believed that co-teaching led to reciprocal learning experiences in which co-teachers learned and benefited from one another.

- Many teachers reported increased cooperative skills among students without disabilities in co-taught classes, along with increased social benefits for all students.
- Students with disabilities benefited from additional attention given to them in co-taught classes in terms of academic and social skills.

Finally, these benefits did not come about without much hard work, effective co-teaching skills, and administrative support. Scruggs, Mastropieri, and McDuffie (2007) found that co-teaching worked best among compatible teachers who volunteered to work together and were given adequate planning time, administrative support, and proper training. In a nutshell, when teachers are provided with the skills to collaborate and co-teach and the administrative support, not only do teachers benefit, but more importantly, their students benefit.

THINK BACK TO THE CASE) with Frank and Elizabeth . . .

3. What supports and modifications could Frank use to assist his students' learning?

Frank could use a number of cognitive supports to help his students learn the content. For example, he could use note-taking techniques such as strategic note taking or guided notes to assist students with taking notes. He could also use cognitive organizers to assist students at learning important concepts from the content.

CHAPTER SUMMARY

Effective collaborative teaching, or co-teaching, does not happen overnight. As with any change in teaching, it takes time to develop a collaborative partnership with others. As those partnerships develop, attitudes begin to change among teachers as they co-plan and co-teach lessons. They begin to develop better communication and support skills, and become more adept at problem solving and co-planning, the four key components of effective collaboration and co-teaching.

Initially, the co-taught class has to be developed to reach a balance between the number of students with mild disabilities and regular education students. Typically, the balance never exceeds one-third students with mild disabilities; more typically, co-taught classes have only 10 percent to 20 percent students with mild disabilities and the rest regular education students (consisting of low- to high-achieving students). Moreover, to

help manage this heterogeneous group of students, teachers typically incorporate different groupings, such as classwide peer tutoring or cooperative learning groups. They may teach using different co-teaching models such as station teaching, interactive teaching, alternative teaching, or parallel teaching. Using these different modes of teaching, with supports and modifications in the classroom, teachers can manage and effectively instruct a large heterogeneous group of students.

In those classes where collaboration and co-teaching work well, you can see the defining characteristics of effective collaboration: collaboration is voluntary and involves shared resources; collaboration requires parity; collaboration is based upon mutual goals, shared participation, and decision making; and collaboration involves a shared accountability for outcomes. When teachers first begin to collaborate, they should do so voluntarily;

the strongest collaborative partnerships between teachers usually begin this way. When teachers work together, they often share resources including teaching materials and professional development information. They often develop a mutual respect for each others' teaching skills, and they develop shared decision making, and, over time, mutual goals for what they want to accomplish as a team. Finally, as these teachers continue to work together over the years, they begin to develop a sense of ownership for all of

the students that they teach and, along with this ownership, a shared responsibility for their outcomes.

Co-teachers also begin to modify their instruction to find better ways to help all students learn. They begin to modify their roles and responsibilities with each other and, through co-planning, begin to better understand their roles and responsibilities during co-taught lessons. As teachers become more proficient at co-planning and teaching, they begin to work not as two teachers, but as one team.

KEY TERMS

Alternative Teaching, 465
Collaboration, 440
Interactive Teaching, 464

Parallel Teaching, 465
Parity, 441
Station Teaching, 463

Support Skills, 446

APPLICATION ACTIVITIES

Using information from the chapter, complete the following activities that were designed to help you apply the knowledge that was presented in this chapter.

1. Work with another student and develop a co-taught lesson. List what each person will be doing during the lesson.
2. Using the four models of co-teaching—station teaching, interactive teaching, alternative teaching,

and parallel teaching—design a lesson for each. Note the different responsibilities for individual teachers depending on which model is being used.
3. Look up a research article on collaboration or co-teaching and write a one-page summary about what you learned from it, making note as to whether the critical elements described in this chapter seem necessary for effective co-teaching.

TECHNOLOGY FOR COLLABORATION AND CO-TEACHING

Power of Two
www.powerof2.org

This website provides information about collaboration, consultation, and co-teaching. It provides forums, resources, and links to other websites on collaboration and inclusion.

Inclusive Education
www.uni.edu/coe/inclusion

This website discusses various aspects of inclusion. It discusses legal requirements, teacher competencies, and teaching strategies for making inclusion

successful in schools. It also discusses how to plan for inclusion and how to prepare others in the school for new inclusion programs. Along with these components, the website also provides information about other issues, such as values, and links to other web resources.

Circle of Inclusion
www.circleofinclusion.org

This website provides information about inclusion and, specifically, details on how to create inclusion programs, benefits of inclusion, information about model programs for inclusion, interactive lessons, and other resources.

Center for Effective Collaboration and Practice

http://cecp.air.org

This website provides IEP introductions, procedures, and worksheets for functional behavioral assessment and behavior intervention plans, as well as strength assessments for students. In addition, suggested programs are discussed that are useful for promoting positive student behavior and increasing academic performance.

Visit the book-specific website at www.cengage.com/education/ boyle for a variety of study tools such as web links, tutorial quizzes, glossary/flash cards, bonus material not included in the text, and more.

The premium website offers access to additional materials, including the Video Cases. Go to www.cengage.com/login to register or purchase access.

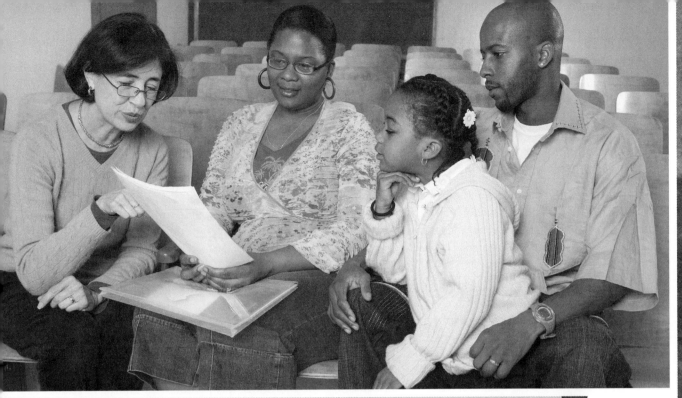

© Michael Newman/PhotoEdit Inc.

Working with Families

14

CHAPTER QUESTIONS

1. How does a student's disability impact a family? In turn, how can a family impact the child with a disability?

2. What are expectations for how special educators will partner with parents?

3. How can schools act to foster home-school partnerships that work?

4. What rights, responsibilities, and roles are available to parents throughout the stages of the special education process?

Do you think that families play a major role in a child's education?
The correct answer is *yes*. Whether the family's influence is positive or negative, and whether the parents participate in "parents' night" and similar school activities or not, families have a profound influence on education. The family is critical for shaping a child's[1] personality. The values that the family communicates about education directly relate to how well a student achieves in school (Winter 2007). Families also play an important role in learning. Literacy skills used in the home and the family's valuation of learning directly influence student skill and motivation. When schools work at cross-purposes with families by challenging the family's values or expecting learning practices that do not match family conventions, students do not learn as well as they could. Conversely, education is enhanced when educators and families work together to plan, implement, and evaluate educational practices. The role of the family is particularly important for students with disabilities.

Family and Disability Impact Each Other

Chapter Question
ALERT

In this section, you will find information that answers a Chapter Question:

1. How does a student's disability impact a family? In turn, how can a family impact the child with a disability?

Although family involvement in education is important for all students, it is particularly important for students in special education. In recognition of the important roles families play in education, the Individuals with Disabilities Education Act (IDEA) requires that parents have the opportunity to participate fully in all phases of the special education process. In the case of early childhood special education, the entire family may be involved in receiving and providing special education services. Parent involvement requires much more than inviting parents to IEP meetings and having an open-door policy. True parent involvement requires forming a partnership with the parents (Winter 2007). The students will benefit from a home-school partnership, but it takes effort to make the relationship work.

CASE 14.1	Charlie's Individualized Education

Case Introduction

As you read the following case, ask yourself what evidence indicates whether Charlie's parent, Mrs. Waters, and the special educator, Rhonda, have a good relationship. Think about how you could replicate the factors that contribute positively to their relationship. Also consider how their relationship impacts Charlie's education.

At the end of the case, you will find case questions. These questions are meant to serve as points for reflection. Of course, if you can answer them immediately, you should do so, but you may want to wait to answer them until you have read the portion of the chapter that pertains to a particular case ques-

tion. Throughout the rest of the chapter, you will see the same questions. When you come to them again, try to answer them based upon that portion of the chapter that you just read.

When Mrs. Waters received an invitation to her son Charlie's IEP annual review meeting, she called Rhonda, Charlie's special education teacher. Mrs. Waters and Rhonda had a good relationship. She told Rhonda that she was generally pleased with how Charlie's homework was going. She and Charlie's father had both been monitoring the quality of Charlie's work, and signing off that he had shown it to them seems to be working well. At last year's IEP meeting, Mrs. Waters and Rhonda agreed that Charlie's homework

---

[1] When referring to students of any age, the IDEA makes reference to *child*. To avoid confusion between referencing laws and regulations and recommended practices, we also use the term *child* in this chapter. Unless otherwise stated, the term is intended to include adolescents as well.

habits were very poor and that his schoolwork was suffering because of it. At that meeting, Charlie insisted that he didn't ever have much homework and that he rarely failed to work on assignments he really did have. Following Rhonda's suggestion at that meeting to institute an assignment notebook and calendar, Charlie's teachers and parents now know to expect him to present his notebook to them daily for signatures. Shortly after they began using the assignment notebook, Charlie revealed to his mother that he was often overwhelmed by his homework.

Rhonda had met with the Waterses and shared some procedures with them for helping Charlie through his homework. The Waterses found her tips helpful, because Charlie's difficulties with following their directions had been frustrating them.

On the phone, Mrs. Waters said that she thought Charlie's writing assignments expected too much of him. She was worried that he was working on too many different skills at once. Rhonda assured Mrs. Waters that they would be able to discuss this at the IEP meeting.

On the day of the meeting, Mrs. Waters arrived a little bit late, due to unexpected traffic. Mr. Waters did not attend; in fact, he had never attended any of Charlie's special education meetings. Rhonda and the director of special education were still in the director's office, meeting about another matter, so Mrs. Waters had to wait several minutes for them.

Once the meeting began, Charlie introduced everyone and, with some prompting from Rhonda, summarized his progress for the year and stated his goals for the upcoming year. Everyone agreed that the homework monitoring system had been going well; Mrs. Waters and Rhonda both praised Charlie for the effort he was putting into monitoring his assignment completion. Even though Charlie argued that he no longer needed the monitoring system, the team agreed to continue its use.

When the subject of writing assignments came up, Mrs. Waters expressed her concern that Charlie was having difficulty doing all that was expected of him. Melinda Orafaci, the English language arts teacher, explained that she wanted her students to appreciate the complexity of composition, so although the students worked on specific skills in class, she wanted them to practice integrating all skills when they did their twice-weekly homework writing assignments. Mrs. Waters also expressed that she thought the expectation for a full-page composition each time was too much for Charlie. Melinda responded that students in Charlie's grade should be able to write "at least" that much. Rhonda broke into the conversation and suggested that she would meet with Melinda to review the writing curriculum expectations and together they could come up with guidelines for how the Waterses could support Charlie's writing at home. She then initiated a discussion about appropriate accommodations for Charlie. All agreed that, if needed, after two months of monitoring Charlie's comfort level and the quality of his writing, Melinda would meet with them again to consider alternatives to the standard assignment. They all agreed to this proposal, as well as to writing messages to one another about Charlie's progress in his assignment notebook.

Rhonda took over a week longer than she promised to write up the IEP following the meeting. Once Mrs. Waters received it in the mail, she was happy to sign and return it.

CASE QUESTIONS

1. What are the indicators that the Waterses have taken a positive view of Charlie's academic potential?
2. Did Rhonda's interactions with Mrs. Waters reflect professional standards for how special educators should interact with parents?

Families benefit from collaborating with schools that provide special education to students. Certainly children with disabilities benefit too, as is the case for Charlie Waters. Conformance with the IDEA requirements for parental involvement is the minimum expectation for special education professionals. Letter-of-the-law compliance is not the same as truly partnering with parents on their child's behalf, however. Although the limits of the law serve to protect educators from having to respond to unrealistic expectations or meet needs that fall outside of the responsibility of schools, truly partnering with parents means engaging in a positive and reciprocal relationship. The trust and respect that Rhonda and Mrs. Waters have for each other is an example of such a relationship. Because they communicated well and respected each other, each listened to the other's contributions, gave useful input, and trusted one another, all of which were to Charlie's benefit.

Although partnerships between schools and parents often go well, at other times, the parties cannot seem to come to agreement or do not communicate at all. The "systems" of schooling and special education can sometimes seem daunting to parents, primarily because of the imbalance of power between families and schools, especially for families that are not from the majority culture (Kalyanpur, Harry, and Skrtic 2000). Thus, special educators and their colleagues need to work not only to comply with special education law but also to recognize the important contribution that parents make to the education process and, further, recognize that parent partnerships need to be invited and nurtured.

The Concept of Family

In the twenty-first century, the average American household is dramatically different from what it was 100 years ago (Hodgkinson 2002); however, the concept of an extended family having responsibility for children is still accurate. Families are not as likely to be the "nuclear family" of the 1950s, which was typified by a married mother and father and 2.5 children per household. Today, approximately 50 percent of children in America live with a single parent for at least part of their childhood (Hodgkinson 2002). The numbers of children being raised by unmarried parents, single fathers, same-sex parents, and grandparents have increased significantly. The percentage of children raised by single mothers is declining. Co-housing, in which a community of two or many more families share collective responsibilities for child supervision, are increasing in popularity (Waxman 2005). Just as was the case 100 years ago, extended family members such as grandparents, aunts and uncles, and older siblings may all have central roles in child rearing, or they may be the primary caregivers in place of parents. Adoption agencies that arrange placements for children and adolescents with disabilities are more likely to place them with gay and lesbian single adults and couples (Brodzinsky, Patterson, and Vaziri 2002). Some children and adolescents legally are not in the care of any family member at all; they are instead wards of the state, a foster family, or a caseworker has legal responsibility for interacting with the school and making legal decisions on those students' behalf.

The IDEA and this book use the term *parent* to mean whoever is a primary caregiver to a child or adolescent. One, two, or more people may fit the label *parent*. In the same regard, families may not be limited to blood relatives or those who live in the same household.

How Family and Disability Impact Each Other

Expectant parents typically do not anticipate having a child with a disability. Although standard medical procedures can detect many forms of mental retardation in utero, they cannot reliably detect it in all cases, and none of the other mild disabilities is detectable even through infancy (except some conditions related to speech and language impairment). Thus, news of a child having a disability most often comes as a surprise. How parents and other family members react to the news of a disability is not standard. Some consider the diagnosis "tragic," regardless of whether the disability is mild or severe, others welcome it as an explanation for phenomena they have been observing (for example, hyperactivity, persistent learning difficulties, schizophrenic tendencies), and some acknowledge its significance while accepting it as simply another life condition (Ho and Keiley 2003; Li and Moore 1998; Roberts, Stough, and Parrish 2002).

Initial reactions to a disability are crucial for how the family will respond. Over time, dealing positively with the disability tends to make it more a routine and accepted aspect of family culture. Although some family members never get over the negative association with disabilities, they come to recognize it as manageable, and to have high expectations for the family member with a disability (Poehlmann et al. 2005). However, in other cases, the stress of not coping with a disability in the family can lead to depression among family members and even the breakup of the family (Ho and Keiley 2003; Lardieri, Blacher, and Swanson 2000; Poehlmann et al. 2005).

Depending upon the nature of a disability, it can have a significant impact on family routine. Siblings can become jealous of what they consider unequal treatment by their parents; the child with the disability can be perceived as someone to "protect" instead of as someone to encourage like any other family member; and routines such as arranging for a babysitter, assigning family chores, and upholding expectations for achieving successes can be altered.

How a mild disability manifests itself strongly relates to family members' reactions (Poehlmann et al. 2005). Children with hyperactivity or inattentiveness can aggravate others in the household because they often seem unfocused, forcing others to complete tasks the children should have. Communicating with a family member with ADHD can also be cumbersome if the individual frequently strays off topic. Likewise, a child with an EBD can cause a great deal of concern for family members, but may also be exasperating either because of withdrawal or acting-out behaviors. Lardieri, Blacher, and Swanson (2000) found that the academic and communication problems of children with LD did not pose a significant problem to either sibling or parent relationships. They did find, however, that when those with LD also presented behavioral problems, siblings reported being less comfortable interacting with them and less accepting of them, and parents reported higher levels of frustration.

Because the occurrence of a disability in a family is not a "normal" (that is, routine) family life event, it can be a source of stress for the family. It can lead to family dysfunction. However, the occurrence of a disability in a family can also be an occasion for family readjustment. Families that include a member with a disability have been found to:

- Adjust emotionally,
- Adjust to the reactions of peers,
- Access community resources,
- Adjust emotionally in relation to the nature of the disability,
- Adjust family and caregiver roles, in accordance with the child's skill development,
- Realize the need for continuous family involvement and care,
- Respond to the financial ramifications of the disability on the family,
- Plan for transitions, including future vocational preparation, and
- Arrange for socialization beyond the family unit (as summarized by Lustig 2002).

These readjustments can be either positive or negative.

Research Evidence

Positive Family Relationships. Parents and other family members can benefit from adopting positive perspectives about disability in their families. Indeed, many do benefit once they get over any initial negative reaction (Muscott 2002; Poehlmann et al. 2005). Muscott (2002) explains that some families have to progress through stages of coping similar to those Kübler-Ross (1969) proposed for how people grieve a death.

Parents who advocate on behalf of their child with a disability develop both a sense of purpose and a realization that they can participate with schools and other service agencies in responding to their child's needs; through such activities, parents come to develop a positive sense of their role as caregiver (originally cited in Lustig 2002). According to Scorgie and Sobsey's (2000) findings from interviews and surveys with parents of children with disabilities, most parents became more confident, assertive, and compassionate, developed stronger relationships with others (including marital bonds and friendships) and empathy in those relationships, and experienced positive adjustments in personal and social perspectives (for example, acceptance of others). Of course those parents likely also experienced stresses not common to parents of children without disabilities. Parents of children with disabilities worry about finding services for their child, providing care for their child, and determining how their child's needs will be met in the future (Lustig 2002).

Effective Responses. The bottom line is that how resilient family members are when a disability is present relates to how well they cope and problem-solve (Lustig 2002). According to Lustig, **problem solving** is "the family's ability to define . . . stressors in terms of manageable components, identify alternative courses of action, and begin to take steps to resolve the component problems and ultimately the problem" (Lustig 2002). For example, family members may become frustrated with a child with ADHD-inattentive who never seems to participate in games or chores without getting distracted. Knowledge that the disability is the cause of the child's behaviors will likely not prevent the family members from becoming frustrated, although that information may be useful for tolerating the behavior. Family members who are able to problem-solve might realize that the length of time waiting to take a turn in a game or the time needed to complete a chore is long enough that the inattentive child can become distracted. Further, the family can examine distracters that may "tempt" the child's inattention. So, in the case of the game, a child might easily become distracted because of enticing game pieces, a television that is on in the background, or other fun objects nearby that divert attention from the game. With this realization, family members can learn to help the child select strategic seating to avoid focusing on the distracters, have some neutral object such as a squish ball to manipulate, or select games that do not require long intervals between taking turns.

In the case of family chores, writing a list of steps on a chalkboard can be helpful (for example, *rake leaves in front yard, lemonade break, bag leaves, transport to compost pile, lunch break, rake leaves in side yard*, and so on). The list should name component tasks that are of short duration and match the child's attention span. The list should also include times to begin the task, scheduled breaks, and times the child can anticipate the task should end.

In addition to developing routines that take into account the child's disability, the family can also collaborate with the child and the school to develop preferred behaviors for the child. In the case of children with ADHD-inattentive, interventions might include teaching them to self-monitor and self-regulate their attention to task by learning to set performance goals, monitor productivity or attention to task, as well as self-administer breaks at appropriate times (Hughes and Boyle 1991). The family members can also learn to monitor and regulate their reactions to the child's inattentive behaviors. They might, for example, discuss their emotional reactions to the behaviors, and set personal goals for how they respond to the behaviors.

Coping is "the family's strategies and behaviors aimed at maintaining or strengthening the stability of the family, maintaining the well-being of the family members, obtaining resources to manage the situation, and initiating efforts to resolve the hardships created by the stressor" (Lustig 2002).

In his study of how parents of children with mild disabilities and more severe disabilities benefited from problem-solving and coping strategies, Lustig (2002) found that those who were able to "reframe" the stresses associated with having a child with a disability led to better family adjustments. To **reframe** means that individuals consider potentially stressful family events positively and consider themselves competent to deal with the events, instead of viewing themselves as passive. Thus, personal perspectives, and not just actions taken, are involved in positive problem-solving and coping strategies.

THINK BACK TO THE CASE) **about Mrs. Waters . . .**

1. What are the indicators that the Waterses have taken a positive view of Charlie's academic potential?

The fact that the Waterses actively participate in Charlie's special education is a strong indicator that they believe in his potential to learn (although some families are not active participants in their child's education they are not uninterested.) Mrs. Waters has goals for Charlie. Even when she was concerned that the writing assignments were too complex for him, she did not suggest that too much was expected of him, only that it was too much all at once. She believed that Charlie could learn the expected skills. If the Waterses had held any pessimistic views of Charlie because of his disability, they have clearly reframed them into more optimistic views of his potential with their support.

Chapter Question
ALERT

In this section, you will find information that answers a Chapter Question:

2. What are expectations for how special educators will partner with parents?

IDEA Expectations for Involving Families in Special Education

"Parent involvement in children's education has been correlated with higher academic achievement, improved school attendance, increased cooperative behavior, and lower dropout rates" (Bryan and Burstein 2004). The IDEA makes a number of references to the roles of families in special education. Prior to passage of the special education law, there were no nationwide provisions for inviting parents to provide valuable information about their child's performance at home. In some cases, parents were not consulted before drastic measures such as medication, sterilization, or institutionalization were committed (D'Antonio 2004). More commonly, their children were tracked into a lower-expectations curriculum in a segregated setting with no input from the parents as to its appropriateness.

In response to this history of parent exclusion, when Congress was preparing the bill that became the Education for All Handicapped Children Act (and after many reauthorizations, is now referred to as IDEA), parent advocacy groups were invited to participate in establishing its parameters. Because of its attention to the needs of families and the impact they have on education, the IDEA has been characterized as promoting "family-centered care, whereby families are fully involved in assessment and intervention decisions for their children" (NJCLD 2007). Thus, the IDEA's emphasis on family involvement stems from recognition of the crucial role parents and other family members can play in special education. Just as a law was necessary to guarantee the right to an appropriate education for children with disabilities, so too do parents require laws to ensure that their positive role in providing special education is not neglected. The IDEA speaks directly to the rights and needs of parents.

Requirements for Family Involvement

Although all six of the major provisions of the IDEA (review Chapter 1) relate to families, two particularly emphasize the role of the family in special education: *Due Process* and *Parent and Student Participation*.

The **due process provision** is a safeguard of parents' (and schools') rights (Bauer and Shea 2003). The legal term means a process for protecting rights that is not arbitrary and is consistent with the law, and a set of formal proceedings that adheres to legal rules and principles. In great detail, the IDEA Regulations specify the due process rights for all parties in all stages of the special education process.

Parents must be informed of their due process rights by the school district. As the wording **parent and student participation** indicates, this IDEA provision specifies that parents must be invited to participate in every stage of special education. Therefore, beginning with the question of whether the child has a disability and may need special education, the parents must give consent for special education procedures and must be invited to join in the process. The IDEA Regulations for parent and student participation are equally as extensive and involved as those for due process. Parents' rights, such as to be included on the IEP team and consent for special education actions, are spelled out in the Regulations.

The IDEA also protects the rights of families by setting expectations for informed consent before a child is assessed for eligibility for special education, including being evaluated for the presence of a disability, enrollment in special education, or major changes made to the students' special education (for example, annual IEP review, change of placement). **Informed consent** requirements from the IDEA are intended "to ensure that the parent:

- Has been fully informed of all information related to the proposed activity (in his native language, or other mode of communication)
- Understands and agrees in writing to carrying out the activity for which his consent is sought
- Understands that giving consent is voluntary and may be revoked at any time
- Understands that revoking consent will not apply to an activity that has already occurred." (Cortiella 2006)

Progress Reports to Parents

To be involved in a child's special education, parents must be informed as to how their child is progressing. In recognition of this need, the IDEA requires that parents be informed of their child's progress at least as often as are parents in general education. Therefore, as often as report cards and/or progress reports are sent home, so too must parents receive reports related to how well the child is progressing on IEP-related goals and activities. It will not suffice to report only to parents via a report card or midterm report card. Although grades over the school year should be indicative of overall progress and parents of children in special education should still receive report cards, these report cards are less likely to directly reflect progress toward an IEP or ITP goal.

The progress report needs to address academic achievement as well as functional performance. Recall that the IDEA and NCLB Act both focus on achievement as an outcome of special and regular education. The portion of the progress report addressing academics should base progress on academic goals within a profile of academic achievement. Using Charlie Waters from Case 14.1 as an example, a report may indicate how well Charlie is progressing in specific goals for composition, accompanying objectives if the team has elected to write them, and how well Charlie is achieving in the language arts curriculum (for example, "Despite difficulties with generating main ideas and topic sentences, which reflects a continuing problem with organizing his thoughts, Charlie has mastered brainstorming content before he begins writing and predetermining the order in which to express that content. Quality of written expression accounts for one-fourth of his quarter grade in language arts; he is averaging C– work in written expression this quarter. Combined with his performance in other aspects of language arts, his quarter grade is C+, an improvement over the previous quarter."). Reports of progress toward goals should be based on multiple objective measures (IDEA 2004), not just teacher observations or test results. The reports should also be in conformance with any format and content expectations agreed upon in the IEP document.

METHODS AND STRATEGIES SPOTLIGHT

Effective Methods for Communicating with Parents

Parent-teacher conferences are just one way that parents and teachers stay connected. Materials can be viewed together, and there are benefits of face-to-face interactions, such as reading one another's expressions and receiving someone's full attention. Although these face-to-face meetings can be beneficial, they can also be inefficient meetings. Scheduling often presents one of the biggest challenges for teachers. These meetings usually have designated end-times, which may preclude having the fuller conversation that everyone would have liked. Also, distractions are bound to occur during the session.

Sending notes back and forth via a student can also be an effective form of communication. Certain content that the parents do not wish to expose their child to precludes this mode. Also, as students sometimes lose things, confidential information is not appropriate for being transmitted in this fashion either. Although sending a brief note to the other party can be effective, the give-and-take of a real-time conversation is lost in this process.

Parents may be willing to converse by telephone or even voice-mail messages (Bauer and Shea 2003), in which case, prearranged times for conversations should be established. These options allow for more flexibility in scheduling meetings. Bauer and Shea also suggest that the educator ask the parents if they are willing to communicate via e-mail. All parties should remember that e-mail is not a secure medium, however. School districts may also prohibit certain identifying information from being communicated over such a public channel.

Standards for Working with Families

Competent educators are sensitive to the needs of their students and their families, including having an appreciation for diverse cultures (Sileo and Prater 1998). They possess knowledge, skills, and attitudes that facilitate their interactions; they also acknowledge the contributions the families make to their own understanding of the child and the school environment (Sileo and Prater 1998).

Educators and other service providers who work with young children are typically expected to be able to work with families and to provide culturally and linguistically sensitive services (NJCLD 2007). Although there is a particular imperative for working with the families of young children, educators of students of all ages should work in partnership with families as well.

They need to be aware of factors that can inhibit effective interactions with families. Typical barriers to parents' participation in their children's schooling include being uncomfortable with the school's conceptualization of parent involvement, limited English proficiency, few experiences with accessing resources to inform their decision making on their child's behalf, and prior negative experiences with schools based on ethic, racial, and cultural backgrounds (Hughes, Schumm, and Vaughn 1999; Salas et al. 2005; Sileo and Prater 1998). In contrast, professionals who are competent in interacting with parents are:

- Aware of their own experiences, values, and attitudes toward diverse groups;
- Aware of the varied cultural, linguistic, and familial backgrounds of their children's families; and
- Culturally responsive in both communications with families and their pedagogical practices. (Sileo and Prater 1998)

The Council for Exceptional Children (CEC) (2009) standards for special education teachers do not include a separate set of standards for working with parents and families; rather, they integrate them among the ten standard areas (see the inside cover of this book). Many of the standards relate to working with families; several explicitly name the expectations for special education teachers to do so (for example, Foundations: "[understand] family systems and the role of families in the educational process" [CC1K7]; Instructional Planning: "involve the individual and family in setting instructional goals and monitoring progress" [CC7S3]). Other standards concerning language and cultural differences, education planning, and collaboration relate to educator-family relationships as well.

The National Association for the Education of Young Children (2001) has published standards for all educators of young children. All five of their core standards include references to working with families and in the home and other natural environments of young children.

THINK BACK TO THE CASE) about Mrs. Waters . . .

2. *Did Rhonda's interactions with Mrs. Waters reflect professional standards for how special educators should interact with parents?*

Case 14.1 does not speak to all of the CEC standards related to working with parents, but it does give several indications of how well Rhonda performed these aspects of her

role. Over time, Rhonda learned about the Waterses' home environment. She found out about Charlie's study habits at home and she learned about how the Waterses were willing and able to support Charlie's education at home. She did not just provide the Waterses with periodic progress reports and otherwise ignore them; rather, she invited Mrs. Waters to contribute ideas about Charlie's education. She listened to Mrs. Waters's concerns and suggestions and worked to incorporate them into her practice. Thus, we do have some indicators that Rhonda exhibited expected skills for collaborating with parents.

It should be noted, however, that Mrs. Waters was kept waiting several minutes when she arrived at the school for the IEP meeting, and this was after she was delayed in arriving. The fact that neither Rhonda nor the special education administrator greeted her reflects poorly on them. This behavior can send the message that they are more important than the parent is or that they are in control of the process. Rhonda was also over a week late in sending the final version of the IEP to Mrs. Waters. Although we can all understand getting behind on paperwork, the Waterses could have interpreted that tardiness as Rhonda's not being as invested in their son's education as she indicates she is in their presence.

Chapter Question
ALERT

In this section, you will find information that answers a Chapter Question:

3. How can schools act to foster home-school partnerships that work?

Families' Relationships with School

Positive home-school partnerships are characterized by "reciprocity, trust, and respect" (Beveridge 2004). Creating welcoming environments or just putting educators and parents in contact with one another is not enough (Salas et al. 2005). Parent participation has a positive impact on student achievement, in both special and general education (Salas et al. 2005). In addition, parent involvement has been reported to:

- Increase parent understanding of school
- Increase parent understanding of their involvement in their child's education
- Promote confidence in parents
- Increase parental involvement
- Engender more positive feelings in parents about their own parenting role
- Increase parents' willingness to participate in school activities
- Increase parent interactions with teachers and administrators (Salas et al. 2005)

"Low-income parents are often perceived by educators as resistant to school efforts to involve them, as poor participators in school events, and as not as committed to their children's school achievement and success as middle-class parents" (Lott 2003). In addition, common perceptions of low-income parents include that they "[are] apathetic and disinterested in their children's education, do not encourage school achievement, and are not competent to help with homework" (Lott 2003). In truth, low-income parents are interested in their children's achievement and wish for involvement in their schools just as much as are parents from other income groups. Further, they typically cite school achievement as the basis for their children's success in life (Lott 2001).

Latino families often perceive schools as unfriendly, and not desiring their involvement (Hughes, Schumm, and Vaughn 1999) because of differences in language and cultural assumptions (Salas et al. 2005). Some Latino parents do not get involved in schools even when their children are having difficulties, because they perceive a lack of communication from the school to indicate that all is well (Goldernberg, as cited in Hughes, Schumm, and Vaughn 1999). Salas et al. (2005) report that some Mexican American families consider education to be the responsibility of schools, so they do not interfere. Latino parents have also reported being uncertain of how to help their children to meet schools' academic expectations, in part because they are not clear as to what those expectations are (Hughes, Schumm, and Vaughn 1999). Harry (1992) found that some Puerto Rican parents also did not consistently participate in the special education process because they were unsure of the purpose of the procedures.

Hughes, Schumm, and Vaughn (1999) found that Latino parents of children with mild disabilities were concerned about their children's limited reading and writing skills and that they wanted to help their children to develop their literacy skills at home. The parents also reported that they were not sure of how to help their children with mild disabilities, but would welcome guidance from school personnel. Latino parents with limited English language proficiency identified that as a primary barrier to helping their children develop their literacy skills, both because it inhibited necessary communication between the parents and the school and because it interfered with guiding their children's English language literacy (Hughes, Schumm, and Vaughn 1999).

Despite the desire for involvement by low-income and Latino parents, their relationships with schools are often fractured. Calls for parent involvement in schooling often appear to be targeted toward middle-class families (Lott 2003). Lott (2003) proposes the following five "prescriptions for change" in how schools relate to low-income families:

- Replace stereotypes with attention to strengths.
- Help parents reduce obstacles to school involvement.
- Expand the role of parents in schools.
- Increase informal communication.
- Help administrators in providing leadership. (Lott 2003)

According to Salas et al. (2005), schools can engage in the following six areas of "best practices" to foster better home-school partnerships with Mexican American families:

- Do not assume or stereotype about family linguistic abilities, acculturation, socioeconomic status, education, experiences, and the like.
- Develop credibility and trustworthiness,
- Understand the literacy proficiency of families, both for English language and special education jargon (see also Smith 2001).
- Determine parents' language of comfort for communications and use it.

- Consider the family's acculturation and how that may account for their goals and interaction styles.
- Do not assume that parents know what educators expect of them or that they are comfortable partnering with the school.

Salas et al. (2005) note that developing such bonds as trustworthiness and credibility takes time.

Levine and Trickett (2000) also identified positive responses that school systems can make to the obstacles of participation that low-income families face; they suggest "offering child care, transportation and evening times for parent-teacher conferences; providing translators and bilingual school personnel; and enhancing cultural sensitivity of school personnel through professional development activities" (see also Smith 2001). Low-income parents typically prefer informal contacts with school to more formal organized, scheduled meetings (Lott 2003).

Parents who feel welcomed by schools consider themselves to have been invited to be involved, to have been treated with respect—including communicating in a comfortable language, and having their opinions valued (summarized from original sources cited in Lott (2003). Lott (2003) suggests that schools should adopt open-school, open-classroom policies to be accessible.

Home and community visits can result in teachers realizing that they share values and expectations with families (Lott 2003). Further, families are a potential wealth of information and resources. Home-school relationships can help both families and school staff to understand one another's strengths and goals, as well as to work in concert on the child's behalf (Hughes, Schumm, and Vaughn 1999). Schutz (2006) wisely warns, however, that such visits require engaging in a careful and detailed process that can sometimes be unrealistic for many teachers. He notes that, without proper supports, home visits can become "voyeurism," and can serve to reaffirm teachers' deficit views of those they have gone to observe. Weekly newsletters and "telephone trees" facilitate communications among schools and parents (Good et al. 1997).

Smith (2001) warns that education "jargon" can also discourage parents from meaningful participation in the special education planning process. He notes that parents may be confused by everyday terminology for special educators, such as *ITP, resource room,* and *mainstreaming.* Statistical information from standardized testing might also be confusing.

To help confront the many barriers to productive relationships between parents and schools, the IDEA (2004) requires that a designated **service coordinator** be provided to families of all students in special education. That individual has a responsibility for facilitating communication between the family and the multidisciplinary team. That individual also performs the function of informing families of service agencies in their state that may provide services to them and their child (NJCLD 2007).

Parent Communication to Schools

Parents should remember that communication is a "two-way street." Although schools exist to serve families, families engaged in a relationship with the school have obligations to provide information, even if it is simply to communicate that they do not understand something. Bauer and Shea (2003) note that parents should expect to communicate to the school about how the child has been and is developing. Parents should also monitor their child's educational progress. Through monitoring, parents will be better informed about what they should share with schools and what things they may want clarification on.

Some ways of communicating are more effective than others. Part of effective communication is being prepared to communicate. Being prepared includes having proper information and being sure of the purpose of communicating. Cortiella (2006) has provided a useful "checklist" for parents to facilitate effective home-school communications (see Box 14.1). Schools could share the checklists with parents as one way of indicating they are open to parent involvement. Educators should be aware of the types of information parents may wish for and reasons for parents to communicate to them. With that knowledge, they can help the parents keep track of needed information and be prepared to respond to parents in ways consistent with the parents' purpose for communicating.

Cortiella (2006) also recommends that parents keep a **communications log** to keep track of communications with educators. Educators would be wise to

---

BOX 14.1

PARENT CHECKLIST FOR HOME-SCHOOL COMMUNICATIONS

It's important to establish and maintain strong home-school communications to get the best help for your child. Use this checklist as a guide to get you started.

- Keep communications open with your child's teacher, and listen carefully if she describes problems with aspects of your child's learning. If you think the problems are serious enough to require special attention, ask the teacher if alternate instructional approaches might help address the problem and ask if any have been tried.
- Keep track of the instructional practices used to help address your child's problems and record how well they assisted your child's learning.
- Ask about the availability of research findings that show the effectiveness of the instructional practices or behavioral programs being used.
- Discuss whether there are cultural factors that might make a difference. If so, explain your child's background so the teacher and other educators can understand your child's behavior and actions. The information provided by parents and family members can be crucial to understanding a child's learning difficulties.
- Try to understand the way your child learns and be able to communicate what you think will help the teacher better understand your child's specific learning style. Observe and provide all the information you can to help the educators develop a better understanding of it.
- Find out if supplementary educational services such as tutoring are available at your child's school and investigate the programs to see if any would benefit your child.

Source: Reprinted with permission from C. Cortiella, *IDEA Parent Guide: A Comprehensive Guide to Your Rights and Responsibilities Under the Individuals with Disabilities Education Act (IDEA 2004).* New York: National Center for Learning Disabilities, 2006.

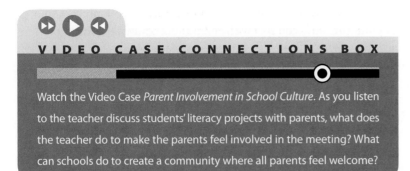

keep a similar log of their communications with parents. Cortiella suggests that contents of the log include the following:

- "Records of meetings and their outcomes
- Dates you sent or received important documents
- Dates you gave the school important information
- Dates of suspension or other disciplinary action
- Notes on telephone conversations (including dates, person with whom you spoke, and a short description of the conversation)."

Developing a Partnership with Parents

Bauer and Shea (2003) have developed a five-stage model for forming effective partnerships with parents. Following the stages of the model, the teacher and parents each identify their goals for partnership and intended involvement in their child's education, as well as monitor how well their partnership is working (see Figure 14.1).

In Phase 1, the teacher and parents meet for the first time. The teacher works to establish a positive relationship in this first meeting. The content of the meeting is an "assessment" of the parents' perceptions of their child and the child's education. Looking at the child's IEP and related documents like progress reports or an ITP can be helpful. The conversation can be conducted much like an interview. The parents' willingness and ability to participate in all aspects of their child's education should be assessed. Thus, educators should ask questions

FIGURE 14.1

Bauer and Shea's Model for Partnership with Parents

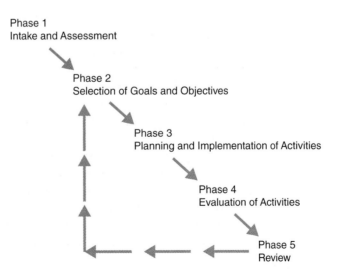

Source: Reprinted with permission from A. M. Bauer and T. M. Shea, *Parents and Schools: Creating a Successful Partnership for Students with Special Needs.* Upper Saddle River, NJ: Merrill/Prentice Hall, 2003.

about sharing in IEP goal setting, participating in interventions at home or homework monitoring, and comfort with communication with the school.

The goals that are established in Phase 2 are parent goals for participation and outcomes of the partnership. The needs that the parents and teacher identify from reviewing assessment data together become the goals. Outcome goals are not just for parents, but for the student and teacher as well.

Once goals are established, just as in the IEP goal and objective development process, activities are planned and the plans are implemented (Phase 3). The activities may include parents and family members giving or sharing information and working at home to implement interventions with the child, or working to educate the parent, for example.

Evaluation of activities is Phase 4 of the model. It includes evaluating whether activities are occurring as planned and whether parties are participating in them as planned. The content of activities is also evaluated. Whether the party in question (student or adult) learned what was expected is also determined.

Finally, in Phase 5 (review), the teacher and parents meet to review the goals, plan, and implementation and evaluation. They also set goals to begin the cycle again.

Although seemingly an involved process, following Bauer and Shea's five phases can ensure that parents and teachers partner effectively. These activities are not one in the same with the IEP planning meeting; they can serve to either help prepare for that meeting or to set interaction plans based on the outcomes of IEP planning.

TIPS FOR GENERALIZATION

Collaborating with Culturally and Linguistically Diverse Parents

Many parents are not actively involved in their child's education due to language and cultural barriers. To build positive relationships with parents from culturally diverse backgrounds, educators must both prevent and remove barriers to parent participation and respond to the parents' needs for support (Matuszny, Banda, and Coleman 2007).

Matuszny, Banda, and Coleman (2007) propose that teachers develop a "progressive plan" to establish and maintain such a relationship. That plan is enacted over the cycle of the school year. In *Phase 1: Initiation*, the educators and parents should meet each other in a social context. Matuszny et al. suggest that the meeting be relaxed and festive, with the goal to create a personal relationship, not to "get down to business." They suggest that the event include food and music, but remind planners to be considerate of cultural and religious orthodoxies when planning. Ideally, Phase 1 will occur before the school year begins.

Following establishment of initial acquaintanceships at the start of the school year, the focus in *Phase 2: Building the Foundation* is on building trust between the family and educators. Useful activities include providing and sharing information, giving parents choices, and inviting parental input to the decision-making process (Matuszny, Banda, and Coleman 2007). Families should visit their child's classroom to observe how it is organized and run. The educators and parents should also discuss how to communicate with each other and what arrangements will be convenient when meetings are required. Importantly, activities for building the foundation should focus on learning from the parents about how the classroom culture does or does not coincide with their culture (for example, as Matuszny, Banda, and Coleman point out, some religions do not include celebrating birthdays or particular holidays).

In *Phase 3: Maintenance and Support*, the relationship that has been established is both maintained and nourished. This phase requires that the educators continue to respect the culturally based traditions and preferences of the parents as they interact. Part of doing so is to maintain "informational equity," which means that educators share information (such as new and relevant test data or evolved insights about the child's learning) as soon as they have it.

Although the progressive plan never ends but rather continues year after year, the final phase, *Phase 4: Wrap-Up and Reflection*, involves the teacher and parents jointly reflecting on their relationship and considering what worked well and what needs to be changed. With all of the focus on the student, it is easy to neglect the quality of the relationship between the mutually concerned adults. Even parents who will not be affiliated with the same teacher the following year will benefit from the wrap-up assessment, as it will yield useful information for them to carry to the next educator with whom they should collaborate.

Johnson and Noga (1998, cited in Bauer and Shea 2003) identified several ways in which communications can block effective relationships. They caution that offering advice instead of offering suggestions is intimidating, and false reassurances can be disingenuous. They also point out that misdirected questions interfere with the progress of conversations, and changing the subject suggests disinterest. Moreover, clichés should be avoided because they call the validity of the conversation into question. Finally, minimizing feelings, jumping to conclusions, and interrupting all send the message to shut down productive conversation. Bauer and Shea (2003) add that listening is an essential skill that is nonetheless often overlooked in conversations.

Opportunities for Parent Involvement in the Special Education Process

Family-centered approaches to education and social services are commonly advocated (Hoffman et al. 2006). Parents should be involved at every stage of the special education process. They are valuable information resources, and they have the capacity to make important education decisions (for example, Dewey, Crawford, and Kaplan 2003).

Early Childhood Special Education

IDEA (2004) includes the mandate that services for children age birth to three are provided in a "natural environment" whenever possible. Home and child care settings are typically thought to be natural environments, particularly for children with mild disabilities. The purpose of this mandate is consistent with the overall purpose of early childhood education, which is to ensure that young children receive the best educational foundation they can early on, to minimize the negative effects of disabilities and delayed education.

Because mild disabilities are often not detectable in early childhood, and even when they are, their future impact across childhood and adolescence can only be estimated, early childhood special education needs to take a comprehensive approach. Still, it would be unrealistic to attempt to address all

Chapter Question
ALERT

In this section, you will find information that answers a Chapter Question:

4. What rights, responsibilities, and roles are available to parents throughout the stages of the special education process?

possible skills with intensity. Evaluations should be conducted to determine areas that require targeted intense instruction in an overall comprehensive curriculum. A comprehensive evaluation of a young child's status and needs related to education involves an integrated assessment of functioning in the following:

- Cognition, including perceptual organization, memory, concept formation, attention, and problem solving;
- Communication, including speech/language form, content, and use for receptive and expressive purposes;
- Emergent literacy, including phonological and print awareness, and numeracy, including number recognition and number concepts;
- Motor functions, including gross-, fine, and oral motor abilities;
- Sensory functions, including auditory, haptic, kinesthetic, and visual systems; and
- Social-emotional adjustment, including behavior, temperament, affect, self-regulation, play, and social interaction. (NJCLD 2007)

Young children have limited attention and sitting tolerance, so it is impractical to think of administering the types of testing batteries that may be used in elementary or secondary education. Furthermore, a more accurate assessment of young children's knowledge and skills will come from observing them in their normal routines. Systematic observations conducted in the early childhood years may include both formal (for example, standardized protocols) and informal procedures. Multiple observations should be made, using multiple procedures and instruments, and in multiple contexts. Children should be observed in their natural environments, and parents and other caregivers with whom they normally interact should be involved in collecting the data. With knowledge of the young child's needs within the functioning areas identified by the NJCLD, educators, caregivers, and parents can partner to address the child's most crucial needs.

Parents and educators or caregivers can use early childhood special educators' knowledge of effective curricular practices to determine jointly how to develop the child's skills within natural contexts. This process will involve parents' direct participation in planning, intervening, and monitoring progress. Among the services that should be provided is help in enhancing the home for language and literacy development (NJCLD 2007). For example, the National Early Literacy Panel (2008) has identified the following areas as indicators of appropriate literacy development for young children:

- Oral language
- Alphabetic knowledge
- Child's ability to write own name
- Phonological sensitivity
- Invented spelling
- Concepts about print
- Rapid naming

Children can develop skills in those literacy areas by engaging in conversation and games with parents and caregivers who know how to model, prompt, and correct a child's performance. The parents also need to understand the literacy goals for their children, so that they can gauge what skills are a priority, how long skill development may take, and when it will be time to introduce new skills of concern to them, for example.

Caregivers of young children and family members should have access to supports, including the following:

- Helping families and caregivers to recognize, understand, and accept the child's problems;
- Selecting programs that meet the child's individual needs;
- Locating parent support networks and programs;
- Finding a service provider or agency whose treatment philosophy is congruent with the family's preferences;
- Identifying appropriate interventions and resources available within public or private preschool programs; and
- Facilitating the child's development in the home and childcare environment. (NJCLD 2007)

The IDEA includes requirements for assessment of family outcomes for early intervention special education programs. Areas of appropriate outcomes from effective early intervention include families (a) understanding their child's strength and needs, (b) awareness of their rights, (c) ability to advocate for themselves and their child, (d) participation in their child's education, (e) receiving needed support, and (f) ability to access community services beyond (but including) public special education (Bailey et al. 2006).

The Special Education Process

Table 14.1 presents the major stages of the special education process and identifies ways in which parents can be involved at each stage. Both legally required participation and pedagogically and socially appropriate practices are listed. (Table 14.2 in this chapter represents parallel information for the RTI model associated with learning disabilities.) A number of activities appropriate for involving parents may rely on the special educators but are not typically their responsibility. An example is "child find" activities required by the IDEA (more on this later). To fulfill its child find obligations, the state typically requires local education agencies to participate in providing information to parents and other community members. A special educator might be asked to contribute to a newsletter, speak at an informational session, or be available to talk to concerned parents, but these are not the typical responsibilities of special education teachers.

Early Intervening. Early intervening should not be confused with "early intervention." The latter refers to services provided to infants, toddlers, and young children. *Early intervention* is intended to help children get off to the best start possible in life. Head Start is an example of an early intervention program. When early intervention is provided as a special education service, the child must be enrolled in special education. The concept of early intervening is quite similar, so it is easy to confuse the two labels, especially when early intervening is applied to preschoolers. **Early intervening** means to provide intervention as soon as a possible need is detected. Instead of waiting to collect extensive documentation of a learning difficulty or for an evaluation to document that a disability exists, intervention is provided immediately. Technically, early intervening is not a

TABLE 14.1: Parent Information and Participation in the Traditional Special Education Model

Early Intervening*	Parent consultation
	Participation at home
	Progress reports
Child Find	Information and resources about disabilities
	Information and resources about special education
Pre-referral	Parent consultation
	Progress reports
Referral	Written notification
	Procedural Safeguards document
Screening	Written notification
	Parent consultation
	Written parent consent
Evaluation	Written notification
	Procedural Safeguards document
	Parent consultation
	Written parent consent
	Data and information shared comprehensible for parents
	Information and resources about disabilities
	Information and resources about special education
Determination Meeting	Written notification
	Procedural Safeguards document
	Advance invitation to schedule the meeting
	Advance invitation to identify need for language interpreter or accommodations
	Data and information shared comprehensible to parents
	Parent collaboration
IFSP*/IEP/ITP Development	Written notification
	Procedural Safeguards document
	Advance invitation to schedule the meeting
	Advance invitation to identify need for language interpreter or accommodations
	Data and information shared comprehensible to parents
	Parent consent
	Parent collaboration
Exploration of Alternatives to Special Education (for students found ineligible for special education)	
Intervention and Progress Monitoring	Participation at home
	Homework monitoring or assistance
Annual Review / Triennial Reevaluation	Procedural Safeguards document
ITP/SOP Development	Procedural Safeguards document

*Although not a special education service, up to 15 percent of special education funds may be used to support early intervening. The intention of early intervening is to support struggling students in general education environments, with particular emphasis on grades K-3 (IDEA 2004).
*Individualized Family Service Plan

special education service, and, in fact, may be thought of as a step to prevent the need for special education (for example, Fuchs et al. 2003).

Parents can play a vital role in early intervening. They can help to provide services at home, or at least support those educators use. Parents often will need to be trained in the procedures they are asked to follow at home (Kutash et al. 2002; Sileo and Sileo 1996; Zhang and Bennett 2003). In fact, an important aspect of early intervening, or any stage of education involving parent participation, is preparing parents and supporting them in their roles. In the spirit of collaboration, parents should be asked to identify the level and types of involvement to which they may be able to commit (Bauer and Shea 2003; Sileo and Sileo 1996). Periodically, an educator should review the parents' activities to make sure they continue to be reliable with what had been planned.

Parents can fully collaborate with educators during early intervening by sharing their observations about the child's performance. By describing the home environment and how the child fits in the home routine, parents can supply important information that relates to how well a skill will be learned (for example, a child with an EBD who is being taught self-regulation strategies for undesirable behaviors may be excused for such behaviors at home instead of expected to self-regulate). Because of their intimate knowledge of their child, parents should also be enlisted to review evidence related to how an intervention is working. In addition to collecting data, they can report on their perceptions of how well the child is progressing and help to think about whether the child is making sufficient progress. Recall that Mrs. Waters from Case 14.1 was able to share valuable observations about Charlie's homework-completion trends, and later made observations about his frustration level with writing composition assignments. Rhonda would not have been aware of either situation without Mrs. Waters's collaboration.

So that parents can fully contribute to the collaborative effort on behalf of their child, they should receive progress reports throughout the early intervening process. The educator and parents can set the schedule for the reports as well as discuss an appropriate format. The reports might be in the form of casual conversations when the parents come to pick up the child, they may be scheduled phone conversations or one-on-one meetings, or they may be written notes or summaries of CB-M data collected across sessions. In addition to providing parents with data they need to participate in the early intervening collaboration, progress reports are a useful tool to demonstrate to parents that the school cares about their interests in their child. Remember, among the reasons that parents report low levels of involvement in their child's education is that they did not believe school staff valued their input or even believed that the parents were concerned about their child's education (Harry 1992; Salas et al. 2005).

Child Find. The very first opportunity for some parents to become involved in special education is through the child find activities of a state or local school district. In accordance with the **child find** requirements of the IDEA, state-level education agencies have an obligation to "identify, locate, and evaluate" (NJCLD 2007) children who may eventually require special education or related services. Many states, in turn, require local education agencies (for example, school districts) to participate. The intent of the child find mandate is to ensure that interventions are provided to a child as soon as possible. Although the benefits of early intervention can only be estimated, they include minimizing the negative impact of a disability on a child and the family (Heward 2006). Children with emotional disturbances may receive instruction in coping strategies, and their parents can be informed of pharmaceutical options in the early childhood years, for example. Those with mental retardation may begin to receive intensive instruction in literacy and functional skills so that they may have initial successes in both of those areas. In the case of children under the age of three, services may also be extended to family members as needed. Without child find, parents may not have realized their child had a disability or that special education supports were available prior to the child entering school; some may not have realized the benefits of early intervention.

With the exception of some instances of mental retardation and EBD, the mild disabilities cannot be detected prenatally or in infancy. However, because some disabilities co-occur with others, the risk for specific mild disabilities can be noted for some children and early detection can occur (see Roberts, Stough, and Parrish 2002). The child find requirements include a responsibility on the school agency's part to partner with pediatricians, day care and preschool providers, and social service agencies to be on the lookout for children at risk for disabilities or with probable special education needs. This responsibility includes informing the service providers with guidelines on what may indicate a disability.

Pre-referral. When a parent, teacher, or student perceives a difficulty with academics or functional performance, pre-referral is an appropriate response. Recall from Chapter 2 that **pre-referral** is the process of trying to resolve the difficulty by collecting information about the student's difficulties and modifying instruction based on that data to see if the problem can be removed. By engaging in pre-referral activities, you may realize that you simply need to modify instructional practices somewhat or revisit concepts and skills assumed to be prior knowledge.

The IDEA does not require that parents be notified when educators engage in pre-referral strategies and conferences. Still, informing the parents may be appropriate, if not at least on the outcomes initially. Should the pre-referral indicate that a referral is warranted, parents would be surprised to learn that educators had a concern and they were not informed. This could result in the start of a poor relationship between parties. Further, the information gathered during the pre-referral process may be useful in the referral stage; however, the fact that the parents did not participate in contributing, selecting, or reviewing the data is problematic.

Just as parents should be informed of pre-referral strategies and consulted about their child, they should also be informed and consulted about the progress of pre-referral activities. The collection of the valuable insights of parents should not end when interventions begin (in this case, pre-referral strategies). Parents can report on how pre-referral activities are impacting a student at home. Of course, parents may also have suggestions on alterations to attempt based on the progress being made in the pre-referral stage.

When parents are informed about pre-referral activities, they can also be consulted as information resources. Family background and child history information can be very valuable to understanding the profile of an infant, child, or adolescent. Parents will be able to report on events that happen outside of school. They may have insights on their child's social status, or they may see evidence of cognitive processing and literacy skills not commonly exhibited in preschool settings. The family may be experiencing economic hard times, the parents may be going through a divorce, or the child may only begin homework late at night, due to the family's routine. All such factors could cause a professional to suspect a disability, when in fact the student does not have one. Conversely, professionals may not believe they are seeing indicators of a disability if they are not familiar with factors outside of schooling.

VIDEO CASE CONNECTIONS BOX

Watch the Video Case entitled *Communicating with Parents: Tips and Strategies for Future Teachers.* List three tips that teachers give to establish good lines of communication with parents. List three other actions that teachers could take to communicate effectively with parents.

Referral. For the same reasons parental consultation is a good idea in pre-referral, parent consultation is also beneficial during the referral stage. At the **referral** stage, someone—an educator or a parent typically—makes an official declaration that a disability is suspected or known to exist and that the option of special education should be investigated. Parental input can also be useful for narrowing down the probable type of disability.

In addition to being a good idea, parental notification is a requirement of the IDEA. Educators must provide written notice to the parents that they have made a referral for an evaluation. No action may be taken toward disability evaluation or consideration of special education enrollment until the parent has provided written consent. This requirement is in keeping with the due process and parent and student participation provisions of the IDEA.

Screening. "The identification process includes (1) screening, (2) examination for the presence of risk indicators and protective factors, (3) systematic observations, and, if indicated, (4) a comprehensive evaluation" (NJCLD 2007).

A **screening** in special education is an informal assessment of *potential* for having a disability (Pierangelo and Giuliani 2009). The information it yields can inform instruction, in addition to indicating whether investigating the presence of a disability may be warranted. The child find requirements require screening children for possible disabilities or at-risk status when necessary.

Screening should include looking for both risk indicators and protective factors (NJCLD 2007). **Risk indicators** are situations such as low APGAR[2] scores, living in poverty, and failure to meet developmental milestones. **Protective factors** are those that may help prevent onset of a disability or buffer its impact;

---

[2]The APGAR test is given to newborns immediately after their birth to assess their physical health and whether immediate medical intervention is needed; the acronym stands for <u>a</u>ctivity and muscle tone, <u>p</u>ulse, <u>g</u>rimace response, <u>a</u>ppearance, and <u>r</u>espiration.

examples include quality health care, language-rich home environments, and access to related services. The information on risk indicators and protective factors will be useful to the educators and parents as they consider whether there is reasonable concern about the possible presence of a disability. Parents are primary sources of information about risk indicators and protective factors. They should provide information related to the prenatal development of the child and perinatal events relevant to disability status (for example, premature birth, anoxia). School districts may have forms listing questions about the birth experience, home environment, and developmental milestones. Also, meeting with parents to interview them about the information can provide valuable information (Bauer and Shea 2003). A meeting can also begin a positive relationship between the two parties.

Evaluation. Once again, the parents can be helpful collaborators in selecting evaluation tools, scheduling evaluations at optimal times, providing data, and interpreting the significance of what is found. To protect parents, the due process and parent and student participation provisions of the IDEA provide explicit guidelines on how they must be involved and informed throughout the evaluation process.

Parents can provide information on the child's English language ability and likely sitting tolerance for certain tests; they can even advise as to whether the test administrator should be male or female. All such information can be useful to collecting the most reliable profile of a child. The same types of background information on birthing events, early milestones, and the home environment, as well as on prior evaluations and diagnoses that may have been provided at an earlier stage can be essential information in evaluating for the presence of a disability. Dewey, Crawford, and Kaplan (2003) found that when parents contributed observational data, the accuracy of psychometric testing-centered evaluation for ADHD in children was improved. They noted that the parents assessed for different aspects of child functioning than the tests could be used to measure.

Once evaluation data has been collected, it must be analyzed consistent with the operational criteria for specific disabilities referenced in the IDEA. Unless the student satisfies the definitional criteria for one of the 13 disability categories served by the IDEA, the student will not be eligible for special education services, regardless of educational needs (see Stanovich 1999; 2005) (Section 504 services may be an option). Although parents should supply data and participate in reviewing it, they may not understand the operational criteria or agree with what a narrow reading of the data indicates. Parents should be informed about the specific disability in question and related conditions (for example, the distinctions between learning disabilities and mental retardation are minor in cases of students who are close to cutoff levels). Because parents may also be concerned with whether or not their child will be eligible for special education, information about special education enrollment and services should be provided. With that information, parents may be better able to understand the evaluation findings and their significance (for example, why they might ask for clarification of why mental retardation was found instead of a learning disability, and whether they may wish to pursue further evaluation).

Eligibility Determination. At the **eligibility determination meeting,** the parents are joined by professionals knowledgeable about the child's possible special education needs. The educators typically include a school administrator, a school psychologist (or other individual qualified to interpret evaluation results), special educators, and general educators. So, the participants in an eligibility determination meeting are typically the same as those who may participate in IEP meetings. Other individuals may also attend at the invitation of the parents or school district if they have knowledge or expertise regarding the child. A translator is provided if needed. It is efficient if those who participate in the eligibility determination meeting include all those who would be required to participate in IEP meetings, and if all agree the child is (a) eligible for special education and (b) needs or would benefit from special education, they may then begin to plan for that special education (that is, begin to plan the IEP). The IEP meeting does not have to be rushed into, however. The IDEA (2004) requires that, once eligibility is determined, the school district must provide written notification of that and an IEP meeting must be scheduled so that an IEP can be developed within 30 days.

The data shared at the determination meeting must be presented in a format that is meaningful to parents. Some may be confused by distinctions between achievement and intelligence tests for example, or may not understand what various subtests assess. Statistical language and concepts may also be confusing; for example, parents may not know what a percentile score indicates and, even once explained, they may not understand why such a comparison is appropriate. Smith (2001) advises that parents should be able to consider whether the evaluation results are an accurate reflection of their child's skills and abilities. Therefore, not only do they need to have the evaluation process and data explained to them, but they should also be comfortable that other data they consider relevant is taken into account (Sileo and Sileo 1996; Zhang and Bennett 2003).

Disagreements are almost inevitable in a group planning process, especially one as complex and emotional as planning a student's special education. Smith (2001) suggests that the "best, fastest, and least costly" resolution of a conflict is via informal problem solving. Keeping in mind that the ultimate goal of interacting is to secure a quality education for a child is also useful in keeping the collaborative process on track. An impartial third party can sometimes bring disagreeing parties back to the process. However, the IDEA calls for a more formal dispute resolution process when needed (see Figure 14.2). **Due Process hearings** follow when less formal mediation procedures are unsuccessful. The IDEA Regulations provide very specific guidelines for due process hearings (see Cortiella [2006] for a useful summary of the process, including major activities and obligations at each stage). Although parents and schools never lose their legal rights, the IDEA now requires that parties engage in a **resolution session** after

FIGURE 14.2

Stages of Due Process

Less formal ◀————————————————————————▶ More formal

Mediation > Due process complaint > Resolution session > Due process hearing > Civil suit

Source: Reprinted with permission from C. Cortiella. *IDEA Parent Guide: A Comprehensive Guide to Your Rights and Responsibilities Under the Individuals with Disabilities Education Act (IDEA 2004).* New York: National Center for Learning Disabilities, 2006.

a **due process complaint** has been filed by either party, but before proceeding to a due process hearing. The decisions arrived at through the resolution session may be legally binding.

IFSP/IEP Development. Parent consent to enrolling a child in special education is a required first step in IFSP and IEP development. Educators should not think of obtaining parental consent as a mere formality, however. It begins a long-term process of home-school collaboration. There are a number of benefits to parents collaborating to develop the IEP; they include increases and improvements in the following:

- Teachers' awareness of the child's in-school and out-of-school environments
- Parents' knowledge of their child's in-school environment
- Communication between parents and educators
- Educators' overall understanding of the child
- Education goal(s) attainment (Smith 2001)

In inviting parents to the determination meeting, school staff should extend the same courtesies and legally required rights that they have in other interactions with the family. Thus, educators should provide written prior notice, inquire as to whether a language translator or accommodations will be needed, and inform the parents of the purpose of the meeting, its time and location, their rights (the Procedural Safeguards document), who will be in attendance, and their right to include others who are knowledgeable about the child's educational needs. As Smith (2001) notes, the communication to the parents must be in a language and format they can comprehend.

When parents participate in identifying goals for their child, the prospect for them being able to support those goals at home increases (Smith 2001). Once the IEP team has identified educational goals (and objectives) and corresponding instructional plans, they next need to discuss where services will be provided and by whom—the placement decision. You and your school staff colleagues may think of placement for services in terms of efficiency for scheduling and professional expertise. Parents are likely to be more concerned with their child's safety, social status, transportation, and implications for future placements, in addition to being concerned with educational processes and outcomes (Smith 2001).

The meeting should conclude with setting plans for maintaining open communications between the school and the families (Smith 2001). Appropriate activities for setting such plans include restating all participants' roles following the meeting and agreeing on acceptable communication channels. Examples of useful communication channels include student assignment notebooks, in which parents and teachers may write notes to one another; specification of when progress reports will be provided and the expected content; schedules for communicating further following progress reports; and agreement on how often phone calls and e-mails can be processed. Smith further suggests that "thanking the parents, family members, and advocate is paramount in emphasizing that their active participation is a valued and essential part of the decision-making process" (5).

| CASE 14.2 | **Parent Participation in Implementing the IEP** |

Case Introduction

Now that you have worked through the first case in this chapter, you should feel comfortable addressing issues in a second case. You are going to read about another child in the Waters family, Amanda, who has recently been enrolled in special education. As you read the case, reflect on the nature of the relationship that Mrs. Waters has with the educators who work with Amanda, compared to the one she had with Rhonda in Case 14.1. Also, ask yourself if the plans Mrs. Waters and the teachers develop reflect a collaborative partnership.

Charlie's younger sister, Amanda Waters, was identified as having mild mental retardation near the end of the last school year, and an IEP was developed. Although Amanda received some special education services over the summer, the IEP was not fully implemented until the fall of the school year. Amanda entered second grade in the fall. Because both Amanda's special education teacher and general classroom teacher were newly hired by the district over the summer, Mrs. Waters wanted to meet them at the beginning of the year, both to establish personal contact and to review the IEP that had been developed before either of them was hired. Bernie Orblanski, the second grade classroom teacher, was beginning his first year of teaching. Olivia Mendoza had one prior year as a special educator in another district, where she had also worked as a fourth-grade-teacher for three years previously.

At the meeting, Mrs. Waters was disheartened by her realization that Bernie didn't seem to understand much about special education or his role in it. He also appeared to be unfamiliar with some of the intervention practices they discussed. Olivia, fortunately, was much more prepared to talk about special education procedures, and she had some ideas for interventions that Mrs. Waters liked.

Among the annual goals for Amanda were that she develop specific reading literacy and math numeracy skills, as well as the functional performance skill of dressing herself (the IEP team had agreed that she may not be able to master tying shoes, but that they would work toward that goal anyway). Olivia suggested using a greater reliance on Direct Instruction approaches in reading and mathematics than the IEP team had discussed last spring. She explained to Mrs. Waters that research evidence has supported the practices as likely to be effective in building foundational skills for children with mild mental retardation. Olivia promised to locate some information on the practices to share with Mrs. Waters.

Bernie did not appear to have much knowledge about Direct Instruction practices, so Olivia offered to help him incorporate them into his whole-class teaching routine and to work on them more intently with Amanda during in-class co-teaching and the pullout sessions specified on Amanda's IEP.

Mrs. Waters asked how she and her husband could support the Direct Instruction activities. Olivia said that the Waterses could participate by monitoring Amanda's homework and practicing specific skills with Amanda. Olivia said that she would work out a procedure for informing the Waterses of specific skills that needed to be practiced. She noted that previously practiced skills could always be reviewed, and promised she would provide tips on how to conduct the practice sessions. Mrs. Waters related that she and her husband were experienced at working with Charlie in collaboration with his teachers, so they would be willing to be as involved as they possibly could be. Olivia seized upon this information and suggested that the Waterses participate in a schedule of C-BM data collection and charting with her and Bernie.

Although Mrs. Waters did not say so, she was concerned that Bernie was too inexperienced to teach Amanda; she also wished that Olivia had more years of experience as a special educator. With those concerns in mind, she requested that progress reports and follow-up meetings among the three be held at the end of each month through November; following this, she requested receiving progress reports halfway through each academic quarter in addition to the end of each quarter—which is what the IEP team previously agreed to. Bernie enthusiastically agreed and also offered to write weekly notes to Mrs. Waters. Olivia said that she would be pleased to participate in the more frequent reporting intervals as well, but noted that she would have to consult with the special education director about changes in procedure from what was stated in the IEP.

CASE QUESTIONS

1. Did the circumstances and content of the meeting among Mrs. Waters, Olivia, and Bernie reflect development of a collaborative home-school partnership?

2. How can the Waterses play a more integral role in Amanda's education than simply monitoring her academic progress and homework practices?

3. What role can the Waterses play in progress monitoring, including making instructional and curricular decisions based on the data collected?

The meeting among Mrs. Waters, Olivia, and Bernie proved to be very beneficial. In addition to establishing contacts with one another, the three were able to review goals for Amanda and to discuss how they could work together to support Amanda's achievement. Thanks to Mrs. Waters's initiative, they progressed from simply getting to know one another to establishing a plan for collaborating. Their approach to establishing the goals for their relationship and how they would interact with one another was a bit more haphazard than the model proposed by Bauer and Shea (2003), but they did get off to a good start. Mrs. Waters has some concerns about what kind of a year Amanda will have based on her initial impressions of Olivia and Bernie, but she can feel more confident about how things should go because they made plans. All parties must now adhere to the plans and be forthcoming whenever they think a change will be needed.

THINK BACK TO THE CASE about Amanda . . .

1. *Did the circumstances and content of the meeting among Mrs. Waters, Olivia, and Bernie reflect development of a collaborative home-school partnership?*

Mrs. Waters had the idea to call the meeting. Although this can be a sign of a positive relationship because she was comfortable approaching the school, it would have been more appropriate if the teachers or special education director had contacted the Waterses. Doing so would have demonstrated their willingness to reach out to the family. New teachers are very busy, they may not have been on contract before the first week of the new school year, and large caseloads may make this an unrealistic goal; however, without Mrs. Waters's initiative, Amanda's teachers would have been strangers to her, and the specific details as to how Amanda's IEP goals should be addressed and the roles the Waterses could play would all have been ignored.

In the meeting, both the teachers and Mrs. Waters offered ideas for the other parties to consider; they all also responded to each other's contributions by giving their perspectives, and by problem-solving how they could work together. So, although the educators are remiss for not having initiated a partnership, the plans they jointly set laid the foundation for a collaborative relationship.

Intervention. Many parents, like the Waterses, are interested in supporting their child's education. They want a say in whether their children are enrolled in special services and updates on how well their children are progressing, as well as to more literally participate in educating their children.

Parents should be told about the education services their child will receive. In special education, that communication is partially accomplished through the requirements for parent participation in IEP development and for their written consent to enact the IEP. Parents should also be informed as to how well their children are performing in their education. Special education responds to this need through the required progress reports and an annual IEP review. Much more can be done to enhance parents' participation, however.

Supporting Interventions at Home. Ample research evidence supports that students benefit from multiple practice opportunities to learn new skills or information (Kame'enui et al. 2002; Swanson and Deshler 2003). Ideally, the practice will be distributed over time and integrated with related skills or content (Kame'enui et al. 2002). Working on academic content at home can be a useful way for students to get the additional practice that they need.

Parents should be asked about their willingness to participate in supporting interventions at home. They should be asked how much time they can devote, what types of skills they are prepared to support, and what communication assistance they may need (for example, English language, how to provide appropriate feedback) (Bauer and Shea 2003; Bryan and Burstein 2004; Salas et al. 2005).

Just as using homework to introduce new concepts or skills is not generally effective (review Chapter 10), asking parents to introduce new academic content at home may also not be appropriate. Parents can, however, monitor student practice. They can quiz students, ask students to model and practice think-aloud skills, and participate with the student to problem-solve assigned tasks.

METHODS AND STRATEGIES SPOTLIGHT

Interviewing Parents about their Participation in Their Child's Education

The word *interview* connotes one person answering questions that another person reads off of a clipboard. The interview with parents should be far more conversational. As Salas et al. (2005) note, the teacher should give information during the "interview conversation" too, as well as welcome the parents to ask questions and raise other topics.

Bauer and Shea (2003) advise that an interview with a parent can function much like an "intake interview," where educators seek to gain necessary information about students. They note that the initial interview can:

- Establish a positive working relationship between teacher and family members;
- Review and discuss the child's program;
- Review and discuss related services and accommodations;
- Review and discuss the role of parents;
- Introduce the parents to engagement in their child's education. (71)

In the case of parents who are uncomfortable with participating in interviews, the teacher can ask if they would be willing to complete interest forms on which the parents indicate their interest and comfort level discussing a variety of topics, such as their feelings about their child and the disability, how children develop and learn, and areas in which help is desired.

Homework. In addition to generally supporting interventions by practicing them at home and signaling their importance, parents can play a major role in homework. When parents assist their children with homework, completion rates increase; in turn, increased homework relates to improved academic achievement (Bryan and Burstein 2004). As Lott (2001) cautioned in the case of low-income parents, however, many parents may not be sure of how to help their children with homework, or even of the expectation to do so.

THINK BACK TO THE CASE about Amanda Waters . . .

2. *How can the Waterses play a more integral role in Amanda's education than simply monitoring her academic progress and homework practices?*

Mrs. Waters volunteered that she and her husband are willing and able to help Amanda with studying at home. Olivia introduced the idea of using Direct Instruction practices, which Mrs. Waters liked and Bernie was willing to support. Olivia also offered to supply Mrs. Waters with information about Direct Instruction and to prepare a system to communicate with the Waterses about Amanda's lesson objectives. She will also need to make sure that the Waterses understand the principles of Direct Instruction and that they are able to implement them in a format consistent with how Amanda is taught at school. A training session may be necessary to make that happen. At that session, Olivia will have the responsibility of making sure that the integrity of the Direct Instruction approach is maintained, but also for truly collaborating with the Waterses to determine the particulars of how the activities will transpire.

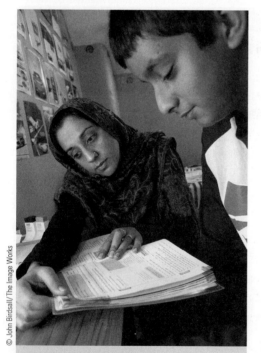

Parents can play a significant role in their child's education. To be effective there must be open communications between home and school and the parties should consult with each other to make sure they are consistent in their practices.

As with supporting interventions in general, teachers and parents should communicate about the parents' roles and expectations for them related to homework. Parents can report to teachers on how well homework is going for their child. Not only can they report back their impressions of how well the child performed but they can report observations on study habits, the child's thought processes, and frustration levels associated with the assigned tasks. For example, parents often note differences in homework expectations between teachers and between grade levels (Bryan and Burstein 2004). These are all examples of information that educators would have difficulty gleaning were it not for open communications with parents.

Progress Monitoring. Although the IDEA requirements for progress reports call for periodically informing parents of their child's progress toward achieving goals, progress monitoring presumes an ongoing process of collecting and analyzing data to indicate how well a student is progressing in all lessons. Progress monitoring is not necessarily distinct from intervention. The data collected for progress monitoring comes from interventions and should be used to inform intervention practices.

Perhaps the best established example of progress monitoring in special education practice is curriculum-based measurement (C-BM) (Deno 1985; 2003a; 2003b). Using C-BM procedures, samplings of student progress in a lesson or unit are collected at regular intervals. When Amanda Waters is working on literacy, numeracy, or dressing skills, for example, the educators can assess and record how well, how consistently, or how quickly she performs targeted skills. For academic interventions, quick one-minute probes of skill performance are typically administered every three days or weekly (review Chapter 2). The data collected is plotted on a graph so that the teacher, parents, and student can also monitor progress.

Parents can participate in administering CB-M probes and charting their child's performance. When they do so, a chart of home performance can supplement a chart of in-school performance.

Of course, sharing C-BM data with parents is a useful way to communicate with them about their child's progress. Specific data points and trends can be discussed, which should help both parties feel assured they are talking about the same phenomena. It also enhances the probability that both parties will interpret the meaning of the data in the same way. In addition, when parents have access to C-BM data, they are better informed about skills and content to practice with their child beyond the homework assignments the student receives.

THINK BACK TO THE CASE about Amanda Waters . . .

3. *What role can the Waterses play in progress monitoring, including making instructional and curricular decisions based on the data collected?*

Just as is the case for preparing the Waterses to participate in Direct Instruction with Amanda, Olivia should be prepared to train the Waterses in the procedures for C-BM, as well as the rationale for the approach. They can keep records of Amanda's progress on specific literacy, numeracy, and dressing skills. They can share the data they collect and chart with Olivia, who can likewise share data that she collects and charts at school. Through their communications the Waterses and Olivia can consider whether Amanda is benefiting from the Direct Instructional practices both in school and at home. They can analyze trends in her performance between the two settings to determine whether they need to focus more on skill generalization or regular review of pre-skills, for example.

Annual Review and Triennial Reevaluation. As discussed in Chapter 1, in addition to the annual review of the IEP, a triennial review must be conducted to update the IEP team on the student's current disability condition and how it impacts the child's academic learning and functional performance. A collaborative partnership with parents can facilitate annual and triennial reviews. In advance of the meeting, parents should be consulted regarding the agenda and the major topics for discussion (Cortiella 2006; Smith 2001). They should be advised to identify their level of satisfaction with the child's education to date and their goals for the coming year. Having this type of information can facilitate devoting more of the meeting time to planning. Parents should be clearly informed that they will be able to state their information within the meeting and that no decisions will be made in advance of the session. Because the balance of power in the special education process can seem to pit the school against the parents (Kalyanpur, Harry, and Skrtic 2000; Salas et al. 2005), educators should also be willing to share their perspectives in advance of the meeting.

According to the IDEA, parents also need to be informed as to who will be present at the review meeting, by both name and position. The parents are also welcome to bring along professionals knowledgeable about their child's education needs.

ITP or SOP Development. Expectations to notify and inform parents properly of IFSP/IEP meetings are no different for the transition meeting to develop an individualized transition plan (ITP) or meeting to develop a summary of performance (SOP) document (review Chapter 12). The concept of inviting parents to participate in determining the need for either document, as well as to participate in setting priorities for them, actually crafting the document, and monitoring implementation are no different than for other special education meetings and processes either. Parents must be informed of the purpose and their rights, they must be invited to participate, and they must be informed of progress as it is monitored. Also, the same principle previously reviewed for ensuring more than minimal compliance with such requirements holds as well.

Because the purpose of developing an ITP or SOP is to help prepare for the student's life beyond K-12 school and special education, educators should take care to ensure that parents and the student are clearly informed on the factors they should be considering. For example, many of the services and protections received via the auspices of the IDEA will no longer be available. Parents need to understand what other laws apply and whether insurance plans can be a resource, for example. Parents may also need assistance in thinking about what factors should be considered via ITP or SOP development.

RTI. In the case of students who are engaged via a responsiveness to intervention (RTI) approach (review Chapter 1), the parents must be furnished with a **written intervention plan** (see Table 14.2). The purposes for providing an intervention plan parallels the purposes of various communications to parents in the pre-referral, referral, and IEP stages of the traditional special education process. That is, it is designed to inform the parents of what is being done with their child and why, as well as to provide advance notice of how the parents will be informed throughout the RTI process. Contents of a written intervention plan should include:

"A description of the specific intervention;
The length of time (such as number of weeks) that will be allowed for the
      intervention to have a positive effect;
The number of minutes per day the intervention will be implemented (such as
      30 to 45 minutes);
The persons responsible for providing the intervention;
The location where the intervention will be provided;
The factors for judging whether the student is experiencing success;
A description of the progress monitoring strategy or approach, such as C-BM,
      that will be used;
A progress monitoring schedule." (Cortiella 2006)

Although RTI models do not typically require providing progress monitoring reports to parents when their children enter into Tier 2 or 3 interventions, common sense dictates that parents would value being informed and that they may have useful input. Furthermore, knowing that interventions at a particular tier have not been successful may be important to parents, because parents have the right to refer their child for traditional evaluation of a possible learning disability at any time.

TABLE 14.2: Parent Information and Participation in the RTI Model*

Universal Screening	
Tier 1: Classwide or Schoolwide Intervention	Written intervention plan Parent consultation Progress reports
Tier 2:	
Tier 3:	
Evaluation**	Written notification Procedural Safeguards document Parent consultation Written parent consent Data and information shared is comprehensible to parents Information and resources about disabilities Information and resources about special education
Determination Meeting	Written notification Procedural Safeguards document Advance invitation to schedule the meeting Advance invitation to identify the need for language interpreter or accommodations Data and information shared is comprehensible to parents Parent collaboration
IEP/ITP Development	Written notification Procedural Safeguards document Advance invitation to schedule the meeting Advance invitation to identify the need for language interpreter or accommodations Data and information shared is comprehensible to parents Parent consent Parent collaboration

*RTI model based on NJCLD (2007).
**Parents may request a formal disability evaluation for special education determination at any time in the RTI process.

Parents also need to be informed of their right to request a formal evaluation for the presence of a disability at any stage of the RTI process. The Procedural Safeguard document should make this option clear to the parents, including informing them on the implications of both RTI and full evaluation. Parents may be confused as to whether participation in RTI is the same as enrollment in special education. It is not, except in the case of versions where one of the tiers constitutes special education enrollment (typically Tier 3, or following the student's failure to respond to effective interventions in Tier 3, although special education enrollment is not an automatic outcome). Although the IDEA does allow states to experiment with incorporating RTI data into the formal evaluation process, designation of a learning disability and enrollment in special education still require parental consent and participation. Remember that the RTI option is only available for those with possible LD, not the other mild disabilities.

Much like the pre-referral and intervention stages of the traditional special education model, progression through the tiers of RTI models will be most efficient if parents are informed and welcomed to participate. Whatever the interventions used in the RTI tiers, parents can still participate by practicing skills at home and observing their child's performance. So that they are fully informed, they should receive progress reports at regular intervals, at least whenever a student is moved to another tier or the RTI model is ceased. Because practices associated with C-BM are frequently used in RTI models (Kavale et al. 2008), parents should receive progress reports at frequent intervals.

CHAPTER SUMMARY

Families come in many different configurations. They differ in culture and values. Having a child or adolescent in the family with a disability can be a source of stress for some families. Special education services can help families when they work together with the school to provide a student with an appropriate education. In the case of special education for the first two years of life, family members may receive services that will indirectly benefit the child as well.

The IDEA provides for the involvement of parents in their child's special education. The six major provisions of the IDEA each relate to a role for the family. Families can provide valuable information to educators about their child's development and learning experiences at home. Families can also partner with educators to help students extend learning to home, including supporting them in succeeding at homework. The IDEA also clearly states that parents must be invited to be active participants in planning and providing special education.

True family involvement is a complex process. Ideally, schools and parents will enter into a collaborative partnership where they truly value one another's skill and expertise. For such a partnership to work, educators must be careful to respect the needs of parents. By partnering at every stage of the special education process, students are more likely to receive a successful education that is relevant to their life in school and beyond.

KEY TERMS

Child Find, 491

Communications Log, 484

Coping, 477

Due Process Complaint, 496

Due Process Hearings, 495

Due Process Provision, 478

Early intervening, 489

Eligibility Determination
   Meeting, 495

Informed Consent, 478

Parent and Student Participation, 478

Pre-referral, 492

Problem Solving, 476

Protective Factors, 493

Referral, 493

Reframe, 477

Resolution Session, 495

Risk Indicators, 493

Screening, 493

Service Coordinator, 483

Written Intervention Plan, 502

APPLICATION ACTIVITIES

Using information from the chapter, complete the following activities that were designed to help you apply knowledge that was presented in this chapter.

1. Ask a parent (even your own) to share with you examples of how she or he has been included or excluded from the student's education process. You do not need to locate the parent of a student in special education for this application activity, but that might be even more instructive for you.

2. Select an instructional approach or activity that you know well (or one of the many presented in this text). Develop a "lesson plan" for teaching the procedures to a parent, and pay attention to what types of learning experiences she or he will need to have to learn the procedures.

3. Review the CEC standards (see the inside cover of this text) and identify those that relate to parent and family partnerships. For each standard you locate, list at least one skill you are sure you can do to meet that standard.

4. Role-play an IEP meeting with your classmates (or attend an actual meeting if that is possible) and observe how, even in the simulation, the parent(s) and educators interact. Pay particular attention to the power dynamics (see, for example, Kalyanpur, Harry, and Skrtic 2000) and consider ways that parents may have felt valued or intimidated in the process.

TECHNOLOGIES FOR WORKING WITH FAMILIES

A number of websites exist to inform teachers or parents about special education. The following can be valuable resources for you.

National Association for the Education of Young Children

www.naeyc.org

The NAEYC website includes information on effective practices for early childhood education. It is appropriate for both parents and educators. Among the information available on the site are standards for early childhood educators.

NCLD's Parent Center

www.ncld.org/content/view/827/527

The National Center for Learning Disabilities' Parent Center is a ready resource of information for parents related to special education.

LD OnLine

www.Ldonline.org

With a primary emphasis on learning disabilities and attention deficit/hyperactivity disorder, this site has a wealth of information about effective practices. It also includes sections where parents can communicate directly with each other or with an expert (similar features for children, students, and adults with disabilities are also included).

My Child's Special Needs

www.ed.gov/parents/needs/speced/edpicks .jhtml

This section of the U.S. Department of Education website provides links to resource documents and other websites related to a variety of aspects of special education. Basic information about disabling conditions can also be found.

 Visit the book-specific website at www.cengage.com/education/ boyle for a variety of study tools such as web links, tutorial quizzes, glossary/flash cards, bonus material not included in the text, and more.

The premium website offers access to additional materials, including the Video Cases. Go to www.cengage.com/login to register or purchase access.

References

Ackerman, P., C. Holloway, P. Youngdahl, and R. Dykman. 2001. The double-deficit theory of reading disability does not fit at all. *Learning Disabilities Research & Practice* 16:152–60.

AD/HD and the Military. n.d. National Resource Center on AD/HD. http://www.help4adhd.org/en/living/workplace/military (accessed December 7, 2007).

Adams, M. J. 1990. *Beginning to read: Thinking and learning about print.* Cambridge, MA: MIT Press.

Al Otaiba, S., and D. Fuchs. 2002. Characteristics of children who are unresponsive to early literacy intervention: A review of the literature. *Remedial and Special Education* 23(5):300–16.

Allsopp, D. H. 1999. Using modeling, manipulatives, and mnemonics with eighth-grade math students. *Teaching Exceptional Children* 32(2):74–81.

Anderson, J. 1990. *Cognitive psychology and its implications.* San Francisco: Freeman and Company.

Andrews, S. P., and J. R. Slate. 2002. Public and private prekindergarten programs: A comparison of student readiness. *Educational Research Quarterly* 25:5,974.

Austin, J. L., M. Lee, and J. E. Carr. 2004. The effects of guided notes on undergraduate students' recording of lecture content. *Journal of Instructional Psychology* 31(4):91–6.

Al Otaiba, S., and M. Rivera. 2006. Individualized guided oral reading fluency instruction for students with emotional and behavioral disorders. *Intervention in School and Clinic* 41:144–9.

Albert, L. R., and J. J. Ammer. 2004. Lesson planning and delivery. In *Teaching content to all*, ed. B. K. Lenz, D. D. Deshler, and B. R. Kissam. Boston, MA: Allyn & Bacon.

Algozzine, B., D. Browder, M. Karvonen, D. Test, and W. Wood. 2001. Effects of interventions to promote self-determination for individuals with disabilities. *Review of Educational Research* 71:219–77.

Allbritten, D., R. Mainzer, and D. Ziegler. 2004. Will students with disabilities be scapegoats for school failures? *Educational Horizons* 82:153–60.

Allington, R. L. 1983. Fluency: The neglected reading goal. *The Reading Teacher* 36:556–61.

Allington, R. L. 2002. What I've learned about effective reading instruction. *Phi Delta Kappan* 83:740–47.

American Psychiatric Association. 1994. *Diagnostic and statistical manual of mental disorders*, text revision: DSM-IV-TR. 4th ed. Washington, DC: American Psychiatric Association.

American Psychiatric Association. 2000. *Diagnostic and statistical manual of mental disorders.* 4th ed., text rev. Washington, DC: American Psychiatric Association.

Americans with Disabilities Act of 1990. Pub. Law no. 101-336, 104 Stat. 327.

Amundson, S., and M. Weil. 1996. Prewriting and handwriting skills. In *Occupational therapy for children*, ed. J. Case-Smith, A. S. Allen, and P. N. Pratt, 524–41. St. Louis, Michigan: Mosby-Year Book.

Applegate, M., K. Quinn, and A. Applegate. 2002. Levels of thinking required by comprehension questions in informal reading inventories. *The Reading Teacher* 56:174–80.

Aram, D. M., and N. E. Hall. 1989. Longitudinal follow-up of children with preschool communication disorders. *School Psychology Review* 18:487–501.

Arbona, C. 2000. The development of academic achievement in school-aged children: Precursors to career development. In *Handbook of counseling psychology,* 3rd ed., eds. S. D. Brown and R. W. Lent, 270–309. New York: Wiley and Sons, Inc.

Arends, R. I. 1998. *Learning to teach.* Boston: McGraw-Hill.

Arndt, S. A., M. Konrad, and D. W. Test. 2006. Effects of the "self-directed IEP" on student participation in planning meetings. *Remedial and Special Education* 27(4):194–207.

Aronson, E., N. Blaney, C. Stephan, J. Sikes, and M. Snapp. 1978. *The jigsaw classroom.* Beverly Hills, CA: Sage.

Association for Childhood Education International. 2000. Program standards for elementary teacher preparation. Association for Childhood Education International. http://www.acei.org/Part1.htm (accessed May 8, 2008).

Association on Higher Education and Disability (AHEAD). 2008. AHEAD Best Practices: Disability Documentation in Higher Education. http://www.ahead.org/resources (accessed May 8, 2008).

Atkinson, R., and R. Shiffrin. 1968. Human memory: A proposed system and its control processes. In *The psychology of learning and motivation,* ed. K. Spence and J. Spence, 90–197. New York: Academic Press.

Ausubel, D. 1963. *The psychology of meaningful verbal learning.* New York: Grune & Stratton.

Ausubel, D., J. D. Novak, and H. Hanesian. 1968. *Educational psychology: A cognitive view.* 2nd ed. New York: Holt, Rinehart, & Winston.

Ayres, A. J. 1972. Improving academic scores through sensory integration. *Journal of Learning Disabilities* 5:336–43.

Ayers, W. 2006. Hearts and minds: Military recruitment and the high school battlefield. *Phi Delta Kappan* 87:594–9.

Baca, L. M., and H. T. Cervantes. 2003. *The bilingual special education interface.* 4th ed. Upper Saddle River, NJ: Prentice Hall.

Bailey, D. B., M. B. Bruder, K. Hebbeler, J. Carta, M. Defosset, C. Greenwood, L. Kahn, S. Mallik, J. Markowitz, D. Spiker, D. Walker, and L. Barton. 2006. Recommended outcomes for families of young children with disabilities. *Journal of Early Intervention* 28:227–51.

Baker, S., R. Gersten, and D. Scanlon. 2002. Procedural facilitators, cognitive strategies: Tools for unraveling the mysteries of comprehension and the writing process and providing meaningful access to the general curriculum. *Learning Disabilities Research & Practice* 17:65–77.

Baker, S. K., D. C. Simmons, and E. J. Kame'enui. 1998. Vocabulary acquisition: Research bases. In *What reading research tells us about children with diverse learning needs: Bases and basics*, ed. D. C. Simmons and E. J. Kame'enui, 183–218. Mahwah, NJ: Erlbaum.

Baltodano, H. M., P. J. Harris, and R. B. Rutherford. 2005. Academic achievement in juvenile corrections: Examining the impact of age, ethnicity and disability. *Education and Treatment of Children* 28:361–79.

Bandura, A. 1977. *Social learning theory.* Upper Saddle River, NJ: Prentice Hall.

Bangert-Drowns, R. L. 1993. The word processor as an instructional tool: A meta-analysis of word processing in writing instruction. *Review of Educational Research* 63(1):69–93.

Barkley, R. 2000. *Taking charge of ADHD: The complete, authoritative guide for parents.* NY: Guilford Press.

Barkley, R. A., M. Fischer, L. Smallish, and K. Fletcher. 2006. Young adult outcome of hyperactive children: Adaptive functioning in major life activities. *Journal of American Academy of Child and Adolescent Psychiatry* 45:192–202.

Barron, K. E., S. W. Evans, L. E. Baranik, Z. N. Serpell, and E. Buvinger. 2006. Achievement goals of students with ADHD. *Learning Disability Quarterly* 29:137–58.

Barsch, R. 1967. *Achieving perceptual-motor efficiency.* Everett, WA: Special Child Publications.

Bauer, A. M., and T. M. Shea. 1999. Inclusion 101: How to teach all learners. *Report, no. ED432843.* Baltimore, MD: Paul H. Brookes Publishing Co.

Bauer, A. M., and T. M. Shea. 2003. *Parents and schools: Creating a successful partnership for students with special needs.* Upper Saddle River, NJ: Merrill/Prentice Hall.

Beder, H., and P. Medina. 2001. *Classroom dynamics in adult literacy education* (NCSALL Report #18). Cambridge, MA: National Center for the Study of Adult Learning and Literacy.

Belkin, A., and G. Bateman, eds. 2003. *Don't ask, don't tell: Debating the gay ban in the military.* Boulder, CO: Lynne Rienner Publishers.

Bell, M. A. 2002. Why use an Interactive Whiteboard? A baker's dozen reasons! http://Teachers.Net (accessed April 7, 2008).

Berninger, V. W. 2003. Preventing written expression disabilities through early and continuing assessment and intervention for handwriting and/or spelling problems: Research into practice. In *Handbook of learning disabilities,* ed. H. L. Swanson, K. R. Harris, and S. Graham, 345–63. New York: The Guilford Press.

Berninger, V. W., R. D. Abbott, D. Whitaker, L. Sylvester, and S. B. Nolen. 1995. Integrating low- and high-level skills in instructional protocols for writing disabilities. *Learning Disability Quarterly* 18:293–309.

Berninger, V., K. Vaughan, S. Graham, R. Abbott, S. Abbott, A. Brooks, and E. Reed. 1997. Treatment of handwriting problems in beginning writers: Transfer from handwriting to composition. *Journal of Educational Psychology* 89:652–66.

Bernstein, D., and E. Tiegerman-Farber. 1997. *Language communication disorders in children.* Boston, MA: Allyn & Bacon.

Berry, G. C. 1999. Development and validation of an instructional program for teaching post-secondary students with learning disabilities to take and study notes. Ph.D. dissertation, University of Kansas, from Dissertations & Theses: Full Text database, no. AAT 9946088 (retrieved May 22, 2008).

Best Buddies. 2007. http://www.bestbuddies.org/site/c .ljJ0J8MNIsE/b.1162355/k.BF9F/Intro.htm (accessed May 1, 2008).

Beveridge, S. 2004. Pupil participation and the home-school relationship. *European Journal of Special Needs Education* 19(1):3–16.

Bhattacharya, A. 2006. Syllable representation in written spellings of sixth and eighth grade children. *Insights on Learning Disabilities* 3:43–61.

Bhattacharya, A., and L. C. Ehri, 2004. Graphosyllabic analysis helps adolescent struggling readers read and spell words. *Journal of Learning Disabilities* 37:331–48.

Birman, B. F., K. C. Le Flock, A. Klekotka, M. Ludwig, J. Taylor, K. Walters, W. Andrew, and Kwang-Suk Yoon. 2007–2008. *State and local implementation of the* No Child Left Behind Act. *Volume II—Teacher quality under* NCLB: *Interim report.* Washington, DC: U.S. Department of Education, ERIC Documents Reproduction Services, no. 497 970.

Bisaillon, J., and I. Clerc. 1999. A computer writing environment for professional writers and students learning to write. *Journal of Technical Writing & Communication* 29:185–203.

Blachowicz, C., and P. Fisher. 2000. Vocabulary instruction. In *Handbook of reading research,* ed. M. Kamil, P. Mosenthal, P. Pearson, and R. Barr, 502–523. Mahwah, NJ: Lawrence Erlbaum Associates.

Blackorby, J., and M. Wagner. 1996. Longitudinal postschool outcomes of youth with disabilities: Findings from the national longitudinal transition study. *Exceptional Children* 62(5):399–413.

Blalock, G., C. Kochhar-Bryant, D. Test, P. Kohler, W. White, J. Lehmann, D. Bassett, and J. Patton. 2003. The need for comprehensive personnel preparation in transition and career development: DCDT position statement. *Career Development for Exceptional Individuals* 26:207–26.

Bond, N. 2007. Questioning strategies that minimize classroom management problems. *Kappa Delta Pi Record* Fall:18–21.

Borkowski, J. G. 1992. Metacognitive theory: A framework for teaching literacy, writing, and math skills. *Journal of Learning Disabilities* 25:253–7.

Bos, C. S. 1988. Process-oriented writing: Instructional implications for mildly handicapped students. *Exceptional Children* 54:521–7.

Bos, C. S. and P. Anders. 1987. Semantic feature analysis: An interactive strategy for facilitating learning from text. *Learning Disabilities Focus* 3:55–9.

Bos, C. S., and P. Anders. 1990. Effects of interactive vocabulary instruction on the vocabulary learning and reading comprehension of junior high learning disabled students. *Learning Disability Quarterly* 13:31–42.

Bos, C. S., and P. L. Anders. 1992. Using interactive teaching and learning strategies to promote text comprehension and content learning for students with learning disabilities. *International Journal of Disability, Development, and Education* 39:225–38.

Bos, C. S., P. Anders, D. Filip, and L. Jaffe. 1989. The effects of an interactive instructional strategy for enhancing reading comprehension and content area learning for students with learning disabilities. *Journal of Learning Disabilities* 6:384–90.

Bottge, B. A. 2001. Reconceptualizing mathematics problem solving for low-achieving students. *Remedial and Special Education* 22(2):102–12.

Boulineau, T., C. Fore, S. Hagan-Burke, and M. Burke. 2004. Use of story-mapping to increase story-grammar text comprehension of elementary students with learning disabilities. *Learning Disability Quarterly* 27:105–21.

Bounds, M., and A. Gould. 2000. Reasons students with disabilities drop out. *Journal for Vocational Special Needs Education* 23:3–9.

Bowman, M., and R. Treiman. 2002. Relating print and speech: The effects of letter names and word position on reading and spelling performance. *Journal of Experimental Child Psychology* 82:305–40.

Boyle, J. R. 1996. The effects of a cognitive mapping strategy on the literal and inferential comprehension of students with mild disabilities. *Learning Disability Quarterly* 19(2):86–98.

Boyle, J. 1996. Thinking while note taking: Teaching college students to use strategic note taking during lectures. In *Innovative learning strategies: Twelfth yearbook*, ed. B. G. Grown, 9–18. Newark, DE: International Reading Association.

Boyle, J. R. 2000. The effects of a Venn diagram strategy on the literal, inferential, and relational comprehension of students with mild disabilities. *Learning Disabilities: A Multidisciplinary Journal* 10(1):5–13.

Boyle, J., and C. Hughes. 1994. Effects of self-monitoring and subsequent fading of external prompts on the on-task behavior and task productivity of elementary students with moderate mental retardation. *Journal of Behavioral Education* 4:439–57.

Boyle, J. R., and T. Seibert. 1998. The effects of a phonological awareness strategy on the reading skills of elementary students with learning disabilities. *Learning Disabilities: A Multidisciplinary Journal* 8(3):145–53.

Boyle, J. R., and M. Weishaar. 1997. The effects of expert-versus student-generated cognitive organizers on the reading comprehension of high school students with learning disabilities. *Learning Disabilities Research & Practice* 12(4):228–35.

Boyle, J. R., and M. Weishaar. 2001. The effects of a strategic note-taking technique on the comprehension and long term recall of lecture information for high school students with LD. *Learning Disabilities Research & Practice* 16(3):125–33.

Boyle, J. R., and N. Yeager. 1997. Blueprints for learning: Using cognitive frameworks for understanding. *TEACHING Exceptional Children* 29(4):26–31.

Bradley, D., and D. Switlick. 1997. From isolation to cooperation in teaching. In *Teaching students in inclusive settings: From theory to practice*, ed. D. Bradley, M. King-Sears, and D. Tessler-Switlick, 225–51. Boston: Allyn & Bacon.

Bray, N. W., K. L. Fletcher, and L. A. Turner. 1997. Cognitive competencies and strategy use in individuals with mental retardation. In *Ellis' handbook of mental deficiency, psychological theory, and research*, ed. W. W. Maclean, 3rd ed., 197–217. Mahwah, NJ: Erlbaum.

Bremer, C., A. Clapper, and D. Deshler. 2002. *Improving word identification skills using Strategic Instruction Model (SIM) strategies*. Minneapolis, MN: National Center on Secondary Education and Transition.

Brodzinsky, D. M., C. J. Patterson, and M. Vaziri. 2002. Adoption agency perspectives on lesbian and gay prospective parents: A national study. *Adoption Quarterly* 5(3):5–23.

Browder, D., W. Wood, D. Test, M. Karvonen, and B. Algozzine. 2001. Reviewing resources on self-determination: A map for teachers. *Remedial and Special Education* 22:233–44.

Brown, A. S. 1990. A review of recent research on spelling. *Educational Psychology Review* 2:365–97.

Brownell, M. T., A. Adams, P. Sindelar, N. Waldron, and S. Vanhover. 2006. Learning from collaboration: The role of teacher qualities. *Exceptional Children* 72(2):169–85.

Bruner, J. 1983. *Child's talk.* New York: W.W. Norton & Co.

Bryan, T., and K. Burstein. 2004. Improving homework completion and academic performance: Lessons from special education. *Theory Into Practice* 43:213–9.

Bryan, T., and K. Sullivan-Burstein. 1997. Homework how-to's. *Teaching Exceptional Children* 29(6):32–7.

Bryant, D., B. Bryant, and D. Hammill. 2000. Characteristic behaviors of students with LD who have teacher-identified math weaknesses. *Journal of Learning Disabilities* 33:168–77.

Bryant, D. P., M. Goodwin, B. Bryant, and K. Higgins. 2003. Vocabulary instruction for students with learning disabilities: A review of the research. *Learning Disability Quarterly* 26:117–28.

Buck, G. H., E. A. Polloway, A. Smith-Thomas, and K. W. Cook. 2003. Prereferral intervention processes: A survey of state practices. *Exceptional Children* 69(3):349–60.

Bulgren, J. A. 2006. Integrated content enhancement routines: Responding to the needs of adolescents with disabilities in rigorous inclusive secondary content classes. *Teaching Exceptional Children* 38(6):54–8.

Bulgren, J. A., D. D. Deshler, and J. B. Schumaker. 1993. *The concept mastery routine*. Lawrence, KS: Edge Enterprises, Inc.

Bulgren, J., D. Deshler, J. Schumaker, and B. K. Lenz. 2000. The use and effectiveness of analogical instruction in diverse secondary content classrooms. *Journal of Educational Psychology* 92:426–41.

Bulgren, J. A., M. F. Hock, J. B. Schumaker, and D. D. Deshler. 1995. The effects of instruction in a paired associates strategy on the information mastery performance of students with learning disabilities. *Learning Disabilities Research & Practice* 10:22–37.

Bulgren, J. and B. K. Lenz. 1996. Strategic instruction in the content areas. In *Teaching adolescents with learning disabilities: Strategies and methods*, ed. D. D. Deshler, E. S. Ellis, and B. K. Lenz, 2nd ed., 409–73. Denver, CO: Love Publishing.

Bulgren, J. A., B. K. Lenz, M. McKnight, B. Davis, B. Grossen, J. Marquis, D. Deshler, and J. B. Schumaker. 2002. *The educational content and outcomes for high school students with disabilities: The perceptions of regular education teachers. Research report*, ERIC Documents Reproduction Services, no. ED469287. University of Kansas, Institute for Academic Access.

Bulgren, J. A., J. G. Marquis, D. D. Deshler, J. B. Schumaker, B. K. Lenz, B. Davis, and B. Grossen. 2006. The instructional context of inclusive secondary general education classes: Teachers' instructional roles and practices, curricular demands, and research-based practices and standards. *Learning Disabilities: A Contemporary Journal* 4(1):39–65.

Bulgren, J. A., J. G. Marquis, B. K. Lenz, J. B. Schumaker, and D. D. Deshler. Forthcoming. Effectiveness of question exploration to enhance students' written expression of content knowledge and comprehension. *Reading & Writing Quarterly*.

Bulgren, J. A., and D. Scanlon. 1997/1998. Teachers' instructional routines and learning strategies that promote understanding of content-area concepts. *Journal of Adolescent & Adult Literacy* 41:292–302.

Burgio, L., T. Whitman, and M. Johnson. 1980. A self-instructional package for increasing attending behavior in educable mentally retarded children. *Journal of Applied Behavior Analysis* 13:443–59.

Burke, J. 2001. Southern Regional Education Board. Technology standards for students. http://www.sreb.org/programs/EdTech/pubs/pubsindex.asp (accessed July 6, 2007).

Burks, M. 2004. Effects of classwide peer tutoring and the number of words spelled correctly by students with LD. *Intervention in School and Clinic* 39(5):301–4.

Burns, E. 2006. *IEP-2005*. Springfield, IL: Thomas.

Burns, M. 2005. Using incremental rehearsal to increase fluency of single-digit multiplication facts with children identified as learning disabled in mathematics computation. *Education and Treatment of Children* 28:237–49.

Butler, D. 1998. The strategic content learning approach to promoting self-regulated learning: A report of three studies. *Journal of Educational Psychology* 90:682–97.

Butler, F., S. Miller, K. Crehan, B. Babbitt, and T. Pierce. 2003. Fraction instruction for students with mathematics disabilities: Comparing two teaching sequences. *Learning Disabilities Research & Practice* 18:99–111.

Cain, K., and J.V. Oakhill. 1999. Inference making and its relation to comprehension failure. *Reading and Writing* 11:489–503.

Cain, K., J. Oakhill, and K. Lemmon. 2004. Individual differences in the inference of word meanings from context: The influence of reading comprehension, vocabulary knowledge, and memory capacity. *Journal of Educational Psychology* 96:671–81.

Calderon, M. 2007. *Teaching reading to English language learners, grades 6–12: A framework for improving achievement in the content areas.* Thousand Oaks, CA: Corwin Press.

Calhoon, M. B., and L. S. Fuchs. 2003. The effects of Peer-Assisted Learning Strategies and Curriculum-Based Measurement on the mathematics performance of secondary students with disabilities. *Remedial and Special Education* 24:235–46.

Calhoon, M. B., S. Al Otaiba, D. Greenberg, A. King, and A. Avalos. 2006. Improving reading skills in predominately Hispanic Title 1 first-grade classrooms: The promise of peer-assisted learning strategies. *Learning Disabilities Research & Practice* 21:261–72.

Callahan, J. F., L. H. Clark, and R. D. Kellough. 1998. *Middle and secondary school students: Meeting the challenge. Teaching in the middle and secondary schools.* 6th ed. Frontin, NJ: Simon and Schuster Company.

Cameto, R. 2005. *How are we preparing youth with disabilities for the transition to early adulthood? Findings from the National Longitudinal Transition Study-2.* Albuquerque, NM: National Center on Secondary Education and Transition, Capacity Building Institute.

Cantrell, R. J., J. Fusaro, and E. Dougherty. Exploring the effectiveness of journal writing on learning social studies: A comparative study. *Reading Psychology* 21:1–11.

Carnine, D. 2000. *Why education experts resist effective practices (and what it would take to make education more like medicine)*, no. ED442804. Washington, DC: Thomas Ford Foundation.

Carnine, D., A. Jitendra, and J. Silbert. 1997. A descriptive analysis of mathematics curricular materials from a pedagogical perspective. *Remedial and Special Education* 18:66–81.

Carnine, D., J. Silbert, and E. J. Kame'enui. 1990. *Direct instruction reading.* 2nd ed. Columbus, OH: Merrill.

Carnine, D. W., J. Silbert, and E. J. Kame'enui. 1997. *Direct instruction reading.* 3rd ed. Upper Saddle River, NJ: Merrill/Prentice Hall.

Carnine, D. W., J. Silbert, E. J. Kame'enui, S. G. Tarver, and K. Jungjohann. 2006. *Teaching struggling and at-risk readers: A direct instruction approach.* Upper Saddle River, NJ: Prentice Hall.

Carnine, L., and D. Carnine. 2004. The interaction of reading skills and science content knowledge when teaching struggling secondary students. *Reading & Writing Quarterly* 20:203–18.

Carr, E., and D. Ogle. 1987. K-W-L plus: A strategy for comprehension and summarization. *Journal of Reading* 30:628–31.

Carskadon, M. A., C. Vieira, and C. Acebo. 1993. Association between puberty and delayed phase preference. *Sleep* 16(3):258–62.

Carter, E. W., K. L. Lane, M. R. Pierson, and B. Glaeser. 2006. Self-determination skills and opportunities of transition-age youth with emotional disturbance and learning disabilities. *Exceptional Children* 72:333–46.

Cartledge, G., R. Gardner, and D.Y. Ford. 2009. *Diverse learners with exceptionalities: Culturally responsive teaching in the inclusive classroom.* Upper Saddle River, NJ: Merrill.

Cass, M., D. Cates, M. Smith, and C. Jackson. 2003. Effects of manipulative instruction on solving area and perimeter problems by students with learning disabilities. *Learning Disabilities Research & Practice* 18:112–20.

Cass, R. J., D. Scanlon, and C. Walther-Thomas. 2006. Secondary teachers' knowledge and beliefs about LD. In *Proceedings of the 14th annual world congress on learning disabilities*, ed. G. Sideridis and D. Scanlon. Weston, MA: Learning Disabilities Worldwide.

CAST. *AspireREADER 4.0*. http://www.cast.org/products/ereader/index.html (retrieved October 24, 2006).

Catts, H. W., and A. G. Kamhi. 2005. *The connections between language and reading disabilities.* New York: Lawrence Erlbaum Associates.

Cavalier, A. R., R. P. Ferretti, and C. M. Okolo. 1994. Technology and individual differences. *Journal of Special Education Technology*. 12:175–81.

Cawley, J., R. Parmar, T. E. Foley, S. Salmon, and S. Roy. 2001. Arithmetic performance of students: Implications for standards and programming. *Exceptional Children* 67:311–28.

Chalk, J., S. Hagan-Burke, and M. Burke. 2005. The effects of self-regulated strategy development on the writing process for high school students with learning disabilities. *Learning Disability Quarterly* 28:75–87.

Chall, J. S. 1983. *Stages of reading development.* New York: McGraw-Hill.

Chall, J. S., and S. A. Stahl. 1982. Reading. In *Encyclopedia of educational research,* ed. H. E. Mitzel. 5th ed., 1535–59. New York: Free Press.

Chambers, D. L. 1996. Direct modeling and invented procedures: Building on students' informal strategies. *Teaching Children Mathematics* 3(2):92–5.

Chandler, S. K., T. Czerlinsky, and P. Wehman. 1993. Provisions of assistive technology: Bridging the gap to accessibility. In *ADA mandate for social change,* ed. P. Wheman, 117–33. Baltimore: Paul H. Brooks Publishing.

Chard, D., and S. Dickson. 1999. Phonological awareness: Instructional and assessment guidelines. *Intervention in School and Clinic* 34:261–70.

Child Trends Databank. 2007. High school dropout rates. http://www.childtrendsdatabank.org/indicators/1HighSchoolDropout.cfm (accessed November 18, 2008).

Cobb, B., P. L. Sample, M. Alwell, and N. R. Johns. 2006. Cognitive-behavioral interventions, dropout, and youth with disabilities: A systematic review. *Remedial and Special Education* 27(5):259–75.

Coleman, M., and J. Webber. 2002. *Emotional and behavioral disorders: Theory and practice.* 4th ed. Boston, MA: Allyn & Bacon.

Cook, B., and M. Semmell. 1999. Peer acceptance of included students with disabilities as a function of severity of disability and classroom composition. *Journal of Special Education* 33:50–61.

Cook, B. G., Tankersley, M., and Landrum, T. J., eds. (forthcoming). Determining evidence-based practices in special education [special issue]. *Exceptional Children.*

Cook, L., and M. Friend. 1995. Co-teaching: Guidelines for creating effective practices. *Focus on Exceptional Children* 28(3):1–16.

Cooper, H., and B. Nye. 1994. Homework for students with learning disabilities: The implications of research for policy and practice. *Journal of Learning Disabilities* 27:470–9.

Cortiella, C. 2006. *IDEA parent guide: A comprehensive guide to your rights and responsibilities under the Individuals with Disabilities Education Act (IDEA 2004).* New York: National Center for Learning Disabilities.

Council for Accreditation of Counseling and Related Educational Programs. 2009. http://www.cacrep.org/ (accessed November 18, 2008).

Council for Exceptional Children (CEC). Forthcoming. CEC knowledge and skill base for all entry-level special education teachers of students with exceptionalities in individualized general curriculums. *What Every Special Educator Must Know: Ethics, Standards, and Guidelines for Special Educators.* 6th ed. Arlington, VA: Council for Exceptional Children.

Council for Exceptional Children. 2003. *What every special educator must know: Ethics, standards, and guidelines for special educators.* 5th ed. Arlington, VA: Council for Exceptional Children.

Council for Exceptional Children. 2007. *Federal outlook for exceptional children: Fiscal year 2008.* Arlington, VA: Council for Exceptional Children.

Coutinho, M. J., D. P. Oswald, and A. M. Best. 2006. Differences in outcomes for female and male students in special education. *Career Development for Exceptional Individuals* 29(1):48–59.

Craig, F. I., and R. S. Lockhart. 1972. Levels of processing: A framework for memory research. *Journal of Verbal Learning and Verbal Behavior* 11:671–84.

Cramer, R. L. 2004. *The language arts.* Boston, MA: Allyn & Bacon.

Cratty, J. 1994. Inspiration—On the way to better ideas. *Computer* 27:81–2.

Crawford, D. B., and D. Carnine. 2000. Comparing the effects of textbooks in eighth-grade U.S. history: Does conceptual organization help? *Education and Treatment of Children* 23:387–422.

Crawford, L., R. Helwig, and G. Tindal. 2004. Writing performance assessments: How important is extended time? *Journal of Learning Disabilities* 37:132–43.

Creaghead, N. 1992. *Classroom language intervention: Developing schema for school success.* Buffalo, NY: Edcom Associates.

Crowley, S. J., C. Acebo, and M. A. Carskadon. 2007. Sleep, circadian rhythms and delayed phase in adolescence. *Sleep Medicine* 8:602–12.

Crutchfield, M. D. 2003. What do the CEC standards mean to me? Using the CEC standards to improve my practice. *Teaching Exceptional Children* 35(6):40–5.

Cummings, R., C. D. Maddux, and J. Casey. 2000. Individualized transition planning for students with learning disabilities. *The Career Development Quarterly* 49:60–72.

Cunningham, P. 1980. Applying a compare/contrast process to identifying polysyllabic words. *Journal of Reading Behavior* 12:213–23.

Cunningham, P. M. 1987. Polysyllabic word strategies for content-area reading. *Clearing House* 61:42–5.

D'Antonio, M. 2004. *The state boys rebellion.* New York: Simon & Schuster.

Damon, W., and E. Phelps. 1989. Critical distinctions among three approaches to peer education. *International Journal of Educational Research* 13:9–20.

Davila, R., M. Williams, and J. MacDonald. 1991. U.S. Department of Education, Office of Special Education and Rehabilitative Services. *Clarification of policy to address the needs of children with attention deficit disorder within general and/or special education.* Memorandum of September 16, 1991.

Davis, B., J. Caro, and D. Carnine. 2006. Using technology to access the general education curriculum. In *Teaching adolescents with disabilities,* ed. D. D. Deshler and J. B. Schumaker, 187–233. Thousand Oaks, CA: Corwin Press.

Davis, M. 2001. *Arrest patterns into adulthood of adolescents with serious emotional disability.* Tampa, FL: University of South Florida, Tampa, Research and Training Center for Children's Mental Health. ERIC Documents Reproduction Services, no. ED 465248.

Day, J. C., and E. C. Newburger. 2002. *The big payoff: Educational attainment and synthetic estimates of work-life earnings. Special Studies. Current Population Reports,* no. ED467533. Washington, DC: Bureau of the Census (DOC).

Day, S. L., and B. J. Edwards. 1996. Assistive technology for postsecondary students with learning disabilities. *Journal of Learning Disabilities* 29(5):486–492, 503.

Delacato, C. H. 1959. *The treatment and prevention of reading problems.* Springfield, IL: Charles C. Thomas Co.

De La Paz, S. 1997. Strategy instruction in planning: Teaching students with learning and writing disabilities to compose persuasive and expository essays. *Learning Disability Quarterly* 20:227–48.

De La Paz, S., and S. Graham. 2002. Explicitly teaching strategies, skills, and knowledge: Writing instruction in middle school classrooms. *Journal of Educational Psychology* 94:687–98.

Deno, S. 1985. Curriculum-based measurement: The emerging alternative. *Exceptional Children* 52:219–32.

Deno, S. 1992. The nature and development of curriculum-based measurement. *Preventing School Failure* 36(2):5–10.

Deno, S. 2003a. Curriculum-based measures: Development and perspectives. *Assessment for Effective Intervention* 28(3–4):3–12.

Deno, S. 2003b. Developments in curriculum-based measurement. *Journal of Special Education* 37(3):184–92.

Deno, S., D. Marston, and P. Mirkin. 1982. Valid measurement procedures for continuous evaluation of written expression. *Exceptional Children* 48:368–71.

Deshler, D. D., G. R. Alley, M. M. Warner, and J. B. Schumaker. 1981. Instructional practices for promoting skill acquisition and generalization in severely learning disabled adolescents. *Learning Disability Quarterly* 4:415–21.

Deshler, D. D., and J. A. Bulgren. 1997. Redefining instructional directions for gifted students with disabilities. *Learning Disabilities: A Multidisciplinary Journal* 8:121–32.

Deshler, D., and J. Schumaker. 2006. *Teaching adolescents with disabilities: Accessing the general education curriculum.* Thousand Oaks, CA: Corwin Press.

Deshler, D. D., J. B. Schumaker, J. A. Bulgren, B. K. Lenz, J. E. Jantzen, G. Adams, D. Carnine, B. Grossen, B. Davis, and J. Marquis. 2001. Making learning easier: Connecting new knowledge to things students already know. *Teaching Exceptional Children* 33(4):82–5.

Deshler, D. D., J. B. Schumaker, B. K. Lenz, J. A. Bulgren, M. F. Hock, M. J. Knight, and B. J. Ehren. 2001. Ensuring content-area learning by secondary students with learning disabilities. *Learning Disabilities Research & Practice* 16:96–108.

Deshler, D. D., J. B. Schumaker, and P. C. McKnight. 1997. *The Survey Routine.* Lawrence, KS: University of Kansas.

DeSimone, J. R., and R. S. Parmar. 2006. Middle school mathematics teachers' beliefs about inclusion of students with learning disabilities. *Learning Disabilities Research & Practice* 21:98–110.

De Valenzuela, J. S., and L. Baca. 2004. Procedures and techniques for assessing the bilingual exceptional child. In *The bilingual special education interface,* ed. L. M. Baca and H. T. Cervantes. 4th ed., 184–203. Upper Saddle River, NJ: Pearson.

Dewey, D., S. G. Crawford, and B. J. Kaplan. 2003. Clinical importance of parent ratings of everyday cognitive abilities in children with learning and attention problems. *Journal of Learning Disabilities* 36:87–93.

Diana v. State Board of Education, Civil Action, no. C70 37RFP (N.D. Cal. January 7, 1970 and June 18, 1973).

Dickinson, D. L., and R. I. Verbeek. 2002. Wage differentials between college graduates with and without LD. *Journal of Learning Disabilities* 35:175–85.

Dieker, L. A. 2001. What are the characteristics of "effective" middle and high school co-taught teams for students with disabilities? *Preventing School Failure* 46(1):14–23.

Dieker, L. A., and W. W. Murawski. 2003. Co-teaching at the secondary level: Unique issues, current trends, and suggestions for success. *The High School Journal* 86:1–13.

Dimino, J., R. Gersten, D. Carnine, and G. Blake. 1990. Story grammar: An approach for promoting at-risk secondary students' comprehension of literature. *Elementary School Journal* 91(1):19–32.

Division on Career Development and Transition. 2000. *Transition-related planning, instruction, and service responsibilities for secondary special educators.* DCDT Fact Sheet (March).

Dixon, R. C. 1991. The application of sameness analysis to spelling. *Journal of Learning Disabilities* 24:285–310.

Dodge, E. P. 2004. Communication skills: The foundation for meaningful group intervention in school-based programs. *Topics in Language Disorders* 24:141–50.

DoD Directive 6130.3. 2003. *Physical standards for appointment, enlistment, or induction.* http://www.dtic.mil/whs/directives/search.htm (accessed January 15, 2009).

DoD Instruction 1332.38. 2006. *Physical disability evaluation.* http://www.dtic.mil/whs/directives/search.htm (accessed January 15, 2009).

DoD Instruction 1304.26. 2007. *Qualification standards for enlistment, appointment, and induction.* http://www.dtic.mil/whs/directives/search.htm (accessed January 15, 2009).

Dolch, E. W. 1936. A basic sight vocabulary. *The Elementary School Journal* 36:456–60.

Dolch, E. W. 1939. *A manual for remedial reading.* Champaign, IL: Garrard Press.

Donahue, M., R. Pearl, and T. Bryan. 1980. Learning disabled children's conversational competence: Responses to inadequate messages. *Applied Psycholinguistics* 1:387–403.

Dounay, J. 2007. High school graduation requirements: Mathematics. Denver, CO: Education Commission of the States. http://mb2.esc.org/reports/Report.aspx?id=900.

Dowhower, S. 1989. Repeated reading: Research into practice. *The Reading Teacher* 42(7):502–7.

Dowker, A. 2003. Young children's estimates for addition: The zone of partial knowledge and understanding. In *The development of arithmetic concepts and skills,* ed. A. J. Baroody and A. Dowker, 243–65. Mahwah, NJ: Erlbaum.

Drame, E. R. 2002. Sociocultural context effects on teachers' readiness to refer for learning disabilities. *Exceptional Children* 69:41–53.

Dunn, C., D. Chambers, and K. Rabren. 2004. Variables affecting students' decisions to drop out of school. *Remedial and Special Education* 25:314–23.

Dunn, L. M. 1968. Special education for the mildly retarded—Is much of it justifiable? *Exceptional Children* 35:5–22.

Dynarski, M., and P. Gleason. 2002. How can we help? What we have learned from recent federal dropout prevention evaluations. *Journal of Education for Students Placed At Risk* 7(1):43–69.

Dzaldov, B., and S. Peterson. 2005. Book leveling and readers. *Reading Teacher* 59:222–9.

Edens, K., and E. Potter. 2007. The relationship of drawing and mathematical problem solving: "Draw for Math" tasks. *Studies in Art Education: A Journal of Issues and Research in Art Education* 48:282–98.

Edgar, E. 2005. Bending back on high school programs for youth with learning disabilities. *Learning Disability Quarterly* 28(2):171–3.

Education of the Handicapped Act Amendments of 1983. Pub. Law no. 98-199.

Ehri, L. 1995. Phases of development in learning to read words by sight. *Journal of Research in Reading* 18:116–25.

Ehri, L. 1998. Grapheme-phoneme knowledge is essential for learning to read words in English. In *Word recognition in beginning literacy,* ed. J. Metsala and L. Ehri, 3–40. Mahwah, NJ: Lawrence Erlbaum.

Ehri, L. C. 2003. *Systematic phonics instruction: Finds of the National Reading Panel.* Paper presented at the invitational seminar organized by the Standards and Effectiveness Unit, Department for Education and Skills, British Government (March).

Ehri, L. C., S. Nunes, S. Stahl, and D. Willows. 2001. Systematic phonics instruction helps students learn to read: Evidence from National Reading Panel's meta-analysis. *Review of Educational Research* 71:393–447.

Ehri, L. C., and C. Robbins. 1992. Beginners need some decoding skill to read words by analogy. *Reading Research Quarterly* 27:13–26.

Eisenman, L. T. 2007. Self-determination interventions: Building a foundation for school completion. *Remedial and Special Education* 28:2–8.

Elbaum, B., J. S. Schumm, and S. Vaughn. 1995. *Students' perceptions of grouping formats for reading instruction.* Paper presented at the annual meeting of the American Educational Research Association, San Francisco.

Elksnin, L. K., and N. Elksnin. 1996. Strategies for transition to employment settings. In *Teaching adolescents with learning disabilities: Strategies and methods,* ed. D. D. Deshler, E. S. Ellis, and B. K. Lenz, 2nd ed., 475–578. Denver CO: Love Publishing.

Elksnin, N., and L. Elksnin. 2001. Adolescents with disabilities: The need for occupational social skills training. *Exceptionality* 9(1–2):91–105.

Elliott, S. 1994. *Creating meaningful performance assessments: Fundamental concepts.* Reston, VA: Council for Exceptional Children.

Ellis, E. S. 1989. A metacognitive intervention for increasing class participation. *Learning Disabilities Focus* 5:36–46.

Ellis, E. S. 1992. *The vocabulary LINCing routine.* Lawrence, KS: Edge Enterprises.

Ellis, E. S. 1996. Reading strategy instruction. In *Teaching adolescents with learning disabilities,* ed. D. D. Deshler, E. S., Ellis, and B. K. Lenz, 2nd ed. Denver, CO: Love Publishing.

Ellis, E. S. 1998. *The framing routine.* Lawrence, KS: Edge Enterprises.

Ellis, E. S., and G. Colvert. 1996. Writing strategy instruction. In *Teaching adolescents with learning disabilities: Strategies and methods,* ed. D. D. Deshler, E. S. Ellis, and B. K. Lenz, 2nd ed., 61–125. Denver, CO: Love Publishing.

Ellis, E. S., D. D. Deshler, B. K. Lenz, J. B. Schumaker, and F. L. Clark. 1991. An instructional model for teaching learning strategies. *Focus on Exceptional Children* 23(6):1–24.

Ellis, E. S., and A. W. Graves. 1990. Teaching rural students with learning disabilities: A paraphrasing strategy to increase comprehension of main ideas. *Rural Special Education Quarterly* 10:2–10.

Ellis, E. S., and B. K. Lenz. 1990. Techniques for mediating content-area learning: Issues and research. *Focus on Exceptional Children* 22(9):1–16.

Engelmann, S. 1980. *Direct instruction.* Englewood Cliffs, N.J: Educational Technology Publications.

Engelmann, S., D. Carnine, O. Engelmann, and B. Kelly. 2002. *Connecting Math Concepts.* DeSoto, TX: SRA/McGraw-Hill.

Engelmann, S. and D. Steely. 2002. *Direct Instruction: Corrective Mathematics.* DeSoto, TX: SRA/McGraw-Hill.

Englert, C., and T. Mariage. 1990. Send for the POSSE: Structuring the comprehension dialog. *Academic Therapy* 25:472–87.

Englert, C. S., and T. V. Mariage. 1991. Making students partners in the comprehension process: Organizing the reading "POSSE." *Learning Disability Quarterly* 14:123–38.

Englert, C. S., Y. Zhao, K. Dunsmore, N. Y. Collings, and K. Wolbers. 2007. Scaffolding the writing of students with disabilities through procedural facilitation: Using an Internet-based technology to improve performance. *Learning Disability Quarterly* 30:9–29.

Englert, S. E., E. H. Heibert, and S. S. Stewart. 1985. Spelling unfamiliar words by an analogy strategy. *Journal of Special Education* 19:291–303.

Englert, S. E., and T. V. Mariage. 1991. Shared understandings: Structuring the writing experience through dialogue. *Journal of Learning Disabilities* 24:330–42.

Englert, S. E., and T. E. Raphael. 1988. Constructed well-formed prose: Process, structure, and metacognitive knowledge. *Exceptional Children* 54:513–20.

Englert, S. E., T. E. Raphael, K. L. Fear, and L. M. Anderson. 1988. Students' metacognitive knowledge about how to write informational texts. *Learning Disability Quarterly* 11:18–46.

Epstein, M. H., E. A. Polloway, R. M. Foley, and J. R. Patton. 1993. Homework: A comparison of teachers' and parents' perceptions of the problems experienced by students identified as having behavioral disorders, learning disabilities, or no disabilities. *Remedial and Special Education* 14:40–50.

Faulkner, H. J., and B. A. Levy. 1994. Fluent and nonfluent forms of transfer in reading: Words and their message. *Psychonomic Bulletin and Review* 6:111–16.

Federal Register. 59(131), February 10, 1993.

Federal Register. 71(156), August 14, 2006. Rules and Regulations.

Feldman, D., L. Kinnison, R. Jay, and R. Harth. 1983. The effects of differential labeling on professional concepts and attitudes toward the emotionally disturbed/behaviorally disordered. *Behavioral Disorders* 8:191–8.

Ferri, B. A., N. Gregg, and S. J. Heggoy. 1997. Profiles of college students demonstrating learning disabilities with and without giftedness. *Journal of Learning Disabilities* 30(5):552–9.

Figueroa, R. A. 2005. Dificultades o Desabilidades do Aprendizaje? *Learning Disability Quarterly* 28:163–7.

Finnis, J. 2004. Myths and facts of learning technology. *Technology & Learning Magazine.* http://www.techlearning.com/story/showArticle.php?articleID=22101447 (accessed July 7, 2007).

Fisher, D., and G. Ivey. 2005. Literacy and language as learning in content-area classes: A departure from "every teacher a teacher of reading." *Action in Teacher Education* 27(2):3–11.

Flavell, J. 1976. Metacognitive aspects in problem solving. In *The nature of intelligence.* Hillsdale, NJ: Erlbaum.

Flavell, J. H. 1979. Metacognition and cognitive monitoring: A new area of cognitive-developmental inquiry. *American Psychologist* 34:906–11.

Fletcher, J., G. R. Lyon, L. Fuchs, and M. Barnes. 2007. Learning disabilities: From identification to intervention. New York: The Guilford Press.

Flores, D., P. Schloss, and S. Alpers. 1995. The use of a daily calendar to increase responsibilities fulfilled by secondary students with special needs. *Remedial and Special Education* 16:38–43.

Flower, L. 1985. *Problem-solving strategies for writing.* New York: Harcourt Brace.

Flowers, C., D. Browder, and L. Ahlgrim-Delzell. 2006. An analysis of three states' alignment between language arts and mathematics standards and alternate assessments. *Exceptional Children* 72:201–15.

Foegen, A. 2008. Algebra progress monitoring and interventions for students with learning disabilities. *Learning Disability Quarterly* 31:65–78.

Forness, S. R., and J. Knitzer. 1992. A new proposed definition and terminology to replace "serious emotional disturbance" in the Individuals with Disabilities Education Act. *School Psychology Review* 21:12–20.

Frank, A. R., and P. L. Singleton. 2000. Young adults with mental disabilities—Does transition planning make a difference? *Education and Training in Mental Retardation and Developmental Disabilities* 35:119–34.

Frank, A. R., D. P. Wacker, T. Z. Keith, and T. K. Sagen. 1987. The effectiveness of a spelling study package for learning disabled students. *Learning Disabilities Research* 2:110–7.

Freeman, B., and L. Crawford. 2008. Creating a middle school mathematics curriculum for English-language learners. *Remedial and Special Education* 29:9–19.

Friel-Patti, S. 1999. Specific language impairment: Continuing clinical concerns. *Topics in Language Disorders* 20:1–13.

Friend, M., and W. Bursuck. 1996. *Including students with special needs.* 1st ed. Boston: Allyn & Bacon.

Friend, M., and W. D. Bursuck. 1999. *Including students with special needs: A practical guide for teachers.* 2nd ed. Boston: Allyn & Bacon.

Friend, M., and W. Bursuck. 2006. *Including students with special needs: A practical guide for classroom teachers.* 4th ed. Boston: Allyn & Bacon.

Friend, M., and L. Cook. 1992. The new mainstreaming. *Instructor* 101(7):30–2.

Friend, M., and L. Cook. 2000. *Interactions.* New York: Longman.

Fritzche, B. A., S. A. McIntire, and A. P. Yost. 2002. Holland type as a moderator of personality-performance predictions. *Journal of Vocational Behavior* 60:422–36.

Fry, E. B. 1968. A readability formula that saves time. *Journal of Reading* 11:513–6.

Fry, E. 1980. The new instant word list. *Reading Teacher* 34:284–9.

Fry, E., D. Fountoukidis, and J. Polk. 1985. *The new reading teacher's book of lists.* Englewood Cliffs, NJ: Prentice Hall.

Fuchs, D., L. S. Fuchs, P. G. Mathes, and E. A. Martinez. 2002. Preliminary evidence on the social standing of students with learning disabilities in PALS and no-PALS classrooms. *Learning Disabilities: Research & Practice* 17(4):205–15.

Fuchs, D., L. Fuchs, P. H. Mathes, and D. C. Simmons. 1997. Peer-assisted strategies: Making classrooms more responsive to diversity. *American Educational Research Journal* 34:174–206, no. EJ545455.

Fuchs, D., D. Mock, P. Morgan, and C. L. Young. 2003. Responsiveness-to-Intervention: Definitions, evidence, and implications for the learning disabilities construct. *Learning Disabilities Research & Practice* 18:157–71.

Fuchs, L. S., D. L. Compton, D. Fuchs, K. Paulsen, J. D. Bryant, and C. L. Hamlett. 2005. The prevention, identification, and cognitive determinants of math difficulty. *Journal of Educational Psychology* 97:493–513.

Fuchs, L. S., and D. Fuchs. 2001. Principles for sustaining research-based practice in the schools: A case study. *Focus on Exceptional Children* 33(6):1–14.

Fuchs, L., and D. Fuchs. 2005. Peer-Assisted Learning Strategies: Promoting word recognition, fluency, and reading comprehension in young children. *Journal of Special Education* 41:93–9.

Fuchs, L. S., D. Fuchs, R. Finelli, S. J. Courey, and C. L. Hamlett. 2004. Expanding schema-based transfer instruction to help third graders solve real-life mathematical problems. *American Educational Research Journal* 41:419–45.

Fuchs, L. S., D. Fuchs, C. L. Hamlett, N. B. Philips, and J. Bentz. 1994. Classwide curriculum-based measurement: Helping general educators meet the challenge of student diversity. *Exceptional Children* 60:518–37.

Fuchs, L., D. Fuchs, C. Hamlett, L. Walz, and G. Germann. 1993. Formative evaluation of academic progress: How much growth can we expect? *School Psychology Review* 22:27–48.

Fuchs, L. S., D. Fuchs, S. R. Powell, P. M. Seethaler, P. T. Cirino, and J. M. Fletcher. 2008. Intensive intervention for students with mathematics disabilities: Seven principles of effective practice. *Learning Disability Quarterly* 31:79–92.

Fuligni, A. J., and C. Hardway. 2006. Daily variation in adolescents' sleep, activities, and psychological well-being. *Journal of Research on Adolescence* 16:353–78.

Fulk, B., and K. King. 2001. Classwide peer tutoring at work. *Teaching Exceptional Children* 34(2):49–53.

Fulk, M., and M. Stormont-Spurgin. 1995. Spelling interventions for students with disabilities: A review. *The Journal of Special Education* 28:488–513.

Gagne, E. 1985. *The cognitive psychology of school learning.* Boston: Little, Brown and Company.

Gammill, D. M. 2006. Learning the write way. *The Reading Teacher* 59:754–62.

Gamoran, A., and M. Weinstein. 1998. Differentiation and opportunity in restructured schools. *American Journal of Education* 106:385–415.

Gardynik, U. M., and L. McDonald. 2005. Implications of risk and resilience in the life of the individual who is gifted/learning disabled. *Roeper Review* 27(4):206.

Garmston, R. 1997. *The presenter's fieldbook: A practical guide.* Norwood, MA: Christopher-Gordon Publishers.

Garrison, L., O. Amaral, and G. Ponce. 2006. Unlatching mathematics for English language learners. *National Council of Supervisors of Mathematics* 9(1):14–24.

Gartner, A., and D. K. Lipsky. 1987. Beyond special education: Toward a quality system for all students. *Harvard Educational Review* 57(4):367–95.

Gaskins, I. W. 2005. *Success with struggling readers: The benchmark school approach.* New York: Guilford Press.

Gately, S. E., and F. J. Gately. 2001. Understanding coteaching components. *TEACHING Exceptional Children* 33(4):40–7.

Geary, D. 2004. Mathematics and learning disabilities. *Journal of Learning Disabilities* 37:4–15.

GED Testing Services. 2002. *Who passed the GED? GED 2002 statistical report.* Washington, DC: American Council on Education.

Gerber, M. 2005. Responses to tough teaching: the 2% solution. *Learning Disability Quarterly* 28:189–90.

Gerber. P. J., R. Ginsberg, and H. B. Reiff. 1992. Identifying alterable patterns in employment success for highly successful adults with learning disabilities. *Journal of Learning Disabilities* 25(8):475–87.

Gerber, P. J., L. A. Price, R., Mulligan, and I. Shessel. 2004. Beyond transition: A comparison of the employment experiences of American and Canadian adults with LD. *Journal of Learning Disabilities* 37:283–91.

Gersten, R. 1991. The eye of the beholder: A response to "Sociomoral atmosphere . . . A study of teachers' enacted interpersonal understanding." *Early Childhood Research Quarterly* 6:529–37.

Gersten, R. 1992. Passion and precision: Response to "curriculum-based assessment and direct instruction: Critical reflections on fundamental assumptions." *Exceptional Children* 58:464–67.

Gersten, R., and D. Chard. 1999. Number sense: Rethinking arithmetic instruction for students with math difficulties. *Journal of Special Education* 33:18–28.

Gersten, R., D. Chard, and S. Baker. 2000. Factors enhancing sustained use of research-based instructional practices. *Journal of learning Disabilities* 33:445–57.

Gersten, R., L. Fuchs, J. Williams, and S. Baker. 2001. Teaching reading comprehension strategies to students with learning disabilities. *Review of Educational Research* 71:279–320.

Getman, G. 1965. *The visuomotor complex in the acquisition of learning skills.* In Learning Disorders, ed. J. Hellmuth. Seattle, WA: Special Child Publications.

Gettinger, M., N. D. Bryant, and H. Fayne. 1982. Designing spelling instruction for learning disabled children: An emphasis on unit size, distributed practice, and training for transfer. *The Journal of Special Education* 16:439–48.

Gibb, G. S., and T. T. Dyches. Forthcoming. *Guide to writing quality individualized education programs.* 2nd ed. Boston, MA: Allyn & Bacon.

Gibbs, D., and E. Cooper. 1989. Prevalence of communication disorders in students with learning disabilities. *Journal of Learning Disabilities* 22:60–3.

Gilabert, R., G. Martinez, and E. Vidal-Abarca. 2005. Some good texts are always better: Test revision to foster inferences of readers with high and low prior background knowledge. *Learning and Instruction* 15:45–68.

Gill, S. R. 2002. Responding to readers. *The Reading Teacher* 56:119–21.

Gillies, R. M., and A. F. Ashman. 2000. The effects of cooperative learning on students with learning difficulties in the lower elementary school. *Journal of Special Education* 34(1):19–27.

Ginsburg, H. P. 1997. Mathematics learning disabilities: A view from developmental psychology. *Journal of Learning Disabilities* 30(1):20–33.

Giordano, G. 1990. Strategies that help learning disabled students solve verbal mathematical problems. *Preventing School Failure* 35:24–8.

Gleason, M. M. 1999. The role of evidence in argumentative writing. *Reading & Writing Quarterly* 15:81–106.

Gleason M., D. Carnine, and N. Vala. 1991. Cumulative versus rapid introduction of new information. *Exceptional Children* 57(4):353–8.

Goldstein, D. E., C. Murray, and E. Edgar. 1998. Employment earnings and hours of high school graduates with learning disabilities through the first decade after graduation. *Learning Disabilities Research & Practice* 13:53–64.

Gonzalez, N., R. Andrade, M. Civil, and L. Moll. 2001. Bridging funds of distributed knowledge: Creating zones of practices in mathematics. *Journal of Education for Students Placed at Risk* 6:115–32.

Good, T., and J. Brophy. 1994. *Looking into classrooms.* New York: Harper Collins College Publishers.

Good, T. L., and J. E. Brophy. 2003. *Looking in classrooms.* 9th ed. Boston, MA: Allyn & Bacon.

Good, T. L., A. R. Wiley, R. E. Thomas, E. Stewart, J. McCoy, B. Kloos, G. D. Hunt, T. Moore, and J. Rappaport. 1997. Bridging the gap between schools and community: Organizing for family involvement in a low-income neighborhood. *Journal of Educational and Psychological Consultation* 8:277–96.

Goodlad, J. 1984. *A place called school.* New York: McGraw-Hill.

Goodman, J. I., and M. L. Duffy. 2007. Using "BUGS" to increase student participation. *TEACHING Exceptional Children Plus* 3(4) Article 3. http://excholarship.bc.edu/education/tecplus/vol3/iss4/art3 (accessed June 21, 2007).

Gordon, C., and C. Braun. 1983. Using story schema as an aid to reading and writing. *The Reading Teacher* 37:116–21.

Gordon, J., S. Vaughn, and J. S. Schumm. 1993. Spelling interventions: A review of literature and implications for instruction for students with learning disabilities. *Learning Disabilities Research & Practice* 8:175–81.

Gormley, S., C. Hughes, L. Block, and C. Lendman. 2005. Eligibility assessment requirements at the postsecondary level for students with learning disabilities: A disconnect with secondary schools? *Journal of Postsecondary Education and Disability* 18:63–70.

Graham, S. 1999. Handwriting and spelling instruction for students with learning disabilities: A review. *Learning Disability Quarterly* 22:78–98.

Graham, S., V. Berninger, and N. Weintraub. 1998. The relationship between handwriting style and speed and legibility. *Journal of Educational Research* 91:290–7.

Graham, S., and K. R. Freeman. 1986. Strategy training and teacher- vs. student-controlled study conditions: Effects on LD students' spelling performance. *Learning Disability Quarterly* 9:15–22.

Graham, S., and K. R. Harris. 1988. Instructional recommendations for teaching writing to exceptional students. *Exceptional Children* 54:506–12.

Graham, S., and K. R. Harris. 1989. Improving learning disabled students' skills at composing essays: Self-instructional strategy training. *Exceptional Children* 56:201–14.

Graham, S., and K. R. Harris. 1992. Self-instructional strategy development. *LD Forum* 16:15–23.

Graham, S., and K. R. Harris. 1993. Teaching writing strategies to students with learning disabilities: Issues and recommendations. In *Strategy assessment and instruction for students with learning disabilities,* ed. L. S. Meltzer, 271–323. Austin, TX: Pro-Ed.

Graham, S., and K. R. Harris. 1996. Self-regulation and strategy instruction for students who find writing and learning challenging. In *The science of writing,* ed. C. M. Levy and S. Ransdell, 347–60. Mahwah, NJ: Lawrence Erlbaum.

Graham, S., K. Harris, and C. Loynachan. 1994. The spelling for writing list. *Journal of Learning Disabilities* 27:210–4.

Graham, S., K. R. Harris, C. A. MacArthur, and S. Schwartz. 1991. Writing and writing instruction for students with learning disabilities: Review of a research program. *Learning Disability Quarterly* 14:89–114.

Graham, S., and C. MacArthur. 1988. Improving learning disabled students' skills at revising essays produced on a word processor: Self-instructional strategy training. *Journal of Special Education* 22(2):133–52.

Graham, S., C. MacArthur, S. Schwartz, and T. Paige-Voth. 1992. Improving the compositions of students with learning disabilities using a strategy involving product and process goal setting. *Exceptional Children* 58:322–35.

Graham, S., and D. Perin. 2007. A meta-analysis of writing instruction for adolescent students. *Journal of Educational Psychology* 99:445–76.

Graham, S., and N. Weintraub. 1996. A review of handwriting research: Progress and prospects from 1980 to 1994. *Educational Psychology Review* 8:7–87.

Graham, S., N. Weintraub, and V. Berninger. 2001. Which manuscript letters do primary grade children write legibly? *Journal of Educational Psychology* 93:488–97.

Graves, D. H. 1983. *Writing: Teachers and children at work.* Exeter, NH: Heinemann.

Greenwood, C. R., C. Arreaga-Mayer, C. A. Utley, K. M. Gavin, and B. J. Terry. 2001. Classwide peer tutoring learning management system. *Remedial and Special Education* 22(1):34–47.

Greenwood, C. R., and J. Delquadri. 1995. Classwide peer tutoring and the prevention of school failure. *Preventing School Failure* 39(4):21–5.

Greenwood, C., J. C. Delquadri, and J. J. Carta. 1999. *Together we can! Classwide Peer Tutoring to improve basic academic skills.* 2nd ed. Frederick, CO: Sopris-West.

Greenwood, C., J. Carta, and L. Maheady. 1991. Peer tutoring programs in the regular education classroom. In *Interventions for achievement and behavior problems,* ed. G. Stoner, M. Shinn, and H. Walker, 179–200. Silver Spring, MD: National Association of School Psychologists.

Gresham, F., K. Lane, D. MacMillan, and K. Bocian. 1999. Social and academic profiles of externalizing and internalizing groups: Risk factors for emotional and behavioral disorders. *Behavioral Disorders* 24:231–45.

Gresham, F. M., and D. L. MacMillan. 1997. Social competence and affective characteristics of students with mild disabilities. *Review of Educational Research* 67:377–415.

Gresham, F. M., G. Sugai, and R. H. Horner. 2001. Interpreting outcomes of social skills training for students with high-incidence disabilities. *Exceptional Children* 67:331–44.

Grigal, M., A. Dwyre, and H. Davis. 2006. Transition services for students aged 18–21 with intellectual disabilities in college and community settings: Models and implications of success. *Information Brief* 5(5).

Grigg, W., P. Donahue, and G. Dion. 2007. *The nation's report card: 12th-grade reading and mathematics 2005,* no. NCES 2007.468. U.S. Department of Education, National Center for Education Statistics. Washington, DC: U.S. Government Printing Office.

Gunning, T. G. 2000. *Creating literacy instruction for all children.* Boston: Allyn & Bacon.

Haager, D. 2007. Promises and cautions regarding using response to intervention with English language learners. *Learning Disability Quarterly* 30:213–8.

Hackney, C. 1993. *Zaner-Bloser handwriting.* Columbus, OH: Zaner-Bloser.

Hall, K., B. Sabey, and M. McClellan. 2005. Expository text comprehension: Helping primary-grade teachers use expository text to full advantage. *Reading Psychology* 26:211–34.

Hallahan, D. P., J. W. Lloyd, J. M. Kauffman, M. Weiss, and E. A. Martinez. 2005. *Learning disabilities: Foundations, characteristics, and effective teaching.* 3rd ed. Boston: Allyn & Bacon.

Halpern, A. 1985. Transition: A look at the foundations. *Exceptional Children* 51:479–86.

Halpern, A. 1993. Quality of life as a conceptual framework for evaluating transition outcomes. *Exceptional Children* 59:486–98.

Halpern, A. S., P. Yovanoff, B. Doren, and M. R. Benz. 1995. Predicting participation in postsecondary education for school leavers with disabilities. *Exceptional Children* 62:151–64.

Hamill, L. B. 2003. Going to college: The experiences of a young woman with Down syndrome. *Mental Retardation* 41:340–53.

Hammill, D., and S. Larsen. 1974. The effectiveness of psycholinguistic training: A reaffirmation of position. *Exceptional Children* 44:402–14.

Hanich, L., N. C. Jordan, D. Kaplan, and J. Dick. 2001. Performance across different areas of mathematical cognition in children with learning difficulties. *Journal of Educational Psychology* 93:615–26.

Harbour, W. S. 2004. The 2004 AHEAD survey of higher education disability service providers. Waltham, MA: Association on Higher Education and Disability.

Hardy, L. 2004. A new minority 50 years after "Brown." *Education Digest: Essential Readings Condensed for Quick Read* 70(1):23–8.

Harniss, M. K., D. W. Carnine, J. Silbert, and R. C. Dixon. 2007. Effective strategies for teaching mathematics. In *Effective teaching strategies that accommodate diverse learners,* ed. M. D. Coyne, E. J. Kame'enui, and D. W. Carnine, 3rd ed. Upper Saddle River, NJ: Pearson Prentice Hall.

Harris, A. J., and E. R. Sipay. 1990. *How to increase reading ability.* New York: Longman.

Harris, K., and S. Graham. 1996. Memo to constructivists: Skills count too. *Educational Leadership* 53(5):26–9.

Harris, K., R. Reid, and S. Graham. 2004. Self-regulation among students with LD and ADHD. In *Learning about learning disabilities,* ed. B.Y. L. Wong, 3rd ed. 167–95. Orlando, FL: Academic Press.

Harry, B. 1992. An ethnographic study of cross-cultural communication with Puerto Rican-American families in the special education system. *American Educational Research Journal* 29:471–94.

Harry, B., and J. Klingner. 2006. *Why are so many minority students in special education? Understanding race and disability in schools.* New York: Teachers College Press.

Harry, B., J. Klingner, and J. Hart. 2005. African American families under fire. *Remedial and Special Education* 26:110–2.

Hart, D., J. Mele-McCarthy, R. H. Pasternack, K. Zimbrich, and D. R. Parker. 2004. Community college: A pathway to success for youth with learning, cognitive, and intellectual disabilities in secondary settings. *Education and Training in Developmental Disabilities* 39:54–66.

Hartley, J. 1983. Note taking research: Resetting the scoreboard. *Bulletin of the British Psychology Society* 36:13–14.

Hasbrouck, J. E., and G. Tindal. 1992. Curriculum-based oral reading fluency forms for students in grades 2 through 5. *Teaching Exceptional Children* 24:41–4.

Hastings, R. P., and S. Graham. 1995. Adolescents' perceptions of young people with severe learning difficulties: The effects of integration schemes and frequency of contact. *Educational Psychology* 15(2):149–60.

Hawking, S. 1988. *A brief history of time.* New York: Bantam Books.

Hayes, J. 1996. A new framework for understanding cognition and affect in writing. In *The science of writing,* ed. C. M. Levy and S. Ransdell, 1–28. Mahwah, NJ: Lawrence Erlbaum.

Hayes, J. R., and L. S. Flower. 1980. Identifying the organization of writing process. In *Cognitive processes in writing,* ed. L. W. Gregg and E. R. Steinberg, 3–30. Hillsdale, NJ: Lawrence Erlbaum.

Hecht, S. A., K. J. Vagi, and J. K. Torgesen. 2007. Fraction skills and proportional reasoning. In *Why is math so hard for some children?* ed. D. B. Berch and M. M. M. Mazzocco, 121–32. Baltimore, MD: Brookes Publishing.

Hecker, L., and E. U. Engstrom. 2005. Assistive technology and students with dyslexia. In *Multisensory teaching of basic language skills,* ed. J. R. Birsh. Baltimore, MD: Brookes Publishing.

Henderson, C. 2001. *College freshmen with disabilities: A triennial statistical profile.* Washington, DC: American Council on Education/HEATH Resource Center.

Hergenhahn, B. R., and M. H. Olsen. 2001. *An introduction to theories of learning.* Upper Saddle River, NJ: Prentice Hall.

Herrero, E. A. 2006. Using Dominican oral literature and discourse to support literacy learning among low achieving students from the Dominican Republic. *International Journal of Bilingual Education and Bilingualism* 9:219–38.

Heshusius, L. 1991. Curriculum-based assessment and direct instruction: Critical reflections on fundamental assumptions. *Exceptional Children* 57:315–28.

Hetzroni, O. E., and B. Shrieber. 2004. Word processing as an assistive technology tool for enhancing academic outcomes of students with writing disabilities in the general classroom. *Journal of Learning Disabilities* 37:143–54.

Heward, W. M. 2006. *Exceptional children: An introduction to special education.* 8th ed. Upper Saddle River, NJ: Merrill/Prentice Hall.

Hicks-Coolick, A., and D. P. Kurtz. 1997. Preparing students with learning disabilities for success in postsecondary education: Needs and services. *Social Work in Education* 19:31–43.

Hiebert, E., and C. Fisher. 2005. A review of the National Reading Panel's studies on fluency: The role of text. *The Elementary School Journal* 105:443–60.

Higgins, K., and R. Boone. 1990. Hypertext computer study guides and the social studies achievement of students with learning disabilities, remedial students, and regular education students. *Journal of Learning Disabilities* 23(9):529–40.

Higgins, K., R. Boone, and T. Lovitt. 1996. Hypertext support for remedial students and students with learning disabilities. *Journal of Learning Disabilities* 29(4):402–12.

Higgins, K., and M. Raskind. 2005. The compensatory effectiveness of the Quicktionary Reading Pen II © on the comprehension of students with learning disabilities. *Journal of Special Education Technology* 20(1):31–40.

Hill, J. W., and K. L. Coufal. 2005. Emotional/behavioral disorders: A retrospective examination of social skills, linguistics, and student outcomes. *Communication Disorders Quarterly* 27:33–46.

Hitchcock, C., A. Meyer, D. H. Rose, and R. Jackson. 2002. Providing new access to the general education curriculum. *Teaching Exceptional Children* 35(2):8–17.

Hitchings, W. E., D. A. Luzzo, P. Retish, M. Horvath, and R. Ristow. 1998. Identifying the career development needs of college students with disabilities. *Journal of College Student Development* 39(1):23–32.

Hitchings, W. E., P. Retish, and M. Horvath. 2005. Academic preparation of adolescents with disabilities for postsecondary education. *Career Development for Exceptional Individuals* 28:26–35.

Ho, K. M., and M. K. Keiley. 2003. Dealing with denial: A systems approach for family professionals working with parents of individuals with multiple disabilities. *The Family Journal: Counseling and Therapy for Couples and Families* 11:239–47.

Hodgkinson, H. 2002. Demographics and teacher education: An overview. *Journal of Teacher Education* 53:102–5.

Hoffman, L., J. Marquis, D. Poston, J. A. Summers, and A. Turnbull. 2006. Assessing family outcomes: Psychometric evaluation of the Beach Center Family Quality of Life Scale. *Journal of Marriage and Family* 68:1,069–83.

Hogan, K., and M. Pressley. 1997. Scaffolding scientific competencies within classroom communities of inquiry. In *Scaffolding student learning Instructional approaches and issues,* ed. K. Hogan and M. Pressley, 74–107. Louiseville, Quebec, CA: Brookline Books.

Hohn, R. 1994. *Classroom learning and teaching.* Boston: Allyn & Bacon.

Holland, J. L. 1985. *Making of vocational choices: A theory of vocational personalities and work environments.* 2nd ed. Englewood Cliffs, NJ: Prentice Hall.

Holland, J. L. 1997. *Making vocational choices.* 3rd ed. Odessa, FL: Psychological Assessment Resources.

Holum, A., and J. Gahala. 2001. North Central Regional Educational Laboratory. Critical issue: Using technology to enhance literacy instruction. http://www.ncrel.org/sdrs/areas/issues/content/cntareas/reading/li300.htm (accessed July 6, 2007).

Honig, M. I., and T. C. Hatch. 2004. Crafting coherence: How schools strategically manage multiple, external demands. *Educational Researcher* 33(8):16–30.

Horn, L., K. Peter, and K. Rooney. 2002. Profile of undergraduates in U.S. postsecondary institutions: 1999–2000. Statistical analysis report, no. NCES 2002–168. Washington, DC: National Center for Education Statistics, U.S. Department of Education, Office of Educational Research and Improvement. http://www.ncld.org/index.php?option=content&task=view&id=433.

Horton, S.V., R. A. Boone, and T. C. Lovitt. 1990. Teaching social studies to learning disabled high school students: Effects of a hypertext study guide. *British Journal of Educational Technology* 21:118–31.

Horton, S.V., T. C. Lovitt, and C. C. Christensen. 1991. Note taking from textbooks: Effects of a columnar format on three categories of secondary students. *Exceptionality* 2:19–40.

Hudson, R. F., H. B. Lane, and P. C. Pullen. 2005. Reading fluency assessment and instruction: What, why, and how? *The Reading Teacher* 58:702–14.

Hughes, C. 1996. Memory and test-taking strategies. In *Teaching adolescents with learning disabilities,* ed. D. D. Deshler, E. S. Ellis, and B. K. Lenz, 2nd ed., 209–66. Denver: Love Publishing.

Hughes, C. A., and J. R. Boyle. 1991. Effects of self-monitoring for on-task behavior and task productivity on elementary students with moderate mental retardation. *Education and Treatment of Children* 14:96–111.

Hughes, T. A., and L. D. Fredrick. 2006. Teaching vocabulary with students with learning disabilities using classwide peer tutoring and constant time delay. *Journal of Behavioral Education* 15(1):1–23.

Hughes, C., M. S. Rodi, S. W. Lorden, S. E. Pittken, K. R. Dereer, B. Hwang, and C. Xinsheng. 1999. Social interactions of high school students with mental retardation and their general education peers. *American Journal on Mental Retardation* 104:533–44.

Hughes, C. A., K. L. Ruhl, J. B. Schumaker, and D. D. Deshler. 2002. Effects of instruction in an assignment completion strategy on the homework performance of students with learning disabilities in general education classes. *Learning Disabilities Research & Practice* 17:1–18.

Hughes, C. A., J. Salvia, and D. A. Bott. 1991. The nature and extent of test-wiseness cues in seventh and tenth grade classroom tests. *Diagnostique* 2–3:153–63.

Hughes, C. A., J. B. Schumaker, and D. D. Deshler. 2005. *The essay test taking strategy.* Lawrence, KS: University of Kansas.

Hughes, C. A., J. B. Schumaker, D. D. Deshler, and C. Mercer. 1988. *The test-taking strategy.* Lawrence, KS: Excel Enterprises.

Hughes, M. T., J. S. Schumm, and S. Vaughn. 1999. Home literacy activities: Perceptions and practices of Hispanic parents of children with learning disabilities. *Learning Disability Quarterly* 22:224–35.

Hughes, C. A., and J. O. Smith. 1990. Cognitive and academic performance of college students with learning disabilities: A synthesis of the literature. *Learning Disability Quarterly* 13:66–79.

Hughes, C. A., and S. K. Suritsky. 1994. Note-taking skills of university students with and without learning disabilities. *Journal of Learning Disabilities* 27:20–4.

Hurst, D., D. Kelly, and D. Princiotta. 2004. *Issue brief: Educational attainment of high school dropouts 8 years later,* no. NCERS 2005–2006. Washington, DC: U.S. Department of Education, National Center for Education Statistics.

Hutchinson, N., J. Freeman, and D. Berg. 2004. Social competence of adolescents with learning disabilities: Interventions and issues. In *Learning about learning disabilities,* ed. B.Y. L. Wong, 3rd ed., 415–38. San Diego, CA: Elsevier Academic Press.

Idol, L. 1987. Group story mapping: A comprehension strategy for both skilled and unskilled readers. *Journal of Learning Disabilities* 20:196–205.

Idol, L. 1988. Johnny can't read: Does the fault lie in the book, the teacher, or Johnny? *Remedial and Special Education* 9:8–25.

Idol, L. 2006. Toward inclusion of special education students in general education: A program evaluation of eight schools. *Remedial and Special Education* 27:77–94.

Idol, L., and V. Croll. 1987. Story mapping training as a means of increasing reading comprehension. *Journal of Learning Disabilities* 10:214–29.

Individuals with Disabilities Education Act (IDEA). 1997. Public Law no. 94-102. [20 U.S.C. §§ 1400 et seq.]

Individuals with Disabilities Education Improvement Act (IDEIA). 2004. Public Law no. 108-446, 118 Stat. 2647 [Amending 20 U.S.C. §§ 1400 et seq.]

Institute of Education Sciences. What Works Clearinghouse. 2006. http://www.whatworks.ed.gov (accessed November 18, 2006).

International Reading Association/National Council of Teachers of English. 1996. *Standards for the English Language Arts.* Newark, DE/Urbana, IL: International Reading Association/National Council of Teachers of English.

Internet world stats: Usage and population statistics. 2008. Internet usage statistics: The internet big picture. http://www.internetworldstats.com (retrieved November 18, 2008).

Isaacs, A., and W. Carroll. 1999. Strategies for basic fact instruction. *Teaching Children Mathematics* 5:508–15.

Isaacson, S. 1989. Role of secretary vs. author: Resolving the conflict in writing instruction. *Learning Disability Quarterly* 12:209–17.

Ishii-Jordan, J. J. 2000. Behavioral interventions used with diverse students. *Behavioral Disorders* 25:299–309.

ISTE Technology Foundation standards for all students. http://www.iste.org/standards (accessed June 25, 2007).

Jaksa, P. Attitude: Living well with ADD and learning disabilities. Uncle Sam Doesn't Want You! http://www.additudemag.com/additude/article/801.html (accessed December, 7, 2007).

Jakulski, J., and M. A. Mastropieri. 2004. Homework for students with disabilities. In *Research in secondary schools: Advances in learning and behavioral disabilities*, ed. T. E. Scruggs and M. A. Mastropieri, 77–122. Oxford, UK: Elsevier.

Janiga, S. J., and V. Costenbader. 2002. The transition from high school to postsecondary education for students with learning disabilities: A survey of college service coordinators. *Journal of Learning Disabilities* 35:462–8.

Jenkins, J. R., P. S. Dale, P. E. Mills, and K. N. Cole. 2006. How special education preschool graduates finish: Status at 19 years of age. *American Educational Research Journal* 43:737–81.

Jenkins, J. R., L. S. Fuchs, P. van den Brock, C. Espin, and S. L. Deno. 2003a. Accuracy and fluency in list and context reading of skilled and RD groups: Absolute and relative performance levels. *Learning Disabilities Research & Practice* 18:237–45.

Jenkins, J. R., L.S. Fuchs, P. van den Brock, C. Espin, and S. L. Deno. 2003b. Sources of individual differences in reading comprehension and reading fluency. *Journal of Educational Psychology* 95:719–29.

Jitendra, A. 2002. Teaching students math problem-solving through graphic representations. *TEACHING Exceptional Children* 34:34–8.

Jitendra, A. K., L. L. Edwards, G. Sacks, and L. A. Jacobson. 2004. What research says about vocabulary instruction for students with learning disabilities, *Exceptional Children* 70:299–322.

Jitendra, A., C. M. DiPipi, and N. Perron-Jones. 2002. An exploratory study of schema-based word-problem-solving instruction for middle school students with learning disabilities: An emphasis on conceptual and procedural understanding. *Journal of Special Education* 36(1):23–38.

Jitendra, A. K., M. M. Salmento, and L. A. Haydt. 1999. A case analysis of fourth-grade subtraction instruction in basal mathematics programs: Adherence to important instructional design criteria. *Learning Disabilities Research & Practice* 14(2):69–79.

Johns, J. L. 1981. The development of the Revised Dolch List. *Illinois School Research and Development* 17:15–24.

Johnson, D. W., R. T. Johnson, and E. J. Holubec. 1991. *Cooperation in the classroom*. Edina, MN: Interaction Book Company.

Johnson, D. W., R. T. Johnson, and E. J. Holubec. 1993. Active Learning: *Cooperation in the classroom.* 6th ed. Edina, MN: Interaction Book Company.

Johnson, D., R. Johnson, and E. Holubec. 1998. *Cooperation in the classroom.* 7th ed. Boston: Allyn & Bacon.

Johnson, L. J., and J. Noga. 1998. Key collaboration skills. In *Early childhood education: Blending theory, blending practice*, ed. L. J. Johnson, M. J. LaMontagne, P. M. Elgas, and A. M. Bauer, 19–43. Baltimore: Paul H. Brookes.

Johnston, P. H. 1997. *Knowing literacy: Constructive literacy assessment.* York, ME: Stenhouse Publishers.

Jordan, N. C., and L. B. Hanich. 2003. Characteristics of children with moderate mathematics deficiencies: A longitudinal perspective. *Learning Disabilities Research & Practice* 18:213–21.

Kahlenberg, R. D. 2001. Learning from James Coleman. *Public Interest* 144:54–72.

Kalyanpur, M., B. Harry, and T. Skrtic. 2000. Equity and advocacy expectations of culturally diverse families' participation in special education. *International Journal of Disability, Development and Education* 47:119–36.

Kame'enui, E. J., D. W. Carnine, R. C. Dixon, D. C. Simmons, and M. D. Coyne. 2002. *Effective teaching strategies that accommodate diverse learners.* 2nd ed. Columbus, OH: Merrill.

Kaplan, J. S. 1995. *Beyond behavior modification: A cognitive-behavioral approach to behavior management in the school.* 3rd ed. Austin, TX: PRO-ED.

Karvonen, M., D. W. Test, W. M. Wood, D. Browder, and B. Algozzine. 2004. Putting self-determination into practice. *Exceptional Children* 71:23–41.

Katims, David S., and S. Harris. 1997. Improving the reading comprehension of middle school students in inclusive classrooms. *Journal of Adolescent & Adult Literacy* 41:116–8.

Katzir, T., Y. Kim, M. Wolf, B. O'Brien, B. Kennedy, M. Lovett, and R. Morris. 2006. Reading fluency: The whole is more than the sum of the parts. *Annals of Dyslexia* 56:51–82.

Kauffman, J. 1997. *Characteristics of emotional and behavioral disorders of children and youth.* Upper Saddle River, NJ: Prentice Hall.

Kauffman, J. 2002. *Education deform: Bright people sometimes say stupid things about education.* Lanham, MD: Scarecrow Education.

Kauffman, J. M. 2003. Appearances, stigma, and prevention. *Remedial and Special Education* 24(4):195–7.

Kauffman, J., and D. P. Hallahan. 2005. *Special education: What is it and why we need it.* Boston: Allyn & Bacon.

Kavale, K. A., and S. R. Forness. 1999. *Efficacy of special education and related services.* Washington, DC: AAMR.

Kavale, K. A., and S. R. Forness. 2000. What definitions of learning disability say and don't say: A critical analysis. *Journal of Learning Disabilities* 33:239–56.

Kavale, K. A., J. M. Kauffman, R. J. Bachmeier, and G. B. LeFever. 2008. Response-to-Intervention: Separating the rhetoric of self-congratulation from the reality of specific learning disability identification. *Learning Disability Quarterly* 31:135–50.

Kavale, K. A. and P. D. Mattson. 1983. Meta-analysis of perceptual-motor training. *Journal of Learning Disabilities* 16:165–73.

Kellogg, R. T. 1996. A model of working memory in writing. In *Cognitive processes in writing,* ed. L. W. Gregg and E. R. Steinberg, 57–72. Hillsdale, NJ: Lawrence Erlbaum.

Kenny, M. E., L. Gualdron, D. Scanlon, E. Sparks, D. L. Blustein, and M. Jernigan. 2007. Urban adolescents' constructions of supports and barriers to educational and career attainment. *Journal of Counseling Psychology* 54:326–43.

Kerr, M. M., and C. M. Nelson. 2002. *Strategies for managing behavior problems in the classroom.* 4th ed. Upper Saddle River, NJ: Pearson Education.

Kiewra, K. A. 1985. Students' note-taking behaviors and the efficacy of providing instructor's notes for review. *Contemporary Educational Psychology* 10(4):378–86.

Kiewra, K. A., R. E. Mayer, M. Christensen, S. Kim, and N. Risch. 1991. Effects of repetition on recall and note taking: Strategies for learning from lectures. *Journal of Educational Psychology* 83:120–3.

Kim, A., S. Vaughn, J. K. Klingner, A. L. Woodruff, C. K. Reutebuch, and K. Kouzkanani. 2006. Improving the reading composition of middle school students with disabilities through computer-assisted collaborative strategic reading. *Remedial and Special Education* 27(4):235–49.

Kim, A., S. Vaughn, J. Wanzek, and S. Wei. 2004. Graphic organizers and their effects on the reading comprehension of students with LD: A synthesis of research. *Journal of Learning Disabilities* 37:105–19.

King-Sears, M., C. Mercer, and P. Sindelar. 1992. Towards independence with keyword mnemonics: A strategy for science vocabulary instruction. *Remedial and Special Education* 13:22–33.

King-Sears, P. E. 2005. Are you highly qualified? The plight of effective special educators for students with learning disabilities. *Learning Disability Quarterly* 28:187–8.

Kissam, B., and B. K. Lenz. 1994. *Pedagogies for diversity in secondary schools: A preservice curriculum.* Lawrence, KS: University of Kansas.

Klamm, K. 1990. An analysis of academic performance, self-concept, social integration, adaptive behavior, and consumer satisfaction in elementary class within a class alternative service delivery model for students with learning disabilities. *Dissertation Abstracts International, 51* (12A), 4085 (UMI No. AAG9110887).

Kliebard, H. M. 1992. Constructing a history of the American curriculum. In *Handbook of research on curriculum,* ed.

P. W. Jackson, 157–184. New York: Macmillan Publishing Company.

Kline, F., J. Schumaker, and D. Deshler. 1991. Development and validation of feedback routines for instructing students with learning disabilities. *Learning Disability Quarterly* 14:191–207.

Kloosterman, P., and F. K. Lester. 2004. *Results and interpretations of the 1990 through 2000 mathematics assessments of the National Assessment of Educational Progress.* Reston, VA: National Council of Teachers of Mathematics.

Knackendoffel, E. 2005. Collaborative teaming in the secondary school. *Focus on Exceptional Children* 37(5):1–16.

Kochar-Bryant, C. and M. V. Izzo. 2006. Access to post-high school services: Transition assessment and the summary of performance. *Career Development of Exceptional Individuals* 29:70–89.

Kohler, P. D. 1998. Implementing a transition perspective of education: A comprehensive approach to planning and delivering secondary education and transition services. In *Beyond high school: Transition from school to work,* ed. F. R. Rusch and J. G. Chadsey, 179–205. Belmont, CA: Wadsworth Publishing Co.

Kohn, A. 2002. Poor teaching for poor kids. *Language Arts* 79:251–5.

Kohn, A. 2006. *The homework myth: Why our kids get too much of a bad thing.* Cambridge, MA: De Capo.

Konefal, J., and J. Folks. 1984. Linguistic analysis of children's conversational repairs. *Journal of Psycholinguistic Research* 13:1–11.

Kortering, L., P. Braziel, and J. Tompkins. 2002. The challenge of school completion among youth with behavior disorders: Another side of the story. *Behavioral Disorders* 27:142–54.

Koscinski, S. T., and D. L. Gast. 1993. Use of constant time delay in teaching multiplication facts to students with learning disabilities. *Journal of Learning Disabilities* 26(8):533–44, 567.

Krinsky, R., and S. Krinsky. 1996. Pegword mnemonic instruction: Retrieval times and long-term memory performance among fifth-grade children. *Contemporary Educational Psychology* 21:193–207.

Kroesbergen, E. H., and J. E. H. Van Luit. 2003. Mathematics interventions for children with special educational needs: A meta-analysis. *Remedial and Special Education* 24(2):97–114.

Kübler-Ross, E. 1969. *On death and dying.* New York: Touchstone.

Kuder, S. J. 2003. Teaching students with language and communication disabilities. Boston, MA: Allyn & Bacon.

Kuhn, M. R., and S. A. Stahl. 2000. *Fluency: A review of developmental and remedial practices.* Ann Arbor, MI: Center for the Improvement of Early Reading Achievement.

Kutash, K., A. J. Duchnowsil, W. C. Sumi, Z. Rudo, and K. M. Harris. 2002. A school, family, and community collaborative program for children who have emotional disturbances. *Journal of Emotional and Behavioral Disorders* 10:99–107.

Kytle, R. 1970. Pre-writing by analysis. *College Composition and Communication* 21:380–5.

LaBerge, D., and S. J. Samuels. 1974. Toward a theory of automatic information processing in reading. *Cognitive Psychology* 6:293–323.

Laing, S., and A. Kamhi. 2003. Alternative assessment of language and literacy in culturally and linguistically diverse populations. *Language, Speech, and Hearing Services in Schools* 34:44–55.

Lambros, K., S. Ward, K. Bocian, D. MacMillan, and F. Gresham. 1998. Behavioral profiles of children at risk for emotional and behavioral disorders: Implications for assessment and classification. *Focus on Exceptional Children* 30(5):1–16.

Langner, E. J. 1997. *The power of mindful learning.* Reading, MA: Addison-Wesley.

Lardieri, L. A., J. Blacher, and H. L. Swanson. 2000. Sibling relationships and parent stress in families of children with and without learning disabilities. *Learning Disability Quarterly* 23:105–16.

Larry P. v. Riles. Civil Action, no. 6-71-2270, 343 F. Supp. 1036 (N.D. Cal., 1972).

Larson, S. C. 1976. The validity of perceptual test: The debate continues. *Journal of Learning Disabilities* 9(6):334–7.

Latham, P. H., and P. S. Latham. The armed forces and attention deficit/hyperactivity disorder. Attention Deficit Disorder Association and Learning Disabilities. http://www.add.org/articles/armedforces.html (accessed December 7, 2007).

Lauth, G., B. Heubeck, and K. Mackowiak. 2006. Observation of children with attention-deficit hyperactivity (ADHD) problems in three natural classroom contexts. *British Journal of Educational Psychology* 76:385–404.

Lazarus, B. D. 1991. Guided notes, review, and achievement of secondary students with learning disabilities in mainstream content courses. *Education and Treatment of Children* 14(2):112–27.

LD OnLine. Gifted and LD. (2008). WETA. http://www.ldonline.org/indepth/gifted (accessed May 1, 2008).

Learning Disabilities Association of America. 1999. Speech and Language Milestone Chart. http://www.ldonline.org/article/6313 (accessed May 1, 2008).

Learning Disabilities Association of Minnesota. 2004. Multi-syllabic instruction. *NetNews* 4, 2–4.

Lee, C. M., and R. F. Jackson. 1992. *Faking it: A look into the mind of a creative thinker.* Portsmouth, NH: Heinemann.

Lee, C., and R. Jackson. 2001. *What about me? Strategies for teaching misunderstood learners.* Portsmouth, NH: Heinemann.

Lee, H. J., and L. M. Herner-Patnode. 2007. Teaching mathematics vocabulary to diverse groups. (What works for me.) *Intervention in School and Clinic* 43(2):121–26.

Lee, J., W. Grigg, and P. Donahue. 2007. *The nation's report card: Reading 2007,* no. NES 2007–496. National Center for Education Statistics, Institute of Education Sciences, U.S. Department of Education, Washington, DC.

LeFever, B. G., M. S. Villers, A. L. Morrow, and E. S. Vaughn. 2002. Parental perceptions of adverse educational outcomes among children diagnosed and treated for ADHD: A call for improved school/provider collaboration. *Psychology in the Schools* 39:63–71.

Lenz, B. K., G. R. Alley, and J. B. Schumaker. 1987. Activating the inactive learner: Advance organizers in the secondary content classroom. *Learning Disability Quarterly* 10:53–67.

Lenz, B. K., J. A. Bulgren, J. B. Schumaker, D. D. Deshler, and D. J. Boudah. 1995. *The content enhancement series: The unit organizer routine.* Lawrence, KS: Edge Enterprises.

Lenz, B. K., D. D. Deshler, and B. R. Kissam. 2004. *Teaching content to all: Evidence-based inclusive practices in middle and secondary schools.* Boston, MA: Pearson Education, Inc.

Lenz, B. K., E. S. Ellis, and D. Scanlon. 1996. *Teaching learning strategies to adolescents and adults with learning disabilities.* Austin, TX: Pro-Ed.

Lenz, B. K., R. Marrs, J. Schumaker, D. Deshler, and D. Boudah. 1993. *The lesson organizer routine.* Lawrence, KS: Edge Enterprises.

Lenz, B. K., and C. Hughes. 1990. A word identification strategy for adolescents with learning disabilities. *Journal of Learning Disabilities* 23:149–63.

Lenz, B. K., J. Schumaker, D. Deshler, and J. Beals. 1984. *Learning strategies curriculum: The word identification strategy.* Lawrence, KS: University of Kansas.

Lenz, B. K., J. B. Schumaker, D. D. Deshler, and J. A. Bulgren. 1998. *The course organizer routine.* Lawrence, KS: Edge Enterprises.

Leong, C. K. 1995. Effects of on-line reading and simultaneous DECtalk aiding in helping below average and poor readers comprehend and summarize text. *Learning Disability Quarterly* 18:101–16.

Levine, E. B., and E. J. Trickett. 2000. Toward a model of Latino parent advocacy for educational change. *Journal of Prevention & Intervention in the Community* 20:121–37.

Lewis, R., A. Graves, T. Ashton, and C. Kieley. 1998. Word processing tools for students with learning disabilities: A comparison of strategies to increase text entry speed. *Learning Disabilities Research & Practice* 13:95–108.

Li, L., and D. Moore. 1998. Acceptance of disability and its correlates. *The Journal of Social Psychology* 138:13–25.

Liberman, I., D. Shankweiler, and A. Liberman. 1989. *The alphabetic principle and learning to read.* Bethesda, MD: National Institute of Child Health and Human Development.

Lidgus, C., and S. Vassos. 1996. Increasing achievement of at-risk students through the use of metacognitive strategies, no. ED 399704. U.S. Department of Education.

Lindstrom, L. E., and M. R. Benz. 2002. Phases of career development: Case studies of young women with learning disabilities. *Exceptional Children* 69(1):67–83.

Lipsky, D. K. 2005. Are we there yet? *Learning Disability Quarterly* 28(2):156–8.

Lipson, M., and K. Wixson. 1997. *Assessment and instruction of reading and writing disability: An interactive approach.* 2nd ed. Reading, MA: Addison Wesley, Longman.

Little, M. E., and D. L. Hahs-Vaughn. 2007. The implementation of content enhancement routines for improved content literacy for middle and secondary social studies students. *Journal of Personnel Evaluation in Education* 20:261–80.

Locke, E. A. 1977. An empirical study of lecture note taking among college students. *Journal of Educational Research* 71:93–9.

Lopes, J. A., I. Monteiro, V. Sil, R. B. Rutherford, and M. M. Quinn. 2004. Teachers' perceptions about teaching problem students in regular classrooms. *Education & Treatment of Children* 27:394–419.

Lott, B. 2001. Low-income parents and the public schools. *Journal of Social Issues* 57:189–206.

Lott, B. 2003. Recognizing and welcoming the standpoint of low-income parents in the public schools. *Journal of Educational and Psychological Consultation* 14:91–104.

Lovett, M. W., L. Lacerenza, and S. L. Borden. 2000. Putting struggling reading on the PHAST track: A program to integrate phonological and strategy-based remedial reading instruction and maximize outcomes. *Journal of Learning Disabilities* 33:458–76.

Lovett, B. J., and L. J. Lewandowski. 2006. Gifted students with learning disabilities: Who are they? *Journal of Learning Disabilities* 39(6):515–27.

Lowery-Corkran, E. 2006. *Academic experiences of students with learning disabilities at private, highly selective liberal arts institutions.* Doctoral Dissertation. Chestnut Hill, MA: Lynch School of Education, Boston College.

Lustig, D. C. 2002. Family coping in families with a child with a disability. *Education and Training in Mental Retardation and Developmental Disabilities* 37:14–22.

Lyon, G. R., and L. C. Moats. 1997. Critical conceptual and methodological considerations in reading intervention research. *Journal of Learning Disabilities* 30(6):578–88.

MacArthur, C. 1988. The impact of computers on the writing process. *Exceptional Children* 54:536–42.

MacArthur, C. A. 1998. Word processing with speech synthesis and word prediction: Effects on the dialogue journal writing of students with learning disabilities. *Learning Disability Quarterly* 21(2):151–66.

MacArthur, C. A., and A. R. Cavalier. 2004. Dictation and speech recognition technology as test accommodations. *Exceptional Children* 71(1):43–58.

MacArthur, C., and S. Graham. 1987. Learning disabled students' composing under three methods of text production: Handwriting, word processing, and dictation. *The Journal of Special Education* 21:22–42.

MacArthur, C. A., and J. B. Haynes. 1995. Student assistant for learning from text (SALT): A hypermedia reading aid. *Journal of Learning Disabilities* 28(3):50–9.

MacArthur, C. A., J. A. Haynes, D. B. Malouf, K. Harris, and M. Owings. 1990. Computer assisted instruction with learning disabled students: Achievement, engagement, and other factors that influence achievement. *Journal of Educational Computing Research* 6(3):311–28.

MacArthur, C., S. Schwartz, and S. Graham. 1991. Effects of a reciprocal peer revision strategy in special education classrooms. *Learning Disabilities Research & Practice* 6:201–10.

Maccini, P., and J. C. Gagnon. 2006. Mathematics instructional practices and assessment accommodations by secondary special and general educators. *Exceptional Children* 72:217–34.

Maccini, P., and C. A. Hughes. 1997. Mathematics interventions for adolescents with learning disabilities. *Learning Disabilities Research & Practice* 12:168–76.

Maccini, P., C. A. Mulcahy, and M. G. Wilson. 2007. A follow-up of mathematics interventions for secondary students with learning disabilities. *Learning Disabilities Research & Practice* 22:58–74.

MacMillan, D. and G. Siperstein (2001). *Learning disabilities as operationally defined by schools. Executive summary.* U.S. Department of Education, Office of Special Education Programs. Washington, DC. ERIC Documents Reproduction Services (ED 458 759).

Madaus, J. W. 2006. Employment outcomes of university graduates with learning disabilities. *Learning Disabilities Quarterly* 29:119–31.

Madaus, J. W., S. Bigaj, S. Chafaleous, and B. Simonsen. 2006. What key information can be included in a comprehensive summary of performance? *Career Development for Exceptional Individuals* 26:90–9.

Madaus, J. W., and S. F. Shaw. 2006. The impact of the IDEA 2004 on transition to college for students with learning disabilities. *Learning Disabilities Research & Practice* 21:273–81.

Magiera, K., C. Smith, N. Zigmond, and K. Gebauer. 2005. Benefits of co-teaching in secondary mathematics classes. *TEACHING Exceptional Children* 37(3):20–4.

Maheady, L., M. K. Sacca, and G. F. Harper. 1988. Classwide peer tutoring with mildly handicapped high school students. *Exceptional Children* 55(1):52–9.

Mann, L. and D. Sabatino. 1985. *Cognitive processes in remedial and special education.* Rockville, MD: Aspen Publications.

Mann, P. H., P. A. Suiter, and R. M. McClung. 1992. *A guide to educating mainstreamed students.* 4th ed. Boston: Allyn & Bacon.

Maras, P., and R. Brown. 2000. Effects of different forms of school contact on children's attitudes toward disabled and non-disabled peers, *British Journal of Educational Psychology* 70:337–51.

Margolis, H., and J. Free. 2001. Computerized IEP programs: A guide for educational consultants. *Journal of Educational and Psychological Consultation* 12:171–8.

Margolis, V. H., and C. A. Michaels. 1994. Technology: The personal computer as a resource tool. In *Transition strategies for persons with learning disabilities,* ed. C. A. Michaels. San Diego: Singular.

Mariage, T. 2001. Features of an interactive writing discourse: Conversational involvement, conventional knowledge and internalization in "Morning Message." *Journal of Learning Disabilities* 34:172–96.

Marston, D., P. Muyskens, M. Lau, and A. Canter. 2003. Problem-solving model for decision making with high-incidence disabilities: The Minneapolis experience. *Learning Disabilities Research & Practice* 18(3):187–200.

Mastropieri, M., and T. Scruggs. 1997. Best practices in promoting reading comprehension in students with learning disabilities. *Remedial and Special Education* 18:197–213.

Mastropieri, M. A., and T. E. Scruggs. 2002. *Effective instruction for special education.* 3rd ed. Austin, TX: Pro-Ed.

Mastropieri, M. A., and T. E. Scruggs. 2007. *The inclusive classroom: Strategies for effective instruction.* 3rd ed. Columbus, OH: Prentice Hall/Merrill.

Mastropieri, M., T. Scruggs, and B. Fulk. 1990. Teaching abstract vocabulary with the keyword method: Effects on recall and comprehension. *Journal of Learning Disabilities* 23:92–107.

Mastropieri, M., T. Scruggs, and J. Graetz. 2003. Reading comprehension instruction for secondary students: Challenges for struggling students and teachers. *Learning Disability Quarterly* 26:103–16.

Mastropieri, M. A., T. E. Scruggs, J. Graetz, J. Norland, W. Gardizi, and K. McDuffie. 2005. Case studies in co-teaching in the content areas: Successes, failures, and challenges. *Intervention in School and Clinic* 40(5):260–70.

Mastropieri, M. A., T. E. Scruggs, V. Spencer, and J. Fontana. 2003. Promoting success in high school world history: Peer tutoring versus guided notes. *Learning Disabilities Research & Practice* 18(1):52–65.

Mather, N. 1992. Whole language reading instruction for students with learning disabilities: Caught in the cross fire. *Learning Disabilities Research & Practice* 7:87–95.

Mathes, P. G., D. Fuchs, L. S. Fuchs, A. M. Henley, and A. Sanders. 1994. Increasing strategic reading practice with Peabody classwide peer tutoring. *Learning Disabilities Research & Practice* 9:44–8.

Matuszny, R. M., D. R. Banda, and T. J. Coleman. 2007. A progressive plan for building collaborative relationships with parents from diverse backgrounds. *TEACHING Exceptional Children* 39(4):24–31.

Mayer, R. 1987. Learnable aspects of problem solving: Some examples. In *Applications of cognitive psychology: Problem solving, education, and computing*, ed. D. E. Berger, K. Pezdek, and W. P. Banks. Hillsdale, NJ: Erlbaum.

Mayer, R. 2004. Should there be a three-strikes rule against pure discovery learning? The case for guided methods of instruction. *American Psychologist* 59:14–9.

Mayes, S., S. Calhoun, and S. Lane. 2005. Diagnosing children's writing disabilities: Different tests give different results. *Perceptual and Motor Skills* 101:72–8.

McDonnell, J., and B. Laughlin. 1989. A comparison of backward chaining and concurrent chaining strategies in teaching community skills. *Education and Treatment in Mental Retardation* 24:230–8.

McMaster, K. L., and D. Fuchs. 2002. Effects of cooperative learning on the academic achievement of students with learning disabilities: An update of Tateyama-Sniezek's review. *Learning Disabilities Research & Practice* 17:107–17.

McMaster, K. L., D. Fuchs, and L. S. Fuchs. 2006. Research on peer-assisted learning strategies: The promise and limitations of peer-mediated instruction. *Reading & Writing Quarterly* 22(1):5–25.

McMaster, K., D. Fuchs, L. S. Fuchs, and D. L. Compton. 2002. Monitoring the academic progress of children who are unresponsive to generally effective early reading intervention. *Assessment for Effective Intervention* 27(4):23–33.

McMullen, R. C., M. E. Shippen, and H. L. Dangel. 2007. Middle school teachers' expectations of organizational behaviors of students with learning disabilities. *Journal of Instructional Psychology* 34(2):75–80.

McNamara, D. S., and W. Kintsch. 1996. Learning from texts: effects of prior knowledge and text coherence. *Discourse Processes* 22:247–88.

McNaughton, D., C. A. Hughes, and K. Clark. 1994. Spelling instruction for students with learning disabilities—implication for research and practice. *Learning Disability Quarterly* 17:168–85.

McPartland, J. 1994. Dropout prevention in theory and practice. In *School and students at risk: Context and framework for positive change*, ed. R. Rossi, 255–76. New York: Teachers College Press.

Medcalf-Davenport, N. 2003. Questions, answers, and wait-time: Implications for assessment of young children. *International Journal of Early Years Education* 11:245–53.

Meese, R. L. 2001. *Teaching learners with mild disabilities: Integrating research and practice.* 2nd ed. Belmont, CA: Wadsworth/Thomson Learning.

Mehring, T. A., and S. E. Colson. 1990. Motivation and mildly handicapped learners. *Focus on Exceptional Children* 22(5):1–14.

Meichenbaum, D. 1977. *Cognitive-behavior modification: An integrated approach.* New York: Plenum Press.

Meichenbaum, D., and J. Goodman. 1971. Training impulsive children to talk to themselves: A means of developing self-control. *Journal of Abnormal Psychology* 77:115–26.

Mellard, D., and P. Lancaster. 2003. Incorporating adult community services in students' transition planning. *Remedial and Special Education* 24(6):359–68.

Mellard, D., D. Scanlon, B. Kissam, and K. Woods. 2005. Adult education instructional environments and interaction patterns between teachers and students: An ecobehavioral assessment. *Literacy and Numeracy Studies* 14:49–68.

Meltzer, L., T. Katzir-Cohen, L. Miller, and B. Roditit. 2001. Impact of effort and strategy use on academic performance: Student and teacher perspectives. *Learning Disability Quarterly* 24:85–98.

Meltzer, L., and K. Krishnan. 2007. Executive function difficulties and learning disabilities: Understandings and misunderstandings. In *Executive function in education: From theory to practice*, ed. Lynn Meltzer. New York: Guilford Press.

Mercer, C. D., and S. P. Miller. 1992. Teaching students with learning problems in math to acquire, understand, and apply basic math facts. *Remedial and Special Education* 13:19–35.

Mercer, C. D., and P. D. Pullen. 2005. *Students with learning disabilities.* Upper Saddle River, NJ: Prentice Hall.

Merrell, K. W., and T. M. Wolfe. 1998. The relationship of teacher-rated social skills deficits and ADHD characteristics among kindergarten-age children. *Psychology in the Schools* 35:101–9.

Merriam-Webster. 1991. *Webster's ninth new collegiate dictionary.* Springfield, MA: Merriam-Webster.

Miller, A. D., S. W. Hall, and W. L. Heward. 1995. Effects of sequential 1-minute time trials with and without intertrial feedback and self-correction on general and special education students' fluency with math facts. *Journal of Behavioral Education* 5:319–45.

Miller, G. A. 1956. The magical number seven, plus or minus two: Some limits on our capacity for processing information. *Psychological Review* 63:81–97.

Miller, J. F., J. Heilmann, A. Nockerts, A. Iglesias, L. Fabiano, and D. J. Francis. 2006. Oral language and reading in bilingual children. *Learning Disabilities Research & Practice* 21:30–43.

Miller, P. W. 2005. Body language in the classroom. *Techniques: Connecting Education and Careers* 80(8):28–30.

Miller, S. P., and C. D. Mercer. 1991a. *Addition facts 0-9.* Lawrence, KS: Edge Enterprises.

Miller, S. P., and C. D. Mercer. 1993. Using mnemonics to enhance the math performance of students with learning disabilities. *Intervention in School and Clinic* 28:105–10.

Miller, S. P. 1996. Perspectives on mathematics instruction. In *Teaching Adolescents with Learning Disabilities,* ed. D. D. Deshler, E. S. Ellis, and B. K. Lenz, 2nd ed., 313–67. Denver, CO: Love Publishing.

Miller, S. P., and P. J. Hudson. 2006. Helping students with disabilities understand what mathematics means. *TEACHING Exceptional Children* 39:28–35.

Miller, S. P., and C. D. Mercer. 1997. Educational aspects of mathematics disabilities. *Journal of Learning Disabilities* 30(1):47–56.

Mills, C. J., and L. E. Brody. 1999. Overlooked and unchallenged: Gifted students with learning disabilities. *Knowledge Quest* 27(5):36–40.

Milsom, A., and M. T. Hartley. 2005. Assisting students with learning disabilities transitioning to college: What school counselors should know. *Professional School Counseling* 8:436–41.

Mirenda, P., K. Turoldo, and C. McAvoy. 2006. The impact of word prediction software on the written output of students with physical disabilities. *Journal of Special Education Technology* 21:5–12.

Moje, E. B., K. M. Ciechanowski, K. Kramer, L. Ellis, R. Carrillo, and T. Collazo. 2004. Working toward third space in content area literacy: An examination of everyday funds of knowledge and discourse. *Reading Research Quarterly* 39:38–70.

Moll, I. 2004. Towards constructivist Montessori education. *Perspectives in Education* 22:37–49.

Moll, L. C., C. Amanti, D. Neff, and N. Gonzalez. 1992. Funds of knowledge for teaching: Using a qualitative approach to connect homes and classrooms. *Theory Into Practice* 31(2):132–41.

Montague M. 2003. Teaching division to students with learning disabilities: A constructivist approach. *Exceptionality* 11:165–75.

Montague, M., and B. Applegate. 1993. Middle school students' mathematical problem solving: An analysis of think-aloud protocols. *Learning Disability Quarterly* 16:19–30.

Montague, M., and C. S. Bos. 1986. The effect of cognitive strategy training on verbal math problem-solving performance of learning disabled adolescents. *Journal of Learning Disabilities* 19:26–33.

Montague, M., and C. S. Bos. 1990. Cognitive and metacogntive characteristics of eighth-grade students' mathematical problem solving. *Learning and Individual Differences* 2:371–88.

Montague, M., and D. van Garderen. 2003. A cross-sectional study of mathematics achievement, estimation skills, and academic self-perception in students of varying ability. *Journal of Learning Disabilities* 36(5):437–48.

Moran, M. R. 1980. An investigation of the demands on oral language skills of learning disabled students in secondary classrooms. *Research report,* no 1. Lawrence: University of Kansas Institute for Research on Learning Disabilities.

Moran, M. 1981. Performance of learning disabled and low achieving secondary students on formal features of paragraph-writing task. *Learning Disability Quarterly* 4:271–80.

Morgan, P. L., and G. D. Sideridis. 2006. Contrasting the effectiveness of fluency interventions for students with or at risk for learning disabilities: A multilevel random coefficient modeling meta-analysis. *Learning Disabilities Research & Practice* 21(4):191–210.

Mortweet, S. L., C. A. Utley, D. Walker, H. L. Dawson, J. C. Delquadri, S. S. Reddy, C. R. Greenwood, S. Hamilton, and D. Ledford. 1999. Classwide peer tutoring: Teaching students with mild mental retardation in inclusive classrooms. *Exceptional Children* 65:524–36.

Mull, C. A., and P. L. Sitlington. 2003. The role of technology in the transition to postsecondary education of students with learning disabilities. *The Journal of Special Education* 37:26–32.

Mull, C., P. L. Sitlington, and S. Alper. 2001. Postsecondary education for students with learning disabilities: A synthesis of the literature. *Exceptional Children* 68:97–118.

Munk, D. D., and W. D. Bursuck. 2001. Preliminary findings on personalized grading plans for middle school students with learning disabilities. *Exceptional Children* 67:211–34.

Murphy, J., C. Hern, and R. Williams. 1990. The effects of the copy, cover, compare approach in increasing spelling accuracy with learning disabled students. *Contemporary Educational Psychology* 15:378–86.

Murray, C., D. Goldstein, S. Nourse, and E. Edgar. 2000. The postsecondary school attendance and completion rates of high school graduates with learning disabilities. *Learning Disabilities Research & Practice* 15(3):119–27.

Murray, C., and J. Naranjo. 2008. Poor, black, learning disabled, and graduating: An investigation of factors and proceses associated with school completion among high-risk urban youth. *Remedial and Special Education* 29:145–60.

Muscott, H. S. 2002. Exceptional partnerships: Listening to the voices of families. *Preventing School Failure* 46:66–9.

Nagel, D., J. Schumaker, and D. Deshler. 1986. *The FIRST-letter mnemonic strategy.* Lawrence, KS: Edge Enterprises.

Nathan, R. G., and K. E. Stanovich. 1991. The causes and consequences of differences in reading fluency. *Theory Into Practice* 30:176–84.

Nation, K. 2005. Connections between language and reading in children with poor reading comprehension. In *The connections between language and reading disabilities,* ed. H. W. Catts and Alan. G. Kamhi, 41–54. Mahwah, NJ: Lawrence Erlbaum Associates.

Nation, K., and M. Snowling. 1997. Assessing reading difficulties: The validity and utility of current measures of reading skill. *British Journal of Educational Psychology* 67:359–70.

National Association for the Education of Young Children. 2001. NAEYC standard for early childhood professional preparation: Initial licensure programs. Washington, DC: NAEYC. http://naeychq.naeyc.org/texis/search/?query=standard&btnG=Search&pr=naeyc.

National Center for Educational Statistics. 2002. Projection of education statistics to 2012. http://nces.ed.gov/pubsearch/index.asp?PubSectionID=1&HasSearched=1&pubspagenum=1&sort=3&order=0&L1=&L2=&searchstring=Projection+of+education+statistics+to+2012&searchtype=AND&searchcat2=&searchcat=title&pagesize=15&searchmonth=11&searchyear=2006&datetype=%3C%3D&pubtype=&surveyname=&surveyid=&centername=NCES&center=NCES (accessed November 6, 2008).

National Center on Educational Restructuring and Inclusion (NCERI). 1995. *National study of inclusive education.* National Center on Educational Restructuring and Inclusion, Graduate School and University Center, City University of New York.

National Collaborative on Diversity in the Teaching Force. 2004. Assessment of diversity in America's teaching force: A call to action. http://ww.nea.org/teacherquality/images/diversityreport.pdf (accessed November 6, 2008).

National Council for Accreditation of Teacher Education. Program standards for elementary teacher preparation. Association for Childhood Education International. 2000. http://www.acei.org/Part1.htm.

National Council of Teachers of English and the International Reading Association. 1996. *Standards for the English Language Arts.* Newark, DE and Urbana, IL: National Council of Teachers of English and the International Reading Association.

National Council of Teachers of Mathematics (NCTM). 1991. *Professional standards for teachers of mathematics.* Reston, VA: NCTM.

National Council of Teachers of Mathematics. 2000. *Principles and standards for school mathematics.* Reston, VA: NCTM.

National Early Literacy Panel. 2008. A synthesis of scientific research on young children's early literacy development. Ohio Department of Education, Early Childhood Conference. http://www.famlit.org/site/c.gtJWJdMQIsE/b.2133427 (accessed November 23, 2008).

National Immigration Law Center. 2004. *Facts about immigrant participation in the military.* Washington, DC: National Immigration Law Center.

National Institute of Mental Health. 2006. Attention deficit deficit-hyperactivity disorder. http://www.nimh.nih.gov/healthinformation/adhdmenu.cfm (accessed June 26, 2006).

National Joint Committee on Learning Disabilities. September 18, 1989. *Letter from NJCLD to member organization. Topic: Modifications to the NJCLD definition of learning disabilities.* Washington, DC: NJCLD.

National Joint Committee on Learning Disabilities. 2005. NJCLD Position Paper: Responsiveness to Intervention and Learning Disabilities. *Learning Disability Quarterly* 28:249–60.

National Joint Committee on Learning Disabilities. 2007. Learning disabilities and young children: Identification and intervention. *Learning Disabilities Quarterly* 30:63–72.

National Joint Committee on Learning Disabilities. 2007. The documentation disconnect for students with learning disabilities: Improving access to postsecondary disability services. *Learning Disability Quarterly* 30: 265–274.

National Reading Panel. 2000. *Teaching children to read. An evidence-based assessment of the scientific research literature on reading and its implications for reading instruction.* Washington, DC: National Institute of Child Health and Development.

National Research Center for AD/HD. 2008. AD/HD and the Military. National Resource Center on AD/HD. http://www.help4adhd.org/en/living/workplace/military (accessed May 7, 2008).

National Research Council. 1996. *National Science Education Standards.* Washington, DC: National Committee on Science Education Standards and Assessment, National Research Council.

National Research Council. 2001. *Scientific inquiry in education.* Washington, DC: National Academy Press.

Neal, L. I., A. D. McCray, G. Webb-Johnson, and S. T. Bridgest. 2003. The effects of African American movement styles on teachers' perceptions and reactions. *Journal of Special Education* 31:49–57.

Neisser, U. 1967. *Cognitive psychology.* New York: Appleton-Century-Crofts.

Nesher, P., and P. Teubal. 1975. Verbal cues as interfering factors in verbal problem solving. *Educational Studies in Mathematics* 6:41–51.

Newman, L. 2005. *Parents' satisfaction with their children's schooling, facts from OSEP's national longitudinal studies.* Department of Education, Office of Special Education Programs.

No Child Left Behind Act. U.S. Code 20 (2001), U.S.C. § 6301 et seq.

Nodine, B., E. Barenbaum, and P. Newcomer. 1985. Story composition by learning disabled, reading disabled, and normal children. *Learning Disability Quarterly* 8:167–79.

Nolet, V., and M. J. McLaughlin. 2000. *Accessing the general curriculum: Including students with disabilities in standards-based reform.* 1st ed. Thousand Oaks, CA: Corwin Press.

Norman, D. A. 1982. *Learning and memory.* New York: W. H. Freeman and Company.

Nowicki, E. A., and R. Sandieson. 2002. A meta-analysis of school-age children's attitudes towards persons with physical or intellectual disabilities. *International Journal of Disability, Development and Education* 49:243–65.

Obiakor, F. E. 2007. *Multicultural special education: Culturally responsive teaching.* Upper Saddle River, NJ: Merrill Prentice Hall.

Ochoa, T. A., and S. E. Eckes. 2005. Urban youth in correctional facilities. *Education and Urban Society* 38:21–34.

O'Conner, R., J. Jenkins, N. Leicester, and T. Slocum. 1992. *Teaching phonemic awareness to young children with disabilities: Blending, segmenting, and rhyming.* Paper presented at the American Educational Research Association annual conference in San Francisco (April).

Odom, S., E. Brantlinger, R. Gersten, R. Horner, B. Thompson, and K. Harris. 2005. Research in special education: Scientific methods and evidence-based practices. *Exceptional Children* 71(2):137–48.

Office of Special Education and Rehabilitative Services. May 30, 2007. U.S. Department of Education. www.ed.gov/about/offices/list/osers.index.html (accessed May 6, 2008).

Ogle, D. 1986. K-W-L: A teaching model that develops active reading of expository text. *The Reading Teacher* 39:564–70.

Okolo, C. 2006. Content-area applications. *Journal of Special Education Technology* 21: 48–51.

O'Melia, M. C., and M. S. Rosenberg. 1994. Effects of cooperative homework teams on the acquisition of mathematics skills by secondary students with mild disabilities. *Exceptional Children* 60(6):538–48.

O*NET online. http://online.onetcenter.org/ (accessed May 7, 2008).

Orfield, G., D. Losen, J. Wald, and C. Swanson. 2004. *Losing our future: How minority youth are being left behind by the graduation rate crisis*. Cambridge, MA: Civil Rights Project at Harvard University.

O'Shea, L., P. Sindelar, and D. O'Shea. 1985. The effects of repeated readings and attentional cues on reading fluency and comprehension. *Journal of Reading Behavior* 17:129–41.

Palincsar, A. S., and A. L. Brown. 1984. The reciprocal teaching of comprehension-fostering and comprehension-monitoring activities. *Cognition and Instruction* 1:117–75.

Palincsar, A. S., and N. K. Duke. 2004. The role of text and text-reader interactions in young children's reading development and achievement. *Elementary School Journal* 105:183–97.

Palmer, S., and M. L. Wehmeyer. 1998. *A teacher's guide to the use of the self-determined learning model of instruction: Early elementary version*. Arlington, TX: the ARC of the United States.

Pardo, L. S. 2004. What every teacher needs to know about comprehension. *The Reading Teacher* 58:272–80.

Parmar, R. S., J. F. Cawley, and R. R. Frazita. 1996. Word problem-solving by students with and without mild disabilities. *Exceptional Children* 62:415–29.

Paxton-Burrsma, D., and M. Walker. 2008. Piggybacking: A strategy to increase participation in classroom discussions by students with learning disabilities. *TEACHING Exceptional Children* 40:28–34.

Pearl, R., and T. Bryan. 1994. Getting caught in misconduct: Conceptions of adolescents with and without learning disabilities. *Journal of Learning Disabilities* 27:193–7.

Pearson, P. D., and D. D. Johnson. 1978. *Teaching reading comprehension*. New York: Holt, Rinehart, & Winston.

Perie, M., W. Grigg, and G. Dion. 2005. *The nation's report card: mathematics 2005*, no. NCES 2006-453. U.S. Department of Education, Washington, DC: U.S. Government Printing Office.

Penfield, W. 1969. Consciousness, memory, and man's conditioned reflexes. In *On the biology of learning*, ed. K. Pribram. New York: Harcourt, Brace & World.

Perfetti, C. 1985. *Reading ability*. New York: Oxford University Press.

Perfetti, C., and M. Marron. 1995. *Learning to read: Literacy acquisition by children and adults*. Philadelphia, PA: National Center on Adult Literacy.

Phelps, L. A., and C. Hanley-Maxwell. 1997. School-to-work transitions for youth with disabilities: A review of outcomes and practices. *Review of Educational Research* 67(2):197–226.

Phillips, L. M. 1988. Young readers' inference strategies in reading comprehension. *Cognition and Instruction* 5:193–222.

Pierangelo, R., and G. A. Giuliani. 2009. *Assessment in special education: A practical approach*. 3rd ed. Upper Saddle River, NJ: Pearson.

Pikulski, J., and D. Chard. 2005. Fluency: Bridging between decoding and reading comprehension. *The Reading Teacher* 58:510–9.

Pinnell, G., J. Pikulski, K. Wixson, J. Campbell, P. Gough, and A. Beatty. 1995. *Listening to children read aloud: Data from NAEP's integrated reading performance record (IRPR) at grade 4*. Washington, DC: Office of Educational Research and Improvement, US Department of Education.

Poehlmann, J., M. Clements, L. Abbeduto, and V. Farsad. 2005. Family experiences associated with a child's diagnosis of fragile X or Down syndrome: Evidence for disruption and resilience. *Mental Retardation: A Journal of Practices, Policy and Perspectives* 43(4):255–67.

Polloway, E. A., M. H. Epstein, W. D. Bursuck, M. Jayanthi, and C. Cumblad. 1994. A national survey of homework practices of general education teachers. *Journal of Learning Disabilities* 27:500–9.

Polloway, E. A., M. H. Epstein, W. D. Bursuck, T. W. Roderique, J. McConeghy, and M. Jayanthi. 1994. Classroom grading: A national survey of policies. *Remedial and Special Education* 15:162–70.

Polloway, E. A., R. J. Foley, and M. H. Epstein. 1992. A comparison of the homework problems of students with learning disabilities and non-handicapped students. *Learning Disabilities Research & Practice* 7:203–9.

Polloway, E. A., and T. E. C. Smith. 2000. *Language instruction for students with disabilities*. Denver: Love Publishing Co.

Pomplun, M. 1997. When students with disabilities participate in cooperative groups. *Exceptional Children* 64(1):49–58.

Popham, W. J. 2006. Content standards: The unindicted co-conspirator. *Educational Leadership* 64:87–8.

Poplin, M. 1988. Holistic/constructivist principles of teaching/learning: Implications for the field of learning disabilities. *Journal of Learning Disabilities* 7(21):401–16.

Poplin, M., and S. M. Rogers. 2005. Recollections, apologies, and possibilities. *Learning Disability Quarterly* 28(2): 159–62.

Porter, J. 1974. Research report. *Elementary English* 51:144–51.

Poteet, J. A. 1979. Characteristics of written expression of learning disabled and non-learning disabled elementary school students. *Diagnostique* 4(1):60–74.

Prater, M. A. 1993. Teaching concepts: Procedures for the design and delivery of instruction. *Remedial and Special Education* 14:51–62.

Prescott-Griffin, M., and N. Witherell. 2004. *Fluency in focus*. Portsmouth, NH: Heinemann.

Pressley, M. 1991. Can learning disabled children become good information processors? How can we find out? In *Subtypes of learning disabilities*, ed. L. Feagans, E. Short, and L. Meltzer, 137–62. Hillsdale, NJ: Erlbaum.

Pressley, M. 2001. Comprehension instruction: What makes sense now, what might make sense soon. *Reading Online* 5(2). http://www.readingonline.org/ (accessed October 20, 2008).

Pressley, M. 2002a. Metacognition and self-regulated comprehension. In *What research has to say about reading instruction,* ed. A. E. Farstrup and S. J. Samuels, 3rd ed. Newark, DE: International Reading Association.

Pressley, M. 2002b. *Reading instruction that works.* 2nd ed. New York: The Guilford Press.

Price, L., P. Gerber, and I. Shessel. 2002. Adults with learning disabilities and employment: A Canadian perspective. *Thalamus: The Journal of the International Academy for Research in Learning Disabilities* 20:29–40.

Price, N., and L. Goodwin. 1980. Individualized education programs: A cost study. *Exceptional Children* 46:446–54.

Proctor, C. P., P. Uccelli, B. Dalton, and C. E. Snow. Forthcoming. Understanding depth of vocabulary and improving comprehension online with bilingual and monolingual children. *Reading & Writing Quarterly.*

Putnam, J. W. 1993. *Cooperative learning and strategies for inclusion: Celebrating diversity in the classroom.* Baltimore, MD: Paul H. Brookes Publishing Company.

Putnam, M. L., D. D. Deshler, and J. S. Schumaker. 1993. The investigation of setting demands: A missing link in learning strategy instruction. In *Strategy assessment and instruction for students with learning disabilities,* ed. L. S. Meltzer, 325–54. Austin, TX: Pro-Ed.

Quinn, M. M., R. B. Rutherford, P. E. Leone, D. M. Osher, and J. M. Poirier. 2005. Youth with disabilities in juvenile corrections: A national survey. *Exceptional Children* 71:339–45.

Rack, J. P., M. J. Snowling, and D. Olson. 1992. The nonword reading deficit in developmental dyslexia: A review. *Reading Research Quarterly* 27:28–53.

Rademacher, J. A., J. B. Schumaker, and D. D. Deshler. 1996. Development and validation of a classroom assignment routine for inclusive settings. *Learning Disability Quarterly* 19:163–78.

Rademacher, J. A., J. B. Schumaker, D. D. Deshler, and B. K. Lenz. 1998. *The quality assignment routine.* Lawrence, KS: Edge Enterprises.

Rafoth, M. A., and T. Foriska. 2006. Administrator participation in promoting effective problem-solving teams. *Remedial and Special Education* 27(3):130–5.

Ramasamy, R., M. L. Duffy, and J. L. Camp, Jr. 2000. Transition from school to adult life: Critical issues for Native American youth with and without learning disabilities. *Career Development for Exceptional Individuals* 23(2):157–71.

Rasinski, T. 2003. *The fluent reader.* New York: Scholastic.

Rasinski, T., and N. Padak. 2004. *Effective reading strategies: Teaching children who find reading difficult,* 3rd ed. Upper Saddle River, NJ: Pearson.

Raskind, M. H. 1994. Assistive technology for adults with learning disabilities: A rationale for use. In *Learning disabilities in adulthood: Persisting problems and evolving issues,* ed. J. Gerber and H. B. Reiff. Boston, MA: Andover Medical Publishers.

Raskind, M. H., R. J. Goldberg, E. L. Higgins, and K. L. Herman. 1999. Patterns of change and predictors of success in individuals with learning disabilities: Results from a twenty-year longitudinal study. *Learning Disabilities Research & Practice* 14:35–49.

Raskind, M. H., and E. Higgins. 1995. Effects of speech synthesis on the proofreading efficiency of postsecondary students with learning disabilities. *Learning Disability Quarterly* 18(2):141–58.

Ratey, J. J., E. Hallowell, and A. Miller. 1997. Psychosocial issues and psychotherapy in adults with attention deficit disorder. *Psychiatric Annals* 27:582–7.

Rea, P. J., V. L. McLaughlin, and C. Walther-Thomas. 2002. Outcomes for students with learning disabilities in inclusive and pullout programs. *Exceptional Children* 68:203–22.

Reder, S. 1995. Synthetic estimates of Iowa's substate adult literacy proficiencies. Report no. ED385714, 31pp.

Reese, L., H. Garnier, R. Gallimore, and C. Goldenberg. 2000. A longitudinal analysis of the ecocultural antecedents of emergent Spanish literacy and subsequent English reading achievement of Spanish-speaking students. *American Educational Research Journal* 37:633–62.

Rehabilitation Act, U.S. Code 29 (1973, as amended), § 794 (Section 504).

Reid, D. K., and M. G. Knight. 2006. Disability justifies exclusion of minority students: A critical history grounded in disability studies. *Educational Researcher* 35:18–23.

Reid, R., and T. O. Lienemann. 2006. *Strategy instruction for students with learning disabilities.* New York: Guilford.

Reiser, B. 2004. Scaffolding complex learning: The mechanisms of structuring and problematizing student work. *The Journal of the Learning Sciences* 13:273–304.

Reutzel, R. D., and R. B. Cooter. 2004. *Teaching children to read: Putting the pieces together.* 4th ed. Upper Saddle River, NJ: Prentice Hall.

Reutzel, R. D., and R. B. Cooter. 2005. *The essentials of teaching children to read: What every teacher needs to know.* Upper Saddle River, NJ: Prentice Hall.

Rhia, R., and N. Mather. 1995. The return of students with learning disabilities to regular classrooms: A sellout? *Learning Disabilities Research & Practice* 10:46–58.

Riccio, C., J. Gonzalez, and G. Hynd. 1994. Attention-deficit hyperactivity disorder (ADHD) and learning disabilities. *Learning Disability Quarterly* 17:311–22.

Riccomini, P. J. 2005. Identification and remediation of systematic error patterns in subtraction. *Learning Disability Quarterly* 28(3):233.

Rinaldi, C., and J. Samson. 2008. English language learners and response to intervention: Referral considerations. *TEACHING Exceptional Children* 40:6–14.

Ritchey, K., and J. Goeke. 2006. Orton-Gillingham and Orton-Gillingham-based reading instruction: A review of the literature. *The Journal of Special Education* 40:171–83.

Roberts, C. D., L. M. Stough, and L. H. Parrish. 2002. The role of genetic counseling in the elective termination of pregnancies involving fetuses with disabilities. *The Journal of Special Education* 36:48–55.

Roberts, J., and M. Zody. 1989. Using the research for effective supervision: Measuring a teacher's questioning techniques. *NASSP Bulletin* 73:8–14.

Roberts, L. D. 1996. The class within a class model: A study of the effects on academic achievement of regular education students in a middle school setting. *Dissertation Abstracts International, 58* (03A), 0724 (UMI No. AAG9817091).

Robinson, C. S., B. M. Menchetti, and J. Torgesen. 2002. Toward a two factor theory of one type of mathematics disability. *Learning Disabilities Research & Practice* 17:81–9.

Roessler, R. T., and H. M. Kirk. 1998. Improving technology-training services in post secondary education: Perspectives of recent college graduates with disabilities. *Journal of Postsecondary Education and Disability* 13(3):48–59.

Rojewski, J. W. 2002. Career assessment for adolescents with mild disabilities: Critical concerns for transition planning. *Career Development for Exceptional Individuals* 25:73–95.

Rose, D. H., and A. Meyer. 2002. *Teaching every student in the digital age: Universal design for learning.* Alexandria, VA: ASCD.

Rosenblum, S., P. Weiss, and S. Parush. 2004. Handwriting evaluation for developmental dysgraphia: Process versus product. *Reading and Writing: An Interdisciplinary Journal* 17:433–58.

Rowe, M. B., ed. 1976. The pausing principle—two invitations to inquiry. *Journal of College Science Teaching* 5:258–9.

Rowe, M. B. 1980. Pausing principles and their effects on reasoning in science. *New Directions for Community Colleges* 8(3):27–34.

Rowe, M. B. 1986. Wait-time: Slowing down may be a way of speeding up! *Journal of Teacher Education* 37:43–50.

Rubin, A., and B. Bruce. 1985. *Learning with QUILL: Lessons for students, teachers, and software designers.* Reading Report no. 60. Washington, DC: National Institute of Education.

Ruhl, K. L., C. A. Hughes, and A. H. Gajar. 1990. Efficacy of the pause procedure for enhancing learning disabled college students' long and short-term recall of facts presented through lecture. *Learning Disabilities Quarterly* 13:55–64.

Ruhl, K. L., C. A. Hughes, and P. J. Schloss. 1987. Using the pause procedure to enhance lecture recall. *Teacher Education and Special Education* 10:14–8.

Ruhl, K. L., and S. Suritsky. 1995. The pause procedure and/or an outline: Effect on immediate free recall and lecture notes taken by college students with learning disabilities. *Learning Disability Quarterly* 18:2–11.

Rusch, F. R., and F. D. Loomis. 2005. The unfulfilled promise of special education: The transition from education to work for young adults with disabilities. *Exceptional Parent* 35(2):72–4.

Saenz, I. M., L. S. Fuchs, and D. Fuchs. 2005. Peer-Assisted Learning Strategies for English language learners with learning disabilities. *Exceptional Children* 71:231–47.

Safer, N., and S. Fleischman. 2005. How student progress monitoring improves instruction. *Educational Leadership* 62:81–3.

Salas, L., E. J. Lopez, K. Chinn, and E. Menchaca-Lopez. 2005. Can special education teachers create parent partnerships with Mexican American families? Si Se Pueda! *Multicultural Education* 13:52–55.

Salend, S., and M. Gajria. 1995. Increasing the homework completion rates of students with mild disabilities. *Remedial and Special Education* 16(5):271–8.

Salend, S. J., and E. Rohena. 2003. Students with attention deficit disorders: An overview. *Intervention in School and Clinic* 38:259–66.

Salvia, J., and C. A. Hughes. 1990. *Curriculum-based assessment: Testing what is taught.* New York: Macmillan.

Salvia, J., and J. Ysseldyke. 2004. *Assessment.* Boston: Houghton Mifflin.

Samuels, S. J. 1979. The method of repeated readings. *The Reading Teacher* 50(5):376–81.

Samuels, S. J. 2002. Reading fluency: Its development and assessment. In *What research has to say about reading instruction,* ed. A. E. Farstrup and S. Samuels, 166–83. Newark, DE: International Reading Association.

Sandall, S., M. L. Hemmeter, B. J. Smith, and M. McLean. 2005. *DEC recommended practices: A comprehensive guide for practical application in early childhood special education.* Longmont, CO: Sopris West.

Sarkisian, N., M. Gerena, and N. Gerstel. 2007. Extended family integration among Euro and Mexican Americans: Ethnicity, gender, and class. *Journal of Marriage and Family* 69:40–54.

Saski, J., P. Swicegood, and J. Carter. 1983. Notetaking formats for learning disabled adolescents. *Learning Disabilities Quarterly* 6:265–72.

Scanlon, D. 1996. Social skills strategy instruction. In *Teaching adolescents with learning disabilities,* ed. D. D. Deshler, E. S. Ellis, and B. K. Lenz. Denver, CO: Love Publishing.

Scanlon, D. 2002. PROVE-ing what you know: Using a learning strategy in an inclusive classroom. *Teaching Exceptional Children* 34:48–54.

Scanlon, D. 2003. Learning strategies expected in content-area inclusion. *Developmental Disabilities Bulletin* 31:11–41.

Scanlon, D. Forthcoming. Introduction to the issue: Tools that support literacy education. *Reading & Writing Quarterly.*

Scanlon, D., R. Cass, A. Amtzis, and G. Sideridis. Forthcoming. Procedural facilitation of propositional knowledge in the content-areas. *Reading & Writing Quarterly.*

Scanlon, D., D. Deshler, and J. B. Schumaker. 1996. Can a strategy be taught and learned in secondary inclusive classrooms? *Learning Disabilities Research & Practice* 11(1):41–57.

Scanlon, D. J., G. Z. Duran, E. I. Reyes, and M. A. Gallego. 1992. Interactive semantic mapping: An interactive approach to enhancing LD students' content area comprehension. *Learning Disabilities Research & Practice* 7:142–6.

Scanlon, D., M. Gallego, G. Duran, and E. Reyes. 2005. Interactive staff development supports collaboration when learning to teach. *Teacher Education and Special Education* 28:40–51.

Scanlon, D., and D. F. Mellard. 2002. Academic and participation profiles of school-age dropouts with and without learning disabilities. *Exceptional Children* 68:239–58.

Scanlon, D., J. B. Schumaker, and D. D. Deshler. 1994. Collaborative dialogues between teachers and researchers to create educational interventions: A case study. *Journal of Educational and Psychological Consultation* 5:69–76.

Scarborough, H. S. 2005. Developmental relationships between language skills and learning to read. In *The connections between language and reading disabilities,* ed.

H. W. Catts and Alan. G. Kamhi, 55–76. Mahwah, NJ: Lawrence Erlbaum Associates.

Schatschneider, C., C. Carlson, D. Francis, B. Foorman, and J. Fletcher. 2002. Relationship of rapid automatized naming and phonological awareness in early reading development: Implications for the double-deficit hypothesis. *Journal of Learning Disabilities* 35:245–56.

Scheeler, M. C., K. L. Ruhl, and J. K. McAfee. 2004. Providing performance feedback to teachers: A review. *Teacher Education and Special Education* 27:396–407.

Schoen, L., and L. D. Fusarelli. 2008. Innovation, NCLB, and the fear factor: Leading 21st-century schools in an era of accountability. *Educational Policy* 22:181–203.

Schoenfeld, A. 2002. Making mathematics work for all children: Issues of standard, testing, and equity. *Educational Researcher* 31:13–25.

Schreiber, P. 1991. Understanding prosody's role in reading acquisition. *Theory Into Practice* 30:158–64.

Schreiner, M. B. 2007. Effective self-advocacy: What students and special educators need to know. *Intervention in School and Clinic* 42:300–4.

Schumaker, J. B., J. A. Bulgren, D. D. Deshler, and B. K. Lenz. 1998. *The recall enhancement routine.* Lawrence, KS: University of Kansas.

Schumaker, J. B., P. Denton, D. Deshler. 1984a. *The learning strategies curriculum: The paraphrasing curriculum.* Lawrence, KS: University of Kansas.

Schumaker, J., P. Denton, and D. Deshler. 1984b. *The Paraphrasing strategy.* Lawrence, KS: Edge Enterprises Inc.

Schumaker, J. D., D. Deshler, G. Alley, M. Warner, F. Clark, and S. Nolan. 1982. Error monitoring: A learning strategy for improving academic performance. In *Coming of age,* ed. W. M. Cruickshank and J. W. Lerner, 170–83. Syracuse, NY: Syracuse University Press.

Schumaker, J. D., J. B. Nolan, and D. D. Deshler. 1985. *The error monitoring strategy: Instructor's manual.* Lawrence, KS: University of Kansas.

Schumaker, J. D., and J. Sheldon. 1985. *The sentence writing strategy.* Lawrence, KS: Edge Enterprises Inc.

Schumm, J. S., and S. Vaughn. 1991. Making adaptations for mainstreamed students: General education teachers' perspectives. *Remedial and Special Education* 12(4):18–27.

Schumm, J. S., S. Vaughn, D. Haager, J. McDowell, L. Rothlein, and L. Saumell. 1995. Regular education teacher planning: What can students with learning disabilities expect? *Exceptional Children* 61:335–52.

Schunk, D. 2004. *Learning theories: An educational perspective.* 4th ed. Upper Saddle River, NJ: Pearson.

Schutz, A. 2006. Home is a prison in the global city: The tragic failure of school-based community engagement strategies. *Review of Educational Research* 76:691–743.

Schwartz , R., and T. Raphael. 1985. Concept of definition: A key to improving students' vocabulary. *The Reading Teacher* 39:198–205.

Scorgie, K., and D. Sobsey. 2000. Transformational outcomes associated with parenting children who have disabilities. *Mental Retardation* 38:195–206.

Scruggs, T. E., and M. A. Mastropieri. 1990. Mnemonic instruction for students with learning disabilities: What it is and what it does. *Learning Disability Quarterly* 13:271–9.

Scruggs, T. E., and M. A. Mastropieri. 1992. *Teaching test-taking skills: Helping students show what they know.* Cambridge, MA: Brookline Books.

Scruggs, T. E., and M. A. Mastropieri. 1996. Teacher perceptions of mainstreaming/inclusion, 1958–1995: A research synthesis. *Exceptional Children* 63:59–74.

Scruggs, T., M. Mastropieri, and J. Levin. 1986. Can children effectively reuse the same mnemonic pegwords? *Educational Communication and Technology* 34:83–8.

Scruggs, T. E., M. A. Mastropieri, and K. A. McDuffie. 2007. Co-teaching in inclusive classrooms: A metasynthesis of qualitative research. *Exceptional Children* 73(4):392–416.

Searcy, S., and S. A. Maroney. 1996. Lesson planning practices of special education teachers. *Exceptionality* 6(3):171–87.

Searlman, A., and D. Herrmann. 1994. *Memory from a broader perspective.* New York: McGraw-Hill.

Sears, N. C., and D. M. Johnson. 1986. The effects of visual imagery on spelling performance and retention among elementary students. *Journal of Educational Research* 79:230–3.

Seethaler, P. M., and Fuchs, L. S. 2006. The cognitive correlates of computational estimation skill among third-grade students. *Learning Disabilities Research & Practice* 21(4):233–43.

Seidenberg, M. S. 1997. Language acquisition and use: Learning and applying probabilistic constraints. *Science* 275:1599–1603.

Shannon, P. 1993. Letters to the editor: Comments on Baumann. *Reading Research Quarterly* 28:86.

Shannon, T. R., and E. A. Polloway. 1993. Promoting error monitoring in middle school, students with LD. *Intervention in School and Clinic* 28:160–4.

Share, D. L., and K. E. Stanovich. 1995. Cognitive processes in early reading development: A model of acquisition and individual differences. *Issues in Education: Contributions from Educational Psychology* 1:1–57.

Shavelson, R. J., and L. Towne, eds. 2002. *Scientific research in education.* Washington, DC: National Academy Press.

Shaywitz, S. E., and B. A. Shaywitz. 1988. Attention deficit disorder: Current perspectives. In *Learning disabilities,* ed. J. F. Kavanagh and T. J. Truss, 369–523. Parkton, MD: York.

Shefelbine, J., L. Lipscomb, and A. Hern. 1989. Variables associated with second, fourth, and sixth grade students' ability to identify polysyllabic words. In *Cognitive and social perspectives for literacy research and instruction,* ed. S. McCormick and J. Zutell. Chicago: National Reading Conference.

Sherin, B., and K. Fuson. 2005. Multiplication strategies and the appropriation of computational resources. *Journal for Research in Mathematics Education* 36(4):347–95.

Sideridis, G. D., and C. R. Greenwood. 1996. Evaluating treatment effects in single-subject behavioral experiments using quality-control charts. *Journal of Behavioral Education* 6:203–11.

Sileo, T. W., and M. A. Prater. 1998. Preparing professionals for partnerships with parents of students with disabilities: Textbook considerations regarding cultural diversity. *Exceptional Children* 64:513–28.

Sileo, T. W., and A. P. Sileo. 1996. Parent and professional partnerships in special education: multicultural considerations. *Intervention in School and Clinic* 31:145–53.

Siperstein, G., J. Leffert, and M. Wenz-Gross. 1997. The quality of friendships between children with and without learning problems. *American Journal on Mental Retardation* 102:111–25.

Sitlington, P. L. 1996. Transition to living: The neglected component of transition programming for individuals with learning disabilities. *Journal of Learning Disabilities* 29:31–9.

Sitlington, P. L., and A. R. Frank. 1999. Life outside of work for young adults with learning disabilities. *The Journal for Vocational Special Needs Education* 22(1):3–22.

Skinner, B. F. 1957. *Verbal behavior.* Edgewood Cliffs, NJ: Prentice Hall.

Skinner, M. E. 1998. Promoting self-advocacy among college students with learning disabilities. *Intervention in School and Clinic* 33:278–83.

Skinner, M. E., and B. D. Lindstrom. 2003. Bridging the gap between high school and college: Strategies for the successful transition of students with learning disabilities. *Preventing School Failure* 47:132–7.

Skinner, M. E., and S. J. Schenk. 1992. Counseling the college-bound student with a learning disability. *The School Counselor* 39:369–76.

Skrtic, T. M. 2005. A political economy of learning disabilities. *Learning Disabilities Quarterly* 28(2):149–55.

Slavin, R. E. 1990. *Cooperative learning: Theory, research, and practice.* Englewood Cliffs, NJ: Prentice Hall.

Slavin, R. E. 1991. Synthesis of research on cooperative learning. *Educational Leadership* 48(5):71–82.

Smith, C., and J. Hofer. 2003. *The characteristics and concerns of adult basic education teachers.* NCSALL Report No. 26. Cambridge, MA: National Center for the Study of Adult Learning and Literacy.

Smith, G. 1999. Teaching a long sequence of behavior using whole task training, forward chaining, and backward chaining. *Perceptual and Motor Skills* 89:951–65.

Smith, S. W. 2001. *Involving parents in the IEP process.* ERIC Digest E611. Arlington, VA: ERIC Clearinghouse on Disabilities and Gifted Education (ED 455658).

Smith, T. E. C. 2001. Section 504, the ADA, and public schools. *Remedial and Special Education* 22(6):335–43.

Smith, T. E. C., C. A. Dowdy, E. A. Polloway, and G. E. Blalock. 1997. *Children and adults with learning disabilities.* Boston, MA: Allyn & Bacon.

Smolkin, L. B., and C. A. Donovan. 2003. Supporting comprehension acquisition for emerging and struggling readers: The interactive information book read-aloud. *Exceptionality* 11:25–38.

Snow, C., M. Burns, and P. Griffin. 1998. *Preventing reading difficulties in young children.* Washington, DC: National Academy Press.

Snowling, M. J. 2005. Literacy outcomes for children with oral language impairments: Students' vocabulary. *The Reading Teacher* 39:198–205.

Snowman, J. and R. Biehler. 2006. *Psychology applied to teaching.* 11th ed. Boston: Houghton Mifflin.

Sparks, S. 2000. Classroom and curriculum accommodations for Native American students. *Intervention in School and Clinic* 35:259–63.

Spencer, V. G., T. E. Scruggs, and M. A. Mastropieri. 2003. Content area learning in middle school social studies classrooms and students with emotional or behavioral disorders: A comparison of strategies. *Behavioral Disorders* 28:77–93.

Stacy, R. 2001. *Complex responsive processes in organizations: Learning and knowledge creation.* London: Routhledge.

Stahl, S. 1986. Three principles of effective vocabulary instruction. *Journal of Reading* 29:662–671.

Stahl, S. 2006. Understanding shifts in reading and its instruction. In *Reading research at work: Foundations of effective practice,* ed. K. Dougherty Stahl and M. McKenna, 45–75. New York: Guilford Press.

Stanovich, K. E. 1999. The sociopsychometrics of learning disabilities. *Journal of Learning Disabilities* 32:350–61.

Stanovich, K. E. 2005. The future of a mistake: Will discrepancy measurement continue to make the learning disabilities field a pseudoscience? *Learning Disability Quarterly* 28:103–6.

Stecker, P. M. 2006. Using Curriculum-based measurement to monitor reading progress in inclusive elementary schools. *Reading & Writing Quarterly* 22:91–97.

Stein, M., D. Carnine, and R. Dixon. 1998. Direct instruction: Integrating curriculum design and effective teaching practice. *Intervention in School and Clinic* 33:227–34.

Stein, M., J. Silbert, and D. Carnine. 1997. *Designing effective mathematics instruction: A direct instruction approach.* 3rd ed. Upper Saddle River, NJ: Merrill/Prentice Hall.

Stein, M., C. Stuen, D. Carnine, and R. Long. 2001. Textbook evaluation and adoption. *Reading & Writing Quarterly: Overcoming Learning Difficulties* 17:5–24.

Stephenson, J., C. Brown, and D. Griffin. 2008. Electronic delivery of lectures in the university environment: An empirical comparison of three delivery styles. *Computers & Education* 50:640–51.

Stevenson, J. 2003. Best wishes, Ed. *Reading,* grade 2. Hightstown, NJ: McGraw-Hill.

Stodden, R. A., and P. Dowrick. 2000. The present and future of postsecondary education for adults with disabilities. *Impact* 13(1):4–5.

Stowell, J. R., and J. M. Nelson. 2007. Benefits of electronic audience response systems on student participation, learning, and emotion. *Teaching of Psychology* 34:253–8.

Strangman, N., and T. Hall. 2003. Text transformations. National Center on Accessing the General Curriculum. Wakefield, MA. http://www.cast.org/publications/ncac/ncac_textrans.html (retrieved July 15, 2007).

Stubbe, D. E. 2000. Attention-deficit/hyperactivity disorder overview: Historical perspective, current controversies, and future directions. *Child & Adolescent Psychiatric Clinics of North America* 9:469–79.

Sturm, J. M., and S. A. Clendon. 2004. Augmentative and alternative communication, language, and literacy: Fostering the relationship. *Topics in Language Disorders* 24:76–91.

Summers, J. A., L. Hoffman, J. Marquis, A. Turnbull, D. Poston, and L. L. Nelson. 2005. Measuring the quality of family-professional partnerships in special education services. *Exceptional Children* 72(1):65.

Suritsky, S. K. 1992. Note taking approaches and specific areas of difficulty reported by university students with learning disabilities. *Journal of Postsecondary Education and Disability* 10(1):3–10.

Suritsky, S. K., and Hughes, C. A. 1996. Notetaking strategy instruction. In *Teaching adolescents with learning disabilities,* ed. D. D. Deshler, E. S. Ellis, and B. K. Lenz, 2nd ed., 267–312. Denver, CO: Love Publishing Company.

Swanson, H. L. 1999. Reading comprehension and working memory in learning disabled readers: Is phonological loop more important than the executive system? *Journal of Experimental Child Psychology* 72:1–31.

Swanson, H. L., and M. Beebe-Frankenberger. 2004. The relationship between working memory and mathematical problem solving in children at risk and not at risk for serious math difficulties. *Journal of Educational Psychology* 96:471–91.

Swanson, H. L., and D. Deshler. 2003. Instructing adolescents with learning disabilities: Converting a meta-analysis to practice. *Journal of Learning Disabilities* 36:124–35.

Swanson, H. L., and M. Hoskyn. 1998. Experimental intervention research on students with learning disabilities: A meta-analysis of treatment outcomes. *Review of Educational Research* 68:277–321.

Swanson, H. L., and M. Hoskyn. 2001. Instructing adolescents with learning disabilities: A component and composite analysis. *Learning Disabilities Research & Practice* 16:109–19.

Swanson, H. L., M. Hoskyn, and C. Lee. 1999. *Interventions for students with learning disabilities: A meta-analysis of treatment outcomes.* New York: Guilford Press.

Swanson, H. L., C. Howard, and L. Sáez. 2006. Do different components of working memory underlie different subgroups of reading disabilities? *Journal of Learning Disabilities* 39:252–69.

Swanson, H. L., L. Sáez, and M. Gerber. 2004. Do phonological and executive processes in English learners at risk for reading disabilities in grade 1 predict performance in grade 2? *Learning Disabilities Research & Practice* 19:225–38.

Swanson, H. L., L. Saez, M. Gerber, and J. Leafstedt. 2004. Literacy and cognitive functioning in bilingual and nonbilingual children at or not at risk for reading disabilities. *Journal of Educational Psychology* 96:3–18.

Sweeney, W. J., A. M. Ehrhardt, R. Gardner III, L. Jones, R. Greenfield, and S. Fribley. 1999. Using guided notes with academically at-risk high school students during a remedial summer social studies class. *Psychology in the Schools* 36(4):305–18.

Switlick, D. 1997. Curricular modifications and accommodations. In *Teaching students in inclusive settings: From theory to practice,* ed. D. Bradley, M. King-Sears, and D. Tessler-Switlick, 225–51. Boston, MA: Allyn & Bacon.

Tang, S. 1995. A comparison of trends in living arrangements for white and black youth. *Western Journal of Black Studies* 19:218–23.

Tatayama-Sniezek, K. M. 1990. Cooperative learning: Does it improve the academic achievement of students with handicaps? *Exceptional Children* 56:426–37.

Taymans, J., and S. Lynch. 2004. Developing a unit planning routine. In *Teaching content to all,* ed. B. K. Lenz, D. D. Deshler, and B. R. Kissam, 162–94. Boston, MA: Allyn & Bacon.

Teicher, M., Y. Ito, C. Glod, and N. Barber. 1996. Objective measurement of hyperactivity and attentional problems in ADHD. *Journal of the American Academy of Child & Adolescent Psychiatry* 35:334–42.

Terrill, M. C., T. E. Scruggs, and M. A. Mastropieri. 2004. SAT vocabulary instruction for high school students with learning disabilities. *Intervention in School and Clinic* 39:288–94.

Test, D. W., C. H. Fowler, D. M. Brewer, and W. M. Wood. 2005. A content and methodological review of self-advocacy intervention studies. *Exceptional Children* 72(1):101.

Test, D. W., and M. Neale. 2004. Using the self-advocacy strategy to increase middle graders' IEP participation. *Journal of Behavioral Education* 13:135–45.

Tetreault, D. R. 2005. Administrative technology: New rules, new tools. *T.H.E. Journal* 32:39–43.

Therrien, W. J. 2004. Fluency and comprehension gains as a result of repeated readings: A meta-analysis. *Remedial and Special Education* 25:252–61.

Thomas-Presswood, T. N., and D. Presswood. 2008. *Meeting the needs of students and families from poverty: A handbook for school and mental health professionals.* Baltimore, MD: Paul H. Brookes.

Thompson, J. R., J. P. Bakken, B. M. Fulk, and G. Peterson-Karlan. 2004. North Central Regional Educational Laboratory. Using technology to improve the literacy skills of students with disabilities. http://www.learningpt.org/pdfs/literacy/disability.pdf (accessed July 6, 2007).

Thompson, S. J., A. B. Morse, M. Sharpe, and S. Hall. 2005. *Accommodations manual: How to select, administer, and evaluate use of accommodations for instruction and assessment of students with disabilities.* 2nd ed. Washington, DC: Council of Chief State School Officers.

Thornhill, S., M. Asensio, and C. Young. 2002. *Video streaming: A guide for educational development.* Manchester, England: Click and Go Video.

Thousand, J., R. Villa, and A. Nevin. 2006. The many faces of collaborative planning and teaching. *Theory Into Practice* 45:239–49.

Thurlow, M. L., J. L. Elliott, and J. E. Ysseldyke. 1998. *Testing students with disabilities: Practical strategies for complying with district and state requirements.* Thousand Oaks, CA: Corwin Press.

Thurlow, M. L., S. S. Lazarus, S. J. Thompson, and A. B. Morris. 2005. State policies on assessment participation and accommodations for students with disabilities. *Journal of Special Education* 38:232–40.

Thurlow, M., and S. Thompson. 2003. *Inclusion of students with disabilities in state and district assessments.* ED, no. 480 047 (18 pp.).

Tickle, L. 2005. The crucible of the classroom: A learning environment for teachers or a site of crucifixion? In *Teaching professional development in changing conditions,* ed. D. Beijaard, P. C. Meijer, G. Morine-Dershimer, and H. Tillema, 61–77. Netherlands: Springer.

Tindle, K., P. Leconte, L. Buchanan, and J. Taymans. 2005. Transition planning: Community mapping as a tool for teachers and students. *Research to practice brief* 4(1):1–5. Minneapolis, MN: U.S. Department of Education, Office of Special Education Programs: National Center of Secondary Education and Transition.

Todis, B. 1996. Tools for the task? Perspectives on assistive technology in educational settings. *Journal of Special Education Technology* 13:49–61.

Topping, K. J. 2005. Trends in peer learning. *Educational Psychology* 25:631–45.

Torgesen, J. K. 1982. The learning disabled child as an inactive learner: Educational implication. *Topics in Learning and Learning Disabilities* April:45–52.

Torgesen, J. K., A. W. Alexander, R. K. Wagner, C. A. Rashotte, K. K. S. Voeller, and T. Conway. 2001. Intensive remedial instruction for children with severe reading disabilities: Immediate and long-term outcomes from two instructional approaches. *Journal of Learning Disabilities* 34:33–58.

Torgesen, J. K., W. E. Dahlem, and J. Greenstein. 1987. Using verbatim text recording to enhance reading comprehension in learning disabled adolescents. *Learning Disabilities Focus* 3:30–8.

Torgesen, J., S. Morgan, and C. Davis. 1992. Effects of two types of phonological awareness training on word learning in kindergarten children. *Journal of Educational Psychology* 84:364–70.

Tournaki, N. 2003. The differential effects of teaching addition through strategy instruction versus drill and practice to students with and without learning disabilities. *Journal of Learning Disabilities* 36(5):449–58.

Trainor, A. 2005. Self-determination perceptions and behaviors of diverse students with LD during the transition planning process. *Journal of Learning Disabilities* 38:233–49.

Trammel, D. L., P. J. Schloss, and S. Alper. 1994. Using self-recording, evaluation, and graphing to increase completion of homework assignments. *Journal of Learning Disabilities* 27(2):75–81.

Troia, G., and S. Graham. 2002. The effectiveness of a highly explicit, teacher-directed strategy instruction routine: Changing the writing performance of students with learning disabilities. *Journal of Learning Disabilities* 35:290–305.

Troia, G., S. Graham, and K. Harris. 1999. Teaching students with learning disabilities to mindfully plan when writing. *Exceptional Children* 65:235–52.

Troiano, P. T. 2003. College students and learning disability: Elements of self-style. *Journal of College Student Development* 44:404–19.

Tseng, M., and S. Cermak. 1993. The influence of ergonomic factors and perceptual-motor abilities on handwriting performance. *American Journal of Occupational Therapy* 47:919–26.

Turnbull, R., N. Huerta, and M. Stowe. 2006. *The Individuals with Disabilities Education Act as amended in 2004.* Upper Saddle River, NJ: Pearson.

Tyler, J. H. 2002. *So you want a GED? Estimating the impact of the GED on the earnings of dropouts who seek the credential.* NCSALL Research Brief. Boston, MA: National Center for the Study of Adult Learning and Literacy. ERIC Documents Reproduction Services, no. ED471 978.

U.S. Department of Education. 2003. *Twenty-fifth annual report to Congress on the implementation of the Individuals with Disabilities Education Act.* Washington, DC: U.S. DOE.

U.S. Department of Education. 2004. *Twenty-sixth annual report to Congress on the implementation of the Individuals with Disabilities Education Act.* Washington, DC: U.S. DOE.

U.S. Department of Education. 2006a. Proven methods: Questions and answers on No Child Left Behind. http://www.ed.gov/nclb/methods/whatworks/doing.html (accessed December 15, 2006).

U.S. Department of Education. 2006b. *Twenty-eighth annual report to Congress on the implementation of the Individuals with Disabilities Education Act.* Washington, DC: U.S. DOE.

U.S. Department of Education. 2007. Individuals with Disabilities Education Act (IDEA) data. Washington, DC: U.S. DOE.

U.S. Department of Education. Institute of Education Sciences. National Center for Education Statistics. 2003. *The nation's report card: Writing 2002*, NCES 2003–529, by H. R. Persky, M. C. Daane, and Y. Jin. Washington, DC: U.S. DOE.

U.S. Department of Education, National Center for Education Statistics. 2001. Teacher preparation and professional development: NCES 2001-008, by B. Parsad, L. Lewis, and E. Farris. Washington, DC: U.S. DOE.

U.S. Department of Education, Office of Special Education and Rehabilitative Services. 2006. *26th annual report to Congress on the implementation of the Individuals with Disabilities Education Act, 2004,* vol. 1. Washington, DC: U.S. DOE.

U.S. Department of Labor. 2000. Bureau of Labor Statistics. *Occupational outlook handbook, 2000–01 edition,* February.

Uberti, H. Z., T. E. Scruggs, and M. A. Mastropieri. 2003. Keywords make the difference! Mnemonic instruction in inclusive classrooms. A classroom application. *Teaching Exceptional Children* 35(3):56–61.

Uhry, J., and J. Shepherd. 1993. Segmentation/spelling instruction as a part of a first-grade reading program: Effects on several measures of reading. *Reading Research Quarterly* 28:218–33.

Van Reusen, A. K., C. S. Bos, J. B. Schumaker, and D. D. Deshler. 2002. *The self-advocacy strategy: For education & transition planning.* Lawrence, KS: Edge Enterprises.

Vaughn, S., C. S. Bos, and J. S. Schumm. 2000. *Teaching exceptional, diverse, and at-risk students in the general education classroom.* 2nd ed. Boston, MA: Allyn & Bacon.

Vaughn, S., and L. S. Fuchs. 2003. Redefining learning disabilities as inadequate response to instruction: The promise and potential problems. *Learning Disabilities Research & Practice* 18:137–46.

Vaughn, S., R. Gersten, and D. J. Chard. 2000. The underlying message in LD intervention research: Findings from research syntheses. *Exceptional Children* 67(1):99–114.

Vaughn, S., M. Reiss, L. Rothlein, and M. Hughes. 1999. Kindergarten teachers' perceptions of instructing students with disabilities. *Remedial and Special Education* 20:184–91.

Vaughn, S., and J. S. Schumm. 1994. Middle school teachers' planning for students with learning disabilities. *Remedial and Special Education* 15:152–61.

Vaughn, S., J. Schumm, B. Jallad, J. Slusher, and L. Saumell. 1996. Teachers' views of inclusion. *Learning Disabilities Research & Practice* 11:96–101.

Veit, D., T. Scruggs, and M. Mastropieri. 1986. Extended mnemonic instruction with learning disabled students. *Journal of Educational Psychology* 78:300–8.

Vellutino, F. R., D. M. Scanlon, and G. R. Lyon. 2000. Differentiating between difficult-to-remediate poor readers: More evidence against the IQ-Achievement discrepancy definition of reading disability. *Journal of Learning Disabilities* 33:223–238.

Venable, G. P. 2003. Confronting complex text: Readability lessons from students with language learning disabilities. *Topics in Language Disorders* 23:225–40.

Verschaffel, L., and E. de Corte. 1997. Teaching realistic mathematical modeling in the elementary school: A teaching experiment with fifth graders. *Journal for Research in Mathematics Education* 28:577–601.

Vockell, E., and D. Fiore. 1993. Electronic gradebooks: What current programs can do for teachers. *Clearing House* 66:141–6.

Vygotsky, L. 1978. *Mind and society: The development of higher psychological processes.* Cambridge, MA: Harvard University Press.

Wagner, D. 1991. *National longitudinal transition study of special education students.* A special report prepared for the Office of Special Education, U.S. Department of Education.

Wagner, M. 1991. *Dropouts with disabilities: What do we know? What can we do?* Menlo Park, CA: SRI International.

Wagner, M., and J. Blackorby. 1996. Transition from high school to work or college: How special education students fare. *The Future of Children: Special Education for Students with Disabilities* 6(1):103–20.

Wagner, M., and J. Blackorby. 2002. Disability profiles of elementary and middle school students with disabilities. SEELS (Special Education Elementary Longitudinal Study), no. ED 00CO0017. U.S. Department of Education.

Wagner, M., and R. Cameto. 2004. The characteristics, experiences, and outcomes of youth with emotional disturbances. A report from the national longitudinal Transition Study-2, 3(2). *NLTST Data Brief, 3*(2). National Center of Secondary Education and Transition, University of Minnesota.

Wagner, M., C. Marder, J. Blackorby, R. Cameto, L. Newman, P. Levine, and E. Davies-Mercier. 2003. *The achievements of youth with disabilities during secondary school.* A report from the National Longitudinal Transition Study-2 (NLTS2). Menlo Park, CA: SRI.

Wagner, M., L. Newman, R. Cameto, P. Levine, and N. Garza. 2006. *An overview of findings from Wave 2 of the National Longitudinal Transition Study-2 (NLTS2).* National Center for Special Education Research. Menlo Park, CA: SRI International.

Wagner, R. K., D. J. Francis, and R. D. Morris. 2005. Identifying English language learners with learning disabilities: Key challenges and possible approaches. *Learning Disabilities Research & Practice* 20(1):17–23.

Walther-Thomas, C., L. Korinek, V. L. McLaughlin, and B. T. Williams. 2000. *Collaboration for inclusive education.* Boston: Allyn & Bacon.

Walton, P., L. Walton, and K. Felton. 2001. Teaching rime analogy or letter recoding reading strategies to prereaders: Effects on prereading skills and word reading. *Journal of Educational Psychology* 93:160–80.

Ward-Lonergan, J. M., B. Z. Liles, and A. M. Anderson. 1998. Listening comprehension and recall abilities in adolescents with language learning disabilities and without disabilities for social studies lectures. *Journal of Communication Disorders* 31:1–32.

Washington, J. A. 2001. Early literacy skills in African-American children: Research considerations. *Learning Disabilities Research & Practice* 16:213–21.

Waxman, G. S. 2005. Who lives in cohousing: Personality and preferences of cohousing residents. California Institute of Integral Studies. *Dissertation Abstracts International: Section B: The Sciences and Engineering* 66(5-B):2883.

Weaver, C. 2002. *Reading process and practice.* Portsmouth, NH: Heinemann.

Webb-Johnson, G. 2002. Are schools ready for Joshua? Dimensions of African-American culture among students identified as having behavioral/emotional disorders. *International Journal of Qualitative Studies in Education* 15(6):653–71.

Wehmeyer, M. L. 1996. Student self-report measure of self-determination for students with cognitive disabilities. *Education and Training in Mental Retardation and Developmental Disabilities* 31(4):282–93.

Wehmeyer, M. L. 2007. Self-determination. In *Quick-guides to inclusion: Ideas for educating students with disabilities*, ed. M. F. Giangreco and M. B. Doyle, 2nd ed., 61–74. Baltimore, MD: Paul H. Brookes Publishing Co.

Wehmeyer, M. L., M. Agran, and C. A. Hughes. 2000. A national survey of teachers' promotion of self-determination and student-directed learning. *Journal of Special Education* 34:58–68.

Wehmeyer, M. L., M. Agran, S. Palmer, D. Mithaug, and C. Blanchard. 1998. *A teacher's guide to the use of the self-determined learning model of instruction: Adolescent version.* Arlington, TX: The ARC of the United States.

Wehmeyer, M. L., S. B. Palmer, M. Agran, D. E. Mithaug, and J. E. Martin. 2000. Promoting causal agency: The self-determined learning model of instruction. *Exceptional Children* 66:439–53.

Wehmeyer, M., and M. Schwartz. 1997. Self-determination and positive adult outcomes: A follow-up study of youth with mental retardation or learning disabilities. *Exceptional Children* 63:245–55.

Weiss, M. P. 2004. Co-teaching as science in the schoolhouse: More questions than answers. *Journal of Learning Disabilities* 37:218–33.

Weiss, M. P., and F. J. Brigham. 2000. Co-teaching and the model of shared responsibility: What does the research support? In *Advances in learning and behavioral disabilities: Educational interventions*, vol. 14., ed. T. E. Scruggs and M. A. Mastropieri, 217–45. Oxford, UK: Elsevier.

Welch, M. 1992. The PLEASE strategy: A metacognitive learning strategy for improving the paragraph writing of students with mild disabilities. *Learning Disability Quarterly* 15:119–28.

Welsch, R. 2007. Using experimental analysis to determine interventions for reading fluency and recalls of students with learning disabilities. *Learning Disability Quarterly* 30:155–29.

White, B., and J. Frederiksen. 2005. A theoretical framework and approach for fostering metacognitive development. *Educational Psychologist* 40:211–23.

White, T. 2005. Effects of systematic and strategic analogy-based phonics on grade two students' word reading and reading comprehension. *Reading Research Quarterly* 40:234–55.

Wiest, D. J., E. H. Wong, J. M. Cervantes, L. Craik, and D. A. Kreil. 2001. Intrinsic motivation among regular, special, and alternative education high school students. *Adolescence* 36(141):111–26.

Wiig, E. H., and E. M. Semel. 1984. *Language assessment and intervention for the learning disabled.* Columbus, OH: Merrill.

Wilby, P. 2004. Teach the language of tolerance. *Times Educational Supplement,* Issue: 4588, 23.

Will, M. C. 1984. Let us pause and reflect—but not too long. *Exceptional Children* 51(1):11–6.

Will, M. C. 1986. Educating children with learning problems: A shared responsibility. *Exceptional Children* 52:411–5.

Williams, J. M., and E. O'Leary. 2001. What we've learned and where we go from here. *Career Development for Exceptional Individuals* 24:51–71.

Williamson, P., J. McLeskey, D. Hoppey, and T. Rentz. 2006. Educating students with mental retardation in general education classrooms. *Exceptional Children* 72:347–61.

Willoughby, S. S. 1990. *Mathematics education for a changing world.* Alexandria, VA: Association for Supervision and Curriculum Development.

Wilson, B. 1996. Instructor manual: Wilson reading system. Milbury, MA: Wilson Language Training Corporation.

Wilson, C. L., and P. T. Sindelar. 1991. Direct instruction in math word problems: Students with learning disabilities. *Exceptional Children* 57:512–9.

Wilson, G., C. Michaels, and H. Margolis. 2005. Form versus function: Using technology to develop individualized educational programs for students with disabilities. *Journal of Special Education Technology* 20:37–46.

Winter, S. M. 2007. *Inclusive early childhood education: A collaborative approach.* Upper Saddle River, NJ: Prentice Hall.

Witzel, B. S., C. D. Mercer, and M. D. Miller. 2003. Teaching algebra to students with learning difficulties: An investigation of an explicit instruction model. *Learning Disabilities Research & Practice* 18:121–31.

Witzel, B. S., P. J. Riccomini, and E. Schneider. 2008. Implementing CRA with secondary students with learning disabilities in math. *Intervention in School and Clinic* 43:270–6.

Wodrich, D. L. 2000. *Attention-deficit/hyperactivity disorder: What every parent wants to know.* 2nd ed. Baltimore, MD: Paul H. Brookes Publishing Co.

Wolf, M. 2007. *Proust and the Squid: The story and science of the reading brain.* New York: Harper Collins.

Wolf, M., and P. Bowers, P. 1999. The 'Double-Deficit Hypothesis' for the developmental dyslexias. *Journal of Educational Psychology* 91:415–38.

Wolf, S. A. 1998. The flight of reading: Shifts, in instruction, orchestration, and attitudes through classroom theatre. *Reading Research Quarterly* 33:382–415.

Wolfson, A. R., and M. A. Carskadon. 1998. Sleep schedules and daytime functioning in adolescents. *Child Development* 69(4):875–87.

Wong, B. Y. L. 1991a. Assessment of metacognitive research in learning disabilities: Theory, research, and practice. In *Handbook on the assessment of learning disabilities,* ed. H. L. Swanson, 265–84. Austin, TX: PRO-ED.

Wong, B. Y. L. 1991b. *Learning about learning disabilities.* San Diego, CA: Academic Press.

Wong, B. Y. L. 1996. *The ABCs of learning disabilities.* San Diego, CA: Academic Press.

Wong, B. Y. L. 1997. Research on genre-specific strategies for enhancing writing in adolescents with learning disabilities. *Learning Disability Quarterly* 20:140–59.

Woodward, A., and D. L. Elliot. 1990. Textbook use and teacher professionalism. In *Textbooks and schooling in the United States. Eighty-ninth yearbook of the National Society for the Study of Education, part I,* 179–93. Chicago: University of Chicago Press.

Woodward, J. 2006. Developing automaticity in multiplication facts: Integrating strategy instruction with timed practice drills. *Learning Disability Quarterly* 29:269–89.

Woodward, J., and C. Brown. 2006. Meeting the curricular needs of academically low-achieving students in middle grade mathematics. *Journal of Special Education* 40:151–9.

Woodward, J., and L. Howard. 1994. The misconceptions of youth: Errors and their mathematical meaning. *Exceptional Children* 61:126–36.

Woodward, J., and M. Montague. 2002. Meeting the challenge of mathematics reform for students with LD. *Journal of Special Education* 36:89–101.

Wraga, M., M. Helt, E. Jacobs, and K. Sullivan. 2006. Neural basis of stereotype-induced shifts in women's mental rotation performance. *Social Cognitive and Affective Neuroscience* (Dec. 8).

Yampolsky, S., and G. Waters. 2002. Treatment of single word oral reading in an individual with deep dyslexia. *Aphasiology* 16:455–71.

Yopp, H. K., and H. Yopp. 2000. Supporting phonemic awareness development in the classroom. *The Reading Teacher* 54:130–55.

Ysseldyke, J. 1973. Diagnostic-prescriptive teaching: The search for aptitude-treatment interactions. In *The first review of special education,* ed. L. Mann and D. A. Sabatino, 1–37. New York: Grune and Stratton.

Yuill, N. M., J. Oakhill, and A. J. Parkin. 1989. Working memory, comprehension ability and the resolution of text anomaly. *British Journal of Psychology* 80:351–61.

Zabel, R. H., and F. A. Nigro. 1999. Juvenile offenders with behavioral disorders, learning disabilities, and no disabilities: Self-reports of personal, family, and school characteristics. *Behavioral Disorders* 25(1):22–40.

Zehler, A. M., H. L. Fleischman, P. J. Hopstock, M. L. Pendzick, and T. G. Stephenson. 2003. *Descriptive study of services to LEP students and LEP students with disabilities,* no. 4. Arlington, VA: U.S. Department of Education, Office of English Language Acquisition (OELA).

Zentall, S. S. 2007. Math performance of students with ADHD: Cognitive and behavioral contributors and interventions. In *Why is math so hard for some children?* ed. D. B. Berch and M. M. M. Mazzocco, 219–43. Baltimore, MD: Paul H. Brookes.

Zhang, C., and T. Bennett. 2003. Facilitating the meaningful participation of culturally and linguistically diverse families in the IFSP and IEP process. *Focus on Autism and Other Developmental Disabilities* 18(1):51–9.

Zionts, L. T., S. M. Shellady, and P. Zionts. 2006. Teachers' perceptions of professional standards: Their importance and ease of implementation. *Preventing School Failure* 50:5–12.

Zoino-Jeannetti, J. A. 2006. *"It would turn the lights on in your head": Perceptions and experiences of learning of women enrolled in an adult education program.* Doctoral Dissertation, UMI Microform no. 3238850. Chestnut Hill, MA: Boston College.

Credits

Chapter 1:

p. 1: photos_alyson/Taxi/Getty Images; p. 22: ©Will Hart/PhotoEdit Inc

Chapter 2:

p. 37: ©Michael Newman/PhotoEdit Inc; p. 55: ©Ellen B. Senisi

Chapter 3:

p. 73: Ragnar Schmuck/fStop/Getty Images; p. 88: ©John Birdsall/The Image Works

Chapter 4:

p. 113: ©Michael Newman/PhotoEdit Inc; p. 128: Andreanna Seymore/Stone/Getty Images; p. 137, left: Ned Frisk Photography/Corbis Images RF/Jupiter Images; p. 137, right: Jenny Solomon/Shutterstock Images

Chapter 5:

p. 147: Sylva Villerot/Photononstop/Jupiter Images; p. 168: Image Source/Getty Images

Chapter 6:

p. 183: ©Bob Daemmrich/The Image Works; p. 194: ©Mary Kate Denny/PhotoEdit Inc

Chapter 7:

p. 221: ©Jonathan Nourok/PhotoEdit Inc; p. 238: ©Ellen B. Senisi

Chapter 8:

p. 257: ©David Young-Wolff/PhotoEdit Inc; p. 274: ©Dan Atkin/Alamy

Chapter 9:

p. 295: ©AGStockUSA, Inc./Alamy; p. 315: Picturenet/Blend Images/Getty Images

Chapter 10:

p. 333: Lisa Pines/Photonica/Getty Images; p. 351: Corbis RF/Jupiter Images

Chapter 11:

p. 373: Creatas Images RF/Jupiter Images; p. 380: ©WizCom Technologies

Chapter 12:

p. 397: Thinkstock Images RF/Jupiter Images; p. 404: ©vario images GmbH & Co.KG/Alamy

Chapter 13:

p. 437: ©Robin Sachs/PhotoEdit Inc; p. 447: Nicholas Prior/Taxi/Getty Images

Chapter 14:

p. 471: ©Michael Newman/PhotoEdit Inc.; p. 500: ©John Birdsall/The Image Works

Index

Note: *Italic* page numbers indicate figures, tables, and boxed material.